OXFORD CONSTITUTIONAL THEORY

Series Editors:

Martin Loughlin, John P. McCormick, and Neil Walker

Religion, Law, and Democracy

OXFORD CONSTITUTIONAL THEORY

Series editors:
Martin Loughlin, John P. McCormick, and Neil Walker

Oxford Constitutional Theory has rapidly established itself as the primary point of reference for theoretical reflections on the growing interest in constitutions and constitutional law in domestic, regional and global contexts. The majority of the works published in the series are monographs that advance new understandings of their subject. But the series aims to provide a forum for further innovation in the field by also including well-conceived edited collections that bring a variety of perspectives and disciplinary approaches to bear on specific themes in constitutional thought and by publishing English translations of leading monographs in constitutional theory that have originally been written in languages other than English.

ALSO AVAILABLE IN THE SERIES

New Constitutional Horizons
Towards a Pluralist Constitutional Theory
Cormac Mac Amhlaigh

Constitutional Ratification without Reason
Jeffrey A. Lenowitz

Legitimation by Constitution
A Dialogue on Political Liberalim
Frank Michelman and Alessandro Ferrara

Authoritarian Liberalism and the Transformation of Modern Europe
Michael Wilkinson

Constitutionalism and the Paradox Principles and Rules
Between the Hydra and Hercules
Marcelo Neves

Constituent Power in the European Union
Markus Patberg

Constitutional and Political Theory
Selected Writings
Ernst-Wolfgang Böckenförde
Edited by Mirjam Künkler and Tine Stein

Constituent Power and the Law
Joel Colón-Ríos

Law and Revolution
Legitimacy and Constitutionalism after the Arab Spring
Nimer Sultany

After Public Law
Cormac Mac Amhlaigh, Claudio Michelon, Neil Walker

Europe's Functional Constitution
A Theory of Constitutionalism Beyond the State
Turkuler Isiksel

Constitutionalism
Past, Present, and Future
Dieter Grimm

Unconstitutional Constitutional Amendments
The Limits of Amendment Powers
Yaniv Roznai

Euroconstitutionalism and its Discontents
Oliver Gerstenberg

Popular Sovereignty in Early Modern Constitutional Thought
Daniel Lee

Religion, Law, and Democracy

Selected Writings

Ernst-Wolfgang Böckenförde
Professor Emeritus, University of Freiburg
and
Former Judge of the Federal Constitutional Court of Germany

Edited by
Mirjam Künkler
Research Professor, Netherlands Institute for Advanced Study
and
Tine Stein
Professor of Political Theory, University of Göttingen

VOLUME II

OXFORD
UNIVERSITY PRESS

OXFORD
UNIVERSITY PRESS

Great Clarendon Street, Oxford, OX2 6DP,
United Kingdom

Oxford University Press is a department of the University of Oxford. It furthers the University's objective of excellence in research, scholarship, and education by publishing worldwide. Oxford is a registered trade mark of Oxford University Press in the UK and in certain other countries

First Edition published in 2020
First published in paperback 2022

Published in the United States of America by Oxford University Press
198 Madison Avenue, New York, NY 10016, United States of America

British Library Cataloguing in Publication Data

Data available

Library of Congress Cataloging in Publication Data

Data available

ISBN 978–0–19–881863–2 (Hbk.)
ISBN 978–0–19–285703–3 (Pbk.)

DOI: 10.1093/oso/9780198818632.001.0001

The translation of this work was supported by Geisteswissenschaften International—Translation Funding for Humanities and Social Sciences from Germany, a joint initiative of the Fritz Thyssen Foundation, the German Federal Foreign Office, the collecting society VG WORT and the Börsenverein des Deutschen Buchhandels (German Publishers & Booksellers Association).

Preface

Ernst-Wolfgang Böckenförde passed away on 24 February 2019. Family, friends, and colleagues travelled from far and wide to pay their last respects at his funeral, held near Freiburg im Breisgau.

As might be expected, former colleagues and students praised his intellectual brilliance, his originality, his discipline, his loyalty, his many contributions to public life in Germany and his ethos in office—as a scholar, constitutional court judge, and public intellectual. But one of the more surprising aspects of the event was the speech given by a local politician of the Social Democratic Party who reminded the audience of 'Böckenförde the citizen'. As soon as he moved to the small village of Au in 1976 upon accepting a professorship at the University of Freiburg, Böckenförde joined the local choir and the music association. He was a frequent participant in church fairs and town festivals and an ardent interlocutor, asking his neighbours about the ebbs and flows of local public life from kindergarten construction to zoning plans, and, of course, offering his own opinions. In short, Böckenförde lived 'in the neighbourhood'. To locals, he was the 'Verfassungsrichter zum Anfassen' (the constitutional court judge at your fingertips). Living in the neighbourhood was one of his ways of working on behalf of the 'integration' of society, one of the phenomena he was fascinated by and grappled with most: how to create understanding in society, relations, exchange, solidarity, cohesion, and in the end 'agreement on the things that cannot be voted upon', a phrase coined by jurist Adolf Arndt that Böckenförde cited frequently. After all, Böckenförde was deeply convinced that democracy cannot survive unless the citizens of that democracy as a political community work continuously towards agreement on those things that lie beyond the ballot box.

Three years have passed since the publication of the first volume of English translations of Böckenförde's writings, containing many of his articles on legal and constitutional issues. Just before the publication of the first volume, we convened two international conferences whose contributions were later published in three special journal issues: 'The Secular State, Constitution, and Democracy: Engaging with Böckenförde' in *Constellations: An International Journal of Critical and Democratic Theory* 25(2) (2018); 'Böckenförde beyond Germany' in the *German Law Journal* 19(2) (2018); and 'Böckenförde as an Inner-Catholic Critic', in the *Oxford Journal of Law and Religion* 7(1) (2018).

Many excellent scholars from the fields of law, political theory, and history contributed to the conferences and to these later publications. The international exchanges also elicited the insight that Böckenförde's work enjoyed surprising reception literatures in languages other than German. This led to a further conference, convened in February 2019, on the reception of Böckenförde's work in Japan, Korea, Latin America, and Southern and Eastern Europe. Contributions to this third conference were published as Beiheft Nr. 24, titled 'Die Rezeption der Werke Ernst-Wolfgang Böckenfördes in international vergleichender Perspektive', of the journal *Der Staat*, a journal Böckenförde had co-founded in 1962.

As we prepared the publication of this volume, brilliant friends and colleagues once again provided immeasurable help with comments and advice. They include David Abraham, Markus Böckenförde, Dieter Gosewinkel, Michael J. Hollerich, Olivier Jouanjan, Oliver Lepsius, Reinhard Mehring, Ulrich K. Preuß, and Julian Rivers. We are deeply grateful to them.

Ernst-Wolfgang Böckenförde shared his thoughts on the selection of articles for both volumes and until the end of 2018 was available to meet with us and communicate in other ways whenever we sought clarification. We are very grateful for those opportunities. In April 2017 we convened a launch of Volume I for him at the University of Freiburg, an event which many of his former colleagues at the university as well as other legal scholars and practitioners attended, and which appeared to give him great pleasure.

Other launch events were held at New York University Law School, the Humboldt University Berlin, Uppsala University, the University of Kiel, the Institute for Human Sciences in Vienna, the London School of Economics and Political Science, and at conferences of the German Studies Association and the International Society for Public Law. We thank our colleagues who hosted these events and discussed Böckenförde's writings there with us, including Robert Alexy, Andreas von Arnauld, Peter Carl Caldwell, Iain Cameron, Sabino Cassese, Max Edling, Dieter Gosewinkel, Ludger Hagedorn, Michaela Hailbronner, Anna Jonsson Cornell, Olivier Jouanjan, Mattias Kumm, Martin Loughlin, Aline-Florence Manent, Johannes Masing, Ralph Michaels, Kai Möller, Christoph Möllers, Jo Eric Khushal Murkens, Claus Offe, Julian Rivers, Mark Edward Ruff, Sascha Somek, Guglielmo Verdirame, Rainer Wahl, and Christian Waldhoff.

As with Volume I, we have been fortunate to employ the services of Thomas Dunlap for the translation. Due to the range of topics and multiple disciplinary perspectives involved, the translation was a particularly challenging one. We thank Thomas Dunlap for mastering this task so skilfully.

We thank Oxford University Press, especially Eve Ryle-Hodges and Imogen Hill, for guiding this publication along with such generous dedication and support. We further thank Geisteswissenschaften International for partially funding the translations for this volume, and Verena Frick and Sven Altenburger, both of the University of Göttingen, for their assistance in the preparation of this volume.

Wherever it seemed necessary, we have inserted annotations (indented and marked with Latin numerals) that include further explanations on the context of German or European politics and history. A comprehensive list of Ernst-Wolfgang Böckenförde's publications is included in the appendix, as well as the laudatio given by former Federal President Joachim Gauck on the occasion of awarding Böckenförde the Grand Cross of Merit of the Federal Republic of Germany.

As this project comes to an end, we marvel at the intellectual journey Ernst-Wolfgang Böckenförde has moved us to undertake. It has been an honour and inspiration, not only to work closely with his texts and to try to understand better how he reconciled his identities as a social democrat, a political liberal, and a Catholic reformer, but also to enter into conversation with so many of his explicit and implicit interlocutors. These work in disciplines as diverse as legal theory, legal history, constitutional law, legal education, social history, Catholic theology, Catholic social thought, canon law, political theory, intellectual history, social policy, sociology, comparative politics, philosophy, legal ethics, and diverse geographies. The conversations will continue as Böckenförde continues to move his readers into profound intellectual engagement. We are grateful to him, as we editors are to each other, for the exciting journey travelled together.

Mirjam Künkler and Tine Stein, December 2019.

Table of Contents

Translator's Note xi
by Thomas Dunlap

Freedom in Religion, Freedom in the State: Ernst-Wolfgang Böckenförde on Religion, Law, and Democracy 1
by *Mirjam Künkler*

PART I: CATHOLIC CHURCH AND POLITICAL ORDER

Böckenförde on the Relation of the Catholic Church and Christians to Democracy and Authoritarianism 46
by *Mirjam Künkler and Tine Stein*

Chapter I. The Ethos of Modern Democracy and the Church [1957] 61

Chapter II. German Catholicism in 1933: A Critical Examination [1961] 77

Chapter III. Types of Christian Conduct in the World during the Nazi Regime [1965/2004] 105

Chapter IV. Religious Freedom between the Conflicting Demands of Church and State [1964–79] 115

PART II. STATE AND SECULARITY

Böckenförde on the Secular State and Secular Law 138
by *Mirjam Künkler and Tine Stein*

Chapter V. The Rise of the State as a Process of Secularization [1967] 152

Chapter VI. The Fundamental Right of Freedom of Conscience [1970] 168

Chapter VII. Remarks on the Relationship between State and Religion in Hegel [1982] 199

Chapter VIII. The Secularized State: Its Character, Justification, and Problems in the Twenty-first Century [2007] 220

PART III. ON THE THEOLOGY OF LAW AND POLITICAL THEORY

Böckenförde on the Relationship Between Theology, Law, and Political Theory 238
by *Mirjam Künkler and Tine Stein*

Chapter IX. Political Theory and Political Theology: Comments on their Reciprocal Relationship [1981] 248

Chapter X. Reflections on a Theology of Modern Secular Law [1999] 259

Chapter XI. A Christian in the Office of Constitutional Judge [1999] 280

Chapter XII. On the Authority of Papal Encyclicals: The Example of Pronouncements on Religious Freedom [2006] 288

PART IV. BASIC NORMS AND THE PRINCIPLE OF HUMAN DIGNITY

Böckenförde on the Right to Life, Human Dignity, and its Meta-positive Foundations 308
by *Mirjam Künkler and Tine Stein*

Chapter XIII. Abolition of Section 218 of the Criminal Code? Reflections on the Current Debate about the Prohibition of Abortion in German Criminal Law [1971] 318

Chapter XIV. Human Dignity as a Normative Principle: Fundamental Rights in the Bioethics Debate [2003] 339

Chapter XV. Will Human Dignity Remain Inviolable? [2004] 354

PART V. BÖCKENFÖRDE IN CONTEXT

Chapter XVI. Biographical Interview with Ernst-Wolfgang Böckenförde [2011] 369

Appendix 1: *List of Original Titles* 395

Appendix 2: *Ernst-Wolfgang Böckenförde: List of Publications* 397

Appendix 3: *Address given by Federal President Joachim Gauck on the Occasion of Awarding the Grand Cross of the Order of Merit of the Federal Republic of Germany to Prof. Dr. Ernst-Wolfgang Böckenförde on 29 April 2016 at Schloss Bellevue* 445

Index 449

Translator's Note

This project has been a team effort from beginning to end. Translating legal German into English is a notoriously difficult task. I am grateful that I was able to draw on some previous translations by J. A. Underwood. Mirjam Künkler and Tine Stein read each chapter very carefully and made many crucial improvements. I was very fortunate, indeed, to have had such conscientious and skilled collaborators.

Thomas Dunlap, February 2018

Freedom in Religion, Freedom in the State

Ernst-Wolfgang Böckenförde on Religion, Law, and Democracy[1]

Mirjam Künkler

I. INTRODUCTION

The freedom of the individual can always only be defended as the freedom of all. Thus argued Ernst-Wolfgang Böckenförde at the age of thirty-one, in an article he himself later referred to as the article that most shaped his thinking.[2] He wrote this apropos the Catholic Church's approach to democracy in the postwar years before Vatican II,[3] which he regarded as driven by instrumentalist considerations. The Church was willing to accept majority rule only as long as the areas relevant to its own interests (education, value debates, the Church's status vis-à-vis the state) remained beyond the reach of majority rule. What is more, it claimed religious freedom for itself, without being willing to grant the same rights to other religions. Böckenförde had particular trouble understanding such a position as a lawyer. How can one expect to enjoy a right that one is not willing to grant to others, he asked.[4]

Freedom is a cornerstone in Böckenförde's thinking, but what does it entail precisely? For Böckenförde, it is first and foremost individual freedom, and it must be protected against both state power and societal power. State power must be limited by a democratic constitution with strongly enshrined personal

[1] This chapter has benefited from numerous discussions with my friend and colleague Tine Stein, as well as our past joint publications. I thank her as well as Peter C. Caldwell, Michael Hollerich, Otto Kallscheuer, and Joachim Wieland for excellent comments.

[2] Ernst-Wolfgang Böckenförde, 'German Catholicism in 1933', *CrossCurrents* 11 (1961), pp. 283–303, included as Chapter II in this volume. See in this regard in particular his reflections on the article in 'Vorbemerkung', in Ernst-Wolfgang Böckenförde, *Kirche und christlicher Glaube in den Herausforderungen der Zeit*, 2nd ed. (Münster: LIT Publishing House, 2007), p. 114.

[3] The Second Vatican Council (Vatican II) fundamentally redefined the Church's doctrinal position in several areas, notably regarding the issue of religious freedom. See more extensively note 120.

[4] Ernst-Wolfgang Böckenförde, 'Religionsfreiheit als Aufgabe der Christen [1965]', in Böckenförde 2007 (note 2), pp. 197–212.

Religion, Law, and Democracy. Ernst-Wolfgang Böckenförde, Oxford University Press (2020). © E.W. Böckenförde, M. Künkler, and T. Stein 2020. DOI: 10.1093/oso/9780198818632.003.0001.

rights and liberties. 'The law-based state [*Rechtsstaat*],' Böckenförde writes, 'is aimed at the demarcation and restriction of state power in the interest of the freedom of the individual.'[5] As he outlined in his article 'Securing Freedom Against Societal Power', it is also the state's role to protect the individual against the violation of his or her freedom by societal groups.

Based on this dual role assigned to the state, one might conclude then that the state is the supreme guarantor of freedom for Böckenförde.

On the one hand, this is certainly the case, and Böckenförde is Hegelian in regarding the liberal state, in particular the rule of law, as the necessary environment in which individual freedom can be enjoyed. This is so because only thanks to a rule of law can individual freedom be guaranteed against encroachment by others and state power itself. Moreover, the kind of freedom the liberal state ensures is not merely freedom from oppression, but it must also include the creation of possibilities in which the individual can pursue self-realization, should he or she choose to do so.[6]

Böckenförde goes beyond Hegel when he argues that self-realization can only be possible in a state where in the final analysis people are subject to the rules they have had the possibility to generate and shape, that is, a liberal democracy. It is here that Böckenförde draws heavily on the legal scholar Herman Heller.[7] For the state *emanates from the people* and is first and foremost an 'organized unity of action and taking effect' (*organisierte Handlungs- und Wirkeinheit*). It provides the procedures and channels for social forces to determine policy. Moreover, it is only through citizen participation and representation that the state enjoys legitimacy.

Böckenförde is also a statist in his position on how to deal with the counteracting forces of capitalism and democracy. In several writings, Böckenförde emphasized that the guarantee of private property in the German Basic Law had to be understood as balancing liberal guarantees on the one hand with limits on those guarantees emanating from societal or public needs on the other.[8] A concept of the state according to which fundamental rights restrict

[5] 'Der Rechtsstaat zielt stets auf die Begrenzung und Eingrenzung staatlicher Macht im Interesse der Freiheit der Einzelnen', in Ernst-Wolfgang Böckenförde, 'Entstehung und Wandel des Rechtsstaatsbegriffs', in Horst Ehmke and Carlo Schmid (eds.), *Festschrift für Adolf Arndt zum 65. Geburtstag* (Hamburg: Europäische Verlagsanstalt, 1969), pp. 53–76; published in English as 'The Origin and Development of the Concept of the *Rechtsstaat*' in Ernst-Wolfgang Böckenförde, *State, Society and Liberty: Studies in Political Theory and Constitutional Law*, transl. by Jim Underwood (New York: Berg Publishers, 1991), pp. 47–70.

[6] Ernst-Wolfgang Böckenförde, 'The State as an Ethical State', included as Chapter III in volume I of this edition, Ernst-Wolfgang Böckenförde, *Constitutional and Political Theory: Selected Writings*, ed. Mirjam Künkler and Tine Stein (Oxford: Oxford University Press, 2017), pp. 86–107.

[7] Hermann Heller, *Gesammelte Werke*, 2nd ed., vol. II. (Tübingen: Mohr Siebeck, 1992 [1928]). On the extent to which Böckenförde's concept of the state relies on Hermann Heller, see Mirjam Künkler and Tine Stein, 'Böckenförde's Political Theory of the State', in volume I of this edition, pp. 38–53; and Olivier Jouanjan, 'Between Carl Schmitt, the Catholic Church, and Hermann Heller: On the foundations of democratic theory in the work of Ernst-Wolfgang Böckenförde', *Constellations: An International Journal of Critical and Democratic Theory* 45 (2) (2018), pp. 184–195.

[8] 'Eigentum, Sozialbindung des Eigentums, Enteignung', in Konrad Duden, Helmut R. Külz et al. (eds.), *Gerechtigkeit in der Industriegesellschaft*. Rechtspolitischer Kongreß der SPD, Mai 1972 in Braunschweig.

state action, he wrote about the Basic Law, is at the same time constrained by a concept of the state according to which constitutional principles entail the duty to provide social services. Constitutionally guaranteed freedom could not be enjoyed unless specific material needs were met first. If liberty were to be guaranteed to all rights holders, specific societal and legal framework conditions had to be provided for, the most important of which was 'the *constant relativization of societal inequality* that arises continually from the exercise of liberty'. The Basic Law in fact imposed a 'social state as a binding constitutional principle on par with that of the *Rechtsstaat*',[9] he argued.

On the other hand, Böckenförde is not exclusively a statist, and here again, his position draws in part on Hegel. For the liberal state needs binding forces that 'hold it'. In Hegel, this is an abstract *Geist*—attitudes and dispositions that support the liberal state. Böckenförde grounded these attitudes and dispositions in societal forces and individuals. Like Hegel, he referred to this as an 'ethos' that needed to feed the commons. These binding forces needed to emanate from the citizenry and the citizenry's willingness to continually work with one another to formulate and secure the public good. Thus, Böckenförde's entire state theory stands and falls with the ethos that emanates from society and that is needed to sustain the state. As he formulated in his often-quoted dictum: 'the liberal, secularized state is sustained by conditions it cannot itself guarantee'.[10]

What are the sources of this social ethos, in Böckenförde's eyes? Religion, that is personal faith, can be an important source and it was certainly the major source for his own motivation to take on public responsibility as a scholar, judge, and public intellectual.[11] But beside religion, 'philosophical, political and social movements can strengthen ... the willingness to not always look out for one's own benefit only, but to act companionably and in solidarity with others'.[12] Moreover, and this is a crucial point that has been overlooked by some of his readers, he insists that religion can be a source for a democratic ethos only if it is placed in the service of the common good, not of particular religious goals, and not of the interests of individual religious groups,[13] a point taken up again towards the end of this introduction.

Further, it is only in the secular state, wrote Böckenförde in 1957, that Christianity can be 'a religion of freedom' (again implicitly referencing Hegel).[14]

Dokumentation, C. F. Müller (1972), pp. 215–231. This article was also included in his 1976 Suhrkamp compilation but unfortunately was the only article not included when the collection was published in English in 1991.

[9] 'Grundrechtstheorie und Grundrechtsinterpretation', *Neue Juristische Wochenschrift* (1974), pp. 1529–1538; published in English as 'Fundamental Rights: Theory and Interpretation', Chapter XI in volume I of this edition, p. 288. Emphasis in the original.

[10] 'Die Entstehung des Staates als Vorgang der Säkularisation', in s.ed., *Säkularisation und Utopie. Ebracher Studien. Ernst Forsthoff zum 65. Geburtstag*, Stuttgart: Kohlhammer, 1967, pp. 75-94; included in this volume as Chapter V, 'The Rise of the State as a Process of Secularization'.

[11] See his article 'A Christian in the Office of Constitutional Judge', Chapter XI in this volume.

[12] Ernst-Wolfgang Böckenförde, 'Freiheit ist ansteckend'. *die tageszeitung*, 23 September 2009, p. 4.

[13] Böckenförde 1961 (note 2).

[14] Ernst-Wolfgang Böckenförde, 'Das Ethos der modernen Demokratie und die Kirche', *Hochland* 50(1) (1957), pp. 4–19, included as Chapter I in this volume.

At a time when official Catholicism still tried to assert its role as part of the state (in many Latin American countries as well as of course Franco's Spain), Böckenförde rejected that argument. With his commitment to the secular state, he stood apart from the mainstream in the Church at the time. Only in the secular state, according to Böckenförde, can citizens develop the free commitment to act in accordance with their religious convictions and not because it is backed by the punitive framework of the state. In other words, only the separation of law and morality enables believers to act truly morally.

Following his personal motto *'civis simul et christianus'* (a democratic citizen while also a Christian), Böckenförde sought to shape public life as a Catholic and he sought to contribute to the reform of Catholicism from his position as a democratic citizen. Böckenförde remained an inner-Catholic critic throughout his life. At the beginning of his career stands an analysis of Catholic complicity in the rise of the Nazi state, and at the end of his career a public intervention on the failure of the Church in dealing with cases of sexual abuse.[15] In both cases, he criticized the Church for prioritizing itself over concern for the people, and for subordinating core Christian values to the *raison d'être* of the institution of the Church.

Just before his passing, Böckenförde had decided that instead of flowers, those wishing to mourn him should donate funds to Donum Vitae, an organization he had helped co-found that provided ethical counselling to women considering to undertake an abortion. The creation of Donum Vitae had caused a serious conflict with the Vatican, which accuses the organization of indirectly abetting the German state's relatively permissive abortion regulations.[16] Even from beyond his grave, Böckenförde sought to represent a different kind of Catholicism: one where respect for people's individual conscience came first.

The collection presented here, the second of two volumes, brings together Böckenförde's essays on issues of religion, ethos, and the Catholic Church in relation to law, democracy, and the state, while the first volume presented a selection of his essays in constitutional and political thought. Volume II is organized in four parts, containing three to four articles each and arranged in historically ascending manner: on the Catholic Church and Political Order (Part I), on the State and Secularity (Part II), on the Theology of Law and Political Theory (Part III), and on Basic Norms and the Principle of Human Dignity (Part IV). All articles feature annotations by the editors, providing background information on historical, cultural, and theoretical contexts. Each of the four parts is preceded by a short introduction by the editors that includes brief outlines of the articles and the context in which they were written. The last chapter consists

[15] Ernst-Wolfgang Böckenförde, 'Das unselige Handeln nach Kirchenraison', *Süddeutsche Zeitung* 29 April 2010. 'The main concern is that the sanctity of the institution is not endangered – this maxim is the real scandal and the reason for the crisis.'

[16] According to a declaration by the German bishops of 20 June 2006, Church staff are prohibited from participating in Donum Vitae, and all other Catholics involved in ecclesiastical councils, committees, associations, and organizations are requested to renounce any senior cooperation with the association.

of excerpts of the biographical interview that historian and legal scholar Dieter Gosewinkel conducted with Böckenförde in 2009/2010.[17]

Section II of this introductory chapter provides an abridged overview of Böckenförde's academic career and public engagement (a fuller version is contained in the Introduction to Volume I). Section III offers an overview and periodization of his academic writings in seven phases from 1957 to 2012. Section IV presents some of his key writings and positions as an inner-Catholic critic, as a theorist of the place of ethos in the public order, and as a thinker of 'open encompassing neutrality' between religion and state. Section V offers a reflection on the cover images Böckenförde chose for the two volumes, before the conclusion closes with brief remarks on Böckenförde's view of religion in democracy compared to other theorists of democracy and secularism.

II. A BIOGRAPHICAL SYNOPSIS

Böckenförde grew up in the Central German town of Kassel with seven siblings. His father was a forester and his mother a housewife. Among the books he said that formed him were Dante's *Divina Commedia* and writings by the Austrian novelist Adalbert Stifter and the German poet Reinhold Schneider (a Catholic anti-war writer). Apart from that, his family's library included works of philosophy, economics, sociology, and law, and a subscription to the Catholic intellectual monthly magazine *Hochland*.[18]

At the age of thirteen years he had a tram accident, as a result of which he lost half his left leg. Partly as a consequence of this accident, his travel activities were limited, and unlike some of his colleagues of similar academic stature, such as Robert Alexy or Dieter Grimm, he did not spend long sojourns at foreign universities. His travels led him frequently to Austria, Italy, and Poland, but seldom further afield, the only exception being trips to Pakistan and the USA, and an extensive lecture tour to Japan which he undertook in 1996 after retiring from the Federal Constitutional Court and the university.

Böckenförde's studies were unusual in that he decided to pursue not only one, but two university degrees, which he then also followed up with two doctoral dissertations in two separate disciplines, law and history, followed by a habilitation in law.[19] In both doctoral dissertations he chose a conceptual perspective: In the dissertation in law of 1956, he examined the public understanding of law,

[17] The 170 page-long interview was published in 'Biographisches Interview', in Ernst-Wolfgang Böckenförde, *Wissenschaft, Politik, Verfassungsgericht. Aufsätze von Ernst-Wolfgang Böckenförde* (Berlin: Suhrkamp, 2011), pp. 307–486. Selections are published here in Chapter XVI, as well as in Volume I.

[18] *Hochland* was a Catholic cultural magazine that published contributions by authors regardless of their denomination and was viewed with scepticism by the Catholic Church for its independence, critical spirit, and anti-denominationalism.

[19] For Böckenförde's academic biography, see in more detail Mirjam Künkler and Tine Stein, 'State, Constitution and Law. Ernst-Wolfgang Böckenförde's Political and Legal Thought in Context', in volume I of this edition, pp. 1–35.

tracing the differentiation between formal and substantive notions of law from the nineteenth century to the Weimar Republic. Against the background of conceptual history Böckenförde showed what the changing meaning of concepts could reveal about changing power constellations, in this case the relationship between monarchy and popular sovereignty.[20] In his history dissertation of 1960, Böckenförde examined the models of constitutionalism that emerged over the course of the nineteenth century and how the concept of 'constitution' evolved from a mere juridical contract into a political category, transforming the meaning of a political community which bound itself legally.[21]

How concepts of law changed meaning against the backdrop of evolving societal and respective power constellations remained a major theme in Böckenförde's work throughout his career.

After completing his habilitation[22] in law in 1964 on 'Organizational Power in the Realm of Government. An Inquiry into the Public Law of the Federal Republic of Germany',[23] Böckenförde was appointed professor of public law in Heidelberg. He became dean of the faculty and in 1969 moved on to the newly founded University of Bielefeld, and then later to Freiburg (1977–95), where he remained until his retirement, exempt from professorial duties during his tenure as constitutional judge (1983–1996). The denominations of these professorships extended to the areas of Public Law, Constitutional History, Legal History, and Philosophy of Law.

Two discussion circles brought the young Böckenförde into communication with some of the leading political thinkers in the early Federal Republic. The first was the Collegium Philosophicum, convened by the philosopher and Hegel expert Joachim Ritter.[24] Ritter's postwar work on Hegel had at its center the problem of the place of the state after the age of democratic revolutions: it

[20] He did so through the prism of the statutory basis requirement for encroachment (*Gesetzesvorbehalt*): the idea that the executive may not encroach upon the citizens' fundamental rights unless the legislature passes a law permitting such encroachment. With the introduction of the legal concept of the statutory basis requirement for encroachment, the balance between monarchy and popular sovereignty had shifted in favour of the latter. Ernst-Wolfgang Böckenförde, *Gesetz und gesetzgebende Gewalt. Von den Anfängen der deutschen Staatsrechtslehre bis zur Höhe des staatsrechtlichen Positivismus* (Berlin: Duncker & Humblot, 1958).

[21] Ernst-Wolfgang Böckenförde, *Die deutsche verfassungsgeschichtliche Forschung im 19. Jahrhundert. Zeitgebundene Fragestellungen und Leitbilder* (Berlin: Duncker & Humblot, 1961).

[22] To become eligible for a professorship in Germany, it used to be the case that an applicant needed to have a doctorate and a second major work, usually in the same field, i.e. the habilitation (combined with the venia legendi, the authorization to teach the subject at university level). Nowadays a second book is widely regarded as equivalent to the formal habilitation, although many scholars still seek the formal acquisition of a habilitation as well. To have two doctorates like Böckenförde is rather unusual and testifies to his broad intellectual interests.

[23] Ernst-Wolfgang Böckenförde, *Die Organisationsgewalt im Bereich der Regierung. Eine Untersuchung zum Staatsrecht der Bundesrepublik Deutschland* (Berlin: Duncker & Humblot, 1964).

[24] Joachim Ritter, professor in Münster, was one of the most influential German philosophers of the postwar period. He edited the 13-volume 'Historisches Wörterbuch der Philosophie', a standard work in the discipline of philosophy. Böckenförde contributed three entries: 'Normativismus' in *Historisches Wörterbuch der Philosophie*, ed. Joachim Ritter and Karlfried Gründer, vol. VI (Basel/Stuttgart: Schwabe, 1984), p. 931f.; 'Ordnungsdenken, konkretes', in ibid, pp. 1311–1313; and 'Rechtsstaat', in: *Historisches Wörterbuch der Philosophie*, ed. Joachim Ritter and Karlfried Gründer, vol. VIII (Basel/Stuttgart: Schwabe, 1993), pp. 332–342.

posed the questions of how to combine an openness to the people's will with political order in the early, conservative and skeptical years of the Federal Republic. While a graduate student in Münster, Böckenförde was invited to join the Collegium. The introduction to Hegel, in particular Hegel's idea of the state, would profoundly shape Böckenförde's subsequent intellectual development. Beyond the philosophical formation, the Collegium Philosophicum also had a lasting sociological impact: here Böckenförde met future colleagues, such as philosopher Robert Spaemann, who would become occasional co-authors and lifelong companions.

While Ritter's group focused on philosophical thinking, another circle influenced Böckenförde's development and career as a legal scholar by bringing him into contact with leading legal thinkers, who were also concerned with democracy and the state but more skeptical of democratic claims. This was the 'Ebrach summer seminar', a twoweek seminar convened every year by legal scholar Ernst Forsthoff in Ebrach village in Upper Franconia.[25] Here aspiring legal scholars were invited to discuss their papers with established ones—and Carl Schmitt was a regular participant. Böckenförde's groundbreaking article on 'The Rise of the State as a Process of Secularization' as well as Schmitt's 'The Tyranny of Values' go back to lectures given at Ebrach.[26]

Among the participants in Ebrach was also conceptual historian Reinhart Koselleck, later Böckenförde's colleague at the University of Heidelberg, where the two taught a course in legal history together. Koselleck, too, was concerned with the relationship between freedom, democracy, and the coercive force of both state and society in his early work. Both later moved to the newly founded University of Bielefeld, and Böckenförde contributed an article to Koselleck's opus magnum *Geschichtliche Grundbegriffe* (basic historical concepts), one of the foundational works of conceptual history.[27]

These ideas about freedom and the state, the social prerequisites for democracy, and even the underlying concern of the conservative liberal intellectuals from the early republic about the limits to the state in a democracy provided some of the key themes for Böckenförde's entire intellectual life. Indeed, Böckenförde actively embodied some of the problems that they brought up, such

[25] Ernst Forsthoff (1902–1974) was a German scholar of constitutional and administrative law, teaching over the course of his career at the universities of Frankfurt am Main, Hamburg, Königsberg, Vienna, and Heidelberg. Like Carl Schmitt (Forsthoff's mentor) and many other German legal scholars, he welcomed the Third Reich and worked on an ideological justification of the totalitarian state. But unlike many other legal scholars, Forsthoff distanced himself from the regime still during the Nazi period and was banned from teaching in 1942. Different from Carl Schmitt, he was ultimately permitted to resume teaching in the Federal Republic and returned to his professorship at the University of Heidelberg in 1952. Forsthoff was a leading drafter of the Constitution of Cyprus and served as the president of the Supreme Constitutional Court of Cyprus from 1960 to 1963.

[26] Sergius Buve (ed.), *Säkularisation und Utopie; Ernst Forsthoff zum 65. Geburtstag* (Stuttgart: Kohlhammer, 1967, Series: Ebracher Studien).

[27] 'Organ, Organismus, Organisation, politischer Körper' (sections VI–IX), in *Geschichtliche Grundbegriffe. Historisches Lexikon zur politisch-sozialen Sprache in Deutschland*, vol. 4, ed. Otto Brunner, Werner Conze, and Reinhart Koselleck (Stuttgart: Klett-Cotta, 1978), pp. 561–622.

as the relationship between a community of believers constituting only part of society with the claim of the state to represent the entire society: the problem of church and state in an inescapably pluralist democracy. Böckenförde was unusual in that he combined normative orientations which at his time were associated with different sociopolitical communities in Germany.[28] On the one hand, he was a devout Catholic and active in the lay organizations of the Church.[29] But while most Catholics until the late 1970s would have associated themselves with the Christian Democrats (the party of the chancellors Konrad Adenauer, Helmut Kohl, later Angela Merkel), Böckenförde joined the Social Democratic Party in 1967 (the party of the chancellors Willy Brandt, Helmut Schmidt, and later Gerhard Schröder). And while Böckenförde no doubt was a statist (like Carl Schmitt), he combined this with a strong political liberal orientation. On the one hand, he regarded the state as the guarantor of societal peace, but on the other hand he was always apprehensive of state encroachment into citizens' private lives. In the late 1970s, for example, when West Germany was shaken by a number of murders, kidnappings, and assaults committed by leftist terrorists (most notoriously, the Red Army Faction), he made a name for himself by writing extensively about the erosion of the rule of law that was justified with reference to the war against leftist terrorism.[30] And elsewhere he commented 'the order of freedom must set itself apart from the order of unfreedom also—and especially—by the methods of its defense'.[31]

On the constitutional court, where he served from 1983 to 1996 across the great transformation of German reunification in 1990, Böckenförde contributed to several groundbreaking decisions, including on asylum, abortion, nuclear disarmament, conscientious objection to military service, taxation, and party financing. With eleven dissenting opinions, he was one of the highest dissenters in the court's history.[32] Extraordinarily, in two cases, his minority opinions became the bases for later majority decisions.

[28] For his profiles as a political liberal, a Catholic, and a social democrat, see Mirjam Künkler and Tine Stein, 'State, Constitution and Law. Ernst-Wolfgang Böckenförde's Political and Legal Thought in Context', in volume I of this edition, pp. 1–35.

[29] He was an advisor to the executive committee of German Catholics, the most important institution of lay Catholicism in Germany. Its tasks include organizing the biennial Catholic *Kirchentag* (Church Day), discussing pending issues with the German conference of bishops, and representing lay Catholicism in public.

[30] Ernst-Wolfgang Böckenförde, 'The Repressed State of Emergency', Chapter IV in volume I of this edition, pp. 108–132. In this context, he also devised a possible constitutional amendment that would constitutionalize an internal state of emergency (the Basic Law only recognizes a state of emergency necessitated by natural disaster), arguing that this would better preserve the rule of law than the prevalent practice of dealing with such emergencies through executive measures. See section III. 4. below and in more detail Mirjam Künkler and Tine Stein, 'Böckenförde's Political Theory of the State,' in volume I of this edition, pp. 38–53. His proposal fell on deaf ears then, but the debate has been revived in 2020 in the context of the state's dealing with the Covid-19 crisis, which is overwhelmingly managed through executive measures without parliamentary consultation, let alone authorization.

[31] Böckenförde 2017 (1978) (note 6), p. 100.

[32] In two of his dissenting opinions, his social democratic leanings come particularly to the fore. One was his take on party financing, where he argued that a law that made donations to political parties deductible for juridical persons, including corporations, violated the equality principle of the Basic Law's Article 3, as

Böckenförde's writings have received wide reception in the academic world. Aside from four *Festschrifts*,[33] several monographs[34] and edited volumes[35] have been published about his work. He has received numerous prizes and awards, as well as five honorary doctorates, three in law and two in Catholic theology.[36] More than eighty of his articles have been translated into foreign languages, and his work enjoys extensive reception literatures in Italy, Poland, Japan, and Korea.[37]

would deductible donations by natural persons at a level exceeding the median income. He also dissented in the case regarding the net wealth tax, where the majority had ruled that the fundamental right to property, in connection with other basic rights, imposed a general upper limit on taxation. In the majority's view, the cumulative burden of all income and net wealth taxes must not exceed 50% of net imputed earnings. Although he strongly defended the right to property otherwise, Böckenförde did not subscribe to the view of a constitutionally mandated upper limit on taxation. In his academic writings, Böckenförde explicitly and implicitly lamented that Article 14 Section 2 of the Basic Law, according to which 'property entails obligations; its use shall also serve the public good' did not find sufficient reflection in the public regulation of private property. On this, see also section III.3 below.

[33] The *Festschrifts* are Rolf Grawert (ed.), *Offene Staatlichkeit: Festschrift für Ernst-Wolfgang Böckenförde zum 65. Geburtstag* (Berlin: Duncker & Humblot), 1995; Rainer Wahl and Joachim Wieland (eds.), *Das Recht des Menschen in der Welt. Kolloquium aus Anlass des 70. Geburtstages von Ernst-Wolfgang Böckenförde* (Berlin: Duncker & Humblot), 2002; Christoph Enders and Johannes Masing (eds.), *Freiheit des Subjekts und Organisation von Herrschaft. Symposium zu Ehren von Ernst-Wolfgang Böckenförde anlässlich seines 75. Geburtstages* (Der Staat, Beiheft 17) (Berlin: Duncker & Humblot, 2006); Johannes Masing and Joachim Wieland (eds.), *Menschenwürde – Demokratie – Christliche Gerechtigkeit. Tagungsband zum Festlichen Kolloquium aus Anlass des 80. Geburtstags von Ernst-Wolfgang Böckenförde* (Berlin: Duncker & Humblot, 2011).

[34] For the monographs, see Norbert Manterfeld, *Die Grenzen der Verfassung: Möglichkeiten limitierender Verfassungstheorie des Grundgesetzes am Beispiel E.-W. Böckenfördes* (Berlin: Duncker & Humblot, 2000); Johanna Falk, *Freiheit als politisches Ziel. Grundmodelle liberalen Denkens bei Kant, Hayek und Böckenförde* (Frankfurt a.M.: Campus, 2006); Cosima Winifred Lambrecht, *Das Staatsdenken von Ernst-Wolfgang Böckenförde: Analogien und Diskrepanzen zu dem Werk 'Der Begriff des Politischen' von Carl Schmitt* (Universitätsverlag Chemnitz, 2015); and Jonas Pavelka, *Bürger und Christ. Politische Ethik und christliches Menschenbild bei Ernst-Wolfgang Böckenförde* (Freiburg: Herder, 2015).

[35] The edited volumes are Hermann-Josef Große Kracht and Klaus Große Kracht (eds.), *Religion—Recht—Republik. Studien zu Ernst-Wolfgang Böckenförde* (Paderborn: Schöningh, 2014); and Reinhard Mehring and Martin Otto (eds.), *Voraussetzungen und Garantien des Staates. Ernst-Wolfgang Böckenfördes Staatsverständnis* (Nomos: Baden-Baden, 2014). Apart from numerous obituaries that were published following his passing in February 2019, the *Verfassungsblog* in May 2019 convened a review with ten commentaries on Böckenförde's legacy.

[36] Böckenförde received honorary doctorates from the Law Schools of the Universities of Basel (1987), Bielefeld (1999), and Münster (2001), and from the Faculties of Catholic Theology of Bochum University (1999), and Tübingen University (2005). In 1970 he became a member of the North-Rhine Westphalian Academy of Sciences and in 1989 corresponding member of the Bavarian Academy of Sciences and Humanities. He has received the Reuchlin Award of the City of Pforzheim for outstanding work in the humanities (1978), the order of merit of the state of Baden-Württemberg (2003), the Guardini Award of the Catholic Academy in Bavaria for work in the field of the philosophy of religion (2004), the Hannah-Arendt Prize for Political Thought (2004), the Sigmund Freud Prize for scholarly prose (2012), and the Grand Cross of Merit (2016), one of the highest tributes the Federal Republic of Germany can bestow on individuals for services to the nation. Böckenförde was Knight Commander of the Pontifical Equestrian Order of St. Gregory appointed by John Paul II (1999).

[37] For an overview of the translations and their reception, see Mirjam Künkler and Tine Stein (eds.), *Die Rezeption der Werke Ernst-Wolfgang Böckenfördes in international vergleichender Perspektive*, Beihefte zu »Der Staat«, vol. XXIV (Berlin: Duncker & Humblot, 2020).

III. BÖCKENFÖRDE: INNER-CATHOLIC CRITIC, CONSTITUTIONAL HISTORIAN, SOCIAL DEMOCRAT, POLITICAL LIBERAL, CONSTITUTIONAL THEORIST

Böckenförde from the beginning pursued two different publication tracks, publishing his religion- and church-related articles mostly with the Freiburg-based Herder publishing house, which specializes in religion and the humanities, and his legal writings with Suhrkamp (after having published his two doctoral monographs and his habilitation with Duncker & Humblot, the publisher also of Hans Kelsen, Carl Schmitt, and Rudolf Smend).

In 1973 and in 1976, just nine and twelve years respectively after he had become full professor at the age of thirty-four, Böckenförde published two collections of his most important essays. It was a rather early age to publish the first instalment of one's 'canon'.[38] The first collection brought together his essays on religion and was published with Herder, the second collection his essays on law, published with Suhrkamp. Between 1988 and 1991, while a judge on the Federal Constitutional Court (1983–1996), Böckenförde published the second instalment of his canon. The 1973 collection was extended into three volumes published between 1988 and 1990, again with Herder,[39] and the 1976 collection was expanded to two volumes, both published with Suhrkamp in 1991.[40] A third instalment followed in 2004, when Böckenförde published a final collection of his writings on religion with the LIT Publishing House (a second expanded edition appeared in 2007),[41] and another volume in political and constitutional theory with Suhrkamp in 1999.[42] His legal writings received a fourth acknowledgement with a final Suhrkamp collection published in 2011, which also contained an extensive biographical interview that historian and legal scholar Dieter Gosewinkel had conducted with Böckenförde in 2009/2010.[43]

Throughout his career, then, Böckenförde distinguished between the readership he addressed in his persona as a Catholic and the readership he addressed as a legal scholar, choosing for each audience the publishers and outlets that would ensure the best possible positioning and dissemination of his arguments.

[38] *Kirchlicher Auftrag und politische Entscheidung* (Freiburg: Rombach (Herder Verlag), 1973); and *Staat, Gesellschaft, Freiheit. Studien zur Staatstheorie und zum Verfassungsrecht* (Frankfurt: Suhrkamp, 1976).

[39] *Schriften zu Staat, Gesellschaft, Kirche. Vol. 1: Der deutsche Katholizismus im Jahre 1933. Kirche und demokratisches Ethos* (Freiburg: Herder, 1988); *Vol. 2: Kirchlicher Auftrag und politisches Handeln. Analyse und Orientierungen* (Freiburg: Herder, 1989); *Vol. 3: Religionsfreiheit. Die Kirche in der modernen Welt* (Freiburg: Herder, 1990).

[40] *Recht, Staat, Freiheit. Studien zur Rechtsphilosophie, Staatstheorie und Verfassungsgeschichte* (Frankfurt: Suhrkamp, 1991). *Staat, Verfassung, Demokratie. Studien zur Rechtsphilosophie, Staatstheorie und Verfassungsgeschichte* (Frankfurt: Suhrkamp, 1991).

[41] *Kirche und christlicher Glaube in den Herausforderungen der Zeit. Beiträge der politisch-theologischen Verfassungsgeschichte 1957–2002* (Münster: LIT Verlag, 2004), with a revised and expanded edition published in 2007.

[42] *Staat, Nation, Europa. Studien zur Staatslehre, Verfassungstheorie und Rechtsphilosophie* (Frankfurt: Suhrkamp, 1999).

[43] *Wissenschaft, Politik, Verfassungsgericht. Aufsätze von Ernst-Wolfgang Böckenförde. Biographisches Interview von Dieter Gosewinkel* (Berlin: Suhrkamp, 2011).

Taking a longitudinal view, Böckenförde's academic work can be organized roughly into seven broad phases, each with different thematic foci, and establishing different components of his later reputation. There are certainly cross-cutting themes and articles that thematically fall into a different phase, not least because writing activity is also a function of publication requests. Nevertheless, a periodization does emerge, partly also coinciding with his changing institutional affiliations. In Section IV below, the first phase will be elaborated in greater detail, as nearly all the major elements in his thinking on the relationship between religion, law, and democracy, and on Catholicism take form in this phase.[44]

1. *On the Church's need for internal reform*

The first phase lasted from about 1956 to 1965. Böckenförde completed his doctorate in law in 1956, his doctorate in history in 1960, and his habilitation in 1964. Also in 1964, he was appointed full professor of public law at the University of Heidelberg where he stayed until 1969.

Strikingly, his published essays in this first phase do not connect directly to his doctoral theses or his habilitation. Instead, they deal predominantly with the Catholic Church and establish him as an inner-Catholic critic. The phase begins with his article on 'The Ethos of Modern Democracy and the Church' published in 1957 and ends with his commentary on the Declaration of Religious Freedom, promulgated at the conclusion of the Second Vatican Council in 1965. Years later, Böckenförde reflected on the fact that the writings in this period were perceived by the Church as those of a dissenter, as even antagonistic to the Church, when he had intended to write as a constructive voice for reform from within.[45] In the course of the 1970s, this perception changed and the scepticism of his work gave way to appreciation, culminating in the late 1990s and 2000s to his being awarded two honorary doctorates in Catholic theology. He also noted years later that his writings in favour of personal freedom and against Catholic natural law as a basis for state law earned him the reputation in Church circles of being a 'lefty', a label to which he objected as reductionist.[46]

The major outlines of his views on the Catholic Church's needs for internal reform, his vision for its role in a democratic state, and his general model of democratic religion–state relations all took form during this period and were never fundamentally altered in his later work. Particular aspects would be deepened, such as in his writings on the necessary distinction between state and society in the early 1970s and the undesirability for societal institutions to aspire

[44] Many of his writings from the fifth phase were included in volume I of this edition, as well as three from the sixth phase, and two each from the third and fourth.

[45] See 'On the Authority of Papal Encyclicals: The Example of Pronouncements on Religious Freedom', published in English as Chapter XII in this volume.

[46] See Böckenförde (note 17), pp. 396f.

to state-like institutional forms (as some in the 'total democratization' movement of the 1970s demanded). He later elaborated in greater detail on the role religions can exercise in democracy, but the basis for his work on religion–state relations was laid in this first phase.

2. *Historicizing the law and the state*

The second phase lasted from about 1965 to 1970. It comprised his appointment at the University of Heidelberg (1965–1969), where in 1967/1968 he also served as dean of the law faculty. During this phase, most of Böckenförde's articles were concerned with the development of the concepts of law, rule of law, and constitutionalism from the nineteenth into the twentieth century. Nearly all of the essays written in this period are of a historical-conceptual nature.

In this period, Böckenförde returned to his two PhD dissertations, particularly the one in history, which he now complemented with several shorter studies of how legal concepts evolved and interacted with social reality in the nineteenth century. In the 1965 article 'The School of Historical Jurisprudence and the Problem of the Historicity of Law', written for the Festschrift for Joachim Ritter, Böckenförde highlighted the fact that concepts of law were always embedded in a particular context and thus in a particular legal culture. In doing so, however, he rejected the approach of the School of Historical Jurisprudence for reducing history to a space within which a natural development of an ethnic or national 'spirit' [*Volksgeist*] unfolds. He connected this 'organic' notion of legal development with the organic state theories that he criticized already in his 1961 article on the Catholic Church and the rise of the Nazis. His belief that law could not function unless supported by an underlying ethos willing to implement such law—a qualitatively different approach to the foundations of law—was then further developed in his article 'The Concept of Law in its Historical Evolution. Outline of a Problem' of 1968.[47] These essays shifted focus away from a 'national spirit' allegedly to be found in law to the pluralistic views and political conflicts that developed law. Böckenförde developed these ideas further in his studies of nineteenth-century constitutionalism as an unstable balance of power between assembly and monarch, in his essays 'The German Type of Constitutional Monarchy in the Nineteenth Century' of 1967, and 'Constitutional Problems and Constitutional Development of the Nineteenth Century' of 1971.[48] Into this

[47] 'Die Historische Rechtsschule und das Problem der Geschichtlichkeit des Rechts', in Ernst-Wolfgang Böckenförde and Joachim Ritter (eds.), *Collegium Philosophicum. Studien. Joachim Ritter zum 60. Geburtstag* (Basel: Schwabe, 1965), pp. 9–36, published in English as 'The School of Historical Jurisprudence and the Problem of the Historicity of Law' in Ernst-Wolfgang Böckenförde, State, *Society and Liberty: Studies in Political Theory and Constitutional Law* (New York: Berg Publishers, 1991), pp. 1–25; 'Der Rechtsbegriff in seiner geschichtlichen Entwicklung. Aufriß eines Problems', *Archiv für Begriffsgeschichte* 12 (1968), pp. 145–165.

[48] 'Der deutsche Typ der konstitutionellen Monarchie im 19. Jahrhundert', in Werner Conze (ed.), *Beiträge zur deutschen und belgischen Verfassungsgeschichte im 19. Jahrhundert* (Stuttgart: Klett, 1967), pp. 70–92, published in English as 'The German Type of Constitutional Monarchy in the Nineteenth Century' in Ernst-Wolfgang Böckenförde (ed.), *State, Society and Liberty: Studies in Political Theory and Constitutional Law* (New York: Berg

period also fall his articles 'The Rise of the State as a Process of Secularization', first given as a talk in October 1964 and then published in the Festschrift for Ernst Forsthoff in 1967; and 'The Origin and Development of the Concept of the *Rechtsstaat*' published in the Festschrift for the Social Democratic politician and intellectual Adolf Arndt in 1969, which lays out the development of the concept of the Rechtsstaat since Kant. Finally, in October 1969 he gave his trendsetting talk on 'The Fundamental Right of Freedom of Conscience', published the following year.[49] The article, one of the most important of his career, contains three themes he would later develop more fully, all of which have become hallmarks of his thought.[50]

As Reinhard Mehring has commented, the disposition in favour of liberal democracy that Böckenförde had outlined and proposed to Catholics in his early writings from 1957 to 1965 was now becoming embedded in an emerging historical-constitutional theory.[51] In this phase, Böckenförde intellectually took up Carl Schmitt, and engages with the latter's work, but from a very different normative starting point than Schmitt.[52] Since 1957 Böckenförde had developed a strong commitment to liberal democracy, partly fed by his reading of the social democratic jurist Hermann Heller, the sociologist and economist Lorenz von Stein, and his exchanges with Franz Schnabel, his doctoral advisor in history, also a social democrat. Unlike Schmitt, Böckenförde had come to embrace modernity for its achievements in bringing about the state as a structure capable of securing inner and outer peace (the state as a *Friedenseinheit*, a peace-providing framework). As he wrote in his 1964 Ebrach talk, there was no way back beyond the Declaration of the Rights of Man of 1789. He called on the Catholic Church to come to terms with the breakthroughs of constitutionalism, individual rights, and the secular nature of the modern state, and to relinquish any absolute claims on the design of the public order. And he held the Catholic Church to account for helping the Nazi seizure of power in 1933. By the time Böckenförde set out to work on Schmittian themes in constitutional and legal theory, he had become a committed democrat, calling on Catholics to support democracy with all their resources by prioritizing the public good over particular Catholic pursuits.

Publishers, 1991), pp. 87–114; 'Verfassungsprobleme und Verfassungsbewegung des 19. Jahrhunderts. Ein Überblick', in *Juristische Schulung* (1971), pp. 560–566, published in English as 'Constitutional Problems and Constitutional Development of the Nineteenth Century' in Ernst-Wolfgang Böckenförde (ed.), *State, Society and Liberty: Studies in Political Theory and Constitutional Law* (Berg Publishers, 1991), pp. 71–86.

49 'Die Entstehung des Staates als Vorgang der Säkularisation', in Buve (note 26), pp. 75–94 published in English as Chapter V in this volume; Böckenförde 1969 (note 10); 'Das Grundrecht der Gewissensfreiheit', *Veröffentlichungen der Vereinigung der Deutschen Staatsrechtslehrer* 28 (1970), pp. 33–88, published in English as Chapter VI in this volume.

50 See Mirjam Künkler and Tine Stein, 'Böckenförde on the Secular State and Secular Law' in this volume.

51 Reinhard Mehring, 'Von der diktatorischen "Maßnahme" zur liberalen Freiheit. Ernst-Wolfgang Böckenfördes dogmatischer Durchbruch in Heidelberg', *Juristen Zeitung* 60 (2015), pp. 860–865.

52 In more detail, Mirjam Künkler and Tine Stein, 'Carl Schmitt in Ernst-Wolfgang Böckenförde's Work: Carrying Weimar constitutional theory into the Bonn Republic', *Constellations: An International Journal of Critical and Democratic Theory* 25(2) (2018), pp. 225–241.

Inspired no doubt by his regular visits to Catholic student societies in the German Democratic Republic (GDR), a second thematic focus emerged during this period, one spawned by contemporaneous politics: the consolidation of the partition of Germany and its consequences in domestic and international law. In 1967, Böckenförde published his first monograph since his 1964 habilitation: a short treatise on the concept of law in communism (*Die Rechtsauffassung im kommunistischen Staat*), where he, after dissecting the meaning of constitutional concepts of the GDR, analysed without reservation the political functionalization of law and its complete subordination to the larger political goals of regime consolidation and survival.[53] In the book Böckenförde also took up the question of the 'German people' as a legal concept, in particular whether there was continuity in the legal identity between the German Reich and Federal Republic of Germany, and whether the Federal Republic of Germany exclusively represented all of Germany and all Germans in international law, a view promoted as the 'identity theory'.[54] Here and in a separate article, Böckenförde vehemently rejected the exclusive identity theory, and pleaded for a recognition of the GDR by West Germany (as Chancellor Brandt did shortly later in 1969).[55] Marking his break with an older, conservative tradition, Böckenförde published his rejection of the identity theory, a theory Carl Schmitt supported, in the Festschrift for Schmitt in 1968 ('The division of Germany and German citizenship').[56]

It is also in this period that Böckenförde became a member of the Social Democratic Party (SPD). Considering his deep anchoring in Catholicism, it was unlikely that Böckenförde would find his way to the SPD, a party that, due to its secularist position and as a political arm of the left-wing workers' movement, counted few Catholics in its ranks in the 1950s. But the SPD undertook a remarkable transformation in 1959 when at its party convention in Bad Godesberg it shed its identity as a 'Weltanschauungspartei', a party with a comprehensive doctrine. This opened the way, Böckenförde reminisced later, to reconcile his Catholic faith with membership in the party.[57] In 1965, not yet a member, he was

[53] *Die Rechtsauffassung im kommunistischen Staat*, 3rd ed. (Munich: Kösel, 1968, first published 1967).

[54] Consequential with regard to the identity theory was also the 1968 'memorandum on Poland' published by the 'Bensberger Kreis', a group of Catholics, among them Böckenförde, who argued that a lasting European peace arrangement could not be achieved without a reconciliation between (West) Germany and Poland and that Germany should give up on all territorial claims towards Poland. The memorandum played an important role in preparing the 'Ostpolitik' of Chancellor Willy Brandt, a groundbreaking reorientation in West German foreign policy towards rapprochement with the Eastern bloc. The official position of West Germany under Brandt became that of a partial legal identity of the Federal Republic with the German Reich, a position Böckenförde supported.

[55] As Mehring also reminds his readers, while on the Federal Constitutional Court, Böckenförde participated in the *Teso* Decision of October 1987, which guaranteed one citizenship of all of Germany and endowed the Federal Republic with the legitimacy to protect GDR citizens in third countries. This became relevant when GDR citizens fled to West German embassies in Hungary, Poland, and Czechoslovakia in the summer of 1989 just before the Berlin wall came down. See Mehring (note 51).

[56] 'Die Teilung Deutschlands und die deutsche Staatsangehörigkeit', in Hans Barion et al. (eds.), *Epirrhosis. Festgabe für Carl Schmitt zum 80. Geburtstag. Vol. 2* (Berlin: Duncker & Humblot, 1968), pp. 423–463.

[57] Böckenförde mentions how the persuasive argumentation of jurist Adolf Arndt, one of the driving forces behind the SPD's decision to abandon its ideological character, played a role in convincing Böckenförde to join the party. See Böckenförde (note 17), p. 408f.

invited to participate in the party's first congress on legal politics in Heidelberg, and two years after joining the party in 1967 became a member of its committee on legal policies, occasionally also advising the SPD party executive.[58]

3. The social Liberal

Böckenförde's discussion of the concept of law in communism can be seen as the bridge leading over to the third phase of his intellectual development, which was dedicated to writings on the relationship between rule of law and economic inequality. It lasted from about 1971 to 1975 and coincided with his time as professor at the University of Bielefeld from 1969 to 1976. In contrast to the second phase in which Böckenförde produced groundbreaking historically oriented articles, the early 1970s were characterized by dogmatic writings on the relationship of the rule of law to the social state, and the interpretation of fundamental rights in the Basic Law that follows from this.

Among the most important writings from this period is his 'The Significance of the Distinction between State and Society in the Democratic Welfare State of Today' of 1972.[59] In a way, Böckenförde expanded on the historical article 'Lorenz von Stein as Theorist of the Movement of State and Society towards the Welfare State', and laid out the dogmatic implications of the differentiation between state and society,[60] relying extensively also on Joachim Ritter's work.[61] For some theorists, like Rudolf Smend and his later followers in the Federal Republic (many of them Social Democrats), the modern world involved the end of a clear distinction between state and society as both were part of a process of 'integrating' a political community. Against Smend's integration theory, Böckenförde insisted, referencing Hermann Heller, that state and society must be differentiated conceptually lest the grounds were laid for a possible encroachment of the state into societal spheres that could in the final analysis escalate into a new totalitarianism.[62] This distinction allowed both the democratic state

[58] See Böckenförde (note 17), pp. 409f.

[59] Böckenförde extended this the following year to a short monograph titled *Die verfassungstheoretische Unterscheidung von Staat und Gesellschaft als Bedingung der individuellen Freiheit* (Opladen: Westdeutscher Verlag, 1973).

[60] 'Lorenz von Stein als Theoretiker der Bewegung von Staat und Gesellschaft zum Sozialstaat', in Historisches Seminar der Universität Hamburg (ed.), *Alteuropa und die moderne Gesellschaft. Festschrift für Otto Brunner* (Göttingen: Vandenhoeck & Ruprecht, 1963), pp. 248–277, published in English as 'Lorenz von Stein as Theorist of the Movement of State and Society towards the Welfare State', in his *State, Society, Liberty* (New York: Berg Publishers, 1991), pp. 115–145.

[61] Compare Joachim Ritter, *Hegel und die Französische Revolution* (Köln-Opladen: Westdeutscher Verlag, 1957).

[62] Böckenförde pointed out that the primary instruments of the rule of law state to ensure the well-being of all citizens and preclude the escalation of economic inequality were taxation and the social responsibility that comes with property. See Joachim Wieland, 'Zum Sozialstaatsprinzip bei Ernst-Wolfgang Böckenförde', *VerfassungsBlog*, 8 May 2019, https://verfassungsblog.de/zum-sozialstaatsprinzip-bei-ernst-wolfgang-boeckenfoerde/, DOI: https://doi.org/10.17176/20190517-144018-0. In Germany, the two relevant taxes were property tax and inheritance tax, of which the state did not make sufficient use, however. Instead, it had over time drastically increased the value added tax which disproportionately burdens the consumption of the less

and society to flourish, as in a liberal order both relied on one another: the legal order, and the state more generally, could not survive unless supported by society, and the flourishing of society in turn required rights and liberties that were secured by state institutions.

Lorenz von Stein was also the key reference point in the articles he published on the public use of private property and Article 14 Section 2 of the Basic Law, according to which 'property entails obligations. Its use shall also serve the public good.' In 'Property, the Social Binding of Property, Expropriation,' an exposition of constitutional law from 1972,[63] Böckenförde reminded municipalities that their organization of land must be oriented towards the public good. Regarding the issue of expropriation, he demonstrated in detail that the Parlamentarischer Rat when drafting Article 14 Section 3 of the Basic Law[64] had intended not to require a full compensation for the market value, but to take into account also the services the state provided through the provision of infrastructure and social insurances. In several writings, Böckenförde emphasized that the guarantee of private property in the Basic Law had to be understood as balancing between liberal guarantees and demands emanating from societal or public needs.[65] Implicitly taking a position in the Forsthoff–Abendroth Controversy of the 1950s, in which Ernst Forsthoff argued that the Basic Law prioritized the rule of law, while Wolfgang Abendroth[66] argued that it prioritized a social state, Böckenförde wrote that the Basic Law imposed a 'social state as a binding constitutional principle on par with that of the *Rechtsstaat*'.[67] Going beyond Abendroth, Böckenförde saw the social state not only emanating as a necessary state function from Article 20 Section 1, but even more so from Article 1 with the principle of human dignity, which the state not only had to respect but also protect. The link for Böckenförde was once again freedom:

well-off strata in society and thus cannot serve the purpose of redistribution. Additionally, the EU member states' competition regarding business tax (which the Court of Justice of the European Union (EUCJ) supports with its basic freedom jurisprudence) has led to lower levels of business taxes collected across the board, thus further depriving states of the capability to make the kind of public sector investments that would lessen the impact of economic inequality.

[63] Böckenförde (note 8). This article was also included in his 1976 Suhrkamp compilation but unfortunately the only article not included when the collection was published in English in 1991.

[64] Article 14 Section 3 states: 'expropriation shall only be permissible for the public good. It may only be ordered by or pursuant to a law that determines the nature and extent of compensation. Such compensation shall be determined by establishing an equitable balance between the public interest and the interests of those affected. In case of dispute concerning the amount of compensation, recourse may be had to the ordinary courts'.

[65] 'Wider die Bauland-Spekulation. Vorschläge zu einer Reform des Bodennutzungsrechts', *Die Zeit* 19 (12 May 1972), p. 54.

[66] The controversy crystallized in an exchange between Schmitt's disciple Ernst Forsthoff and Marxist legal scholar Wolfgang Abendroth (under whose guidance Jürgen Habermas later wrote his habilitation). For a summary of the controversy, see Michael Stolleis, *Geschichte des öffentlichen Rechts in Deutschland*, vol. IV (Munich: C.H. Beck, 2011), pp. 281f.

[67] Böckenförde (note 9).

> The state is now bound to intervene in the 'free' processes of society, to continuously modify the social inequality to which society is forever giving rise, and even to exercise (overall) control over the development and affluence of society as the (social) foundation of liberty for all. The object of this is not, of course, to override the liberty of the individual and of free society, but to underpin both freedoms socially in the light of economic and social circumstances and trends—on the basis, that is to say, of the state's mission to support and guarantee the liberty of the individual and a free society.[68]

Böckenförde believed that Lorenz von Stein had analysed the internally degenerative dynamics of capitalism like few others and demonstrated that, if left to its own, capitalism through its necessary creation of inequality destroyed democracy in the long term, unless regulated by the state and rechannelled into a social market economy. Böckenförde also suggested that while Karl Marx' proposals to solve this predicament were unacceptable, his analysis was nevertheless accurate (and largely congruent with von Stein's).[69]

When asked in 2010 to reflect on his successes and failures, Böckenförde replied that he regarded his lack of success in changing the discourse around the *Rechtsstaat-Sozialstaat* debate as his greatest failure. The view that the enjoyment of individuals' rights depends on certain material conditions being met first, and that the creation of these conditions falls into the competencies of the state, at least the German state based on Article 14 of the Basic Law, had not sufficiently taken hold, he regretted.[70]

Between 1973 and 1976 he wrote several articles that stressed how the social state was 'a binding constitutional principle on a par with that of the *Rechtsstaat*'. He connected this idea with a theory of fundamental rights that required action by the state.[71] A concept of the state according to which fundamental rights restrict state action, he wrote, is at the same time constrained by a concept of the state according to which normative principles included in the constitution entail the duty to provide social services. 'Freedom,' Böckenförde observed, 'necessarily means the acceptance of social inequality.' However, if liberty is to be guaranteed for all, 'specific societal and legal framework conditions (including those of an institutional and societal-structural nature)' are required and '(t)he most important of these framework conditions is the *constant relativization of societal inequality* that arises continually from the exercise of

[68] Böckenförde (note 9). Extract from Chapter XI in volume I of this edition, p. 288.

[69] Regarding Böckenförde's reading of Marx, and the extent to which Böckenförde's assessment of the social state differed from Forsthoff's, see Peter C. Caldwell, 'Capitalism's Threat to Political Stability and Social Policy as a Solution: Reflections on Ernst-Wolfgang Böckenförde's Political Theory of the Welfare State' in Mirjam Künkler and Tine Stein (eds.), *Understanding Böckenförde* (forthcoming).

[70] Böckenförde (note 17), p. 485. See here Chapter XVI, p. 393.

[71] 'Die Methoden der Verfassungsinterpretation – Bestandsaufnahme und Kritik', *Neue Juristische Wochenschrift* 29(46) (1976), pp. 2089–2099; 'Die politische Funktion wirtschaftlich-sozialer Verbände und Interessenträger in der sozialstaatlichen Demokratie. Ein Beitrag zum Problem der "Regierbarkeit"', *Der Staat* 15 (1976), pp. 457–483.

liberty'.[72] Although it is not the state's responsibility to equalize individual differences in human capacities and dispositions, there is solid normative ground, Böckenförde suggested, for the argument that the state had to moderate the social inequality arising from these differences.

The articles from the third phase show Böckenförde as a truly 'social–liberal' political thinker, since he did not relinquish liberty for equality or vice versa, but argued for a strong state that was simultaneously responsible for and capable of guaranteeing individual liberty while also compensating for social and economic inequality.

4. *The political Liberal*

The fourth phase of Böckenförde's work lasted from about 1976, when Böckenförde joined the University of Freiburg, to 1981 and was defined by his work on state theory and militant democracy. He left the imperative of the social state to one side[73] and dedicated himself to a new body of questions bearing on the rule of law, namely what the core purpose of the state is and how the democratic state ought to deal with those citizens who reject it. These questions emanated from the political circumstances of the time, specifically the *Grundwertedebatte* (debate on core values)[74] and the rise of leftist militant groups, at the forefront the Red Army Faction (RAF).

Partly as a response to the reforms in family law and criminal law undertaken during the chancellorship of Willy Brandt (regarding, inter alia, divorce, abortion, and homosexuality), certain commentators on the right diagnosed an erosion of values (*Werteverfall*) in West German society. When Helmut Schmidt became chancellor in 1974, the Catholic bishops in particular called on Schmidt to show 'moral leadership' and re-orient the state's purposes towards conveying a unitary disposition (de facto of what they considered to be Christian values) to the public. Böckenförde had been consulted by the chancellor on an appropriate response to the Catholic Church and thus Böckenförde, together with the Jesuit scholar Oswald von Nell-Breuning, came to draft the chancellor's core speech on

[72] Freiheitssicherung gegenüber gesellschaftlicher Macht', in Diether Posser and Rudolf Wassermann (eds.), *Freiheit in der sozialen Demokratie. 4. Rechtspolitischer Kongreß der SPD vom 6. bis 8.6.1975 in Düsseldorf. Dokumentation* (Karlsruhe: C. F. Müller, 1975), pp. 69–76, published in English as 'Protection of Liberty against Societal Power: Outline of a Problem', Chapter XII in volume I of this edition, p. 294. Emphasis in original.

[73] Hermann-Josef Große Kracht speaks in this context even of '*abgebrochene Aufbrüche*', of aborted departures. See his 'Freiheitsrechtliche Kapitalismuskritik und der Etatismus der sozialen Demokratie. Ernst-Wolfgang Böckenförde als Theoretiker des Sozialstaates im Kontext konservativen Staatsrechts, sozialdemokratischer Politik und katholischer Soziallehre', in Hermann-Josef Große Kracht and Klaus Große Kracht (eds.), *Religion—Recht—Republik. Studien zu Ernst-Wolfgang Böckenförde* (Paderborn: Schöningh, 2014), pp. 91–120, here p. 103.

[74] The *Grundwertedebatte* took place in the context of debates over legal reform in particular of abortion and divorce, but encompassed a far broader field of issues, all revolving around the core question: to what extent should the state provide for a shared ethos in society, to what extent should its actions and policies aim to represent a certain worldview?

the matter, titled 'Ethos and Law in State and Society' (1976).[75] In it, Chancellor Schmidt rejected the idea that the state could, or should, beyond enforcing the constitution, impose certain values from above. The state needed to be neutral with regard to worldviews, he emphasized, and value debates should take place within society. The speech caused much controversy, as conservatives accused the chancellor of being too reserved, and as indirectly contributing to the public erosion of values.

Böckenförde took up the question of the ethical state again in 1978, when he asked whether the core functions of the state ought to go beyond providing for security and liberty.[76] While he rejected the Aristotelian expectation that the public order must promote the good life (eudaemonia), he did argue that the state ought to create conditions in which citizens have the opportunity for self-realization, should they wish to pursue it. But the state could not identify with particular worldviews without violating the very liberalism on which it was founded. 'Against the inappropriate attempt to seek the realization of intellectual and moral content through the state in the demand for a uniform attitude, one should recall that it was part of the intellectual-moral substance of the modern state that it dispensed with making a uniform political disposition, a uniform faith, or a uniform ideology its obligatory foundation—and in this very way inscribing the subjectivity and distinctiveness of individuals into its law.'[77] Along similar lines, he published an essay in the *Frankfurter Allgemeine Zeitung* a few months later directed at the 'Radicals Decree',[78] in which he insisted that a truly liberal state could only prosecute citizens for violations of the law, but not for their political inclinations and sympathies.[79] This implied that a liberal state could not demand from its citizens loyalty and fidelity of political conviction,

[75] 'Ethos und Recht in Staat und Gesellschaft', speech given by German Chancellor Helmut Schmidt at the Catholic Academy on 23 May 1976. Böckenförde also drafted the Welcome Address of the Chancellor at the Biennial Catholics Day in 1982.

[76] See *Der Staat als sittlicher Staat* (Berlin: Duncker & Humblot, 1978), published in English as Chapter III of volume I of this edition. He supplemented the article with other writings on his state theory during this period: 'Der vernünftige Staat – Aufgaben und Grenzen,', *Deutsches Allgemeines Sonntagsblatt* 20, (14 May 1978), p. 10; 'Der Staat als Organismus. Zur staatstheoretischen Diskussion in der Vormärzzeit,', *Neue Zürcher Zeitung*, 16/17 December 1978, p. 61, later expanded as 'Der Staat als Organismus. Zur staatstheoretisch-verfassungspolitischen Diskussion im frühen Konstitutionalismus,' in Böckenförde (note 40), pp. 263–272; and Böckenförde (note 27).

[77] Chapter III of volume I of this edition, p. 101.

[78] The 'Radicals Decree' (*Radikalenerlass*), issued by Chancellor Willy Brandt in 1972, made it impossible for members and former members of the Communist Party and other political parties judged to be anti-constitutional to become public servants. This affected professions across all social milieux, from university professors and schoolteachers to caretakers in public buildings and bus drivers. The discriminatory regulations remained in place until ten to fifteen years later when several federal states (*Bundesländer*) consecutively loosened the impact of the secret service pre-employment screenings. It was in this context that German intellectuals increasingly feared that the over-emphasis on security had done irreparable damage to the country's once liberal democracy. The decree became a topic at the meeting of the SPD party executive the day after Böckenförde's 1978 speech, but this apparently did not change party policy at that time. See Böckenförde (note 17), p. 429.

[79] 'Verhaltensgewähr oder Gesinnungstreue? Sicherung der freiheitlichen Demokratie in den Formen des Rechtsstaates', *Frankfurter Allgemeine Zeitung* (8 December 1978), pp. 9–10. Böckenförde elaborated

and, to stay true to its liberalism, had to tolerate even those rejecting the liberal democratic order.

Between 1978 and 1981, Böckenförde published a series of articles debating appropriate state responses to the RAF and other violent groups that threatened the state order at the time. State responses were governed by the 1968 Emergency Acts, a series of statutes approved in a heated debate just a decade before. These acts, he argued, actually posed a greater threat to the rule of law. Instead, he proposed anchoring a state of emergency in the Basic Law;[80] constitutional law, as opposed to mere statutory law, should determine the conditions under which emergency action was permissible. In 'The Repressed State of Emergency' (Chapter IV in volume I of this edition) Böckenförde laid out how the Emergency Acts had given rise to questionable practices on the part of the security services (installing eavesdropping devices that violated the confidentiality of attorney–client privileges during the meetings between RAF prisoners and their lawyers, and wiretapping of the private apartment of a nuclear physicist under suspicion of collaborating with terrorists). He expounded why a constitutional provision for a tightly regulated state of emergency would be less rights-eroding than the contemporaneous Emergency Acts, which he suggested went further in providing a blanket authorization to state practices than even the Enabling Act of 1933, which had granted Hitler almost unlimited power. Böckenförde argued in favour of a constitutional amendment that would provide for the possibility of a declared state of emergency, and in 1981 he published a blueprint of such clauses.[81] His position did not prevail, partly because many still viewed the emergency powers embodied in Article 48 of the Weimar Constitution as having paved the way for the ascendance of the Nazi regime while preserving constitutional continuity.[82]

The articles written in this phase, especially those on the state of emergency, the radicals decree and on the rights of those citizens opposing liberal democracy, manifest Böckenförde's strongest stances in political liberalism. It is here that he writes 'The order of freedom must set itself apart from the order of unfreedom also—and especially—by the methods of its defense'[83] and in the

on his critique of the Radicals Decree in Ernst-Wolfgang Böckenförde, 'Rechtsstaatliche politische Selbstverteidigung als Problem', in Friedrich-Ebert-Stiftung, *Extremisten und öffentlicher Dienst* (Baden-Baden, 1981), pp. 9–33.

[80] See Ernst-Wolfgang Böckenförde, 'Der verdrängte Ausnahmezustand', *Neue Juristische Wochenschrift* (1978), pp. 1881–1890), included as Chapter IV in volume I of this edition, pp. 108–132.

[81] Ernst-Wolfgang Böckenförde, 'Ausnahmerecht und demokratischer Rechtsstaat', in Hans-Jochen Vogel, Helmut Simon, and Adalbert Podlech (eds.), *Die Freiheit des Anderen. Festschrift für Martin Hirsch* (Baden-Baden: Nomos, 1981), pp. 259–272. For a counterargument, see Gertrude Lübbe-Wolff, 'Rechtsstaat und Ausnahmerecht. Zur Diskussion über die Reichweite des § 34 StGB und über die Notwendigkeit einer verfassungsrechtlichen Regelung des Ausnahmezustandes', *Zeitschrift für Parlamentsfragen* 11 (1980), pp. 110–125, and Böckenförde's rejoinder 'Rechtsstaat und Ausnahmerecht. Eine Erwiderung', *Zeitschrift für Parlamentsfragen* 4 (1980), pp. 591–595.

[82] Compare also Böckenförde (note 17), p. 428.

[83] 'The State as an Ethical State', Chapter III, in volume I of this edition, p. 100.

biographical interview with Dieter Gosewinkel, he notes 'it is important that the so-called enemies of freedom do not lose their rights. They must be restrained, but must not be placed outside the guarantee of freedom.'[84] Remarkably, none of these articles were adopted in his canonical collections (mentioned at the beginning of this Section III), even though Böckenförde considered 'The State as an Ethical State' and 'The Repressed State of Emergency' among his most important articles (both are included in volume I of this edition).[85] Partly as a result of their absence from the Suhrkamp compilations, it has only been recently that the political Liberal in Böckenförde's work has once again received more attention in Germany.

5. *Political theology and constitutional dogmatics*

Böckenförde published on questions of religion and the Church throughout his career, but in the early 1980s he again dedicated himself with more attention to specifically religious topics. He published on the political theology of John Paul II in 1980, on the Federal Constitutional Court decision regarding school prayer, and on Bishops' attempts to influence the electoral behaviour of believers.[86] He also published his widely cited articles on Carl Schmitt's political theology and the relation between state and religion in Hegel.[87] On these, see the introductions to Parts II and III of this volume.

In December 1983 Böckenförde was appointed judge in the second senate of the Federal Constitutional Court, where he continued to serve until the summer of 1996. While he refrained from other public engagements at this time, he continued to publish actively. His focus in this fifth phase became the constitution. While on the court, he published half a dozen widely cited articles on constitutionalism, many of which have been translated into several foreign languages. He also wrote his most elaborate work on democratic theory, 'Democracy as a Constitutional Principle', which built fundamentally on the article that started his career, 'The Ethos of Modern Democracy'.[88] Many

[84] See 'Biographical Interview', Chapter XVII in volume I of this edition, p. 386.

[85] Mirjam Künkler, 'Böckenförde and the State of Emergency' in Mirjam Künkler and Tine Stein (eds.), *Understanding Böckenförde* (forthcoming).

[86] 'Das neue politische Engagement der Kirche. Zur 'politischen Theologie' Johannes Pauls II', *Stimmen der Zeit* issue 4 (1980), pp. 219–234; 'Der "Wahlhirtenbrief" 1980. Eine Anfrage an die deutschen Bischöfe', (co-authored with Franz Böckle, Bernhard Stöckle and Hans F. Zacher) *Herder-Korrespondenz* 34(11) (1980), pp. 570–573; and 'Zum Ende des Schulgebetsstreits. Stellungnahme zum Beschluß des BVerfG vom 16.10.1978', *Die Öffentliche Verwaltung* 33 (1980), pp. 323–327.

[87] 'Politische Theorie und politische Theologie. Bemerkungen zu ihrem gegenseitigen Verhältnis', *Revue européenne des sciences sociales* 19(54/55) (1981), pp. 233–243. 'Bemerkungen zum Verhältnis von Staat und Religion bei Hegel', *Der Staat* 21 (1982), pp. 481–503.

[88] 'Demokratie als Verfassungsprinzip', in Josef Isensee and Paul Kirchhof (eds.), *Handbuch des Staatsrechts der Bundesrepublik Deutschland. Vol. 1 Grundlagen von Staat und Verfassung* (Heidelberg: C. F. Müller, 1987), pp. 887–952. See also 'Demokratische Willensbildung und Repräsentation', in Josef Isensee and Paul Kirchhof (eds.), *Handbuch des Staatsrechts der Bundesrepublik Deutschland. Vol. 2 Demokratische Willensbildung. Die Staatsorgane*

of the articles from this period are included in volume I of this edition and have been discussed in detail there.[89] Here three will be highlighted.

Among his most prominent from this period is his 1986 article on the 'Constituent Power of the People', which has been translated into seven languages.[90] It particularly reverberated in work on democratic theory and constitutional design. Building on Emmanuel Joseph Sieyès' distinction between *pouvoir constituant* and *pouvoirs constitués*, the core contribution of the article lay in Böckenförde's discussion of the relationship between the legitimacy of a constitution and the democratic motivations of those involved in the constitution-making process—what is sometimes referred to as the question of 'ownership' of the constitution by the people. Without the latter, Böckenförde suggested, no constitution, however well designed, will have much of a chance of being implemented. His Hegelian concern for the binding forces that 'hold' the state once again came to the fore here. '(N)o supra-positive law and no idea of political order becomes concretely effective unless a historical-political force appropriates them, presents them as its own beliefs and ideas, and acts on their behalf'. What is required of a *pouvoir constituant* is 'a living awareness of justice, efficacious ideas of order, and a formative ethico-political will ... in short, a 'spirit' that can and does take shape in institutions, regulations, and procedures. If that is lacking, even the best-justified postulates cannot bring about the validity of something that is not alive as a separate spirit in the people or the nation.'[91]

In 'Democracy as a Constitutional Principle', Böckenförde laid out his theory of democracy in the modern state. In the end, he argued, all political decisions must be traced back to the demos and must be legitimized by the democratic citizenry. This 'chain of legitimation' back to a popular decision might be long,

des Bundes (Heidelberg: C. F. Müller, 1987), pp. 29–48. The article has been translated into Italian, Korean, Portuguese, Spanish, and Arabic.

[89] For individual articles and their translations, see the following footnotes. Apart from those discussed, volume I of this edition includes from this fifth period also the following four articles: 'Geschichtliche Entwicklung und Bedeutungswandel der Verfassung', in Arno Buschmann et al. (eds.), *Festschrift für Rudolf Gmür zum 70. Geburtstag am 28.7.1983* (Bielefeld: Gieseking, 1983), pp. 7–19), included as Chapter VI ('The Historical Evolution and Changes in the Meaning of the Constitution'). The article was translated into Italian, Polish, Japanese, Korean, and English. Further, 'Der Begriff des Politischen als Schlüssel zum staatsrechtlichen Werk Carl Schmitts', in Helmut Quaritsch (ed.), *Complexio Oppositorum. Über Carl Schmitt. Vorträge und Diskussionsbeiträge des 28. Sonderseminars 1986 der Hochschule für Verwaltungswissenschaften Speyer* (Berlin: Duncker & Humblot, 1988), pp. 283–299, published as Chapter II ('The Concept of the Political: A Key to Understanding Carl Schmitt's Constitutional Theory'); 'Grundrechte als Grundsatznormen. Zur gegenwärtigen Lage der Grundrechtsdogmatik', *Der Staat* 1 (1990), pp. 1–31, published as Chapter X ('Fundamental Rights as Constitutional Principles: On the Current State of Interpreting Fundamental Rights'); and 'Begriff und Probleme des Verfassungsstaates', in Rudolf Morsey, Helmut Quaritsch, and Heinrich Siedentopf (eds.), *Staat, Politik, Verwaltung in Europa. Gedächtnisschrift für Roman Schnur* (Berlin: Duncker & Humblot, 1997), pp. 137–149, published as Chapter V ('The Concept and Problems of the Constitutional State').

[90] *Die verfassunggebende Gewalt des Volkes. Ein Grenzbegriff des Verfassungsrechts* (Frankfurt: Metzner, 1986), included as Chapter VII in volume I of this edition ('The Constituent Power of the People: A Liminal Concept of Constitutional Law'). The article was translated into Italian, French, Japanese, Korean, English, Spanish, and Portuguese.

[91] Chapter VII, 'Constituent Power of the People' in volume I of this edition, p. 184.

but must not be interrupted in a democracy. The article was translated into Italian, Spanish, Portuguese, Korean, and Arabic, and has been cited several times by the Federal Constitutional Court, inter alia on the suffrage of foreigners (BVerfGE 83, 37; 83; 60), on the laws regarding state organization (BVerfGE 93; 37; 107; 59), and it has shaped the court's overall approach to the EU and EU law (BVerfGE 89; 155; 123; 267).

Another key article of his was published a year later, on the 'Critique of the Value-Based Grounding of Law'.[92] Taking a position contrary to post-war West German constitutional jurisprudence, particularly the 1958 *Lüth* decision, according to which values of the Basic Law radiate into all other areas of law (including those governing relations between citizens, not only between citizen and state), Böckenförde warned '[t]he value-based conception of the constitution means a reach toward a new totality: the constitution is no longer limited to its traditional subject matter, [instead] its value-creating standardizations are universal and extend into all areas of social life. The constitution encompasses the whole of society and—as a structure and system of values—advances an absolute claim to validity, one that reaches into all areas of the law.'[93]

Böckenförde explained that the attempt to ground law in values was per se arational since there was no coherent and no non-ambivalent way of identifying meta principles with which values could be placed into hierarchies. Discursive mediation was impossible when values were appealed to, since appealing to values was nothing other than grasping intuitive sentiments about a priori facts of the ethical world. Modern societies were necessarily plural societies with disagreement over values and over what values should be prioritized. Since a rational method for introducing a hierarchical order of values was not in sight, legal norms with their general claim to validity could not be based on values. Separately, Böckenförde feared that a value-based jurisprudence opened the gate for the positivization of the subjective opinions of judges and legal scholars. Their views on the question of which values ought to be protected by the law and which values ground legal norms would then be ranked higher than others, which would ultimately result in nothing less than legal positivism by today's rating. If rights were to be seen as grounded in values, then the lack of a rational method for defining the superiority of one value over another would ultimately lead to decisions on competing rights based on wavering consensuses defined by those who prevail in societal value debates.[94] In sum, one can say that while Böckenförde laid the groundwork for his constitutional

[92] Chapter IX in volume I of this edition.

[93] See Chapter VI in volume I, 'The Historical Evolution and Changes in the Meaning of the Constitution', p. 167.

[94] 'Zur Kritik der Wertbegründung des Rechts. Überlegungen zu einem Kapitel "Rechtsphilosophie"', in Reinhard Löw (ed.), *OIKEIOSIS. Festschrift für Robert Spaemann* (Weinheim: VCH Verlagsgemeinschaft, 1987), pp. 1–21, published in English as 'Critique of the Value-Based Grounding of Law', Chapter IX in volume I of this edition.

theory in his historical works of the 1960s, his constitutional dogmatics were fully developed in the second half of the 1980s while he served on the Federal Constitutional Court.

6. *Europeanization and nationalism*

After 1990, Böckenförde turned his gaze to topics of Europeanization and nationalism.[95] This work tied in with his regular participation in talks taking place in the papal summer residence at Castelgandolfo (south of Rome), which were designed to facilitate exchanges on democracy and Europe's future among Catholics on both sides of the Iron Curtain. The talks were convened by Krzysztof Michalski, the spiritus rector of the Vienna-based Institute for Human Sciences (IWM).[96] Böckenförde took part seven times,[97] and it was to no small extent due to these personal meetings that his writings began to be translated extensively into Polish, his work falling onto fertile ground among proponents of the 'Open Church' in Poland, which called on Church officials to give up their siege mentality and enter into earnest discussions with others, including Jews.[98]

[95] Three essays on these topics are included in volume I: 'Staatsbürgerschaft und Nationalitätskonzept' in Böckenförde (note 42), pp. 59–67, included as Chapter XIV ('Citizenship and the Concept of Nationality'); *Welchen Weg geht Europa?* (Munich: Carl Friedrich von Siemens-Stiftung, 1997), included as Chapter XVI ('Which Path is Europe Taking?'); and 'Die Zukunft politischer Autonomie. Demokratie und Staatlichkeit im Zeichen von Globalisierung, Europäisierung und Individualisierung', in Martin Meyer and Georg Kohler (eds.), *Die Schweiz – für Europa? Über Kultur und Politik* (Munich: Carl Hanser Verlag, 1998), pp. 63–90, included as Chapter XV ('The Future of Political Autonomy: Democracy and Statehood in a Time of Globalization, Europeanization, and Individualization'). Other essays from this period are 'Nationen und Nationalstaaten. Die Ordnung Europas am Scheideweg', in Hilmar Hoffmann and Dieter Kramer (eds.), *Das verunsicherte Europa. Römerberggespräche Frankfurt 1992* (Frankfurt: Anton Hain, 1992), pp. 77–88; 'Die Nation – Identität in Differenz', in Krzysztof Michalski (ed.), *Identität im Wandel. Castelgandolfo-Gespräche. Vol. 6* (Stuttgart: Klett-Cotta, 1995), pp. 129–154; and 'Europa und die Türkei. Die europäische Union am Scheideweg?' *Forum Kommune* 23(1) supplement (2005), pp. X–XI, XIII–XX.

[96] Michalski built up a network of European intellectuals at the Vienna institute before and after the fall of the Berlin Wall in 1989, including the priest and philosophy professor Józef Tischner from Kraków, an important figure in Solidarnosc and a friend of Karol Wojtyla's, later Pope John Paul II. It was also at the IWM, on whose academic advisory board Böckenförde served for many years, that Böckenförde and Edward Shils led a series of Jewish–Christian exchanges, which culminated in their jointly edited volume *Jews and Christians in a Pluralistic World* (London: Weidenfeld & Nicolson, 1991).

[97] Böckenförde's lectures there included 'The Image of Man from the Perspective of Today's Legal Order' (1983), 'The Crisis of the Legal Order: The State of Emergency' (1985), 'The Social and Political Ideas of Order of the French Revolution' (1991), and 'The Nation – Identity in Difference' (1994). A participant reports from the experience: 'A federal constitutional judge of West German democracy held keynote speeches at the papal court on questions of the regulatory policy of future Europe: the image of man in the legal system, the concept of the nation, the regulatory ideas of the French Revolution and the state of emergency.' See Otto Kallscheuer, 'Folgenlose Lektüre? Zur Böckenförde-Rezeption in Polen und Italien', in Künkler and Stein (note 37), pp. 85–93, here p. 86.

[98] On the extensive reception of his work in Poland, see Joanna Byrska, 'Die Rezeption des politischen und konstitutionellen Denkens Ernst-Wolfgang Böckenfördes in Polen', in Künkler and Stein, ibid., pp. 69–84.

Böckenförde was a proponent of European integration, regarding it as desirable first and foremost from a political point of view as a peace process. But he formulated several cardinal warnings about the way the process was being conducted.[99] In retrospect, Böckenförde's warnings appeared almost prophetic. They chiefly concerned the issue of democracy internal to the EU, the weakness of European cultural policy, the tensions arising from discrepancies between European economic and fiscal policies, and the issue of diverging views between EU member states as to the ultimate purposes of integration.

Böckenförde defended the idea of a 'multi-goal Europe' at a time when even uttering the possibility of a 'multi-speed Europe' was highly unpopular among pro-European publics. Some saw in the idea an insult to the members who had just joined, others suspected in the phrase the hidden desire among the economically stronger countries to share only some privileges of EU membership with new candidates, but not all; in other words, to 'cherry pick'. But Böckenförde's reasoning was rather different. Those advocating an 'ever-closer union' (especially Germany and France at the time) would need to accept that other member states, notably Britain, might never wish to pursue the same political goals. Therefore, Böckenförde insisted, it did not help to simply aim at a 'multi-speed Europe'. One also needed to acknowledge the reality of multiple goals among EU member states. One should therefore open different EU treaty mechanisms to different audiences and drop the goal of an ever-closer union for all members. For example, he proposed that Turkey might eventually join the Euro group and thus the currency union, but stay out of the political union of the EU.[100] Britain on the other hand could be allowed to opt out of those mechanisms aiming at a closer political union, while remaining economically integrated.

Böckenförde also underlined the democracy-eroding forces emanating from the lack of synchronicity between the political integration and the economic integration following the Maastricht Treaty of 1992. While EU member states were less and less capable of regulating their internal markets (as this competency had shifted to the EU level), they remained nevertheless responsible for labour market policy and distributive social policy in the eyes of the national voter. A legitimacy deficit would arise: the member states would still be seen as responsible for the common good of their citizens, but national governments would no longer be sovereign to set up restraints for

[99] For a summary of Böckenförde's main positions regarding the European Union and the enlargement process, see Mirjam Künkler and Tine Stein, 'Ernst-Wolfgang Böckenförde, the European', *Verfassungsblog*, May 2019.

[100] See his four articles, 'Which Path is Europe Taking?' (1997) (note 95); The Future of Political Autonomy: Democracy and Statehood in a Time of Globalization, Europeanization, and Individualization (1998) (note 95); Ernst-Wolfgang Böckenförde, 'Conditions for European Solidarity', in Krzysztof Michalski (ed.), *What Holds Europe Together?* (Budapest: Central European University Press, 2005), pp. 30–41; and Ernst-Wolfgang Böckenförde, 'Nein zum Beitritt der Türkei', *Frankfurter Allgemeine Zeitung* (10 December 2004), p. 1.

the common market. The Euro crises and the political crises ensuing in their wake, especially in Greece, Portugal, and Italy, would prove Böckenförde's warnings true.

7. Constitutional courts, human dignity, and biotechnologies

After Böckenförde retired from the Federal Constitutional Court in Karlsruhe in 1996, he continued to publish productively for almost another twenty years. Whereas he had refrained from commenting on the court itself while in office, he now published several articles on constitutional court jurisprudence. He also took up his engagement as public intellectual again, writing and lecturing on a range of hotly debated issues, from bioethical questions, abortion, pre-implantation diagnosis and prenatal genetic testing in the light of human dignity, to the broad field of politics and religion.

On constitutional courts and their jurisdiction, Böckenförde pointed out that even though constitutional courts had been the rising stars of the post-war period, on a comparative scale constitutional adjudication still had 'far less backing within the legal system itself than regular adjudication. [Since it is] active at the level of the political system, it must make institutional provisions for the recognition of its decisions, and it is highly dependent on their acceptance.'[101] He explored in depth the tensions arising from the necessary lack of oversight of constitutional court judges and compared various models in place in different jurisdictions of recruitment and other mechanisms, such as term limits, to somewhat manage the risks of constitutional court judges overstepping their competencies. He also dedicated much space to discussing the relationship between the constituent power of the people on the one hand and the finality of constitutional court decisions on the other. In this context, Böckenförde remarked, the Polish system post-1990 offered a noteworthy model, where in the case of a constitutional court veto of legislation, the legislature had the power to override the veto by a supermajority, thus engaging in constitutional reform and acting as an ongoing constituent power. Whereas in the latter, the constitution is the expression of popular sovereignty, in most other cases the finality of constitutional court decisions is an expression of limits imposed on popular sovereignty.

Even more so than constitutional courts, the topic of human dignity in light of new biomedical developments became a focal point of Böckenförde's interests in the 2000s and 2010s. One of his articles became a cornerstone of

[101] 'Die Überlastung des Bundesverfassungsgerichts', *Zeitschrift für Rechtspolitik* 29 (1996), pp. 281–284; 'Zur Idee der Verfassungsgerichtsbarkeit im demokratischen Staat', *Justizblatt* 50(10) (3 July 1996; 'Verfassungsgerichtsbarkeit. Strukturfragen, Organisation, Legitimation', *Neue Juristische Wochenschrift* 52(1) (1999), pp. 9–17, published in volume I as Chapter VIII, 'Constitutional Jurisdiction: Structure, Organization, and Legitimation'.

the German bioethical debate, causing a heated exchange among legal scholars and politicians alike. In his essay provocatively titled 'Human Dignity was Inviolable', published in 2003 in the *Frankfurter Allgemeine Zeitung*,[102] Böckenförde criticized a new interpretation of Article 1 of the Basic Law that had been published in one of the leading constitutional commentaries, the 'Maunz-Dürig'. Here legal scholar Matthias Herdegen laid the ground for an understanding of human dignity as being very open to different interpretations, depending on the specific circumstances of the case such as the stage of prenatal development. Böckenförde regarded this opinion as not only shaking the constitutional foundation of the Basic Law but as entirely relativizing any concept of human dignity by effectively allowing humans to judge who is likely to live a life worth living. Accordingly, Böckenförde argued here and in several follow-up articles for a rather restrictive bioethical policy, including a prohibition on pre-implantation genetic diagnosis.[103]

Into this period also fall his articles on how the secular state can be theologically justified, the relationship between religion and the state in the face of great diversity in worldviews,[104] his reflections on what it meant to be a Catholic in the office of constitutional judge, and on the authority of papal encyclicals,[105] all of which are included in this volume.

Böckenförde also published two more monographs, the very substantial *History of the Philosophy of Law and the State from Antiquity to the Middle Ages* in 2002[106] and, returning to his own profession, *Of the Ethos of the Jurists* in 2010.[107]

[102] Ernst-Wolfgang Böckenförde 'Die Würde des Menschen war unantastbar', *Frankfurter Allgemeine Zeitung* (3 September 2003), pp. 33–35. See also the longer version 'Bleibt die Menschenwürde unantastbar?' *Blätter für deutsche und internationale Politik* 10 (2014), pp. 1216–1227, included in this volume as Chapter XV, 'Will Human Dignity Remain Inviolable?'

[103] Chapter XIV, 'Human Dignity as a Normative Principle: Fundamental Rights in the Bioethical Debate' [2003]. For one of his last articles regarding the prohibition of pre-implantation genetic diagnostic testing, see Ernst-Wolfgang Böckenförde, 'Einspruch im Namen der Menschenwürde', *Frankfurter Allgemeine Zeitung* (15 March 2011). Interestingly, at the height of the bioethical debate between 1999 and 2003, Jürgen Habermas made a related intervention, arguing that the normative self-understanding of humankind according to which humans are free and equal requires the idea that all humans, including unborn life, should be seen and treated as those persons they will eventually become. Jürgen Habermas, *Die Zukunft der menschlichen Natur. Auf dem Weg zu einer liberalen Eugenik?* (Frankfurt am Main: Suhrkamp, 2001).

[104] Chapter X, 'Reflections on a Theology of Modern Secular Law [1999]'; Chapter VIII, 'The Secularized State: Its Character, Justification, and Problems in the Twenty-First Century [2007]'.

[105] Chapter XI, 'A Christian in the Office of Constitutional Judge [1999]'; Chapter XII, 'On the Authority of Papal Encyclicals: the Example of Pronouncements on Religious Freedom [2006]'.

[106] *Geschichte der Rechts- und Staatsphilosophie. Antike und Mittelalter* (Tübingen: Mohr-Siebeck, 2002), published in Portuguese as *História da Filosofia do Direito e do Estado - Antiguidade e Idade Média*, trans Adriana Beckman Meirelles, (Porto Alegre: Sérgio Antonio Fabris Editor, 2012).

[107] Ernst-Wolfgang Böckenförde, *Vom Ethos der Juristen* (Berlin: Duncker & Humblot, 2010), 2nd ed. with corrections in 2011.

In 2005 Böckenförde received his last (of five) honorary doctorates. It was awarded by the Faculty of Catholic Theology of the University of Tübingen and Böckenförde used the occasion to address the question of the relationship between papal authority and the plurality of voices inside the Church. In his speech titled 'On the Authority of Papal Encyclicals: The Example of Pronouncements on Religious Freedom', Böckenförde showed that irrespective of their authority and authenticity, encyclicals have always been open to revision, and church dogma evolved in contradictory manner, even though the opposite has regularly been asserted within the Church. But Böckenförde noted with concern that the reformed code of canon law of 1983 places severe limitations on inner-Catholic discussion about doctrine, in that its reformed Article 752 has introduced 'the duty of obedience of the intellect and will' even to the non-infallible parts of the papal magisterium. (The code of 1917 had noted only 'the duty to avoid' all errors bordering on heresy.) Böckenförde commented that 'if this norm is taken seriously . . . a person's own contrary understanding is utterly irrelevant . . . every public questioning and criticism, also in the form of scholarly discussion, is ruled out'.[108] Not only (as Böckenförde pointed out) does this lead to a situation where canon law determines theology, and not theology canon law. It also risks to invalidate the officially upheld principle of freedom of conscience as the new point of departure of every position taken by the church in public debate. Furthermore, it ignores the communio structure of the Church and the fact that all authority relations are themselves dependent on the contextual relationships of the community of believers. Papal authority cannot free itself from this, lest it end up being perverted into an ecclesiological system of power. But as a way forward, Böckenförde pointed out that since the code of canon law is the product of the papal legislator and not the papal magisterium, it can in fact be criticized. Thus the self-inflicted loss of interpretive space by the papal legislator could at least be challenged.[109]

IV. ON THE CHURCH, ETHOS, AND THE SECULAR STATE

Section IV presents some of Böckenförde's key writings and positions as an inner-Catholic critic (1), as a theorist of the place of ethos in the public order (2), and as a thinker of 'open encompassing neutrality' between religion and state (3). Böckenförde coined the term 'open encompassing neutrality' in

[108] Chapter XII in this volume, 'On the Authority of Papal Encyclicals: The Example of Pronouncements on Religious Freedom [2006]', p. 303.

[109] Interestingly, in the speech Böckenförde also reminded his listeners of the theological concept of the *sensus fidelium* as a justification for internal criticism, highlighting its potential power long before Pope Francis introduced a theological commission on it. *Sensus fidelium* (sense of the faithful) is laid down in *Lumen Gentium* 12, which states: 'The entire body of the faithful, anointed as they are by the Holy One (1 John 2, 20.27) cannot err in matters of belief.' The status of *sensus fidelium* could enable, if not a reconciliation, then at least a dialogue between the magisterial authority and the plural voices within the Church. Böckenförde relied here on the analyses of his older brother Werner Böckenförde (1928–2003), a theologian and canon lawyer.

juxtaposition to distancing neutrality, to emphasise that a religiously neutral state need not impose a strict separation between religion and state, but may be based on an open or amicable separation of politics and religion that does not prioritize freedom from religion at the cost of freedom to religion.

1. *Böckenförde as an inner-Catholic critic*

Throughout his career, Böckenförde was concerned with both freedom and democracy and the Catholic Church's—*his* church's—relationship to both. His work from 1957-1965 challenged the Church's distanced relationship to democracy, and even further implicated parts of the Church in National Socialism. These early works contained sharp analyses of the Catholic Church and of its views on natural law. In his article 'The Ethos of Modern Democracy and the Church' (1957), he vehemently criticized the Catholic Church's stance on democracy and human rights and called on it to embrace the principles of religious freedom and secular authority as part of modernity.[110] In a second article, 'Natural Law against the Background of Today' (1958), he developed a comprehensive critique of the Church's adherence to natural law thinking, which, he suggested, had caused Catholics to mistake specifically Catholic interests with the public good as such.[111] In a third article, titled 'German Catholicism in 1933' (1961), he provided the first inquiry into the Church's calamitous relationship with the Nazi regime.[112] The article was one of the first works to be published in post-war West Germany that forced the Church to face the demons of the past and set in motion several research programmes on the topic, both inside and outside the Church. In a further article, 'Religious Freedom as a Mandate for Christians. A Jurist's Thoughts

[110] Ernst-Wolfgang Böckenförde, 'Das Ethos der modernen Demokratie und die Kirche', *Hochland* 50(1) (1957), pp. 4–19, included as Chapter I in this volume.

[111] Ernst-Wolfgang Böckenförde, 'Naturrecht auf dem Hintergrund des Heute', *Archiv für Rechts- und Sozialphilosophie* 44 (1958), 94–102. His critique was further expanded in an article co-authored with Robert Spaemann, 'Die Zerstörung der naturrechtlichen Kriegslehre. Erwiderung an P. Gustav Gundlach SJ', in: *Atomare Kampfmittel und christliche Ethik. Diskussionsbeiträge deutscher Katholiken* (Munich: Kösel, 1960), 161–196. Böckenförde and Spaemann reacted to the influential Catholic social theorist Gustav Gundlach who suggested that the idea of a nuclear war could be justified by Catholic just war theory if such a war was waged to protect a Catholic state. Böckenförde and Spaemann rejected this claim and suggested moreover that the contemporary NATO strategy of massive retaliation contradicted Christian teachings on just war. The ensuing discussion was of particular acuity as the nuclear armament of the Bundeswehr was being considered in the Bundestag at the time. The two young scholars elucidated that according to Catholic teachings, a Catholic soldier could not in good conscience execute any order given in connection with the deployment of nuclear weapons if deployed against a conventional attack or with the aim of deterrence. The exchange caused an uproar both inside the German Catholic Church and the German military establishment. Due to the careful argumentation of Böckenförde and Spaemann, however, Gundlach's position was ultimately no longer tenable and he himself ceased making the argument, though he never recanted it.

[112] Ernst-Wolfgang Böckenförde, 'German Catholicism in 1933', *CrossCurrents* 11 (1961), pp. 283–303, included in a new translation as Chapter II in this volume.

on the Discussions of the Second Vatican Council' (1964/1965),[113] Böckenförde pleaded for Catholics to accept a religiously neutral state, which would imply also that natural law be confined to the realm of the ethical and not be placed at the basis of state law.

As Böckenförde disclosed late in his life, he was dismayed to see that for many years the Catholic Church appeared to view him as a dissenter, even at times as an opponent, when what he sought to be was an engaged voice 'from within' for the sake of truth and reform.[114] All four of the mentioned articles were targeted at Catholic audiences, and two were published in a Catholic magazine (*Hochland*).[115] In 'The Ethos of Modern Democracy and the Church', published before Vatican II, Böckenförde outlined why Catholics should embrace the secular democratic state for the sake of their own spiritual well-being: indeed he argued that the secular democratic state was the *only* political regime in which it was possible to live a truly Catholic life out of free choice and conviction. While by the 1950s the Catholic Church appeared to have formally accepted the empirical reality that many believers lived in democracies that were ruled by majority decisions, the Catholic Church's official position was still that this majority principle could not apply in areas of particular concern to the Church, including family law (in particular, questions of marriage, birth control, sexuality) and education.

In 'Natural Law against the Background of Today', Böckenförde examined the disposition of Catholics to the common good in the late nineteenth and early twentieth centuries. In the aftermath of the *Kulturkampf* of the 1870s,[116] German Catholics had felt excluded from an increasingly liberal public sphere. Compared to other citizens (predominantly Protestant), they were viewed

[113] Ernst-Wolfgang Böckenförde, 'Religionsfreiheit als Aufgabe der Christen. Gedanken eines Juristen zu den Diskussionen auf dem Zweiten Vatikanischen Konzil', *Stimmen der Zeit* 90(9) (1964/65), pp. 199–212.

[114] My 'undertaking ... was initially accompanied more by criticism than approval – let me recall merely the medium-sized earthquake that my essay about German Catholicism in 1933 caused among the Catholic-ecclesiastical public. A change in the direction toward respect and in part – though at first still hesitant – approval came with the various contributions on religious freedom, the first of which was written during the debates of the Vatican Council ["Religionsfreiheit als Aufgabe der Christen", 1965], and those dealing with the political mandate of the Church [1969, 1973, 1980/84, 1983]. Eventually there were discussions as between equals, coupled with growing recognition by the discipline of theology.' See this volume, Chapter XII, p. 288.

[115] This major occupation as an inner-Catholic Critic also applies to his 1967 article on the rise of the state as a process of secularization. Jan-Werner Müller lays this out in great detail in 'What the Dictum Really Meant and What It Might Mean for Us', *Constellations: An International Journal of Critical and Democratic Theory* 45(2) (2018), pp. 196–206.

[116] The *Kulturkampf* (culture war) was a struggle of Chancellor Bismarck's government against the Catholic Church concerning the role and power of Catholic institutions in predominantly Protestant Prussia. Bismarck enacted a series of anti-Catholic laws, including the disbanding of Catholic organizations, confiscation of church property, and banishment or imprisonment of clergy. The *Kulturkampf* was in the long term unsuccessful and the discriminating laws were eventually repealed. However, the term was still used in the Weimar Republic to refer to (factual or putative) discrimination of Catholics, and the example of the resistance exhibited by the Catholic Church during the Kulturkampf was invoked later to ask why it had done so little to resist its suppression by the Nazi regime.

as reactionary and 'ultramontane', i.e. harbouring loyalties to Rome rather than their motherland. Throughout the later years of the German Empire and then the Weimar Republic, they lived lives of inner emigration—seeing the Church as their true home and seeking the guidance of the Church for their behaviour towards the state and their fellow citizens. Political action usually meant defending the interests and rights of the Church; it did not mean, as it should have, according to Böckenförde, taking the Catholic faith as an ethical inspiration to address issues of public concern. Due to this state of introversion, pious Catholics concentrated on the inner workings of the Church, on religious practice, and on religious education (all *bona particularia* (particular goods) as opposed to common goods), building up the conviction that as long as these areas were under the aegis of the Church, Catholics could live under any public order. It is out of this (misguided) logic, Böckenförde explains, that parts of the Catholic Centre party and the Prussian Episcopate had rejected in the spring of 1918 the democratization of the inegalitarian Prussian Three-Class franchise, fearing that this would result in a loss of the majority needed to protect Church privileges, especially its control over religious schooling. Overall, Böckenförde diagnosed and criticized, instead of seeing public life as a whole, Catholics reduced their gaze to particular Catholic interests only. The adherence to natural law thinking removed Catholics from the public square and made them unfit to be democratic citizens, in that it caused believers to prioritize the interests of the Church over their interests as citizens of a larger demos.

In 'The Catholic Church in 1933' Böckenförde laid bare the assumptions and priorities that had guided the political outlook of the vast majority of Church officials between 1933 and 1945, leading to the effective endorsement of the Nazi seizure of power on the part of the Catholic Church in Germany.[117] Going through numerous speeches and private letters of Catholic dignitaries and leaders of Catholic associations, Böckenförde concluded that they paved the way for the rise of fascism—not alone, of course, and not always intentionally, but nevertheless they did. Böckenförde blamed the officials' failure to a large extent on their fascination with 'organic' theories of society and economy, which fit with traditional Catholic moral theology's reliance on natural law argumentation. The distance of Catholics to the modern state and the fact that the Catholic Church never came to accept modern democracy doctrinally (a step only undertaken later with the Second Vatican Council) caused a narrowing of

[117] Böckenförde recalled in 2009: '[In preparation of writing the 1961 article] I sat in the archive [of the Swiss Catholic journal *Ecclesiastica*]. There I came across some things. At first, I couldn't believe what I was seeing. It became surprisingly clear to me that these were exactly the positions that I had fundamentally criticized in my [1957] democracy essay. . . That is also why I structured the [1961] essay as a case study, in order to spell out and reinforce that the traditional theory of [natural law of] the Church was untenable. [My essay] was not supposed to be only a historical account, but a case study in order to demonstrate something theoretically and systematically by way of historical events.' See Chapter XVI of this volume, p. 374.

Catholic leaders' judgment of public affairs. Böckenförde's article, published when he was thirty-one, was considered so explosive that several of his mentors advised against publishing it, or urged him to wait until he had secured a tenured faculty position.[118] Böckenförde published it nevertheless, and a back and forth between him and several critics ensued, excerpts of which were published in subsequent issues of the same magazine. Ultimately, the Committee for Contemporary History, which the Catholic Church felt compelled to convene in order to probe the accuracy of Böckenförde's claims, validated his account in all major points. (The Committee expanded its research later and is still active today.)

These three articles sealed what Böckenförde still regarded at the end of his life as his major achievement vis-à-vis the Church: an internal engagement on the part of the German Catholic Church with its own history and a defence of the secular state from within a Catholic perspective: 'I still claim credit for this today. I was able to persuade [German] Catholicism that one's own freedom can be defended only as part of the general freedom.'[119]

The fourth article in this phase, 'Religious Freedom as a Mandate for Christians. A Jurist's Thoughts on the Discussions of the Second Vatican Council', was written to inform the ongoing discussions of the Council on the question of religious freedom.[120] The laity of Catholics had long de facto accepted living in secular, non-Christian states and sharing equal citizenship with non-Catholics and non-believers. But from the viewpoint of Catholic canon law, such positions were still untenable. According to the Catholic magisterium, Catholics were still required to live in Christian states (not just nominally Christian-majority states, but states where political authority was Catholic and where Catholic norms were implemented by state authority). The Second Vatican Council was reconsidering all of this: it was putting long-standing Catholic doctrine to debate. In his article, Böckenförde identified as the Church's key approach to religious freedom the tolerance theory of 1315, reaffirmed by Pope Pius XII as late as 1953, according to which 'religious error had no objective right even to exist', and as a consequence of which religious freedom was something to be tolerated but, in the final analysis, not to be accepted. Böckenförde gave expression to his bewilderment with the position of the Church, according to which it claimed freedom of religion for itself but was not prepared to grant this to others. He

[118] Mirjam Künkler and Tine Stein, 'State, Law and Constitution: Ernst-Wolfgang Böckenförde's Political and Legal Thought in Context', in volume I of this edition, pp. 1–36.

[119] Biographical interview, Chapter XVI of this volume, p. 377.

[120] The Second Vatican Council (Vatican II) fundamentally redefined the Church's doctrinal position in a number of areas, notably on the issue of religious freedom. As late as 1886, Pope Leo XIII had reaffirmed that only a state based on the Christian faith was truly legitimate and that religious liberty and freedom of conscience were illegitimate deviations from Christian natural law (encyclical 'Immortale Dei'). By contrast, in its 'Declaration on Religious Freedom' (Dignitatis Humanae), the Second Vatican Council recognized that the human person's right to religious freedom should be acknowledged in constitutional law as a civil right.

had particular trouble comprehending this position as a jurist. Applied as such, Böckenförde wrote, the tolerance theory was not a legal principle, but 'a power principle'.[121]

The election of Pope John XXIII in 1963, a champion of the equality of persons irrespective of religious conviction, who declared 'We were all made in God's image, and thus, we are all God-alike', facilitated a rethinking on these matters. The 'Declaration on Religious Freedom' (*Dignitatis Humanae*) for the first time grounded religious freedom in the dignity of the human person as such, which by implication would need to be extended beyond Catholics. The Church thereby abandoned the goal for Christians to live in a Christian public order and facilitated a vision of Christianity as a 'religion of freedom'.[122]

Some of Böckenförde's arguments regarding the necessity for Catholics to accept the religiously neutral state for their own good (only a religiously neutral state facilitates embracing faith out of a position of freedom) can be found as well in the 'Declaration on Religious Freedom'. While arguing for the supremacy of secular state law over religious law, and against the idea that natural law could lie at the basis of state law, Böckenförde championed the importance of natural law as a source for ethical reasoning. In other words, religious norms could and should inform the individual's behaviour in private and public, but could not be made mandatory for citizens to follow (as religious law when enforced by the state would necessarily do). Religion, according to Böckenförde, can only be embraced fully from a position of free choice, free from state and societal pressures.

2. *Ethos, we-consciousness, sense of belonging*

In 1978 Böckenförde penned an article on 'The State as an Ethical State', in which he asked, drawing on Hegel's concept of '*sittliche Substanz*', or ethical substance, whether the state should provide a guiding ethos to the citizenry.[123] Böckenförde answered in the negative. In his widely quoted thesis, 'The liberal, secularized state is sustained by conditions that it cannot itself guarantee', he pointed to the problem that the modern democratic state cannot resort to imposing values or worldviews on its citizens without undermining the very liberalism on which it is founded.[124] '*Sittliche Substanz*' was no doubt

[121] 'A maxim of law applies by its nature universally, not only for me, but also against me. A legal principle that seeks to exclude this mutuality is not a legal principle but a power principle.' See Chapter IV in this volume, p. 126.

[122] Georg Wilhelm Friedrich Hegel, *Vorlesungen zur Philosophie der Religion* [1821–1831], vol. II (Stuttgart: Glockner, 1959), p. 207.

[123] Böckenförde (note 6).

[124] See Chapter V in this volume. On the eve of his election as Pope, Cardinal Ratzinger publicly discussed Böckenförde's dictum with Jürgen Habermas. The dialogue was published as Joseph Ratzinger and Jürgen

crucial for public life, but it had to emanate first and foremost from within society.[125]

What are its sources? 'Philosophical, political and social movements can strengthen the sense of commonality in the populace and the willingness to not always look out for one's own benefit only, but to act companionably and in solidarity with others,' he wrote.[126] Further, religion can be such a source, but he insisted (and this is missed by some of his readers), only if it is placed into the service of the common good, not of particular religious goals, or the interests of individual religious groups.[127]

The consensus on a society's fundamental values 'of its way of life and its political organization' is based on the implied and trusted agreement about 'that which cannot be voted upon' (*das Unabstimmbare*), about the foundations of society and politics that obviously cannot be violated.[128] No state can survive purely on the basis of guaranteeing constitutional liberties: it also needs a genuine democratic political culture, which can only emanate if citizens trust that others will consider them full members of the polity no matter whether they are in the majority or minority at any given time. Unlike Jürgen Habermas, Böckenförde did not believe that joint participation in the democratic process alone was sufficient for this agreement to emerge and sustain itself.

Böckenförde describes this agreement also in terms of a we-consciousness, or what sociologist Ralf Dahrendorf has called a 'sense of belonging'.[129] It consists of

Habermas, *The Dialectics of Secularization. On Reason and Religion* (San Francisco: Ignatius Press, 2007). Unlike Böckenförde, Ratzinger sees religion and natural law as the only real sources capable of sustaining democracy.

[125] 'It is not the state that must prescribe and make obligatory a way of life; on the contrary, [the democratic state] must be sustained by basic attitudes within society.' Böckenförde, 'Biographisches Interview', Chapter XVII of volume I of this edition, p. 384.

[126] Ernst-Wolfgang Böckenförde, 'Freiheit ist ansteckend', *die tageszeitung*, 23 September 2009, p. 4.

[127] See Chapter II of this volume. Böckenförde also explained that when religious groups had in the past used the democratic process to promote their own worldviews, this had been at the expense of the quality and longevity of democracy. 'The inner strength of a democratic state depends more on the democratic loyalty which different political groups have to each other than on the realization of certain demands of natural law.' Ernst-Wolfgang Böckenförde, 'Kirchliches Naturrecht und politisches Handeln', in Franz Böckle and Ernst-Wolfgang Böckenförde (eds.), *Naturrecht in der Kritik* (Mainz: Matthias-Grünewald-Verlag, 1973), pp. 96–125, here p. 102.

[128] Ernst-Wolfgang Böckenförde, 'Noch einmal: Das Ethos der modernen Demokratie und die Kirche. Erwiderung', *Hochland* 50(5) (1958), pp. 409–421, here page 41. Here he draws on Arnold Arndt, a social democratic jurist who deeply impressed him and was a major force in Böckenförde joining the social democratic party (SPD). See Ernst-Wolfgang Böckenförde, 'Begegnung mit Adolf Arndt', in Claus Arndt (ed.), *Adolf Arndt zum 90. Geburtstag. Dokumentation der Festakademie in der Katholischen Akademie Hamburg* (Bonn: Friedrich Ebert Stiftung, 1995), pp. 32–39. For Arndt's notion of the *Unabstimmbare*, see Adolf Arndt, 'Christentum und freiheitlicher Sozialismus', in Horst Ehmke and Carlo Schmid (eds.), *Adolf Arndt, Politische Reden und Schriften* (Bonn: JHW Dietz Verlag, 1976), pp. 113–133.

[129] See Ralf Dahrendorf, 'Freiheit und Soziale Bindungen. Anmerkungen zur Struktur einer Argumentation', in Krzysztof Michalski (ed.), *Die liberale Gesellschaft. Castelgandolfo-Gespräche 1992* (Stuttgart: Klett-Cotta, 1992). Earlier in his career, Böckenförde had, like Hermann Heller, referred to this as societal (or relative) homogeneity, but due to the multiple misunderstandings this created, later shifted to the terms 'we-consciousness' and 'sense of belonging'. Dahrendorf agrees with Böckenförde that *Verfassungspatriotismus* is too thin to create cohesion in society and he also agrees that this cohesion cannot be created or imposed by the state but needs

the shared visions of how to live together that bind the people to one another that prompt them to work towards a common good. Böckenförde borrows the idea from the social-democratic legal scholar of the Weimar period Herman Heller, who described it thus:

> In fact, the real intellectual basis of parliamentarism is not the belief in public discussion as such, but the belief in a common ground for discussion, and therefore the chance of fair play for the domestic political opponent, with whom agreement is believed to be possible to the exclusion of brute force.[130]

This we-consciousness is a marker for societal cohesion. It is in perennial need of re-construction and in democratic politics needs to be created in society (through communication, participation in shared activities, exchange of views, etc.) and cannot be imposed by the state.

One might interject here and point out that societal cohesion, or we-consciousness, can emerge in multiple ways: as a 'sense of belonging' created by similar ethos, a single stream of ethics and consciousness that connects us to each other in a singular humanity. Or it may emerge as a sense of coexistence, which is a belief that there are different ethics we have, but we agree to coexist without believing in, or even trying to develop through dialogue, any notions of common ethic. The latter would be more of a tolerance of others' ethics rather than an agreement with them—a coexistence of multiple humanities on the basis of a modus-vivendi pluralism.

Böckenförde certainly subscribes to a coexistence of multiple humanities, as it is a sign, in his view, of a democratic society that it can accommodate different worldviews. But precisely because of this diversity, it is important that society continuously work towards creating agreement on the things that cannot be voted upon. Without the societal processes that force people to engage across the multiple divides of divergent worldviews, democracy will erode from within. Modern democratic life requires a commitment that binds people to one another. After all, it means (in his view) being willing to pay (potentially high) taxes so as to alleviate poverty in one's society and to enable everyone to live a life in dignity. It means being resistant to corruption, for the opposite would contribute to an erosion of the public good. And of course, it means in the ultimate analysis to be willing to die for one another in the case of war. All of these very demanding, indeed existential, concessions require a strong bond with the other members of the same political community.

to emanate voluntarily from within civil society. Unlike Böckenförde, Dahrendorf emphasizes the importance of this cohesion not only for the functioning of democracy but also for capitalism (*Marktwirtschaft*) and unlike Böckenförde, he believes the most fertile ground for a strong civil society is a thin state.

130 Hermann Heller, 'Politische Demokratie und soziale Homogenität', in Hermann Heller, *Gesammelte Werke*, 2nd ed., vol. II (Tübingen: Mohr Siebeck, 1992 [1928]), pp. 421–433, here p. 427. David Dyzenhaus comments that Heller 'was merely pointing out that the belief in the worth of public discussion requires a belief in the existence of a social and political foundation for such discussion which makes it possible to live with the result of such discussion, even when it is not to one's liking'. David Dyzenhaus, *Legality and Legitimacy. Carl Schmitt, Hans Kelsen, and Hermann Heller in Weimar* (Oxford: Clarendon Press, 1997), p. 191.

Ethos, ethics, *Sittlichkeit* have been recurrent themes in Böckenförde's work. When Böckenförde, upon retiring from the constitutional court, was meant to receive the highest honour of the Federal Republic of Germany for his public service, he politely declined. In his own words, he had merely performed duties emanating from the office entrusted to him.[131] Böckenförde has written not only about the ethos of democracy, but also the ethos of the public, the ethos of the Church, and the ethos of lawyers.[132] In the end, every democracy can only be as good as the public ethos (created by societal forces) that sustains it.

3. *State, secularity, and open encompassing neutrality*

In his writings on religion and state, Böckenförde underlines that the 'secularized state has no religion and does not represent one', 'the acceptance, organization, and exercise [of religion] are no longer a state matter, nor is religion guided and directed by the state. The secularized state ... foregoes any form of religious sovereignty, and it no longer lends its power to enforcing religion or religious demands.'[133] Böckenförde argues in favour of a model he calls 'open encompassing neutrality' of the state towards religion: an amicable and liberal separation of religious and political authority, defined in a manner that accommodates positive religious freedom (the freedom to profess a religion) as much as negative religious freedom (the freedom not to profess a religion).[134]

Böckenförde conceives the relationship between law, politics, and religion in the frame of fundamental rights: he regards freedom of conscience not only as one of the key human rights, but as the most important human right, as it gives the individual autonomy to distinguish between good and evil, and to act accordingly. Religious freedom means for Böckenförde the right to have or not to have a religious faith (freedom of belief), to affirm this faith privately or openly and to advocate or not advocate it (freedom to profess), to exercise or not exercise one's religion publicly (freedom of worship), and to join or not join

[131] Quoted also in the address given by Federal President Joachim Gauck on the occasion, see Appendix 3 in this volume.

[132] See Ernst-Wolfgang Böckenförde, 'The Ethos of Modern Democracy and the Church' [1957], Chapter I of this volume; Böckenförde 1958 (note 128), pp. 409–421; ''The State as an Ethical State', Chapter III in volume I of this edition; Ernst-Wolfgang Böckenförde, 'Ethische und politische Grundsatzfragen zur Zeit', *Herder Korrespondenz* issue 7 (1981), pp. 342–348; Böckenförde 1988 (note 39); Ernst-Wolfgang Böckenförde, 'Staatliches Recht und sittliche Ordnung', in Hermann Fechtrup, Friedbert Schulze, and Thomas Sternberg (eds.), *Aufklärung durch Tradition. Symposion der Josef Pieper Stiftung zum 90. Geburtstag von Josef Pieper* (Münster: LiT-Verlag, 1995), pp. 87–107; Ernst-Wolfgang Böckenförde, *Recht, Sittlichkeit, Toleranz* (Ulm: Humboldt Studienzentrum, 2001); Böckenförde (note 107).

[133] Chapter VIII in this volume, p. 221.

[134] Alfred Stepan's model of the 'Twin Tolerations' is largely congruent with this view, but in Böckenförde the legal manifestations of this relation between religion and state are thought out in much greater detail. Alfred Stepan, 'The World's Religious Systems and Democracy: Crafting the Twin Tolerations', in Alfred C. Stepan, *Arguing Comparative Politics* (New York: Oxford University Press, 2001), pp. 213–253.

together in religious communities (religious freedom of association).[135] The correlate to these individual rights is the open and overarching principle of the state's neutrality towards religion and other worldviews. This principle entails, first and foremost, a prohibition for the state to justify law on religious grounds. Furthermore, it entails the dissociation of political authority from religious authority, and requires of the state to not privilege religion over non-religion and one religious faith over another.

In his article 'The Secularized State: Its Character, Justification, and Problems in the twenty-first century' (2007), Böckenförde explicitly contrasts his concept of an open encompassing neutrality—the state's neutrality toward religions that remains at the same time open to them and encompassing religious views—with a neutral state that distances itself from religion ('distancing neutrality'). The latter 'tends toward consigning and confining religion to the private and private-social sphere. . . [It] shapes the legal system in a purely secular way and turns away religious aspects as irrelevant and private.' Occasionally, he invokes the laïcist French model in this context. Open encompassing neutrality, by contrast, 'additionally accords [religion] room to develop in the public sphere, for example in the school, educational institutions, and in what is summarily referred to as the public order—though, of course, it does so without any form of identification. . . [It] seeks to create a balance, in that affirming and leading a life in accordance with religion, to the extent that it is compatible with the secular goals of the state, is permitted also within the public sphere by the legal system and is incorporated into the latter.'[136] While distancing neutrality champions negative religious freedom (the freedom not to be religious), open encompassing neutrality, he argues, aims for a balancing of negative and positive religious freedom, in particular the right to live one's life in accordance with one's religion's tenets.

Böckenförde suggests that it is to a large extent from nonidentification (with a particular religion) that the modern state draws its legitimacy towards all of its citizens in their plurality of worldviews. This means that individuals are protected by the constitution in their peculiarity and uniqueness, and that for this protection to be truly meaningful it needs to extend into the public sphere. Citizens must have confidence 'in the untouchability of their peculiarity'. Böckenförde writes, 'individual specialness, in order to be able to unfold as specialness, is dependent on entering into institutions that are sustained and guided by the state, which is the case above all in the areas of upbringing and schooling'.[137] Drawing on Adalbert Podlech (who wrote his habilitation with Böckenförde), he distinguishes between the 'polity [*Gemeinwesen*]' as the totality

[135] Ernst-Wolfgang Böckenförde, 'Bekenntnisfreiheit in einer pluralen Gesellschaft', in Böckenförde 2007 (note 41), pp. 439ff, here p. 442. See furthermore Chapter VI of this volume. Also Ute Sacksofsky, 'Ernst-Wolfgang Böckenförde's Oeuvre on Religious Freedom Applied to Recent Decisions of the European Court of Human Rights', *German Law Journal* 19(2) (2018) (Special issue—Statism, Secularism, Liberalism Ernst-Wolfgang Böckenförde Beyond Germany), pp. 301–320.

[136] See Chapter VIII in this volume, p. 223.

[137] Chapter VI of this volume, p. 185, note 62.

of the citizens on the one hand, and the *Hoheitsgewalt* (sovereign activity) of the state on the other, in order to suggest that where the state exercised its *Hoheitsgewalt* it needs to be neutral with regard to religion and other worldviews, whereas in the *Gemeinwesen* the individual citizen needs to be able to express his or her peculiarity and specialness. It is this distinction that enables Böckenförde to argue in favour of permitting individual officials to wear religious garb in the *Gemeinwesen*, such as schools, but not in courthouses, which is where the state exercises its *Hoheitsgewalt*.

In courtrooms, where the state engages in a sovereign activity (*Hoheitsfunktion*) the display of crucifixes could be perceived by individuals as an infringement on their freedom of conscience, and they should therefore be removed. Here distancing neutrality towards religion ought to be applied.

Unlike courtrooms, schools are not, however, institutions of the state as an entity of power, Böckenförde suggests. Rather, they are intermediary institutions that connect state and society. Public schools are a 'means through which the state fulfils its duty of civic education, not indoctrination'. This allows for a qualitatively different regulation of the presence of religious symbols, namely one of open encompassing neutrality that enables citizens to show themselves as religious or non-religious beings at their own pleasing, including in wearing religious garb.[138]

Böckenförde applied his argument to the deliberative processes of public life, too. In the 2000s, Jürgen Habermas famously argued that citizens could expect co-citizens to engage with their religiously justified reasonings in public deliberation, even if the latter did not share these—an argument that Böckenförde had already developed in the 1960s. But Habermas also introduced a *translation proviso* for political processes at the parliamentary level where, he argued, religious arguments would need to be translated into secular rationality in order to count. Böckenförde examined the possible tension between religious and secular commitments in a 1999 article titled 'A Christian in the Office of Constitutional Judge', in which he looked back on his years on the constitutional bench. In this office he was exclusively bound by the secular state law and the *bonum commune*—the common good of the entire citizenry. Particularist concerns or interests, such as those of a Catholic, had no place in the inner deliberative process, Böckenförde concluded. This was the logic he had applied as a judge on the constitutional court. Interestingly, unlike with other oaths during his career, he insisted on taking this particular oath of office on the bible. As he explained, he invoked God here to help him find the strength to keep religion out of his reasoning while serving on the constitutional bench.[139] As

[138] Sacksofsky (note 135).

[139] See Chapter XI in this volume. Distinguishing the swearing-in as professor from that of the constitutional judge (both civil service positions), he comments in the biographical interview (Chapter XVI, p. 388) '[as constitutional court judge I swore with religious affirmation] [b]ecause I believe that especially this entirely independent and unchecked office depends on the morality of the individuals who exercise it. That is why I consider it legitimate that the religiously neutral state in this case lays claim to a person's inner powers of commitment, even if this is formally voluntary. The oath for regular civil service positions does not have this specific meaning. That is also why I left out the religious affirmation when I was sworn in as a professor.'

a public official, one was accountable to the entire demos, he went on, and as such could not allow oneself to formulate positions based on a particularist identity. Böckenförde was adamant: Religion can and should inform the individual ethos, but religious reasons cannot guide a decision-making process the results of which apply to all citizens, regardless of their inner convictions.

V. WHY THOMAS MORE?

Böckenförde personally selected the illustrations for both covers of this edition. For volume I, he chose Shakespeare's *King Lear*, as drawn by the Austrian artist Oskar Kokoschka (1886–1980). It was perhaps above all a warning of the calamity bound to happen when a ruler lost his way. The inner ethos is a core theme in Böckenförde's work, who repeatedly suggested that any public service is only as strong as the inner ethos of the individual who sustains it.

The theme of the inner ethos is also the connection to the cover image gracing volume II. Here, Böckenförde chose a portrait of Thomas More (1478–1535), as painted by Hans Holbein the Younger (1497–1543). Both King Lear and Thomas More are figures from British history and myth. Did Böckenförde select them perhaps also with a view to honouring the publisher? What is more, he chose two British themes as painted by Germanic painters. Did he undertake a conscious attempt at underlining commonalities and relations, or was it coincidence? Böckenförde had otherwise only few references to Britain in his overall work, as scholars from France and to a lesser extent Italy were much more formative in his thinking. But then there is of course Thomas Hobbes, whose work influenced Böckenförde perhaps on a level comparable only to Georg Wilhelm Friedrich Hegel, Carl Schmitt, and Hermann Heller.

While King Lear is a tale of vanity, betrayal, and desperate human indignity, Thomas More symbolizes rectitude, and unfailing loyalty to God. As Lord Chancellor, More had been an exemplary public servant, who remained true to his inner conviction even in the face of death, while King Lear succumbed to forces that tore him apart. Can one deduce a connection to the themes of the volumes: the image of a flawed and failing leader for a volume on constitutionalism and rule of law; and the image of an exemplary public servant for a volume on religion? A fallen leader whose failures could not have had such devastating consequences if some semblance of constitutionalism had existed, here? A servant to God whose legacy lives off his refusal to place King above faith, there?[140]

The sketch of More drawn by Holbein hung in Böckenförde's office at home and was the only image in the room without references to his family. Underneath the image, More's last words were printed, addressed to the English people before his beheading by King Henry VIII's executioner: 'I call

[140] Although we also initially suggested other possible illustrations for the covers, Böckenförde was rather determined regarding his choices.

you to witness, brothers, that I die in and for the faith of the Catholic Church; the King's loyal servant, but God's first.'

Regarding his own sense of what it means to be a *civis simul et christianus*, Böckenförde remained inspired until the end of his life by More as a legal thinker, philosopher, Humanist and Christian. More stood for the fulfilment of duty and indomitability, and Böckenförde no doubt admired More's refusal to betray his conscience and faith in favour of the King, even at the cost of his own life. Böckenförde went so far as to suggest that it was due to freedom of conscience that the modern state had to become neutral with regard to religion and other worldviews, and in that regard, freedom of conscience was the key to all modern freedoms.[141]

There are only a few references to More in Böckenförde's writings, and his *History of the Philosophy of Law and the State: from Antiquity to the Middle Ages* (2002) does not include More (it went up to Martin Luther). In his classic article on the freedom of conscience (1969), Böckenförde does not mention More, although a discussion of More's stance on the matter would have lent itself to the topic. But in his 1978 article 'The State as an Ethical State' he opens with the following words:

> The European humanists in the first half of the sixteenth century, whether theologians like Erasmus and Melanchthon or jurists like Johannes Reuchlin and Thomas More, directed their attention not only to humanistic-philosophical education and a humanistic way of life, but also to the political order of their time, and some placed themselves in its service. Reuchlin was a judge of the Swabian League for twelve years, thus participating in one of the efforts to establish a permanent system of peace in the [Holy Roman] Empire, and Thomas More was Lord Chancellor to the King of England for a number of years. They were not yet able to achieve the state as a lasting order of peace, but they laid the groundwork for it through their ideas and actions.[142]

Böckenförde's first born is called Thomas. One of Böckenförde's Italian translators, publishers, and intellectual interlocutors, Michele Nicoletti, recalled how Böckenförde remarked on a visit to Trento, speaking Italian: 'My son, too, like yours, is called Thomas / Tomaso. Not in memory of Thomas Aquinas—no, in memory of Thomas More.'

Nicoletti also believes that part of Böckenförde's felt connection to More was as a jurist. Böckenförde remarked to him that theologians usually failed to understand matters of the state and power, but that jurists did—and that as a Catholic intent on shaping public life, one would be better served to train as a legal scholar than as a theologian.[143] ('*Silete Theologi in munere alieno*,' warned Albericus Gentilis.[144])

[141] Böckenförde 1970 (note 49).

[142] Böckenförde (note 6), p. 86.

[143] Nicoletti also recalls speaking about his research on Karl Neundörfer and remarking that among all the German Catholic theologians of his time, he was the only one to be perceptive of and to accurately analyse at his time the problems facing Weimar parliamentarism and their relations to the topic of Church and state. This, Böckenförde replied, was not so surprising as Neundörfer was a jurist. He, as opposed to the theologians not trained in law, was well equipped to do so.

[144] 'Theologians, keep silence about matters that are outside your area of expertise.'

But it is not only the themes of faith and ethos that bound Böckenförde to More. There is also the question of economic distribution. More writes of his ideal of a Christian humanism and social justice in his Utopia:

> When I consider any social system that prevails in the modern world, I can't, so help me God, see it as anything but a conspiracy of the rich to advance their own interests under the pretext of organizing society. They think up all sorts of tricks and dodges, first for keeping safe their ill-gotten gains, and then for exploiting the poor by buying their labour as cheaply as possible. Once the rich have decided that these tricks and dodges shall be officially recognized by society—which includes the poor as well as the rich—they acquire the force of law. Thus, an unscrupulous minority is led by its insatiable greed to monopolize what would have been enough to supply the needs of the whole population.[145]

The perceptiveness that democracy requires also underlying economic conditions for people to exercise their rights, and the sense that Christianity demanded engagement also for economic justice strongly resonated with Böckenförde.

VI. CONCLUSIONS: *CIVIS SIMUL ET CHRISTIANUS*

Ernst-Wolfgang Böckenförde (1930–2019) was one of Europe's foremost public law scholars and a major public commentator on issues of diverse theoretical and practical import, ranging from legal theoretical debates about the rule of law and constitutional democracy, the state of exception, and the place of values in grounding the law, to normative discussions about the deployment of nuclear missiles, the regulation of abortion, asylum, EU enlargement, counter-terrorism, genetic engineering, and the capitalist globalized economy. As laid out elsewhere,[146] Böckenförde writes as a social democrat, a Catholic, and a liberal. It is not only these plural normative commitments that make Böckenförde an unusual thinker. It is also the originality of his theoretical contributions towards understanding, legitimizing, and criticizing the secularized democratic constitutional state that make him invaluable for contemporary democratic and constitutional theory as well as for reflections on secularization.

A key idea in Böckenförde's work is that democracy requires 'implicit agreement on those things that cannot be voted upon'. At a most basic constitutional level, these are the unamendable clauses of a Constitution—they are not subject to electoral majorities, they are 'off the agenda', they cannot be contested. Beyond those constitutional clauses there are wide-ranging conventions that we assume others in the polity will abide by. Böckenförde underlined time and again the fact that legal provisions are only as strong as the democratic culture that sustains them. No democratic state can create or uphold 'the implicit agreement about those things that cannot be voted upon' by means of

[145] Thomas More, *Utopia* (1516), transl. by Paul Turner (London: Penguin Books, 1965), p. 130.

[146] Mirjam Künkler and Tine Stein, 'State, Law, and Constitution: Ernst-Wolfgang Böckenförde's Political and Legal Thought in Context', in volume I of this edition, pp. 1–35.

coercion. In his widely quoted 1967 thesis 'The liberal, secularized state is sustained by conditions it cannot itself guarantee', he pointed to the problem that the modern constitutional state, as a necessarily secularized state, cannot resort to imposing certain values or worldviews on its citizens without undermining the very liberalism on which it is founded. The rule of law and democratic procedures, according to Böckenförde, cannot be sustained in the long term unless they are carried by people who consider themselves part of the same demos and work towards a shared democratic culture. This culture needs to be created from within society, and all the state can do is create the structural conditions in which these exchanges over values can take place in peace and safety.

As an inner-Catholic critic, Böckenförde spent significant energies early in his career to show how the practices of the Catholic Church in post-war Germany of embracing the democratic process to further its own worldview (e.g. calling from the pulpit on voters to elect particular candidates, trying (unsuccessfully) to meddle in the curriculum of state schools) had undermined the ability of Catholic believers to open themselves fully to democratic citizenship. A democratic culture, according to Böckenförde, significantly depends on citizens' ability and desire to work across religious, economic, and political divides to create a we-consciousness, to find agreement on those things that lie beyond the ballot box and motivate citizens to work towards the *common* good, not to prioritize the interests of particular groups if that risked diminishing other citizens' de facto rights.

A state that is not neutral in religious and other worldviews by definition favours those sharing the worldview such a state promotes and is therefore ultimately incompatible with democratic politics. But a state that *is* neutral in religious and other worldviews need not impose a strict separation between religion and state, as some of the world's constitutions do. Instead, Böckenförde holds, it may be based on an open or amicable separation of politics and religion that does not prioritize freedom from religion at the cost of freedom to religion. Precisely because of the neutrality of the state in religious matters, it is important to be as sensitive to positive freedom of religion as to negative freedom. For this reason, for example, Böckenförde rejects headscarf bans for teachers and endorses the establishment in Germany of Islamic public holidays to complement the extant Christian ones.

Böckenförde shares with most democratic theorists, including US philosopher John Rawls and German philosopher Jürgen Habermas, the insistence on the neutrality of the liberal democratic state with regard to religion and other worldviews. Indeed, Rawls' postulate to 'take the truths of religion off the political agenda' finds unreserved resonance in Böckenförde.[147] But overall, with his view that a secular state need not insist on the privatization of religion, but instead can and should still grant space for religion to express itself in public life (as long as this does not violate the state's neutrality), his democratic theory is closer to that of Indian political theorist Rajeev Bhargava and Canadian

[147] John Rawls, *Political Liberalism* (New York: Columbia University Press, 1993), p. 151.

philosopher Charles Taylor.[148] All three believe in certain forms of accommodation and recognize that different religions require different arrangements. Yet while Böckenförde criticizes models that seek to relegate religion to the private sphere, he considers the other extreme as equally illiberal: the courting of particular religious groups or religious interpretations by state institutions, however implicit.[149]

Böckenförde is also not a communitarian. While he does regard religious freedom to be not only an individual right but also a group right, in both instances this right is subject to the liberal constitutional order. Thus, differing from Bhargava, for example, Böckenförde would argue that the state is *required* (and not only empowered) to interfere in cases of discrimination that are undertaken in the name of religion. Böckenförde would also not share Bhargava's and Will Kymlicka's view that the administration of religious personal law by the state is compatible with democratic politics and human rights, unless citizens are able to easily opt out of religious law without facing potential political, social, economic, or cultural disadvantages. In the end, Böckenförde's view of the democratic state is one in which the equal rights of citizens are not up for debate or relativization, while communitarian approaches leave open arrangements of religious autonomy which are likely to shield religions from state intrusion even where they discriminate on the basis of religion, class / caste, ethnicity, or gender.

In the final analysis, Böckenförde is a theorist of freedom more than belonging: 'One's own freedom can be defended only as part of the general freedom,' he wrote in 2002.[150] Arguments for rights and freedoms framed in the context of a particular community can only be sustainable in the long term if one is willing to grant these same rights and freedoms to others in the same political space.

148 For a comparison between Böckenförde and Bhargava, see Mirjam Künkler and Tine Stein, 'Ernst-Wolfgang Böckenförde on Law, Religion, and Democratic Models of Secularism', in Anupama Roy and Michael Becker (eds.), *Dimensions of Constitutional Democracy: India and Germany* (Singapore: Springer, 2020), pp. 67–90.

149 Böckenförde mentions the example of Turkey in this regard, which under the mantle of *laiklik* greatly interferes in the religious landscape of the country. But the privileging of the religious right by the US judiciary in some states would also fall into this category.

150 Ernst-Wolfgang Böckenförde, 'Vorbemerkung', in Böckenförde (note 41), pp. 113–114, here p. 114.

PART I

CATHOLIC CHURCH AND POLITICAL ORDER

Böckenförde on the Relation of the Catholic Church and Christians to Democracy and Authoritarianism

Mirjam Künkler and Tine Stein

Part I of the volume brings together Böckenförde's earliest writings from the late 1950s to the mid-1960s. They cover his democratic theory (Chapter I), his documentation of the failure of German Catholicism during the rise of the Nazi regime (Chapter II), Böckenförde's reflections on the possibilities and limits of Christian conduct in authoritarian and totalitarian contexts (Chapter III), and on the dogmatic revolution that resulted in the recognition of religious freedom on the part of the Catholic Church in 1965 (Chapter IV). Taken together, the articles lay the basis for Böckenförde's attempt to reorient—through internal criticism—church doctrine and practice towards the principle *civis simul et christianus*: the idea that Catholic beliefs and interests can be reconciled with political liberalism and commitment to the political community even if that community is not Catholic, but a religiously pluralistic one. Years later, Böckenförde reflected on how some of his early writings resulted in his image as a stark critic of the Catholic Church, which only gradually transformed into an appreciation on the part of German Catholicism of his efforts to transform the church from within.[1]

Böckenförde penned his first article, titled 'The Ethos of Modern Democracy and the Church' at the age of twenty-seven while pursuing his second doctorate in history at the University of Munich (having completed his doctorate in law in Münster the year before). The article features a passionate call on the Catholic Church to accept democracy on substantive, not just instrumental, grounds and to grant Catholic believers independence in their electoral choices.

[1] My 'undertaking ... was initially accompanied more by criticism than approval—let me recall merely the medium-sized earthquake that my essay about German Catholicism in 1933 caused among the Catholic-ecclesiastical public. A change in the direction toward respect and in part—though at first still hesitant—approval came with the various contributions on religious freedom, the first of which was written during the debates of the Vatican Council ["Religionsfreiheit als Aufgabe der Christen", 1965], and those dealing with the political mandate of the Church [1969, 1973, 1980/84, 1983]. Eventually there were discussions as between equals, coupled with growing recognition by the discipline of theology.' See Chapter XII of this volume, p. 288.

Religion, Law, and Democracy. Ernst-Wolfgang Böckenförde, Oxford University Press (2020). © E.W. Böckenförde, M. Künkler, and T. Stein 2020. DOI: 10.1093/oso/9780198818632.003.0002.

Böckenförde wrote the article against the backdrop of the upcoming 1957 federal elections, during the preparations of which Catholic priests and church leaders had called upon believers to vote for the Christian Democratic Union (CDU).[2] Böckenförde staunchly opposed such meddling in believers' political choices. Moreover, he regarded the political content of the pastoral letters as symptomatic of the Church's instrumental view of democracy. The church accepted democratic procedures as long as they proved to be suitable vehicles to further its interests, but believed, according to Böckenförde, that it could opt out of democratic decision-making processes and majority rule every time areas of life were concerned which it regarded as part of its own purview, especially in the realm of family law and education. Böckenförde reminded readers that the Catholic bishops had been prepared to publicly reject the West German Basic Law of 1949 unless it would concede to parents the right to insist on denominational schools for their children.[3]

But beside his appeal to the Church to embrace democracy on substantive grounds, Böckenförde in this article also lays out his democratic theory. In section II of the article, subtitled 'Structural Features of Modern Democracy', he explains why majority rule means that there cannot be specific areas of morality which one societal actor, such as the Church, seeks to withdraw or withhold from public deliberation. If it is concerned about becoming subject to majority-supported policies deeply at odds with its own normative positions, it needs to enter public discussion and win the argument:

> Democracy means equality in the rights of political participation. . . Precisely the right of the majority to make decisions that are binding on the social whole, to possess legitimacy, rests on the fact that it competes with the minority for political leadership, and that the latter has the absolute equal opportunity to become the majority itself. All political groups have the same right to exist, and a given minority is always a potential majority. . . Democracy requires a genuine willingness to compromise, not as a tactical manoeuvre because one is not (yet) strong enough to govern alone, but as a genuine concession and renunciation because one accords also to one's political opponent the right to have his own political convictions.[4]

Böckenförde goes on to lay out what he considers to be the three cornerstones of democracy, namely majority rule, individual liberty, and equality, whereby the latter two constrain the first. Equality here means political equality: the equal right of every citizen to vote and run for political office. It does not establish social equality, although Böckenförde notes that political equality is a precondition to social equality, and that the achievement of social equality is

[2] The Christian Democratic Party (together with its ally the Christian Social Union in Bavaria) did win an absolute majority in September that year, the only time in the Federal Republic's history.

[3] Instead, mixed schools were widely adopted where Protestant and Catholic children would learn together, except in weekly religion classes (usually about two hours a week), when they would be separated to follow (nondevotional) instruction in their own denomination.

[4] Chapter I of this volume, p. 66.

a continual democratic task. Both political equality and individual liberty guard majority rule from degenerating into majority despotism.[5]

Returning to the concerns of the Catholic Church, Böckenförde clarifies that the triad of majority decision-making, political equality, and individual liberty make up the formal values of democracy, but not the content of governance. The latter is subject to the democratic process, such as the protection of marriage and the family, and it is here that the Church as a societal actor may enter the public realm to take part in generating consensus around certain values and work towards translating these into policies. Of course, this bears the risk of politicization for the Church and the Church must decide how to deal with this risk. In Böckenförde's view, it would be well advised 'to secure Christian values and convictions in a more lasting way than through temporary, majority-bound, and therefore contested institutionalizations'.[6] He advises the Church not to become a partisan player but to concentrate on supporting the citizens' ethos by facilitating dialogue, public education, and service for the common good.

His main point, to which he returns in the next article on 'German Catholicism in 1933', is that the formal values of democracy alone will not suffice to sustain constitutional politics. What is required is an *ethos* among the citizenry and its leaders to remain committed to these formal values. The first goal of every citizen therefore must be to ensure that the structural features of democracy are guaranteed and safeguarded, not that his or her personal values are politically realized. The Catholic Church failed in this task in 1933, he concludes. 'Looking back, what was required in 1933, was to support the political group that promised to offer the staunchest resistance to National Socialism on the basis of a liberal order, even if it did not recognize the confessional school or did not fully respect the natural law conception of property.'[7] Because the Catholic Church prioritized the latter in 1933, it contributed to the demise of Weimar democracy.

Franz Josef Schöningh, the editor of the Catholic magazine *Hochland* in which this article was published, regarded Böckenförde's intervention as so important that he placed the article at the opening of the fiftieth anniversary issue of the magazine[8] and used the preface to reflect on the place and role of Catholics in the young democracy.[9] Apparently, some Catholic intellectuals, among which Schöningh counted himself, felt unease with a broader Catholic complacency amidst a seemingly flourishing economy and democracy. A self-contentedness

[5] '[E]lectoral equality, freedom of association and assembly, freedom of personal and political opinions, including freedom of the press, are inseparable from democracy, and as fundamental democratic rights form the internal limits to every will of the majority, regardless of whether or not they are derived from constitutional routes' (Chapter I, this volume, p. 67).

[6] Chapter I of this volume, p. 75.

[7] Ibid., p. 68.

[8] Böckenförde's article elicited a wide public debate and the journal published several of his critics in the following edition, together with Böckenförde's rejoinder: 'Noch einmal: Das Ethos der modernen Demokratie und die Kirche. Erwiderung', *Hochland* 50(5) (June 1958), pp. 409–421. The article was translated into Polish in 1994 and 1999 and into Italian in 2007.

[9] For a summary of Schöningh's reflections, see annotation III in the biographical interview (Chapter XVI) in this volume.

had taken hold which seemed to put a cloak of silence over the Catholic Church's role during Nazism, wrote Schöningh. But Catholics should not fool themselves into thinking that the political dominance of Catholic elites in the 1950s was somehow a reflection of, or even thanks to, an allegedly particularly strong stance of resistance against the Nazis. There had been no such particularly strong stance, Schöningh insisted: most Catholic organizations imploded like houses of cards in 1933, not after intense struggles characterized by fierce resistance but after 'a single gust of wind'. It was time for Catholics to face this past and draw lessons for contemporary challenges.

Böckenförde took up this challenge with his article 'German Catholicism in 1933', included here as Chapter II. It is the article Böckenförde regarded as his most important historiographic writing.[10] A few years earlier, the Constitutional Court in Karlsruhe had faced a landmark court case over whether the Reichskonkordat of 1933, an agreement between Hitler and the Pope that guaranteed the Church far-reaching autonomy in education and its internal organization, remained legally binding in post-war West Germany. The case was initiated over the question of whether public schools could be segregated by denomination, as the Concordat made possible. The court ruled that education was a matter for the Länder, but it also ruled that the Reichskonkordat still applied.[11] The case and the public debates it provoked set in motion an evaluation of the Church's role during the rise of the Nazi regime. Böckenförde had read and been very impressed by historian Rudolf Morsey's writings on the demise of the Centre Party[12] and set out to investigate the behaviour of Catholic associations and networks during the last months of the Weimar Republic. Had they been complicitous in, perhaps even aided, the legal power grab of the Nazis in 1933, as some voices in the public controversy appeared to suggest? In his biographical interview Böckenförde looks back: 'Morsey's very well-documented account was a kind of revelation for me. That is how I found my way to the pastoral letters and the pronouncements by Catholic organizations. I sat in the archive ... [and at] first, I couldn't believe what I was seeing. It became surprisingly clear to me that these were exactly the positions that I had fundamentally criticized in my essay ["Ethos of Modern Democracy" of 1957].'[13]

In 'German Catholicism in 1933', which, like the previous article he published in *Hochland*, Böckenförde went through numerous speeches and private letters of Catholic dignitaries and leaders of Catholic associations to gauge their attitude towards the concordat. His conclusion: they paved the way for the rise of fascism—not alone and not necessarily or always knowingly, but nevertheless, they did. Böckenförde blamed this to a large extent on their fascination with

[10] It was translated into English and published in the same year as 'German Catholicism in 1933', *Cross Currents* 11 (1961), pp. 283–304.

[11] Federal Constitutional Court Decision of 26 March 1957. BVerfGE 6, 309 2 BvG 1/55.

[12] Rudolf Morsey, 'Die Zentrumspartei', in Erich Matthias and Rudolf Morsey (eds.): *Das Ende der Parteien 1933* (Düsseldorf: Droste, 1960), pp. 281–453.

[13] Chapter XVI in this volume, p. 374.

'organic' theories of society and economy, which fit with traditional Catholic moral theology's reliance on natural law argumentation. The distance of Catholics to the modern state and the fact that the Catholic Church never came to accept modern democracy doctrinally (a step only undertaken later with the Second Vatican Council) caused a narrowing of Catholic leaders' judgment of public affairs.

Böckenförde structured the article as a case study which sought to make a theoretical point by way of historiographic examination. He explained that instead of seeing public life as a whole, Catholics came to reduce their gaze to particular Catholic interests only. In the aftermath of the *Kulturkampf*, German Catholics had felt excluded from an increasingly liberal public sphere; compared to other citizens, they were viewed as reactionary and 'ultramontane', harbouring loyalties to Rome rather than their motherland. Throughout the later years of the Empire and then the Weimar Republic, they lived lives of inner emigration—seeing the Church as their true home and seeking the guidance of the Church for their behaviour towards the state and their fellow citizens. Political action usually meant defending the interests and rights of the Church; it did not mean, as it should have according to Böckenförde, taking the Catholic faith as an ethical inspiration to address issues of public concern. Due to this state of inner emigration, pious Catholics concentrated on internal Church matters, on religious practices, and on religious education (all *bona particularia*), building up the conviction that as long as these arenas were under the aegis of the Church, they could live under any public order. The *bona particularia* of special relevance to the Church, Böckenförde writes, were taken for the *bonum commune*: Particular Catholic concerns were taken as the common good. It is out of this logic, for example, that parts of the Catholic Centre party and the Prussian Episcopate had rejected in the spring of 1918 the phasing out of the Prussian Three-Class franchise, fearing that this would result in a loss of majorities needed to retain current arrangements on the Church and religious schooling. The concordat that Hitler offered promised to put an end to the normative struggles around Church independence and religious education by guaranteeing Catholics indefinite autonomy in the issues of religion, Church life, and schooling. Accordingly, Cardinal Faulhaber cried out in delight to Hitler: 'What the old parliaments and parties failed to accomplish in sixty years, your statesmanlike farsightedness has realized world-historically in six months'.[14]

Böckenförde's diagnosis that Catholics mistook Catholic affairs for the common good and that they were willing to sacrifice the democratic constitution of the Weimar Republic in exchange for autonomy in those policy areas they cared about prompted him to formulate his famous plea that freedom can only be defended as the freedom of all.[15]

[14] Cited by Böckenförde in Chapter II of this volume, pp. 98f.

[15] 'Vorbemerkung', in Ernst-Wolfgang Böckenförde, *Kirche und christlicher Glaube in den Herausforderungen der Zeit*, 2nd ed. (Münster: LIT Publishing House, 2007), p. 114.

The concordat was representative of a larger Vatican policy under Pope Leo XIII, which consisted of working with political regimes through treaties that guaranteed Catholic rights in education and Church life irrespective of the form of government in place—a political heedlessness that Böckenförde criticized as irresponsible. But, as Böckenförde showed, it was not only the rise of the Nazis that Catholic dignitaries accepted. He also documented their remarkable lack of alarm over the persecution of their fellow Jewish countrymen and -women, a topic to which Böckenförde returned decades later in his article 'The Persecution of German Jews as a Case of Civic Betrayal' (1997).[16] He recounts how a pastor had asked Cardinal Faulhaber to issue a critical statement with regard to the boycott of Jewish businesses that the government had proscribed in April 1933. In his response, Faulhaber wrote: 'There are far more important issues of current concern for the authorities of the Church, because schools, the Catholic associations, and issues such as sterilization are even more important for Christianity in our homeland.'[17]

Although Böckenförde meticulously documented Catholic leaders' enthusiasm for Hitler, it was not this part of the essay that provoked particular controversy. Instead, it was the second part of the article, where he laid out the reasons for Catholic leaders' complicity in the demise of the Weimar Republic. Within three weeks, the first print run of the *Hochland* issue was sold out and the magazine printed 3,000 more copies. In a following issue, the magazine featured the comments of several of his critics together with his rejoinder.[18]

His critics accused Böckenförde of having cited Church leaders out of context and exaggerating the extent to which Catholic officials embraced the new regime. In his rejoinder, always matter-of-fact in tone, Böckenförde insisted that his sources spoke for themselves and he supported all his major points with added documentation. As if to provoke the ire of the Church leadership further, he also specified that his evidence cast light not on the behaviour of Catholic believers and pastors in general, but on the majority of Church leaders and dignitaries, on the leaders of Catholic associations and Catholic intellectuals. The debate spread beyond *Hochland* to leadings newspapers and magazines where proponents of Böckenförde's theses and defendants of the church exchanged fiery arguments.[19] In the end, the Catholic Church saw itself

[16] Included as Chapter XIII in volume I of this edition: Ernst-Wolfgang Böckenförde, *Constitutional and Political Theory: Selected Writings*, ed. Mirjam Künkler and Tine Stein (Oxford: Oxford University Press, 2017).

[17] Böckenförde quoted this sentence in a book review he wrote in 1966 where he had discussed some recent publications on the Catholic Church and the National Socialist regime: 'Kirche und Politik. Zu einigen Neuerscheinungen über das Verhältnis der katholischen Kirche zum "Dritten Reich"', *Der STAAT* 2 (1966), pp. 225–238, here p. 233.

[18] 'Der deutsche Katholizismus im Jahre 1933. Stellungnahme zu einer Diskussion', *Hochland* 54 (1962), pp. 215–245.

[19] Two recent publications review the debates that Böckenförde's article triggered: Thomas Brechenmacher (ed.), *Das Reichskonkordat 1933. Forschungsstand, Kontroversen, Dokumente* (Paderborn: Schöningh, 2007), and Mark E. Ruff, *The Battle for the Catholic Past in Germany, 1945–1980* (Cambridge: Cambridge University Press, 2017).

compelled to convene a committee of historians, what came to be known as 'the Committee for Contemporary History', to investigate the matter. The Committee eventually vindicated Böckenförde in all major points. Over the following decades, it evolved into a major research institution inside the Catholic Church, which continues its work to this day. Böckenförde had achieved no less than set in motion a process of critical reflection and scientific probing within the German Catholic Church.[20]

In addition to having instigated discussions inside the Church with both his 1957 and 1961 articles, Böckenförde opened a public dispute on a third front, regarding Catholic perspectives on nuclear armament. His articles on the topic are not included in this volume, which makes their mention even more important to grasp the scope of his engagement with and criticism of Catholic positions early in his career. His interventions on the topic took place in three publications, all co-authored with the philosopher Robert Spaemann, with whom he had been a member of Joachim Ritter's Collegium Philosophicum in Münster. Böckenförde and Spaemann reacted to a speech delivered by the influential Catholic social theorist Gustav Gundlach[21] at the Catholic Academy in Munich in 1960. There, as well as elsewhere later, Gundlach suggested that the idea of a nuclear war could be justified by Catholic just war theory. Reinterpreting—misleadingly, as many contemporaries pointed out—Pope Pius XII's writing *Bellum iustum*, Gundlach argued that nuclear war could generally be justified if waged to protect the Christian faith. Pius XII, by contrast, who was engaged in re-interpreting and updating St Augustin's (354–430) just war theory, had just not rejected outright the idea of nuclear war if freedom, dignity, and faith of a people were under threat of being entirely annihilated.

Böckenförde and Spaemann called Gundlach's interpretation of Pius XII's *Bellum iustum* 'the destruction of natural law theory of war'.[22] The matter became particularly testy when the former pastor of the Catholic student congregation in Münster, Egon Schmitt, invited the two to elaborate on their critique in the journal *Militärseelsorge* [military chaplaincy], which he edited.[23] The journal was widely read among high-ranking officers in the German military and the article provoked fierce debate. Among other matters, Böckenförde and Spaemann suggested that the contemporary NATO strategy of massive retaliation contradicted Christian teachings on just war. The ensuing discussion was of

[20] See for example Ruff 2017 (note 19), p. 86, who comments 'Earning him reprimands and acidulous remarks from prominent names in the ecclesia and political Catholicism, this article spawned a historical controversy so charged that it helped alter the institutional landscape of research into the Catholic past.'

[21] The Jesuit Gustav Gundlach (1892–1963) was an influential Catholic social theorist and close advisor of the popes Pius XI and Pius XII, whose social teachings were highly influenced by German Jesuit thought. Gundlach served as professor at the Pontifical Gregorian University in Rome.

[22] Ernst-Wolfgang Böckenförde and Robert Spaemann: 'Die Zerstörung der naturrechtlichen Kriegslehre. Erwiderung an Pater Gustav Gundlach SJ', in Rudolf Fleischmann et al. (eds.), *Atomare Kampfmittel und christliche Ethik. Diskussionsbeiträge deutscher Katholiken* (Munich: Kösel, 1960), pp. 161–196.

[23] Ernst-Wolfgang Böckenförde and Robert Spaemann, 'Christliche Moral und atomare Kampfmittel', *Militärseelsorge. Zeitschrift des Katholischen Militärbischofsamts* 3 (1961), pp. 267–301.

particular acuity as the nuclear armament of the Bundeswehr was being considered in the Bundestag at the time. Egon Schmitt offered the two authors space for a rejoinder to their critics, which led to attempts—ultimately unsuccessful—by the Federal Ministry of Defence to censor this particular issue of the journal.[24] Sensing a lack of support from the Catholic leadership, particularly the Catholic military bishop, Schmitt resigned his editorship. As Dieter Gosewinkel points out in the biographical interview, the implications of Böckenförde and Spaemann's argument amounted to nothing short of elucidating that a Catholic soldier could not in good conscience execute any order given in connection with the deployment of nuclear weapons if deployed to counter conventional attacks.[25] Despite the potential explosiveness of this argument, the debate remained largely confined to theorists inside the Church and the military. But, as Böckenförde notes in the interview, inside the Church, Gundlach's position was history. No longer could any serious participant in the debate hold on to a similar position.

Since 1961, Böckenförde had been regularly invited to Catholic Student Societies in the GDR, where saint's day activities were often structured as events of public discussion and debate with speakers invited from all over Germany, including the West. In the autumn of 1961, he was a guest at the Catholic Students Society in Leipzig, where his article on 'German Catholicism in 1933' was discussed as well as questions on the rule of law. The construction of the Berlin wall, which had begun merely weeks earlier, made many students realize that they might spend their entire life in the GDR with diminished possibilities for emigration. This affected their professional choices. Could one still pursue the goal of becoming a lawyer if the political regime in which one was going to work was likely to be a non-democratic one? And how overtly political could one afford to be in the here and now, if exit to West Germany was no longer a viable option? Böckenförde was so impressed and agitated by these discussions that he dedicated a monograph to 'the concept of law under communism' a few years later.[26]

In May 1965, he was invited to speak at saint's day activities again, this time at the Catholic Student Society (KSG) of East Berlin. About 450 students attended the event to which three speakers had been invited.[27] Unusually, Böckenförde gave two lectures. The first dealt with the prosecution in West Germany of crimes committed during Nazism, a lecture which led to discussions implicitly comparing West and East German transitional justice policies. Böckenförde on the one hand laid out how the high requirements of proving

[24] Ernst-Wolfgang Böckenförde and Robert Spaemann, 'Noch einmal. Atomare Kampfmittel und christliche Ethik', *Militärseelsorge. Zeitschrift des Katholischen Militärbischofsamts* 4 (1962), pp. 213–229.

[25] 'Biographisches Interview', in Ernst-Wolfgang Böckenförde, *Wissenschaft, Politik, Verfassungsgericht* (Berlin: Suhrkamp, 2011), p. 399.

[26] Ernst-Wolfgang Böckenförde, *Die Rechtsauffassung im kommunistischen Staat* (Munich: Kösel, 1967).

[27] In the audience was the student Wolfgang Thierse (b. 1943), who in reunified Germany became a prominent SPD politician and Speaker of Parliament from 1998 to 2005. When Böckenförde's 1965 address was published for the first time in 2004, Böckenförde dedicated the publication to Thierse.

guilt, which are part of a rule of law state and which he strongly believed in, often made it difficult to sentence individuals who were likely culpable. On the other hand, he also expounded the normative difficulty of deciding where precisely guilt was to be located when crimes were grounded in long chains of command, and of deciding on the amount of guilt at every level when the carrying out of crimes was undertaken by a multitude of contributing offices and functions, from the masterminds of the Holocaust to the conductors of deportation trains. The Stasi (the East German security service, *Staatssicherheit*), which meticulously documented the meeting, appeared to be particularly interested in how students reacted to his discussions of prosecution under rule of law requirements.[28] In his second lecture, the one included in this volume as Chapter III, 'Types of Christian Conduct in the World during the Nazi Regime', Böckenförde addressed the possibility of exhibiting a genuinely Christian comportment in the context of authoritarian rule. He sought to address the question without naming the GDR and without giving the Stasi overt reason to interfere with his visit. Nevertheless, the implications were not lost on the Stasi, which noted in its documentation that Böckenförde was addressing the Nazi era with allusion to the here and now ('unter Anspielung auf die Jetzt-Zeit').[29]

In his address, Böckenförde laid out six types of behaviour drawing on historical examples. He is clear from the outset that no type of conduct is immune from incurring guilt.

The first type consists of a position that prioritizes adherence to religio-natural law over everything else. Politics are viewed as temporal and ultimately meaningless. As he laid out in the 1933 article, Böckenförde regarded this type as most widespread within the German Catholic Church. Here he gives the example of the German Cardinal Bertram, who welcomed the Reich Concordat of 1933, guaranteeing the Church ostensible autonomy in return for its embrace of the Nazi regime. The consequence of this was that the Church could be exploited by the Nazis for political purposes and thus became complicitous in the rise and consolidation of their rule.

A second type describes political engagement for the Nazi regime with the expectation of being able to create a better, Christian-authoritarian order. It was particularly members of the Catholic nobility and Catholic intellectuals who exhibited this kind of behaviour, he writes, overall a small segment of society.

[28] The documentation was discovered after the end of the GDR. It is discussed in Peter-Paul Straube, *Katholische Studentengemeinde in der DDR als Ort eines außeruniversitären Studium generale* (Leipzig: Benno, 1996), Document 55, p. 372 ff, Blätter (ZAIG 1059 Bl. 1–8). Document 55 consists of eight pages on the event. See also Thomas Brose, 'Offensichtliche Anspielung. Böckenförde 1965 in Ost Berlin: Religion und Staat', *FAZ*, 17 June 2015. Brose notes that many reputable scholars were invited to give lectures at the Catholic Student Societies in Leipzig, Dresden, and Berlin at that time and that these (including Karl Rahner, Johann Baptist Metz, Heinrich Böll, Luise Rinser, Hans Maier, Robert Spaemann, and Böckenförde) were usually announced anonymously as 'N.N.', so as not to provoke more far-reaching interference on the part of East German state authorities.

[29] See Straube (note 28), p. 5.

These Catholics 'were instrumentalized as useful idiots, but soon pushed out of whatever positions of influence they may have held'.[30]

A third type describes a widely prevalent position of negotiating the trade-off between behaving as much as possible in an apolitical manner, not 'exposing oneself' unnecessarily on the one hand, and not acting against one's conscience on the other. Böckenförde provides an example from his own memory as a child: whether to join the required activities of the *Jungvolk* on Sunday morning or to go to church instead, which could, however, be interpreted as active resistance and raise suspicion. This type of conduct was not simple conformism, for adherents of this attitude did try to follow Christian precepts wherever possible. But it involved an inner emigration from the world, and was focused primarily on one's own salvation, not on any societal commitment. Böckenförde is clear that this type of conduct often involuntarily buttressed the Nazi regime.

A fourth type consisted of a deliberate and active oppositional stance that was individual-based and not organized: supporting the persecuted, e.g. hiding those sought by the Gestapo. But to do so could also mean performing one's role within the Nazi regime. Böckenförde gives the example of a party functionary who was key to formulating the race laws in a manner that those of mixed descent were categorized as 'Aryans', not Jews. He notes that the moral dilemmas of both a Weberian ethics of conviction and an ethics of responsibility come into view here: was this functionary's behaviour 'in line with an ethics of responsibility to avoid the threat of something worse? Or would it have been the responsible thing to do not to participate, and to let the law become as radical as possible, so that the Jews living in Germany would have immediately realized what they were facing?'[31]

As a fifth type Böckenförde identifies open oppositional activity, of which he observes three variations: First, the public defence of fixed principles, such as exhibited in Franz Graf von Galen's resignation from the Prussian *Landtag*, after his Centre Party had voted for the Prussian Enabling Act. His resignation speech clearly pointed to the consequences of such an act by which parliament relinquished its own right to legislate. A second variation of this type consisted of acts of active political resistance, organized clandestinely, with the consequent risks to oneself and one's family. Böckenförde names the acts of the resistance fighters of 20 July 1944 as examples of this type of conduct. A third variation 'manifested itself as simple, publicly visible Christian protest', such as the actions of Sophie and Hans Scholl in Munich, and the sermons of the bishop of Münster, Clemens August Graf von Galen, who criticized the euthanasia program. Even if not successful, many of these actions continue to resonate today as a testimony and symbol of resistance to injustice. It involved the abdication of life plans and a readiness to bid farewell to the world, creating 'an invulnerability that was not impaired by the threats and actions of those in power'.[32]

[30] Chapter III of this volume, p. 108. [31] Chapter III of this volume, p. 110. [32] Ibid., p. 112.

A final form of conduct was that of the Christian as partisan. Böckenförde gives the example of Kurt Gerstein, a member of the (Protestant) Confessing Church who rose to key positions in the SS organization and, once tasked with organizing the chemical supplies for extermination camps, was able to hold back large quantities. He also passed on reports in 1942 about the extermination activities to various offices inside the Catholic Church, especially the Apostolic Nunciature, as well as to Swedish diplomats and the Dutch resistance. Böckenförde notes that it is impossible to know or even estimate to what extent the machinery of destruction was impeded by Gerstein's actions. After the war, Gerstein was unable to persuade the French authorities that he had been an internal partisan and was put on trial, during which he committed suicide.

Böckenförde notes that weighing up different kinds of evil was a key consideration in choosing between these types of conduct and criticizes that Christian moral doctrine had very little to offer a believer by way of orientation.

The last article in this part is devoted to the principle of religious freedom, which the Catholic Church officially embraced for the first time in its history during the final meeting of the Second Vatican Council on 7 December 1965. When the respective declaration, 'De Libertate Religiosa', was first published in German, it was Böckenförde who was asked to write the introduction to it.[33] Böckenförde views the declaration as nothing less than 'the Church's recognition, justification, and development of a principle that makes it possible for persons of different faiths to coexist in freedom under a system that is acceptable to all'.[34] From a doctrinal point of view, 'De Libertate Religiosa' put the issues to rest that had triggered the confessional wars between Catholics and Protestants: namely, the question of tolerance and religious freedom, 'the great path of suffering for western Christendom'. With the declaration, the Church reconciled the right of truth and the claim to individual freedom on the basis of a person's right to liberty, which it grounded in natural law and theology.

While the Council was convening and before it completed drafting 'De Libertate Religiosa', Böckenförde had published an article in which he sought to illustrate that, from the viewpoint of the legal scholar, the so-called theory of tolerance of 1315, reaffirmed by Pope Pius XII as late as 1953, was untenable.[35] According to the latter, 'religious error had no objective right even to exist', and as a consequence religious freedom was something to be tolerated but, in the final analysis, not to be accepted. Böckenförde noted later that many of the claims and demands he had outlined in that first article of 1964/65

[33] Ernst-Wolfgang Böckenförde, 'Einleitung zur Textausgabe der "Erklärung über die Religionsfreiheit" ', in *Erklärung über die Religionsfreiheit* (Latin and German) (Münster: Aschendorff, 1968), pp. 5–21.

[34] Chapter IV of this volume, p. 116.

[35] Ernst-Wolfgang Böckenförde, 'Religionsfreiheit als Aufgabe der Christen. Gedanken eines Juristen zu den Diskussionen auf dem Zweiten Vatikanischen Konzil', *Stimmen der Zeit* 90(9) (1964/65), pp. 199–213.

were addressed and partly resolved in 'De Libertate Religiosa'.[36] In particular, Böckenförde had given expression to his bewilderment with the position of the Church, according to which it claimed freedom of religion for itself but was not prepared to grant this to others. He had particular trouble comprehending this position as a jurist. Applied as such, the tolerance theory was not a legal principle, but a 'power principle', Böckenförde wrote.[37]

The election of Pope John XXIII in 1963, a champion of equality who declared 'We were all made in God's image, and thus, we are all Godly alike', facilitated a re-thinking on these matters. 'De Libertate Religiosa' for the first time grounded religious freedom in the dignity of the human person as such, which by implication would need to be extended beyond Catholics. The Church thereby abandoned the goal for Christians to live in a Christian public order and facilitated a vision of Christianity as (what Hegel calls) a 'religion of freedom'.[38]

In the article included here, which is based on a 1979 lecture and brings together sections of those earlier two writings with reflections drafted nearly fifteen years after 'De Libertate Religiosa',[39] Böckenförde reminds readers that up until the eighteenth century the punishment for those considered blasphemers was death. This was the principle applied by the Catholic Church (Thomas Aquinas justified that those following a false belief be put to death 'even if they do not endanger others'), but most reformers during the reformation took it on as well. The Protestant theologians Martin Luther and Philip Melanchthon retained these same positions once the question was about the preservation of their own denominations. Luther indeed suggested that Anabaptists deserved death by stoning, and John Calvin in Geneva extended responsibility for blasphemy even to those not holding false beliefs but protecting those who did, because, as he put it, 'by concealing a crime one becomes an accomplice.'

It was only the humanists Erasmus of Rotterdam and Johannes Reuchlin who departed from these positions by arguing that the only effective weapon against deviance was the power of persuasion through rational argument. The Peace of Augsburg of 29 September 1555 was the first testament to institutionalize a legal recognition of more than one justified claim to truth: Its maxim '*cuius regio eius religio*' (whose land, his religion) imparted to the Imperial estates of the Holy Roman Empire the freedom to decide between Catholicism and Lutheranism (later also Calvinism) in their own territories. The Union of Utrecht and the Treaty of Westphalia went further by tying religious freedom not to the ruler,

[36] 'Vorbemerkung' in Ernst-Wolfgang Böckenförde, 'Bekenntnisfreiheit in einer pluralen Gesellschaft', in Ernst-Wolfgang Böckenförde, *Kirche und christlicher Glaube in den Herausforderungen der Zeit. Beiträge zur politisch-theologischen Verfassungsgeschichte 1957–2002*, 2nd ed. (Münster: LIT Publishing House, 2007), p. 194.

[37] 'A maxim of law applies by its nature universally, not only for me, but also against me. A legal principle that seeks to exclude this mutuality is not a legal principle but a power principle' (Chapter IV of this volume, p. 126).

[38] Georg Wilhelm Friedrich Hegel, *Vorlesungen zur Philosophie der Religion*, vol. II (Stuttgart: Glockner, 1959), p. 207.

[39] The article was published in Polish in 1994, in Japanese in 1999, in Korean in 2002, and in Italian in 2007.

but for the first time to the individual. A change in the ruler's denomination no longer required his subjects to follow. The individual-based conception of religious freedom thereby also opened the door to the recognition of rights of religious dissenters.

A further step towards recognizing religious freedom was undertaken when the Prussian Civil Code of 1794 as the first of its kind acknowledged the autonomy of the individual in matters of faith, and as such espoused a private freedom of religion:

> The notions of citizens about the state and God and divine things, the faith and the inner service to God, cannot be the subject of compulsory laws. Every resident in the state must be granted full freedom of religion and conscience. Nobody is obligated to accept prescriptions from the state with regard to his private opinion in matters of religion.[40]

Böckenförde reminds his audience that despite these advances in state law, as late as the nineteenth century and into the twentieth, the Catholic Church still strictly rejected religious freedom as an external right within the framework of the state's legal system. Later, it declared it at most an evil to be tolerated, acceptable in certain situations for the sake of higher good, but as late as 1953, Pius XII still proposed that error had no right to exist before truth. Only with the 1965 Declaration on Religious Freedom by the Second Vatican Council did the Catholic Church make a positive and, in its justification, final about-turn. The external right to religious freedom was accepted, not merely as a given but was explicitly justified positively as grounded in the dignity of the human person (*ipsa dignitate personae humanae*). Whereas all pre-Council declarations (as well as the writings of most early Protestant thinkers) reduced man to a simple object of religious truth as administered by the church, the declaration of 1965 for the first time accepted the autonomous liberty of every individual irrespective of questions of religion. The objective of state law, in this entirely new understanding on the part of the magisterium, was no longer to ensure individual salvation and the defence of eternal truths. Instead, state law became divorced from questions of religion and is seen as a necessary system to guarantee liberty and societal peace. The pathway to this new understanding was through the realization of reciprocity: the Church, while morally upholding its understanding of truth, signalled its readiness to relinquish the privileges it had traditionally enjoyed in Catholic countries, since these might hinder the secular state's mission to guarantee religious freedom for all its citizens.

Böckenförde makes it clear that the impulses for such a radical change in dogma must be found outside the official Church. 'When it comes to religious freedom ... we owe its origins not to the churches, or theologians, or even Christian natural law, but its theoretical preparation to the Christian Humanists and later to the Enlightenment thinkers, and its practical realization to the modern state, to jurists, and to secular rational law.'[41]

[40] Cited by Böckenförde in Chapter IV of this volume, p. 120.

[41] Chapter IV of this volume, p. 121.

In fact, it was partly the Soviet countries' inversion of the traditional Catholic tolerance theory that prompted the sea change in 1965. The principle 'no one must be coerced into accepting the Catholic faith' had been part of Catholic doctrine since 1315, but it did not of course grant the individual the freedom to adopt other faiths, or to renounce Catholicism once it had been adopted. Soviet constitutions turned the tolerance principle on its head by guaranteeing 'the freedom of anti-religious propaganda' to all citizens. The golden rule of Matthew 7.12 had been used against the Church.

Böckenförde is not shy to point out how radically the 1965 declaration departs not only from long-held positions inside the Church but even from recent affirmations of dogma. The 1965 declaration stands 'not only in tension but direct contradiction' to Pius IX's syllabus of 1864, his encyclical 'Quanta Cura' of 1864, and to Pope Leo XIII's encyclical 'Libertas' of 1888. It also stands, according to Böckenförde, against all hitherto extant interpretations of natural law. Close to the end of the article, and in a manner that appears rather parenthetical but whose implications are explosive, Böckenförde calls on the Catholic Church to 'clarify whether the Syllabus and the mentioned encyclicals themselves articulated prohibitions contrary to natural law, or whether Christian natural law has such an inherent range of variation that completely contrary and mutually exclusive statements of natural law are possible with respect to the same question within the space of one hundred and forty years.'[42] What contemporary scholars such as Josef Isensee designated a 'Copernican Revolution' of the Church's official teachings was never acknowledged as such by the Church.

Böckenförde here gets at the fundamental question of how the Church can come to diametrically opposed positions when the acknowledged bases on which the magisterium is built have not been altered. A recent observer summarized it thus: 'There is a topos in the magisterium which may appear peculiar to outsiders. Innovations are never acknowledged as such but are portrayed as organic developments and evolutions of the tradition. Following this logic, there are no historical ruptures, only continuities.'[43]

Looking back, Böckenförde regarded 'De libertate religiosa' as the most important declaration among all of Vatican II. It enabled Catholics to embrace the secular state on substantive grounds, not being forced to merely tolerate it because one happened to live in it. As such, the Declaration fulfilled one of his most important calls of the 1957 article 'The Ethos of Modern Democracy and the Church': the Church accepted the fundamental principle of reciprocity and acknowledged that it could no longer demand privileges for itself from the public order that it was not also prepared to grant to others.

[42] Chapter IV of this volume, p. 134.

[43] Jörg Ernesti, *Papst Leo XIII. Papst und Staatsmann* (Freiburg: Herder, 2019), p. 172.

I

The Ethos of Modern Democracy and the Church [1957]

I. THE ETHOS OF MODERN DEMOCRACY AS A PROBLEM OF THE COMMON GOOD

A Protestant writer recently asserted that modern democracy is a fundamentally unresolved problem for theology as well as the Church,[1] and that there is some uncertainty over what stance one should take towards it.[1] A Catholic, meanwhile, would be more inclined to invoke the rich tradition of his own moral theology and social ethics, which is said to have always included questions about the organization of state and society in its reflections. But if that same Catholic consulted the discussions in the standard textbooks and manuals, he would find very little concrete information. In an effort to preserve the requisite neutrality towards the various forms of government, those discussions do not go beyond a general doctrine of principles. They propagate the Aristotelian schema of types of government, from which they conclude with respect to democracy that the individuals in it, as the bearers of the power of the state, and the representatives they elect have a special obligation to the common good and are responsible for making it a reality according to the degree of their influence.[2] The common good itself, however, remains an abstract and static concept; for the most part it is only roughly circumscribed, but is never concretely specified in terms of the various structural forms of the state and society. This fails to solve the real task

[1] Editors' Note: This was Böckenförde's very first publication, published at the age of twenty-seven. He wrote it in the context of the political campaigns leading up to the 1957 federal elections, during which Church leaders had repeatedly recommended believers to vote for the conservative party, the Christian Democratic Union (CDU). Böckenförde objected to the Church identifying with a particular party or political group, and moreover felt the Church was still not ready to accept fundamental elements of the democratic process.

[1] See Hans Hermann Walz, 'Die Christenheit und die demokratische Gesellschaft', *Zeitwende* (February 1957): 85.

[2] At least in Bernhard Häring, *Das Gesetz Christi* (Freiburg–Munich, 1954), we find the beginning of a concrete treatment. Johannes Messner, *Naturrecht* (Innsbruck–Vienna, 1950), deals with democracy in more detail. However, he offers primarily a sociological-political description and critique and posits a picture of democracy that is oriented towards Anglo-American conditions, where democracy and liberalism have become conjoined into an entity all its own, and which therefore applies to the democracy of continental Europe only with qualifications.

Religion, Law, and Democracy. Ernst-Wolfgang Böckenförde, Oxford University Press (2020). © E.W. Böckenförde, M. Künkler, and T. Stein 2020. DOI: 10.1093/oso/9780198818632.003.0003.

of political ethics, that of establishing a standard for evaluating practical political action, one that is concrete enough, beyond all casuistry, to serve as a guide for a person's conscience. Providing such a solution invariably requires concretizing the concept of the common good, which means determining the factors and behaviours that sustain a specific governmental and social order and allow it to flourish externally and internally. Of course, such a concretization is not possible simply on the basis of supreme principles, whose general validity always comes at the price of a lack of specificity, but only on the basis of an insight into the inner structural laws of the various forms of political order.

Every state form—if the label is understood not merely in formal terms—has its specific ethos. The order it represents does not arise automatically out of something given a priori. Rather, in the final analysis it is—also to the extent that it emerges historically and organically—a product of human shaping. It is the objectification of certain ideas about human coexistence, grounded in reflections about human reason and in decisions freely made. Since this is an order among human beings, that is to say, an ethical-personal entity, a certain ethos is 'inserted into it' from the very outset and presupposed as a sustaining principle—in such a way that the observance of this ethos makes possible the existence of this state form in the first place and therefore constitutes the core of its concrete common good.

This ethos is human and historical. If one seeks to grasp its content, one cannot proceed from ideals that are prefixed to reality as a norm. Instead, one must cleave to reality itself, to the inner structure of the concrete organizational form of the state. Humans insert this ethos into this organizational form as a structural element as part of their organizing and formative actions.

Two things follow from this. First: the question about the ethos of democracy must be posed in concrete terms. The topic of our reflections must not be the ethos of democracy as such, but the ethos of modern continental European democracy. It makes a difference to the spirit of democracy whether it arises out of a long and steady tradition, or is the result of a revolution; whether it emerges out of the religious responsibility of Puritan communities, or out of autonomous thinking in the sense of Rousseau and Kant.

Second: it is entirely possible that this ethos does not in every respect accord with the demands posited by a Christian-natural law image of the state. For it grows out of deliberations of reason and out of decisions freely made, and like those it is therefore subject to the possibility of true and false, of good and evil.

But does this not from the outset cast into question the value and ethical relevance of such an ethos? How, the objection goes, can an ethos be the core substance of the common good and binding as a yardstick if it is not clearly oriented itself towards ideas of order based in natural law, and may even be influenced by bad human thinking and desires?—One should not take this objection lightly. It springs from the innermost core of an ahistorical worldview, one that is at play within traditional social ethics to this day as the legacy of scholasticism.[3]

[3] The problem is examined more closely in the imaginative exposition by Werner Schöllgen, 'Ethik und Ethos', in *Festschrift für Fritz Tillmann* (Düsseldorf, 1949), especially pp. 424ff.

Reality, or the situation that the active human being encounters, is conceived in purely abstract terms, as an 'object' isolated from the past and the future, open to any kind of configuration like some malleable substance. All that matters is implementing the objectively valid principles in each case. This notion, as plausible as it may appear at first glance, fails to grasp the essential historicity of every form of state-political order. We can act within and shape the social realm only on the basis of what is historically already given. Our circumstances and the possibilities of our actions are largely predetermined by the thoughts and action of humans who have gone before and who live with us; but as with all things, what flows together ineradicably here is everything that grows out of human freedom: right and wrong, merit and blame. Thus it is definitely not in our hands to realize a just order in the here and now all at once; rather, all we can do is to take smaller or larger steps towards or away from such an order. For that reason it may be necessary, precisely for the sake of the common good, to respect also less perfect or even contestable political structural forms, provided they do not directly contravene human dignity and divine law; and to place oneself loyally on the ground of their ethos, instead of hollowing them out from the inside for the sake of realizing absolute values and thus surrendering them to the enemies of human order.[4] In this regard, as in all other things, the Christian must not be rigidly dogmatic, but must accept things as they are with the requisite soberness.

II. STRUCTURAL FEATURES OF MODERN DEMOCRACY

Modern democracy is the consistent attempt to establish and erect all state order and authority from below, that is, on the basis of the individual human being. All the formulas that are used to characterize democracy—such as 'the unity (identity) of the governing and the governed' (Franz Schnabel,[II] Carl

[4] It is essentially the same idea when Thomas Aquinas states that an inherently unjust law, which is not binding as such, could be binding for the purpose of avoiding unrest or rebellion, because everyone had to be ready and willing to forego his own good for the common good. He draws the inviolable boundary (only) when it comes to the violation of divine law. See Summa theol. I, II, qu. 96 art. 4.

[II] Franz Schnabel (1887–1966) was a historian best known for his (unfinished) four-volume work on the history of nineteenth-century Germany. He was one of the few historians in the Weimar Republic who believed in parliamentary democracy and defended it in his writings. Partly because of this, he lost his professorship in Karlsruhe under the Nazis. After the war he was appointed professor of history at the University of Munich (1947), where Böckenförde completed his dissertation in history as his advisee in 1960. Schnabel received several honorary doctorates and was an honorary member of the British Historical Association and of the American Historical Association. As a liberal, Schnabel remained an outsider in his profession for a long time. He acknowledged the positive influence of the French Revolution on German political culture, interpreted Lorenz von Stein as a liberal thinker (as Böckenförde did later), promoted the historiography of culture and technology beside political history, and prioritized European over German/national perspectives. Besides his university career, he was also an author of schoolbooks, drawing on his experience as a Gymnasium (secondary school) teacher, as which he had started his career.

Schmitt[III]), 'government of the people, by the people, and for the people' (Abraham Lincoln), 'identity of the subject and object of governance' (Hans Kelsen[IV]), 'All state authority is derived from the people' (Article 20, Basic Law)—have this in common: the social order is to be created by those subject to it. Its substance is determined, not by a superordinated authority independent of its acceptance by the governed, but by the understanding and will of the governed themselves. Democratic constitutions are constructed on this idea. The people choose their representatives; the latter form the government; the 'will of the state', that is, laws and ordinances, are created in the interplay with the government and under the influence of public opinion and the most diverse interest groups, which in turn are established on the basis of individuals. Such an order receives its inner meaning from the notion that human beings are by nature good, created and capable of giving themselves the laws governing their conduct, and that an internal harmony arises automatically from the interplay of individual interests and goals. The champions of modern democracy were animated by this notion, and it formed the basis of their arguments.

The intellectual roots of this conception are easy to discern: they are found in the modern idea of autonomy and individualism, as well as in the optimistic image of humankind propagated by the Enlightenment. For all theoreticians of the law of reason, especially for Rousseau and—following him—Kant, the core problem of the order of the state was how to reconcile the autonomy of the individual with the (unquestioned) necessity of an obligatory social order. Both thinkers grounded the state in the social contract as the idea 'by which alone the legitimacy of the state can be conceived' and they elevated into an indispensable demand that nobody is bound by laws 'other than those to which he himself has given his consent'. It is from this that modern democracy derives its principled legitimacy which transcends every consideration of expediency. Because a social order is absolutely indispensable, the original individual-autonomous freedom undergoes a metamorphosis and returns as the democratic freedom of each individual to participate in determining the social order. That the autonomy of

III Carl Schmitt (1888–1985) was a professor of public law from 1921 to 1945 at various German universities. A brilliant legal and political thinker with a keen sense for power, Schmitt played a decisive role in laying the legal groundwork for the demise of the Weimar Republic and the rise of the Nazi regime. Because of this role, he never again gained a position at any German university after the war. Böckenförde regularly met Schmitt from the mid-1960s until Schmitt's death in 1985. On the relationship between Böckenförde and Schmitt, see 'Biographical Interview with Ernst-Wolfgang Böckenförde [Dieter Gosewinkel]', Chapter XVII of volume 1 of this edition, pp. 369ff; Mirjam Künkler and Tine Stein: 'Carl Schmitt in Ernst-Wolfgang Böckenförde's Work: Carrying Weimar Constitutional Theory into the Bonn Republic', *Constellations* 25 (2018), pp. 225–241; and Mirjam Künkler and Tine Stein, 'State, Constitution and Law. Ernst-Wolfgang Böckenförde's Political and Legal Thought in Context', in volume I of this edition, pp. 1–35.

IV Hans Kelsen (1881–1973) was an Austrian legal philosopher who in the Weimar Republic's legal debates represented a neo-Kantian defence of legal positivism. He fled the Nazi regime in 1933 and eventually became a professor at the University of California, Berkeley, defending a 'pure theory of law'. Hans Kelsen, *Introduction to the Problems of Legal Theory: A Translation of the First Edition of the Reine Rechtslehre or Pure Theory of Law*, trans. Bonnie Litschewski Paulson and Stanley L. Paulson (Oxford: Oxford University Press, 1992, reprinted 2004).

the individual is transferred in the process to the community is a consequence of the principle itself, though from a historical perspective it derived its special legitimation from the conviction—arising from Calvinism—that the people as such cannot go wrong (Cherbury, Rousseau).

The second structural element of modern democracy alongside the modern idea of liberty is equality. With that, modern democracy is part of a larger historical context. As we learn from Alexis de Tocqueville, the development towards equality within society and the state is a dominant theme of modern history. It takes place against the backdrop of historical events in a process that is difficult to discern clearly and can hardly be stopped. By way of the dissolution of fairly straightforward aristocratic and corporative orders based on personal rule and dependency, through the progressive replacement of the rule of persons by the 'rule of norms' (laws), it leads to legal, political, and social equality. It was promoted above all by the Christian doctrine of the equality of all human beings before God, by rationalism's conception of man, which derived the equality of all human beings from the reason with which all were endowed, and by the politics of the absolutist kings, who set out to force all estates and corporations into the same status devoid of political rights.

The equality that modern democracy demands and realizes is political, but not social (even though political equality creates all the preconditions for social equality). It is not a few who are to govern, but the people as a whole, all citizens of the state, and they should do so in the same manner. Democracy means equality in the rights of political participation. This finds its clearest expression in universal and equal suffrage, whose triumphal march is unstoppable once the ground of democracy has been won, and against which—as reality has repeatedly confirmed—no legitimate democratic argument can be found, in spite of all the obvious problems.—Everyone has the same opportunity to rise politically, he must only find enough people to support him. Unlike what is found in a monarchy, any qualitative difference between the rulers and the ruled is precluded. The political leader is created by those he leads and from among their midst; he does not govern on the basis of his own self, but because and as long as he is accepted as the leader by those he leads. He must face competition over this leadership and step down as soon as a competitor wins the confidence of the governed in his stead. The universal right to stand for office, equal access to public offices, the periodic election of the popular representation within relatively short periods of time, the entire parliamentary governmental system, that is, the dependence of the government on the confidence of the parliament and its responsibility towards him: these are all an expression of this principle and find their legitimacy in it.

In this way, free and equal citizens support the rule and tolerate it only as free and equal citizens, as a well-known professor of public law put it.[5] The connection between and mutual constraint of these principles determine the innermost structural law and structural ethos of modern democracy.

[5] Hermann Jahrreiss, *Mensch und Staat* (Cologne-Berlin, 1957), p. 95.

If democratic freedom is to apply to all, a change of the existing order requires not the will of a few, but at least the consent of the majority. If it is fewer, those who oppose change would be disadvantaged; in the reverse case, the same would hold for those who support change. Equality demands the same thing. If all citizens have the same rights of political participation (which also means: equal opportunity to exert political influence), every political opinion must be seen as equally important; qualitative differentiations must not exist. The old distinction between *pars sanior* and *pars maior*[V] derived from canon law cannot endure before the form of modern democracy. On the basis of democratic equality, to the extent that we are talking about the legal effect, voices can only be counted, but not weighted.

Thus, the majority principle is not merely a technical makeshift for democracy, but is structurally appropriate to it. That does not imply, however, that democracy simply means majority rule or majority absolutism, as its opponents often contend. Just as freedom and equality establish the majority principle, they also constrain it. If every political conviction must be seen as legally equal and all citizens are entitled to the same democratic freedom, the very nature of these principles prohibits the majority—in concrete terms: the political groups holding power—from establishing itself as absolute. Precisely the right of the majority to make decisions that are binding on the social whole, to possess legitimacy, rests on the fact that it competes with the minority for political leadership, and that the latter has the absolute equal opportunity to become the majority itself. All political groups have the same right to exist, and a given minority is always a potential majority. Moreover, it is part of freedom and equality that no one claims sole validity for his own political convictions and denies that the political conviction of the opponent is worth discussing or has the democratic right to exist. (That does not mean he must believe that it promotes the common good or is at least relatively correct within the context of a general relativism). This entails in general, but especially in situations when coalitions are formed, a genuine willingness to compromise, not as a tactical manoeuvre because one is not (yet) strong enough to govern alone, but as a genuine concession and renunciation because one accords also to one's political opponent the right to have his own political convictions.

Here we have now in fact arrived at the ethical foundation of modern democracy—at the very inner core, as it were. On the one hand, democracy requires that everyone is inwardly ready to loyally accept, for the sake of the order of the whole, the decisions of the majority for as long as they are in force, even if he does not approve of them. On the other hand, such an attitude can be expected only if the ruling groups do not assert themselves absolutely legally or ideologically, but leave also to the opponent the same democratic freedom and the same opportunity to win political power. Here we encounter the constitutional element of modern democracy, the objective basis of justice that is

[V] *pars maior*: the numerically superior party; *pars sanior*: the party that has greater insight into divine will.

preserved in the face of all autonomy and all functionalism.[6] Democracy and the *Rechtsstaat* (state governed by the rule of law) occupy different levels and affect different things: democracy affects the bearers and form of state governance, the *Rechtsstaat* affects the substance and scope of state governance. It is in that core area, however, where the form necessarily goes beyond the 'formal' if it does not wish to be a coercive system, that the two come into contact: electoral equality, freedom of association and assembly, freedom of personal and political opinions, including freedom of the press, are inseparable from democracy, and as 'fundamental democratic rights' form the internal limits to every will of the majority, regardless of whether or not they are derived from constitutional routes.

However, these basic democratic rights do not guarantee a specific content of governance; instead, they secure the equal freedom to create new content or preserve the existing one. Still, precisely therein lies the difference between democracy and (majority) dictatorship. For this is where it becomes evident that modern democracy is not merely a value-neutral technique for the formation of the political will, one that is also open to every majority absolutism—this is how it was widely understood in public law doctrine of the Weimar period. Instead, it is a system of political order that has its own value foundation in the principles of democratic freedom and political equality, and which is entitled to defending that foundation against internal enemies. It is entirely in this spirit that the Federal Constitutional Court recently justified the prohibition of the KPD [German Communist Party] not on the grounds that this party denied the system of private property or religious freedom, but on the grounds that its goals and activities were incompatible with the democratic principles of freedom and equality.[VI] Incompatible because that party claims the sole and absolute validity for its political conviction (Marxism-Leninism), and because it sees in the political opponent merely the enemy who should be stripped of his rights at the earliest possible opportunity.[7]

The structural ethos of modern democracy thus relates essentially to formal values; this does not yet establish, but merely makes possible, a specific content of governance, such as private property, occupational freedom, the protection of marriage and the family. That accords with the origin of modern democracy in the idea of autonomy: only freedom and equality are institutionalized;

[6] In this sense Carl Schmitt, *Legality and Legitimacy* (Durham, NC: Duke University Press, 2004), especially pp. 30–33.

[VI] In 1956 the Federal Constitutional Court ruled the Communist Party (KPD) to be unconstitutional. According to Article 21 Section 2 Basic Law 'parties that, by reason of their aims or the behaviour of their adherents, seek to undermine or abolish the free democratic basic order or to endanger the existence of the Federal Republic of Germany shall be unconstitutional'. Earlier, in 1952, the court had already ruled the Socialist Reich Party (SRP), an openly neo-nationalist-socialist party, to be unconstitutional. See for a summary, interpretation, and a translation of the main passages of both cases Donald P. Kommers and Russell A. Miller: *The Constitutional Jurisprudence of the Federal Republic of Germany*, 3rd ed. (Durham, NC: Duke University Press, 2012), pp. 286–292.

[7] *Entscheidungen des Bundesverfassungsgerichts*, vol. V (Tübingen, 1956), pp. 198–200, 224–227.

in terms of content, democracy contains only what individuals and groups—in the final analysis, the people as a whole—insert into it through disposition, attitude, and discernment. Montesquieu, to whom we owe many insights into the nature and conditions of the state order, saw this connection when he said that the principle on which democracy is built was virtue. Precisely because the democratic order is constituted from the very bottom up, from the individual, it depends, like no other state form, on what the individual brings to it. Therein lies its possibility, but also its constant peril.

In spite of what is in this sense its 'formal' character, this ethos, as an ethos that is structurally necessary, forms the core of all common good in every modern democracy. This entails two things. First: all other things that make up the concrete common good of the state community must be built upon this foundation, and they must not cast into question that foundation for the sake, perhaps, of some higher values. It is a general experience that higher values can be realized without risk and in a lasting way only if the foundation (of lower values) on which they rest is secured. After all, what did all the constitutional protections avail the Weimar democracy once the foundation, the democratic loyalty of the political groups, ceased to exist?—Second: as long as this core of the common good is preserved, the state is in principle still 'in order', even if a lot of other things might happen that are detrimental to the common good.

To put it in concrete terms: for democracy, a fair electoral law is more critical than a good education law (even if that is also very important). And the worst that can happen to democracy is not an inadequate realization of natural law demands, but measures and manipulations that curtail the political opponent's freedom of opposition and the equal opportunity to gain political power, even if these measures are implemented (in good conscience) in an effort to realize 'absolute values'. The crucial point is that these things are all seen in the right proportion, not only in the realm of theoretical reflections, but likewise in the realm of practical action, when it comes to the political decisions of the voters, the popular representatives, and the government. A political decision that wishes to be truly beneficial to the common good must be oriented towards this framework of the concept of the common good. This implies in general terms that what is demanded in the sense of a political decision of conscience cannot be determined abstractly, according to timeless criteria of the concept of the common good such as 'recognition of natural law', but only historically and concretely. Looking back, what was required in 1933, then, was to support the political group that promised to offer the staunchest resistance to National Socialism on the basis of a liberal order, even if it did not recognize the confessional school or did not fully respect the natural law conception of property. What the common good demanded was, first and foremost, to protect a liberal-democratic order as such against the emerging dictatorship of National Socialists.

It is understandable that various objections are raised against the developed structural image of modern democracy. They are directed primarily against the 'formal' conception of democracy, which is said to be fundamentally Rousseauist. And—connected to this—against the far-reaching separation of democracy and the *Rechtsstaat*, which, it is argued, fails to grasp the boundaries that are drawn a priori by the idea of law for every bearer of state authority, including the people; moreover, that separation is also refuted by reality, in Switzerland and the USA, for example. Democracy, it is said, can receive its meaning only from the realization of material values and the guarantee of governance in accordance with reason, otherwise it is detrimental to the common good.[8]

In response, it must be pointed out that my concern here is not to show how modern democracy is supposed to be (and can be), nor to provide an intellectual justification for it. Instead, the sole aim is to show what it is, namely a form of political order that is historically evolved and shaped by a specific spirit. To be sure, democracy should always be a constitutional democracy and lead to governance that accords with reason. However, the question is whether democracy is inherently a constitutional democracy, or whether its being thus is not a constant demand whose fulfilment depends on the people's constitutional thinking and desire and its political discernment. Anyone who evaluates the institutions and the political reality of modern democracy (one can point, for example, to the race question in South Africa, the Black issue in the USA, and the highly emotional character of electoral campaigns everywhere) will be forced to realize two things. First, democracy and the *Rechtsstaat* are very different things, and the nature of modern democracy lies much more in voluntarism than in the 'rule of reason'. Second, however, democracy does not turn into a dictatorship simply because it leaves certain substantive demands unfulfilled. Moreover, one must beware of devaluing democracy and its ethos rashly because they are merely 'formal'. Neither Weimar democracy nor the Austrian republic perished because they were insufficiently constitutional, but rather because—in addition to other circumstances—many political groups and functionaries lacked precisely that 'formal' ethos of democracy.

Finally, as far as Switzerland and the USA are concerned, one must not overlook—leaving aside that here, too, ideality and reality diverge—that democracy arose in those countries on different intellectual foundations. We did not receive democracy from religious motives that sprang from Puritan-Calvinist roots, but by way of Rousseau, the French Revolution, and the modern notion of equality, as part of a movement that was initially focused, not on service to a common task, but on a desire to possess (*Habenwollen*) and the dismantling of traditional authorities. Much of what was brought into democracy in Switzerland and the USA from the outset and became institutionally consolidated through long practice is something we must still achieve.

[8] Similarly Johannes Messner, *Naturrecht*, p. 525, when he sees the nature of democracy in the greatest possible application of reason. But he is then compelled to admit right away that fictive elements always come into play in the process, and these need to be curtailed.

III. THE CHRISTIAN AND THE ETHOS OF MODERN DEMOCRACY

The consequences that arise from the structural picture that I have laid out for the stance of the Christian within and towards modern democracy seem initially distressing. One should say this openly and not gloss over it for reasons of expediency of whatever kind. The political thinking and desire of the Christian, especially the Catholic Christian, is oriented toward substantive values, not towards a formal constitution. He is concerned with the order and shaping of governmental and societal life out of the principles that arise from revelation and natural law, and from their application, insofar as they concern the societal sphere. By contrast, questions about the form of government are of secondary importance. The Christian tends to answer those questions depending on the extent to which a given form of government ensures or facilitates the realization of these valid principles. Moreover, a deep chasm separates him from the intellectual origins of modern democracy. Through his faith he knows that human beings are bound to the immutable norms of the divine order of the world and bear original sin, which is why he will always oppose the modern idea of autonomy and the image of humankind propagated by the Enlightenment. Added to this is an ambivalent relationship to modern ideas of freedom, though it is probably grounded less in dogma than in theological doctrines.[VII] Shaped in part by centuries of authoritative systems, European Christianity's value system accords a much higher place to 'good order' and to virtue than it does to individual freedom. Asserting and preserving the order of truth with all means of power also against opponents and those who hold different ideas, and exercising a certain coercion to virtue vis-à-vis one's fellow human beings, continues to be seen as service to the Kingdom of God. By contrast, respect for the individual's freedom to make decisions, which also entails the risk of a less perfect order, carries the odium of indifferentism. Does truth not possess a higher right than the majority? Must this democratic ethos, if followed to its logical conclusion, not invariably lead to a profound relativism, and eventually turn all social order into the mere sum of purely functional rules of interaction? This raises the precise question: to what extent can the (Catholic) Christian, if he is sincere, be a loyal democrat?

In this relationship to democracy a distinction is commonly made between a realm of conscience and a realm of expertise. In the realm of expertise—meaning: as far as the relative autonomy of the areas of cultural expertise extends—the only thing that supposedly matters is the objective correctness of a decision, and that is largely a question of expertise, experience, and discernment, about which there can be different opinions. To that extent, the majority principle and a willingness to compromise are permissible. But in the realm of

[VII] With 'dogma' Böckenförde refers to official Church doctrines which until the paradigm shift of Vatican II had denied individual freedom. In contrast, 'theological doctrines' here denote systematic interpretations of the Bible based on the common methodologies used in this discipline.

conscience, the argument goes, a Christian can neither enter into compromises nor accept as obligatory majority decisions that run counter to his conviction; this is where every democracy encounters its immutable boundaries.

While this differentiation does narrow the problem to a more restricted area and thereby defuses it somewhat, it does not yet resolve it (or only in a negative sense). For in democracy, the refusal to compromise in the realm of conscience remains fundamentally unchallenged only as long as the worldview of a people is sufficiently homogenous to preclude questions of conscience from being pulled into the political discussion. Moreover, one cannot draw a sharp line between the realm of conscience and the realm of expertise, because the religious and natural law principles that belong to the realm of conscience exert a formative effect on the realm of expertise, as is particularly evident in the areas of marriage and family law, the educational system, and the law governing state–church relations.

If a Christian adopts this distinction, the result is that he will sometimes think democratically, and sometimes autocratically. To the extent that he sees the realm of conscience threatened, compromises and coalitions become tactical manoeuvres for him, mere means to an end, and he is inwardly no longer willing to accord the political opponent the equal opportunity to attain power, the primordial right of democracy.

Without becoming aware of it, he thus succumbs to a friend–foe attitude: while the opponent is supposed to remain untouched in his person, substantively—in this case: politically—he must be removed and his influence must be eliminated. But that attitude must invariably corrode every state—and especially a democratic one—from the inside. The historical accomplishment of the modern state lies precisely in the fact that it overcame the friend–foe groupings of the feudal era (feuds) and of the confessional civil wars, gradually turning human beings who waged war on one another for religious or political reasons into 'civilized' citizens living peacefully under a shared order. Any approximation to a situation of civil war, however disguised, therefore threatens its very existence. And a *democratic* state order can afford such an attitude least of all. Rather, if it wishes to survive, it presupposes a *partnership* in the relationship among political groups and opponents. How else but through partnership can loyalty and a state consciousness arise on the ground of freedom and equality, and how else can one justify state authority and sovereignty that was initially completely dismantled in the wake of the process of democratization? One of the—sometimes painful—experiences of history is that there is no going back. Once the grounds of autonomy and of the modern idea of freedom have been reached, authority and sovereignty cannot be justified against them, but only through them, that is, from a shared inner affirmation.

Such a partnership, however, means a great deal: namely, allowing every person who does not himself advance a claim to exclusivity and thereby negate partnership from the outset to be a subject with equal rights, whatever his attitude and political goals may be beyond that. This leads back to the structural ethos of modern democracies. But it also shows that this cannot be simply dismissed as relativism. Rather, in positive terms it entails the unconditional acceptance of one's fellow humans as persons, in other words, an ethos of personal partnership also in the politico-social realm. Should there not lie in that also for Christians a possible political attitude that is worth pondering in greater detail? Moreover, beyond the safeguarding of the few minimum conditions of an external social order, is coercion on behalf of the good and the order of truth truly the final theological point of reference, seeing that God Himself, all disappointments notwithstanding, time and again entered into the risk of freedom with us humans?

Such a stance, however, would also call for a changed attitude towards politics. The immediate goal of political action would not be the realization of absolute postulates of justice (by way of autocratic commands), but the facilitation of the peaceful coexistence of emancipated human beings under a shared order that is in some way acceptable to all. While such an order requires the foundation of justice, the emphasis has noticeably shifted. It would require foregoing a few conventional expectations against the state order that are regarded as indispensable; compromise and agreement would be given an entirely different function. It would not matter so much that the state by itself compels demands of natural law, but that it keeps open for its citizens the possibility to live in accordance with them. Moreover, many forms of thinking and behaviour from the time of the denominational state and of the Christian authoritarian state would no longer fit into this picture of political action. The state that was neutral with regard to denominations would no longer appear as a potentially possible concession in the sense of the lesser evil, but as a legitimate political goal, because it allows everyone to live according to his conviction and protects him within it.[9] The pronouncement by Frederick the Great, that in his state 'everyone can go to heaven in his own way' is usually considered by Christians an expression of freethinking and indifferentism, and it may well have been written out of such an attitude. But as the maxim of *state* action it has a definitely positive core, one that is often overlooked. Moreover, in its day it was by no means put forth as a carte blanche for irreligiosity, but as a rejection of a Protestant assault on Catholic schools that had been set up in Potsdam for the children of Catholic soldiers.

However, an inner affirmation of modern democracy is easier and entails a smaller risk in a state in which the Christian faith still determines public life (at least by way of tradition), as in England, or where a positive liberalism prevails, as in the USA, than in states split by different worldviews and additionally burdened by the legacy of a cultural war. On the other hand, Christians run the risk of failing to grasp the opportunity that the principle of democratic freedom offers them. For the question remains whether, under the conditions of an open and secularized society, which is simply part of our politico-social reality, questions extending into the realm of conscience cannot be resolved in the best and most lasting way if Christians take modern democracy seriously—which does

[9] On this, see also Richard Egenter, 'Staat, Toleranz und Konfessionen', *Hochland* (April 1954): 305.

not mean that they would have to consider it the best or even only possible form of government—and place themselves loyally on the ground of its ethos: that is to say, they demand for themselves only what they are willing to concede to everyone who thinks differently. Does that not make them more credible and unassailable in their demands?

IV. THE CHURCH AND THE ETHOS OF MODERN DEMOCRACY

Unlike the individual Christian, the Church—here and in what follows I am talking chiefly about the official [Catholic] Church—does not stand directly within the sphere of political decisions and responsibility. At the same time, it cannot do what a culturally militant liberalism demands, namely withdraw from public life into a merely private, apolitical sphere. Its mission and task, to proclaim the Word of God to humankind and to bring about the salvation of the faithful, imposes on it an obligation to bring the commandments of God and the immutable ethical norms to the conscience of all humans, including the powerful in the state and society, and to that extent it assumes an office of guardian for the orders of the world. So much for the principle. The way in which the Church can and should exercise that mandate depends on the changing historico-political context; and it must be determined by the Church in each instance on the basis of a correct understanding of the prevailing reality.

The traditional stance of the Church in and towards the state took shape in Europe at a time when the states were monarchies and Christian authoritarian states. Throne and altar were the guarantors and the real bearers of public order. Moreover, the monarchical state was structurally dependent on the blessing and the benevolent attitude of the Church (for the authority of the ruler by the Grace of God, the blessing of the Church was the strongest, indeed, the indispensable, pillar). It was thus in that state's own interest to be a Christian state. For that reason, it bound the Church institutionally to itself in the form of the state Church, while at the same time it liked to lend it its secular arm, and was generally willing (and compelled) to follow admonitions from the Church. In Prussia and in the German Empire, dismantling the *Kulturkampf*[VIII] soon proved an imperative of the reason of state. For the Church this created an ambivalent situation: it wore the golden fetters of being a state church, but within the context of that bond it could confront the state and its government with its own authority, and if need be even peremptorily, and lend emphasis to its demands and admonitions by withholding its blessing.

VIII The *Kulturkampf* (culture war) was a struggle of Chancellor Bismarck's government against the Catholic Church in the 1870s concerning the role and power of Catholic institutions in predominantly Protestant Prussia. Bismarck enacted a series of anti-Catholic laws, including the disbanding of Catholic organizations, confiscation of church property, and banishment or imprisonment of clergy. The discriminating laws, some of which were not repealed until fifty years later, left Catholics deeply alienated from the public order as well as the majority culture for decades to come.

In modern democracy the situation is fundamentally different. The democratic society, which builds its state from the bottom up, on the will of those who are subject to state authority, does not—politically speaking—require the blessing of the Church. It does encounter the Church and must reckon with it as an important factor of public opinion, and it may also strive to arrive at some amicable arrangement with it, but structurally it is not dependent upon it. To that extent the democratic state—seen as an institution—is religiously indifferent. For the Church this means liberation from the fetters and constraints of being a state Church, but also the loss of its position of power within the state.

Within this changed reality, the Church can exercise its office and pursue its mandate only by utilizing the special opportunities to bring influence to bear in order to push through with their help the demands it deems necessary. What this looks like in practical terms is that it seeks to influence the pluralistic groups contending for power in the state and supports those that are close to its demands or embrace them. It instructs its faithful to give their vote only to those candidates who are willing to advocate for these demands (the 'Christian principles'). It also calls upon the faithful to engage in protests and demonstrations to lend weight to the Christian demands vis-à-vis opposing groups or the government.

From the perspective of democracy there is inherently no objection to this path, as the Church is merely using its democratic right, which is open to every other group in the same way. But the Church must be cognizant of the inner consequences that arise from this. If it makes use of the democratic rights in this way, it no longer confronts the democratic state as a—in the final analysis—incommensurable partner on a higher level. Instead, figuratively speaking, it enters into the state, onto the ground of the pluralistic democratic society, and in so doing submits itself to the structural laws of the democratic order. It cannot complain if outsiders place it on a par with other pluralistic groups such as unions and interest groups, and it must accept it when the political opponents of the groups it supports also see it as a political opponent. But above all: if, with democratic right, it supports certain political groups, it must also run the risk that these groups will lose, and it must make its peace with that. For there is one thing it cannot do, once it has entered onto the ground of democracy, without losing all its credibility in the political realm: to use democracy as long as a majority is achieved, but in case of a defeat, to revert to the natural law position and invoke its incommensurable position.

Anyone who is familiar with the structure and practice of the Church's political thinking knows that this will always be a critical point for the Church. Not only because its own constitution is grounded on authority and obedience, and because it has been accustomed for centuries to confront the state partner authoritatively, but also for principled reasons: because it does not feel that it is able to foreswear fundamental concerns in favour of the ethos of a political structure. The course of the battle over schools inside and outside Germany offers an instructive example.[IX] On the ground of democracy, the Church gets

[IX] The Catholic Church initiated and supported political claims of a parents' 'natural' (here: God-given) right to decide on the education of their children (*Elternrecht*) and thus to insist on their

into the situation, with a certain kind of inevitability, of either losing its standing among the groups of democratic society and being accused of dishonesty (a charge that also makes up the core of what is labelled on the outside as clericalism), or of being unfaithful to its own mandate, as it understands it. This never completely resolvable antinomy also explains the inner affinity of the Church for authoritarian regimes, as long as it believes that they rest on a Christian basis. That became especially clear, for example, in Austria in 1934.[X]

All of this raises the question of whether the most appropriate path for the Church may not be different from the one described here: namely, that it does not make use of the special possibilities that modern democracy makes available, but always confronts the democratic society as a partner with its own mission and mandate, and from this vantage point (and the special authority this bestows) exercises its office as admonisher and guardian. That does not entail a renunciation of political efficacy, as such a renunciation would be unacceptable. But it would mean that the Church remains aloof as far as possible from the conflicts between the political groups (thus releasing its faithful into complete political autonomy), seeks the same kind of contact to all political groups to arrive at an acceptable modus vivendi with all of them, and remains open to them all, in order to infuse into them the religio-political impulses that it is able to impart to political work.

To be sure, this path means foregoing some (tactical) immediate successes and some supporting positions for it presupposes the affirmation of pluralistic society and thus of a state that is institutionally not Christian. On the other hand, however, it offers the chance to secure Christian values and convictions in a more lasting way than through temporary, majority-bound, and therefore contested institutionalizations. For in a democratic society the real safeguard lies not in such institutionalizations, but in the positive-liberal attitude of those in power and of the people themselves, in that everyone, out of respect for the freedom of the other, respects every genuine conviction (and thus also the Christian one) and allows it to flourish. A Church that is 'apolitical' to this extent, which exercises its office as guardian and watcher beyond day-to-day politics independent from (and freely vis-à-vis) *all* groups and is not branded a political power bloc, has much better prospects to be heard also by those who are inwardly removed from it and recognize its legitimate demands. And a Church that behaves this way, while maintaining its own position, can summon also its ideological opponent to the democratic ethos with credibility and inner legitimation and demand adherence to it.

right to send their children to confessional schools (which moreover ought to be state-funded). In the early days of the Federal Republic of Germany this battle over schools almost endangered the adoption of the Basic Law.

[X] The Austrian Catholic Church welcomed and supported the authoritarian turn from the first republic to a fascist regime. In 1933, Chancellor Engelbert Dollfuß, a leading figure in the dissolution of the republic, presented his programme for a 'Christian state' at the Catholic Church Day in Vienna. In 1934, a concordat between the Vatican and Austria was signed, with which the Catholic Church's support for Austro-fascism was legitimated by the Pope.

Of course, one should not idealize the political realities, and the Christian least of all. A democratic stance also presupposes multilateralism, and in the final analysis partnership is only possible if the Other, too, wishes to be a partner. One can hardly use democratic loyalty and an appeal to the democratic ethos to oppose a closed power block that asserts itself absolutely, such as a militant and undemocratic socialism. Again and again there can be situations in which a Church that sees itself as a partner to democratic society has no choice but to intervene in the contest between the political groups. But there is a fundamental difference whether such an approach is the *ultima ratio*, after all other efforts have failed, or whether it becomes the rule and serves to provide political support in a particular direction.

Finally, it is important to return this entire issue to its appropriate system of ethical principles. For here, too, we are dealing with the concrete common good of a concrete state, which is always merely the best that is historically feasible, not a fixed abstraction, and which is in no way exhausted by the mere preservation of Christian values. It is not simply a question of practical prudence how the Church carries out its mission for the world, whether it leaves behind obsolete positions and ways of thinking, and to what extent it accepts the democratic ethos. In the spirit of Christian political ethics, what applies here, as well, is the yardstick of a properly understood appropriateness; but the latter cannot be concretely defined without taking into account historical reality, with respect to its negative sides too. The issue is not to defend or condemn modern democracy, but to see it for what it is, and then do what is right.

II

German Catholicism in 1933

A Critical Examination [1961]

It is not through silence that we can carry away the burden of the past, but by expressing what has happened, and by thereby honoring the attendant circumstances.

Federal President Heinrich Lübke on the National Day of Mourning 1960

When the Nazi regime, after twelve years in power, ended in utter military and political collapse in the spring of 1945, it was for German Catholics—as for Protestant Christians—the hour of liberation from an ever more oppressive persecution.[I]

On the whole, German Catholics, led and fortified by their bishops and clergy, had resisted this pressure bravely and in the process proved committed opponents of National Socialism. As a result, in the political rebuilding after the war significant responsibility fell on them almost by default, further enhanced by the trust that the three victorious Western powers frequently accorded them. Understandably enough, this situation was not suited to raising and examining the question whether and to what extent Catholics and their spiritual leaders might have helped to consolidate Nazi rule in its early stages and had offered their own cooperation. German Catholicism was content with its demonstrated opposition to the Nazi system, and seized the new opportunities for exerting influence without hesitation and without taking a closer look at its own past. And no one else was interested in doing so, either.[1]

[I] Editors' Note: The article was published in English translation in the same year: 'German Catholicism in 1933', *Cross Currents* 11 (1961), 281–303. The present text is a new translation. We thank Christoph Kösters from the Committee for Contemporary History for sound advice regarding the annotations pertaining to Catholic intellectuals and organizations.

[1] The debates over the continued validity of the *Reichskonkordat* were equally unsuited to setting in motion an unbiased clarification of the actual events, even if they provided a sustained stimulus to the discussion. On this see, on the one hand, K. D. Bracher, *Nationalsozialistische Machtergreifung und Reichskonkordat* (Wiesbaden, 1956), and, on the other hand, Ernst Deuerlein, *Reichskonkordat* (1956), and R. Leiber, S.J., 'Zu Karl Dietrich Bracher, Nationalsozialistische Machtergreifung und Reichskonkordat' (unpublished).

Religion, Law, and Democracy. Ernst-Wolfgang Böckenförde, Oxford University Press (2020). © E.W. Böckenförde, M. Künkler, and T. Stein 2020. DOI: 10.1093/oso/9780198818632.003.0004.

Now that expert historical examination has made an abundance of material accessible and has shed light on many events that were previously obscured,[2] there is even greater urgency to openly raise the question about the conduct of German Catholicism in 1933. This is independent of whether the findings that emerge will be seen as agreeable or disagreeable at this time. The duty to historical truth brooks no gradations, and in the end the cause one is interested in is always best served by not avoiding the truth. Of course, in times of open or concealed ideological enmities, every objective statement and every objective argument can be misused as a poisoned weapon. But anyone who would consider a critical word of reflection within the Catholic Church as opportune only if it could not be used against it by an enemy would have to wait until the end of time: for it is one of the laws of the life of the Church that it never lacks for enemies.

It is therefore not the intent of these pages to level belated accusations in one direction or another and in this way 'come to terms' with the past; the disguised civil war of the [post-war] political purges has already sufficiently complicated the objective engagement with the Nazi period. Rather, the only goal can be to report what happened truthfully and to get to the bottom of fallacies to which contemporaries succumbed at the time. From this one can most readily draw lessons and consequences for the present and the future.[3]

I. HOW DID THE CHURCH AND CATHOLICS ACT IN 1933?

On the eve of the crisis year 1933, German Catholicism presented itself as a social group solidly united on the basis of a religion and worldview, organized into numerous occupational and professional organizations, and bound by a common political will. It had left the ghetto status of former times far behind, and had achieved a respectable and acknowledged position in social and political life. Ever since the days of the *Kulturkampf*,[II] its political representation, and to a large extent also its political home, was the Zentrumspartei [Centre Party] (later also the Bayerische Volkspartei [Bavarian People's Party, BPP]). Through this party it had become one of the pillars of the democratic-parliamentarian state of Weimar, which was now in crisis.

[2] Rudolf Morsey, 'Die Deutsche Zentrumspartei', in Matthias and Morsey, eds., *Das Ende der Parteien 1933* (Düsseldorf, 1960); Ludwig Kaas, *Tagebuch*, 7–20 April 1933, and *Briefwechsel zum Reichskonkordat*, ed. Rudolf Morsey, *Stimmen der Zeit*, vol. 166 (September 1960), pp. 422ff., vol. 167 (October 1960), pp. 11ff. On Morsey's essay see Karl Buchheim, 'Warum das Zentrum unterging', *Hochland* (October 1960): 15–27, and S.J. Robert Leiber, 'Reichskonkordat und Ende der Zentrumspartei', *Stimmen der Zeit* 167 (December 1960), pp. 213–223.

[3] The fate of the Zentrumspartei (Centre Party) in 1933 was recounted by Karl Buchheim (see note 2), which is why this question is left aside here.

[II] The *Kulturkampf* (culture war) was a struggle of Chancellor Bismarck's government particulary against the Catholic Church in the 1870s concerning the role and power of Catholic institutions in predominantly Protestant Prussia. Bismarck enacted a series of anti-Catholic laws, including the disbanding of Catholic organizations and orders, confiscation of church property, and banishment or imprisonment of clergy. Some of the discriminating laws were not repealed until fifty years later.

Within the political leadership of German Catholicism, and this deserves special consideration, the episcopate and the clergy played a dominant role. This was one legacy of the *Kulturkampf*. During that conflict, Catholics, faced with a state that was threatening their right to a religious life, had rallied closely around their bishops and priests, who were most directly exposed to the state's persecution; ever since, they saw them as their true leaders also in the secular-political realm. Of course, this did not become immediately apparent as long as the founding generation of the Centre Party[III] was politically active, but it did become increasingly noticeable from the turn of the century. This circumstance invested the pronouncements from their spiritual leaders almost invariably with special authority and efficacy; moreover, securing religio-cultural freedom and the effectiveness of the Church was the overriding political goal. As time went on, the clergy that was active in the Centre Party gradually took on more and more of a leadership position. The dominant role in the party of the ecclesiastical element (which had begun with the party congress of 1928 and was especially acute during the crisis years of 1932/33)[4] was therefore not the expression of a clerical claim to leadership brought to the party from the outside. Instead, it was entirely in keeping with the internal situation of German Catholicism as it had developed since the *Kulturkampf*. 'Under their [the bishops'] guidance we cannot go wrong': these words of a brave parliamentarian from the Centre Party in the days of May 1933 characterize the expectation that was alive within the Catholic laity toward its spiritual leaders. Of course, German Catholics could have no inkling that it was precisely these leaders who would call upon them to affirm and support the Nazi state.

What made this call all the more surprising was that as late as the beginning of 1933, as well as immediately after the *Machtübernahme*, German Catholicism seemed a firm and unshakable opponent of the Nazi movement. The bishops

[III] The Centre Party was founded in 1870 by lay Catholics as a political force to combat Bismarck's anti-Catholicism policies. During the Kaiserreich, the party won a quarter of the seats in the Reichstag, and by the beginning of the Weimar Republic had become the second-largest party. In exchange for certain promises by the Nazis for the rentention of particular constitutional institutions (such as parliamentary rights) and specific governmental guarantees (such as religious instruction in public schools), and also in light of immense pressures against its personnel (extending even to death threats), the Centre Party voted in favour of the Enabling Act in 1933 (*Ermächtigungsgesetz*) and thus made possible the formally legal transfer of power to Chancellor Adolf Hitler. Its support for the Enabling Act did not shield the party from mounting Nazi pressure in the course of the *Gleichschaltung* in 1933, with arrests of Centre Party leaders, the firing of civil servants who were members of the Centre Party, and the like. Like other political parties, the Centre Party was forced to dissolve in summer 1933 and immediately thereafter a bill was passed installing a one-party state. After World War II, efforts to re-establish the Centre Party failed. Instead, prominent politicians of the former party, such as Konrad Adenauer, mayor of Cologne during the Weimar Republic, established a new Christian party, the 'Christian Democratic Union' (CDU), which was deliberately bi-denominational, thus integrating Catholics and Protestants.

[4] In 1928, Prelate Kaas had been elected party chairman; in 1932/33, the leadership of the Centre Party group in the Reichstag was in ecclesiastical hands (this was Prelate Kaas; the *chairmanship* was now formally in the hands of the parliamentarian Perlitius), as was that of the Prussian *Landtag* group (Prelate Lauscher) and that of the Baden *Landtag* group (Prelate Föhr). The chairman of the Bavarian People's Party group in the Reichstag was Prelate Leicht.

had denounced the erroneous views of the Nazi movement, had warned against its danger, and had declared support for the goals of the NSDAP—and in many cases also mere membership in the party—as impermissible.[5] This condemnation went so far that in some dioceses, active National Socialists or even all party members (as in Mainz) were excluded from receiving the sacraments and church burial. The Centre Party and the Bavarian People's Party (BPP) conducted the campaign for the election on 5 March 1933, in sharp opposition to the National Socialists. And despite the considerable impediments they were already suffering at the hands of the press and the government, they were largely able to defend their vote share and win 92 Reichstag seats (out of a total of 647).

The political situation after the March election was as follows: the Centre Party and the BPP had been displaced from their key position in parliament, because the NSDAP and the German National People's Party together held the absolute majority of the votes and could therefore govern without them. However, in conjunction with the SPD, the Centre Party and the Bavarian People's Party constituted a considerable minority, which was able to block the two-thirds majority required for constitutional changes and thus had it within its power to prevent the attempt by the new government to abrogate the Weimar Constitution. When it came to the efforts by the National Socialists to internally stabilize and legally expand their dictatorial rule, it therefore mattered a great deal whether German Catholicism and its political representatives were willing to defend the Weimar Constitution and to block an anti-democratic government from taking legal control of all levels of the state. Of course, this presupposed a willingness to counteract the weariness of democracy promoted by years of crisis and by certain concrete manifestations of political life, on the understanding that it was not merely some institution or another that was at stake, but the very substance of the parliamentary-democratic state. Although the election of 5 March 1933 had given Hitler the chance to establish authoritarian rule, that rule was by no means legally and politically unassailable.

This is where the facts and documents marshalled by Morsey speak a clear language.[IV] As early as 6 March, Prelate Kaas, as the chairman of the Centre Party, without sounding out the party first, made an offer to Vice-Chancellor

[5] The individual pronouncements are recorded in *Ecclesiastica: Archiv für zeitgenössische Kirchengeschichte*, ed. the Katholische Internationale Presseagentur (KIPAJ) (Freiburg, Switzerland), Issue 13, No. 6 (2 November 1933), p. 57f. We are talking about the decision of the episcopal ordinariate of Mainz on September 1930, the New Year Eve's declaration of Cardinal Bertram in 1930, the instruction of the Bavarian bishops of 10 February 1931, the decrees of the bishops of the Cologne ecclesiastical province of 5 March 1931, and of the bishops of the Paderborn ecclesiastical province of 10 March 1931, and the statement by the bishops of Berlin of 20 March 1931. How clearly these warnings and admonitions from the bishops were understood is revealed by, among other things, the special issue of the Centre Party publication 'Der Weckruf' in April 1931 (Issue 7, No. 4).

[IV] Historian Rudolf Morsey was the first to thoroughly investigate the Centre Party's behaviour at the end of the Weimar Republic and in the early Nazi years. Morsey's article 'Die Deutsche Zentrumspartei', in Rudolf Morsey and Erich Matthias: *Das Ende der Parteien* (Düsseldorf: Droste, 1960), pp. 281–453) was an initial starting point for Böckenförde to undertake his research on the role of the Catholic Church in 1933.

von Papen[V] to draw a line under the past and indicated his willingness to cooperate (Morsey, pp. 355–356). During deliberations within the party leadership and parliamentary delegation, Kaas then argued forcefully in favour of accepting the Enabling Act [*Ermächtigungsgesetz*], and in the end he was able to prevail. In the process there were sharp disagreements with Brüning,[VI] who clearly recognized the fundamental importance of the act for suspending the Weimar Constitution. To that end, Brüning vigorously opposed the acceptance of the Enabling Act for legal and political reasons, a stance that was supported by such prominent party politicians as Bolz, Joos, Wirth, Helene Weber, and others.[6]

The intensity of the disagreement between Kaas and Brüning is revealed by the notes that Karl Bachem recorded in April 1933 (Morsey, pp. 434–435). According to Bachem, Brüning emphasized that the Centre 'could not go along with and legitimize this development, which rested, if not on a formal, certainly on a substantive breach of the law and introduced a complete confusion of legal terms. He argued that the Weimar Constitution was still rightly in effect, and the Centre had to adhere to it as a 'constitutional party'. Bachem commented on this quarrel as follows: 'Thus two irreconcilable positions confronted each other: the clear, principled one of Brüning, and the more or less opportunistic one of Kaas.'

The only explanation of why Brüning eventually did go along with the majority decision led by Kaas and voted for the Enabling Act in the

V Franz von Papen (1879–1969) was a member of the Prussian parliament for the Centre Party 1921–1928 and 1930–1932. In June 1932 he became chancellor of Germany, ruling to a large extent through emergency provisions in accordance with Article 48 Weimar Constitution, signed by president Hindenburg. Six weeks into his tenure, Papen also made himself Reich Commissioner of Prussia, the largest of the German states, after his government initiated a military shutdown of Berlin, accusing Prussia's ruling Social Democrats of being in league with the Communists. After new elections in November 1932, which the National Socialists won, Papen made a deal with Hitler and president Hindenburg, according to which Hindenburg would appoint Hitler as chancellor, but Papen, as vice-chancellor, would nominate the majority of the cabinet. This deal led to Hitler's appointment on 30 January 1933, who quickly marginalized Papen and non-Nazi ministers in the cabinet. For the next seven weeks until the Enabling Act was passed which de facto gave Hitler free reign, Hitler largely ruled on the basis of emergency decrees, including just five days after his appointment the Decree for the Protection of the German People, allowing the police to take people into 'protective custody' without charges. Papen stayed on as vice-chancellor until July 1934, was then appointed ambassador to Austria (1934–1937) and to Turkey (1939–1944). After the war Papen was tried for war crimes in the International Military Tribunal of Nuremberg but eventually aquitted. A West German denazification court sentenced him to eight years of hard labour, of which he served four.

VI Heinrich Brüning (1885–1970), leading politician of the Centre Party, served as Chancellor from 1930 to 1932. President Hindenburg who issued presidential emergency decrees enabled Brüning to pursue a rigid austerity programme during the world economic crisis. After he failed to prevail over Prelate Kaas in the inner-party discussions, Brüning himself joined the parliamentary group's vote in favour of the Enabling Act. Under growing pressure from the Nazi regime, he then organized the imminent dissolution of the Centre Party. Brüning fled Germany in 1934 and then resided in the United States during and after the war, where he taught as a professor of government at Harvard University. During the last years of his professional career he held a professorship for political science at the University of Cologne from 1951 to 1955.

6 See Morsey, pp. 357–366; on the deliberations of the party delegation on 23 March, pp. 362–365.

session of the Reichstag was probably excessive loyalty to the party and the parliamentary group.

In negotiations with Hitler, Prelate Kaas won the inclusion of a number of assurances into the government declaration that concerned the relationship between Church and state, schools, and the irremovability of judges; moreover, one could think that accepting the Enabling Act was the best chance of restraining the far-reaching Emergency Decree of 28 February 1933, and of keeping civil servants from the Centre Party in their jobs. But in return for these hopes and assurances, the fulfilment of which was not backed by any guarantees, the Centre Party and the BPP voluntarily lent a hand in the parliament eliminating itself legally and thus abandoning the foundations of the democratic constitution. The SPD remained true to itself and the constitution and voted against the Enabling Act.

Evidently, what mattered to Prelate Kaas and the majority of the Centre Party and the BPP politicians was to find an arrangement with the new regime, provided the latter was willing to make certain concessions in areas of special importance to Catholics (church and school policy) and remained open to Christian influence. That seemed more important than defending the democratic-parliamentary state, on the ground of which they had stood for twelve years. As we now know from Kaas's diary entries, which have been published in *Stimmen der Zeit*,[VII] he travelled to Rome on the very day following the adoption of the Enabling Act (March 24) to discuss the new situation with the cardinal state secretary.[7] And when, following a private meeting with Hitler on 2 April, he journeyed to Rome the second—and final—time on 7 April, he told von Papen[VIII] that he fully accepted the new state of affairs created by Hitler's statements on cultural policy in his speech to the Reichstag. Nothing, he maintained, could contribute more to the internal consolidation of the authoritarian regime than the continued pursuit of the policy announced in that speech; he therefore placed himself on the side of positive cooperation 'out of inner conviction'.[8] Subsequently, Prelate Kaas, in close contact with the cardinal state secretary, inserted himself into the negotiations over the Concordat, which began as early as 9 April. While the Centre Party came under increasing pressure from the measures of the National Socialists, Prelate Kaas, in a telegram on Hitler's

[VII] *Stimmen der Zeit. Zeitschrift für christliche Kultur* (Voices of the time. Magazine for Christian Culture) is a Jesuit journal established in 1865, focusing on the reconciliation of the Catholic faith with modernity.

[7] Prelate Kaas's first trip to Rome, which was not unimportant for the problem of the Reich Concordat and the end of the Centre Party, is entirely skipped over by R. Leiber, S.J. (see note 2).

[VIII] Prelate Kaas and Vice-Chancellor von Papen met on the train to Rome. Officially, von Papen was en route to a private skiing trip in the Alps but in fact he was on a secret government mission to offer Rome a treaty guaranteeing the rights of the Catholic Church (*Reichskonkordat*) if it declared its acceptance of the Nazi regime. Kaas and von Papen met in the dining car on 8 April 1933 and had discussions on the matter. Once in Rome, the Vatican authorized Kaas, who was known for his expertise in church–state relations, to negotiate the draft of the terms with von Papen. The Concordat was signed on 20 July 1933 and ratified on 10 September 1933.

[8] Kaas, *Tagebuch*, note 2, p. 426f.

birthday on 20 April, gave [Hitler] assurances of his 'unswerving cooperation'.[9] The political representative of German Catholicism, in the interest of securing the Church's concerns on cultural policy, had thus internally already decided the fate of the party he led (which Brüning did not take over until the beginning of May) in favour of stabilizing the Nazi regime.[10]

Prelate Kaas was not alone in this stance towards the Nazi regime. In some places in the Catholic press, there had already been a willingness before 20 March 1933 to recognize the new 'authority' of the Nazi government, towards which no further attitude of opposition was to be taken.[11] Of fundamental importance was the subsequent declaration of the Fulda Conference of Bishops, which had already been published on 28 March, five days after the approval of the Enabling Act. This declaration, in view of Hitler's statements in the Reichstag speech on 23 March, withdrew the long-established, resolute 'general warnings and prohibitions' about a collaboration with the NSDAP, and admonished Catholics to be loyal towards the 'legitimate authority', even though not one point of the Nazi party programme had been changed.[12] With that, the situation created by the acceptance of the Enabling Act had been legitimized also 'spiritually', and a political opposition of the Catholics to the new regime had been stripped of internal backing.[13]

The path that had thus been embarked upon had to lead rapidly to a progressive rapprochement with the Nazi regime. For in order to preserve the assurances on church and cultural policy held out by the government and so as not to diminish the Christian influence, it was necessary to support the new regime fully and to try and guide it from within through active cooperation. A certain duality therefore characterized the subsequent conduct of the German bishops. On the one hand, they acted on behalf of the existing civil servants, especially

[9] The telegram read as follows: 'On this day I send sincere blessings and the assurance of unwavering cooperation in the great work of creating an internally united, socially pacified, and externally free Germany' (Morsey, p. 379).

[10] In a letter of December 1947, Brüning speaks of the 'more than sinister politics' of Prelate Kaas. On the attitude of the cardinal state secretary and other Vatican prelates concerning the cooperation of the Catholics with the new state, see, for one, the report by the Bavarian envoy Baron von Ritter of 24 April 1933 (Kaas, *Tagebuch*, p. 430, note 34), whose credibility is supported by the diary of Prelate Kaas, and, on the other hand, the discussion by R. Leiber, S.J. (see note 2), pp. 214–217.

[11] Thus, for example, Alphons Nobel, *Der Katholik im neuen Reich* (Augsburg, 1933), p. 10. This was a reprint of the leading articles from the *Augsburger Postzeitung*. See also Morsey, p. 354, note 10.

[12] See *Germania* 88 (29 March 1933); *Ecclesiastica* 13, p. 458. After an explicit reference to Hitler's declaration guaranteeing Catholic doctrine of faith and the existing concordats, we read: 'Without repealing the condemnation of certain religio-ethical errors contained in our earlier measures, the episcopacy therefore believes that it can entertain the confidence that the above-described general prohibitions and warnings no longer need to be considered necessary. Catholic Christians for whom the voice of the Church is sacred need no special admonition at this point in time to show loyalty to the legitimate authority ... ' In this context it is remarkable that Vice-Chancellor von Papen had paid a visit to Cardinal Bertram, the chairman of the Fulda conference of bishops, on 18 March 1933 (Morsey, p. 357).

[13] According to Robert Leiber, S.J. (note 2), p. 217, Cardinal State Secretary Pacelli's immediate reaction to the declaration of the bishops was as follows: 'Why did the bishops have to accommodate the government so quickly? If they had to do so, could they not have waited another month?'

those from the Centre Party, and demanded freedom and autonomy for church organizations;[14] on the other hand, the Catholic laity heard from them a growing number of calls for cooperation with the 'new state' and a positive integration into it. Not an inconsiderable number of Catholics, especially those who were still committed opponents of the Nazi regime, may have understood these calls as primarily tactical; on the whole, however, there is no denying that these calls had an important effect within the Catholic and general public. All the more so since the Centre Party had become for the time being virtually leaderless when Prelate Kaas travelled to Rome without having previously resigned the chairmanship of the party (Morsey, pp. 370f., 377ff.).

As early as 25 April, Archbishop Gröber of Freiburg left no doubt at the diocesan synod that the Catholics 'must not reject the new state, but must affirm it positively and work with it unswervingly'.[15]

In a speech in Beuthen on 4 May Cardinal Bertram declared that the new government not only wanted to tolerate the Catholic Church, but placed the greatest importance 'on the Church developing its powers in the life of the people'. From this awareness sprang the 'elation' with which the Catholics engaged in their cooperation.[16]

On 5 May the Bavarian bishops published a joint pastoral letter, which characterized the programme of the new government as a willingness to move towards a spiritual, moral, and economic renewal of the nation and called upon the cooperation of all those who loved their fatherland: 'No one may now, out of discouragement or bitterness, stay on the sideline and grumble; no one who is genuinely willing to cooperate must be sidelined out of bias and narrow-mindedness.'[17]

This was followed on 3 June by the programmatic joint pastoral letter from all German bishops. The above-mentioned duality is expressed here with particular clarity. On the one hand, the principles of the Nazi state, especially the exceedingly strong emphasis on authority, are affirmed; on the other hand, certain intentions and methods of the NSDAP are rejected, and a number of demands are raised on behalf of the freedom of the Church and the Catholic organizations and their ability to work effectively. The concluding passage then contains the following lines: 'Beloved diocesans! When we, the German bishops, put forth the enumerated demands, this does not contain a hidden reservation towards the new state. Under no circumstances do we wish to deprive the state of the powers of the Church, and we may not do so, because only the

[14] See the proclamation of the bishops of the East German church province of 13 April 1933, and of the church province of the Upper Rhine of 15 April 1933 (*Ecclesiastica*, 13, p. 457f.); also the decision by the Fulda Conference of Bishops on 31 May 1933, on the question of youth organizations, which said, among other things: 'The Church rejects a state view in which the entire youth should be encompassed and educated exclusively by the state, in school and outside school, as incompatible with Church doctrine.' See *Die junge Front* 2(26) (25 June 1933).

[15] *Ecclesiastica*, 13, p. 475.

[16] See *Die junge Front*, 3, No. 2 (14 January 1934).

[17] *Ecclesiastica*, 13, p. 459.

power of the people and the power of God, which flows inexhaustibly from the life of the church, can save and elevate us.'[18]

As Morsey reports (p. 393), this pastoral declaration was followed by a wave of resignations from the Centre Party.

There was, of course, also a different stance, one that strikes us today as a lonely beacon of political clear-sightedness and courageous resoluteness. Franz Graf von Galen,[IX] a delegate to the Prussian *Landtag*, who had already urged Brüning in March not to vote for the Enabling Act, resigned his mandate after the *Landtag* group of the Centre Party, under the leadership of Prelate Lauscher, had decided unanimously to accept what he believed was the even more far-reaching Prussian Enabling Act.[X] He publicly justified his move by saying that it was impossible for him to voluntarily renounce the constitutional tasks assumed by his mandate, and thereby take on shared responsibility for the laws passed on the basis of the enabling authority.[19]

Support for the Nazi regime from the German bishops reached its high point at and after the signing of the Reich Concordat in July 1933.[20] Hitler was

[18] *Germania*, No. 159 (12 June 1933); *Ecclesiastica*, 13, p. 468. The section on authority states: 'In addition to the heightened love for the fatherland and the *Volk* (people), our time is characterized by a surprisingly strong emphasis on authority and by the implacable demand for the organic integration of individuals and corporate bodies into the totality of the state. In this it proceeds from the standpoint of natural law that no community flourishes without authority, and that the willing integration into the *Volk* and obedient subordination to the lawful leadership of the *Volk* guarantee the restrengthening of the power of the *Volk* and of national greatness.' Following a reference to the value and meaning of authority within the Church, we read further: 'It is therefore by no means difficult for us Catholics to appreciate the new, strong emphasis on authority within the German state, and to subordinate ourselves with the kind of willingness that is characterized not only as a natural virtue, but also as a supra-natural one, because we see in every human authority a reflection of divine rule and a participation in the eternal authority of God.'

[IX] Franz Graf von Galen (1879–1961) was a member of the Prussian parliament (*Landtag*) for the Centre party in 1932–1933. His brother is Clemens August Graf von Galen (see annotation XV).

[X] The *Landtag* was the parliament of the Free State of Prussia, by far the largest of the German states within the Weimar Republic, formed in 1918 after the dissolution of the Kingdom of Prussia. With a Nazi majority, it passed its own Enabling Act on 18 May 1933, which ended Prussia's existence as a state and transformed it into a mere administrative unit of the Reich. Executive and budgetary power had already de facto been transferred to the Reich level earlier.

[19] The statement was published in *Germania*, No. 143 (26 May 1933] and in the entire provincial press of the Centre Party. The crucial passages stated: 'If I now lay down my mandate to the Prussian *Landtag*, I believe that by doing so I can at this time best comply with the obligations imposed upon me by this confidence... I myself believed that I could not voluntarily renounce the possibility of fulfilling the tasks assumed with the mandate. Through the passage of the constitution-altering law, this renunciation by the elected representatives was bindingly stipulated, and in the process the co-responsibility for all laws passed on the basis of the enabling power was imposed upon them. In my view, keeping the mandate after this decision was impossible.' Within the Centre Party group in the Prussian *Landtag*, which included a number of prominent individuals, Graf von Galen was alone in his decision; however, we know the MP Letterhans stayed away from the *Landtag* on voting day, so he would not be compelled to cast his vote in line with the decision of the party group.

[20] Within the Catholic public, the conclusion of the Reich Concordat was generally celebrated as an epochal event and most warmly welcomed. Among the many voices that could be listed, see, for example, Eduard Hegel, 'Gedanken zum Reichskonkordat', *Zeit und Volk* I, pp. 25ff.; and Ivo Zeiger, S.J., 'Das Reichskonkordat', *Stimmen der Zeit* 126 (1933/34), pp. 1ff. Zeiger saw the Concordat as something 'very great' and as the expression of a 'shifting of thinking' in the field of religious and Church policy. The Enabling Act now took on for him a special legitimation, because it had created the preconditions for the will of the government to assert itself unhindered by the 'excrescences of the parliamentary system' (p. 2–3).

evidently seen quite unreservedly as the new authority, in spite of earlier, resolute warnings and even though his support for the murderers of Potempa[XI] could hardly be forgotten; he was thus seen as capable of entering into agreements, and one was willing to take his words as the pronouncements of a statesman. Continuing to harbour doubts about the goals of the new regime therefore seemed to lack any justification. The episcopal declarations and the statements by heads of orders and the leaders of associations and organizations (including, for example, the Görres Society[XII]) often went far beyond diplomatic consideration and traditional accommodation. However, so as not to form an erroneous judgment, one must bear in mind that the full scope of Hitler's criminality was at that time still outside the realm of experience.

In his letter of thanks [for the completion of the concordat] which Cardinal Bertram composed in the name of the Fulda Conference of Bishops, he emphasized that the episcopacy of all the dioceses in Germany, as soon as it became possible thanks to Hitler's statements, had immediately expressed the 'sincere and joyful willingness' to cooperate with the new government, 'which has made the promotion of the Christian education of the people, the defence against godlessness and immorality, the sense of sacrifice for the common good, and the protection of the rights of the Church the lodestar of its work'.[21]

Cardinal Faulhaber concluded his handwritten letter, which was animated by the highest appreciation for Hitler's 'world-historical' deed, with this assurance: 'For us it comes sincerely from the heart: may God preserve our Reich chancellor for our people'; he explicitly emphasized what a 'great deed' this handshake with the papacy meant for Germany's standing 'in the West and the East and before the entire world'.[22]

In a thanksgiving mass on the occasion of the signing of the Concordat, Archbishop Gröber admonished the flock not to lose faith in the good will of the leader of the state; he had the 'unshakable confidence' that the Führer would stand firmly by his word. Some time later he reiterated that he was standing 'unreservedly' behind the Reich government and the new Reich.[23] Similarly, Bishop Berning of Osnabrück declared the following on the occasion of his swearing in as

[XI] On 9 August 1932, a Communist miner and trade unionist from the Silesian village of Potempa was beaten to death by five uniformed Nazi Stormtroopers. The five murderers were sentenced to death, but under emergency powers their sentences were commuted to life imprisonment in September 1932. In March 1934 all five were released from prison under a general Nazi amnesty of anyone who had committed a crime 'for the good of the Reich during the Weimar Republic'.

[XII] The Görres Gesellschaft [Görres Society] is a learned society for the advancement of the arts and sciences ('zur Pflege der Wissenschaften'), whose goal is to foster interdisciplinarity and exchange between different disciplines, based in the Catholic tradition and ethics. It was founded in 1876 in Koblenz in honour of Catholic publicist and historian Joseph Görres (1776–1848), who was an early advocate for freedom of the Catholic Church from state interference. It was dissolved by the Nazis in 1941 and founded anew in 1948.

[21] The text in *Ecclesiastica*, 13, p. 322, and in A. Kupper, 'Zur Geschichte des Reichskonkordats', *Stimmen der Zeit* 163 (1958/59), p. 367.

[22] Full text in Kupper (note 21), p. 367–368.

[23] On the one hand *Germania*, no. 225 (17 August 1933), *Zeit und Volk* I, p. 221; on the other hand, *Ecclesiastica*, 13, p. 475. It is difficult to reconcile these statements with the claim by R. Leiber, S.J., p. 219, that Archbishop

a Prussian state councillor: 'The German bishops have long since affirmed the new state, they have not merely promised to recognize its authority, as goes without saying for every Catholic. We serve the state with ardent love and all our powers.'[24]

The same tenor was found in appeals and declarations by the bishops Bornewasser of Trier, Kaller of Ermland, the auxiliary bishops[XIII] Baumann in Paderborn and Burger in Freiburg, and by the capitular vicar[XIV] Steinmann of Berlin.[25]

The German episcopacy may have believed that it would guide the Nazi regime and the inner upheaval of 1933 in the direction of Christian-authoritarian state and thus change everything for the better. However, it discovered very quickly just how much it had become the prisoner of its own policy. Immediately after the March elections, Hitler had already recognized, with his unique political instinct, that a real incursion into the Catholic segment of the population in favour of National Socialism could only be achieved 'if the curia dropped the two parties [Centre and BPP]' (Morsey, p. 354). He then worked consistently towards this goal, whereby it did not matter to him at all whether it was the Vatican or the German bishops who 'dropped' them.

When the German bishops, for the sake of hoped-for and proffered guarantees on church and cultural policy and in order to preserve 'Christian' influence, readily placed their authority onto the scale—even though the church did not face an immediate external or internal emergency—in favour of a Nazi regime that was not yet consolidated, and in some cases energetically promoted the signing of the Concordat, they not only helped (intentionally or not) to stabilize the Nazi regime, but also tied their own hands. They were now committed for a long time to the profession of loyalty they had issued, for the simple reason that they did not wish to provide any cause to put the realization of the Concordat at risk, an agreement which the Nazi regime did not take all that seriously in the first place.

Gröber had assessed the effect of the Concordat with cool deliberation in July 1933, concluding that it would at least give the church in Germany a few months of truce.

[24] *Ecclesiastica*, 13, p. 477; *Zeit und Volk* I, p. 441.

[XIII] An auxiliary bishop is appointed at the request of the diocesan bishop to support him in his pastoral and administrative tasks. An auxiliary bishop is a titular bishop of sees that no longer exist and he does not possess the right of succession (see for the latter can 403 Codex Iuris Canonici/1983 and can 350 § 3 CIC/1917).

[XIV] A capitular vicar is a diocesan administrator.

[25] Bishop Bornewasser on the Feast of Christ the King in 1933 in Trier Cathedral: 'We have entered into the new Reich with head held high and firm steps, and we are willing to serve it with the deployment of all the powers of our body and soul' (*Ecclesiastica*, 13, p. 477). Bishop Kaller concluded his appeal for collaboration with the rebuilding of the Reich, the economy, and youth work with the appeal: 'Activists is what we want to be' ('Unsere katholischen Aufgaben heute', *Zeit und Volk* I, pp. 91–93). Auxiliary Bishop Baumann spoke, in *Zeit und Volk* I, p. 688, of the 'self-evident' integration into the new state and the 'equally self-evident' cooperation in the rebuilding of our people; auxiliary Bishop Burger declared: 'The goals of the Reich government have long since become the goals of our Catholic Church' ('Unser Wille zur Tat', *Zeit und Volk* I, p. 181f.). Capitular Vicar Steinmann said at the Catholic youth conference in the Neukölln stadium on 20 August 1933: 'What we have all hoped and striven for has become fact. We have one Reich and one Führer, and we follow this Führer loyally and conscientiously' (*Ecclesiastica*, 13, p. 476).

Thus, the plebiscite and Reichstag elections on 12 November 1933, saw in most dioceses proclamations from the pulpit—including from the newly appointed Bishop of Münster, Clemens August Graf von Galen,[XV] the future 'Lion of Münster'—which encouraged votes in favour of the Reich government, in part also in favour of the NSDAP.[26]

However, the declaration by the Bavarian bishops deviated from the others in that it already contained a slightly critical undertone and explicitly released the vote with respect to the Reichstag election; the publication of this document was suppressed by the Nazis.[27]

The joint pastoral letter in June 1934, which already contained serious admonitions and barely concealed criticism of the new anti-Christian statements and claims of National Socialism, was not read out, so as not to impede the renewed negotiations about the implementation of the Reich Concordat.[28]

In this context it therefore deserves to be mentioned that as far as we know, Heinrich Brüning was the only prominent Catholic politician who had expressly warned the Vatican against signing the Reich Concordat.[29]

However, it was not only the bishops who affirmed the Nazi regime in 1933 and called for supporting it. On the one hand, the Catholic laity, honestly convinced of the principles of the policy of the Centre Party, was hesitant in following the new current of the times. And not a few Catholic intellectuals and politicians, the likes of Konrad Adenauer, Heinrich Brüning, P. Gustav Gundlach, Josef Schmidlin, and Georg Schreiber, soon ended their public activity in the Catholic sphere and withdrew into quiet opposition. On the other hand, however, a group of spiritual leaders was beginning to speak out, and

[XV] Clemens August Graf von Galen (1878–1946), Bishop of Münster in 1933, and appointed as cardinal in 1946, was an early public and harsh critic of the national socialist religion policy and an outspoken opponent of the Nazi euthanasia programme. In August 1941 he criticized in a number of pastoral letters and sermons the state's persecution of church personnel and the killing of the disabled. After the 1938 Night of Broken Glass he asked the rabbi of Münster how he coud help. Nevertheless, he never spoke out in public against the deportation and the mass murder of Jews. He was beatified in 2005.

[26] Although the declaration by Cardinal Bertram on 9 June 1933, which was adopted also by the archdiocese of Cologne (*Ecclesiastica*, 13, pp. 478–479), emphasizes the freedom to cast one's vote freely on purely political matters, it goes on to admonish the faithful: 'Yet everyone should be cognizant of the obligation to support the authority of the government to the best of one's knowledge and conscience' (*Germania*, No. 309 (9 November 1933)). The appeal from the bishop of Münster, which was joined by the bishops of Osnabrück and Freiburg and the capitular vicar in Berlin, had the same thrust. We read there: 'It seems to us ... a patriotic [*vaterländische*] duty to keep the love and loyalty for the German fatherland and people, as before so also in the current fateful hour, and to demonstrate unity with the other *Volk* comrades on November.' (The text in P. Weinberger, 'Kirche und Drittes Reich im Jahre 1933', *Werkhefte katholischer Laien* (1958), p. 58, also in *Germania*, No. 309 (9 November 1933)).

[27] See *Ecclesiastica*, 13, p. 480; there also references to the suppression of the appeal. Also, Deuerlein, *Reichskonkordat*, p. 138f.

[28] See W. Gurian, *Der Kampf um die Kirche im Dritten Reich* (Lucerne, 1936), p. 101f.; Bracher, Sauer, and Schulz, *Die Nationalsozialistische Machtergreifung* (Opladen, 1960), p. 345.

[29] See Morsey, p. 406. The statement by R. Leiber, S.J., p. 219, that nobody who was asked advised against the signing of the Concordat refers only—and this must not be overlooked—to those who were asked, namely asked 'in Rome'.

although their number was initially small, their echo quickly grew louder and they found the way forward and upward in no time. They sought to defend the principles of the new order, to identify more or less fundamental convergences between Catholic and Nazi thinking, and to conceptualize the beginnings of the Nazi Reich as a great and positive historical turning point. Leaving aside some individual differentiations, the common element was a deeply rooted anti-liberalism that gave rise automatically to a rejection of democracy and modern society, and a penchant for authoritarian government, Führerdom, and an 'organic national order'. This was joined by the declared enmity toward Bolshevism, which was regarded as a direct threat, and anger about widespread 'public immorality'.[30]

This new leadership stratum also found strong expression in published sources, which comes as no big surprise, given the tenor of the times. Journals and publication series were set up, which regarded it as their task to serve 'the building of the Third Reich out of the united forces of the National Socialist state and Catholic Christianity'.[31]

However, from the multitude of voices that spoke up, one must not draw a direct inference about the overall internal state of German Catholicism. We are no longer able today to determine the extent to which these voices found a positive echo or went unheard. Those who held different views had a much more difficult time expressing them openly. At the same time, it would be wrong to discount the importance of these voices [in favour of the Nazi regime] for the mental climate and the public opinion within German Catholicism: too large was their number, too prominent their authors, and too obvious the inner congruence with the pronouncements of the bishops.

From within the camp of professional theologians, it was above all Michael Schmauz[XVI] and Josef Lortz[XVII] who, on the basis of the anti-liberal Catholic

[30] The fight against godlessness, Bolshevism, and 'public immorality' also appeared in nearly all episcopal pronouncements as the special achievement—in some cases even as the 'salvific work'—of the Nazi regime, which deserved the gratitude and cooperation of the Catholics. See especially the pastoral letter of the Bavarian bishops on 5 May 1933 (note 17), the joint pastoral letter of 3 June 1933 (note 18), the address by Bishop Bornewasser (note 25), and that of the Bamberg Archbishop von Hauck (*Zeit und Volk* I, p. 1045).

[31] Thus explicitly the series *Reich und Kirche* (Verlag Aschendorff, Münster). The journals were: *Deutsches Volk*, published by several chairmen of Catholic journeymen associations and the professors Wilhelm Schwer and Theodor Brauer, and the weekly *Zeit und Volk* (Verlag Kösel-Pustet), at the editorial helm of which were Axel Emmerich (Edgar Alexander) and H. J. Krumbach. The co-editor and publishing director, Paul Siebhertz, saw in Hitler the 'man with the strong sense of responsibility', and he considered it 'the duty of conscience to make every effort to support the Reich Chancellor in the realization of his governing programme' (*Zeit und Volk* I, pp. 7–8). A. Emmerich resigned from the journal after only ten issues, because, as he reported, the advocacy of Catholic principles had been made impossible for him as a result of the influence exerted by third parties on the content of the journal. See E. Alexander, *Der Mythos Hitler* (Zurich, 1937), p. 387.

[XVI] Michael Schmaus (1897–1993) was a Catholic priest and professor of dogmatics during the Nazi regime, first at the University of Münster (from 1933), later at the University in Munich (1946–1965), as president of which he served at one point (1951–1952). In a denazification trial he was first classified as a 'follower', but this was later changed to 'non-affected', making it possible for him to resume his post at the university.

[XVII] Josef Lortz (1887–1975) was a Catholic priest and professor of church history at the State Academy Braunsberg in East Prussia (1929–1933) and later at the University of Münster (1933–1945). He too

ideas about authority and totality, sought to build a bridge between Catholicism and National Socialism.[32] National Socialism seemed to Schmaus the radical opposite of liberalism and Bolshevism, against whose perversions it was reasserting the 'nature-given orders and realities'. 'The tablets of National Socialist Oughts and of Catholic imperatives are, of course, on different levels of being, the former on the natural, the latter on the supra-natural level... But they point in the same direction.' Schmaus did not believe that the totalitarian claim of the Nazi state was dangerous, since it had been given its authentic interpretation by the Reich Concordat.[33]

Recognizing precisely this totalitarian claim and saying a 'complete yes' to National Socialism was the demand issued by J. Lortz. Of course, he may have been thinking more of an authoritarian regime than of the totalitarian one that soon became reality. Like Schmaus, Lortz noted fundamental affinities between Catholicism and National Socialism, and he believed that he could see in the latter a movement of awakening against at least six centuries of corruption, a movement of awakening that, at its deepest, also prepared the path to being a believer.[34]

For Jakob Hommes,[XVIII] the complete affirmation of National Socialism arose out of the idea of a comprehensive cultural and national renewal as the realization of natural law. In his eyes, National Socialism's will as it pertained to the state, the economy, and culture was the 'breakthrough of full natural law' and meant the 're-establishment of the organic constitution of the community and culture, the return to the natural order and the order of creation', and thus the uniquely German form of the occidental movement of renewal against liberalism and rationalism.[35] Hommes was not alone in this view; the much-invoked reverence for creation and predefined orders, which was supposedly

was permitted to resume his university career after the war and became professor of 'history of occidental religions' in 1950 at the University of Mainz.

[32] The writings by M. Schmaus, J. Lortz, and J. Pieper referenced below appeared in the series 'Reich und Kirche'.

[33] Michael Schmaus, *Begegnungen zwischen katholischem Christentum und nationalsozialistischer Weltanschauung* (Münster, 1933), p. 31, see also p. 22.

[34] Josef Lortz, *Katholischer Zugang zum Nationalsozialismus kirchengeschichtlich gesehen* (Münster, 1933) ('Reich und Kirche'), pp. 5, 21f., and 26. A few years later, after 1936, Lortz removed the final chapter of his 'Geschichte der Kirche' [History of the Church], which affirmed National Socialism, from the new editions.—Convergences between the Catholic and the Nazi worldviews were also sought by the theologians: Karl Eschweiler, *Die Kirche im neuen Reich* (Deutsches Volkstum, 1933), pp. 451ff., though on the whole he was more restrained and not unaware of possible points of danger. By contrast, Hugo Schnell, *Der katholische Mensch im totalen Staat* (Zeit und Volk I, pp. 273ff.) saw precisely in the totalitarian claim of the Nazi state the Christian element within National Socialism.

[XVIII] Jakob Hommes (1898–1966) was a philosopher, who in 1954 became professor at the Philosophical-Theological Academy of Regensburg. From 1931 to 1954 he worked at the Herder publishing house.

[35] Jakob Hommes, 'Katholisches Staats- und Kulturdenken und Nationalsozialismus', *Deutsches Volk* I, pp. 285ff.); 'Nationalsozialismus, Katholizismus und Staatslexikon', ibid., pp. 342ff. Hommes believed it would be interesting and attractive to show 'how many National Socialist ideas are contained in the encyclicals of the popes from the perspective of natural law' (p. 346).

characteristic of the Catholic believer, now assumed an astonishingly concrete form.[36] The already-mentioned defensiveness against Bolshevism did the rest to have men like Hommes see National Socialism as a natural ally and protector.[37]

The corporatist-authoritarian social order and the social policy carried out by the Nazi regime also met with widespread approval and was interpreted as the triumph over the class conflict in favour of an occupational order grounded in natural law, as the encyclical *Quadragesimo anno*[XIX] had recommended. Theodor Brauer,[XX] in particular, explained and defended the societal and social policy of the Third Reich in this sense.[38] Even Josef Pieper,[XXI] whose opposition to National Socialism as a worldview [*Weltanschauung*] was never in doubt, believed he could ascertain that here the convergence of the basic ideas 'truly extends into the core of the Christian social ethic and into the shared fountainhead of all socio-political drives of the National Socialist state'.[39]

Another path to the positive embrace of and support for the Nazi state led via a theological valorization and interpretation of the idea of the Reich to a theologico-political ideology of the Reich. It was widespread above all within the Catholic youth movement, among the German Benedictines, and among Catholic academics. The ideological background was spelled out by the universalism of Othmar Spann[XXII] and the quest for community and

[36] See, for example, Axel Emmerich (Edgar Alexander), 'Überwindung des Liberalismus', *Zeit und Volk* I, pp. 110ff.); Wilhelm Spael, 'Der Katholik in der neuen Staatwirklichkeit', ibid., pp. 637ff.; Heinrich Lützeler, 'Der europäische Sinn der deutschen Wende', ibid., pp. 672ff.; the editorial report 'Nationalsozialismus und Katholizismus', *Deutsches Volk* I, pp. 309ff.; Wilhelm Reinermann, 'Von der nationalen Revolution zur nationalen Volksgemeinschaft', ibid., pp. 29ff.

[37] Recognition of the Bolshevic danger also led F. A. Kramer, the future founder of the *Rheinischer Merkur*, to affirm and legitimize the Nazi seizure of power. See Volk und Zeit I, pp. 188–191, esp. p. 191.

[XIX] *Quadragesimo anno* was issued by Pope Pius XI in 1931, on the fortieth anniversary of the encyclical *Rerum Novarum* issued by Pope Leo XIII. Both encyclicals deal with the negative social implications of industrial capitalism, the latter addressing the situation of workers, the former arguing for a societal order founded on the principles of solidarity and subsidiarity.

[XX] Theodor Brauer (1880–1942) was a scholar of Catholic social ethics and active in the Catholic workers' and Christian Trade Union movement. Since 1923 he held a professorship at the Technical Academy of Karlsruhe and after 1928 was Director of the Research Centre for Social Sciences in Cologne. In 1937 he emigrated to the USA where he became professor of economics at the Catholic college of St. Thomas (at Saint Paul in Minnesota).

[38] See the various essays by Theodor Brauer in the journal *Deutsches Volk*, 1 and 2, as well as his pamphlet *Der Katholik im neuen Reich. Seine Aufgabe und sein Anteil* (Munich, 1933). By contrast, the essay by Gustav Gundlach, S.J., 'Fragen um die berufsständische Ordnung', *Stimmen der Zeit* 125 (1933), pp. 127–137, contained a fairly clear warning against equating Nazi social policy and the occupational order.

[XXI] Josef Pieper (1904–1997) was a Christian Catholic philosopher and from 1959 professor at the University of Münster, whose work focused on the thought of Thomas Aquinas and Plato.

[39] Josef Pieper, *Das Arbeitsrecht des neuen Reiches und die Enzyklika Quadragesimo anno* (Münster, 1934) (Reich und Kirche), p. 6. Remarkably enough, the author withdrew the tractate two months later. In October 1934 he published the tractate *Vom Sinn der Tapferkeit* in which Pieper came out against the falsification of the basic concepts of ethics by National Socialism.

[XXII] Othmar Spann (1878–1950) was an Austrian economist, sociologist, and philosopher who held a professorship at the University of Vienna until 1938, when he was forced to resign (despite having been a NSDAP member since 1930). He rejected parliamentary democracy and instead advocated the establishment of a corporatist state. His universalist approach opposed individualism,

wholeness that was alive in the youth movement. The 'Reich' appeared to be the real Catholic—because holistic—form of political order, as the integration of the political world into the order of salvation, and thus as the Christian-Catholic counter-position to the modern, individualistic, and secularized state. In this view, Reich policy was Catholic policy, and the Reich of Adolf Hitler meant a departure, and the possibility of a new, organic-holistic and substantively Christian order: a transition out of the interregnum that had been in place since 1803, on towards a new definitivum.[XXIII] Here the *imperium* and the *sacerdotium*, as the Concordat affirmed, would be liberated once again to fulfil their true task and unfold their true power.[40] [XXIV] Thus here, too, we find the call for positive cooperation with the Nazi state and integration into it.[41]

Similar considerations had also played a role in the creation of the association 'Kreuz und Adler' [Cross and Eagle], which took place at the beginning of April 1933 under the patronage of [Vice-Chancellor] von Papen. The association wanted to bring together conservative Catholics on a non-partisan basis as a counterweight to the Centre and to prevail upon them to collaborate in the building of the new Reich. Among its members were Catholic noblemen such as Ferdinand Freiherr von Lüninck, professors such as Otto Schilling, Theodor Brauer, and Karl Hugelmann, journalists such as Emil Ritter, as well as Eugen Kogon, Albert Mirgeler, and others.[42]

The highly respected abbot of Maria Laach,[XXV] Ildefons Herwegen, carved out a special role for himself as the interpreter of a religious transfiguration of the Führer principle and of the order built on the volkish forces of

liberalism, and Marxism and regarded the state as the ultimate vehicle for human self-actualization. Spann is considered a major thinker of Austrofascism.

XXIII Contractually, *definitivum* as a final version, as opposed to a *provisorium*.

40 See A. Mirgeler, 'Die deutschen Katholiken und das Reich', *Schildgenossen* 13, pp. 53–56.; Robert Grosche, 'Der Kampf um den Reichsgedanken im politisch-geistigen Leben der Gegenwart', *Deutsches Volk* I, pp. 91ff., esp. 96–98; Robert Grosche, 'Die Grundlagen einer christlichen Politik der deutschen Katholiken', *Schildgenossen*, 13, pp. 46–52.; Friedrich Muckermann, S.J., 'Volk, Führer und Reich', *Zeit und Volk* I, pp. 183–184; Damasus Winzen, O.S.B., 'Gedanken zu einer "Theologie des Reiches"', *Catholica* 2 (1933), pp. 97ff., esp. 112–115.

XXIV See preamble of the Concordat: 'guided by the common desire to consolidate and promote friendly relations existing between the Holy See and the German Reich, willingly to endorse the relationship between the Catholic Church and the State for the entire area of the German Reich in a manner that satisfies both'.

41 This was the purpose especially of the *Dritte Soziologische Studientagung* des *Katholischen Akademikerverbands* in Maria Laach, 21–23 July 1933; see on this the report by F. A. Freiherr von der Heydte, which is characterized by an inner approval, 'Katholizismus, Nationalsozialismus und Reichsidee', *Zeit und Volk* I, pp. 207ff. Its concluding sentence read: 'Out of all lectures and talks at the meeting spoke the consciousness of the responsibility towards church and *Volk* ... and the purposeful will to serve the *Volk* and to serve the Reich in the National Socialist state and in the National Socialist movement.'

42 See *Deutsches Volk* I, p. 68, and Morsey, p. 373, note 39.

XXV Maria Laach is a Benedictine abbey in the Eifel region in the Rhineland, built in the eleventh and twelfth centuries. Already during the Weimar Republic Maria Laach had become a centre for right-wing Catholicism.

blood and soil.[XXVI] He repeatedly called upon Catholics to participate in this order:[43]

> 'The *Volk* and state have become one again through the deed of the Führer Adolf Hitler. Because the Führer, out of the loneliness of service and sacrifice, borne by an unswerving faith in the German *Volk*, has brought the latter once again to a joyful affirmation of itself, he has grown into the millions.' 'The faith of the Führer in the *Volk* is answered by the followership of the *Volk*. The loyal following of all towards the One creates a new experience of community, which allows our *Volk* to return to the ultimate roots of its unity: to blood, soil, and fate.'[44]

It was thus by no means unusual when Franz von Papen, in his widely regarded speech in Cologne ahead of the November elections in 1933, called upon the Catholics to show loyal followership to the Führer and to collaborate in the building of the new Christian Reich that was under way.[45]

If the call for a positive collaboration in the Nazi state thus resounded from all sides, the concrete practical repercussions could not be long in coming. The conduct of the Catholic journeymen associations (*Gesellenvereine*)[XXVII] and Catholic student organizations provides a telling example. Already during the early summer of 1933, they reshaped their organizations in line with the Führer principle and explicitly embraced the principles and form of the new order.

At the German Journeymen Meeting (*Deutscher Gesellentag*)[XXVIII] in Munich in June 1933, General Secretary J. Nattermann interpreted the building of the new

XXVI P. Ildefons Herwegen (1874–1946) joined the Order of Saint Benedict in 1895, was ordained in 1901 and in 1913 became abbot of Maria Laach abbey.

43 Thus at a rally in Cologne at the end of May 1933 (see Morsey, p. 390) and in a lecture in Bonn (see *Zeit und Volk* I, p. 275).

44 Ildefons Herwegen, O.S.B., 'Deutsches Heldentum in christlicher Verklärung', *Deutsches Volk* I, pp. 121–125, 122.

45 F. von Papen, *Der 12. November 1933 und die deutschen Katholiken* (Münster, 1934) (Reich und Kirche). Carl Schmitt followed a special path in affirming and supporting the Nazi state in 1933. He was neither a representative of Christian natural law nor did he stand on the ground of the organic state doctrine or Reich ideology. In 1931/32, in his capacity as a constitutional law scholar, he had legally defended the authoritarian government of the presidential cabinets for being—in his view—the last chance of the Weimar Constitution. Now, following the passage of the Enabling Act, he justified and defended the new order of the consolidating Nazi rule. In a sharp turn against the 'democratic functionalism' of Weimar and the abstraction and substantive emptiness of the bourgeois *Rechtsstaat*, he highlighted the new trinity of 'state, movement, *Volk*' as the characteristic political order of the German people, in which a substantive justice and a thinking in terms of concrete orders [*konkretes Ordnungsdenken*] was once again becoming effective in opposition to the liberalistic dissolution. The relevant publications are listed in their entirety in the bibliography compiled by P. Tommissen, *Festschrift für Carl Schmitt* (Berlin, 1959)].

XXVII Catholic journeymen associations were founded in the middle of the nineteenth century by the journeymen's Father Adolph Kolping (see annotation XXIX) as societies supporting young travelling craftsmen in their moral and professional development. Rapidly, the *Gesellenvereine* increased at the turn of the century to a number of more than one thousand with 80,000 journeymen members and 120,000 master-craftsmen members. Aside from religious instruction, the societies offered free classes in skilled crafts and trades, and in building one's own business.

XXVIII Where Vice-Chancellor von Papen delivered a welcome speech in front of an audience of about 20,000, stressing that he and *Reichskanzler* Hitler would guarantee the free development of the Christian faith. The SA ('Sturmabteilung', the paramilitary wing of the NSDAP) smashed this assembly, beating up the journeymen who were easily recognizable by their orange shirts.

Reich as God's call from German nature for the decisive blow against Bolshevism. 'Once again the German nation has seized the shield of the holy Empire against unbelief and paganism. Once again, the German *Volk* has been faithful to its old calling. This, German youth, is how I interpret our present hour.' A short time later, on the occasion of the great Kolping pilgrimage[XXIX] to Trier in August 1933, he declared that Chancellor Adolf Hitler and Journeymen Father Adolf Kolping could join hands in their various tasks, and he emphasized 'once again' that he was delighted 'when true, loyal Kolping sons become equally loyal SA and SS men'.[46]

The newly appointed leader of the Unitas Association (*Unitas-Verband*)[XXX], Erbprinz Karl zu Löwenstein, demanded at the general assembly of the Unitas Association in the summer of 1933 the 'honest readiness to collaborate with the best efforts in the great tasks of the new time'. He repeatedly affirmed, without reservation, the new task of the student associations: that of being educational communities for the Nazi state and to realize a piece of the national educational work of National Socialism.[47]

Similarly, the Union of German Catholic Student Associations (*Kartellverband deutscher katholischer Studentenvereine*) and the Ring of German Catholic Fraternities (*Ring katholischer deutscher Burschenschaften*) proclaimed at their merger into the Catholic Fraternity (*Katholische Burschenschaft*) at the beginning of September 1933: 'We want the *Burschenschaft* because we want the unity of Catholic and German students under National Socialist goals.'[48] [XXXI]

XXIX Adolph Kolping (1813–1865) was a Catholic priest who founded the Catholic journeymen associations (later named Kolping Society), which provided social services for workers in the rising industrial capitalist economy. Today, the Kolping Society is one of the largest social service institutions in the Catholic Church with about 275,000 members. The Kolping Society maintains educational and recreational institutes that support families (such as holiday homes for groups) and youth. Kolping communities also organize pilgrimages to various Christian sites.

46 Johannes Nattermann, 'Gott und Volk. Ansprache auf der ersten Kundgebung des deutschen Gesellentags', *Deutsches Volk* I, pp. 161–164, 163. The address in Trier: *Zeit und Volk* I, p. 228. Before that, General Praeses Monsignior Hürth had said, among other things: 'This morning I saw a picture that moved me deeply. It shows an SS man who helps a sick woman up the steps to the Holy Robe, where she was seeking solace and healing. Is not this a symbol?' (ibid.). See, finally, the decision by the Central Assembly of the Catholic Journeymen Associations of 18/19 September 1933 [*Kolpingblatt*, 1 October 1933]. It proclaimed the willingness to serve the German *Volk* and its Reich; it suggested that under the leadership of the People's Chancellor Adolf Hitler, much was being realized that accorded with the goals and wishes of Adolf Kolping.

XXX The *Unitas-Verband*, founded in the middle of the nineteenth century, is the oldest Catholic association of academics and students, uniting several students' organizations of various universities.

47 See the report about the 69th General Assembly of the Unitas Association in Frankfurt/Main, in *Unitas* 73, pp. 120–121; also, Erbprinz zu Löwenstein, 'Der Unitas-Verband in der deutschen Studentenfront', *Unitas* 73, p. 119f.; idem, 'Der Verband in der Zeitenwende', *Unitas* 74, p. 1f.; 'Bericht über die südwestdeutsche Führertagung des UV', *Germania* 310 (10 November 1933).

48 *Germania* 248 (9 September 1933).

XXXI The Union of German Catholic Student Associations was founded in the 1860s. In 1933 many of its members welcomed the idea of a '*Großdeutschland*' proclaimed by the Nazis. Thus, the merging of the Union with the Ring of German Catholic Fraternities (an association of five fraternities which had split off in the 1920s from the Unitas Association) into the Catholic German Fraternity in September 1933 promoted by the Nazi regime in the course of the *Gleichschaltung* did not

For the Bund Neudeutschland (Federation New Germany), the Bundesthing[XXXII] in Freiburg at the beginning of August 1933 meant the 'breakthrough to an inner, profound affirmation of the National Socialist state on the basis of spiritual engagement', after it had previously already adjusted positively to the new 'state without parties'.[49]

At the plebiscite and the Reichstag elections on 12 November 1933, the leadership of the associations issued calls that presented voting in the spirit of the Führer as self-evident or a duty. Especially clear was the declaration by Forschbach, the leader of the Union of Catholic German Student Fraternities (UCF, *Cartellverband der katholischen deutschen Studentenverbindungen*),[XXXIII] 'All men of the UCF must rally happily to the banners of Adolf Hitler in this momentous time. Whoever does not vote "Yes" on the plebiscite on November 12 and does not vote for the Reichstag list of the NSDAP violates his oath as a *Bursche*, because he is betraying his fatherland and *Volk* in the hour of greatest danger.'[50]

It was only consistent when the UCF and the Catholic Fraternity (*Katholische Burschenschaft*), at the beginning of 1934, also gave up the denominational principle as 'no longer grounded in the new state' and when, at the assembly of the UCF in April 1934, every chapter leader, by name, was placed under obligation to stand for the Nazi state and its Führer, as well as for the educating of all members of the UCF in the National Socialist spirit.[51]

However, it deserves to be mentioned that quite a few members of the Catholic student organizations renounced their membership because of this growing *Gleichschaltung*.

instigate much opposition. The Catholic German Fraternity had to drop its Catholic principles in 1934 and was eventually dissolved in 1938.

XXXII Federation New Germany was a Catholic organization founded after World War I by Jesuits as part of the Catholic branch of the Weimar Republic's *Jugendbewegung* (the youth movement had emerged at the turn of the century as a cultural and educational movement with numerous associations focusing on outdoor activities). It was affiliated with the Centre Party. In 1933, the members of the Federation met at the *Bundesthing* (Federal Thing, 'thing' being an old German word for assembly or gathering).

49 See Heinrich Jansen-Cron, 'Das Bundesthing', *Leuchtturm: Monatsschrift der neudeutschen Jugend* 27 (1933), pp. 134–135, and 'Leitsätze Neudeutsche Jugend und neuer Staat', ibid., pp. 136–138. The formulation of these principles was preceded by lectures by Professor Franz Schnabel on the history of the Reich over the last few centuries, and by Max Müller on National Socialism and the Reich of the present with a subsequent discussion.

XXXIII The Union of Catholic German Student Fraternities is another German umbrella organization of Catholic fraternities, founded in the late nineteenth century.

50 *Germania* 306 (6 November 1933). The declaration of the leader of the Catholic Fraternity, Hank, was as follows: 'The Katholische Burschenschaft affirms the political Führer idea embodied in the person of the People's Chancellor Adolf Hitler, in which the spirit of the discord and contentiousness of the liberal party state is overcome and the unity of our *Volk* has been accomplished in the great German liberation and awakening movement of National Socialism. That is why the Katholische Burschenschaft stands united and emphatically behind the Führer, after he called upon the entire nation to affirm his policy on November 12.'

51 The declaration about the abandonment of the denominational principle appeared in *Academia*46 (March/April, 1934); on the Cartell Assembly in Münster, ibid., 47, pp. 3–4.

In the face of this general affirmation of and support for the Nazi regime, openly dissenting voices are not found in the Catholic public after March 1933. This is not surprising. Once the Nazi regime had the necessary instruments of power in its hands, it was no longer willing to tolerate a real opposition, and public Catholic voices of opposition had even less of a chance, as they would not only have stood against the new rulers, but would have had to turn against authoritative declarations of the bishops and the vast majority of public Catholic opinion. To be sure, there were many who thought differently, not least among the pastoral clergy, who often knew the new rulers from direct experience and their backgrounds, but in this situation they could express themselves only through silence.

However, the 'hidden' opposition that was still possible in 1933 was on the whole quite sparse. At least the weekly *Die junge Front*, with Johannes Maaßen[XXXIV] at the helm, remained fairly restrained towards the Nazi regime and did not shy away from indirect criticism, especially until the signing of the Concordat;[52] several issues were banned by the authorities. *Hochland*[XXXV] also maintained the line of hidden opposition and granted the name Hitler no influence on its pages, then or later.[53] By contrast, *Stimmen der Zeit* abandoned its initial restraint from about June 1933 and called for a recognition of the given facts and cooperation with the new state.[54]

Of course, the present account, which is limited deliberately to the year 1933, cannot report on the brave resistance that both clerics and laypeople offered to the Nazi tyranny in later years, when the attacks on religion, the Church, and freedom became ever more frequent. Or how several of those who have appeared here as resolute champions of the Nazi regime in 1933 subsequently, following a better understanding, switched to the camp of the secret or open opposition. That is why emphatic reference should be made here to the hall

XXXIV Johannes Maaßen (1902–1949) was a journalist who first worked for the journal of the Centre Party *Germania* and from 1932 until its prohibition in 1936 for the weekly *Junge Front*, renamed in 1935 as *'Michael'*. This magazine of the Catholic Young Mens Association (*Katholischer Jungmännerverband Deutschlands*) was distributed door to door with a circulation of up to 300,000.

52 See especially the article 'Gleichschaltung?' by J. M. (No. 19, 5.7.1933) and the article 'Juden in Deutschland' by the same author (No. 21, 5.21.1933), who very courageously stood up for the upstanding Jews. The attitude of the German Catholics and their spiritual leaders on the Jewish question in 1933 and later is in urgent need of a closer study.

XXXV The magazine *Hochland* was founded by Catholic journalist and editor Carl Muth (1867–1944). It was published between 1903 and 1941, then banned during the Nazi regime, and published again from 1946 to 1971. It was the leading journal in German Catholic spiritual and intellectual life, independent of (and critically regarded by) the Church. The articles, written not only from Catholic points of view, but also from interdenominational, or even secular perspectives, dealt with topics in various areas of knowledge, literature, and art.

53 For example, after the signing of the Concordat, *Hochland* published, instead of the hymns of praise to the Reich Concordat that were heard everywhere, an essay about the Napoleonic Concordat of 1801 and its political and historical ramifications—in essence an unmistakable warning (31/3 (December 1933), pp. 242–254).

54 Thus Max Pribilla, S.J., 'Nationale Revolution', *Stimmen der Zeit* 125 (1933), pp. 156ff., especially 159–163. Also M. Preis, S.J., 'Die Staatsverfassung im totalen Staat', ibid., 125, pp. 145ff., and Ivo Zeiger, S.J., 'Das Reichskonkordat', ibid., 126, pp. 1ff. (see above note 20).

of fame of Catholic resistance, which includes a number of bishops, led by Cardinal Faulhaber and Bishop Graf von Galen, many concentration camp inmates, and countless nameless persecuted believers; it is in no way diminished by the conduct in 1933 described here. However, it would be equally wrong and an all-too-easy way out to cover up the events of 1933 by invoking that resistance and the persecution that was suffered, or by closing one's eyes to a thoughtful examination of these events.

II. REASONS BEHIND THE BEHAVIOUR OF THE CHURCH AND THE CATHOLICS

The question that needs to be objectively clarified is this: how could it be that the important ecclesiastical and spiritual leaders of German Catholicism in 1933 saw in Hitler and the Nazi state the trailblazers to a comprehensive renewal and called emphatically for positive collaboration and support for the Nazi regime?

That question is not adequately answered if one points to the possibility of error that accompanies all human understanding and especially political understanding, and if one admits to such an error. Although tactical considerations may have played a part in the episcopal pronouncements, in other statements—and in part also in these pronouncements—the affirmation of and support for the Nazi regime was justified in such principled and 'Catholic' terms that one must ask about the *internal* reasons for the 'susceptibility' of German Catholicism to the Nazi regime in 1933, if one does not want to impute opportunism from the outset. To what extent, alongside such internal reasons, opportunism may in fact have also played a concrete part can be determined only on the basis of sources that are not yet accessible.

Since the beginning of the modern, secularized world, the Catholic believer has stood in constant tension to it. The forms of order which that world has brought forth, the modern state and modern society, have remained internally alien to him from the outset. They were no longer his world, and he never felt truly at home within them. For German Catholics, this general tension received special reinforcement and a specific colouring from the experience of the *Kulturkampf*. During that conflict, German Catholics had been—in spiritual and existential terms—pushed out of the state as well as society. The state in which they lived ceased to be in any way their 'home', and in a society characterized increasingly by liberalism, they were considered backward and ultramontane. The response by Catholics was inner emigration out of the state and society. They sought and found their politico-societal locus *outside* state and society in the Church, and from that locus they determined their political action *within* the state. Since that time, standing up together for the rights of religion and the Church was—in the final analysis—the decisive reason that brought the Catholics together for political action and set them apart from other political groups. Politically, too, the believing Catholic made his decisions primarily as a member of the Church, not as a citizen of the state, once an alternative between the two had emerged; his relationship to the state was a broken one. The numerous affirmations of the national state must not obscure this *inner* condition. In truth, they confirm it.

The result of this situation was that in the political thinking of the Catholics, the realms of religion, Church, and school constituted the real core of the common weal, of good political order, against which all other areas receded in importance. Added was the fact that those areas had a direct connection to natural law, something that further boosted their principled importance in the political vision and rendered them fundamentally inaccessible to compromises. Thus a specific narrowing of political consciousness emerged among the Catholics, one that robbed them increasingly of the capacity of judging and deciding—in serious cases—in a genuinely political fashion, namely out of the whole and oriented towards the whole. For by imputing to certain areas of the politico-social order a claim to absoluteness grounded in natural law, they elevated them above and isolated them from all other areas. The starting point of political decision-making was no longer the whole of the political order in its unity and historical conditionality, but certain partial goods—however important—that were separated out of the context of the whole. These 'bona particularia' [particularist goods] were equated with the substance of the bonum commune [common good], and that meant that all other goods were by comparison of lesser importance and could be relinquished if need be.

Hitler's assurances that he wished to preserve friendly relations between Church and state, and his willingness to enter into a concordat about areas of Church and state (for Hitler merely a political calculation), thus touched German Catholicism in its most vulnerable place and had to become for it, politically speaking, a fatal temptation. As late as the spring of 1918, a segment of the Centre Party group and of the Prussian episcopacy, especially Cardinal von Hartmann [Cologne], had rejected the proposal for the abolition of Prussia's three-class franchise, on the grounds that ecclesiastical and educational concerns would be endangered in view of the changing majority situations.[55]

Now the conflict was that much sharper. Was not the offer being made to legally secure and guarantee the 'natural law' areas of politics, the freedom of Church and school? The goal on which Catholics had been fixated for decades, which their political representation—the Centre Party—had failed to achieve, which neither the Empire nor the Republic had fulfilled for them, suddenly seemed to have moved within their grasp. Compared to this, what did the abrogation of the Weimar Constitution, the foreseeable end of the political parties, and the restrictions on political freedom matter? Cardinal Faulhaber's proclamation in his letter of thanks to Hitler upon the signing of the Concordat—'What the old parliaments and parties failed to accomplish in sixty years, your

[55] On this see Karl Bachem in *Geschichte der Zentrumspartei*, vol. 8 (1931), p. 239f.; also, *Der Interfraktionelle Ausschuß 1917/18*, edited by E. Mathias and R. Morsey (Düsseldorf, 1959), vol. 2, p. 560f.

statesmanlike farsightedness has realized world-historically in six months'[56]—encapsulates the political attitude of German Catholicism, an attitude on the basis of which it inevitably failed to grasp the real state-political task.

This, precisely, is also the attitude that speaks from the diary entries of Prelate Kaas, and which alone is probably able to explain what is—from the vantage point of the Weimar Constitution—his more than questionable behaviour. The result of the unresolved *Kulturkampf* situation and the fixation of political thinking on the natural law 'bona particularia' was that the crucial leaders of German Catholicism were not so much unwilling as incapable, in the situation that prevailed in the spring and summer of 1933, to act primarily in a state-political manner instead of merely with a concern for matters of Church and cultural policy. The state-political insight and responsibility that men like Brüning, the *Landtag* delegate Graf von Galen, Joos, Letterhaus, and a few others displayed in spite of this deserve to be highlighted. However, on the whole it was no coincidence that they were unable to prevail. One must not underestimate the fact that the parliamentary leadership positions within the Centre Party and the BPP were largely in the hands of prelates, who, by virtue of their ecclesiastical profession, were much more susceptible to the danger of seeing politics primarily as a means for securing ecclesiastical-cultural concerns, and to looking upon a political party of the Catholics as a vanguard of the Church in the world.

The tragic situation of the Weimar Republic is revealed here once again in all its starkness. From the beginning, the Weimar Republic—as its end would show—had no serious and committed defenders of its political substance, which rested on a political and ideological compromise. It had only followers who, in the final analysis, confronted it with inner reservations, and who wished to use the neutrality and openness of the constitution as a way of eventually abrogating that compromise. The Social Democrats embraced the constitution because and in so far as it was open to Socialism: 'Republic, that's not much, Socialism is the goal' was E. Bernstein's well-known slogan.[XXXVI] Conservative groups rejected the constitution as such and tolerated it at most as a transition to a restoration of the monarchy. The crisis of 1933 then revealed that a comparable reservation prevailed also among the Catholics: 'Republic, that is not much, denominational school and "Christian" state is the goal.' A republic that is dependent on such followers cannot survive a serious crisis.

The absence of a willingness to become active on behalf of the Weimar state in its crisis was also furthered by the natural law doctrine of the state as it was and is taught to Catholics. In the form it was given by the Neo-Scholasticism that began with Leo XIII, this state doctrine knows the distinction between the suprahistorical natural law principles of the state order, and the concrete forms of state and constitution that are not dependent on natural law and thus subject to historical change, and towards which it is neutral. The upshot of this distinction is that the natural law principles detached from historical forms and orders

[56] See *Stimmen der Zeit*, vol. 163, p. 367.

[XXXVI] Note the rhyme in German: 'Republik, das ist nicht viel, Sozialismus ist das Ziel!'

bear all normativity and obligatoriness, while these concrete historical forms and orders are pushed aside into the realm of the 'historically accidental' or 'mere factual', the 'inherently' insignificant, and are thus emptied of normative content. When push came to shove, it was not worth fighting for them with all one's power. The declaration of neutrality towards whatever form the state takes, first explicitly formulated by Pope Leo XIII, gives expression to this relationship. Fundamentally, only what is directly demanded by natural law principles deserves full personal commitment.

What this means, then, is that the sense for historical and political legitimacy and continuity is invariably lost, and with it also the capacity for history-related political action. The doctrine of the 'normative power of the factual', strictly rejected in theory, sees here a potent resurrection in practice. For one was willing to immediately recognize 'given facts', be it a revolution, be it the electoral victory of a party hostile to the constitution—after all, it is all taking place in the realm of the historically accidental and changeable—provided the possibility of realizing the natural law principles was preserved.[57] But what revolutionary concerned about consolidating his power will not initially concede that possibility? Thus, in every historically decisive moment, a partial or complete political paralysis is inevitable. Every bond of loyalty to a concrete form of government or constitution, however solid, will prove empty as soon as it is put to the test. Calm is the citizen's first duty—provided one has the sense that natural law remains secure or will be secured.[58]

In the application of these principles, German Catholics let the monarchy fall in 1918 without lifting a finger, and in 1933 they marshalled no serious defence of the parliamentary-democratic state they had helped to create. The moment Hitler pretended to respect 'Christian principles' Catholics—leaving aside their weariness of democracy—were, already by virtue of their political principles, drained of the energy to defend the Weimar state. Loyalty to the existing, historical constitution had no grounding in natural law. Hitler seemed like the 'legitimate authority' with a claim to loyalty and obedience, to some extent as soon as he assumed the reins of government, but certainly following his Reichstag speech on 23 March 1933. That was something the German

[57] In this context belongs also the scholastic topos of the 'tyrannus a titulo', the ruler who has come to power illegitimately, to whom one could not offer any resistance as long as he successfully exercised the tasks of one in authority. A concrete effect emanated from the essay by M. Preis, S.J., 'Die Staatsverfassung im totalen Staat', *Stimmen der Zeit* 125 (1933), pp. 145ff. We read there: 'Precisely the clear awareness of the historical conditionality of all state theories can obligate him [the Catholic] objectively and ethically to dissolve the—once necessary—bond with antiquated forms of political life, and to test and prove the formative political power of his principles in a new situation[!].' As a result, the author accommodated himself fully to the 'new situation' of the total state as early as June 1933 and looked at the state and the basic features of its constitution 'as the necessities of state demand today in the light of natural law principles'.

[58] In essence, if with a positive cast, this is also expressed in Pius XI's letter of response to the German bishops to their joint pastoral letter of 3 June 1933. It says: 'Nor is there any doubt that Catholic men, precisely out of their religion, which they profess with fidelity and zeal, will engage in every nation in honest, loyal, and lasting cooperation with the public authorities, as long as the rights of God and the church remain whole and inviolate' (*Junge Front*, 2 No. 40, 10.1.193)].

bishops explicitly declared only five days later, on 28 March. This also explains the appalling lethargy that seized the Centre Party after 23 March and clung to it until the end. The Centre was literally caught in the middle.

Still, the two-fold bias, one arising from the *Kulturkampf* situation, the other from the a-historical natural law doctrine of the state, is not sufficient by itself to explain the widespread affirmation and support of the Nazi regime by German Catholicism in 1933. Instead, one must look for the most decisive impulse behind it in the deeply rooted anti-liberalism that had been characteristic of Catholic thinking since the nineteenth century, and probably still is to this day.

Historically, this anti-liberalism is a result of the defence against and an overcoming of the Enlightenment within the Church.[59] Initially it was religious in character and was directed against the principled critique of religion, revelation, and dogma that was being advanced within the framework of reason. But through the influence of the Restoration and Romanticism, this anti-liberalism soon turned into a political stance, as well. These origins explain why it adopted from the outset the intense opposition to the 'ideas of 1789' and the forms of order based on it that was characteristic of the Restoration and Romanticism. In the process, this anti-liberalism received special legitimation from the papal condemnation of Lamennais ['Mirari vos' 1832], which impacted not only liberalism as a worldview, but also 'liberal Catholicism' as a political movement.[60]

Those opposed to the individualism of the Enlightenment, which manifested itself in the theory of the social and state contract, in the doctrine of popular sovereignty, and in the liberation of the individual from traditional orders and ethical bonds, set up the theory of the 'organic' order that adhered to 'realities given by nature' and was based on authority, genuine community, and a system based on [occupational] estates. This seemed like the truly 'Christian' and natural order in opposition to the assault of the 'modern' world pushing for emancipation. Substantively, this organic theory was—in origin and content—one that sought to preserve or restore the pre-revolutionary and pre-liberal structures of life. The more historical development advanced along the path laid down by the ideas of 1789, the more anachronistic and divorced from reality this theory appeared. Eventually ending up as a pure counter-ideology to the individualistic and autonomist vision of the Enlightenment, it remained closely bound to the latter in this very negation. What seemed to Enlightenment theory as progress and achievement, and thus as the true accomplishments of the nineteenth century, had to present itself as decay and dissolution from an 'organic' point of view.

In this way, Catholic political thinking gradually lost any impartiality and openness towards historical reality and the problems contained therein. One

[59] See Franz Schnabel, *Deutsche Geschichte im neunzehnten Jahrhundert*, vol. 4: Die religiösen Kräfte (Freiburg, 1951), pp. 44–56; 164–202.

[60] We know today that this condemnation of 'liberal Catholicism' came about also, and especially, at the urging of Metternich, who saw the security of the restored monarchies threatened by this movement. See Schmidlin, *Papstgeschichte der neuesten Zeit*, vol. 1 (Munich, 1933), pp. 559–560.

no longer proceeded from the given, concrete reality, in order to recognize and shape what was possible within it; instead, one measured this reality a priori against one's own theory, which was thoroughly alienated from it. Reality was then to be thoroughly reshaped on the basis of this theory. That is the internal thought process of every ideology. The 'theory' became accordingly ever more ideological and abstract. Beginning with World War I, it invigorated and renewed itself chiefly through the 'organic' state doctrines of Romanticism, which experienced a remarkable renaissance thanks to Othmar Spann and his universalist school. And the idea of a revival of the 'Reich', newly put forth by the liturgical movement and the Catholic youth movement, now also found a place within it.[XXXVII] This idea meant once again an escape from the concrete problems and alternatives raised by the modern state and modern society.

In the end, Catholic political thinking was thus living largely out of a principled negation of at least two hundred years of historical reality. Opinions might diverge on the justification for such a relationship to history. But if one stands in opposition to two hundred years of historical development and historical incontrovertibility, one cannot simultaneously seek to formulate and implement practical politics, which, after all, cannot avoid historical realities. This will invariably lead to illusions or catastrophes. Around 1933, wide circles of German Catholicism had attained an ideological bias and disconnection from reality that caused them to see in the Nazi movement a welcome ally in the struggle against the 'pernicious liberal spirit' and for a Christian order that achieved the 'full realization of natural law'—simply because that movement thought of itself as very emphatically anti-liberal and anti-Marxist and employed numerous words from 'organic' thinking. Wherever one found in Nazi terminology the same words and phrases, such as 'national order in keeping with nature', 'corporatist-organic state structure', 'community bondedness', '*Volkstum* [peoplehood]', 'authority', or 'Reich', one presupposed that they referred to the same thing and believed that one was witnessing the departure towards a new and better order, one that was correcting centuries of old errors.

The mismatch with historical reality could not have been any greater. The 'organic' unity of the pre-Revolution orders had separated once and for all into 'society' and 'state' through the turning point of 1789. Civil-liberal society had formed in emancipation from the old orders, a society in which the individual is set free from antiquated bonds, in which all people are recognized as bearers of inviolable individual rights and are called upon to pursue their free economic and personal self-realization on the basis of liberty and equality. At the same time, the state existed as the necessary counterpart: as the bearer of sovereign

[XXXVII] On Spann, see annotation XXII. The demands of the liturgical movements and the youth movements of the 1920s folded well into Spann's universalist approach in which equality and unity took on such a prominent place, insofar as the former sought to cultivate religiosity in the private rather than public realm (the full integration of prayer into the chores of daily life) and the latter demanded the concentration of Catholic life in the parish (as opposed to its fragmentation in associations and other societal groups).

power and authority, its task is to protect the concrete ways of life and to constrain the unshackled individualism of society so as not to expose the individual helplessly to the rhythm of acquisition and consumption. Even though state and society are in many ways concretely linked, this 'split' [*Entzweiung*] as such has been irreversible ever since.[61] If one does not wish to tolerate the structural coexistence of 'state' and 'society', there are only two alternatives: either to dissolve the state into society, which gives complete leeway to the society of needs and consumption and subordinates the individual to its functional laws; or to abolish society through the state, which simultaneously abrogates the rights of the person and individual liberty. The first is the path taken by liberalism and Marxism—of course in fundamentally different ways; the second is the path of fascism.

Hegel was the first thinker who recognized this fundamental reality of the modern world that came into being once and for all in 1789, and he described its internal necessity in his *Rechtsphilosophie* [Philosophy of Law].[62] He believed that henceforth the coexistence of freedom and order was possible only in the existence side by side of state and society. And in spite of all the pantheism and worship of the state of which he was accused, he emphasized that the possibility of this side-by-side existence was conditioned by the efficacy of the Christian faith. For it was only and precisely the Christian faith that was able, on the one hand, to acknowledge internally the freedom and subject status of all human beings, which is the foundation of modern society; and, on the other hand, to affirm an overarching authority that preserved ethical principles.[63] One cannot say that the development of the last 150 years has refuted this insight of Hegel's.

Without realizing it in their ideological bias, the leaders of German Catholicism, who advocated an 'organic' order that overcame liberal society, thus became influential trailblazers of the fascist revolt against 'society' that began in Germany in 1933. In that sense their original alliance with the Nazi system has a certain consistency. The final result, however, would be exactly the opposite of what they were striving for—namely, the even more uncontested autocracy of the liberal society they opposed. For as a result of the Third Reich, all concepts of statehood, authority, and suprapersonal order were so perverted and devalued that it proved impossible in 1945 to constitute the state as anything other than the servant of an unshackled economic and acquisitive society. This, of course, has removed all the institutional obstacles to the realization of the tendency of modern society to establish itself as a totality and to subordinate everything else to its functionality.

This context, finally, reveals also the tragic role of the pastoral pronouncements in 1933. When it came to the political behaviour of German Catholics, their bishops, with pastoral authority, gave them advice and directives they

[61] See Joachim Ritter, *Hegel und die Französische Revolution* (Cologne-Opladen, 1957).

[62] Ibid.

[63] Hegel, *System der Philosophie*, Teil 3 (Glockner edition, Stuttgart, 1929), §552, pp. 434ff.

would have been better off not following—in terms of state politics, that would have been the right thing to do.[64]

At the same time, this reveals the deep inner problem of the Church's *potestas indirecta*.[XXXVIII] For all the breadth of its competency, as a *potestas indirecta* the Church never has any direct responsibility anywhere. Those Catholics who loyally followed the political advice and directives of their bishops in 1933 had to endure the consequences of their action during de-Nazification in 1945 alone, without being able to publicly ask that their bishops protect and defend them.

All of this should be sufficient cause to rethink the question of the sphere of competency of the pastoral office in political matters, and the question of the political judgment and political self-conception of German Catholicism. It would appear that German Catholicism is today assimilating into society with the same lack of reservations with which it used the state in 1933 against society, and in the process it is once again failing to find the right balance, though this time coming from the opposite direction.[XXXIX] For can one honestly say that the positions and political principles that led to the errors of 1933 have been overcome in German Catholicism today?

[64] See also Friedrich Muckermann, S.J., *Der deutsche Weg* (Zurich, 1946), p. 25. After 1933 he had to 'time and again admire the sure instinct of the Catholic people, which saw things more clearly than did the academics, who recognized the terrible danger much sooner than even the bishops themselves did'.

[XXXVIII] *Potestas indirecta* refers to a doctrine of Catholic state theory according to which the Church still has supreme power, but only vested in spiritual matters.

[XXXIX] Böckenförde is referring to what he conceived as a continually instrumental view of democracy on the part of the Church, using state institutions when opportune to further its influence, but rejecting the democratic state when it regulated matters the Church saw as its exclusive domain. As laid out in his article 'Ethos of Modern Democracy and the Church' (Chapter I in this volume), Böckenförde holds that the Church should accept democracy on substantive grounds and focus its political activities on supporting citizens' ethos (instead of interfering instrumentally in the political process by giving electoral recommendations from the pulpit).

III

Types of Christian Conduct in the World during the Nazi Regime [1965/2004]

The conduct of Christians in the world and towards the world has been an old theme ever since the revelation of God in Jesus Christ was proclaimed to humankind.[1] We are not talking about something marginal, but about the realization of faith in the world. For the Christian faith encompasses also conduct in the world, in the way humans coexist and interrelate; it is not limited to prayer, liturgy, and sacrament. Let us recall only the Ten Commandments, the great hymn on love in the letter of Paul to the Corinthians (I Cor. 13), and the admonition in the Letter to the Romans to honour the existing authority as established by God and to submit to it (Romans 13.1–7).

To that end, the Christian faith conveys *specific* actuating forces, that is to say, independent commandments and impulses for conduct in the world. It is not limited to sanctioning what prevails in any given society; instead, it tends to stand against it and to go beyond it, even though in the history of Christianity there have repeatedly been amalgamations with actual practice and tradition. That is also why an inherently autonomous Christian moral and ethical doctrine exists. It encompasses the normative principles for Christian conduct in the world. Of course, except for a few exceptions, these principles are not inherently concrete statements. Concrete statements and commandments of how to behave take shape out of the experiences of given situations and conflicts: these are related back to the principles, which are thus concretized through the substance of real-life instances. To that extent, the Christian moral doctrine also has the character of an answer: it provides answers to potential life situations that lie within the realm of experiences.

How, then, did Christian morality realize itself under the Nazi regime, how could it realize itself? I am not talking about Christian morality primarily as a

[1] Editors' Note: The article is based on a public address Böckenförde gave to students in East Berlin in May 1965 on the occasion of the saint's day of the Catholic Student Society. Implicit in his remarks is a reflection on the possibility of exhibiting a genuinely Christian comportment in the context of authoritarian rule, here concretely the GDR. Among the 450 people in the audience was Wolfgang Thierse, the later president of the German Bundestag (speaker of parliament, 1998–2005) in reunified Germany. Böckenförde dedicated the article to him when he published the text for the first time in 2004.

Religion, Law, and Democracy. Ernst-Wolfgang Böckenförde, Oxford University Press (2020). © E.W. Böckenförde, M. Künkler, and T. Stein 2020. DOI: 10.1093/oso/9780198818632.003.0005.

system of norms, but as a lived attitude, carried by the impetus of the Christian message. A Christian frequently found himself in situations for which there were no experiences to draw upon. Fascism introduced something fundamentally new: the totalitarian politicization of all realms and contexts of life, the state taking hold of the entire person down to his innermost core, without the recognition of any kind of private sphere or of principles that stand on their own. All processes of life were incorporated into the racist-fascist ideology and completely functionalized relative to it, and individual human beings were accordingly placed under a totalitarian obligation. With that, the conduct and behaviour of individuals moved into a new dimension: they had no escape or refuge from the political and from their functionalization towards the political, even if they wished to be deliberately non-political. Conduct and behaviour, in addition to their immediate meaning and substance, always had a political function and effect, which alone mattered for how the regime judged a person.

The traditional moral doctrine could provide no adequate answer to this situation. As political ethics, it related to behaviour within a community which—for all its substantial particular defects—did seem sustainable in its fundamental order, and was not perverted in its nature. This was the unspoken precondition for its behavioural norms. Now, however, reality was becoming increasingly a totalitarian *malum commune* [common evil], instead of *bonum commune* [common good]. The traditional doctrine of the relationship of Christians to authority thus fell entirely out of sync with the times, reality had slipped from its grasp.

But how did Christians—both those holding ecclesiastical offices and the believing laity—behave in practice? To what extent did they find their own behavioural forms, and what were they? To what extent did they—objectively speaking—fail in this, or prove themselves Christians in a given situation? In what follows I shall ask about *typical* forms of behaviour that occurred and describe and analyse them in detail. In the process I shall leave aside conformism and opportunism, which was also often found among Christians; my interest is in forms of behaviour that were, from the perspective of those involved, based on a conscious Christian motivation and fundamentally Christian attitude.

1. A first type of behaviour is characterized by the fact that a given situation and the political forces at work are seen primarily or even exclusively from a perspective of ecclesiastical institutions, pastoral care, natural law, and cultural policy. Attention is paid only to the religio-natural law realm of principle; as for the rest, one and one's behaviour are 'apolitical' and neutral. A political party and a political regime are recognized as long as, and to the extent to which, they do not violate the laws of God and the teachings of the Church; they are rejected if, and to the extent to which, they do. This accorded with the behaviour of the majority of ecclesiastical office holders before and in 1933, especially also after Hitler's seizure of power, as it did with the behaviour of numerous Catholic politicians.

I will give two representative examples. Cardinal Bertram, the chairman of the Fulda Bishop's Conference, declared the following in his pastoral letter of 15 October 1933, a few months after the conclusion of the Reich Concordat:

> The documents known to all show how the episcopacy has raised its voice, solely for religious reasons, against movements and parties in which rallies and activities included the danger that the emerging political upheaval would have a disruptive and disorienting spill-over effect on the religious and ecclesiastical sphere. The documents show no less that the bishops, as soon as the reorganization of public conditions was a fact, without any change to their fundamental statements, immediately paved a path to peace, when at long last the authoritative declarations provided assurances with sufficient clarity, assurances which, once they are fully and completely realized, will bring about the elimination of the indicated threat.[1]

And as early as 4 April 1933, barely two weeks after the passage of the Enabling Act, a programmatic article entitled 'The Path of the Centre [Party]', which had official character and may have been penned by Prelate Kaas[III] himself, asserted that the substantive character of the Centre Party (the chief political representation of German Catholics) as a worldview endowed it with a special resilience and adaptability 'towards what are merely manifestations of the time'. It allowed the party, 'without endangering the substance of its political heritage', to find the correct realpolitik stance and dutiful attitude of state politics also towards those developments for which it was not responsible.[2]

What was the consequence of this form of behaviour? While subjectively it believed that it could avoid politics, objectively it could not; instead, it merely reduced it to a question of worldview. As a result, it became predictable and calculable for the Nazi regime, especially during the phase of the internal stabilization of power. The regime merely had to leave areas of cultural policy of interest to the Church and morality grounded in natural law untouched for the time being so as not to arouse any political opposition while establishing and consolidating its own power. To that extent, this form of behaviour could be exploited for one's own purposes, which is something the regime in fact did deliberately.

Following the consolidation of the Nazi regime, when the question of power had been decided, this kind of behaviour was focused chiefly—and to this extent consistent with its stance—on working for the freedom of the Church and the possibility of Christians living a religious life. The guiding principle was the well-understood essence of the Church in the sense of the *cura animarum*. This

[1] *Ecclesiastica* 13 (1933), p. 473.

[II] As a member of the Weimar Republic's parliament (*Reichstag*), Prelate Kaas was the (informal) leader of the Centre Party's parliamentary group. He argued successfully in favour of the Enabling Act, whose passing in parliament required the support of the Centre Party. See Chapter II in this volume for his role in the Centre Party's contribution to the demise of the Weimar Republic and its support of Hitler's seizure of power.

[2] *Kölnische Volkszeitung*, 4 April 1933; see Josef Becker, 'Zentrum und Ermächtigungsgesetz 1933', *Vierteljahreshefte für Zeitgeschichte* 1961, pp. 202–207.

entailed, on the one hand, political abstinence and as much loyalty as possible, and, on the other hand, a withdrawal to the legal status guaranteed in the Reich Concordat; the latter was the starting point for petitions and protests, which, of course, accomplished little. An extension of the Church's role as guardian and watchman into a general responsibility was largely held back in favour of defending and possibly securing one's own sphere. No unnecessary dangers were to be created for the flock entrusted to it. Inner resolve was displayed for protecting this realm of one's own, but at the same time an effort was made—out of a sense of pastoral responsibility—to avoid the creation of a martyrdom situation. Meanwhile, the strategy of the Nazi regime for pushing ahead the planned persecution of Christianity and the Church was a policy of small, steadily intensifying steps, the continual restriction of the Church's freedom and effectiveness, and its displacement into the most narrow sphere of worship.

2. A less widespread but nevertheless existing type of behaviour can be characterized as political engagement for the Nazi regime in the early stages. It was not guided by careerism or an inner connection with National Socialism, but—in the face of the decline and death throes of Weimar democracy—by the expectation of being able to create a better, Christian-authoritarian order. Although this was objectively an illusion, and, in retrospect, the expression of political naiveté, subjectively the intentions were sincere. What contributed to this stance not least were an aloofness from democracy and modern, liberal-individualistic society, which certainly existed among Catholics, and opposition to the widespread political conformism of Catholics during the Weimar period. One saw the possibility of a Christian-inspired political activism in the Nazi regime and felt confident that one could influence the direction the regime was taking in a positive way. It was only a small group that embraced this type of behaviour: segments of the Catholic nobility and a number of Catholic intellectuals. For the regime they were welcome as helpers during the initial phase of stabilization; they were instrumentalized as useful idiots, but soon pushed out of whatever positions of influence they may have held. Most soon realized their mistake and also withdrew on their own; not a few of them were later part of the active political opposition to the regime.

3. Another type of behaviour assumed great practical significance in daily life. It was concerned with the simple and consistent fulfilment of religious and professional obligations. Individuals were willing to accept disadvantages that arose from it. Personal conduct against one's conscience was out of the question and intolerable demands on the part of the regime and its office holders were rejected; otherwise, one behaved in a neutral and 'apolitical' fashion.

The basic attitude that came into play here can be described as follows: getting through the times with decency and faithful to oneself, not exposing oneself unnecessarily, being loyal as long as nothing 'contrary to the faith' was being demanded. When applied in practice, this basic stance often led individuals to walk close to the line: can I still do this or go along with it, or do I have to reject it—regardless of the consequences? Here are a few minor examples, some of which concerned me as a youngster: what about participation in the activities of the Deutsche Jungvolk[III] or the Hitler Youth on Sunday morning, which ruled out attending mass? Participation in an attractive Pentecost camp without the possibility of attending church? Musical participation in a 'naming ceremony',[IV] which replaced baptism among ardent followers of National Socialism? Of course, there were also much more difficult questions and constellations.

This basic attitude was widespread among soldiers and officials, but also among the 'common people'. One cannot simply qualify it as conformism, for it was certainly carried by a Christian consciousness. However, it was focused primarily on proving oneself, on one's own salvation, not on a wider commitment. Keeping clear of doing wrong and not denying one's faith was the maxim in this sense; it was a rather passive bourgeois-Christian ethos. Immersing oneself fully in work on behalf of the general order that was in shambles was not considered; it would have meant an existential threat. One stuck with a withdrawal into the inner Christian realm, the inner emigration from the 'world'.

Within this type of behaviour, however, a not unimportant variation developed. A person proceeded from the same basic stance, but went beyond its self-referential focus by taking responsibility also for protecting and preserving the sphere of life in which one stood—whether with respect to the family, subordinates, or employees. Not infrequently this was the reason for joining the party, as a way of immunizing one's own sphere of life and work against harassment and threats from party organs. One did not go out on a limb within the party and was only a formal member, but one did remain head of an agency, for example, thereby securing to some degree one's own professional position, including one's children's education and training, and was able to shield and protect also subordinates and co-workers. Under the roof of party membership one kept one's own area clean and orderly, practised righteousness and an ethos of survival.

The form of behaviour described here posed no threat to the Nazi regime in its two variations. It was not based on any oppositional disposition and no resistance activity. In some way the regime could even derive an advantage from it. Thanks to the decency and personal humanity that were (still) practised by individuals or broadly in certain spheres of life, the regime had a better reputation than it deserved ('It's really not that bad, there are many decent people').

4. Another form of behaviour can be characterized as an oppositional stance that did not just remain internal and passive, but was deliberate and active. It realized itself above all in personal and professional spheres, where it developed clandestine or visible activities, but it did not extend into organized political opposition. These are the people who, if the opportunity arises, throw sand into

III The Deutsche Jungvolk was the youth wing for boys aged ten to fourteen of the Hitler Youth organization. In 1939 membership became compulsory.

IV Note that in the GDR a comparable rite of passage was instituted to replace the Protestant confirmation: the *Jugendweihe* (youth consecration) was established as a secular coming of age ceremony for all fourteen-year-olds and involved a pledge to the goals of the socialist state. Those who did not participate faced serious disadvantages (in school, later admissions to university or vocational training, and applications for housing and cars).

the gears of the system, who work against the goals of the Nazi regime from their position, support the harassed and persecuted within the limits of their possibilities, perhaps even hide them from the Gestapo. To what extent can and should one 'hold one's position' so as to use it as a vantage point for working against the regime? In the process, to what extent must one support or at least tolerate what is repugnant to oneself? What is in that sense still justifiable, for example, for a high-ranking official in a ministry, in order to be able to do something else or prevent certain things? How should and can doctors in institutions for the incurably ill conduct themselves? New boundary problems emerged in all of these questions, especially for the traditional Christian moral doctrine, and the rift between the ethics of conviction and the ethics of responsibility came to the fore very clearly.

Here, too, is an example: the race expert in the Reich Interior Ministry, Dr. Bernard Lösener, was ordered to attend the Reich Party Rally in Nuremberg in 1935 to formulate a law about the future status of the Jews, which Hitler wished to announce there.[3] The treatment of so-called half-Jews had long been a point of contention between the Ministry of the Interior and the authorities of the SS/Party. In terms of their legal status, the Ministry of the Interior wanted to count them among the Aryans, the Party and the SS among the Jews. If Lösener, who had been critical of Nazi racial policy since 1933, did carry out the assignment, he could base it on the more moderate position of his ministry and thus, if Hitler proclaimed it, give it some validity within the Party and the SS. And that is what happened. Was this in line with an ethics of responsibility to avoid the threat of something worse? Or would it have been the responsible thing not to participate and to let the law become as radical as possible, so that the Jews living in Germany would have immediately realized what they were facing and left the country as quickly as possible? The contrast between an ethics of conviction and an ethics of responsibility is only relative, and action taken from an ethics of conviction can certainly also accord with an ethics of responsibility. Of course, this is something one knows only after the fact.

5. There was also a heightened oppositional stance, namely, a direct political opposition motivated by conscious Christian responsibility. In terms of typecasting, it emerged in various forms.

a) One form showed itself in the public defence of fixed principles, combined with the readiness to draw political consequences from it. Here one should mention the example of Franz Graf von Galen, a member of the Prussian Landtag and relative of the future bishop of Münster. When the Centre party group in the Prussian Landtag decided, in May 1933, to vote for the Prussian Enabling Act, a successor law to the Reich Enabling Act with comparable content, he resigned his mandate with a remarkable public justification. It was impossible for him, he declared, by approving this law to voluntarily renounce the possibility of fulfilling the tasks he had taken on with the acceptance of his mandate

[3] Bernhard Lösener, 'Als Pressereferent im Reichsministerium des Innern', *Das Reichsministerium des Innern und die Judengesetzgebung: Vierteljahreshefte für Zeitgeschichte* 9 (1961), pp. 264–313 (272ff.).

and thereby assume co-responsibility for the laws enacted on the basis of the Enabling Act.[4] These were clear words and consistent conduct beyond political tactics and organized resistance. It made clear, at the very beginning of the Nazi regime, the kind of responsibility that was assumed with a global Enabling Act, by which parliament relinquished its own right to legislate.

b) Acts of active political resistance were another form. It meant taking on responsibility for the political whole with the utmost risk to oneself and one's family. Such behavioir consciously left behind the maxim of preserving the bourgeois existence, it joined the dangerous struggle over the right order of political coexistence, combined with giving up a normal life, an action driven in the final analysis also by honour. The prerequisite for this was the inner certainty of one's own conviction and the willingness to sacrifice, to sacrifice also one's own life to care for others. Authentic examples can be found in the ranks of the resistance fighters of 20 July and the Kreisau Circle.[V] Among them was no small number of practising Christians, such as Major General Henning von Treskow, Colonel Graf von Stauffenberg, or—in the Kreisau Circle—the Jesuit father Alfred Delp.

The question that arises with new incisiveness regarding this form of behaviour concerns the possible success and the foreseeable consequences of one's own actions. One stepped—willingly or not—into the dimension of political responsibility and had to take this into account in everything one did. To plan and realize something in this respect that did not turn into irresponsible and inconsiderate action required a lot of knowledge, contacts, and networks; this was from the outset not for everyone.

c) The third form manifested itself as simple, publicly visible Christian protest, some of which was intended to—and in any case did—have a political effect. Here one should mention the Berlin cathedral provost Lichtenberg, the Scholl siblings in Munich, and the euthanasia sermons of the bishop of Münster, Graf von Galen.[VI] This was about the visible testimony of the Christian conscience.

[4] *Germania* No. 143 (26 May 1933); on the context see above No. 4, p. 123, with note 19.

[V] On 20 July 1944 the most serious attack on Hitler's life was made, albeit in vein. The failed attack by Claus Schenk Graf von Stauffenberg led to the execution of more than 200 high-ranking officers in the military and civil administration. The Kreisau Circle, active from 1940 to 1944, was an opposition group initiated by Helmuth James Graf von Moltke. The group regularly met at Moltke's estate in Kreisau (Silesia) and focused on planning Germany's reorganization in a post-Nazi era. Moltke was arrested in 1944 and the group finally dissolved after Claus Schenk Graf von Stauffenberg's failed assassination attempt. Most of the circle's members, including Moltke, were sentenced to death and executed.

[VI] Bernhard Lichtenberg (1875–1943), beatified and granted the title of 'Righteous among the Nations', was a Roman Catholic priest in Berlin who publicly supported those persecuted by the Nazi regime. Arrested in 1941, he was later sent to a concentration camp and died during transportation to Dachau. Sophie (1921–1943) and Hans Scholl (1918–1943) were members of the White Rose, a student resistance group in Munich. After distributing flyers against the Nazi regime and the war on 18 February 1943, they were immediately apprehended. Five days later, they were sentenced to death in a show trial and executed on the same day. The Scholl siblings have been commemorated considerably for their resistance. Clemens August Graf von Galen (1878–1946), Bishop of Münster and

Is it appropriate to raise the question of the potential political success of this kind of behaviour? The sermons of the bishop of Münster had such success to some extent, as the euthanasia actions of the regime were suspended at least in part. The action by the Scholl siblings had no success; it failed to go beyond a demonstration and the actors paid for it with their lives. But was it not justified in its own right, as a testimony and symbol of resistance to injustice, with a power that has continued to resonate? It is precisely as such a symbol that their action is honoured today.

For these two last-named forms of behaviour, the question of manoeuvring and weighing between evils, which had rather marginal importance to Christian moral doctrine, took on a new dimension. Under the conditions of a totalitarian, fascist dictatorship, all actions became and had to become situational. General behavioural rules encompassed reality less and less and ran the risk of becoming empty. Because the action one decides to take is situationally determined, it can serve only as an example, and no longer as a general exemplar. In certain situations and positions, protest and resistance were tantamount to a rather senseless stupidity, as they meant exposure and endangerment; in other situations they represented the sensible or even necessary courageous act. The question of the admissibility of means also arises anew. For example, how far does the duty of truth extend when it comes to dictators and their henchmen? Are they even entitled to a truthful response to their questions? Is not the *reservatio mentalis*[VII] entirely legitimate?

Independent of this one must not overlook what conditions had to exist in those who took such action for their conduct to succeed as arising from the inside, from their personality. These conditions included a kind of dying from the world, bidding farewell to job opportunities and life plans, and a retreat into the interiority of the Christian faith. If this was successful, it created an invulnerability that was not impaired by the threats and actions of those in power, an attitude of readiness that opened up entirely new possibilities of political work while accepting extreme dangers.

6. One final form of behaviour must be mentioned, one that could develop especially under the fascist system and its total politicization: the Christian as partisan. He disappears within the system and its organizations and completely assimilates externally, such that he is not perceived in any sense as an outsider. In this way he seeks to insinuate himself into key levers of power so he can

since 1946 cardinal, was an outspoken opponent of the Nazi euthanasia programme. In a number of pastoral letters and sermons he criticized the state's persecution of church leaders and the killing of the physically or mentally disabled. After the 1938 Night of Broken Glass he asked the rabbi of Münster how he coud help. Nevertheless, he never spoke out in public against the deportation and the mass murder of Jews. He was beatified in 2005.

VII *Reservatio mentalis* is an attitude of inner retention, which means that a person actually does not support his or her statement, even if uttered under oath. The concept goes back to Jesuit doctrine and was heavily criticized by Kant for whom a lie can never be justified.

engage in sabotage from the inside. This was a new and effective form of resistance, though one that carried extreme risk; if it succeeded, it struck the system where it was no longer capable of defending itself. However, a host of preconditions had to be in place for something like this to succeed at all, and it could be only a matter for individual actors. But such individuals did exist, and one of them was Kurt Gerstein, a partisan in SS uniform.[5]

Kurt Gerstein, a member of the (Protestant) Confessing Church who had studied mining and later medicine, stood from the outset in inner opposition to the Nazi regime.[VIII] During the war, in 1941, he decided to enter the Nazi system, specifically the (Waffen) SS as the most powerful organization, as the most likely way of informing himself about terrible and criminal schemes and being able to disrupt or prevent them. He reached key positions and rose to the rank of *SS-Hauptsturmführer*, tasked with, among other things, organizing the chemicals, especially Zyklon B, for the Jewish extermination camps in Poland. Here he was able to hold back large quantities of these chemicals, to set them aside. In the end it has remained unclear to what extent the machinery of destruction was obstructed by his actions. He passed reports about the extermination actions that had got under way, which he himself had observed during inspection visits, to various offices of the Church; indeed, he had difficulties doing so with the Apostolic Nunciature.

What requirements does this kind of behaviour impose? It entails that someone stand completely on his own, living a double life. That requires an inner certainty of faith and great strength of character. How else is it possible not to lose one's personal integrity, given the necessarily full accommodation and assimilation to the environment in which one is working? What is called for is steadfastness independent of receiving gratitude and recognition, at the time or later. For this is part of the nature of the partisan: he remains initially unrecognized and must remain so, and later he is often considered compromised by the outside world. That is what happened to Kurt Gerstein. The story of his activity as a partisan within the SS was not believed; the French, whose prisoner of war he became in the end, considered him a Nazi activist who should be put on trial.

[5] For details, see Jürgen Schäfer, *Kurt Gerstein—Zeuge des Holocaust. Ein Leben zwischen Bibelkreisen und SS* (Bielefeld, 1999). In preparing the lecture, I was able to draw only on the documentation of the so-called Gerstein Report published with an introduction by Hans Rothfels, 'Augenzeugenberichte zu den Massenvergasungen', *Vierteljahreshefte für Zeitgeschichte* 1 (1953), pp. 177–194.

[VIII] Many Protestants had voted for the NSDAP, and the pro-regime 'German Christians', a church-like bureaucracy, had attempted to unify the various Protestant denominations to enable the 'Gleichschaltung' within the Nazi regime. It was against this current that the 'Confessing Church' was created within German Protestantism. Its programmatic foundation was the Barmer Declaration of Faith of 1934, written by Karl Barth with advice from Martin Niemöller. The declaration held that the Church is not an institution of the state, and that state control of the church is doctrinally indefensible. Against the totalitarian ideology of the Nazi regime, the declaration argued for a limitation of the state's purpose and reiterated that government, by divine order, had the task of ensuring justice and peace.

Driven by inner despair, he committed suicide. It was only many years later that the true story of Kurt Gerstein became known.

I have come to the end. The forms of behaviour by Christians under the Nazi regime that I have described here were and are not without problems. And they show one thing: It is not easy being a Christian in such times, and no one is immune from incurring guilt.

IV

Religious Freedom between the Conflicting Demands of Church and State [1964–79]

The year 1965 is a memorable moment in the history of religious freedom.[I] In that year, the principle of religious freedom was accepted by the religious institution that had resisted it most ardently and the longest: the Catholic Church. It happened in the Second Vatican Council's declaration *De Libertate Religiosa*, which was approved by the council fathers on 7 December 1965, and solemnly proclaimed by the Pope at the conclusion of the Council. It is no exaggeration to say that religious freedom won its final victory nearly four hundred years after the end of the Council of Trent.[II] It is no longer a principle that is recognized and implemented only by the legal system of the state, but a principle that is now also ecclesiastically grounded and legitimized by the Catholic Church, as it is by the reformed churches and denominations. The right of truth and the claim to individual freedom, which long stood opposed in ecclesiastical and religious thinking, have been reconciled on the ground of a person's right to liberty (which is grounded in natural law and theology). With this declaration, the Council has not only demanded something for the Church and its believers,

[I] Editors' Note: The article is based on a lecture Böckenförde delivered at the Reuchlin Society in Pforzheim on 19 April 1979. Sections I and II had in large parts already been published at that time in Ernst-Wolfgang Böckenförde, 'Religionsfreiheit als Aufgabe der Christen. Gedanken eines Juristen zu den Diskussionen auf dem Zweiten Vatikanischen Konzil', *Stimmen der Zeit* 90 (1964/65), pp. 199–213, and Sections III and IV in Ernst-Wolfgang Böckenförde, 'Einleitung zur Textausgabe der "Erklärung über die Religionsfreiheit"', in *Erklärung über die Religionsfreiheit (lateinisch und deutsch)* (Münster: Aschendorff, 1968), pp. 5–21. For the purpose of the 1979 lecture, Böckenförde expanded on the historical overview of Section I, highlighting the breakthrough achieved when the humanists Johannes Reuchlin and Erasmus of Rotterdam were the first prominent voices to reject punishments for blasphemy, arguing instead in favour of the power of persuasion through rational argument in matters of religion. By adding this section, Böckenförde implicitly also honoured his host, who in the previous year had awarded him the 'Reuchlin Prize for outstanding scholarly work in the humanities'. His article 'The State as an Ethical State', included as Chapter III in volume I of this edition, was his lecture upon accepting the prize. The present translation is based on the reprint of the article in Ernst-Wolfgang Böckenförde, *Religionsfreiheit. Die Kirche in der modernen Welt* (Freiburg: Herder, 1990), pp. 33–58, with updated references.

[II] The nineteenth ecumenical council of the Catholic Church was held in Trent from 1545 to 1563 and convened in reaction to the emerging inner-Catholic reform and protest movements, against which it defined heresies and laid down other fundamental matters of faith and doctrine. It was the last ecumenical council of the Catholic Church held before 1869 (the so-called First Vatican Council).

Religion, Law, and Democracy. Ernst-Wolfgang Böckenförde, Oxford University Press (2020). © E.W. Böckenförde, M. Künkler, and T. Stein 2020. DOI: 10.1093/oso/9780198818632.003.0006.

but has simultaneously given something to the world: the Church's recognition, justification, and development of a principle that makes it possible for persons of different faiths to coexist in freedom under a system that is acceptable to all.

I.

If we thus find ourselves at a turning point of history, it would be good to review the tension-filled path that religious freedom has charted between the conflicting demands of church and state. Not in the sense of historical remembering, but in the sense of a full recognition of what has come to historical fruition. The question of tolerance and religious freedom was the great path of suffering for western Christendom. After the religious schism had become a reality during the Reformation, Christians of different denominations for centuries denied one another the right to the free exercise of religion. And to that end they tried to use the secular arm of the state and the legal system. One could not imagine how people—orthodox and heretics, Protestants and Papists[III] were supposed to continue living alongside and with each other. People felt an obligation to employ all means to punish and combat apostasy from the true faith and to restore the lost unity; after all, the true religion itself formed an essential foundation of the political system. The tension-laden conflict between religious truth and human freedom that opened up was repeatedly decided in favour of truth and against freedom.

This attitude was widespread not only among Catholics, who were defending their true and traditional religion, but also among the great reformers. Since the introduction of the Inquisition in the twelfth and thirteenth centuries, the curia in Rome had explicitly authorized and participated in handing over 'the stubborn heretic' to the secular powers for judgment and punishment. One of the great medieval theologians, Thomas Aquinas, emphatically justified this process: 'The worldly authority has the right to put heretics to death, even if they do not endanger others, for they are blasphemers against God (*blasphemi in deum*) because they follow a false belief.'[1] Here heresy as such is made punishable as a religious offence, and not only insofar as it represented simultaneously political upheaval in the unitary religio-political world of the Middle Ages. Faith is understood as a kind of legal relationship of loyalty and carries within itself elements of the public cult of the polis, which it had taken over from the ancient world.

The reformers in no way abandoned this doctrine. To be sure, in his early writings Luther defended the freedom of belief and of the Christian conscience, arguing that it was bound only to Scripture. This was aimed against the Catholic territorial sovereigns in a (still) Catholic world. Yet when the issue for Luther was no longer merely the freedom of his own faith against the prevailing forces, but the preservation of the established Protestant denomination and

[III] A partisan backing the side of the pope on a particular issue.

[1] IV Sentent. D. 13 qu 2 art. 3.

tolerance towards deviations within the Protestant faith (brought to light by Zwingli and the Anabaptists),[IV] he and Melanchthon continued to advocate the same principles as the medieval Church:[2]

> But there are other heretics who dare teach matters contrary to the faith as it is clearly founded on the Scriptures and professed by all Christendom, such as the articles which children are taught in the Creed. These heretics presume to teach among other things that Christ is not God, but only man; that he is therefore only a prophet like any other, as the Turks and the Anabaptists maintain. Such people should not be tolerated, but punished as public blasphemers... Moses lays down in this law that such blasphemers, and all false teachers, should be stoned.

We read the following in the memorandum to Landgrave Philip of Hesse on the question of what to do with the Anabaptists the Landgrave had arrested, which was drafted by Wittenberg theologians and signed also by Luther (though he added a moderating comment):[3]

> Everyone is bound to prevent and repress blasphemy according to his status and function. By virtue of this commandment princes and civil authorities have the power and the duty to abolish unlawful cults, and to establish orthodox teaching and worship. The same commandment teaches them, moreover, to repress the public teaching of false doctrines and to punish the obdurate. Concerning this point the text of Leviticus applies (24:16): 'he that blasphemeth the name of the Lord, dying let him die'.

No different, in fact harsher still, were the principles that held in reformed Geneva under Calvin's political theocracy. Time and again, the Geneva reformer impressed upon the worldly authorities their duty to revenge the honour of God insulted by heresies and blasphemies:[4]

> Our sympathy-mongers, who take such great pleasure in leaving heresies unpunished, now see that their fantasy hardly conforms with God's commandment. Afraid lest the Church be blamed for being too severe, they would allow all kinds of errors to spread freely to secure tolerance for one man. But God does not even allow whole towns and populations to be spared, but will have the walls razed and the memory of the inhabitants destroyed and all things frustrated as a sign of his utter detestation, lest the contagion spread. He even gives us to understand that by concealing a crime one becomes an accomplice. Nor is this to be wondered at, since it is here a question of rejecting God and sane doctrine, which perverts and violates every human and divine right.

[IV] Zwingli and the Anabaptists were not considered Protestants by Luther and other reformers, because they took a fundamentally different stance with regard to the doctrine of the real presence of Christ in the Eucharist (which Zwingli rejected). Thus, the question of religious freedom for Luther and Melanchthon was not only about demarcation from Catholicism, but also from other reform movements whose ideas they did not accept.

[2] See Joseph Lecler, S.J., *Toleration and the Reformation*, trans. T. L. Westow (New York, 1960), vol. I, p. 161. The following quotes pp. 161ff. On the interpretation of these passages see also Martin Honecker, 'Martin Luther und die Politik', *Der Staat* 22 (1983), p. 483f.

[3] Honecker (note 2), p. 484.

[4] Lecler (note 2), p. 333. The following quote ibid., p. 334.

And in response to the protestation of Christian love and gentleness, he proclaimed:

> That humanity, advocated by those who are in favour of a pardon for heretics, is greater cruelty because in order to save the wolves they expose the poor sheep. I ask you, is it reasonable that heretics should be allowed to murder souls and to poison them with their false doctrine, and that we should prevent the sword, contrary to God's commandment, from touching their bodies, and that the whole Body of Jesus Christ be lacerated that the stench of one rotten member may remain undisturbed?

There was still a third current, especially during the first decades of the Reformation, which aimed at preventing the threatening schism of Christendom with patient intellectual debate rather than the power of the sword. It was advocated by the Christian humanists, whose spiritual leader was Erasmus and whose circle also included Johannes Reuchlin.[V] Initially it met with a positive reception at the court of Charles V (from his chancellors Gattinara and Granvella) and from a number of German princes. The theological argument put forth by the humanists, in particular Erasmus, had two parts: first, that the spirit of the Gospel was the spirit of love, which would not countenance that the currents of Christianity contending over the truth confronted one another with coercion and force; second, that the religious error in misguided individuals could be not be combatted with fire and sword, but only with patient persuasion, that is to say, with intellectual weapons.[5] Drawing on passages in Isaiah and Matthew, Erasmus wrote:

> Here one hears no mention of tortuous syllogisms, nor of threat and thunderbolts; no mention here of troops armed with steel, nor of bloodbaths and burnings. But you do hear of gentleness, of kindness towards the weak in whom there is still some hope of the fruits of goodness.

As a further justification, he invoked the parable of the weed and the wheat:

> The servants who want to cut out the weeds before the time are those who think that the false apostles and heresiarchs should be suppressed by the sword and by corporal punishment. But the Master of the field does not desire their

[V] Johannes Reuchlin of Pforzheim (1455–1522) was a humanist of the Renaissance era. He studied Latin in the Dominican monastery of his hometown, Greek and Law in Paris, Orléans and Poitiers, and Hebrew in Cesena and Rome. Reuchlin became one of Germany's foremost scholars of Greek and Hebrew. In 1510 he was appointed to a commission of Emperor Maximilian considering the banning of all Jewish books in the country. As the only member of the commission, Reuchlin pleaded against the proposal and instead called for the establishment of two professorships of Hebrew at all German universities. His opposition to the commission's recommendations landed him a summons by the Court of Inquisition, going through several appeals to Rome, where in 1516 he was de facto acquitted. His defences, which his supporters disseminated widely, mobilized public opinion in Germany and France and are said to have helped spark the Protestant Reformation. (His sister's grandson was Philipp Melanchthon, who was highly influenced by Reuchlin and spent much of his youth with the latter. Melanchthon in 1518 assumed the professorship of Hebrew and Greek at Wittenberg, which had originally been established for Reuchlin.)

[5] Lecler (note 2), p. 121.

> destruction, but rather that they should be tolerated in case they should amend and turn from tares into wheat. If they did not amend, the task of chastising them one day should be left to their judge.[6]

With this he had staked out a mediating position, one that advocated tolerance and patience to preserve Christian unity for as long as possible and keep it from fracturing. But its foundation was precisely that this unity was not yet broken or would be wilfully broken. It made no a priori decision of what should be done with the obstinate heretic or apostate who showed no sign of improvement but obduracy and sought to disseminate his heresy. Following a period of religious colloquies and attempts at mediation, it was therefore inevitable that the harsh positions in uncompromising defense of the truth or the pure Gospel eventually (re)gained the upper hand.

What was the consequence of this shared Christian conviction of the requisite intolerance towards every enemy of the true religion or the pure Gospel? A century of ghastly confessional wars in Europe. The Empire, France, the Netherlands, England, Switzerland: in the sixteenth and seventeenth centuries, all became battlefields of a never-ending political struggle over religious truth. Thousands upon thousands lost their lives, offices, honours, and earthly possessions, were driven from home and hearth only because they wished to worship God as dictated by the conviction of their religious conscience. An authority that could have ended the dispute over the truth in an authoritative and binding manner did not exist. Pope and Council, once the highest authorities of a unified Christendom, had themselves become parties to the conflict.

In this hopeless state of affairs, how could one find a path to peace, first of all a path to political peace? The political system began to fall back upon itself, to disconnect itself from its previous unquestioned anchoring in the true religion. It sought its ground and goal independently of religious truth in the establishment and preservation of external peace, public safety, and order. Finally, it turned the very question about the accepted religion—state religion, parity, or tolerance—into a political and no longer a religious matter. Politics addressed the religious question. In the hopeless situation of the confessional wars, the maxim *cuius regio eius religio*,[VI] [7] though it initially contained little religious freedom, was in fact a first step towards a new order of peace that carried within itself the seed of freedom. That may seem perplexing at first glance. Yet once the question of the accepted public religion ceased to be a question of truth that brooked no compromises, but a question of politics, it had been released from the destructive absoluteness which had led to the confessional wars. It was then in principle open to a settlement, also a settlement in the sense of

[6] Erasmus, 'Paraphrases on St. Matthew' 13, 24–30, quoted in Lecler (note 2), p. 122.

[VI] The principle 'whose land, his religion' was the key principle of the Peace of Augsburg of 29 September 1555, which gave the imperial estates of the Holy Roman Empire the freedom of deciding between Catholicism and Lutheranism (later also Calvinism) in their own territories.

[7] See Martin Heckel, 'Cuius regio – eius religio', in his *Staat und Kirche nach den Lehren der evangelischen Juristen Deutschlands in der ersten Hälfte des 17. Jahrhunderts* (Munich, 1968), pp. 227–234.

the demarcation of spheres of freedom, of tolerance, and—finally—religious freedom.

It was in this sense that the subsequent development took place step by step, with some interruptions. To be sure, kings and territorial sovereigns, along with their legal advisors, long clung to the notion that only one religion—at least as an officially recognized one—could exist in a state. But the reason for this was political, that of securing public peace, and no longer religious or theological. The conclusiveness of this foundation depended on the persistence of the actual preconditions. As early as 1598, the King of France made an attempt to tolerate two religions in one state in the Edict of Nantes, an attempt that held up for nearly a century and was undone more by intervention of the Church than political calculation.[8] And in the Empire the first—though very modest—demarcations of spheres of religious liberties had already begun in 1555, in the Peace of Augsburg, a development that was continued in the Peace of Westphalia of 1648.[9] It was a long and often arduous path. But given the claims to exclusivity on the part of the contending religious parties, religious freedom could be achieved only through the state and its political decision-making power. And thus, following a few preliminary stages, it eventually became a reality in the nineteenth century as a right of freedom guaranteed and protected by the state.

On the European continent Prussia set the example for other states. Joseph II's Patent of Toleration of 1781 in Austria had granted only a qualified private exercise of religion to the two Protestant and the Greek-Orthodox confessions in Habsburg lands, but not yet a freedom of religion or general freedom to profess one's faith;[10] the ecclesiastical territories were confessionally closed lordships; in England, Catholics were granted full civic equality only in 1829;[11] and in Sweden, women were still expelled from the country as late as 1859 for having converted to Catholicism.[12] But in the Prussian Civil Code of 1794 we find these memorable sentences:

> The notions of citizens about the state and God and divine things, the faith and the inner service to God, cannot be the subject of compulsory laws.
>
> Every resident in the state must be granted full freedom of religion and conscience.
>
> Nobody is obligated to accept prescriptions from the state with regard to his private opinion in matters of religion.
>
> Nobody shall be discomfitted, held accountable for, mocked, or even persecuted for his religious proclivities.[13]

[8] Leopold von Ranke, *Französische Geschichte*, vol. II (Wiesbaden, 1957), Book 13, Chapter 5, pp. 349–364.

[9] See Wilhelm Kahl, *Lehrsystem des Kirchenrechts und der Kirchenpolitik* (Freiburg and Leipzig, 1894), § 22 (pp. 316ff.); Martin Heckel, 'Augsburger Religionsfriede, II. Juristisch', in *Evangelisches Staatslexikon*, 2nd ed. (Stuttgart, 1975), cols. 93ff.

[10] Inge Gampl, 'Toleranzpatent, österreichisches', in *Evangelisches Staatslexikon* (Stuttgart, 1966), col. 2304f. (no longer in the 2nd ed.).

[11] Julius Hatschek, *Englische Verfassungsgeschichte bis zum Regierungsantritt der Königin Viktoria* (Munich and Berlin, 1913), p. 749f.

[12] Albert Hartmann, *Toleranz und christlicher Glaube* (Frankfurt, 1955), p. 270f.

[13] *Allgemeines Landrecht für die preußischen Staaten*, Teil 2, Titel 11, §§ 1-4.

To be sure, even in Prussia under the Civil Code state guardianship over the churches, the *landesherrliche Kirchenregiment* [rule over the church by the territorial secular authorities], continued; still, the binding principle established here, once made a reality, would invariably result in full religious freedom.

Of course, this is not to deny that the state, too, in contravention of the established principle, once again challenged the religious freedom that had been attained: for example, in the *Kulturkampf*[VII] in Prussia and Germany, in the secularizing laws in France around the turn of the century, and in the Jesuit articles of the Swiss federal constitution—not to mention those countries in which the order of state was destroyed by the totalitarian pretensions of a ruling party.

And yet: when it comes to the religious freedom that Christians, too, regard as self-evident today, we owe its origins not to the churches, or theologians, or even Christian natural law, but its theoretical preparation to the Christian Humanists and later to the Enlightenment thinkers, and its practical realization to the modern state, to jurists, and to secular rational law.

To be sure, the modern state and the jurists who helped shape it had to pay a price to make this path towards religious freedom possible. As early as 1562, on the eve of the Huguenot wars in France, Michel de l'Hôpital, the king's chancellor, had articulated the principle that should and had to become decisive for the new order of things: 'What matters,' he declared in the council of the king, 'is not which is the true religion, but how one can coexist.'[14] The state and public order had to become worldly, had to be secularized, unmoor itself from being anchored in the true religion or any kind of particular religion if it wanted to find a new and universal basis that encompassed all citizens and left behind the irresolvable quarrel between the denominations. In terms of the principle of how this state was constructed, religion could no longer be a legally indispensable element of the political order. The state as such declared itself neutral on the question of religious truth. As a matter of principle, the question of the religious creed became a personal matter of each individual citizen. In this sense, too, religion was 'set free' and a further consequence was its broad displacement into the private and social realm. Karl Marx formulated this with unsurpassed incisiveness in his essays on Bruno Bauer.[15]

There is good reason to ask how differently the order of Europe and the modern state could have developed if the representatives of religious truth four hundred years ago had embraced the very principle of freedom that is

[VII] The *Kulturkampf* (culture war) was a struggle of Chancellor Bismarck's government against the Catholic Church in the 1870s concerning the role and power of Catholic institutions in predominantly Protestant Prussia. Bismarck enacted a series of anti-Catholic laws, including the disbanding of Catholic organizations, confiscation of church property, and banishment or imprisonment of clergy. Some of the discriminating laws were not repealed until fifty years later. As Böckenförde writes in his 1961 article (Chapter II of this volume), the experience left Catholics with a deep sense of alienation towards the state and insecurity towards the public order.

[14] Leopold von Ranke, *Französische Geschichte*, vol. I (Andreas edition) (Wiesbaden, 1957), Book 3, p. 115.

[15] Karl Marx, 'Zur Judenfrage I', in his *Die Frühschriften* (Landshut edition) (Hamburg, 1953), p. 183. English: http://www.marxists.org/archive/marx/works/1844/jewish-question/.

today self-evident also for Christians. The statesmen and jurists who eventually erected the modern state as a worldly, secular, confessionally neutral, and then also religiously neutral state, merely cashed in the bill that the theologians of the Reformation era and the confessional wars had drawn. *Silete theologi in munere alieno* ['let theologians keep silent about matters outside their province']: this pronouncement of Albericus Gentilis, a jurist of international law, was a warning and an impassioned appeal. It was born not from anti-clericalism, but from the affliction of the confessional civil wars. And the much-maligned and often misunderstood sentence of Thomas Hobbes—*auctoritas non veritas facit legem* ['authority, not truth makes law']—belongs into this context. Of course, both pronouncements were addressed to a system in which the universal Christian foundation of the political community was still presupposed. The declaration of neutrality was made towards the quarrelling denominations, not towards Christianity as such.

II.

How did the churches react to this state-driven development towards tolerance and religious freedom? As a Catholic, I may be permitted to examine chiefly the Catholic Church: first, because the fundamental problems emerge most closely here, and, second, because I can speak more freely and unconstrained by ecumenical deference.

1. Until Pope Pius XII's so-called Tolerance Address in 1953, traditional Catholic teaching always effectively rejected the recognition of religious freedom or—which amounts to the same thing—tolerance as a principle. In the process it proceeded from the primacy of truth over freedom, and from the proposition that error as such could not be accorded any right against the truth. Only special reasons with a view towards the common good could allow granting error an existence in spite of this—but this could never be done de jure, as a principle, only de facto, as the acceptance of an evil. This was fundamentally still the same doctrine that had prevailed during the era of the Reformation and Counter-Reformation. In the Council Hall, as well, it was emphatically advocated by several Fathers (a minority, though).[16] However, within this doctrine one can differentiate gradations that are not unimportant.

In its starkest form, it was articulated as late as 1948 by the Roman Jesuit journal *Civiltà cattolica*.[17] The Catholic Church, convinced by its divine prerogatives of being the only true church, had to claim the right of freedom for itself alone, since that right could be accorded solely to the truth, but never to error. Although it would not fight against other religions, it would demand that they be prevented—with just and humane means—from spreading false doctrines.

[16] Especially by Cardinal Ottaviani, at the time the Secretary of the Holy Office, and by Cardinals Siri (Genoa) and Ruffini (Naples); on the disputes within the Council Hall see Pietro Pavan, *Lexikon für Theologie und Kirche*, 2nd ed., vol. 13, pp. 704ff.

[17] *Civiltà cattolica* 99 (1948), vol. 2, p. 33 (4.3.1948).

Thus, in a state in which the majority is Catholic, the Church would demand that error not be granted legal existence. But if the concrete circumstances did not permit the full application of this principle, the Church would demand for itself the greatest possible concessions. At the same time, it would be compelled, as the lesser evil, to accept the legal toleration of other religious communities. Moreover, in some countries the Catholics themselves would be forced to demand full religious freedom for all, where in principle they would have the sole right of existence. In this case the Church does not renounce its thesis, but accommodates itself to the hypothesis, that is, to the actual state of affairs, which real life could not ignore.

So far the author of the *Civiltà cattolica*. His pronouncements are no cause for outrage; the language is clear, the thinking is not devoid of internal logic or backing in older pronouncements by the magisterium—as, for example, especially in Pius IX's syllabus of 1864, points 77 and 78 of which explicitly condemn the public freedom of worship. Without any whitewashing, what becomes clear here is the kind of results to which the principle of the precedence of truth over freedom gives rise if it is consistently applied.

Fundamentally the same position, if somewhat moderated with respect to the possibility of tolerance, was advocated by Cardinal Ottaviani, who held an eminent position within the leadership of the church. He argued that in principle, that is, under normal conditions within a Catholic state, nothing was as obvious as the obligation of state leaders to prohibit false religions. For Ottaviani, this followed from the duty of the state to adopt the true religion as its foundation, and to promote not only the material welfare of its citizens, but also their moral and spiritual well-being.[18] As justification, Ottaviani invoked several statements by Pope Leo XIII. His teachings about the relationship between church and state did in fact adhere fundamentally to the Catholic state as the thesis and the state's special duties towards the true religion, and he always spoke of the public toleration of other religions only as an evil that had to be accepted under certain circumstances.[19] Peter Tischler made this sufficiently clear, with abundant examples, in his comprehensive study of Leo XIII's doctrine of the state.[20]

Ottaviani was not an outsider in this respect. Klaus Mörsdorf's textbook on church law, which was very widely used in Germany, contains the same position in the eleventh edition of 1964, which was published during the deliberations of

[18] Alfredo Ottaviani, *Institutiones juris publici ecclesiastici*, vol. II: *Ecclesia et status*, 4th, expanded edition (Rome, 1960), pp. 46–47, 66–67.

[19] Leo XIII, *Immortale Dei* (1885), c. 36 (Haec quidem) 'The Church, indeed, deems it unlawful to place the various forms of divine worship on the same footing as the true religion, but does not, on that account, condemn those rulers who, for the sake of securing some great good or of hindering some great evil, allow patiently custom or usage to be a kind of sanction for each kind of religion having its place in the State.' ['Revera si divini cultus varia genera eadem iure esse, quo veram religionem, Ecclesia iudicat non licere, non ideo tarnen eos damnat rerum publicarum moderatores, qui, magni alicuius adipiscendi boni aut prohibendi causa mali, moribus atque usu patienter ferunt, ut ea habeant singula in civitate locum.'] English text: http://www.vatican.va/holy_father/leo_xiii/encyclicals/documents/hf_l-xiii_enc_01111885_immortale-dei_en.html.

[20] Peter Tischleder, *Die Staatslehre Leos XIII* (Mönchengladbach, 1923), p. 187f.

the Second Vatican Council. 'The religiously neutral state of the modern era', we read there, 'appears to the Church as a national apostasy. As the faithful guardian of Christian revelation, the Church cannot accord error any kind of rights and must therefore reject the unlimited freedom to profess and worship; however, it does not fail to recognize that the denominationally mixed state is in a different position than the Catholic state of the Middle Ages.'[21]

The third incremental step, which restricted the principle ethically and thereby relativized its validity, though without relinquishing it, refers to what is known as the Tolerance Address of Pius XII. Here the duty to suppress moral and religious errors is subordinated to a higher and universal norm. It is no longer the final norm of action and no longer exists by itself in isolation. Still, in principle this duty is maintained as a universal norm that binds also the holder of state power. The crucial sentences read as follows:[22]

> The duty of repressing moral and religious error cannot therefore be an ultimate norm of action. It must be subordinate to higher and more general norms, which in some circumstances permit, and even perhaps seem to indicate as the better policy, toleration of error in order to promote a greater good. Thus the two principles are clarified to which recourse must be had in concrete cases for the answer to the serious question concerning the attitude which the jurist, the statesman and the sovereign Catholic state is to adopt in consideration of the community of nations in regard to a formula of religious and moral toleration as described above. First: that which does not correspond to truth or to the norm of morality objectively has no right to exist, to be spread or to be activated. Secondly: failure to impede this with civil laws and coercive measures can nevertheless be justified in the interests of a higher and more general good.

Even though certain emphases are placed differently here, the charge often advanced by non-Catholic Christians that the Catholic attitude towards tolerance was in the final analysis an opportunistic one was probably also true of this version of the tolerance theory. For example, non-Catholics or non-Christians who might ask whether Catholics would advocate religious freedom and tolerance also if they represented the overwhelming majority in the state and held the power of the state firmly in their hands, or if the state was a traditionally Catholic one, received no clear answer. After all, Pius XII's toleration thesis, too, did not recognize that the state must, in principle, present itself as a house in which every citizen has the same right to religious life, including the misbeliever or apostate, provided only that he is willing to recognize the state order as such.

2. If one reduces this pre-conciliar church doctrine to its objective core, irrespective of its various shadings, it amounts to a reversal of all natural law that the Church insistently asserted and asserts in other areas. For according to this theory, the subject of the law is not the human being but truth, and thus an abstract concept. The human being has been debased to being the object of this

[21] Klaus Mörsdorf, *Lehrbuch des katholischen Kirchenrechts*, 11th ed. (1964), vol. I, pp. 51–52.

[22] English: http://www.ewtn.com/library/papaldoc/p12ciri.htm.

notion of truth. Right did not belong to the human being qua human being, as the emanation from his existence as a person and an instrument to secure his personal freedom. Instead, it belonged to the human being provided and in so far as he stood within religious and moral truth. Not the human being as such, but truth was in the right. But what does it mean to say 'truth is in the right'? From an earthly perspective it can always mean only the following: right belongs to those who are or deem themselves in possession of the truth, and to the authority that decides about truth. After all, truth does not exist in the abstract in the realm of the earthly world, as an intrinsic essence of its own, but only in the conviction of truth held by concrete human beings. 'Truth is right' thus means concretely, and applied to the order of human coexistence, that only the Church, as the authority that decides concretely about truth, and those who belong to it, are in the right. With this, the universality and mutuality of the law is negated.

This theory was in principle incompatible with society. If the modern state wanted to secure the freedom of its citizens, it had no choice but to oppose this theory and to prevent the church from practising it. That is precisely how it became the pioneer of religious freedom. This socially incompatible character of the traditional doctrine of the Church was not nullified by the fact that the teaching of the Church had always acknowledged that no one must be coerced into accepting the Catholic faith. As securely as the Church advocated and defended this principle (it is explicitly laid down in c. 1315 of the CIC),[VIII] it in no way established fundamental tolerance or religious freedom. For it refers only to the voluntary *acceptance* of the Catholic faith and therefore in no way excludes that it is impossible to freely renounce the faith once it has been accepted. Nor does it rule out that the false faith has no freedom of worship and proselytizing. After all, that kind of constraint does not impose the Catholic faith, but merely prevents erroneous faith from speaking out and spreading.

Modern Communism simply had to adopt the principles of the traditional Catholic tolerance theory and interpret them in the sense of intolerance to create a legitimizing basis for its practice of continual religious persecution without bloodshed and restrictions on religious freedom. One example will illustrate this. Article 124 of the Soviet Constitution of 1936 declared: 'Freedom of religious worship and freedom of anti-religious propaganda is recognized for all citizens.' The content of this article is clear: the error of religious superstition has no right to existence, propaganda, and action against the truth of atheism. The person who is a prisoner to error must be prevented from spreading false teachings; he therefore has no legal status but merely enjoys freedom of worship that is tolerated for the sake of external peace. Only truth, that is, atheism, can claim freedom of propaganda, a full right of existence. The consequences in practice are well known. As irritating and unjust as this situation is,

[VIII] Böckenförde refers here to the Code of Canon Law of 1917, corresponding to Article 748 Section 2 of the revised code of 1983: 'No one is ever permitted to coerce persons to embrace the Catholic faith against their conscience.'

and Cardinal König pointed this out with moving words in the Council Hall,[23] the frightening fact remains that in this instance the Catholic Church is being treated by atheism, which lays claim to the truth, in accordance with the same principles it had proclaimed in its traditional toleration theory for the treatment of error. The Church had to suffer the painful experience that the pronouncement of the Gospel, 'Whatever you wish that others would do to you, do also to them' (Matt. 7.12), the foundation of all earthly justice and perhaps one of the few genuine maxims of natural law, was turned against it.

In the last session of the Council, Cardinal Beran of Prague emphasized this connection with candid and memorable words: 'Thus it would appear that the Catholic Church in my homeland must today suffer a painful atonement for every sin and mistake that was carried out in the past against freedom of conscience in its name, as for example the burning of the priest John Hus, or the external coercion to return to the Catholic faith that was inflicted upon the Czech people in the seventeenth century.'[24]

The order of the law is universal, its nature, as Thomas Aquinas said, is *aequalitas*, appropriateness and mutuality.[25] Thus, a maxim of law applies by its nature universally, not only for me, but also against me. A legal principle that seeks to exclude this mutuality is not a legal principle but a power principle.

III.

The Council's declaration on religious freedom has now left all of this far behind. It has departed from the previous doctrine not merely gradually, but fundamentally. It has found a new basis for the relationship between revealed truth and human liberty, which has stood and stands in the background of all conflicts over religious freedom. As such it has continued the path that Pope John XXIII had already taken in his encyclical 'Pacem in Terris'.

1. The Declaration accepts the right of religious freedom (*ius ad libertatem religiosam*) and understands it as an indispensable external right of the human person for the private and public exercise of religion in accordance with the demands of one's own conscience. This right of freedom is justified not on the basis of a specific subjective state of the person, but out of his inherent nature; according to the Declaration, it is and exists independent of the objective truth of the religious conviction of the individual, and independent of his subjective effort to attain that truth.[26] With that, the principled step has now been taken from the 'right of truth' to the 'right of the person'. The Declaration therefore

[23] See KNA (Catholic News Agency), Sonderdienst Nr. 50, 9.26.64, pp. 2–3.

[24] *Orientierung* (1965), p. 200.

[25] *Summa theologiae* II, II, q. 57, art. 1 ('illud enim in opere nostro dicitur esse iustam quod respondet secundum aliquam aequalitatem alteri'); qu. 58, art. 2 co.

[26] 'Declaratio de libertate religiosa', *Acta Apostolicae Sedis* 58 (1966): 929ff., No. 2: 'Insuper declarat, ius ad libertatem religiosam esse revera fundatum in ipsa dignitate personae humanae, qualis et verbo Dei revelato et ipsa ratione cognoscetur.'

states: 'In consequence, the right to this immunity continues to exist even in those who do not live up to their obligation of seeking the truth and adhering to it, and the exercise of this right is not to be impeded, provided that just public order be observed.'[27]

This sentence marks the legal core of the new doctrine of the Church. In retrospect it is barely possible to gauge what an enormous step the Vatican Council took with this pronouncement. During the Council, even such a staunch defender of religious freedom as Cardinal Bea still believed that this freedom could be justified only by way of the 'error invincibilis' of the conscience that was erring in good faith and the practical impossibility of determining whether an error was deliberate or inadvertent.[28] The Declaration left all of this far behind by recognizing the principle of the legal freedom of the person (and with it an indispensable part of the modern notion of freedom). It deepened this recognition further by justifying it also theologically, namely out of the freedom of the act of faith, which for its own sake presupposes the freedom not to believe.[29] All expectations that non-Catholic Christians and non-Christians, and especially jurists of secular law, could have placed on the Council in this regard were fulfilled by this Declaration. The Church itself has found a new point of orientation in its relationship to the modern world and the specific form of its order, the modern state, a point which, consistently developed, will have a profound impact.

One example of how this principle can be made concrete, which the Declaration itself mentions, may illustrate this. The privileged standing that the Church might enjoy in a traditionally Catholic state is stripped of legitimacy as a matter of principle. After the Declaration, this kind of standing now appears only as a situation produced by special circumstances. Although it is not condemned as such if it exists, it is constrained such that it may not lead to any kind of restriction on the religious freedom of the citizens and other religious communities.[30] This is further underscored by the general demand that government 'see to it that equality of citizens before the law, which is itself an element of the common good, is never violated, whether openly or covertly, for religious reasons'. Specific obligations of the state toward the true religion as such are no longer mentioned here. The religious state no longer appears as a Catholic desideratum. The duties of state power vis-à-vis religion concerns only religious freedom and its realization:

[27] English text: http://www.vatican.va/archive/hist_councils/ii_vatican_council/documents/vat-ii_decl_19651207_dignitatis-humanae_en.html

[28] A. Cardinal Bea, 'Religiöse Freiheit und Wandlungen der Gesellschaft', *Stimmen der Zeit* 173 (1963/64): 321.

[29] 'Declaratio de libertate religiosa' (note 26), Nos. 3 and 10.

[30] Ibid., No. 6: 'Si attentis populorum circumstantiis peculiaribus uni communitati religiosae specialis civilis agnitio in iuridica civitatis ordinatione tribuitur, necesse est ut simul omnibus civibus et communitatibus religiosis ius ad libertatem in re reli- giosa agnoscatur et observetur' ['If, in view of peculiar circumstances obtaining among peoples, special civil recognition is given to one religious community in the constitutional order of society, it is at the same time imperative that the right of all citizens and religious communities to religious freedom should be recognized and made effective in practice.']

> Therefore government is to assume the safeguard of the religious freedom of all its citizens, in an effective manner, by just laws and by other appropriate means.
>
> Government is also to help create conditions favourable to the fostering of religious life, in order that the people may be truly enabled to exercise their religious rights and to fulfill their religious duties" (No. 6).

For the position of the church within and vis-à-vis the state, 'divine prerogatives' are no longer claimed. The Declaration invokes the divine mandate the church received from its establishment by Jesus Christ, from which it derives its claim to freedom in human society. But what is demanded now by virtue of this 'special freedom' is nothing different from what the church is already entitled to as a community of the faithful on the basis of universal religious freedom. Indeed, the Declaration even proceeds from the assumption that the Church in fact receives the legal and consolidated position it requires by dint of its divine mandate only when the principle of religious freedom is not only proclaimed, but fully put into practice (No. 13). What is asserted, and the Declaration says this explicitly, is a concordance between the freedom of the Church and universal religious freedom, which is to be guaranteed to all humans and human societies as an external right. The Church merely claims for itself the rights that any other religious community can invoke. This is, not least, a repeal of the verdict about the separation of state and church on the basis of and within the framework of universal religious freedom, a verdict that Leo XIII had still pronounced so emphatically.[31]

2. Does this mean that the conciliar Declaration has relinquished the truth claim of the Catholic faith and accommodated itself to the agnosticism of which Church teachings have hitherto accused the state? By no means. As emphatically as it accepts religious freedom as a principle of the law, the Declaration simultaneously adheres to the truth claim of the Catholic faith and to humanity's obligation to seek and adopt the true faith: 'On their part, all men are bound to seek the truth, especially in what concerns God and His Church, and to embrace the truth they come to know, and to hold fast to it.'[32]

But does this not once again challenge the principle of religious freedom just now proclaimed, and does the Declaration not therefore suffer from an internal contradiction? Such an assumption would be a fundamental error. For the Declaration makes a clear—and for a doctrinal document of the Church probably the first—distinction between the legal order, on the one hand, and moral obligations, on the other. It consistently speaks of the duty to seek religious truth and hold fast to it as a *moral* obligation (*officium morale; obligatio moralis*),[33] which leaves untouched the external right to religious freedom, which is aimed against encroachments from other people and the power of the state. Not only does this recognition of the distinction between legal sphere and moral sphere

[31] Tischleder (note 20), pp. 318ff.

[32] 'Declaratio' (note 26), No. 1.

[33] 'Declaratio' (note 26), No. 1: *'morali hominum ac societatum officio'*. No. 2: *'morali tenentur obligatione ad veritatem gerendam'*; on this see the clear commentary by P. Pavan in J. Hamer and Y. Conger (eds.), *Die Erklärung über die Religionsfreiheit* (Paderborn, 1967), pp. 170ff.

pave the way for a new understanding of modern law within the thinking of the Church, but it simultaneously allows us to fully recognize the content and scope of religious freedom in the first place, which, after all, is an issue always—and only—as a principle of secular, external law.

Even if the law is by no means completely separated from the moral order, the legal and the moral orders are different in content and goal. The law concerns the relationship of humans to one another and vis-à-vis state power, not the relationship of the human being to God. It does not pertain to eternal salvation and the moral perfection of human beings, but to the external organization of their earthly coexistence. Primarily it is thus not the order of virtue and truth, but of peace and freedom. It is precisely in this way that it allows each person to live in accordance with the truth as he understands it or takes hold of in faith and thus to bring about his salvation. The individual right guaranteed by the legal system is therefore only the delineation and protection of a sphere of liberty against interferences from others and the power of the state, but not the establishment of a freedom from moral-ethical responsibility toward God and the truth. Accordingly, the recognition of the right to religious freedom is by no means a moral carte blanche for individuals to treat the question of religion as they wish or an exemption from their obligation toward the truth. It amounts only to the protection and securing of the external possibility to worship God according to the norms of one's own conscience and to profess one's religion privately and in public—or not to profess it; protection once again from encroachments by others and the power of the state.

The jurists of secular law have always fought for this distinction between the legal and the moral order (which by no means amounts to a complete separation). They now find confirmation that in doing so they did not become methodological atheists, so to speak, but that they acted also as Christians.

On the basis of this distinction between the legal and the moral sphere, it is also possible to reconcile the traditional teaching of the Church (i.e., that error has no right against the truth) with the recognition of religious freedom without the need to abandon one of the two positions. When it comes to the moral conduct of human beings, to the manner in which they make use of their legal freedom, it is certainly correct that error has no right against the truth, and that rights are given only to be exercised in accordance with religious and moral truth. In this sense it is not a specifically Catholic theory, but a principle that every Christian believer—indeed, every human being who acts and thinks in an ethically moral way—will acknowledge. For example, the right of parents to raise their children is guaranteed by the state's legal system as a general right of freedom. However, for Christian parents, in moral terms, this does not establish, with respect to their responsibility to God, a 'right' to raise their children without faith, but only the authority to raise their children as Christians, in accordance with their religious conviction. Morally speaking, error in fact has no right against the truth.

As much as these principles hold in the realm of the moral order, they do not and cannot apply in the realm of the law. If they are transferred to the realm of the law, they have a freedom-destroying effect. What made the traditional Catholic tolerance doctrine untenable was therefore less its principles as such, but rather the fact that these principles were readily translated from the moral sphere to the legal sphere. In the process their effect was freedom-destroying, and when realized in practice, totalitarian. The Declaration (finally) gave up this undifferentiated equating of the legal and the moral order.[34] It has consigned the traditional Church doctrine to the sphere where it is meaningful and where it belongs, the realm of the moral order—while also affirming it there. Viewed in this light, the doctrine can certainly exist in tandem with the recognition of religious freedom. The Declaration can therefore rightly state: 'Religious freedom, in turn, which men demand as necessary to fulfil their duty to worship God, has to do with immunity from coercion in civil society. Therefore it leaves untouched traditional Catholic doctrine on the moral duty of men and societies towards the true religion and towards the one Church of Christ.'[35]

With all of this, the Declaration has not only defended the Church's claim to truth, something one cannot blame it for, but it has simultaneously done something of great importance for the state order, something the state could not do by itself: it has justified external religious freedom and all the consequences that flow from it also inwardly, that is, on the basis of the position of faith and the religious claim to truth. The positive meaning of this for the anchoring of the modern state within the consciousness of its Christian citizens is nearly impossible to gauge. One might get a sense of it by recalling the words of Hegel, who said that it was an empty notion to imagine that individuals acted only in accordance with the sense or letter of the law, and not in accordance with the spirit of their religion, wherein lies their innermost conscience and highest obligation.[36] 'Such laws,' he went on to say, 'even if they have the genuine content, founder on the conscience, whose spirit is different from the spirit of the laws and does not sanction them.'

3. Can one therefore say that with this conciliar Declaration, the principle of religious freedom no longer constitutes a field of conflict between Church and state, but a field of cooperation? I believe that the basic answer is yes. Let us

[34] The traditional Catholic understanding of the law was shaped until very recently by this equating. It proceeded from an undifferentiated moral concept of law. Law was conceived as one segment of the moral order, with no independence of its own with respect to content and goal, as 'the part of morality that deals with the external inter-human conduct that is stringently obligatory'. On this see in greater detail E.-W. Böckenförde, 'Religionsfreiheit als Aufgabe der Christen', in *Kirche und christlicher Glaube in den Herausforderungen der Zeit*, 2nd ed. (Münster: LIT Publishing House, 2007), pp. 1197ff (first published 1965); additional references can also be found there.

[35] 'Declaratio' (note 26), No. 1. Of course, it should be noted that the 'traditional Catholic doctrine' was *not* based only on a moral duty, but—by virtue of the equating of the moral and the legal orders—on a simultaneously moral *and* legal obligation of the individual and society towards the true religion, with all the described consequences for the shape of the state legal system that arose from this. The conciliar text is therefore objectively inaccurate insofar as it obscures the reorientation of Church doctrine and the break with the traditional doctrine still advocated by Pope Leo XIII; see also below, section IV.

[36] G. W. F. Hegel, *Enzyklopädie der philosophischen Wissenschaften* (1830), § 552, Pöggeler-Nidelin ed. (Hamburg, 1959), p. 435f. English translation: *Philosophy of Mind*, translated by W. Wallace and A. V. Miller. Revised with introduction and commentary Michael Inwood (Oxford University Press, 2007).

assume that the conciliar Declaration becomes the maxim, the justifying and simultaneously limiting maxim of the Church's demands upon the state, and that the state, in turn, remains faithful to its orientation towards the freedom and security of all its citizens, a mandate inherent in its very origins and by dint of which it has pushed through religious freedom on its own accord. In that case, while differences of opinion about modalities and subsidies may well exist, there could be no principled differences between churches and the state.

This might seem like a bold thesis: however, so as not to avoid immediate relevancy, let us take the statement in the conciliar Declaration on the school problem as a test case. The Declaration states 1) that the state must recognize the right of parents 'to make a genuinely free choice of schools and of other means of education, and the use of this freedom of choice is not to be made a reason for imposing unjust burdens on parents, whether directly or indirectly'; 2) that the rights of parents are violated 'if their children are forced to attend lessons or instructions which are not in agreement with their religious beliefs, or if a single system of education, from which all religious formation is excluded, is imposed upon all'.[37]

The right of parents to a free choice of schools, which the Declaration derives from the connection between religious freedom and parental educational rights, is aimed primarily at the possibility of separate, non-state schools; the rejection of unjust financial burdens as a result of this freedom of choice makes this abundantly clear. What is decisive, however, is the assertion that no child can be compelled to attend instruction that is not in agreement with the religious beliefs of the parents. Because of its natural right character, this assertion holds for all parents, not only Catholic ones. The result is that a public denominational school cannot be demanded nor set up by the state wherever its establishment, given the concrete educational circumstances, would compel attendance not only by children of one's own faith, but also by those of a minority of the other faith. In this case, the natural right of parents of the respective religious minority as recognized by the Declaration would be violated. Consequently, denominational schools can henceforth be demanded only as schools free of minorities.

With this, Church doctrine has recognized the maxim that is also becoming increasingly established in the state's legal system: namely, that for reasons of religious freedom and freedom to profess, denominational schools with denominational minorities can no longer be operated as educationally all-encompassing denominational schools.[38] [IX] But if this is the case, the

[37] 'Declaratio' (note 26), No. 5.

[38] From the more recent judicature see the decision by the Bavarian Constitutional Court of 10 May 1967: bay. VfGH. In the literature, on the one hand, A. von Campenhausen, *Erziehungsauftrag und Staatliche Schulträgerschaft* (Göttingen, 1967), pp. 179ff.; on the other hand, Alexander Hollerbach, 'Die Kirchen unter dem Grundgesetz', *Veröffentlichung der Vereinigung der Deutschen Staatsrechtslehrer* (VVDStRL) 26 (1968), pp. 95ff. In 1975, the Federal Constitutional Court inferred the confessional character of such schools from the fact that the 'principles of the Christian confession' by which the students are taught and educated should be understood in the sense of a shared cultural heritage, see BVerfGE 41,65 (84f.).

[IX] In all-encompassing denominational schools (*materielle Bekenntnisschulen*) all the teaching content and education is infused with the principles of a particular denomination. The alternative

question arises as to how a state with a denominationally mixed population without self-contained confessional areas should guarantee the possibility of all-encompassing denominational schools except by authorizing and financially supporting non-state denominational schools. All the more so since the state, in its own educational system, must offer all children, without regard to their denomination, the same educational opportunities, and therefore cannot combine the children of the denominational minority into small and underperforming schools, or impose on them an especially long commute to school. Within the framework of the state school system, this leaves only the possibility of operating according to a stringent application principle, though it brings numerous difficulties with it, and as we know from experience, it does not open any great chances for denominational schools.

The result is that the free, non-state Catholic school, which is adequately supported by the state (on the ground of the Church's social doctrine), seems not only a desirable goal, but from the perspective of religious freedom also in some sense the only possible solution for denominationally mixed states.

The limits on the freedom of religion can be seen as another touchstone. Every legal freedom is valid and can only be valid within the boundaries that arise from the necessity of an orderly and peaceful coexistence of the citizens within a state community. Otherwise it would abolish itself as a legal freedom. The Declaration did not shut itself off from this problem, but it has raised the question about the boundaries of religious freedom itself, and on the whole it has resolved it in exemplary fashion. Above all, it resisted the temptation, by falling back on an abstract-metaphysical concept of the common good, to indirectly take back the freedom it previously recognized: the common good is defined in greater detail clearly and unambiguously on the basis of the rights and personal self-realization of the individual.[39] Moreover, when it comes to the legal boundaries of religious freedom, it refers not to a philosophical but to a legal concept, that of public order (*ordre public*). To the jurist it is clear that this concept, too, has its problem and requires substantive elaboration, but that cannot take place outside the judicial frame of reference in which the concept itself is embedded.[40] The Declaration seeks to concretize this concept itself and to

type, which gradually replaced the *materielle Bekenntnisschulen* in the first decades of the Federal Republic, is the inter-denominational or mixed-religion school (*Gemeinschaftsschule*) where pupils belonging to different denominations and religions, as well as agnostics, are educated in the spirit of the common ground between different worldviews.

[39] 'Declaratio' (note 26), No. 6. Different still A. Ottaviani, *Institutiones juris publici ecclesiastici*, 4th ed. (Rome, 1960), vol. I, p. 302, vol. II, pp. 46–47. Life in the true religion is part of the (objectively defined) *bonum commune*, and securing the 'true religion' is therefore a task of the state's legal system.

[40] The *ordre public* includes, on the one hand, the traditions and customs of the country; on the other hand, religious freedom—by virtue of its constitutional recognition—is itself a component of the *ordre public* and must therefore be legally protected against encroachments. The balance must be struck in the sense of the conditions for preserving an orderly and peaceful external coexistence, one that makes possible equal freedom for all.

circumscribe it. Subsequently, and this is of special interest, it adds, as a regulatory and interpretational rule, the presumption for freedom in the sense of the distributive principle in a state under the rule of law:[41] 'For the rest, the usages of society are to be the usages of freedom in their full range: that is, the freedom of man is to be respected as far as possible and is not to be curtailed except when and insofar as necessary.'[42]

This section of the Declaration is repeatedly reminiscent of a textbook on the protection of freedom by a state under the rule of law, and one can readily endorse it, also from the perspective of the liberal state.

IV.

To be sure, in conclusion, having spoken so far of the achievements of the Declaration, one must also talk about its problems. Those problems arise both internally, that is, vis-à-vis the Church, and externally, that is, vis-à-vis the state.

1. Internally, the Declaration, by recognizing individual religious freedom and its corollary, public freedom of worship, stands not only in tension but direct contradiction to Pius IX's Syllabus of 1864, his encyclical 'Quanta Cura' of 1864, and to Pope Leo XIII's encyclical 'Libertas' of 1888. Substantively, the Declaration is the polar opposite of these pronouncements of the papal doctrinal office.[43] The common interpretation today, that the Council has merely developed the previous teachings of the Church more fully, bringing the elements inherent in it to completion, therefore does not hold. Church doctrine as set down in the documents mentioned has simply been repealed by the Declaration. And since the declaration of religious freedom is grounded in an inalienable right flowing from the nature of the human person, it has also been declared as incompatible with natural law. These facts must be acknowledged.[44] The Declaration thus manifests by itself the historicity of doctrinal pronouncements, not only as an abstract possibility, but as a concrete reality, namely at the level of authenticity of the papal encyclicals. I do not wish to anticipate further

[41] Carl Schmitt, *Verfassungslehre*, 4th ed. (Berlin, 1965), pp. 125ff. [42] 'Declaratio' (note 26), No. 7.

[43] See Denzinger, *Enchiridion Symbolorum*, 26th ed. (Freiburg, 1947); No. 1690 (Encyclical Quanta Cura), No. 1777/78 (Syllabus, No. 77/78), No. 1874 (Encyclical Immortale Dei) and No. 1932 (Encyclical Libertas). In the Encyclical Libertas of Leo XIII, the relevant passage reads: 'itaque ex dictis consequitur, nequaquam licere petere, defendere, largiri cogitandi, scribendi, docendi, itemque promiscuam *religionum libertatem*, veluti iura totidem, quae homini natura dederit' ('From what has been said it follows that it is quite unlawful to demand, to defend, or to grant unconditional freedom of thought, of speech, of writing, or of worship, as if these were rights given by nature to man'; No. 42: English text: http://www.vatican.va/holy_father/leo_xiii/encyclicals/documents/hf_l-xiii_enc_20061888_libertas_en.html)

[44] This must be emphatically asserted against the harmonizing interpretive efforts of some modern theologians like R. Aubert, Pavan, and J. C. Murray, who, while recognizing sociological and historical contingencies and developments, nevertheless seek to uphold a continuity of Church teachings; see on this the report by Petrus Huizing, 'Über Veröffentlichungen und Themenstellungen zur Frage der Religionsfreiheit', *Concilium*, 2nd vol. (1966), pp. 621ff. (627f.), and especially J. C. Murray in J. Hamer and Y. Congar (eds.), *Die Konzilserklärung über die Religionsfreiheit* (Paderborn, 1967), pp. 125–165, esp. pp. 126f., 132f., 163f.

interpretation. It must clarify whether the Syllabus and the mentioned encyclicals themselves articulated prohibitions contrary to natural law, or whether Christian natural law has such an inherent range of variation that completely contrary and mutually exclusive statements of natural law are possible with respect to the same question within the space of 140 years.

The Declaration further presupposes that the unity of public order and a specific religion can be only an accidental, not a necessary one. It declares the legal protection of such a unity, which invariably would restrict religious freedom if not abolish it entirely, as contrary to natural law. In so doing it presupposes that the substance of the common good of a politically united people can be determined independent of a religion, indeed, of specific religions. To be sure, this accords with the conditions and possibilities within the framework of European culture and civilization at the stage of emancipation, which was first brought about by the historical workings of the Christian faith and rendered effective within world history. If this socio-cultural basis is now granted universal validity ex post, the ordering forms of the polis religions must be invariably stripped of all legitimation, and thus a verdict must also be pronounced on centuries of Christian-occidental development. One could then speak only of the tragedy of those stages in the historical development of humanity,[45] a response whose limited persuasive power makes the real problem abundantly clear.

2. Externally, vis-à-vis the state, the Declaration raises the problem of the social compatibility of all religions. The Declaration itself presupposes the social compatibility of all religions. It is only under these conditions that one can posit—as the Declaration does—that the freedom of a private and public exercise of religion in accordance with the demands of one's own conscience cannot conflict with the correctly understood public order. This prerequisite likely applies to Christian revelation as it presents itself *today* in the Christian churches, and the Declaration surely had primarily the Christian religion in mind. The faith content and the impulses for action that emanate today from the Christian faith encompass social compatibility, indeed, they virtually demand it and are able to convey themselves to the way the modern world is lived and organized. But does this hold for every religion across the board? The Declaration refrains from defining the concept of religion, which it uses as a fundamental concept.[46] The reasons why it did this remain open. The assumption, in any case, that every serious subjective conviction of conscience about the final questions of human existence and the behaviour norms derived from it is inherently socially compatible, that is to say, that the public order can be

[45] On this see the noteworthy discussion by Johannes Messner, 'Judenschema und Religionsfreiheit', *Die Furche* No. 49 (1965), p. 9.

[46] The problem becomes topical not least with a view towards the so-called Youth Religions [the German government has classified as such the Hare Krishnas and Transcendental Meditation, for example, but also more sinister groups such as Scientology]; on this see now also E.-W. Böckenförde, in *Essener Gespräche zum Thema Staat und Kirche* 19 (1985), pp. 156ff.

constructed smoothly out of subjective convictions of conscience, would be an error that would proceed from demonstrably incorrect hypotheses.

With this, the conciliar Declaration hands this difficult problem unresolved back to the state's legal order. It leads to the question of whether, religious freedom being recognized, one can do without civil tolerance in its true meaning—i.e., as the toleration of something that cannot be legally acknowledged.[47] Formulated in legal terms it means: what are the limits to which Article 4 of the Basic Law is subject? The solution envisaged by the Weimar Constitution, and later adopted also into the Basic Law, namely, that the civil and citizen rights and obligations are neither conditioned nor constrained by the exercise of religious freedom, already presupposes the resolution of the conflict more so than achieving it.[48] The statutory legal order itself must then have absorbed the principle of religious freedom into its substance. The conscientious rejection not only of military service, but also of alternative civilian service,[X] by members of Jehovah's Witnesses, offers a vivid example of this problem.[49] Here the state's legal system is thrown back upon the question about its foundation and the legitimatory ground of its universality and universal applicability. Ever since a theory of modern state law has existed, the legal system has always derived these things from its reasonableness, reasonableness with respect to making possible peace, a secure life, equal freedom, and appropriate prosperity for all. It is on this basis that it has erected its absolute provisions. A state order that—in this sense—satisfies the demand to be an *imperium rationis*, which should not be confused with a realm of realized values, will also have the strength to grant tolerance where it is unable to recognize a right.

For the sake of fairness, however, one must not take lightly the objection of the old theory of tolerance that makes itself heard here: the objection, namely, that this merely displaces the tolerance problem, but in no way resolves it. To be sure, the argument goes, the state has neutralized itself vis-à-vis religion;

[47] Therein lies the real concept of tolerance, which is today often confused with the recognition or guarantee of legal freedom. Tolerance has to do with the acceptance of an evil, is also a question about the weighing between colliding goods; by contrast, legal freedom is an actionable claim, independent of weighing and balancing.

[48] The problem was already correctly seen at the time of the Weimar Constitution by H. Mirbt, 'Glaubens- und Gewissensfreiheit', in Nipperdey, ed., *Grundrechte und Grundpflichten der Reichsverfassung*, vol. II, 1930, p. 350f.

[X] From 1961 onward, West Germany allowed men to sign up to alternative civilian service in lieu of military service, on the basis of conscientious objection. Service would last between six and twenty months. The Jehovah's Witnesses were total objectors, rejecting both military as well as alternative civilian service, which meant they would face criminal proceedings, resulting very often in prison sentences. This only changed in 1996, when Jehovah's Witnesses doctrinally accepted the possibility of alternative civilian service.

[49] On this see E.-W. Böckenförde, 'Das Grundrecht der Gewissensfreiheit', *Veröffentlichung der Vereinigung der Deutschen Staatsrechtslehrer* (VVDStRL), No. 28 (1970), pp. 33ff.; esp. pp. 57–63 [included in this volume as Chapter VI], and the decisions by the Federal Constitutional Court, BVerfGE 23,127 (134); 23,192 (204f.).

it applies intolerance now on a different level, namely the secular level of its world-immanent goals, but here it espouses it with the same severity for which religion was criticized. This objection deserves closer consideration. The response to it presupposes an answer to the question about the bedrock and foundation of the law.

PART II

STATE AND SECULARITY

Böckenförde on the Secular State and Secular Law

Mirjam Künkler and Tine Stein

Part II brings together four articles dealing with aspects of the secularity of the modern state. It opens with one of Böckenförde's most widely cited articles—translated into seven languages—'The Rise of the State as a Process of Secularization' published in 1967, in which he lays out the emergence of the modern state as a process of emancipation from the influence of religious authority that occurred in three distinct stages. Although less well-known internationally, the second article included here is no less important in Böckenförde's intellectual development. It deals with 'The Fundamental Right of Freedom of Conscience' (1970), which Böckenförde regards as the cornerstone of the religiously neutral modern state and as the cardinal individual liberty, from which all others spring. In the third article, 'Remarks on the Relationship between State and Religion in Hegel', written in 1982, Böckenförde reviews Hegel's major writings on questions of religion and the state to guide him in his own quest for the 'inner regulatory forces' and the binding ethos that keep democratic societies together. The interest in this binding ethos and the Hegelian notion of freedom places the article in a direct line with Böckenförde's 1967 secularization essay as well as his 1978 article on 'The State as an Ethical State' (included in volume I). In the fourth article in this part, 'The Secularized State: Its Character, Justification, and Problems in the Twenty-first Century' of 2007, Böckenförde returns to the core ideas of the 1967 secularization essay fifty years later, asking what is the secular state, and how can it deal with a plurality of worldviews? Böckenförde lays out the cornerstones of his views on the desirable relationship between religion and state in contemporary democracy by juxtaposing his concept of 'open encompassing neutrality' vis-à-vis that of 'distancing neutrality', of which he regards the French laïcist model as paradigmatic. The latter 'tends towards consigning and confining religion to the private and private-social sphere' and prioritizes the freedom *from* religion. By contrast, the model of 'open encompassing neutrality' places the freedom *to* (exercise) religion on an equal footing with the freedom from religion and permits the presence of religion in the public sphere (such as the wearing of religious symbols by public school teachers).

Religion, Law, and Democracy. Ernst-Wolfgang Böckenförde, Oxford University Press (2020). DOI: 10.1093/oso/9780198818632.003.0007.

His seminal article on 'The Rise of the State as a Process of Secularization' is based on a talk Böckenförde gave at the 1964 Ebrach Summer School that legal scholar Ernst Forsthoff convened.[1] Böckenförde had just completed his habilitation in law and was about to be appointed professor in Heidelberg, where he stayed (and became dean of the law faculty) until moving on to Bielefeld in 1969. In the article, he distinguishes three relevant stages in the process of secularization by which he understands the gradual release of the political system and its institutions from the oversight and domination of the Church. The eleventh-century Investiture Controversy forms the first stage, during which the analytical differentiation between religion and politics was institutionalized in the competition between throne and altar over the appointment of bishops. The second stage is defined by the Protestant Reformation and the Confessional Wars, during which secular state law wins precedence over religious law. Böckenförde explains how Thomas Hobbes' work is paradigmatic for this breakthrough, in which he made the case that the political order's main concern should be the secular purpose of peace and security rather than ensuring ways of life that might secure subjects' spiritual salvation.[2] Hobbes' argument that the attempt to derive positive law from religious truth should be abandoned paved the way for the interconfessional peace agreements that first enshrined rights of religious toleration. As the third stage, Böckenförde singles out the state's normative commitments to human rights and citizen's rights, which were constitutionalized in the aftermath of the American and French Revolutions.

With the third post-revolutionary stage, which amounts to an enthronement of the autonomous and free individual, new questions arise. Böckenförde asks where the state finds the strength to sustain itself and guarantee 'the inner regulatory forces of liberty that it needs, once the binding power of religion is no longer'?[3] It is this line of thought that leads him to formulate his famous dictum, which has become the most frequently quoted sentence from a scholarly article in German ever since: 'The liberal, secularized state is sustained by conditions it cannot itself guarantee.'[4] How is this formula to be understood? The state cannot guarantee conditions securing its survival because were it to use its instruments of legal coercion and authoritative command to impose democratic norms and worldviews on its citizens, it would violate the very liberalism on which it was founded. Böckenförde's liberalism is grounded in the

[1] It was first published in a 1967 Festschrift for Forsthoff, titled *Säkularisation und Utopie. Ebracher Studien. Ernst Forsthoff zum 65. Geburtstag*. Stuttgart: Kohlhammer, 1967; a collection in which Carl Schmitt's widely cited essay 'The Tyranny of Values' was also published. Since then, Böckenförde's article has been translated into Italian (1985 and 2007), English (1991), Polish (1994), French (2000), Japanese (2003), Korean (2004), and Czech (2006).

[2] On this, see also his 2004 essay, 'Security and Self-Preservation before Justice. The Paradigm Shift from a Natural-Law to a Positive-Law Basis in Thomas Hobbes' System of Law', Chapter I in volume I of this edition, pp. 56–68.

[3] Chapter V, this volume, p. 166.

[4] Ibid., p. 167.

freedom of the individual and the separation of the sphere of the state and the sphere of society.[5] Böckenförde argues that democratically ruled societies are in need of a shared sense of belonging that binds them together so that democratic citizens do not only enjoy their democratic rights but also perform their democratic duties (such as working towards a common good, pay taxes, and if necessary be prepared to die for one another). In a liberal democratic system, this sense of belonging cannot be imposed by the state—it has to emerge from within civil society and from the ethos of individuals-as-citizens that is directed towards the common good. Böckenförde sees no way of winding back the clock to before 1789: the secular state and human rights are an enduring achievement, and this is for the better, including for those Christians who mourn the loss of the Christian state. Christians, in particular Catholics, should 'no longer see this state, in its secularity, as something alien, hostile to their faith, but as a chance for liberty, the preservation and realization of which is also their task'.[6] The historical context of the article, written and revised during the Second Vatican Council 1963–1965, points to Böckenförde's implied addressees. The article was not written to articulate a scepticism toward agnostics, atheists, or believers of other faiths, as a way of praising Christians who truly sustain the state by contrast to other citizens. Rather, his argument was directed precisely in the opposite sense, as a plea to Catholics to accept the legitimacy of the secular state.[7] As such, the article is best understood when read in conjunction with his 1957 article 'The Ethos of Modern Democracy and the Church' (Chapter I in this volume).

The next article, 'The Fundamental Right of Freedom of Conscience', has been described as constituting the liberal core of Böckenförde's constitutional thought.[8] It is based on a lecture he delivered at the most important meeting of German-speaking public law scholars, the *Tagung der Staatsrechtslehrervereinigung,* held in Bern in October 1969.[9] In the article, Böckenförde lays out why he regards freedom of conscience to be the basis of all modern individual liberties, and indeed, as the basis of the modern concept of freedom itself. When read in conjunction with Böckenförde's other

[5] Ernst-Wolfgang Böckenförde, *Die verfassungstheoretische Unterscheidung von Staat und Gesellschaft als Bedingung der individuellen Freiheit* [The differentiation in constitutional theory between state and society as a requirement for individual freedom] (Opladen: Westdeutscher Verlag, 1973).

[6] Chapter V, this volume, p. 167.

[7] Böckenförde highlighted this intention in an interview with Dieter Gosewinkel that illuminated his scholarly and political biography: 'The last section [of the article] should be read as an appeal chiefly to Catholics to see the secularized state no longer as a potential enemy and at a great remove. Rather, they should accept it and become part of it, as an opportunity for them as well, and because it depends also on the powers they can contribute to it. . . The thrust of the essay was that one should no longer entertain reservations and mourn the Christian state, which will not exist again.' See 'Biographical Interview with Ernst-Wolfgang Böckenförde', Chapter XVI of this volume, p. 378.

[8] Reinhard Mehring, 'Von der diktatorischen 'Maßnahme' zur liberalen Freiheit. Ernst- Wolfgang Böckenfördes dogmatischer Durchbruch in Heidelberg', *Juristen Zeitung* 60 (2015), pp. 860–865, here p. 863.

[9] The article was translated in 1991 into English and in 2006 into Italian.

key writings on democratic and legal theory, it becomes apparent that the article contains the kernel for three other core contributions developed later: his insistence on the distinction between state and society directed against the Smend school,[10] his critique of the value-based grounding of law directed against Federal Constitutional Court jurisprudence following the (in)famous *Lüth Decision* of 1958,[11] and his notion of secularity as requiring 'open encompassing neutrality', which he then developed fully in 2007.[12]

The article builds on his work on religious freedom (see Chapter IV in this volume) to argue that only in modernity can religion be chosen freely and the believer be free in her or his belief. The modern state draws its justification from the non-identification with the moral convictions of its citizens and therefore from the distinction between legality and morality. In other words, the state prescribes what is legal (or not), but leaves questions of morality to individual citizens and to society.

Proceeding from Article 4 of the Basic Law, which guarantees freedom of belief and conscience (Article 4 Section 1), freedom to exercise one's religion (Article 4 Section 2), and freedom to conscientiously object to military service (Article 4 Section 3), Böckenförde looks back at the constitutional history of this particular freedom and the different connotations attached to it in West European and German legal documents from the 1500s until 1970.

Freedom of conscience was slowly and progressively carved out as a right emanating from deepening notions of religious freedom gained successively in peace agreements ending the confessional wars in Europe. In the Peace of Augsburg (1555), the formula *cuius regio, eius religio* (whose realm, his religion) gave the ruler the power to determine one denomination for all inhabitants in his territory (Catholic, Lutheran, later also Calvinist). Subjects not willing to convert to the prince's religion could migrate to another territory (*ius emigrandi*), while offenders (those refusing to embrace the prince's religion and staying in the realm) could be deported. In the Union of Utrecht (1579) and in the Treaty of Westphalia (1648), this principle was replaced by a right to religious freedom that for the first time recognized the individual subject as the bearer of this freedom. An individual had the right to choose his religion independent from the ruler, opening the door also to the recognition of rights of religious minorities and religious dissenters.

[10] 'Die Bedeutung der Unterscheidung von Staat und Gesellschaft im demokratischen Sozialstaat der Gegenwart', in *Rechtsfragen der Gegenwart. Festgabe für Wolfgang Hefermehl zum 65. Geburtstag* (Stuttgart: Kohlhammer, 1972), pp. 11–36. Translated into Korean in 1987 and 1992, English in 1991, Japanese in 1999, French in 2000, and Italian in 2007.

[11] 'Zur Kritik der Wertbegründung des Rechts. Überlegungen zu einem Kapitel "Rechtsphilosophie"', in: Reinhard Löw (ed.), *OIKEIOSIS. Festschrift für Robert Spaemann* (Weinheim: VCH Verlagsgemeinschaft, 1987), pp. 1–21. Revised and expanded version published in: Ernst- Wolfgang Böckenförde, *Recht, Staat, Freiheit: Studien zur Rechtsphilosophie, Staatstheorie und Verfassungsgeschichte* (Frankfurt am Main: Suhrkamp, 1991), pp. 67–91. The article was translated into Polish in 1995, French in 1997, and English in 2017.

[12] *Der säkularisierte Staat. Sein Charakter, seine Rechtfertigung und seine Probleme im 21. Jahrhundert* (Munich: Carl Friedrich von Siemens Stiftung, 2007). Translated into Italian in 2007 and into English in this volume.

Yet this still guaranteed the right of an individual to choose between recognized religions only. Freedom of belief and conscience irrespective of the question which religions were recognized by the state was for the first time guaranteed in the Civil Law of Prussia of 1794 (*Allgemeines Landrecht für die preußischen Staaten*), which prohibited harassment or persecution on the grounds of religious opinion. Prussian law in and after 1794 also went far beyond the Treaty of Westphalia in extending rights and exemptions to a multitude of religious groups, including the expressed right to worship in private. It exempted Mennonites and Quakers from military service, exempted sectarians and Jews from the prescribed form of the oath, respected Sabbath observance and marriage according to Rabbinical law, and forbade any direct coercion of an action contrary to a person's notions of religion. Böckenförde notes, 'the basis of this far-reaching tolerance was, on the one hand, a reason-based theory of the state which limited the state to worldly purposes and in so doing accorded a special rank to individual freedom and security, and, on the other hand, the notion and confidence that *all religions were in essential agreement in their teachings about the [public] obligations of the individual*'.[13]

The full freedom of worship (i.e. in private *and* public) for all religious denominations *(Kultusfreiheit)* and freedom of assembly for religious societies *(religiöse Assoziationsfreiheit)* were then first enshrined in German lands in the constitutions of several German Länder during the *Vormärz* era (around 1830–1848) and in the Paulskirche constitution of 1848.[14]

Yet the first constitution in German lands to explicitly render the state neutral in religious matters was the Weimar constitution of 1919. It did not recognize an established church and it no longer endowed the state with the *ius reformandi*, the right to interfere in questions of religious truth or theology. The Basic Law of 1949 included these provisions of the Weimar constitution and furthermore recognized freedom of conscience as a *separate* fundamental right, in addition to freedom of religion and freedom to profess, on the basis of a universal concept of conscience that is neutral with regard to questions of religion or other worldviews.

A major point of Böckenförde's genealogical approach to the freedom of conscience is to demonstrate that in Germanic constitutional history it was the first right enjoyed by the individual against direct coercion of the state in matters of religion, and as such it was enshrined as a defensive right. But it took a long time for it to be disconnected from the right to religious freedom. While the two were coupled in the 1794 Civil Law of Prussia and in most subsequent constitutions, it was only in the Basic Law of 1949 that the freedom of conscience was separated from religion, that is, it was no longer assumed that having a conscience was dependent on being a religious believer. Reviewing the debates of the constituent assembly in 1948–1949, Böckenförde outlines why this

[13] Chapter VI, this volume, p. 182, note 55. Emphasis added.

[14] See Articles 144 (full freedom of faith and conscience), 145 (communal domestic and public exercise of religion), and 147 (free formation of religious societies).

was a significant, but also necessary departure in light of the state's neutrality. 'This universal concept of conscience cannot be defined with recourse to theological or philosophical notions or interpretations of conscience. . . The jurist who took this line would simply become a party to the intellectual debate about conscience, falling short of the duty of neutrality towards religion and other worldviews laid upon him by the constitution.'[15]

Böckenförde takes the opportunity to comment on the Federal Constitutional Court's interpretation according to which the constitution presented an objective order of values, following the 1958 *Lüth Decision*. Böckenförde is strictly opposed to such a view and instead pleads in favour of an understanding of the constitution as providing an ordering frame (*Rahmenordnung*), nothing more and nothing less. The first draft of the Basic Law, written during the Herrenchiemsee convention in 1948, recognized a statutory encroachment by the state in favour of public security, morality [*Sittlichkeit*], and health. This was dismissed by the Parlamentarischer Rat that finalized the constitution in 1949. 'Individual rights to liberty were emphatically understood as *leges speciales* to the universal right to liberty enshrined in Article 2. In line with this basic intention, those spheres of liberty that had been particularly abused and jeopardized by the state during the National Socialist years were granted [by the Parlamentarischer Rat] special protection against possibilities of encroachment; they were to be "inviolable" and "indefeasible".'[16]

The major reference point for the Parlamentarischer Rat was the question of encroachments and limitations, not of values and an order of values.[17] According to Böckenförde, with its interpretation of the constitution as presenting an objective order of values, the Federal Constitutional Court had 'elevated disregard for considerations of historical origin to the status of a tenet'. What is more, it had *reversed* the achievement of enshrining the freedom of conscience in the Basic Law independent of any considerations as to religious or philosophical questions. 'Guaranteed in the context of the *order of values* of the Basic Law, freedom of conscience would protect the very person who, because he conforms to prevailing opinions, has no need of such protection; it would not protect the outsider, the dissident, for whom it has the greatest relevance.'[18]

It is also in this article that Böckenförde first outlines his understanding of the open encompassing neutrality of the state with regard to religion and other worldviews, which presents the cornerstone of his thinking on democratic religion–state relations.[19] He had first outlined this concept in a legal opinion written a year earlier (but published only in 1975).[20] Böckenförde suggests that

[15] Chapter VI of this volume, pp. 193–194.

[16] Chapter VI of this volume, p. 179.

[17] 'The sphere of individual liberty was defined as being in principle unlimited, while the possibility of statutory encroachment was held to be in principle limited, measurable, and controllable.' Ibid., p. 179.

[18] Ibid., pp. 187–188. Emphasis added.

[19] Ibid., p. 185, note 62.

[20] Ernst-Wolfgang Böckenförde, 'Kreuze (Kruzifixe) in Gerichtssälen? Zum Verhältnis von staatlicher Selbstdarstellung und religiös weltanschaulicher Neutralität des Staates', *Zeitschrift für evangelisches Kirchenrecht* (1975), 119–147, at 130–132.

it is to a large extent from nonidentification (with a particular religion) that the modern state draws its legitimacy towards all of its citizens in their plurality of worldviews. This means that individuals are protected by the constitution in their peculiarity and uniqueness, and that for this protection to be truly meaningful it needs to extend into the public sphere. Citizens must have confidence 'in the untouchability of their peculiarity'. Böckenförde writes, 'individual specialness, in order to be able to unfold as specialness, is dependent on entering into institutions that are sustained and guided by the state, which is the case above all in the areas of upbringing and schooling'.[21] Drawing on Adalbert Podlech (who wrote his habilitation with Böckenförde), he distinguishes between the 'polity [*Gemeinwesen*]' as the totality of the citizens on the one hand, and the *Hoheitsgewalt* (sovereign activity) of the state on the other, in order to suggest that where the state exercised its *Hoheitsgewalt* it needs to be neutral with regard to religion and other worldviews, whereas in the *Gemeinwesen* the individual citizen needs to be able to express his or her peculiarity and specialness. It is this distinction that enables Böckenförde to argue later in favour of permitting individual officials to wear religious garb in the *Gemeinwesen*, such as schools, but not in courthouses, which is where the state exercises its *Hoheitsgewalt*.

Böckenförde closes the article by exploring how conscience, once separated from the question of religion, can be understood for judicial purposes in the practical administration of freedom of conscience. Since conscience is internal, it is impossible to probe a stated position of conscience as to its sincerity. This is relevant of course beyond conscientious objection to military service, and extends, for example, also to asylum decisions. It is here that Böckenförde makes extensive reference to the sociologist Niklas Luhmann.[22] Luhmann argued that there is one way for conscience to be accessible from the outside, namely its readiness to persist. This readiness to persist, Böckenförde agrees with Luhmann, brings up the possibility of 'burdensome alternatives' that may be imposed as a reasonable sacrifice on the appellant to conscience. The civilian alternative to mandatory military service (introduced in West Germany in 1961) presented one example of such a 'burdensome alternative'.[23] Böckenförde was one of the first legal scholars to introduce the element of the social effect of the individual's conscience into the normative discourse about fundamental

[21] Chapter VI of this volume, p. 185, note 62.

[22] Incidentally, this is the only article in which he cites Luhmann extensively, possibly because in 1970 when this article is published, Böckenförde is about to join the University of Bielefeld, where Luhmann was appointed in 1968. Böckenförde later sponsored Luhmann's admission to the North Rhine-Westphalian Academy of Sciences, Humanities and the Arts. See Ernst-Wolfgang Böckenförde: 'Laudatio auf Prof. Dr. Niklas Luhmann (217. Sitzung der Rheinisch-Westfälischen Akademie der Wissenschaften am 15.12.1976)', in s.ed., *Jahrbuch 1976 der Rheinisch-Westfälischen Akademie der Wissenschaften* (Opladen: Westdeutscher Verlag, 1977), pp. 70–73. See also 'Biographisches Interview', in Ernst-Wolfgang Böckenförde, *Wissenschaft, Politik, Verfassungsgericht. Aufsätze von Ernst- Wolfgang Böckenförde* (Berlin: Suhrkamp, 2011), p. 355f.

[23] See annotations VI and X in Chapter VI for background information on the further development of the military service and its civil service alternative in the Federal Republic.

rights. His interpretation of the freedom of conscience offered a bridge connecting the normativity of the Basic Law with the sociological fact that there are citizens who have legitimate reasons to reject certain norms of the constitutional polity.[24]

It is the quest for the 'inner impulses and binding forces' on which democracy relies that brings Böckenförde to Hegel, a topic explored in depth in the next article included here, 'Remarks on the Relationship between State and Religion in Hegel'. Individual ethos is a cornerstone of Böckenförde's democratic theory, and the relationship between ethos and freedom a key intellectual concern of his. Individual freedom is not possible unless secured by a constitutional democracy whose endurance in the final analysis depends on the ethos of individual citizens to work towards the common good. Unlike Jürgen Habermas, Böckenförde does not have confidence that rule of law and democratic procedures are sufficient for democracy to survive in the long term. Rather, it requires the continual renewal of citizens to agree on the things that lie beyond the ballot box—agreement on the kind of society they wish to live in and contribute to. Without this agreement, the willingness of citizens to work towards the common good, pay their taxes, serve in public roles, work against corruption, die in defence of their fellow citizens if necessary, will suffer, risking, in turn, the erosion of public institutions. The agreement on the things that cannot be voted upon is beyond state access—the state cannot impose it, nor can it force citizens to engage in the kind of societal exercise that might create this agreement. This, in essence, is the so-called Böckenförde paradox (or dictum): democratic procedures cannot survive without citizen participation, but democracy cannot force citizens to participate in these procedures. Institutions and procedures always only function as well as the individuals who fill these institutions and procedures with meaning. The exercise of citizenship, that is, participation, public service, working for the common good, relies on the inner motivations of people, their inner ethos.

Böckenförde first read Hegel intensively in the Collegium Philosophicum of Joachim Ritter, of which he was a member in his student days in Münster, and Böckenförde indeed can be described as a Hegelian. In 1978, he had penned the article 'The State as an Ethical State' (Chapter IV in volume I of this edition) in which he rejected the idea that the state ought to show ethical leadership (as Catholic bishops demanded at the time in the face of an alleged erosion of values in society), but at the same time affirmed that the state must create the conditions in which the individual is not only free from external threat but also

[24] To quote the quintessential innovation of Böckenförde's concept of the freedom of conscience as summarized by his colleague Adalbert Podlech in the discussion of the Vereinigung der deutschen Staatsrechtslehrer in 1969: 'It is the function of the freedom of conscience to permit the individual to be loyal to the polity in cases in which he/she feels driven to reject a particular norm of this very polity.' See *Veröffentlichungen der Vereinigung der Deutschen Staatsrechtslehrer*, 28 (1970), p. 133. We thank Ulrich K. Preuss for providing us with this quote.

has the possibility for self-realization.[25] In 1982 he then dedicated a separate article to Hegel, included here as Chapter VII, by analysing the relation between religion and state in Hegel's work.

While reviewing Hegel's main writings on religion and state (chiefly, the *Philosophy of Right*, the *Philosophy of Mind*, and the *Philosophy of World History*), Böckenförde asks whether religion should be seen as a foundation of the modern state. The article is divided in four sections. First, Böckenförde reconstructs Hegel's concept of the state. For Hegel, the state is simultaneously universal and historical. It is more than the political system or government—it is the polity in general and the structured form in which the people exist. Moreover, the state is the materialization of the ethical idea as such and the manifestation of how 'truth' in history became reality. In Hegel's view, 'truth' is ultimately God's will in the world. Like many others since, Hegel regarded secularization as a unique long-term effect of the story of Christ—the entering of God into the world and the unprecedented elevation of the individual as the receptacle of God's unconditional love. Different from the philosophy of the ancients, according to Hegel, Christianity holds within it the right of the uniqueness of the subject which in the final analysis can lead, and has led, to the recognition of the right of subjective freedom.[26]

Second, Böckenförde examines how Hegel sees the relationship between state and religion. For Hegel, state and religion are two forms of the same substance: reason. Morality and reason are closely intertwined. Religion is a source of morality for the people, and the state and church are the institutional manifestations of reason. As a consequence, according to Hegel, Christian churches should be protected by the state as the Christian religion is the state's foundation; other religions should be tolerated.

Third, Böckenförde shows that Hegel identifies individual conscience as the core of each person's freedom; however, Hegel denies a right to an aberrant conscience, indicating, in Böckenförde's view, a very limited notion of freedom.

Fourth, Böckenförde discusses Hegel's philosophy in light of the state today with its separation of state and religion. In the secular democratic state, religion is set free. (Conversely by accepting the secular state, Christianity can be a religion of freedom, Böckenförde writes elsewhere.[27]) But since today's state does

[25] The 1978 article is Böckenförde's key work on the state and has been translated into Italian, Polish, English, and Slovenian. Incidentally, in the biographical interview, Böckenförde characterizes the Collegium Philosophicum as an attempt on the part of Ritter to enact a dimension of Hegel's 'State as an Ethical State' in the sense of creating conditions in which all voices will be heard and where these in their plurality are understood to convey a glimpse of reality. See 'Biographisches Interview' (note 3), p. 352.

[26] As Böckenförde reminds his readers, 'No less a thinker than Hegel gave a positive interpretation, from a Christian perspective, of the trend towards secularization in modern European history: it was not the negation but the realization of the essence of the revelation that came into the world with Jesus Christ. And Karl Marx pointed out—critically, given his standpoint—that the emancipation of the state from religion does not do away with or seek to do away with man's true religiousness.' See Chapter V in this volume, p. 165.

[27] Ernst-Wolfgang Böckenförde, 'Vorbemerkung', in Ernst-Wolfgang Böckenförde, *Kirche und christlicher Glaube in den Herausforderungen der Zeit: Beiträge zur politisch-theologischen Verfassungsgeschichte 1957–2002*, 2nd ed. (Münster: LIT Publishing House, 2007), pp. 193–195, here p. 194.

not consider religion as part of its foundation, in Hegel's view it would 'stand freely in the air'. Böckenförde concludes, contrary to Hegel, that only 'agreement on the things that cannot be voted upon' can form the basis to the state, and this brings him back to the importance of citizen engagement in societal activities where this implicit agreement is continuously being (re)created.

In 'The Secularized State: Its Character, Justification, and Problems in the Twenty-first Century' (2007), Böckenförde summarizes his thinking on what constitutes democratic religion–state relations fifty years after he published his 1967 secularization essay. Religious freedom must encompass several dimensions and it must be both an individual and a corporate right. It includes the freedom to have a religion (freedom of belief) as well as not, the freedom to profess a religion as well as not, freedom to exercise one's religion in public (freedom to exercise) as well as not, and the freedom to join religious associations (freedom of religious association) as well as not.[28]

The article is divided into three sections, discussing the character, the justification, and the problems of the secular state respectively, elaborating in particular on the meaning of open encompassing neutrality in the face of growing pluralism with regard to religions and other worldviews.

Böckenförde's term 'open encompassing neutrality' has reached the status of a doctrinal term in discussions about religion and the state in Germany and Europe.[29] It aims to convey a notion of a secular state that is neutral with regard to religion in that it does not identify with any religion, but that is open to religion rather than hostile to it, encouraging religious expression in public life, not banishing it to the private sphere. As mentioned above in the context of Böckenförde's article on the freedom of conscience, Böckenförde believes that the modern state draws its legitimacy towards all of its citizens in their plurality of worldviews from its nonidentification with any particular religion. The nonidentification allows the citizen to feel protected in her or his specialness and pecularity. Citizens must have confidence 'in the untouchability of their peculiarity', and for this untouchability to be meaningful, it must be able to extend into the public sphere as well.

[28] Ernst-Wolfgang Böckenförde, 'Religion im säkularen Staat', in Rainer Isak and Hansjörg Schmid (eds.), *Christen und Muslime in Deutschland. Religion—Gesellschaft—säkularer Staat* (Freiburg: Verlag der Katholischen Akademie, 2003), pp. 11–25, here p. 12, based on G. Anschütz, 'Religionsfreiheit', in G. Anschütz and R. Thoma (eds.), *Handbuch des deutschen Staatsrechts*, vol. II (Tübingen: Mohr, 1932), 675–689.

[29] In the Federal Constitutional Court's jurisprudence on religion the principle of neutrality is explicitly described as 'offen und übergreifend' (Böckenförde's terms, whereby 'übergreifend' is sometimes translated as 'encompassing', sometimes as 'comprehensive'). See, for example, the widely cited headscarf decision of 2003: 'However, the religious and ideological neutrality required of the state is not to be understood as a distancing attitude in the sense of a strict separation of state and church, but as an open and comprehensive one, encouraging freedom of faith equally for all beliefs. Article 4.1 and 4.2 of the Basic Law also contain a positive requirement to safeguard the space for the active exercise of religious conviction and the realization of autonomous personality in the area of ideology and religion (cf. BVerfGE 41, 29(49); 93, 1(16)).' (BVerfG, Judgment of the Second Senate of 24 September 2003, 2 BvR 1436/02, paras. 1–138, here para 43 http://www.bverfg.de/e/rs20030924_2bvr143602en.html). In political theory 'übergreifend' in this context tends to be translated as 'encompassing' rather than 'comprehensive', partly because of the association of the latter term with John Rawls' political theory.

Distancing neutrality 'tends towards consigning and confining religion to the private and private-social sphere. . . [It] shapes the legal system in a purely secular way and turns away religious aspects as irrelevant and private.' Open encompassing neutrality, by contrast, 'additionally accords it room to develop in the public sphere, for example in the school, educational institutions, and in what is summarily referred to as the public order—though, of course, it does so without any form of identification. . . [It] seeks to create a balance, in that affirming and leading a life in accordance with religion, to the extent that it is compatible with the secular goals of the state, is permitted also within the public sphere by the legal system and is incorporated into the latter.'[30] While distancing neutrality champions negative religious freedom (the freedom not to be religious), open neutrality, he argues, aims for a balancing of negative and positive religious freedom (the right to live one's life in accordance with one's religion's tenets).

So what does open encompassing neutrality entail? In practice, the rights and interests of the religious and non-religious need to be weighed on a contextual basis. Building on the mentioned distinction between spaces that are part of the *Gemeinwesen* (the polity at large) and areas where the state exercises its *Hoheitsgewalt* (sovereign activity), Böckenförde outlined different scenarios for the permitted presence of religious symbols in public spaces. Regarding the display of crucifixes in courtrooms, he argued that they could be perceived as an infringement on the individual's right to a religiously neutral state and should therefore be removed.[31] In courtrooms, where the state engages in a sovereign activity (*Hoheitsfunktion*), distancing neutrality towards religion ought to be applied.

Schools, unlike courtrooms, however, are not institutions of the state as an entity of power, but intermediary institutions that connect state and society. Public schools are a 'means through which the state fulfils its duty of civic education, not indoctrination'. The regulation of the presence of religious symbols therefore allowed for a different solution, he suggested: one of open encompassing neutrality that allowed citizens to show themselves as religious or non-religious beings at their own pleasing, including in wearing religious garb.[32]

Böckenförde asks further how the secular state can be justified today. While it emanated historically from the struggle against ecclesiastico-religious claims to supremacy, as he showed in his 1967 secularization article, today the normative justification of the secular state has moved into the foreground as the order

[30] Chapter VIII of this volume, p. 223.

[31] As Manent explains, as courtrooms are places 'where the authority of the state is wielded, the state's symbolic endorsement of a specific religion over others could be perceived as intimidating and potentially coercive by religious (or atheist) minorities'. Aline-Florence Manent, 'Democracy and Religion in the Legal and Political Thought of Ernst-Wolfgang Böckenförde', *Oxford Journal on Law and Religion* 7(1) (2018), pp. 74–96.

[32] Ute Sacksofsky, 'Ernst-Wolfgang Böckenförde's Oeuvre on Religious Freedom applied to recent Decisions of the European Court of Human Rights', *German Law Journal* 19(2) (2018) (special issue—Statism, Secularism, Liberalism Ernst-Wolfgang Böckenförde Beyond Germany), pp. 301–320. Drawing on his argument that individuals are protected by the constitution in their uniqueness, and that for this protection to be truly meaningful it needs to extend into the public sphere, he also argued in favour of instituting a public Muslim holiday in Germany. Ernst-Wolfgang Böckenförde, 'Freiheit ist ansteckend', *die tageszeitung*, p. 4, 23 September 2009.

of human rights. 'Guaranteeing and securing [human rights is] the central task of all state power, its proper and new very purpose.' What was hard won in the eighteenth and nineteenth centuries appears to be self-evident today: that 'the state exists for the sake of the individual, not the individual for the sake of the state'.[33] But also from within religion, a justification of the secular state has emerged, as the only public order where religion can be chosen freely. To illustrate the extraordinary turnabout the Catholic Church undertook in the course of only forty years, from the rejection of the secular state as late as 1953 by Pope Pius XII to Pope John Paul II's explicit call for the secular state in 1998, Böckenförde cites the latter's remarkable statement: 'A modern state cannot make atheism or religion one of its political ordinances. The state, while distancing itself from all extremes of fanaticism or secularism, should encourage a harmonious social climate and a suitable legislation that enables every person and every religious denomination to live their faith freely, [and] to express that faith in the context of public life.'[34]

In the third part of the article, Böckenförde asks what the unifying bond among democratic citizens may be in the face of growing worldview plurality, responding implicitly also to calls that newly arriving immigrants in Germany commit themselves to a Christian *Leitkultur*.[35] Against Cardinal Ratzinger's writings to this effect, Böckenförde responds that a society that understands itself as liberal and democratic must necessarily impart the same rights to all newly naturalized citizens, and that religious freedom as a human right cannot and must not be subject to a cultural reservation. Citizens and groups need not profess their commitment to the democratic secular state for them to enjoy the rights and protections that come with democratic citizenship. He praises the Federal Constitution Court for confirming this very position with regard to Jehovah's Witnesses.[36] In a liberal system, Böckenförde writes, ideas are free. Only violations of the law can be prosecuted, but not normative reservations against the liberal democratic order. For that, after all, is the achievement of the freedom of conscience. Catholics long harboured inner reservations against the secular state, and the same may be true for other groups, religious or not, today. Catholics were 'even allowed to advocate the "Catholic state as a thesis", ... and declare the religiously neutral state of the modern age to be a

[33] Chapter VIII of this volume, p. 224.

[34] John Paul II, sermon in Havana on 25 January 1998; English translation: http://www.ewtn.com/cuba/words.htm. See Chapter VIII, p. 226.

[35] Originally, the term was introduced by the German-Syrian political scientist Bassam Tibi, presenting a normative idea of a common liberal culture in Europe, which he felt should be more assertive in public life, and where rights violations in the name of cultural relativism should not be tolerated. Later, however, the concept was re-ascribed, inter alia by CDU politician Friedrich Merz, to denote a majoritarian notion of a leading Christian culture, into which those of different cultural and religious heritage should assimilate. Cardinal Ratzinger, whom Böckenförde quotes in the article, overwhelmingly used the concept in this latter sense, and it is this sense to which Böckenförde here responds.

[36] BVerfGE 102,370. Ernst-Wolfgang Böckenförde, 'Säkularer Staat und Religion', *MUT. Forum für Kultur, Politik und Geschichte* 484 (2007), pp. 24–35.

"national apostasy", as ... late as 1964'.[37] It is a hallmark of the liberal state that it grants its citizens the right to give expression to such inner reservations.

But what can be the sources of societal cohesion when societies become increasingly plural? Böckenförde explores whether a Roussean civil religion may bind heterogenous societies together, but finds that the loyalty it demands is incompatible with the liberal state, opening the gates instead to the possible emergence of a new kind of fundamentalism. The source of societal cohesion must be the stabilization of an open and secular order itself, out of which grow new bonds within a heterogenous citizenry. For sure, the hands of the state are not tied in this regard, as universal state schooling remains the chief instrument where a democratic culture can be cultivated. But also '[f]reedom-related laws, if they are consistently and impartially applied, are able to generate a new kind of unifying bond across a plural, partly centripetal cultural reality: the commonality of life in and under a legal order that is grounded in reason and inviolable ... the law, not arbitrariness, is the coating of freedom, also and especially under the conditions of partial heterogeneity'.[38]

In the closing paragraphs, Böckenförde returns to the question of persistent reservations against democracy. Muslims have long lived in democratic societies and exercised democratic citizenship. Yet for those wishing to follow their religious school of law faithfully, does the democratic secular state pose a challenge? The Central Council of Muslims in Germany appeared to think so, for it emphasized that whatever reservations Muslims might have, as long as they were in the minority and lived as if in a diasporic situation, Islamic law obliged them to respect the local legal order.[39] Muslim intellectuals within and outside Germany have objected to such a depiction of their religion (also found in human rights documents by other Islamic associations), but the question remains whether democracy can survive in the long term if citizens adhere to worldviews that reject its normative principles.

In a rejoinder to critics of his 1957 essay, Böckenförde had written that a Christian who wished to conscientiously follow Catholic natural law doctrine lived in a situation of real tension in the modern world (prior to Vatican II). On the one hand, Christian natural law suggested specific ways of life and of organizing public order. On the other hand, the Catholic saw himself confronted by other citizens' rightful demand for the respect of their personal freedom, even if that freedom led them to live their lives in erroneous ways from the Catholic viewpoint.[40] This tension was only resolved once the Catholic magisterium reconciled the right of truth and the claim to individual freedom. Muslims who adhere to schools of Islamic law that do not accept the claim to individual freedom and the limitation of religious law to questions of personal ethics (and

[37] Chapter VIII in this volume, p. 235.

[38] Chapter VIII in this volume, pp. 233–234.

[39] Article 10 of the Fundamental Declaration of the Central Council of Muslims in Germany. English version: http://muhammad.islam.de/3037_print.php.

[40] 'Noch einmal: Das Ethos der modernen Demokratie und die Kirche', in Böckenförde (note 27), pp. 27–55, here p. 43.

thus the exclusion from state law) may see themselves confronted by similar tensions. The question therefore, according to Böckenförde, is whether such schools of Islamic law will be reinterpreted to embrace a person's right to liberty. The task is not to excavate individual verses from the Qur'an and Sunna to support ideas of inter-faith tolerance or peace, but to work within the Islamic legal traditions to decide the tension-laden conflict between religious truth and human freedom in favour of human freedom.[41]

Such inner-religious reform processes are best conducted in a free discursive environment where all voices can be heard. For this reason, too, Böckenförde would say, it is important that state neutrality does not mean the restriction of such debates to the private sphere. By contrast, the more such debates are conducted in the public realm and are subjected to public inquiry, the higher the chances that religious groups do not demand rights for themselves they are not also willing to concede to those adhering to other worldviews.

[41] Were Böckenförde to revisit this question fifteen years later, he would find that they are. These endeavours take various approaches in different traditions and schools of thought; to name only a few thoroughgoing ones, from Islamic jurisprudential perspectives, Mohsen Kadivar, *Human Rights and Reformist Islam* (Edinburgh: Edinburgh University Press, 2021); Abdullahi Ahmed an-Na'im, *Islam and the Secular State: Negotiating the Future of Shari'a* (Cambridge, MA: Harvard University Press, 2008); from a sociological perspective, Asef Bayat, *Making Islam Democratic: Social Movements and the Post-Islamist Turn* (Stanford, CA: Stanford University Press, 2007).

V

The Rise of the State as a Process of Secularization [1967]

For our generation, it is part of the stock-in-trade of scholarship that 'state' is not a universal concept.[I] Instead, it denotes a form of political order that emerged in Europe between the thirteenth and the late eighteenth or early nineteenth centuries as a result of specific conditions and impulses of European history. Since that time it has spread throughout the civilized world, detached, as it were, from the concrete circumstances of its origin. Whereas generations of nineteenth-century academics used to speak with blithe assurance of the 'Hellenic state', the 'medieval state', the 'Inca state', or the 'state' in Plato, Aristotle, and Thomas Aquinas, we can no longer do so. We know, particularly since the publication of Otto Brunner's epoch-making *Land und Herrschaft* ['Territory and Dominion'],[1] that the state slowly developed out of the quite unstate-like power structures and relationships of the Middle Ages. We know the stages of that development: first, territorial lordship, a system of various spheres of sovereignty, territorially as yet undefined, converging on the person of the territorial lord;[2] then territorial sovereignty as the essentially territorially defined sovereign dominion of the prince in his land, combining and reinforcing the various titles to power (*jus territorii*);[3] and, finally—in Enlightened Absolutism, the French Revolution, and thereafter—the concentrated, unitary authority of the state, externally sovereign, internally supreme and above the traditional legal order, potentially all-embracing in its authority and facing a society where political hierarchies had been levelled, a society of subjects or citizens (equal before the law).

[I] Editors' Note: This is one of Böckenförde's best-known articles, reprinted in numerous volumes, and translated into English, Italian, French, Polish, Czech, Japanese, and Korean. The article is an expanded and revised version of a lecture he gave in 1964 at the Ebrach summer seminar, on invitation of Ernst Forsthoff.

[1] O. Brunner, *Land und Herrschaft. Grundfragen der territorialen Verfassungsgeschichte im Mittelalter*, 3rd ed. (Brno, Munich, and Vienna, 1943). Before Brunner, see H. Heller, *Staatslehre* (Leiden, 1934), pp. 125ff.

[2] See the description in Brunner, *Land und Herrschaft*, pp. 414ff.

[3] The definition of sovereignty in imperial law as *jus territorii* or *droit de souveraineté* in the Peace of Westphalia, *Instrumentum Pacis Osnabrugense*, VIII §1; see also Zeumer, *Quellensammlung zur Geschichte der Deutschen Reichsverfassung*, 2nd ed. (Tübingen, 1913), p. 416.

Religion, Law, and Democracy. Ernst-Wolfgang Böckenförde, Oxford University Press (2020). © E.W. Böckenförde, M. Künkler, and T. Stein 2020. DOI: 10.1093/oso/9780198818632.003.0008.

That is the emergence of the state as seen in terms of constitutional history. But it is only one aspect of the historical process. The other aspect is no less important: it has to do with the detachment of the political order as such from its spiritual and religious origin and evolution; with its 'becoming secular' in the sense of exiting a world in which religion and politics formed a unity to find a purpose and identity of its own, conceived in secular (political) terms; and, finally, with the separation of the political order from the Christian religion and from any specific religion as its foundation and leaven. This development, too, forms part of the emergence of the state. In fact, without this aspect of the process it is impossible to understand the state as it has evolved and as we see it today, or to grasp the fundamental problems of political order that confront the state of today.

It is customary to label the kind of process involved here 'secularization'. That is acceptable and appropriate as long as, carefully avoiding the myriad ideological associations that cling to the term 'secularization', we understand it in its original sense, which is neutral as regards lawfulness and unlawfulness, legitimacy or illegitimacy.[4] In this sense 'secularization' means simply 'the withdrawal or release of an object, territory, or institution from ecclesiastical and spiritual observance and control'.[5]

I.

At the mention of secularization in the context of the emergence of the state, most people think of the sort of declaration of neutrality on questions of religious truth that was increasingly made and implemented by many statesmen and political thinkers in the face of the seemingly interminable confessional civil wars that rocked Europe in the sixteenth and seventeenth centuries. The idea was to find a new foundation for the political order, to give it new universality that went beyond and was no longer dependent on any one particular religion. The 'declaration of neutrality' finds its most striking expression—ahead of its time—in the words spoken by Michel de l'Hôpital, chancellor to the French king, in the royal council on the eve of the Huguenot war in 1562: the question, he said, was not which was the true religion, but how men could live together.[6] This removal of politics from a pre-existing religious context and from the pursuit of religious objectives laid the foundation for the gradual concession of civic toleration, and for the state's recognition of religious liberty as the first of the citizen's fundamental rights. However, this was not the beginning of the process of secularization, but simply a stage within it. The beginning, the event that first made possible the kind of separation of which l'Hôpital spoke, and at the same time placed it in a historical continuum, reaches back much further.

[4] See H. Lübbe, *Säkularisierung. Geschichte eines ideenpolitischen Begriffs* (Freiburg i. Br., and Munich, 1965), p. 24.

[5] Ibid., p. 23.

[6] L. von Ranke, *Französische Geschichte*, ed. Willy Andreas (Wiesbaden, 1957), vol. I, p. 157.

We must look for it in the Investiture Controversy (1057–1122), the spiritual and political conflict between pope and emperor over the whole future order of Western Christendom that was waged by both sides with the utmost determination. The Investiture Controversy shook the old unitary politico-religious world of the *orbis christianus* to its foundations. Here the distinction between and separation of 'spiritual' and 'temporal'—a key theme of European history ever since—made its first appearance.[7]

The full significance of the Investiture Controversy for the process of secularization becomes apparent only against the background of the unity of the *res publica christiana* that it dissolved and exploded. Not only was that order 'Christian' in the sense that Christianity was the recognized foundation of the political order; it was in itself, in its substance, fashioned in sacred and religious terms. It was a holy order that embraced all spheres of life, with no distinction as of yet between 'spiritual' and 'temporal', 'church' and 'state'.[8] The Holy Roman Empire of the German Nation (the 'Reich') was not founded on the Roman imperial inheritance, though it drew on that inheritance, but on the Christian theology of history and Christian eschatology. It was the realm of the *populus christianus*, the manifestation of the *ecclesia*. As such it was wholly involved in the task of realizing the *regnum Dei* on earth and stemming the assault of evil in the present age (*kat-echon*).[9] Emperor and pope were not representatives respectively of the temporal and spiritual orders; both stood *within* a single *ecclesia* as holders of different offices (*ordines*). The emperor, as overlord and protector of Christendom, was just as much a consecrated, hallowed person (*Novus Salomon*) as the pope; the *res publica christiana* lived in both of them as a politico-religious unity.[10] From the outset, political events were thus bound up with the Christian view of history, from where they derived their direction and justification.

But it was not only in this universal fashion that the Reich represented a unitary politico-religious world; it did so also in terms of concrete institutions, legal actions, and the conduct of daily life. Soon after its emancipation by Emperor Constantine, Christianity had taken over the function and position of the *polis* religion of antiquity, becoming the public cult of the Empire and ordering its life. On the other hand, it had assimilated much of the nature magic- and salvation-oriented religiousness of the Germanic peoples. Both elements strengthened and enhanced the way in which the religious, cultic dimension permeated the whole of existence. In this way, faith itself took the form of a

[7] A. Mirgeler, *Rückblick auf das abendländische Christentum* (Mainz, 1961), pp. 109ff.

[8] On this and what follows, see F. Heer, *Aufgang Europas* (Vienna and Zurich, 1951), with its extensive documentation of sources.

[9] The Reich as *kat-echon*: C. Schmitt, *Der Nomos der Erde im Völkerrecht des Jus publicum europaeum* (Cologne, 1950), p. 29f.

[10] E. Ewig, 'Zum christlichen Königsgedanken im frühen Mittelalter', in *Das Königtum, Vorträge und Forschungen*, 3 (Konstanz and Lindau, 1954), pp. 71ff.; E. Eichmann, *Die Kaiserkrönung im Abendland*, vol. 1 (Würzburg, 1942), pp. 105–108, 109–125.

politico-religious and at the same time legal bond of allegiance to the powerful god-king, Christ. Its true content was the 'fides' of the believer as liegeman and vassal of God; any separation of 'internal' and 'external' was wholly alien to it.

What effect did the Investiture Controversy have on this unitary politico-religious world?

The principle that made the struggle possible and took it beyond a dispute about power by furnishing its intellectual justification was the separation of 'spiritual' and 'temporal'. That separation, elaborated by the young discipline of theological scholarship, became the real intellectual weapon in the Investiture Controversy. Its use meant inevitably that the imperial-ecclesiastical world entity (*reichskirchliche Weltganze*, as Albert Mirgeler called it) that had hitherto existed and in which people lived was dissolved from its innermost core. The holders of the spiritual office claimed everything spiritual, sacred, and holy for themselves and for the *ecclesia* they constituted. That *ecclesia* detached itself, as an autonomous, legally self-constituting, and sacramentally hierarchical institution from the all-embracing unity of the *orbis christianus*—the old *ecclesia*. In fact, this separation was already implicit in the battle-cry *libertas ecclesia*.[11] The emperor, and indeed the office of the ruler as such, was ousted from that new *ecclesia*; it lost its spiritual locus and was discharged into worldliness. The emperor was no longer a consecrated person but a layman like any other believer. As far as the performance of his Christian duties was concerned, he was subject, like anyone else, to the jurisdiction of the spiritual authority, which for its part was not under the jurisdiction of any temporal authority. That was the new *ordo* expressed in the *Dictatus papae*.[12]

The revolution involved here meant more than simply the desacralization of the emperor. Along with him, the political order as such was released from the sacred and sacramental realm; it was quite literally de-sacralized, deconsecrated, and secularized—and consequently set free to pursue its own development as a secular concern. What was intended as a devaluation, a defence against imperial claims to sovereignty in the realm of the *ecclesia*, became, in the inexorable dialectic of historical processes, an emancipation. The Investiture Controversy established politics as a separate, self-contained realm. Politics was no longer capable or in need of a spiritual justification; henceforth it was amenable only to a secular one in terms of natural law.

Incidentally, the break with the old order found striking expression in the behaviour of Gregory VII himself, as P. E. Hübinger has pointed out.[13] After repeated warnings and in the face of continued encroachments, Gregory finally excommunicated the Emperor, and thus also, in terms of the old order, declared him unworthy of holding royal office. In so doing he was essentially

[11] See Mirgeler, *Rückblick*, p. 122.

[12] *Dictatus papae Gregorii VII*, esp. theses XVIII ('Quod [Romanus pontifex] a nemine ipse iudicari debeat') and XII ('Quod illi liceat imperators deponere').

[13] From an unpublished lecture on Gregory VII given in Münster in the spring of 1964.

still operating in the old unitary world, even if his action, like that of Henry III in Sutri, was unusual and appropriate only to an extraordinary situation. However, when he released the royal penitent at Canossa from the ban, he confined himself to the religious, spiritual act of reconciliation with the 'Church'. The removal of the political consequences of the ban—that is, the reinstatement of Henry in his royal office—no longer concerned him as pope; that was the emperor's own affair. The separation of spiritual and temporal was plain to see.

Clearly implicit in that separation was the move towards a (hierocratic) system of ecclesiastical sovereignty. In the definition of relations between the spiritual and the temporal, on which everything now depended, the spiritual was able and indeed obliged—in what was still a self-evidently Christian society—to claim precedence. The temporal ruler was a Christian, and as such he was subject to the Christian commandments, the interpretation and observance of which was the task of the spiritual power. The popes and the canonists of the Curia—leaving aside for the moment the wider, directly political pretensions of Boniface VIII, for example—stressed this logic time and again and sought to apply it in practical politics. Referring to Friedrich Kempf's argument with Walter Ullmann, Hans Barion has shown that the supremacy of the spiritual power evolved precisely by limiting the church's claim to judge only *ratione peccati* and *ratione saluti*.[14] [II] Such a judgment, regardless of all the politico-legal consequences directly bound up with it in a Christian society, demanded full authority. The *ratio peccati* was the only authoritative dictum to which the *ratio ordinis politici* had to subordinate itself a priori, even if the *res* to be judged necessarily belonged to both realms. The Church's head start in institutionalization[15] did its part to enforce its supremacy.

We must not forget, however, that the precondition for the assertion of that supremacy was precisely the recognition of temporality, the secularization of politics as a matter of principle. But that also meant that this relationship could be reversed, namely as soon as the political sphere was able to make people aware of the temporality dictated to it and to assert the *ratio* and the supremacy of the political over the spiritual power. With the same logic by which temporal conduct had been drawn *ratione peccati* into the jurisdiction of the spiritual power, spiritual conduct could—*ratione ordinis politici*—be placed under the jurisdiction of the temporal power. Thomas Hobbes, taking up the major theme of political theology, later offered an impressive exposition of that logic.[16]

[14] H. Barion, in *Zeitschrift der Savigny-Stiftung für Rechtsgeschichte, kanonistische Abteilung*, 46/1960, p. 485, esp. pp. 493ff. Review of F. Kempf: 'Die päpstliche Gewalt in der mittelalterlichen Welt', in *Saggi storici intorno al Papato, dei Professori della Facolta di Storia Ecclesiasticd* (Rome, 1959), pp. 117–169.

[II] *Ratione peccati* and *ratione saluti* refer to matters of sin and of salvation—which politics has no powers to decide on.

[15] Mirgeler, *Rückblick*, p. 127.

[16] See C. Schmitt, 'Die vollendete Reformation', in *Der Staat* 4 (1965), p. 64f.

Ecclesiastical supremacy over the temporal power, on the one hand, and a state church, on the other, were no longer a matter of different systems. Instead, they were essentially two sides of the same coin: the realization in one direction or the other of the possibilities implicit in the separation of 'spiritual' and 'temporal'. Following the Investiture Controversy, the papacy tried for centuries to impose ecclesiastical supremacy. In so doing it played an essential part in the holders of temporal power gaining a heightened awareness of the autonomy and worldliness of the political sphere, and increasingly narrowing the church's lead in institutionalization by developing forms of state power. The examples of the Hohenstaufen and the French kings, among others, exemplify that the early forms of the concept of sovereignty and the territorial consolidation of the sovereign sphere emerged precisely out of the clash with the papal claim to supremacy.

Of course, the outcome of the Investiture Controversy was far more profound in the realm of ideas than what was immediately realized historically and politically. As Mirgeler pointed out,[17] the secularization that actually occurred with the 'spiritual'/'temporal' distinction was obscured by the fact that the new, internally divided Christendom was generally regarded as simply carrying on the old unitary politico-religious entity, and continued to be understood within the traditions of the sacral unity of empire and church. The change at the level of principle notwithstanding, an overlap of *imperium* and *ecclesia* was de facto preserved, especially within the Holy Roman Empire. While the outward forms of the old universe survived for a long time, they became increasingly hollow, of course, as form and content drifted farther and farther apart. Moreover, there was no real possibility, in the minds of the emperor and the temporal rulers, of either the nation as a whole or their temporal rule being and remaining anything but Christian. In this initial stage, secularization had meant only a release from the realm of the sacral and the sanctified, from the immediate orientation (eschatological or incarnatory) towards the Hereafter; it did not entail a release from the religious foundation altogether. The dominions and kingdoms, set free on the path towards worldly politics in the wake of the Investiture Controversy, remained Christian domains and authorities. The Christian religion provided the unquestioned foundation, the shared ground that guaranteed the homogeneity between the rulers and the ruled. Moreover, the movement towards the state, and the emergence—in the fifteenth and early sixteenth centuries—of a political sphere engaged in the pursuit and contest of power,[18] initially took place within this context as well. The event that changed the situation, provoking the crisis that led to the second stage of secularization, was the schism of the Reformation.

[17] Mirgeler, *Rückblick*, pp. 129, 122f.

[18] W. Dilthey, *Gesammelte Schriften*, vol. II (Berlin and Leipzig, 1914), pp. 246ff.; G. Dahm, *Deutsches Recht* (Stuttgart, 1951), p. 266.

II.

Once the religious schism had become a reality, European Christendom confronted the question of how it might be possible for the different confessions to live together within a shared political order. Owing to the importance of the Christian religion for the political order, the conflict was not merely a spiritual, but also a political one. For the two—later, three—confessions, it was a conflict about true belief, about the pure Gospel. And as a struggle over truth, it brooked no compromise. In keeping with the relationship between spiritual and temporal powers as elaborated by theologians and canon lawyers, it was the duty of the temporal power to use its instruments publicly to suppress error and punish heretics. On this point, Roman Catholics, Lutherans, and members of the Reformed Church were in fundamental agreement.[19] The temporal power had to deal not only with seditious heretics, who were at the same time political troublemakers; it was also incumbent upon the authorities to punish non-seditious heretics, for they blasphemed against God.[20] The notion of belief as a quasi-legal relationship of fidelity and the still vital tradition of the *polis* religion barred the way to civic toleration.

This made it inevitable that the religious question in its entirety would become a political matter. Sixteenth- and seventeenth-century Europe was swept by a wave of horrible confessional civil wars. Political and religious interests, commitment to the true faith, and efforts to expand and defend spheres of power clashed incessantly. Alliances formed and re-formed.[21] At three places in Europe, this politico-religious struggle was fought out in exemplary fashion and with different results: in Spain under Philip II, in the Holy Roman Empire in the clash between the emperor and the estates, and in France in the Huguenot wars. Leaving aside the special development in Spain, these confessional civil wars gave rise to the second stage of the secularization process: a state built on and justified in purely temporal and political terms. With its arrival, the separation of religion and politics was also fundamentally decided.

To what extent this development was intended by those involved need not concern us here. What we can say is that it arose out of the logic of the historical situation and the conditions of action it dictated. The distinction between 'spiritual' and 'temporal', first employed by the popes to justify ecclesiastical supremacy, now exerted its force in the direction of the primacy and supremacy of the political sphere. The demands made by the spiritual power upon the temporal power as a result of the schism implied a permanent state of political conflict, for they were inherently and directly temporal and political. Small wonder, then, that the temporal powers, the kings and princes, unless they

[19] Description and sources in J. Lecler, *Geschichte der Religionsfreiheit im Zeitalter der Reformation* (Stuttgart, 1965), vol. I, pp. 148ff., 240–252, 439ff.

[20] Thomas Aquinas, *Commentary on the Sentences*, IV.13.2.3. Luther: see Lecler, *Geschichte der Religionsfreiheit*, vol. I, pp. 249ff. Melanchthon: see *Corpus Reformatorum*, IV.737–740.

[21] For an excellent general treatment see Lecler, *Geschichte der Religionsfreiheit*, vols. I and II.

wished to become enforcers of their own religious party, took spiritual matters into their own hands for the sake of the political order—that is to say, they brought them under their control and jurisdiction and asserted the primacy of politics over religion. A pacified political order bestowing calm and security on nations and individuals could be restored only through the political sphere elevating itself above the demands of the feuding religious parties and emancipating itself from them. We must bear this problem in mind if we are to reach a true understanding of the development of royal power in France, the *cuius regio, eius religio* of the Holy Roman Empire, the territorialism and Erastianism[III] that began to characterize Protestant ecclesiastical jurisprudence as early as the beginning of the seventeenth century,[22] and, finally, the political theology of Thomas Hobbes' doctrine of the state.

Leopold von Ranke described the confessional civil war in France in his *French History*. Those who believe that the desperate situation in France in the second half of the sixteenth century has been deliberately exaggerated in our own day to create an ideology justifying the modern state should go back to Ranke's account and find out what things were really like at the time. France experienced a seemingly never-ending series of military confrontations over the authorization, revocation, renewal, extension, and limitations of various pacification edicts for the Huguenots. Moreover, that conflict was bound up at every turn with the power struggle between the monarchy and the mutinous nobles of the Fronde. Thirty years of varying fortunes turned virtually the entire country into a civil war battlefield.[23] There is no need to describe those wars and their different phases here; what interests us is the emergence of a specifically political kind of thinking in the theories of the state-centred French jurists known as *les Politiques,* and the stabilization and concentration of political power based on those theories.

The *Politiques* proceeded to develop their own specifically political argumentation, which was something quite new in terms of the tradition of Scholastic natural law.[24] They put forward a *formal* concept of peace drawn not from the world of truth, but from its contrast to the civil war. And they accorded that formal concept of peace—meaning an absence of war, outward calm, and security of existence—primacy over the fight for religious truth. Civil war, they

[III] Erastianism stands for the idea that the state has supremacy over the church even in ecclesiastical matters and that therefore sins should be punished by civil authorities and not the church. The term goes back to the writings of Thomas Erastus (1542–1583) and came into use in the context of the debates over state or church supremacy in England in the mid-seventeenth century. Presbyterians used it as a term of abuse for those who urged state supremacy.

[22] See J. Heckel, *Cura religionis, Jus in sacra, Jus circa sacra*, new ed. (Darmstadt, 1962), pp. 44ff., 53f., 67ff.; also M. Heckel, 'Jus circa sacra', in *Evangelisches Staatslexikon* (Stuttgart, 1975), col. 829. The negative assessment of territorialism in ecclesiastical politics in Lecler, *Geschichte der Religionsfreiheit*, vol. II, pp. 381ff., 530ff., does not do justice to this connection.

[23] Von Ranke, *Französische Geschichte*, books 4–6, vol. I, pp. 117–275.

[24] R. Schnur, *Die französischen Juristen im konfessionellen Bürgerkrieg* (Berlin, 1962), esp. pp. 16–23. See also Lecler, *Geschichte der Religionsfreiheit*, vol. II, pp. 109ff.

argued, did not lead to victory or the suppression of heresy, but brought only hatred, poverty, and enmity. Arms were an inappropriate means of overcoming the schism in the faith. For the *Politiques*, formal peace, contrasted to the horrors and sufferings of civil war, was an autonomous, *inherently justified* good. It could be established only by way of national unity, and national unity was possible only where the king's command was obeyed as the supreme law. Only the king, the neutral instance standing above the warring factions, above the citizens, could establish and preserve peace.[25] For the *Politiques*, confessional differences were no longer a matter for the state, but the concern of the Church. The king's job, as Michel de l'Hôpital told Charles IX in a memorandum of 1568, was to ensure that his subjects did not seek to annihilate one another in savage and malicious obduracy; the question of truth was one he could and should not decide.[26] The separation of politics from religion and the assertion of its autonomy prevailed here without much ado, but emphatically so. What did the king give his subjects, de l'Hôpital asked, when, on condition that they loyally observed his law, he left them free to follow their conscience: 'He gives them liberty of conscience, or rather he leaves their consciences at liberty.' And he went on: 'Do you call that capitulating? Is it capitulation when a subject enters into an agreement with you that he acknowledges his sovereign and remains his subject?'[27] The purely secular view of the political power relationships is already complete in this argument. Religion is no longer an essential component of the political order.

When Henry III of Navarre [who later became king of France as Henry IV] converted to Catholicism in order to actualize his claim to the French throne under the *loi salique*, this was not—as might appear on the outside—a victory for 'true religion', but a victory for politics. Henry's action was prompted by reasons of state prudence and political common sense.[28] The king changed his faith to give the country peace at last, a peace that could be achieved in no other way, and to secure the authority of the monarchy. The first thing he did after bringing peace to the country was to establish a legal existence for the Huguenots under the Edict of Nantes (1598).[29] Henceforth, an individual might be a citizen of the kingdom and enjoy full civil rights without belonging to the 'true religion'. The first, substantive separation of church and state was thus a reality. The Edict of Nantes was the first attempt to allow two religions in one state.

It is instructive to compare King Henry IV of France with Henry IV, the Holy Roman emperor. The emperor went to Canossa as a penitent to receive

[25] Schnur, *Die französischen Juristen*, pp. 21–23.

[26] See Lecler, *Geschichte der Religionsfreiheit*, vol. II., p. 111.

[27] Quoted in Lecler, *Geschichte der Religionsfreiheit*, vol. II, p. 112.

[28] Von Ranke, *Französische Geschichte*, vol. I, pp. 265ff.

[29] 'That was the worst thing in the world,' the pope is reputed to have said of the freedom of conscience granted by the edict when the French envoy told him about it; see Lecler, *Geschichte der Religionsfreiheit*, vol. II, p. 183. The edict did indeed mark the end of the old relationship between religion and politics.

papal absolution, the precondition, within a unitary politico-religious world, for returning to royal office. The French king converted to Catholicism and abjured heresy to secure his rule and give the country peace and stability. Despite the similarity between the two chains of events, the roles of conqueror and conquered had been thoroughly reversed.

This remains true even though the principle of a state religion continued to prevail almost everywhere in Europe—including France—for a long time yet. For the decision to have a state religion was not a question of realizing and implementing the truth, but a question of politics. 'Two religions cannot exist in one state' was the argument repeatedly advanced in many quarters, by both theologians and politicians, against toleration and freedom of worship.[30] That may well have been true in many places at the time: after all, people who had lived for centuries within the structures of the public cult-religion had to mature first and become capable of toleration. But it was a political argument rather than a religious one, related to security and order within the state. The whole question was thus released from the unconditional nature of the obligation to truth and made subject to the contingencies and conditions of politics. It was this—and only this—that opened the question up to consideration, to the demarcation of spheres of liberty, indeed, paved the way for toleration. Religion was no longer guaranteed *de jure* but *de facto*, and what guaranteed it was a decision of the political authority. As a logical consequence it was placed under the control of the territorial ruler's governance of the church, indeed, under that of the established state church. The fact that the rulers of the day had no intention of placing themselves and their nascent states outside the pale of Christendom, but were themselves Christian and wished to remain so, in no way lessened the fundamental difference between their world and the world before the schism. For the newly emergent order this Christian identity was an actual, given condition; but it was no longer a necessary one.

The extent to which secularization in this sense determined politics and the state henceforward is clear from Richelieu's *Testament politique*. In it this cardinal of the Roman Church, addressing a very devout prince brought up as a faithful son of the Church, speaks of 'God's government' as the prime foundation for the happiness of the state, and something every ruler had to put into effect.[31] But in what does it consist? Richelieu presupposes the answer as already known, offering no details beyond an exhortation to lead a virtuous and exemplary life. 'God's government', pushed aside into the realm of morality, is left with no tangible content for politics. And so *raison* is proclaimed as the guiding principle of political action. Natural understanding enables everyone to grasp that man, having been created *raisonnable*, may do nothing except through *raison*. Otherwise he would be acting against his nature and hence against the foundations of his own being.[32] The religious connection is now established

[30] See ibid., vol. I, pp. 367, 549; vol. II, pp. 63f., 137f., 143f., 385f.

[31] Cardinal Richelieu, *Testament politique*, ed. Wilhelm Mommsen (Klassiker der Politik) (Berlin, 1926), II.1., p. 164f.

[32] Ibid., II.2.

only indirectly in that man's *raison* is created by God; in its realization, however, it is a law unto itself.

What announced itself on the European continent here, notably in France, as a solution in principle to the relationship between spiritual and secular authority, between religion and politics, received its clearest theoretical expression in the political theory of Thomas Hobbes. It is particularly instructive for our concerns. Hobbes justifies the state as a sovereign decision-making entity that guarantees external peace and security. His starting point is simply and solely human need—in other words, the preservation and protection of the elementary good things of life as they pertain to outward existence. Man's religious destiny and religion as a good of human life are not part of it. '*Salus publica in quo consistit?*' ('What constitutes the safety of the people?'), Hobbes asks in Chapter 13 of *De cive*, which deals with the duties of the ruler. His answer is classic in its trenchancy: '*(1) ut ab hostibus externis defendantur; (2) ut pax interna conservetur; (3) ut quantum cum securitate publica consistere potest, locupletentur; (4) ut libertate innoxia perfruantur*' ['(1) in defence from external enemies; (2) preservation of internal peace; (3) acquisition of wealth, so far as this is consistent with public security; (4) full enjoyment of innocent liberty'].[33] The purely secular, this-worldly objective of the state, independent of religion, is spelled out clearly: to safeguard the conditions in which civic life may be preserved, and to enable citizens to satisfy their individual living requirements. For this purpose the state is established, and to this end it is invested with the *summum imperium* (supreme authority), appointed to make the final decision and therefore equipped with sovereign power. Only through such a sovereign, final decision-making authority, against which none may appeal to his 'private' judgment, can peace and security be achieved and a secure distinction drawn between right and wrong. The state in this sense is the 'minimum condition' for peace and security.

The *rectia ratio* that serves Hobbes as a methodological guide for his justification of the state is no longer a reason inherently determined and directed by belief, but an autonomous, individualistic, goal-oriented reason.[34] That does not mean that Hobbes was an atheist or that his system can only be understood atheistically, as Leo Strauss maintained.[35] Hobbes takes it for granted that the ruler, as the bearer of state power, is a Christian. He incorporates the Christian faith *as such* into the state through his irreplaceable statement that 'Jesus is the Christ'.[36] And yet Hobbes' construct of the state incorporates the principle of

[33] Thomas Hobbes, *Elementa philosophica de cive*, chapter 13.6. English translation: *On the Citizen*, ed. and translated by Richard Tuck and Michael Silverthorne (Cambridge, 1998).

[34] Typical of the definition of 'natural law' in Hobbes is this sentence from *De cive*, chapter 2.1: '*Dictamen rectae rationis circa ea, quae agenda vel omittenda sunt ad vitae membrorumque conservationem, quantum fieri potest, diuturnam*' ('the Dictate of right reason about what should be done or not done for the longest possible preservation of life and limb'). The transition from an ontological reason oriented towards a universal order of purposes to a purposive-functional reason is complete here.

[35] L. Strauss, *Hobbes' politische Wissenschaft* (Neuwied, 1966), pp. 78ff.

[36] Modern Hobbes scholarship has corroborated this; see, for example, Th. Hood, *The Divine Politics of Thomas Hobbes* (Oxford, 1964). See also Carl Schmitt, *Die vollendete Reformation*, pp. 51ff.; Bernard Willms, 'Von der Vermessung des Leviathan, Aspekte neuerer Hobbes-Literatur', *Der Staat* 6 (1967): pp. 255ff., 230ff.

secularization. His justification of the state does not spring from the Christian faith, is independent of it as both cause and objective, and is based purely on human needs and on goal-oriented, individualistic reason. What Hobbes sets out with regard to the Christian nature of this state is the demonstration, by way of excluding contradiction, that this state of reason in which the ruler is a Christian is itself a Christian state. Neither the Gospel nor individual divine commandments say anything against the sovereign power of the ruler and the subject's unconditional duty of obedience, nor against the ruler's competence in spiritual matters.[37] Expressed as a thesis, it means that the state and Christianity can coexist and that recognition of the sovereign decision-making power of the state does not entail any denial of belief; still, this does not nullify the purely temporal, utilitarian justification of the state and definition of its goals, nor does it call their logical consistency into question.

In this second stage of secularization, as well, translating decisions of principle into reality was not a one-time event, but a historical process. The secularizing transformation of the politico-social order took place gradually, and for a long time old and new components coexisted in close proximity.

It was the French Revolution that brought to completion the political state that had emerged from the confessional civil wars and had been prefigured in Hobbes. The 1789 'Declaration of the Rights of Man and of the Citizen'—what Lorenz von Stein called the 'first basic law of the new society'—speaks of the state as a *corps social*. The state is an organization of political power to protect the natural, prior rights and liberties of the individual. Its (very) purpose and justification lie not in its historical origin or divine institutions, not in any service to the truth, but in its relationship to the free, self-determined individual person. Its basis is man *as man*. However, man as he enters into the concept of nature entertained by the law of reason, and from there passes into the principles of the Declaration, is a secular being emancipated from any necessarily religious destiny. Ever since the French Constitution of 1791, the liberties that the state exists to protect and preserve have included freedom of belief and freedom of worship.[38] That renders the state as such neutral with regard to religion, emancipating it from religion. Religion is consigned to the sphere of society, declared a matter for the interests and appreciation of individuals or groups of citizens without being a component of the political order as such. It is freed both from and by the state. Karl Marx saw this structural correlation very clearly: 'Religion,' he wrote, 'is no longer the spirit of the state . . . ; it has become the spirit of civil society . . . It is no longer the essence of community, but the essence of difference. . . It has been ejected from the community as such.'[39] Wherever the state grants its citizens freedom of religion as a basic

[37] See Hobbes, *De cive*, chapter 15; *Leviathan*, part III, chapters 32, 40, 42. In this regard I disagree with the assessment by Willms, 'Vermessung des Leviathan'.

[38] Constitution of 1791, I; the Declaration of the Rights of Man and of the Citizen of August 4, 1789, contained only the guarantee of freedom of religious opinion within the bounds of statutory public order.

[39] K. Marx, 'Zur Judenfrage', *Die Frühschriften*, ed. S. von Landshut (Stuttgart, 1953), p. 183. English translation: http://www.marxists.org/archive/marx/works/1844/jewish-question/

right—and doing so formed part of its 'mandate' from the outset, even if it took some time for that freedom to materialize—these remarks apply. Freedom of religion as a right to liberty embraces not only the right to profess a religion privately and publicly, but also the right not to profess a religion without detriment to the citizen's legal position.[40] It follows that the substance of the universality that the state is supposed to embody and protect can no longer be sought in religion or in a particular faith, but must be found independently of religion in secular goals and common interests. The extent to which freedom of religion is realized is thus a measure of the secularity of the state.

For a long time, the nineteenth century tried to duck these consequences. Against the emancipation of the state from religion implicit in the grant of freedom of religion, the post-1815 Restoration asserted the idea of the 'Christian state'. The 'Christian state' was supposed to halt and even reverse the growing and universally visible trend towards a fundamental secularization. But what did it actually achieve? No more than the imposition of a non-secular veneer over reality, without being in any way able to affect the survival and diffusion of the idea of the state and with it the political principle of secularization. What resulted were makeshifts: monarchy by the grace of God, the alliance of throne and altar, the Holy Alliance, and so on.[41] Christianity became a prop for highly secular transactions, deployed to stabilize power constellations and to sanction specific politico-social circumstances dictated by the times, in an effort to preserve them against efforts to change them. Here again, Marx clearly recognized the principles involved in the process: 'The so-called Christian state is the Christian negation of the state, but by no means the political realization of Christianity.'[42] Indeed, all such attempts to preserve or restore the supposedly institutional-Christian character of the state against its structurally determined secularity and neutrality met with failure. Freedom of religion had the final say not only in the nineteenth century, but also when Germany was re-established as a political entity after 1945, and a Christian state was once again to be established in place of the secularized one.[43] It had to, if the state did not want to give up on itself.

See also E. Weil, 'Die Säkularisierung der Politik und des politischen Ansehens in der Neuzeit', in *Marxismusstudien*, 4th ser. (Tübingen, 1962).

[40] G. Anschütz, 'Die Religionsfreiheit', in G. Anschütz and R. Thoma (eds.), *Handbuch des Deutschen Staatsrechts*, vol. II (Tübingen, 1932), section 106.

[41] On the monarchy by the grace of God, see O. Brunner, 'Vom Gottesgnadentum zum monarchischen Prinzip', in *Das Königtum* (Konstanz-Lindau, 1954), pp. 279ff. (291ff.). When Charles X of France laid his hands on lepers as called for in the coronation ceremony, as a demonstration of the divine healing powers of kings, he wore gloves.

[42] Marx, *Die Frühschriften*, p. 183. English: http://www.marxists.org/archive/marx/works/1844/jewish-question/

[43] The West German state constitutions in the first years after 1945 contained a great many ideological attempts at restoring a 'Christian' state, which are worth a closer examination. The last word of 'religious freedom': *Entscheidung des Bundesverfassungsgerichts*, vol. 19, pp. 206 ff., 226, and A. Hollerbach, 'Das Staatskirchenrecht in der Rechtsprechung des Bundesverfassungsgerichts', *Archiv des öffentlichen Rechts* 92 (1967), p. 99.

III.

Looking back over the development described above, the first question that emerges concerns the objective significance of the secularization process. Did the emergence of the state imply the exclusion of Christianity from a public, world-shaping role, and must the state therefore be seen as a specifically un-Christian or a-Christian form of political organization? Or did the emergence of the state realize a principle of politico-social order that essentially corresponds to the substance of the Christian revelation, but needed to assert itself against the institutionalized powers of Christianity?

What this question boils down to is this: to what extent did the de-sacralization of the political order, the 'desecularization of the spiritual sphere', and the 'despiritualization of the secular sphere'[44] that took place in and through the emergence of the state involve also a *de-Christianization*? It is doubtful whether this question admits of an answer at all, one way or the other. For the answer depends very largely on the interpretation of the secularization process in terms of theology and the philosophy of history, which brings us to Christianity's self-understanding and changing self-interpretation. Is Christianity, in its inner structure, a religion like any other—meaning that its real manifestation is that of the public (*polis*) cult? Or does the Christian faith transcend all previous religions? Do its efficacy and its realization lie precisely in breaking down the sacral forms of religion and the dominance of public worship, and in leading humans to a 'temporal' organization of the world based on reason, leading them to the self-awareness of their liberty? No less a thinker than Hegel gave a positive interpretation, from a Christian perspective, of the trend towards secularization in modern European history: it was not the negation but the realization of the essence of the revelation that came into the world with Jesus Christ.[45] And Karl Marx pointed out—critically, given his standpoint—that the emancipation of the state from religion does not do away with or seek to do away with man's true religiousness.[46] As a personal confession on the part of the individual, and as a social (and to that extent also political) force communicated through the religious beliefs of citizens, the Christian faith is capable of operating also—and especially—in the 'secular' state. In fact, in the secular state religion is set free precisely to operate in this way: freedom of religion is not merely 'negative' but also a 'positive' freedom of belief. However, religion is denied a role in public institutions and a necessary share in the common purpose of the state. Can one say that this alone condemns the Christian faith to losing its universal effectiveness and potential historical power? This question is not meant to be purely rhetorical.

[44] H. Krüger, *Staatslehre*, 2nd ed. (Stuttgart, 1966), p. 44.

[45] G. W. F. Hegel, *Grundlinien der Philosophie des Rechts*, ed. E. Gans (Stuttgart, 1952), section 185, and *Encyklopädie der philosophischen Wissenschaften* (Hamburg, 1830), section 552.

[46] Marx, *Die Frühschriften*, p. 183.

Another question is even more relevant. What is the state's lifeblood, where does it find the strength to sustain itself and guarantee its homogeneity[IV] and the inner regulatory forces of liberty that it needs, once the binding power of religion is no longer and can no longer be essential to it? Up until the nineteenth century, in a world that was interpreted first in sacred and subsequently in religious terms, religion had always been the strongest binding force for the political order and the life of the state. Can morality [*Sittlichkeit*] be established and preserved on a this-worldly, secular foundation? Can the state be built on 'natural ethics'? If not, can the state—irrespective of all of that—live by fulfilling its citizens' eudaemonistic expectations? These questions lead back to a deeper question of principle: To what extent can peoples united in a state live solely on the guarantee of individual liberty, without a unifying bond antecedent to that liberty?

The process of secularization was at the same time a major process of emancipation—the emancipation of the temporal order from traditional religious authorities and obligations. It was brought to completion with the 'Declaration of the Rights of Man and of the Citizen', which set the individual on his own two feet and his liberty. But this raised the fundamental problem of a new integration: the emancipated individuals had to arrive at a new togetherness and homogeneity, lest the state succumb to an inner dissolution, which then gives rise to a total, so-called '*Außenlenkung*' ('otherdirectedness'). This problem was initially obscured because a new unifying force replaced the old one in the nineteenth century—the idea of the nation. The unity of the nation followed the unity from religion, establishing a new homogeneity (though one with a more external-political orientation),[47] within which people continued to live largely out of the tradition of Christian ethics. This national homogeneity sought and found expression in the nation state. By now, the idea of the nation has lost its formative power, and not only in many European countries. In the new states of Asia and Africa, too, its formative power will be temporary. The individualism of human rights, brought to full fruition, liberates people not only from religion, but also, in a further stage, from the (ethnic-folkish [*volkhaft*]) nation as a homogeneity-creating force. After 1945, attempts were made—especially in Germany—to find a new basis of homogeneity in the existence of shared beliefs about values. But if one probes this recourse to 'values' for its communicable content, it proves an exceedingly poor and even dangerous substitute. It opens the door to the subjectivism and positivism of

[IV] Note that homogeneity, a key term for Böckenförde, must not be understood in his work as denoting the opposite of pluralism or heterogeneity, but as a marker for societal cohesion (which he deems necessary to sustain democracy in the long term). In democratic politics, this cohesion needs to be created in society (through communication, participation in shared activities, exchange etc.) and cannot be imposed by the state as that would violate the democratic state's liberal principles.

[47] See the seminal historico-systematic study by E. Lemberg, *Geschichte des Nationalismus in Europa* (Stuttgart, 1950), and his *Nationalismus* (Reinbek, 1964).

the values of the day, which—each laying claim to objective validity—tend to destroy rather than consolidate liberty.[48]

The question about the binding forces thus arises anew and in its true essence: *The liberal, secularized state is sustained by conditions it cannot itself guarantee. That is the great gamble it has made for the sake of liberty.* On the one hand, as a liberal state it can only survive if the freedom it grants to its citizens is regulated from within, out of the moral substance of the individual and the homogeneity of society. On the other hand, it cannot seek to guarantee these inner regulatory forces by its own efforts—that is to say, with the instruments of legal coercion and authoritative command—without abandoning its liberalness, and relapsing, on a secularized level, into the very totalitarian claim it had led away from during the confessional civil wars. The prescribed state ideology, like the revival of the Aristotelian *polis* tradition or the proclamation of an 'objective order of values',[V] abolishes the very separation by which the liberty of the state is constituted.[49] No path leads back across the threshold of 1789 without destroying the state as the order of liberty.

The state can try to circumvent this problem by turning itself into the guarantor of the citizens' eudaemonistic life expectations and seeking to derive from this its sustaining power. But this opens up a field without limits: the state no longer pursues social policy with the intent of safeguarding the existence of its citizens (an indispensable task), but seeks to find in this very activity its 'very purpose' (*Um-Willen*), its legitimizing foundation. The state, no longer trusting the inner binding forces or deprived of them, is then forced onto the path of elevating the realization of the social utopia into its programme. It is doubtful whether this can resolve the fundamental problem it is trying to escape in this way. What will the state fall back on in times of crisis?

And so we must once again join Hegel[50] in asking whether the secularized, temporal state must not also, in the final analysis, be sustained by the inner impulses and binding forces that religious faith imparts to its citizens. Of course, not in such a way that it is turned back into a 'Christian' state, but in such a way that Christians no longer see this state, in its secularity, as something alien, hostile to their faith, but as a chance for liberty, the preservation and realization of which is also their task.

[48] See C. Schmitt, 'Die Tyrannei der Werte', in *Säkularisation und Utopie. Ebracher Studien* (Stuttgart, 1967), pp. 37ff.

[V] The Federal Constitutional Court ruled in 1958 that the Basic Law established an 'objective order of values', enshrined in fundamental rights, which permeated the entire legal system, and were therefore also justiciable in the relations between citizens, not only between citizen and state.

[49] The adoption of the classic *polis* tradition is entirely passed over in W. Hennis, *Politik und praktische Philosophie* (Neuwied, 1963); on this see also Bernard Willms, 'Ein Phoenix zu viel', in *Der Staat* 3 (1964), pp. 488ff. Axiomatically on the problem of the split [Entzweihung], see J. Ritter, *Hegel und die Französische Revolution* (Cologne-Opladen, 1957).

[50] *Encyklopädie der philosophischen Wissenschaften* (1830), §552. The problem of the relationship between the state and religion is discussed here at a level of intellectual reflection unequalled since.

VI

The Fundamental Right of Freedom of Conscience [1970]

If we ask ourselves what the Basic Law regards as the right and proper interpretation of the freedom of conscience guaranteed as 'inviolable' in Article 4,[1] and if we examine the relevant literature and the relevant judicature in search of an answer to our question, we shall quickly be reminded of something Hegel wrote in his *Grundlinien der Philosophie des Rechts* (Elements of the Philosophy of Right):

> The ambiguity associated with conscience therefore consists in the fact that conscience is assumed in advance to signify the identity of subjective knowledge and volition with the true good, and is thus declared and acknowledged to be sacrosanct, while it also claims, as the purely subjective reflection of self-consciousness into itself, the authority [*Berechtigung*] which belongs only to that identity itself by virtue of its rational content which is valid in and for itself.[1]

The ambiguity to which Hegel refers explains why the question of the substance of the freedom of conscience guaranteed under constitutional law not only elicits widely different answers, but raises fundamental questions of its own about the binding character of the state legal system, the ultimate bounds (which cannot be overstepped) of the state's guarantee of liberty, and the legitimation of the modern state and of the *Rechtsstaat*.

Is the state, in the shape of its legal system, in any sort of position to recognize a freedom of the individual conscience that goes beyond the freedom of introspection of the so-called *forum internum*, which of course scarcely needs to be guaranteed by law? Will it not, in so doing, relinquish its universality and its universal validity, the very foundation of its power to keep the peace, particularly in a non-homogeneous society? On the other hand, if it is one of the

[1] Editors' Note: This article is based on a lecture Böckenförde gave at the *Tagung der Staatsrechtslehrervereinigung* in Bern in October 1969, published in 1970. Translated by Thomas Dunlap based on the extant translation by James Underwood. Some footnotes and one section have been omitted with the author's consent (see annotation XIV).

[1] G. W. F. Hegel, *Grundlinien der Philosophie des Rechts*, ed. E. Gans (Stuttgart, 1952), section 137 (pp. 197f.); English translation by H. B. Nisbet, *Elements of the Philosophy of Right* (Cambridge University Press, 1991), p. 165.

Religion, Law, and Democracy. Ernst-Wolfgang Böckenförde, Oxford University Press (2020). © E.W. Böckenförde, M. Künkler, and T. Stein 2020. DOI: 10.1093/oso/9780198818632.003.0009.

aims or *the* aim of the *Rechtsstaat* as well as of liberal democracy to guarantee the liberty of the individual, surely the individual's conscience, the innermost core of his personality, must be inviolable and the state must refrain as a matter of principle from forcing its citizens to go against their consciences. However, there is another aspect to the problem. Can conscience, as the sum total of individual consciences, be taken to constitute an authority on which a state system may seamlessly be erected—the 'voice of God within us', as Christian theologians describe it?[2] Or does a gulf begin to widen here that can be bridged only by conscience taking its bearings from objective ethical and legal norms?[3]

The interpretations of Article 4 of the Basic Law must be seen—even and indeed especially in their divergence—against the background of these questions.[4] There is a good reason for this. The Basic Law does not place the guarantee of freedom of belief and conscience promulgated in Article 4 under any restrictive reservation favouring 'universal laws' or 'civic and political obligations'. This departure from Article 135 of the Weimar Constitution, as well as from the corresponding guarantees in, for example, the Swiss and Austrian constitutions and the European Convention on Human Rights,[5] was not made without premeditation, as I propose to show. This gives our question about

[2] This is an old *topos* of Christian teaching about the conscience, which has its exegetical point of reference in Romans 2:15; see H. Hartmann, *Toleranz und christlicher Glaube* (Frankfurt a. M., 1955), pp. 182, 188; J. Mausbach and P. Ermecke, *Katholische Moraltheologie*, 9th ed., vol. I (Münster, 1959), pp. 158, 161. For a critical view of this understanding of conscience from the theological standpoint, see H. Thielicke, 'Gewissen, Gewissensfreiheit I: Theologisch', in *Evangelisches Staatslexikon* (Stuttgart, 1966), col. 671; also G. Lanzenstiel, ibid., cols. 672f.

[3] Christian theology seeks to evade the *aporia* that opens up here by means of a device that is possible in theological argumentation. On the one hand, it recognizes the individual conscience as the immediate norm and binding authority for concrete ethical and moral action; on the other, it preaches the duty of guiding and forming conscience in accordance with the norms of belief and the teachings of the Church.

[4] For a survey of the various interpretations from the standpoint of 1958, see H. Scholler, *Die Freiheit des Gewissens* (Berlin, 1958), pp. 115–125. If we seek to trace the different kinds of interpretation back to a few basic types, depending on the content they assign to freedom of conscience, we can distinguish the following.

(1) The *restrictive* interpretation: freedom of conscience protects only the so-called *forum internum* and/or the sphere of individual privacy. See esp. R. Zippelius, in *Bonner Kommentar*, Article 4, margin no. 45; Scholler, *Die Freiheit*, pp. 131ff. But see also H. Scholler, 'Gewissen, Gesetz und Rechtsstaat', *Die öffentliche Verwaltung*, 1969, pp. 526ff.

(2) The *extensive* or anarchist interpretation: no one may be forced into a (personal) act against his conscience. See esp. W. Geiger, *Gewissen, Ideologie, Widerstand, Nonkonformismus* (Munich, 1963), pp. 67f., 72f.; A. Arndt, in *Neue juristische Wochenschrift*, 1965 (p. 2196, note on *Entscheidungen des Bundesverfassungsgerichts (BVerfGE)*, 19, 135), 1966 (p. 2205), and 1968 (p.980).

(3) The *functional* or balancing interpretation: see esp. N. Luhmann, 'Die Gewissensfreiheit und das Gewissen', *Archiv des öffentlichen Rechts* 90/1965, 257–286; A. Podlech, *Das Grundrecht der Gewissensfreiheit und die besonderen Gewaltverhältnisse* (Berlin, 1969), esp. pp. 35ff.

[5] Switzerland: Article 49 Section 5 of the *Bundesverfassung* or Federal Constitution, proviso in favour of 'civic duties'; according to the prevailing doctrine, the bar of public order, of approximately equal significance to general laws, applies to all the basic rights, including freedom of conscience. See F. Fleiner and Z. Giacometti *Schweizerisches Bundesstaatsrecht* (1949), pp. 246ff.; J. F. Aubert, *Traité de droit constitutionnel suisse*, vol. II (Neuchâtel, 1967), pp. 633ff. For a critical view see H. Huber, 'Die Grundrechte in der Schweiz', in *Die Grundrechte*, 2nd ed. (Berlin, 1968), vol.I, p. 207.

Austria: Article 14 Section 2 of the *Bundesverfassungsgesetz* or Federal Constitutional Law, specifying national civic duties. See F. Ermacora, *Handbuch der Grundrechte und Grundfreiheiten* (Vienna, 1963), p. 366f.

the fundamental right of freedom of conscience a more immediate and acute relevance. It calls urgently for considerations of principle as to what is, and can be, meant in substance by the freedom of conscience thus guaranteed. How far can a constitution that sees the state as a democratic embodiment of the rule of law actually guarantee the freedom of conscience without placing itself in jeopardy in the process?

I.

Freedom of conscience is firmly anchored in history, not only in terms of its intellectual foundations, but also in its manifestation as a fundamental right. The principle embodied in it is rightly regarded as the basis of our modern rights of individual liberty—indeed, of the modern concept of liberty itself. So our question concerning the substance of the freedom of conscience guaranteed under Article 4 of the Basic Law cannot be posed in the abstract; it has to be framed with due regard to that intellectual and historical continuity.[6]

1. Both Article 135 of the Weimar Constitution and, arising out of it, Article 4 of the Basic Law go back, in terms of external form and the traditions of constitutional law, to the fundamental right of 'freedom of belief and conscience' found in the constitutions of the nineteenth century.[7] At the time, the substance of that fundamental right was clearly defined, though it is scarcely ascertainable from the wording and certainly not from the order of values embodied in those documents; it can be ascertained only in terms of constitutional history, through the development of freedom of conscience itself. The idea of freedom of conscience originated in the denominational and political disputes of the sixteenth and seventeenth centuries. It first appeared in explicit terms in the 1579 Union of Utrecht and subsequently in the Treaty of Westphalia (1648).[8]

European Convention on Human Rights: Article 9.2, permitting such restrictions as 'are necessary measures in a democratic society in the interest of public safety, public order, health, and morality, and the protection of the rights and liberties of others'; see K. J. Partsch, in *Die Grundrechte*, 2nd ed., vol. I/1, p. 425f. Even in the United States, the 'free exercise' clause of the First Amendment, which guarantees freedom of belief and religious freedom, is understood as valid within the limits of public order. See the Supreme Court decision in the case of *Cantwell v. Connecticut*, 310 US 296 (1940); and H. W. Bayer, in *Zeitschrift für ausländisches öffentliches Recht und Völkerrecht*, 24/1964, p. 204.

[6] Incidentally, this is true of the interpretation of the basic rights in general. Ulrich Scheuner, 'Die Religionsfreiheit im Grundgesetz', *Die Öffentliche Verwaltung* (1967), p. 586; idem, 'Pressefreiheit', *Veröffentlichungen der Vereinigung der Deutschen Staatsrechtslehrer VVDStRL* 24 (1965), pp. 45ff, has rightly pointed out that each individual basic right cannot be understood merely as an outgrowth or specialized application of a general main right of freedom; rather, it derives its specific subject matter from the fact that it is a response to particular threats to freedom and the law, and its substance cannot be defined without consideration of this 'historical-constitutional interpretation'. The interpretation presented here follows this methodological starting point.

[7] See the Bavarian constitution of 1818, IV.9.I; the Württemberg constitution of 1819, Articles 24, 27 Section 1; the Baden constitution of 1818, Article 18; the Grand Duchy of Hesse constitution of 1820, Article 22; the Electorate of Hesse constitution of 1832, Article 30; and the Hanover constitution of 1833, Article 30 Section 1.

[8] In the 1579 Union of Utrecht it is recognized as a public-order institute in the Netherlands. See W. Hamel, 'Glaubens- und Gewissensfreiheit', in *Die Grundrechte*, vol. IV/1 (Berlin, 1960), p. 40; J. Kuhn, *Toleranz und*

As a legal concept, it has always had the sense of a defensive right, enjoyed by the individual, against direct coercion in matters of religion. It related exclusively to questions of belief and religion; hence the term *Glaubens- und Gewissensfreiheit* ('freedom of faith and conscience') that later became standard. This was directed against the sovereign prince's religious ban (*Religionsbann*)[II] and the *ius reformandi*, against which a certain sphere of individual liberty was legally defined and safeguarded. To that extent it is true also of German constitutional development that freedom of conscience was the first fundamental right in the precise sense of a secular right of individual liberty[9] that was due to the individual for his own sake, legally emancipated him from certain obligations, and safeguarded the sphere of liberty it provided against encroachments by the sovereign. The substance and scope of that freedom of conscience were admittedly restricted. In substance it related only to freedom from coercion to adopt or retain a particular belief or denomination, to the right to hold (simple) domestic devotions in accordance with one's own religion, and to the so-called *beneficium emigrationis*, the right to emigrate in order to be able to practise one's religion.[10] Moreover, it extended only to adherents of the three Christian

Offenbarung (Leipzig, 1923), pp. 389ff. In the Treaty of Westphalia: *Instrumentum Pacis Osnabrugense*, V.34. See W. Kahl, *Lehrsystem des Kirchenrechts und der Kirchenpolitik* (Freiburg i. B. and Leipzig, 1894), p. 316f.

II The Religionsbann and the *ius reformandi* are among the main principles of the Peace of Augsburg of 1555, giving secular sovereign powers in the Holy Roman Empire the right to regulate ('reform') religious conditions in their territories. The formula *cuius regio, eius religio* (whose realm, his religion) gives the prince the power to determine one denomination for all inhabitants in his territory (Catholic, Lutheran, later also Calvinist). Those inhabitants who do not agree with the prince's religion have the right to leave the country (*ius emigrandi*). By contrast, following the Peace of Westphalia, the conversion of the prince no longer entailed the forced conversion of all of his subjects. Freedom of conscience, recognized in the Union of Utrecht and in the Treaty of Westphalia, refers to the individual as such and is independent from the ruler, opening the door also to the recognition of rights of religious minorities and religious dissenters.

9 Freedom of conscience as (the first) secular right of individual freedom: M. Heckel, 'Parität', *Zeitschrift der Savigny-Stiftung für Rechtsgeschichte, Kanonistische Abteilung* 49 (1963), p. 350, with a critical evaluation of the process. In the well known controversy prompted by G. Jellinek, *Die Erklärung der Menschen- und Bürgerrechte*, 4th ed. (Tübingen, 1927), the question of the historical origin of the French *Déclaration* of 26 August 1789 and the question of the origin of the principle of the modern rights to liberty and its first concretization were insufficiently distinguished from each other; see R. Schnur (ed.), 'Foreword' in *Zur Geschichte der Erklärung der Menschenrechte* (Darmstadt, 1964), pp. x–xi. As regards the second question at issue here, Jellinek's thesis would still appear to be legally justified: freedom of conscience as an individual right goes beyond class differences to bring the immediate individual–state relationship into play and gives expression—for the first time—to the essential, systematic *priority of the individual* and his aims in life vis-à-vis the political authority or the state. See Carl Schmitt, *Verfassungslehre* (Berlin, 1928), p. 157f [*Constitutional Theory* (Durham, NC, 2008), pp. 197ff.] A quite distinct question is whether the intellectual foundations on the basis of which freedom of conscience as a basic right is possible and its realization promoted are of a religious, reformatory kind or relate to natural law and the law of reason; see the contributions of O. Voßler and G. Ritter in Schnur, *Zur Geschichte der Erklärung der Menschenrechte*, and G. Oestreich, 'Zur Entwicklung der Menschenrechte und Grundfreiheiten', in *Die Grundrechte*, 2nd ed., vol. I/1, pp. 48–57.

10 See *Instrumentum Pacis Osnabrugense*, Article V, sections 34, 35, 37; and Kahl, *Lehrsystem*, pp. 316f. With respect to the right of domestic devotions, a distinction was made between *devotio domestica simplex*—simple domestic devotion, that is, without clergy—and *devotio domestica qualificata*, that is, with the involvement of clergy; only the simple domestic devotion was included in freedom of conscience. On the content and manifestations of the *beneficium emigrationis*, which on the one hand could be used on a person's own initiative in order to enjoy 'full' freedom of religious practice in another territory, and on the other constituted a defence against

denominations recognized in the old Reich (the Holy Roman Empire of the German Nation). It was not enjoyed by the members of denominations or sects that were seen as a threat to the political and religious orders equally; they had no protection against the sovereign prince's religious ban or against his right of expulsion.[11] The guiding principle of the constitution of the Reich with regard to the treatment of matters of religion was parity between the recognized denominations, not toleration or freedom of faith.[12]

The first extension of freedom of conscience beyond these limits took place in Brandenburg-Prussia under the influence of the ideas of the Enlightenment and the law of reason. In practical use from the late seventeenth century onwards, it found explicit recognition in Justice Minister Wöllner's religious edict of 9 July 1788 and subsequently in the famous Articles 1–4 and 7–8 of section II, chapter 11 of the General State Laws for the Prussian States [*Allgemeines Landrecht für die preußischen Staaten*], the first German code of law adopted by the Prussian states, on 5 February 1794. The code guaranteed 'complete' freedom of belief and conscience, not only among the religious parties enjoying legal recognition in the Reich, but also for the sects; it ruled out any kind of harassment or persecution on grounds of religious opinion and with it the sovereign prince's right to deport offenders; and it explicitly guaranteed 'interior' and domestic worship.[13] It was this extended, circumscribed version that henceforth

the sovereign's right to deport—*ius reprobationis*—see ibid., p. 317; J. J. Moser, *Von der Landeshoheit im Geistlichen* (Frankfurt a. M. and Leipzig, 1773, repr. Osnabrück, 1967), pp. 861–867; U. Scheuner, 'Die Ausreisefreiheit in der Verfassungsgeschichte und im Verfassungsrecht Deutschlands', in *Festschrift für Richard Thoma* (Tübingen, 1950), pp. 208ff.

[11] *Instrumentum Pacis Osnabrugense*, VII.2 (at the end); J. J. Moser, *Von der Teutschen Religionsverfassung* (Frankfurt a. M. and Leipzig, 1773, repr. Osnabrück, 1967), pp. 28f., 36f. Moser therefore quite logically distinguished between 'freedom of conscience as such', which he saw wholly in terms of a secular right of liberty, such that 'in matters of religion a man may think and act as he likes, without being hindered therein or punished on that account by the spiritual or secular powers', and the 'restricted and qualified' freedom of conscience obtaining in Germany according to which 'anyone, from the highest to the lowest, may profess the Evangelical Lutheran or Reformed religion or the Roman Catholic religion and nothing may be demanded of such a person that is contrary to the principles of his religion' (ibid., pp. 36–37).

[12] Heckel, in *Zeitschrift der Savigny-Stiftung für Rechtsgeschichte, Kanonistische Abteilung*, 49/1963, p. 350.

[13] *Allgemeines Landrecht für die preußischen Staaten*. Section II, chapter 11:

1: The notions held by the citizens of the state concerning God and divine matters, belief, and personal divine service cannot form the object of coercive laws.
2: Every citizen of the state must be allowed complete freedom of belief and conscience.
3: It is the duty of no one to accept the dictates of the state with regard to his private opinion in religious matters.
4: No one shall be troubled, called to account, ridiculed, or persecuted because of his religious opinions.
7: Every head of household may arrange divine worship in his home as he sees fit.
8: He cannot, however, urge members of another religious party to attend such worship against their will.

For a detailed treatment of the extent and content of this guarantee of freedom of belief and conscience—this was the first time the two had been coupled—see Kahl, *Lehrsystem*, p. 318f.; H. Fürstenau, *Das Grundrecht der Religionsfreiheit* (Leipzig, 1891), p. 77f. The degree to which Prussia (notwithstanding the state's continuing supervision over those churches qualified as religious communities) was ahead of the states of its time is revealed, for example, by a comparison with the Patent of Toleration that Joseph II issued in 1781 for the crown lands of the Habsburg Monarchy. The Patent of Toleration granted the followers of the two Protestant denominations and of the Eastern Orthodox faith a qualified private, but in no way public, right

determined the legal concept of freedom of belief and conscience, notably in the written constitutions of the *Vormärz* period and in those of 1848, and it was in this version that freedom of belief and conscience came to be included among the 'civil rights' *(bürgerliche Rechte)* embodied in Article 16 of the Federal Act *(Bundesakte)* of 1 September 1949.[14] The connection with matters of religion remained inherent in it.

However, the demand for freedom of religious activity went beyond the sphere circumscribed by freedom of conscience. With Prussia again taking the lead, during the course of the nineteenth century many German states—and, with the adoption of the Weimar Constitution in 1919, the whole of Germany[15]—added to freedom of belief and conscience full freedom of worship, private and *public,* for all religious denominations *(Kultusfreiheit)* and freedom of assembly for religious societies *(religiöse Assoziationsfreiheit).* With the recognition of these rights, freedom of belief and conscience as a *separate* fundamental right was naturally—in terms of substance—superseded. Compared with universal freedom of religious practice and freedom of religious assembly, it had no substantial significance of its own beyond the fact that it embodied the logically necessary premise of those freedoms and further reinforced something that had come to be taken for granted alongside them: namely, the prohibition of religious coercion by the state. Yet despite this extensive loss of function it was retained in the constitutional texts as a separate fundamental right. Freedom of belief and conscience figured in the Paulskirche Constitution alongside full freedom of worship and freedom of religious assembly,[16] and in the same way it found a place in the Weimar Constitution. This was due partly to a certain traditional element clinging to constitutional texts in the teeth of altered circumstances of constitutional law; but it was also due to the enormous importance accorded to freedom of conscience in the intellectual movements and political debates of the nineteenth century. This had its roots in the idea of the autonomy of the personality as well as in the conception of man's innate freedom of thought and judgement first elaborated in the thinking of European rationalism from the seventeenth century onwards and developed to particularly striking effect in the philosophy of Kant.[17] In that climate, of course, conscience

to the exercise of religion; the legal prohibition against religious sects remained unchanged. In this regard, the Law of 18 June 1782 (quoted in Ignaz Beidtel, *Untersuchungen über die kirchlichen Zustände in den Kaiserlich-Österreichischen Staaten* (Vienna, 1849), p. 84f. stated: 'Furthermore, if a man, a woman, or whoever reports to a *Oberamt* or *Kreisamt* [regional or country office] as a Deist, Israelite, or a so-called *Lampelbruder* [Protestant], he shall, without further inquiry, be given 24 blows or lashes on his behind and sent home. This shall be repeated as often as he returns to report himself, not because he is a Deist, but because he says he is and he does not know what that means.'

[14] See Kahl, *Lehrsystem,* p. 320f.; Fürstenau, *Das Grundrecht,* pp. 110ff.

[15] For a general survey of this development, see Kahl, *Lehrsystem,* pp. 204–236, 322ff.

[16] See Articles 144 (full freedom of faith and conscience), 145 (communal domestic and public exercise of religion), and 147 (free formation of religious societies).

[17] W. Hamel, 'Gewissen, Gewissensfreiheit II: Rechtlich', in *Evangelisches Staatslexikon,* cols 677–679. See also Hamel in *Die Grundrechte,* vol. IV, pp. 41f., 44; K. Schlaich, *Kollegialtheorie, Kirche, Recht und Staat in der Aufklärung* (Munich, 1969), pp. 156–158. For Kant's theory of the autonomy of the (moral) personality see

and freedom of conscience were placed in a different context. Freed from the connection with religious belief, conscience was set up on its own and seen as the last and highest authority of the autonomous personality. In conscience the individual had his organ of moral awareness, was directly in touch with himself, and laid down his own laws of action.[18] Freedom of conscience therefore meant not only freedom to practise one's own religion—over against the sovereign's *jus reformandi;* it also meant freedom of religion and beyond that a more general freedom of the individual to act and be permitted to conduct himself in accordance with his own law as laid down for him by his conscience.[19] It was this freedom of conscience that the Roman Catholic Church opposed so stubbornly in the nineteenth century and concerning which Karl Marx made his derisively critical remarks.[20]

2. To the extent to which it became prevalent in the intellectual climate of the time, this view inevitably gave rise to a fresh question regarding the substance of freedom of conscience in terms of constitutional law.[21] But such a question was also posed, of course, by the changes in constitutional law implicit in the adoption of the Weimar Constitution. By fundamentally doing away with the religious and ecclesiastical sovereignty of the state, the Weimar Constitution, the residual items in Articles 136ff notwithstanding,[22] deprived freedom of

his *Grundlegung der Metaphysik der Sitten*, ed. K. Vorländer, pp. 57ff., and *Kritik der praktischen Vernunft*, ed. K. Vorländer, p. 39 (thesis IV).

[18] Kant's theory of autonomy and conscience is fundamental here. In addition to the references given in note 16, see esp. the 'Tugendlehre', in *Metaphysik der Sitten*, ed. K. Vorländer, introduction XIIb (p. 242f.) and section 13 (pp. 289ff.). Granted, Kant sees conscience as the 'awareness of an inner court of law in man' that has to think of someone other than itself as the judge of its proceedings. However, that other person appears only as a *postulate;* in order that the phenomenon of conscience (as individual court) may be thought of reasonably, it 'may be a real or merely an ideal person that reason creates for itself' (ibid.). The principle of autonomy, of self-legislation in conscience, is retained (see esp. the note on this subject in section 13 of the 'Tugendlehre', pp. 290–291). For opposition to this concept of conscience, see the critical remarks of Hegel in *Grundlinien*, section 135 (p. 194).

[19] In this sense freedom of conscience was chiefly actualized by philosophical liberalism and particular tendencies of political liberalism and the democratic left. On this subject see the article 'Liberalismus' by Paul Pfizer, Liberal opposition leader in the Württemberg lower house, in C. von Rotteck and C. T. Welcker, *Staatslexikon*, vol. IX (Altona, 1841), pp. 713ff, (716ff.). Various statements were made in the debates about basic rights in the Frankfurt National Assembly; see H. Scholler (ed.), *Die Grundrechtsdiskussion in der Paulskirche.*

[20] See the encyclical *Mirari vos,* issued by Gregory XVI on 15 July 1832 (H. Denzinger, *Enchiridion symbolorum*, 33rd, Freiburg i. B., 1965, p. 549f.); the encyclical *Quanta cura,* issued by Pius IX on 8 December 1864 (ibid., pp. 574ff.); Pius IX's *Syllabus errorum* of 1864, nos 78, 79 (ibid., pp. 577ff.); the encyclical *Libertas praestantissimum*, issued by Leo XIII on 20 June 1888 (ibid., pp. 629ff.); and K. Marx, 'Zur Judenfrage', in *Die Frühschriften*, ed. S. von Landshut (Stuttgart, 1953), p. 197f.

[21] Approaches in this regard appear when the Württemberg Constitution of 1819, on the one hand, guarantees everyone (§27), without distinction of religion, 'untroubled freedom of conscience' (in the traditional sense), while, on the other hand, stipulating in §24 that the state secures every citizen 'freedom of the person, freedom of conscience and thought[!], freedom of property and the freedom to emigrate', and when in the *Lehrbuch des Deutschen Staatsrechts* by Meyer-Anschütz (7th ed., 1914–1919), freedom of religion appears in the systematic classification as a subcategory of the 'freedom of intellectual activity' (ancillary to 'freedom of the press').

[22] G. J. Ebers, 'Religionsgesellschaften', in H. C. Nipperdey (ed.), *Die Grundrechte und Grundpflichten der Reichsverfassung*, vol. II (Berlin, 1930), pp. 362ff., 365; G. J. Ebers, *Staat und Kirche im neuen Deutschland* (Munich,

belief and conscience (in the form in which it had existed hitherto) of its point of reference. That point of reference had been the *ius reformandi* embodied in the religious and ecclesiastical sovereignty of the state, against which freedom of belief and conscience carved out a sphere of individual liberty. The Weimar Constitution excluded that *ius reformandi,* along with the whole idea of an established church, from the realm of possible sovereign rights of the state, making the state a strictly secular polity. The question then inevitably arose of whether freedom of belief and conscience ought not also to be 'secularized'. In other words: should the point of departure for freedom of conscience be provided henceforth not by religious conscience as an organ of belief, but by secular conscience as the seat of ultimate, independently formulated, individual convictions about life, released from its religious role?

There was another thing. The Prussian constitution of 1850 had laid down in its Article 14 that, religious freedom notwithstanding, those state institutions that were associated with religious practice should take the Christian religion as their basis.[23] This retention of its 'Christian foundation' represented a reservation against total neutrality with regard to religion and other worldviews on the part of the state.[III] That reservation, too—which in the states with established churches carried even greater weight than it did in Prussia—was in principle removed by the Weimar Constitution, irrespective of that constitution's retention of a special place for the churches. The state was no longer simply denominationally neutral—that is to say, treating Christian denominations equally and tolerating everything else; it was now, as a matter of principle, neutral with regard to any kind of religious faith.[24] This decision, in redefining the spiritual substance of the state, inevitably pushed things in the same direction of a redefinition of freedom of conscience. Now not only religious belief but any kind of conscientious conviction, regardless of its foundation, must enjoy the protection of freedom of conscience. Furthermore, that decision implicitly brought up to date the freedom to *exercise* conscience, because, in the context of the religiously neutral state, which was committed to no substantial principles of order, special importance attached to safeguarding the individual's freedom to live and act in accordance with the convictions of his own conscience. So there was an

1930), pp. 119ff., 131ff. P. Mikat, 'Kirchen und Religionsgemeinschaften', in *Die Grundrechte*, vol. IV, pp. 126ff. (esp. p. 129), gives the dissenting opinions as well.

[23] On the origin, content, and scope of this provision see G. Anschütz, *Die Verfassungsurkunde für den preußischen Staat* (Berlin, 1912), pp. 260ff.

[III] Note that the principle of 'neutrality with regard to religion and other worldviews' for '*religiöse und weltanschauliche Neutralität des Staates*' is a specific German concept which has been elaborated in German jurisprudence in order to accurately define the character of the secular state. It demands that the state does not identify with any particular religion or worldview and that it does not justify law on religious grounds or grounds associated with other worldviews or comprehensive doctrines. Furthermore, it entails the dissociation of political authority from religious authority, and requires of the state not to privilege religion over nonreligion and one religious creed over another.

[24] Ebers, in Nipperdey, *Die Grundrechte und Grundflichten*, vol. II, p. 363.

intrinsic logic at work when, in the debate in the Weimar National Assembly on the subject of the organization of education, nearly all the parties relied heavily on freedom of conscience to justify their very disparate demands,[25] while that same National Assembly, in adopting virtually without discussion the 'complete freedom of belief and conscience' contained in the Paulskirche Constitution, laid down a fundamental right whose substance was hardly understood at all.

3. The constitutional lawyers of the Weimar period attempted to deal with the problem confronting them, although the 'freedom of belief and conscience' of Article 135 of the Weimar Constitution was never systematically discussed. Their task was made easier by the reservation contained in that same article in favour of the general laws of the state. In the Weimar Constitution the former unity of freedom of belief and freedom of conscience is in part indirectly and in part expressly done away with, and the extension to general freedom of action *in accordance with* religion and conscience is universal. In his *Handbuch des deutschen Staatsrechts* ('Handbook of German Constitutional Law') Gerhard Anschütz defines religious freedom as the freedom in law 'to live in accordance with one's religious, irreligious, or anti-religious convictions, doing everything those convictions require and not doing what they forbid'.[26] This not only extends religious freedom to freedom of action but also neutralizes it to universal freedom of conviction. Hermann Mirbt[27] speaks of the freedom 'to form or not to form one's *Weltanschauung* [worldview]' and 'to voice those convictions and act accordingly'. Stier-Somlo,[28] Giese,[29] and G. J. Ebers[30] distinguish freedom of conscience from freedom of faith and freedom to profess, defining

[25] See the debates in the plenum of the National Assembly, 17th and 18th sessions of 28 February and 3 March 1919 (E. Heilfron, *Die deutsche Nationalversammlung im Jahre 1919* (Berlin, n. d.), vol. II, , pp. 938ff., 1109ff., 25th session of 11 March 1919 (ibid., vol. III, pp. 1641ff.), 59th and 60th sessions of 17 and 18 July 1919 (ibid., vol. VI, pp. 4001ff., 4075ff.). See also the minutes of the constitutional committee of the German National Assembly, 19th and 21st sessions of 1 and 3 April 1919, *passim*, and 42nd session of 18 June 1919, esp. pp. 5, 12.

[26] G. Anschütz, 'Religionsfreiheit', in *Handbuch des deutschen Staatsrechts*, vol. II (Tübingen, 1932), p. 681. For Anschütz, *Religionsfreiheit* was an umbrella term for freedom of faith and conscience, freedom of religious practice, and freedom of religious association. This terminology, which Anschütz makes the basis also of his commentary on the Weimar Constitution, goes back to the commentary on Article 12 of the Prussian Constitution of 1850. Here it was suggested by the wording itself, in that Article 12 guaranteed side by side the freedom to profess religion, the association into religious communities, and the shared domestic and public exercise of religion, and specified for all of these freedoms, in Clause 3 under the summary designation 'Religious freedom', the proviso of the civic and political responsibilities. The three named manifestations of religious freedom thus designate, in ascending order, the various stages of the guarantee of religious freedom as they followed each other substantively and historically; see Gerhard Anschütz, *Preußische Verfassung* (note 23), p. 120f. In his commentary on the Weimar Constitution, Anschütz still defined the freedom of faith and conscience in the sense of a limitation to the right to have and profess—or not to profess—a faith or a worldview; see *Die Verfassung des Deutschen Reiches*, 13th ed. (1933), Note I on Article 135.

[27] H. Mirbt, 'Glaubens- und Gewissensfreiheit', in Nipperdey, *Die Grundrechte und Grundpflichten*, vol. II, p. 328.

[28] F. Stier-Somlo, 'Glaubens-, Gewissens- und Bekenntnisfreiheit', in *Handwörterbuch der Rechtswissenschaft*, vol. III (Berlin and Leipzig, 1928), p. 21.

[29] F. Giese, *Die Verfassung des Deutschen Reiches*, 8th ed. (Berlin, 1931), Article 135, n. 1 (p. 286).

[30] Ebers, *Staat und Kirche*, p. 151.

the former as the freedom 'to act in accordance with the moral conscience'—in other words, as a fundamental right to freedom of moral action.

This new and broader interpretation—one might almost say, 'redefinition'—had no practical consequence at first, the guarantee of freedom of conscience being embedded in the reservation of general laws. The liberal statist Anschütz[31] contented himself with the striking formula '*Staatsgesetz geht vor Religionsgebot*' ('The law of the state takes precedence of the dictates of religion'); only laws that were directed against freedom of religion as such were to be excluded—which was of course where the real problem lay, given the redefinition of the substance of the fundamental right. Hermann Mirbt[32] took a more urgent view of the aspect of the matter that has to do with principle and goes back to the problem of the origin of the modern state. This is the fact that not only the state but also religious conviction is given the right to determine outward behaviour, while the state cannot lay down the substance of a religious conviction. Mirbt held that the only possible recourse for the state was—and the words sound as if they were carefully chosen—to 'stress and enforce its right of definition and maintain its indifference in the face of the resultant conflicts with religious beliefs and doctrines' (!);[33] nevertheless, he added that in individual conflicts an attempt must be made 'to bind together the fundamental right of freedom of religion and the fact that everyone is subject to the state legal system in such a way that the existence of neither is placed in jeopardy'.[34]

So constitutional law scholarship in the Weimar period was already being pushed in the direction of the same questions and problems as govern the discussion on the subject of freedom of conscience today. The continuity of the questions and of the kinds of argument used—the historical determinant, as it were—is stronger than it looks at first sight. The reason lies in the matter at issue. Freedom of conscience has accompanied the modern state from the outset; faced with different historical and political situations, the principle of individual liberty implicit in it strives ever more successfully to find fresh embodiments.

II.

This background makes it relevant to ask how far Article 4.I of the Basic Law took over the substance and meaning of Article 135 of the Weimar Constitution, handing down to us unchanged the problems of interpretation that the constitutional lawyers of the Weimar period perceived but in no way solved, and how far Article 4 of the Basic Law gave fresh emphases to freedom of conscience or endowed it with a new and farther-reaching substance.

[31] G. Anschütz, *Die Verfassung des Deutschen Reiches*, 13th ed. (Bern), n. 3 on Article 135.

[32] Mirbt, in Nipperdey, *Die Grundrechte und Grundpflichten*, p. 350f.

[33] Ibid., p. 351.

[34] Ibid., p. 350.

1. If we look first at external indications, we are struck by the fact that Article 4 of the Basic Law has been uncoupled from the provisions regarding the churches and religious societies and clearly stresses a right of individual freedom due to everyone.[IV] The wording, which differs from that of Article 135 of the Weimar Constitution, makes explicit mention of freedom of philosophical creed as well and is aimed not simply at freedom of faith and conscience, but at the *inviolability* of that freedom—in other words, presumably at a special kind of unconditionality. That accords with the absence of the reservation in favour of general laws contained in the Weimar Constitution. Finally, Article 4.III adds the right to refuse military service, basing it not on belief *and* conscience, but on conscience alone. All these things point to a new independence of status for and strengthening of this fundamental right, to a general agreement with the principle of neutrality with regard to religion and other worldviews, and accordingly, in conjunction with the material link between 4.I and 4.III, to an independent guarantee of freedom of conscience alongside freedom of faith and freedom to profess—on the basis, be it noted, of a concept of conscience that is no longer religious but purely secular.

However, we should not place too high a value on such indications alone. That would be to fall prey to the danger of postulating and interpreting the constitution as a kind of legal code, which it is not, and overlooking what at the technical level is its inevitably incomplete and fragmentary nature, as well as the specific manner in which it has been influenced by the historical and political circumstances of its development.[35] If we want to avoid the risk of being misled by accidents of historical development, the interpretative significance of such indications can more fittingly be derived from the extent to which those accidents coincide with the basic normative impulses of the constitution and the constituent authority—what Carl Schmitt calls the fundamental decisions that mould the constitution.[36] One such basic normative impulse that finds repeated expression in the Basic Law, and for which there is evidence in the debates, concerns the relationship between citizen and state that interests us here. It is the recourse to the classical rights of freedom and to the principle of freedom embodied in the liberal *Rechtsstaat* in response to the fundamental infringements of liberty that took place during the National Socialist period.[37]

[IV] Article 4 Basic Law: (1) Freedom of faith and of conscience, and freedom to profess a religious or philosophical creed, shall be inviolable. (2) The undisturbed practice of religion shall be guaranteed. (3) No person shall be compelled against his conscience to render military service involving the use of arms. Details shall be regulated by federal law. (Translated by Christian Tomuschat and David P. Currie, revised by Christian Tomuschat and Donald P. Kommers in cooperation with the Language Service of the German Bundestag, see https://www.gesetze-im-internet.de/Teilliste_translations.html).

[35] See E.-W. Böckenförde, *Die Organisationsgewalt im Bereich der Regierung* (Berlin, 1964), p. 17, and in *Die öffentliche Verwaltung*, 1966, p. 35r.

[36] C. Schmitt, *Verfassungslehre*, 4th ed., Berlin, 1965, pp. 20ff. (esp. p. 23f.) [English: *Constitutional Theory* (see note 8), pp. 75ff.]. See also H. J. Wolff, 'Rechtsgrundsätze und verfassungsgestaltende Grundentscheidungen als Rechtsquellen', in *Gedächtnisschrift für Walter Jellinek* (Munich, 1955), pp. 48ff.

[37] For a thorough treatment see H. von Mangoldt, 'Einleitung zum Grundrechtsabschnitt', *Das Bonner Grundgesetz, Kommentar* (Frankfurt a. M. and Berlin, 1953), pp. 34ff. Von Mangoldt was chairman of the

The state envisaged by the Basic Law exists for the sake of individual liberty and security.[38] Its prime objective is to guarantee rights of individual liberty that are affirmed as human rights antecedent to the state; its duty is to respect and safeguard the dignity of man.[39] In concrete terms this basic definition leads to a reinforcement of the distributive principle embodied in the *Rechtsstaat*;[40] all fundamental rights have the direct force of law (Article 1.III); they are also binding on the legislature, and that obligation is subject to judicial control (93.I); curtailment of them is lawful only to a limited extent and only as expressly permitted (19.I–II). A general reservation in favour of public security, morality [*Sittlichkeit*], and health, as proposed by the Herrenchiemsee draft, was expressly rejected in the debates;[41] the sole admissible statutory encroachments were those which, after very careful consideration, were specified under each fundamental right; the sphere of individual liberty was defined (in accordance with the presumption of freedom implicit in the rule of law) as being in principle unlimited, while the possibility of statutory encroachment was held to be in principle limited, measurable, and controllable.[42] The talk was in fact of encroachments and limitations, not of values and an order of values, and individual rights to liberty were emphatically understood as *leges speciales* to the universal right to liberty enshrined in Article 2.[43] In line with this basic intention, those spheres of liberty that had been particularly abused and jeopardized by the state during the National Socialist years were granted special protection against possibilities of encroachment; they were to be 'inviolable' and 'indefeasible'.

It is consistent with this fundamental constitutional decision in favour of individual liberty (and I must ask the reader's indulgence if I am perhaps taking up too much of his or her time with matters that may be obvious, but with the intrusion of the philosophy of values and value calculations into our

Committee for Questions of Principle of the Parliamentary Council, which among other things discussed the basic rights section; see also his report to the plenary of the Parliamentary Council on the fundamental rights section, in *Parlamentarischer Rat, Schriftlicher Bericht zum Entwurf des Grundgesetzes für die Bundesrepublik Deutschland*, 1949, pp. 5 ff.

[38] See Article 1 Section I of the Herrenchiemsee draft and the relevant opinion in the *Bericht über den Verfassungskonvent auf Herrenchiemsee* (Munich, 1950), p. 21 (3).

[39] Article 1 of the Basic Law to that extent reflects a basic decision by the constitutional authority that—regardless of the question of how far direct legal claims may be derived from Article 1 itself—is an important pointer in any event, but particularly as regards the interpretation of the basic rights section and the individual guarantees conveyed therein. Another authority who takes this line is von Mangoldt, *Das Bonner Grundgesetz, Kommentar*, p. 43f.

[40] On this principle see Schmitt, *Verfassungslehre*, § 12 (pp. 125–128) [*Constitutional Theory* (note 8), pp. 169ff.]; Z. Giacometti, *Allgemeine Lehren des rechtsstaatlichen Verwaltungsrechts* (Zürich, 1960), pp. 1–8, 10f.

[41] K. B. von Doemming, R. W. Füsslein, and W. Matz, 'Entstehungsgeschichte der Artikel des Grundgesetzes', *Jahrbuch des öffentlichen Rechts*, new ser., 1 (1950), p. 178; von Mangoldt, *Das Bonner Grundgesetz, Kommentar*, p. 36f., and 'Parlamentarischer Rat, Schriftlicher Bericht', p. 5r.

[42] See C. Schmitt, 'Inhalt und Bedeutung des zweiten Hauptteils der Reichsverfassung', *Verfassungsrechtliche Aufsätze* (Berlin, 1958), p. 208f.

[43] Von Mangoldt, *Das Bonner Grundgesetz, Kommentar*, p. 38, and 'Parlamentarischer Rat, Schriftlicher Bericht', p. 6f.

interpretation of fundamental rights, and with the Federal Constitutional Court having elevated disregard for considerations of historical origin to the status of a tenet, there has sometimes been a danger that the simple truths of 1949 might be forgotten) that freedom of faith, freedom of conscience, and freedom to profess are guaranteed as inviolable and unconditional in Article 4.1 of the Basic Law. Following the myriad threats to this very freedom in the Third Reich, a sphere of 'natural' individual liberty beyond the reach of any kind of encroachment by the state was now to be guaranteed and safeguarded. 'Faith, conscience, and conviction are free', it says—not without a certain pathos—in many of the constitutions of the individual German states.[44] The words give telling expression to the concurrence of views that was more taken for granted than spelled out in the debates.[45] The individual was to be undisturbed and inviolable in what constituted the inner core of his personality. The conflict so long experienced between the commands of the state and the dictates of God and conscience was no longer to take place. To put it the other way around, the pointed maxim of Gerhard Anschütz—'The citizen is not permitted to give the God in whom he believes greater obedience than he gives the state'[46]—was no longer to serve as a guide for interpreting freedom of faith and conscience. Reservation of general laws and limitations generally were discussed *only* in connection with Article 4.II with respect to the guarantee of public religious practice,[47] and even there the adoption of a limiting clause was eventually turned down. This too was dictated by a normative intention directed at the Third Reich, although it was agreed that certain restrictions (such as a police ban on processions when there

[44] Article 4 of the Bremen constitution; Article 9 of the Hesse constitution; Article 4 of the Saarland constitution; Article 6 Section 1 of the Herrenchiemsee draft. Article 8 of the Rhineland-Palatinate constitution is similar.

[45] It is striking that in the deliberations of the constitutions of the *Länder*, there was hardly ever a debate about guaranteeing freedom of conscience (freedom of faith and freedom of conscience); there was agreement on this from the outset. This consensus can be explained by the shared consciousness of the time (specifically, the intent to preclude threats to liberty as experienced during the Nazi period), which does not rule out that the various political and ideological [*weltanschauliche*] groups sometimes associated different substantive ideas with the notion of freedom of conscience. See, for example, the 'Beratungen des Verfassungsausschusses der bayerischen verfassunggebenden Landesversammlung', *Stenographische Berichte*, vol. 1, p. 208 (9. Sitzung v. 31.7.1946). Likewise, freedom of conscience and the concept of conscience were discussed only briefly in the Parliamentary Council's Committee on Basic Questions; see on this the 'Protokoll' of the 8th and 24th sessions of the Committee on Basic Questions on 7 October and 23 November 1948, respectively. In the 24th session, the MP Dr. Süsterhenn made the comment that when it comes to freedom of belief, freedom of conscience, and freedom to profess a religious or philosophical creed, 'internal decisions' were in play ('Protokoll', p. 4). Which was then picked up by Chairman von Mangoldt with these words: 'We have, first of all, faith and conscience. That is the internal part. We contrast this internal part to the external part, profession [of faith]' (ibid., p. 5). In what way and to what extent this 'internal part', which constitutes the factual situation of conscience, should be protected—of essential importance to the reach of freedom of conscience—is not discussed at all. On the genesis of Article. 4 of the Basic Law, see also Heinrich Scholler (note 4), pp. 110–115.

[46] Anschütz, *Die Verfassungsurkunde*, pp. 229f.

[47] Parliamentary Council, Committee for Questions of Principle, minutes of the 24th session of 23 November 1948, pp. 12–18. Dr Süsterhenn spoke against adoption of a limiting clause; the chairman, Dr. von Mangoldt, spoke for a proviso in favour of general laws.

was a risk of spreading an epidemic) should remain admissible.[48] If we take seriously this basic normative decision, and the conclusions drawn from it, by the constituent authority (and I see no interpretative principle that might dispense interpreters of the constitution from doing so), the interpretation hinted at above emerges as the correct one. The old, congruous concept of freedom of belief and conscience, which had already become problematic in the Weimar Constitution, has indeed been abandoned, and freedom of conscience is guaranteed as a *separate* fundamental right, in addition to freedom of religion and freedom to profess, on the basis of a universal concept of conscience that is neutral with regard to religious or philosophical boundaries. It represents a contradiction of the normative intention of Article 4.I of the Basic Law and of its proven defensive function with regard to the concrete threats to freedom experienced during the National Socialist period to understand it, as Hamel does,[49] as no more than a guarantee of the freedom of the religious or philosophical belief that has its organ in conscience. This is particularly so when the concept of professing [a religion] is formed and realized in the way he describes.[50] In that case the relationship between the various fundamental rights guaranteed in Article 4.I–II is such that they are independent per se but may in practice interlock. The exercise of freedom of faith, freedom to profess, or freedom of worship need not but may (in a particular case) constitute an exercise of freedom of conscience.

2. That raises the question of the *substance* of this independently guaranteed freedom of conscience. It does not seem possible to restrict the freedom of conscience guaranteed under Article 4.I to the so-called *forum internum* and to exclude from it freedom to act on the dictates of conscience.[51] It is admittedly

48 Ibid., p. 12f.; von Doemming, Füsslein, and Matz, in *Jahrbuch des öffentlichen Rechts*, new ser., 1/1950–1951, p. 74f.

49 Hamel, in *Die Grundrechte*, vol. IV, pp. 37–110 (esp. pp. 56, 60ff.). As here, R. Herzog, 'Die Freiheit des Gewissens und der Gewissensverwirklichung', *Deutsches Verwaltungsblatt* (1969), p. 718; Podlech, *Das Grundrecht der Gewissensfreiheit*, pp. 21ff.

50 Hamel, in *Die Grundrechte*, vol. IV, p. 56. Hamel, proceeding on the basis of a value interpretation of the fundamental rights, sees freedom to profess *(Bekenntnisfreiheit)* as existing only 'in respect of professions of faith in absolute powers'. He therefore—quite logically—denies it to sceptics or nihilists. This interpretation, which proceeds from the assumption that a fundamental right has 'a function in the building of the community ... only if and because a value, a common good, finds expression in a fundamental right', causes the constitutional substance of freedom of the fundamental right, which contains primarily a legal exclusion vis-à-vis encroachments by the state and attempts at exerting influence, to disappear. The state becomes the judge and decider of whether or not a worldview is a 'profession', a 'profession of faith in absolute powers', and so on, and whether or not the exercise of the fundamental right still 'manifests a common value'; this no longer guarantees freedom, but only value-laden freedom with the state in charge of defining what constitutes value. Hamel was already opposed by A. Podlech, 'Der Gewissensbegriff im Rechtsstaat', *Archiv des öffentlichen Rechts* 88 (1963), pp. 185–221. Hamel's counter-criticism, 'Die Gewissensfreiheit im Grundgesetz. Eine Erwiderung', *Archiv des öffentlichen Rechts* 89 (1964), pp. 322–335, failed to touch on the decisive point of the controversy.

51 But see Zippelius, in *Bonner Kommentar*, Article 4, margin no. 44; R. Thoma, 'Über die Grundrechte im Grundgesetz für die Bundesrepublik Deutschland', in H. Wandersleb (ed.), *Recht, Staat, Wirtschaft*, vol. III (Düsseldorf, 1951), p. 17f. H. von Mangoldt and H. H. Klein, *Das Bonner Grundgesetz*.vol. I (Frankfurt a. M. and Berlin, 1957), Article 4, n. III.1 (p. 218), is less clear-cut.

tempting to adopt some such restrictive interpretation in order to get round the problem of the absence of reservation and the absence of limitations in Article 4.1. If freedom of conscience is a separate fundamental right, that problem can no longer be solved satisfactorily by way of Article 136 of the Weimar Constitution. It must further be admitted that this reduced freedom of conscience (trimmed down to 'freedom of thought in matters of conscience') would not merely be safeguarding something not subject to the law,[52] since modern technological civilization possesses external means of destroying or incapacitating conscience as *forum internum*. But, if the freedom of conscience of Article 4.1 is to retain any real significance, as intended, conscience cannot be separated from the ability to act in conformity with conscience. Otherwise it would be reduced to a level that any dictator might guarantee, provided only that he refrained from using Orwellian methods. It is too simple to solve the problem of limitations wittingly posed in Article 4 by means of an interpretation that suppresses the problem from the outset.[53] From its earliest beginnings as a legal concept, freedom of conscience has always been oriented towards the freedom to *act in conformity with* conscience. In the sixteenth and seventeenth centuries, freedom of conscience covered not only matters of personal faith, but also a certain minimum context for the practice of that faith in the form of domestic devotions *(Hausandacht)*. The principle inherent in it continued to push it in the direction of further private or public forms of practical activity, and eventually all the way to complete freedom of worship. For J. J. Maser, writing in the late eighteenth century, freedom of conscience also included the freedom to be able to live in accordance with one's notions of religion.[54] Indeed, it was precisely that practical freedom that made it a problem to extend freedom of conscience to sects and to non-Christians, Jews in particular.[55] And in the nineteenth century, when the state's claim to sovereignty reached its fullest extent, the reservation

[52] To that extent the criticism directed by Scholler, *Die Freiheit*, p. 131, at the interpretation of freedom of conscience as a freedom (only) of the *forum internum* is mistaken.

[53] Yet that is what Zippelius does in *Bonner Kommentar*, Article 4, margin nos. 42–44.

[54] This freedom is contained in Moser's definition of freedom of conscience: 'and nothing may be demanded of such a person that is contrary to the principles of his religion' *(Von der Teutschen Religionsverfassung*, p. 37). It was in any case predicated in German political and ecclesiastical jurisprudence as a component of freedom of conscience, which is why, conversely, freedom of conscience was not lightly granted to adherents of other faiths. On this point see M. Heckel, *Staat und Kirche nach den Lehren der evangelischen Juristen Deutschlands in der ersten Hälfte des 17. Jahrhunderts* (Munich, 1968), pp. 63 ff., 168 ff.; Schlaich, 'Kollegialtheorie', pp. 82–84, 154–156.

[55] The granting of freedom of conscience to Christian sects and Jews therefore proceeded with special legal provisions that enabled the persons thus tolerated to live in accordance with their 'notions of religion' *(Religionsbegriffen)*. The Prussia of the *Allgemeines Landrecht* (5 February 1794), for example, exempted Mennonites and Quakers from military service, exempted sectarians and Jews from the prescribed form of the oath *(Allgemeine Gerichtsordnung*, 1.10.317–351), respected Sabbath observance and the Jewish form of marriage *(Edikt betreffend die bürgerlichen Verhältnisse der Juden in dem Preußischen Staate*, 11 March 1812, sections 24–25, in *Gesetzsammlung*, 3rd ed., vol. I, Berlin, 1812/13, p. 17), and forbade any direct coercion of an action contrary to a person's notions of religion *(Allgemeines Landrecht*, §§ 30, 31, II, II). The basis of this far-reaching tolerance was, on the one hand, a reason-based theory of the state which limited the state to worldly purposes and in so doing accorded a special rank to individual freedom and security, and, on the other hand, the notion and confidence that all religions were in essential agreement in their teachings about the obligations of the

inserted into individual constitutions in favour of civic and political obligations confirmed the connection in the very act of negating it.[56] [V]

The possibilities of conflict between law and conscience remained slight, of course, because the state still saw itself in Christian terms and because of the consensus among the Christian denominations with regard to social morality. If it follows logically upon the transition from the old freedom of religion and conscience to freedom of conscience pure and simple (a transition begun under the Weimar Constitution and completed by the Basic Law) that the possibilities of conflict between the law of the state and the exercise of individual conscience have increased, the problem to which this gives rise is still no reason to turn the looked-for extension of freedom of conscience into its opposite by reducing it to the realm of personal feeling.[57] So the freedom of conscience guaranteed by Article 4 of the Basic Law covers not only the freedom to possess a conscience but also the freedom not to have the state—or, to be more precise (following Podlech[58]), the public authority acting in a sovereign manner—keep one from acting in accordance with the dictates and prohibitions of that conscience.[59]

3. This of course raises the problem of how far that kind of freedom can be guaranteed *unconditionally.* Does unconditional freedom of conscience not logically entail relinquishing the validity of the general legal order to the citizen's

individual towards his fellow citizens, that is, they contained the duties of natural morality. On this see above all Gottlieb Suarez, *Vorträge über Recht und Staat* (Cologne and Opladen, 1960), pp. 53–54.

[56] Anschütz (*Die Verfassungsurkunde*, pp. 194ff., and *Die Verfassung*, comment on Article 135) included under freedom of belief and conscience *(Bekenntnisfreiheit)* the right to promote and criticize religious beliefs, the right to choose (free of state interference) what sort of religious education one's children should receive, freedom to decide whether to receive or to give religious instruction, and later also the right (under state law) to secede from the church.

[V] Böckenförde discusses in detail the nineteenth-century legal status of German Jews with regard to civil rights and duties, in 'The Persecution of the German Jews as a Civic Betrayal', Chapter XIII of volume I of this edition, pp. 309–317.

[57] Wolfgang Keim, *Schule und Religion* (Hamburg, 1967), p. 121, makes the crucial point: 'Conscience that may only make decisions for itself without being able to act them out in the world must atrophy in the same way as faith that may not be professed... Conscience is essentially something lived out.' Also insightful is the discussion of freedom of conscience in Hermann von Mangoldt (see note 43), comment 2 on Article 4, which—picking up on his observations in the Parliamentary Council (see above note 51)—posits conscience as the 'internal part', but then almost automatically arrives at its extension into the realm of action: 'What shall be secured by constitutional law is the right to profess a religious faith and to act in accordance with one's moral conscience'). This is also an indication of how little the sporadic statements (quoted above note 51) about conscience as the 'internal part' can be interpreted as the desire of the creators of the constitution in the direction of guaranteeing merely the *forum internum.*

[58] Podlech, *Das Grundrecht der Gewissensfreiheit,* p. 41.

[59] That is the prevailing view in the literature today, though the extent of this freedom of exercise is variously determined. See, for example, von Mangoldt and Klein, *Das Bonner Grundgesetz,* note III.1 on Article 4 (not unequivocal); Hamel, in *Die Grundrechte,* 1st ed., vol. IV, p. 52, and in *Evangelisches Staatslexikon,* col. 682; Geiger, *Gewissen, Ideologie, Widerstand, Nonkonformismus,* pp. 67f., 72f.; Arndt, in *Neue juristische Wochenschrift,* 1965 (p. 2195), 1966 (pp. 2204f.), 1968 (pp. 979f.); U. Scheuner, 'Die Religionsfreiheit im Grundgesetz', *Die öffentliche Verwaltung,* 1967, p. 586f.; Luhmann, in *Archiv des öffentlichen Rechts,* 90/1965, pp. 257f.; Keim, *Schule und Religion,* p. 121; H. Weber, 'Ersatzdienstverweigerung aus Gewissengründen', *Neue juristische Wochenschrift,* 1968, p. 1610; Podlech, *Das Grundrecht der Gewissensfreiheit,* pp. 35ff.; Scholler, in *Die öffentliche Verwaltung,* 1969, p. 528f.; Herzog, in *Deutsches Verwaltungsblatt,* 1969, p. 719f.

private judgement of conscience, thereby de facto abolishing it? Does it not take the *quis judicabit*, which is indispensable for the state's system of peace, from the state and the totality represented in it and return it to the individual, thereby stripping the organs of the state of their capacity to act and their authority, and eventually dissolving the state itself? Does that not leave only two alternatives: either subjecting freedom of conscience to the reservation of the general laws, irrespective of the intention of the creators of the constitution, or restricting its substance from the outset, unless one wants to impute to the Basic Law the intention of promptly dissolving the state it brought into being?

There are two things to be said about this before we go any further. One is that freedom can never, as legal freedom, be absolute and unrestricted; part of the definition of freedom is that it shall be capable of existing alongside the freedom of others. Absolute, unrestricted freedom means only absolute power—power over other people. The second thing to be said is that no constitutional norm may be interpreted in such a way as to offer a legal argument for overthrowing the constitution itself. An interpretation of that kind would be a logical contradiction.

That said, however, the crucial question is whether an interpretation of freedom of conscience that follows the intention of the constituent authority in aiming to protect the inviolability of conscience as far as possible, and that accordingly sets the bounds of freedom of conscience not at general laws or at public order in the traditional sense, but very much farther down the line really does, as many people fear, imply the dissolution of the state and of the rule of law, or, instead, is part of the logic of modern political theory of the state. In terms of the concept of the state that lies at the heart of the liberal *Rechtsstaat*, there can be little doubt that the second answer is the correct one. According to that concept, the state has its purpose or ratio *(Umwillen)* primarily in guaranteeing and safeguarding the human rights of the individual and in securing his liberty and property.[60] Conscience, as the innermost core of the individual's personality and liberty, is a given fact as far as the state is concerned; it is 'inviolable' and therefore to be respected as far as possible.

However, even independently of that, anyone who goes back to modern political theory of the state pure and simple will reach no other conclusion. One of the constituent principles of the modern state is the principle of non-identification or neutrality, as Herbert Krüger has highlighted again.[61] As freedom of conscience stands at the beginning of the freedom of the individual,

[60] Stated in principle in Article. 2 of the *Declaration des droits de l'homme et du citoyen* of 4 August 1789; systematically developed in Schmitt, *Verfassungslehre*, p. 125f. [*Constitutional Theory*, p. 169f.], and *Verfassungsrechtliche Aufsätze*, p. 192.

[61] H. Krüger, *Allgemeine Staatslehre* (Stuttgart, 1964), pp. 178–184. See also the different emphasis of M. Heckel, *Staat, Kirche, Kunst* (Tübingen, 1968), pp. 208ff.; K. Schlaich, 'Zur weltanschaulichen und konfessionellen Neutralität des Staates', *Essener Gespräche zum Thema Staat und Kirche* 4 (1970), pp. 9–43. See also *Entscheidungen des Bundesverfassungsgerichts*, 12, 45 (54), and 19, 206 (216). For the background in terms of intellectual history, see C. Schmitt, 'Das Zeitalter der Neutralisierungen und Entpolitisierungen', *Der Begriff des Politischen*, 3rd ed. (Berlin, 1963), pp. 79–95. Ernst-Wolfgang Böckenförde, 'Die Entstehung des Staates als Vorgang der Säkularisation', in *Säkularisation und Utopie. Ebracher Studien* (Stuttgart, 1967), pp. 75–94. Included in this volume as Chapter V, 'The Rise of the State as a Process of Secularization'.

non-identification (neutrality) stands at the beginning of the modern state; the two things correspond. By progressively dismantling existing identifications, the state paved the way for individual freedom and became literally the common house of all its subjects and citizens. So it is from nonidentification that it very largely draws its legitimacy. However, non-identification consists not only in the fact that the state makes no special feature and no particular moment the substance of its universality, but also in the fact that specialness is able to develop *qua* specialness, having been set free to do so. Non-identification refers not only to an objective neutrality (with respect to demands for identification of religious, ideological, or social provenance) but also, from the individual's point of view, to an encompassing, open neutrality such that, to use Krüger's words, the individual 'knows himself to be untouchable and secure within his state in his individuality as an intellectual and moral personality'.[62] It is this very circumstance—namely, that the individual, faced with unreasonable demands on the part of the state, can feel himself safe in his individuality, in his intellectual and moral personality, and hence particularly in his conscience—that gives the state its authority to command its citizens' absolute loyalty and indeed obedience, to cite Krüger once more.[63]

Thus the state's respect for conscience, the recognition of its inviolability, and the refusal, in instances of conflict, to 'offend' conscience by demanding a *sacrificium conscientiae* do not mean the dissolution of the state and its binding power of decision; rather, they are the precondition and legitimation of the state and its binding power. It is in fact in venturing to the furthermost limits—of seeming weakness—that the state gains its full reality and superiority.

It is open to question, of course, whether in a democracy, which from the outset derives decisions of state from the participation and consent of its citizens, this line of argument does not lose its stringency and justification. In terms of the democratic principle of everyone playing a part in decisions binding on everyone,[64] it would indeed be logical to make every individual without exception subject to those decisions; anything else would mean departing from the democratic identity of all citizens and establishing a privilege. However, a liberal democracy committed to the rule of law, which is the kind of state

[62] Krüger, *Allgemeine Staatslehre*, p. 183. See also Heckel, *Staat, Kirche, Kunst*, p. 208f. The way Krüger expresses himself makes it clear that he, too, is ultimately talking about an *encompassing* neutrality and generality that does not exclude the individual in his peculiarity and uniqueness, but includes and involves him. He rightly points out that the most effective affirmation of the state proceeds from 'confidence in the untouchability of peculiarity' by the state (*Allgemeine Staatslehre*, p. 181). Of course, a neutrality in this sense can no longer be distancing where the individual specialness, in order to be able to unfold as specialness, is dependent on entering into institutions that are (today) sustained and guided by the state, which is the case above all in the areas of upbringing and schooling. Here neutrality must present itself differently, as the guarantee of the possibility for specialness to unfold itself also in the public sphere. Very fruitful for a further discussion of the problem is Adalbert Podlech's distinction between 'polity [*Gemeinwesen*]' as the totality of the citizens, and 'state' as the bureaucratically organized system of (sovereign) decision making (note 4, pp. 78ff.).

[63] Krüger, *Allgemeine Staatslehre*, p. 184.

[64] Pithily expressed by J.-J. Rousseau in *Du contrat social*, 1.6. See also I. Fetscher, *Rousseaus politische Philosophie*, 2nd ed. (Neuwied, 1968), section 8 (esp. pp. 96ff.), and pp. 121f., 135ff.

in which the Basic Law places its faith, derives its justification and its authority not solely from the democratic principle of participation, but also—if not primarily—from the liberal principle of the guaranteeing and safeguarding of individual liberty, a principle that modifies the democratic principle and limits its scope.[65] For the state of the Basic Law, therefore, the argument advanced above retains its relevance.

4. Of course, even a state legal order that respects conscience in this way, guaranteeing its 'inviolability', cannot avoid setting out firm limits that may not be overstepped in the exercise of conscience. It will not, however, find them in general laws[66] [VI] or public order (seen in terms of the law governing the police);[67] nor is the much-cited *Wertordnung des Grundgesetzes* (order of value

[65] Against the many attempts at harmonization on the part of modern constitutional law theory and contemporary political science, it must be reaffirmed that liberalism and democracy are by no means identical in respect to their underlying principle, even though they have a shared field. The principle of the participation of all in political decision-making and in the exercise of the power of the state, that is, the freedom of democratic participation, by no means guarantees ipso facto the freedom of the individual in the sense of individual self-determination. The latter requires the binding determination of the limits of the democratic exercise of power and of majority decision. On this, see, for example, Adolf Arndt, *Neue Juristische Wochenschrift* (1966), p. 2206.

[66] In addition to Thoma, in Wandersleb, *Recht, Staat, Wirtschaft*, vol. III, p. 18, where admittedly this is merely stated rather than argued ('It is of course beyond doubt that ...'), see above all von Mangoldt and Klein, *Das Bonner Grundgesetz*, Article 4, n. III.5 (vol. I, p. 220). See also the judgments of the state supreme courts *(Oberlandesgerichte)*—principally in cases of conscientious objection to alternative service—based on Article 136 Section 1 of the Weimar Constitution: Oberlandesgericht Stuttgart, 8 February 1963 (*Neue juristische Wochenschrift*, 1963, p. 776); Oberlandesgericht Karlsruhe, 25 May 1964 (*Juristenzeitung*, 1964, p. 761); Oberlandesgericht Hamburg, 22 July 1964 (*Monatsschrift für deutsches Recht*, 1965, p. 63); Oberlandesgericht Cologne, 23 June 1965 (*Neue juristische Wochenschrift*, 1965, p. 1448).

[VI] 'Alternative service' in note 66 refers to the mandatory civilian service, set up in 1961, which has to be carried out in case of objection to military service on reasons of conscience. Conscientious objection to military service is guaranteed in Article 4 Section 3 Basic Law: 'No person shall be compelled against his conscience to render military service involving the use of arms. Details shall be regulated by a federal law.' In 2010, the alternative service was suspended in accordance with the suspension of military service and Germany now has an exclusively professional army. In April 1985, during Böckenförde's tenure on the Federal Constitutional Court, the Second Senate affirmed the constitutionality of a law that made the civil service alternative for conscientious objectors longer by five months than the standard military service. Böckenförde, together with judge Mahrenholz, dissented, arguing that the law violated equal treatment for conscientious objectors and treated the right to conscientious objection as a mere interest to be balanced against the state's countervailing interest in maintaining a battle-ready fighting force. As a result of that balancing, as Böckenförde and Mahrenholz wrote, 'the constitution loses the precision of content that makes it possible truly to apply the constitution to the underlying facts; it merely reflects the state of tension without itself containing a decisive norm for its resolution. The result is that there must be a balancing between the elements in tension, which are no longer normatively trumped by the constitution ... the validity and force of constitutional limitations on the exercise of state authority, which are contained in the fundamental rights, are thus lastingly transformed.' BVerfGE, 69, 1 (here p. 63) (1985). On this, see Justin Collings, 'Ernst-Wolfgang Böckenförde on the Federal Constitutional Court', in Mirjam Künkler and Tine Stein (eds.), *Understanding Böckenförde*, forthcoming.

[67] This is predominantly the case in Swiss constitutional law, which sees 'public order' generally as an immanent limit on guarantees provided under the basic rights. See W. Burckhardt, *Kommentar der Schweizerischen Bundesverfassung*, 3rd ed. (Bern, 1932), pp. 443, 446f.; Fleiner and Giacometti, *Schweizerisches Bundesstaatsrecht*, p. 330; Aubert, *Traite de droit constitutionnel suisse*, vol. II, p. 633; and, for a critical view, Huber, in *Die Grundrechte*, 2nd ed., vol. I, p. 207.

of the Basic Law) any more appropriate as a starting-point.[VII] Apart from the inherent irrationality of values and the absence of a rationally recognizable and debatable scale of preference for an order of values,[68] freedom of conscience would then be incorporated in the system of the state as understood in value terms; it would be qualified and assigned to a particular rank within that entity, rather than being in principle antecedent to it and its possibilities of action as a reserve of individual freedom that exists for its own sake.[69] This logic of thinking in terms of values is irrefutable—Rudolf Smend[70] demonstrated it as early as 1927—and the practical consequence of it may be deduced symptomatically from the Federal Constitutional Court's decision 12.1.[71] [VIII] Guaranteed in the

VII Böckenförde is referring implicitly to the (in)famous *Lüth Decision* of 1958, in which the Federal Constitutional Court developed the doctrine that constitutional norms affect the entire legal system and that the fundamental rights entail an 'objective order of values' which radiates into all other spheres of law. See for an English translation of the main passages Donald P. Kommers and Russell A. Miller, *The Constitutional Jurisprudence of the Federal Republic of Germany*, 3rd ed. (Durham, NC: Duke University Press, 2012), pp. 442–448.

68 A. Brecht, *Politische Theorie* (Tübingen, 1959), pp. 155ff., 342ff.; A. Podlech, 'Grundrechte und Staat', *Der Staat* 6 (1967), pp. 349ff., and 'Werte und Wertungen im Recht', *Archiv des Öffentlichen Rechts* 95 (1970).

69 For a thorough treatment of this point see E. Forsthoff, 'Zur heutigen Situation einer Verfassungslehre', in *Epirrhosis. Festgabe für Carl Schmitt*, vol. I (Berlin, 1968), pp. 209–11. For an indication of how destructive of liberty this interpretation of the basic rights can be in the hands of a facile line of argument based on civil law, see E. von Hippel, *Grenzen und Wesensgehalt der Grundrechte* (Berlin, 1965), esp. pp. 19, 25f., 31f. For a strongly rational argument based on constitutional hermeneutics, see F. Müller, *Die Positivität der Grundrechte* (Berlin, 1969).

70 R. Smend, 'Die Freiheit der Meinungsäußerung', *Veröffentlichungen der Vereinigung der Deutschen Staatsrechtslehrer* 4 (1928), pp. 44ff. (esp. pp. 51–53). The subject is the closer definition of the limits of 'general laws' for free speech in line with Article 118 of the Weimar Constitution. Smend defines that generality as 'the generality of those communal values that as such take precedence over the implementations of basic rights originally conceived as individualistic, so that overstepping them is an infringement or abuse of basic rights' (p. 52). This formal definition offers no criterion for determining which communal values enjoy such precedence. Smend goes on to state that 'general laws in line with Article118' are ones 'that take precedence over Article 118 because the social good that they protect is more important than free speech' (p. 52). Alternatively, 'a law limiting free speech is any law deserving to take such precedence of free speech' (p. 53). Everything therefore depends on a question of evaluation. Smend himself points out the oddity of this interpretation: namely, that the only indication of the fact of a legal consequence is 'that it must be a fact justifying the legal consequence' (p. 52). The standard for that evaluation is derived from the moral and cultural value judgement of the time: 'The basic rights take up a position on such questions of constellations of values touching on public life, and it is the function of basic-rights interpretation to point out those questions and the answers to them provided by the basic rights or (as in Articles 118 and 129) attached by the fundamental rights to the moral and cultural value judgement of the time [!]' (p. 53).

71 *Entscheidungen des Bundesverfassungsgerichts*, 12, 1 (4f.). From the standpoint of critical objectivity, the (only) question to be asked in connection with this judgment is whether it would have been the same had the prisoner sought with his offer of cigarettes to persuade his fellow convicts not to leave the church but to join it.

VIII In the *Tobacco-Atheist-Decision* of 1960, the Federal Constitutional Court decided on the constitutionality of a denial of parole. A prisoner had been denied parole on the basis of the fact that he had encouraged fellow inmates to skip the Christian church service in exchange for the consumption of tobacco, which he provided. He argued that the denial of parole was based on a justification that violated individual freedom of belief. The court established that, contrary to the plaintiff's claims, such a violation had not occurred: 'A person who exploits the special circumstances of penal servitude and promises and rewards someone with luxury goods in order to make him renounce his beliefs does not enjoy the benefit of the protection of Article 4 of the Basic Law.' See Kommers and Miller (annotation VII, p. 545).

context of the order of values of the Basic Law, freedom of conscience would protect the very person who, because he conforms to prevailing opinions, has no need of such protection; it would not protect the outsider, the dissident, for whom it has the greatest relevance.

No, the bounds of freedom of conscience that cannot be overstepped are to be placed only where the fundamental, *ultimate aims* of the modern state—the state has such aims *(Zwecke)* and not just a direction *(Sinn)*[72]—are *immediately* threatened: domestic peace, the continued existence of the state and the integrity of its frontiers, the safeguarding of life and liberty, the individual rights requiring absolute protection.[73] Conscience, which demands from the state freedom and unconditional respect for itself, must for its part respect the rights and liberties of others; it must not seek to overrule them or to overrule the state itself. Even when conscience cannot agree to this kind of elementary observance of the social contract and the state is obliged to curb or punish the exercise of conscience (there are not many such cases, thank God), it is still possible for the way in which this is done—and in particular for the nature and severity of the sanctions adopted—to show respect for the conscientious conviction involved, even if one cannot understand or relate to that conviction.[74] For the rest, when it is not a question of that fundamental area that can be abandoned only at the cost of self-contradiction—and that covers the majority of cases—the state does, for the sake of respect for conscience, consent to a 'system of allowances and partial lifting of obligations', as Adolf Arndt aptly puts it.[75] It allows the individual who is obeying his conscience partially to exclude himself from the people at large through passivity (default) in order to avoid sustaining damage to his conscience.

Such allowances are primarily and most unconditionally called for where it is a question of obligations that by their nature can be met only by wholly *personal* action (compulsory military service, obligations under oath).[76] Here the

[72] This is directed mainly at Krüger, *Allgemeine Staatslehre*, pp. 192ff.

[73] A legal definition of the elementary purposes of the state is provided by the *Allgemeines Landrecht*, II.13.1–2. These were developed theoretically in the state contract doctrine of the law of reason. See for example Hobbes, *Elementa philosophica de cive*, 13.7; J. Locke, *Two Treatises on Government*, II.9.124; C. G. Suarez, *Vorträge über Staat und Recht* (Cologne and Opladen, 1960), pp. 7ff.; I. Kant, 'Über den Gemeinspruch', *Werke*, ed. W. Weischedel, vol. VIII (Darmstadt, 1968), p. 153f.

[74] For this kind of differentiation of legal consequences and the type of sanctions for persons who act on grounds of conscience, see above all H. Welzel, 'Gesetz und Gewissen', in *Hundert Jahre deutsches Rechtsleben. Festschrift zum hundertjährigen Bestehen des Deutschen Juristentages* (Karlsruhe, 1960), p. 399. To be practicable, this presupposes a distinction between the person who acts on grounds of conscience and the person who acts out of conviction. For proof that this is possible, see K. Peters, 'Gewissenstäter und Überzeugungstäter', in *Beiträge zur gesamten Strafrechtswissenschaft. Festschrift für Hellmuth Mayer zum 70. Geburtstag* (Berlin, 1967), pp. 257ff. See also Welzel, in *Hundert Jahre deutsches Rechtsleben*, p. 395.

[75] Arndt, in *Neue juristische Wochenschrift*, 1966, p. 2205. Such a partial dispensation does not nullify the (general) validity of the relevant legal norm; the state refrains from applying it in an individual instance recognized as an exceptional case.

[76] Ibid., p. 2205f. U. F. Rühl, *Das Grundrecht der Gewissensfreiheit im politischen Konflikt* (Frankfurt a. M., 1987), p. 255f., cites additional typical cases. Such a partial dispensation does not invalidate the (general) validity of the respective rule, it disregards its application in a case that is accepted as an exception. On refusal to take

conflict for the individual is at its most acute, because it makes a difference, particularly as regards a person's responsibility to his own conscience, whether he is obliged to act against his conscience *personally,* of his own doing, or whether that action or its outcome is brought about through the intervention of someone else (tax foreclosure, substitute consent to a blood transfusion).[77] And it is difficult to imagine cases in which this kind of lifting of obligations to *personal* action would challenge the unrelinquishable sphere of the fundamental aims of the state (compulsory inoculation may represent a borderline case that can still be solved regularly by a concrete exemption being made).[78]

Lest this kind of toleration and partial lifting of obligations become a privilege separating out the appellant to conscience from the equality (and democratic identity) of all citizens, the state legal order can and should impose alternative courses of action wherever possible. It is entitled to do so because the individual's claim to an exemption relates only to the concrete action that offends his conscience, not to a general release without substitute. In terms of respecting the equality of all citizens it is also obliged to do so. This is the fundamental significance—going beyond the important aspects of the practicability of freedom of conscience—of Luhmann and Podlech's call for the formulation of alternative courses of action for positions of conscience.[79] [IX]

This course—making allowances for conscientious objections to the general legal order—is not in fact as new as it might appear. In the history of freedom of conscience, the problem first arose when freedom of belief and conscience was extended to sects that, partly because of their religious convictions, found themselves unable to meet all their legal obligations. Again the Prussia of the *Allgemeines Landrecht* was exemplary here, making such allowances for Mennonites and Quakers, particularly with regard to the performance of military service, while on the other hand depriving them, out of a concern

an oath, see *Entscheidungen des Bundesverfassungsgerichts,* 33, 23 (30ff.); decision of the Federal Constitutional Court, 25 November 1988, in *Europäische Grundrechtszeitschrift,* 1988, p. 566.

[77] See the representations of H. Hirschmann, S.J., in his statement on conscientious objection to military service before the Defence Committee of the German Bundestag; shorthand minutes *(Sonderprotokoll)* of the 94th session of the Defence Committee, 1 June 1956, p. 15. The problem requires further discussion. Herzog, in treating this distinction as parallel to that between passive and active exercise of the right of resistance (in *Deutsches Verwaltungsblatt,* 1969, p. 720r.), misunderstands its nature and meaning. Cases of conscience are much more often concerned with the desire not to do something than with taking particular positive action, and this is established in the structure of decisions in matters of conscience. See below, beginning of section III; and Luhmann, in *Archiv des öffentlichen Rechts,* 90 (1965), p. 282f.

[78] See also Herzog, in *Deutsches Verwaltungsblatt,* 1969, p. 722. For a different view see Welzel, in *Hundert Jahre deutsches Rechtsleben,* p. 398.

[79] Luhmann, in *Archiv des öffentlichen Rechts* 90 (1965), pp. 274f.; Podlech, *Das Grundrecht der Gewissensfreiheit,* pp. 35ff.

[IX] Niklas Luhmann and Adalbert Podlech had called for an equivalence in the burden placed on those fulfilling a given duty and those objecting to do so based on their conscience. It was legitimate, according to Luhmann, to impose a functionally equivalent duty on those who had objected to fulfil a given norm based on their conscience. Even though freedom of conscience could absolve one from fulfilling a given norm, this did not need to imply the exemption also from fulfilling an imposed substitute duty.

for reciprocity and practical justice, of certain civil rights.[80] The code provided explicitly for the possibility of such allowances by laying down (in section II.11.29) that exemptions from certain laws might be granted to the adherents of particular religious opinions only when expressly permitted by the state. True to its principles, it went on, 'If this does not occur, while the adherent of such a religious opinion cannot be forced to do something contrary to his conviction he must accept the disadvantageous consequences that the laws attach to neglect of their observance'.[81] There are similar examples in Baden in 1807 and in Article 27.11 of the Württemberg constitution of 1819.[82] The later nineteenth century had little time for that kind of concrete humanitarianism,[83] falling back with characteristic pomposity on such abstractions as the validity of statute and the sovereignty of the state.[84] But do these *Landrecht* provisions really show a lack of concern for the state, as Anschütz believed?[85] Be that as it may, the legislature of the German Federal Republic itself professed the same spirit of concrete toleration and humanity in the Act of 14 August 1969,[86] when it offered those (namely, Jehovah's Witnesses) who object on grounds of conscience to an alternative to military service a further option, which they could accept, offering release from alternative service.[X] A law that, in the face of the conscientious

[80] This was done in the 1783 '*Gnadenprivilegium* for the Mennonite Communities in the Kingdom of Prussia' issued by Frederick the Great, as well as in the Edict of 30 July 1789, variously reissued, extended to other areas of Eastern Prussia through two Cabinet Orders on 9 July 1840 and 9 November 1843, and confirmed also for Western Prussia through §22 of the Western Prussia Code of Provincial Law of 1844 (GS, p. 106), and in the Cabinet Order of 16 May 1830, for Brandenburg and the western provinces, with a possible extension also to the Quakers. On this see the references in H. Hecker, *Die Kriegsdienstverweigerung im deutschen und ausländischen Recht*, Research Institute for International Law and Foreign Public Law at Hamburg University, Heft 13 (Frankfurt a. M. and Berlin, 1954), p. 9. The underlying concrete humanitarian attitude of enlightened absolutism in Prussia is aptly expressed by Carl Gottlieb Suarez, *Vorträge* (note 73), pp. 55–56.

[81] *Allgemeines Landrecht* §§ 30, 31 II, I 1.

[82] Baden: 'Erstes Konstitutions-Edikt, die kirchliche Staatsverfassung des Großherzogtums Baden betreffend, v. 14.5.1807 [First constitutional edict concerning the ecclesiastical constitution of the Grand Duchy of Baden]', § I; § 27 II; Württemberg Constitution of 1819: 'The full enjoyment of citizen rights is accorded the three Christian denominations. Other Christian and non-Christian believers [*Glaubensgenossen*] can be admitted to participation in the civic rights only in the degree to which they are not impeded by the principles of their religion in the fulfilment of their civic duties.' Examples for some of the states of the Union in North America in Karl Rothenbücher, *Die Trennung von Staat und Kirche* (Munich, 1907), p. 134, and in Hellmuth Hecker (note 80), pp. 30ff.

[83] R. von Mohl, *Das Staatsrecht des Königreiches Württemberg*, vol. I (Tübingen, 1829), p. 321, already regards it as requiring the state, against all its rights and duties, 'to tolerate citizens who do not wish to comply with the things that are generally accepted'.

[84] Kahl, *Lehrsystem*, p. 293; Anschütz, *Die Verfassungsurkunde*, p. 229f. It is significant for the distribution of the positions that the government bill for the military service law of the North German Confederation (9 November 1867; *Bundesgesetzblatt*, 1/1867, p. 131) retained the privileges that obtained in Prussia while the version passed by the North German Reichstag abolished them, whereupon the king decreed in an order-in-cabinet of 3 March 1868 that Mennonites refusing military service should be recruited as non-combatants only; see Hecker, *Die Kriegsdienstverweigerung*, p. 9.

[85] Anschütz, *Die Verfassungsurkunde*, p. 229.

[86] *Bundesgesetzblatt*, 1/1969, p. 1105.

[X] Members of the Jehovah's Witnesses rejected taking part in the civil service alternative to military service because they saw the former only as a technical replacement for military service preparing the country for a future war whereas Jesus, they argued, called for complete pacificism. The total

objector to alternative service, finally solves the problem in the right place, instead of, like the Federal Constitutional Court, working it out through a 'ne bis in idem' [multiple punishments for the same crime, violating the principle 'no legal action can be instituted twice for the same cause of action'],[87] is worthy of a certain respect, giving voice as it does to the spirit of the body politic.[XI]

5. The foregoing considerations make it possible to define more precisely the substance and nature of the freedom of conscience guaranteed in Germany's Basic Law. The real object of the protection provided by freedom of conscience is not 'the freedom to act in accordance with one's moral conscience' *(Handlungsfreiheit gemäss dem sittlichen Gewissen)*.[88] This wording, already current during the Weimar period, may serve as a kind of paraphrase according to which the freedom to exercise conscience also forms part of the substance of freedom of conscience. But it is too vague, too imprecise; it does not comprehend the true centre and orientation of this fundamental right, and it misleadingly approximates freedom of conscience to universal freedom of action. That would inevitably imply an equally broad limiting formula, and the tiresome debate about Article 2.I of the Basic Law would be repeated in different colours.[XII] The object to be protected by, and the nucleus of, the freedom of conscience enshrined in the Basic Law, on the basis of which our definition of

rejection (*Totalverweigerung*) of both military and civilian service led to the imprisonment of over 800 young male Jehovah's Witnesses over several months. In 1969, the Bundestag changed the law (*Lex Jehova* (§ 15 a Zivildienstgesetz) to create the opportunity that a longer work engagement in social services could be recognized to mitigate the legal consequences of a *Totalverweigerung*. (Also, members of Jehovah's Witnesses who did sign up for the civilian service alternative were excluded from the religious community until a change in their internal policy in 1996.)

[87] Decision of 7 March 1968; *Entscheidungen des Bundesverfassungsgerichts* 23 191 (202ff.).

[XI] In its decision of 7 March 1968, the Federal Constitutional Court ruled that a *Totalverweigerer* (someone rejecting the carrying out of both military service and its civilian alternative, such as the Jehovah's Witnesses, see previous annotation) could not be punished twice (first for refusing to complete military service and then again for refusing to complete the civilian alternative to military service), for that would violate the principle of *ne bis in idem*. This also means that if a *Totalverweigerer* received a suspended sentence for refusing to complete military service, the suspension cannot be withdrawn on the basis of his subsequent refusal to complete the civilian service alternative, for that would violate Article 4 Section 3 Basic Law.

[88] Von Mangoldt, *Das Bonner Grundgesetz, Kommentar*, comment 2 on Article 4; S. Süsterhenn and H. Schäfer, *Verfassung von Rheinland-Pfalz* (Koblenz, 1950), comment on Article 8; von Mangoldt and Klein, *Das Bonner Grundgesetz*, comment III.1 on Article 4, even though he equates freedom of conscience and freedom to profess, adopting the old view of Anschütz. Probably similar Arwed Blomeyer, 'Gewissensprivilegien im Vertragsrecht', *JuristenZeitung* (1954), pp. 309–310.

[XII] Böckenförde is referring to a heated debate among constitutional law scholars in the 1960s about the semantic character of Article 2 Section 1 Basic Law: '(1) Every person shall have the right to free development of his personality insofar as he does not violate the rights of others or offend against the constitutional order or the moral law.' Scholars debated whether the article applied to the general right to freedom, with the consequence that the other fundamental rights of the Basic Law would be mere specifications of the general fundamental right of Article 2 Section 1. Or, on the contrary, should it be interpreted as a residual right, which applied only in cases where none of the specified fundamental rights were applicable (e.g. the freedom to leave the country). The distinction has important implications for the limits of the respective freedom. Böckenförde took the latter position, as did the majority of constitutional law scholars.

that freedom must be developed, in fact lie in the guarantee—also hinted at in the wording of Article 4—of the *inviolability* of conscience. Conscience and the exercise of conscience are to be made free and inviolable by allowing conscientious convictions to take shape freely—that is to say, unhindered by measures taken by the public authority—and by ensuring that no one (subject to the limits set out above) can be compelled by the public authority acting in a sovereign manner to behave (through action or by default) in a way that goes against the dictates of his own conscience. On the one hand, that is less than a freedom of action in accordance with conscience; on the other hand, because of the orientation towards unconditionality, it is also more. Not everything that conscience permits and that to that extent happens in accordance with conscience is protected by freedom of conscience; and it is not conscientious *misgivings* but only *dictates* of conscience—conscientious convictions—that activates the defensive claim of the fundamental right [and thus establishes the concrete right not to be coerced into a particular course of action].[89] So the often-quoted example of the Mormons is not in fact a case of freedom of conscience at all: the Mormon's religious convictions, while they allow him to have several wives, do not dictate that he should. Nor does the decision of the Federal Constitutional Court in the *Rag Collection case*[90] touch on freedom of conscience but only on freedom of religious practice.[XIII] A meaningful dogmatics of freedom of conscience, which strives for discriminating solutions, must take this stipulation as its starting point.

Freedom of conscience as thus defined in a way that aims at unconditionality owes its origin, as we have seen, to the principle of toleration, of making allowances; it is also, in a constitution embodying the rule of law, no longer the 'way in' for the rights of liberty but the conclusion and perfection of them. That is what gives it its peculiar quality as a fundamental right. In guaranteeing it, the state is going to the limit; in order not to deprive its citizens of the security of the state even in cases of conflict between law and conscience—which may

[89] See also Arndt, *Neue juristische Wochenschrift*, 1966, p. 2205.

[90] *Entscheidungen des Bundesverfassungsgerichts*, 24 (236ff.); and see P. Häberle, 'Grenzen aktiver Glaubensfreiheit', *Die öffentliche Verwaltung* (1969), pp. 385ff. The decision suffers from the fact that within Article 4 of the Basic Law it does not distinguish freedom of religious practice and freedom of conscience, also with respect to the various articulated limitations (Article 4 Section 2—Article 136 Section 2), therefore allowing space to a problematic expansion of one's own freedom of action at the expense of others, without a precept of conscience targeted specifically at this action being apparent (the giving of alms is possible in a variety of ways). For a critical view see R. Herzog, M. T. Maunz, G. Dürig, and R. Herzog, *Grundgesetz* (Munich, 1988), Article 4, margin nos. 120ff.

[XIII] In the *Rag Collection Case*, decided in 1968 (*Bundesverfassungsgerichtsentscheidung* 24, 236ff.), the Federal Constitutional Court affirmed the constitutional complaint of a Catholic youth association which organized a collection of old clothes and other renewable materials, called 'Aktion Rumpelkammer' (operation storage room), in order to sell these materials and donate the money obtained to young people in less-developed countries. A professional second-hand dealer had sued the Catholic youth association for economic damage. The regional court of Düsseldorf ordered the Catholic youth association to stop the programme. It saw a violation of competition rules because the programme had been advertised during the church service. By contrast, the Federal Constitutional Court ruled that the operation was protected by the free exercise of religion. See Kommers and Miller (annotation VII), pp. 540–543.

easily become extreme cases—it grants them asylum by way of a partial lifting of obligations. Before it can exist, that kind of asylum must be respected as such by both sides, by the state as well as by its citizens; it calls for a high degree of loyalty. Consequently, the exercise of freedom of conscience must also remain subject to the principle of toleration.

Certain things follow from this. First, freedom of conscience is guaranteed only as a *wholly personal* individual right. Unlike freedom of religious practice, it is not guaranteed as a right of groups or of religious societies. Least of all is it a 'way in' for indirect powers. Secondly, freedom of conscience is not a basic right that in itself authorizes propaganda for its exercise—a problem that becomes particularly relevant in connection with Article 4.III of the Basic Law.[91] Anyone making use of it as a political weapon is failing to respect asylum. Finally, it is also from this angle that we must look at the problem of recognition proceedings. Problematical though the effect of such proceedings may be (by what means can conscience be ascertained and controlled from outside?), there can be no doubt about their justification in principle, provided they are directed towards ascertaining the genuine nature—the so-called 'whether'—of the decision of conscience in order to guard against the abuse of positions of conscience. Anyone laying claim to a special legal position with the intention of deviating from the public at large is not entitled to break off communication.[92]

III.

Although we have found the definition of the substance of freedom of conscience, it seems to me that we need to devote a little more attention to the actual object of the protection it affords, namely conscience. Up to now we have always taken conscience for granted as a circumscribed, known entity.

The lawyer faces a certain dilemma here. The Basic Law does not guarantee freedom of conscience only for certain consciences that conform to a legal concept of conscience that he himself has formulated or postulated; it guarantees it for all consciences. It knows no separate legal concept of conscience but refers to conscience as a given reality of social life.[93]

That does not mean that the task of formulating a concept of conscience falls away, because now it is a question of finding a universal concept of conscience, linked to the *phenomenon* of conscience, in order to define such manifestations of it as *Meinung* (opinion), *Überzeugung* (conviction), *Ansicht* (point of view), and so on. This universal concept of conscience cannot be defined with

[91] See A. Köttgen, *Die Grundrechte der Soldaten* (Munich, 1956), p. 74; and the Federal Constitutional Court decision of 25 February 1969 *(Die öffentliche Verwaltung*, 1969, p. 349).

[92] Podlech, *Das Grundrecht der Gewissenfreiheit*, p. 71f.; thus *Entscheidungen des Bundesverwaltungsgerichts*, 9, 97 (99f.), and 14, 146 (149), are correct.

[93] *Entscheidungen des Bundesverfassungsgerichts*, 12, 45 (54); Arndt, in *Neue juristische Wochenschrift*, 1968, p. 779, and in the shorthand report of the proceedings of the German Bundestag, second electoral period, p. 8838 B and C.

recourse to theological or philosophical notions or interpretations of conscience.[94] The jurist who took this line would simply become a party to the intellectual debate about conscience, falling short of the duty of neutrality towards religion and other worldviews laid upon him by the constitution.[95] The recourse to 'general usage' *(allgemeiner Sprachgebrauch)* adopted by the Federal Constitutional Court also seems problematic.[96] And the same can be said of the court's request for information from reference books and dictionaries,[97] in response to which, on the principle of treating a plurality of sources on an equal footing, the *Große Herder* and the *Große Brockhaus* were both consulted without proper attention being paid to the incompatibility of the two definitions. Why is it that a specific (normative) *idea* of conscience—for instance, the one prevailing in society or among particular social groups—cannot even find expression in general usage, let alone in textbooks and dictionaries?

At this point Niklas Luhmann's analysis and description of the *function* of conscience in the context of and on behalf of human personality offers a way forward.[98] Luhmann sees the true function of conscience in maintaining the personality's identity with itself. It takes the form of a controlling agency, ensuring that the ego does not burst the bounds of its own personality, but rather that what starts out as an infinite number of possible ways of behaving is reduced, in its relationship with its environment, to an internally coherent representation of self and style of conduct.[99] Conscience, then, is not permanently in evidence every day; it figures as the source of regulation and requirement wherever the personality, either as a result of behavioural possibilities of its own or as a result of behavioural demands imposed by its environment, is crucially affected in terms of its structure and in terms of the possibility of protecting its own identity.[100]

What are the implications of this functional description for the conceptual understanding of the phenomenon of conscience? Mainly, it seems to me, the following.

First, conscience cannot be understood as something purely personal, an isolated value system of its own; it is in a permanent condition of social

[94] For a general survey of theological and philosophical concepts and interpretations of conscience see J. Stelzenberger, *Syneidesis, Conscientia, Gewissen* (Paderborn, 1963). See also M. Hinzmann, *Die aktuelle Kriegsdienstverweigerung* (Hamburg, 1959), pp. 18–29. On the current theological doctrine of conscience put forward by the Christian denominations see on the one hand H. Thielicke, *Theologische Ethik*, 2nd ed. (Tübingen, 1958), vol. I, pp. 481ff.; and on the other Mausbach and Ermecke, *Katholische Moraltheologie*, vol. I, pp. 157ff., and B. Häring, *Das Gesetz Christi*, 3rd ed. (Freiburg i.B., 1963), vol. I, pp. 215ff. For a more recent treatment, see R. Eckertz, *Die Kriegsdienstverweigerung aus Gewissensgründen als Grenzproblem des Rechts* (Berlin, 1986), pp. 51–113.

[95] See *Entscheidungen des Bundesverfassungsgerichts*, 12, 45 (54f.); also 19, 1 (18) and 206 (216). The Federal Constitutional Court is therefore right in leaving aside the closer discussion of philosophical and theological doctrines of conscience as irrelevant to the legal interpretation of the notion of conscience.

[96] Ibid., 12, 45 (54). [97] Ibid., 7, 242 (246).

[98] Luhmann, *Archiv des öffentlichen Rechts*, 90 (1965), pp. 257–286 (esp. 264–270).

[99] Ibid., pp. 264ff. For a critical view, see Eckertz, *Die Kriegsdienstverweigerung*, pp. 59ff.

[100] Luhmann, *Archiv des öffentlichen Rechts*, 90 (1965), p. 267f.

communication, shaping and constituting itself in terms of its convictions and its opinions out of that condition.[101] That is the basis for the formation of judgements by conscience as an intellectual process. It is also the basis for the way conscience is pre-formed by upbringing at home and in school, for the way in which it is influenced by the ideas and beliefs that are alive in a society, for its sudden 'awakening' as a result of heightened reflection, and, finally, for change, modification, and manipulation of conscientious convictions. It further explains why conscience mainly appears in a defensive mode and why its dictates are chiefly dictates of non-compliance with requests coming from outside. In the case of positive action, conscience itself has the alternatives at its disposal. Principles and dictates usually allow for a variety of positive realizations.[102]

Secondly, as nearly all theories of conscience stress, questions of conscience cannot be limited in any way, either objectively, or in terms of the substance of the dictate of conscience, or in terms of reasons and motives. Because of the control function of conscience, any kind of behaviour critically affecting the integrity and identity of the personality may become a matter of conscience. What kinds of behaviour or what areas of behaviour these are in concrete terms is determined by the individuality of the personality concerned—that is to say, by the 'norms' that sustain its self-image and its identity. Consequently, questions of conscience cannot be restricted to an objective sphere of 'morality' (*Sittlichkeit*);[103] conscientious convictions may express themselves not only in general principles but equally in concrete imperatives tied to given situations,[104] and they may consist of religious as well as of rational or political convictions.[105]

Thirdly, the view that all decisions of conscience are backed by a 'final seriousness' (*letzter Ernst*), an 'unconditionality', and that this is what identifies them[106] is more than simply a characteristic of many theories of conscience; it has its roots in conscience itself. Conscience as a source of dictates, as a 'voice', swings into action only when the personality finds its identity crucially threatened ('I cannot be the sort of person who does that'). A person who lives his life in conformity with the dictates of his conscience and who loyally observes the laws of the state does not make daily decisions of conscience.[107] Conscience

[101] This is underlined by, among others, T. Würtenberger, 'Vom rechtschaffenen Gewissen', in *Festschrift für Erik Wolf* (Frankfurt a. M., 1962), pp. 340ff.

[102] See also Luhmann, in *Archiv des öffentlichen Rechts*, pp. 282f.

[103] Such a restriction, which often also characterizes the moral theologians' teaching on conscience, occurs in *Entscheidungen des Bundesverfassungsgerichts*, 12, 45 (57).

[104] See also Hinzmann, *Die aktuelle Kriegsdienstverweigerung*, pp. 26–29; *Entscheidungen des Bundesverwaltungsgerichts*, 7, 242 (246ff.). For the theological doctrine of conscience see on the one hand Häring, *Das Gesetz Christi*, vol. I, pp. 215ff., and on the other Thielicke, *Theologische Ethik*, vol. II, pp. 520ff., 543ff. *Entscheidungen des Bundesverfassungsgerichts*, 12, 45 (57) tends to reject this.

[105] *Entscheidungen des Bundesverwaltungsgerichts*, 49, 71 (72) partly corrected and clarified earlier decisions: 7, 242 (246f.), and 12, 271 (272f.). See also H. J. Becker, 'Aus der neueren Rechtsprechung des Bundesverwaltungsgerichts zum Recht der Kriegsdienstverweigerung', *Deutsches Verwaltungsblatt* (1981), pp. 111ff.

[106] See above all Welzel, in *Hundertjahre deutsches Rechtsleben*, p. 395 and n. 51; *Entscheidungen des Bundesverwaltungsgerichts*, 7, 242 (244f.); *Entscheidungen des Bundesverfassungsgerichts*, 12, 45 (55).

[107] Rightly pointed out by Arndt, in *Neue juristische Wochenschrift* (1966), p. 2205.

comes into play where there is conflict, not where there is none. So the fear of an 'inflation' of decisions of conscience is at variance with social reality.

Fourthly, the criterion for the presence of a genuine decision of conscience cannot be found in its truth in the form of agreement with universal legal principles, the moral law, general moral awareness, an accepted order of values, or anything of that kind.[108] That would represent a denial of the individuality of conscience,[109] a negation of its freedom and autonomy. The only consciences to be recognized as consciences would be those that were subject to that kind of truth, a truth coming from outside and by no means necessarily inherent in them.[110] A state legal order that sought to draw such a distinction between 'true' and 'false' consciences would be handing itself a yardstick not inferred from conscience itself and therefore forbidden to it in the light of freedom of conscience.[111]

The conclusions that emerge from all this as regards the reality of conscience and a concept of conscience based upon it do not make the fundamental problem concerning the practical administration of freedom of conscience disappear; in fact, they bring it out into the open. Conscience as an intellectual and spiritual process of personality largely—indeed, almost entirely—eludes external supervision and control.[112] Neither by its object, nor by the manner of its motivation, nor by the extent to which it tallies with a given moral order can a stated position of conscience be examined as to its sincerity. Seen in this light, conscience remains inaccessible, a personal secret, and therein lies what may well be its most powerful protection. Given this state of affairs, the way in which the Federal Administrative Court fell back on the overall credibility of the appellant to conscience is understandable;[113] however, it does not solve the problem. Credibility may be evidence of conscience but can hardly be a criterion of it.

Nevertheless, there remains one point at which, according to Luhmann, conscience can be grasped—albeit indirectly—from outside: namely, its readiness to persist.[114] A decision of conscience can be identified by the fact that

[108] For a fundamental treatment of this point, see Eduard Spranger, 'Die Individualität des Gewissens und der Staat', *Logos* 22 (1933), pp. 171–202.

[109] Ibid., esp. pp. 187ff., 193ff.

[110] Such a situation was conjured up by Adolf Arndt in the debate in the Bundestag on section 25 of the Military Service Law *(Wehrpflichtgesetz);* see the shorthand report of the proceedings of the German Bundestag, second electoral period, vol. 31, p. 8838B: 'It would therefore be a disastrous mistake and a constraint incompatible with the Basic Law to seek to establish by law which theological doctrine is the correct one as the fundamental moral view and which conscience hears the right voice and which is wrong. There would then be a temptation for us not to credit the other man's faith because it is not our own, not to accept the other man's conscience as his conscience because it is not our own.'

[111] *Entscheidungen des Bundesverfassungsgerichts,* 12, 45 (56) is fundamental here.

[112] Luhmann, *Archiv des öffentlichen Rechts,* 90 (1965), pp. 276ff.; Herzog, in *Deutsches Verwaltungsblatt,* 1969, pp. 719f. See also Thielicke, *Theologische Ethik,* vol. II, p. 656f.; and *Entscheidungen des Bundesverfassungsgerichts,* 28, 243 (259); 48, 127 (166); 69, 1 (25).

[113] See also *Entscheidungen des Bundesverwaltungsgerichts,* 7, 242 (249); 9, 97 (98f.) and 100 (102); 13, 171 (172f.); 14, 146 (149). For a critical view, see H. H. Klein, *Beweis und Gewissen,* 1972, with further references.

[114] Luhmann, *Archiv des öffentlichen Rechts,* 90 (1965), pp. 283–285.

its seriousness (often spoken of) is no abstract affair but something very concrete: a disposition to stand by the decision arrived at, a refusal to be talked out of it, even a preparedness to put up with disadvantages as a result. The problem of the provision of alternative courses of action crops up again here, this time not from the standpoint of justice and civic equality but in terms of its practical, procedural function. Luhmann rightly speaks of 'burdensome alternatives' imposing a reasonable sacrifice on the appellant to conscience.[115] It is a point of great practical significance. Such alternatives do not attract the person who has other reasons than those of his conscience, and they make it possible to shorten the problematic process of examining conscience or even to do without it. Nor do they discriminate against the appellant to conscience, because at the same time they demonstrate on his behalf to the citizens at large that his actions are dictated by conscience and that he therefore deserves their respect.[116] Finally, they not only protect the state against abuse of the most easily abused of the freedoms that it guarantees; they also protect freedom of conscience itself, because it is most likely to survive if administered in accordance with the principle of toleration that controls it.[XIV]

IV.

And so to my conclusion. Any interpretation of a constitution that seeks to give effect to its underlying meaning in terms of detail as well as generally is faced with the task of avoiding two contradictions. One of them consists in interpreting an individual provision in such a way that, with its help, the constitution as a whole or a substantial part of it may be turned upside down. The other contradiction consists in setting about interpreting a constitutional provision not on the basis of the normal situation postulated by that constitution, but with a view to possible repercussions should that normal situation cease to obtain.[117]

[115] Ibid., p. 284f.; taken up in *Entscheidungen des Bundesverfassungsgerichts*, 48, 127 (170, 173), and 69, 1 (35ff.).

[116] Luhmann, in *Archiv des öffentlichen Rechts* 90 (1965), pp. 284, is correct: 'Here especially we ought to be on our guard against the snares of sympathy; because if we shrink here from demanding any kind of sacrifice, we not only diminish the "value" of conscience; we are also obliged to use other correctives, in particular normative preconceptions regarding acceptable subjects for conscience'.

[XIV] In the original article a further section follows here, dealing with Article 4 Section 3 of the Basic Law, which contains the right to conscientious objection. Conscription was adopted in the Basic Law in 1956 in light of the rearmament of the Federal Republic and the establishment of the German Armed Forces. In 1960 the Federal Constitutional Court affirmed that Article 4 Section 3 applied not only to military service but also to the peace-time preparation for military service and thus the lawfulness of a civil service alternative for conscientious objectors, which was set up institutionally in 1961. With effect from 2011, the alternative service was suspended in accordance with the suspension of military service. With the author's permission, this section has been omitted here.

[117] On the necessary relation between legal norm and the normality that it presupposes see H. Heller, *Staatslehre* (Leiden, 1934), pp. 254ff.; C. Schmitt, *Politische Theologie*, 2nd ed. (Munich, 1934), p. 19f. With regard to the interpretation of Article 4 Section 3 of the Basic Law, Arndt, in *Neue juristische Wochenschrift* (1966), is precise.

Our suggested interpretation of freedom of conscience in the sense of Article 4 of the Basic Law is knowingly based on the normal situation postulated not only by the Basic Law, but by every constitution embodying the rule of law. One element in that normal situation is the fact that the number of consciences that will at one point or another find themselves in conflict with the state's legal system has been shown by experience to be small. Another key element is civic loyalty as expressed, notably, in renunciation of the use of freedom of conscience as a political weapon. If that loyalty is absent and the putative normal situation consequently does not obtain, the resultant exceptional situation cannot be countered by having already, as a precaution, been built into the interpretation of the rights of freedom. That would debase the interpretation of the constitution itself. It is part of the structure of the liberal *Rechtsstaat* that it is sustained by presuppositions that it cannot itself guarantee without jeopardizing its own liberal nature.[118] However, we must not allow that to lead us away either from the principles of the *Rechtsstaat* or from the principles of the modern state in general. The modern state is subject to the law of 'division' (*Entzweiung*) that governs the modern world.[119] It is based not on a revealed truth but on reasonable aims. Following the experiences of the religious civil wars, it sticks deliberately to the realm of *established norms* (*Setzungen*), choosing to stop short of the realm of ultimate truth. For that very reason it is unable to unite its citizens with the power and unconditionality of a manifest truth, but only with the power of its aims. Accordingly, it does not interfere with the ultimate in man, namely his conscience, but respects it. Looked at in this way, freedom of conscience is a principle of the modern state, and especially of the *Rechtsstaat;* it establishes its reason. The state that in this sense can justly lay claim to being an *imperium rationis*—which really ought not to be confused with an empire of realized values—will possess the inner strength to grant tolerance even where it is unable to recognize a right.[120]

[118] Ernst-Wolfgang Böckenförde, 'Entstehung und Wandel des Rechtsstaatbegriffs', in *Festschrift für Adolf Arndt* (Frankfurt, 1969), p. 75f.; see *Recht, Staat, Freiheit*, p. 168f. Thus Herzog, in *Deutsches Verwaltungsblatt* (1969), p. 722, got it right: 'When the really central questions—even, it may be, the question of "order or anarchy"—become the object of conscientious decisions by dissenting groups, one of the most self-evident prerequisites of the democratic constitutional state is removed. . . The constitution as a whole is then reduced *ad absurdum*, and it remains to be seen what form of political coexistence is adequate in such an event.'

[119] J. Ritter, *Hegel und die Französische Revolution* (Cologne and Opladen, 1956).

[120] Hegel, *Grundlinien*, section 270 (p. 354 and note). On this see Hermann Lübbe, 'Gewissensfreiheit und Bürgerpflicht', in *Humanität und Verantwortung. Festschrift für Hans Barth* (Zurich and Stuttgart, 1964), pp. 205ff.

VII

Remarks on the Relationship between State and Religion in Hegel [1982]

For a long time, the question of the relationship between the state and religion was considered settled and insignificant.[I] The state seemed a self-sustaining political entity and community, whose foundation lay in the nation's will and consciousness of political unity. When it needed legitimation that pointed beyond its existence, it derived it from its worldly tasks and purposes. In the 'general theory of the state' and its representative accounts, the relationship between the state and religion was and is to this day not a separate topic:[1] the state, seen in relation to religion, rests in itself; as a modern, secular state it does permit religion and guarantees its freedom as one dimension of the freedom of human beings, whom it binds together into a single entity, but it is neither dependent on religion nor bound to it in its politics.

This certitude—or possibly also: unconcern—stands entirely in contrast to the classical works of political and state theory, which always regarded the question on the relationship between the state or the political system and religion as an important, indeed, in many cases an essential, problem of state-political existence.[2] [II] This certitude has today vanished. The question about the relation between state and religion has taken on new currency, ever since (and in the

[I] Editors' Note: This is an expanded version of a paper Böckenförde delivered at the symposium 'Hegel's Philosophy of Law', convened by the Faculty of Philosophy at the University of Tübingen, 8–10 October 1981, to commemorate the 150th anniversary of Hegel's death.

[1] This holds true for Georg Jellinek's *Allgemeine Staatslehre*, which mentions the unity of political and cultic community that existed in the ancient polis only in the discussion of the Hellenistic state (3rd ed., Berlin, 1914, p. 300f.), but without any further implication. It applies to the *Allgemeine Staatslehre* of Richard Schmidt, 2 vols. (Leipzig, 1901–1903), to Hermann Heller's (unfinished) *Staatslehre* (Leiden, 1934), but also to the sociologically oriented *Staatslehre* of Gottfried Salomon (Berlin, 1931). In Herbert Krüger's *Staatslehre*, 2nd ed. (Stuttgart, 1966), religion appears merely as an object of distancing for the state, be it genetic, because the state is a secular entity (§7), or be it systemic, arising out of the principle of non-identification (§ 34.I).

[2] Let me refer only to Plato's *Politeia*, Cicero's *De legibus*, *De regimine principum* attributed to Thomas Aquinas, also to Thomas Hobbes' *Leviathan* (parts 3 and 4 of which are usually overlooked), Rousseau's *Contrat social*, and not least Hegel's *Rechtsphilosophie*.

[II] With the conflation of 'state-political', Böckenförde seeks to indicate that in analyzing a modern political order, the dimension of 'the political' (in Carl Schmitt's sense) and the state as a specific type of modern political order have to be taken into account conjointly.

Religion, Law, and Democracy. Ernst-Wolfgang Böckenförde, Oxford University Press (2020). © E.W. Böckenförde, M. Künkler, and T. Stein 2020. DOI: 10.1093/oso/9780198818632.003.0010.

degree to which) national-cultural identity has become problematic (not only in Germany) in the face of an unfolding spiritual-ethical pluralism, a technical-industrial system that is becoming dominant, and the loss of the formative power of the national.[3] Is religion, as was believed for centuries, the real sustaining and formative force that guarantees the civilized behaviour and ethos of citizens from which the state lives, or is it replaceable and dispensable as that kind of force? This is a question that has significance and explosiveness especially for our contemporary secularized state that is neutral with respect to religion and worldviews (*religiös-weltanschaulich neutral*).[III] If this state, too, needs a sustaining and supportive foundation in the pre-political realm, where does it possess and find such a foundation?

The obvious answer is that the sustaining foundation lies in the general consensus or in the 'value community' [*Wertegemeinschaft*] that is today frequently invoked.[IV] But what is *their* foundation? Consensus and 'value community' are, first of all, merely terms that neither explain nor justify what they designate. Are we dealing here with things merely posited, with the actualization of a temporal consciousness open to all kinds of transformation and change and devoid of a substance of its own? Are we dealing with the actually existing cultural traditions (which, of course, in turn require a regenerating force in the succession of generations)? Or are we dealing after all, and ineradicably, with religion? If that is so, the question arises as to what consequence this would have for the state that is neutral with regard to religion and worldviews, a state that explicitly rejects having a specific religion, indeed, religion as such, as its foundation. Can it be said and demonstrated that religion does after all have a place in the formation of this state, but in a mediated and externally

[3] The basic values debate that began in the Federal Republic in 1976 [*Grundwertedebatte*] and has been ongoing since can be regarded as one symptom of this loss. For important positions in the *Grundwertedebatte*, see G. Gorschenek (ed.), *Grundwerte in Staat und Gesellschaft* (Munich, 1977); see also A. Paus (ed.), *Werte, Rechte, Normen* (Salzburg, 1978).

[III] The principle of neutrality towards religion and (other) worldviews (*religiös-weltanschauliche Neutralität des Staates*) that Böckenförde invokes here is commonly known in the German philosophical and juridical context as a principle characterizing the state's non-identification with any particular religion or worldview. It demands that the state does not justify law on religious grounds or grounds associated with other comprehensive doctrines. Furthermore, it entails the dissociation of political authority from religious authority, and finally requires of the state not to privilege religion over nonreligion and one religious creed over another. Religions and other worldviews can be viewed here as synonymous with Rawlsian comprehensive doctrines.

[IV] Böckenförde famously rejects the notion that the state can create or lead this *Wertegemeinschaft*. For this, compare his writings on the *Grundwertedebatte* (Chapter III, 'The State as an Ethical State' and Chapter IX 'Critique of the Value-Based Grounding of Law' in volume I of this edition). Instead, he writes, the *Wertegemeinschaft* needs to emanate from society. Böckenförde served as a ghostwriter (together with Oswald Nell-Breuning) for a decisive speech Chancellor Helmut Schmidt delivered in 1976, titled 'Ethos and Law in State and Society', which emphasized that the state needs to be neutral with regard to worldviews. The speech caused much controversy, as the chancellor's position was viewed as too reserved, and as indirectly contributing to the public erosion of values (*Werteverfall*) the Catholic Church diagnosed at a time when the federal government undertook important reforms in family law and regarding women's rights.

invisible form—for example, such that religion in general or a specific religion carries and legitimizes precisely this neutrality with regard to religion and worldviews?[V] Or is the form of the secular state's existence, from the perspective of the pre-political foundations of the state, tantamount in the final analysis to a dance on a volcano?

In what follows, I will probe the question regarding the relation between state and religion on the basis of Hegel's reflections. Hegel was the last of the great state thinkers who systematically addressed and discussed this question within the framework of a philosophical justification of the state and a state theory. And he did not do this abstractly and generally for the relation between the political order and religion as such, but concretely for the relation between the modern European state of his day and Christian religion. That lifts his contribution a priori above being merely of historical interest. The core piece of Hegel's pronouncements on the relation between the state and religion is found in the extensive explanatory note to § 270 of his *Elements of the Philosophy of Right*, which has received scant scholarly attention.[4] This should be supplemented by his *Lectures on the Philosophy of World History* and § 552 of the *Philosophy of Mind*. The *Philosophy of World History* contains the systematic preconditions for the elaborations in *Philosophy of Right*; in the *Philosophy of Mind*, the statements in the *Philosophy of Right* are developed further, and they presuppose them as the foundation. Together the three pieces form Hegel's 'treatise' on the relation between the state and religion.[5]

My observations, which are restricted to a focused presentation and interpretation guided by Hegel's text, followed by a discussion of the problem as it relates to the present, are laid out in four steps. Step one: In the context of the present topic, what does 'state' mean to Hegel, and what is its foundation? Step two: On that basis, what is the relation between state and religion, fundamentally and with respect to current manifestations? Step three: What precisely is the right of (personal) conscience in and towards the state? Step four: What

[V] Talal Asad and Saba Mahmood appear to suggest as much. Böckenförde wrote this article before the publication of their works, and the question he poses here appears to anticipate the debate they instigated on whether the secular state is based in fact on secularity as understood from a decidedly Christian perspective. Their argument that the state is the product of the *Christian* religion surely was already recognized by Hegel, as Böckenförde lays out in the following.

[4] Even the profound account of Hegel's work in Charles Taylor, *Hegel* (Cambridge, 1975), devotes less than half a page to § 270 of Hegel's *Philosophy of Right* and the topic of state and religion addressed there.

[5] In what follows I will cite the *Rechtsphilosophie* (usually only with paragraph references) in the Glockner edition, vol. VII (3rd ed., Stuttgart, 1952) [English: *Elements of the Philosophy of Right*, edited by Alan W. Wood, translated by H. B. Nisbet (Cambridge, 1991), hereafter cited as *Philosophy of Right*], the *Enzyklopädie der philosophischen Wissenschaften im Grundriß* (1830) in the Nicolin and Pöggeler edition (Hamburg, 1959) [English: *Hegel's Philosophy of Mind*, translated from the 1830 Edition, together with the *Zusätze* by W. Wallace and A. V. Miller, with revisions and commentary by M. J. Inwood (Oxford, 2007), hereafter cited as *Philosophy of Mind*]; and the 'Einleitung zur Philosophie der Geschichte' in the Johannes Hoffmeister edition, *Die Vernunft in der Geschichte* (5th ed., Hamburg, 1959) [English: *Lectures on the Philosophy of World History*, translated by H. B. Nisbet (Cambridge, 1975)].

importance does Hegel's definition of the relation between state and religion have for that relation today?

I.

a) When Hegel speaks of the 'state' within the framework of his philosophy, including also his philosophy of law, he has a philosophical, not a legal concept of the state in mind.

1. This concept, as a philosophical one, is universal because it is aimed at an understanding of reality and the truth of reason. Nevertheless, it is a concept related concretely to history, one that encompasses the state in the shape and form that became reality after the French Revolution, the era of the Confederation of the Rhine [1806–1813] and of the Prussian reforms. For Hegel, this combination of universal-philosophical and concrete-historical thinking is possible without internal contradiction because it is part of the basic preconditions (and understanding) of his philosophy that the spirit, rational truth, comes to fruition *in* history (which in no way means *as* history) and develops its forms and institutions; the (essential) concept creates for itself and attains its actuality and reality in history, by means of which the idea, as the unity of existence and concept, realizes itself.[6]

2. The concept 'state' means in Hegel more than the political organization of a society, the 'political system' or the administrative organs acting in a sovereign manner; it is also more than the mere organization of authority [*Herrschaftsordnung*] or 'government' in the sense of Anglo-American political theory. It encompasses what a people as a whole has in common, which is principally a political community, but it incorporates also the spiritual culture, education and knowledge, the public orders of life, and the general public consciousness:

> The spiritual individual, the nation—insofar as it is internally differentiated so as to form an organic whole—is what we call the state. This term is ambiguous, however, for the [concepts of the] state and the laws of the state, as distinct from religion, science, and art, usually have purely political associations. But in this context, the word 'state' is used in a more comprehensive sense, just as we use the world 'realm' to describe spiritual phenomena.[7]

In this sense, the state is for Hegel 'the ethical universe.'[8] Yet he does not fail to see that the state also in this sense does not have an existence independent of the individual, but represents merely the structured form in which a people

[6] For a definition and on the relationship between concept, idea, and existence see Hegel's—brief—discussion in *Philosophy of Right*, §1.

[7] *Philosophy of World History*, p. 96. Similarly, we read in *Philosophy of Right*, §274 that 'the state, as the spirit of a nation [*Volk*], is both the law which *permeates all relations within it* and also the customs and consciousness of the individuals who belong to it'.

[8] *Philosophy of Right*, p. 21.

exists. 'The state itself is an abstraction which has its purely universal reality in the citizens who belong to it; but it does have reality, and its purely universal existence must take on a determinate form in the will and activity of individuals' (Hist., p. 116).[VI]

3. Substantively, the state, as a developed concept that comes to reality in its time, is the 'actuality of concrete freedom' (§ 260). Hegel did not mean this as an abstract hypostatization, but as concretely related to the state of his day. The state is the actuality of concrete freedom through the fact that, on the one hand, it gives its due to the subjectivity and particularity of individuals (in the autonomous family and in the system of civic society), and, on the other hand, binds this subjectivity and particularity into the general, that is, the form of reasonable existence, and maintains it therein. 'The principle of the modern states has enormous strength and depth because it allows the principle of subjectivity to attain fulfilment in the *self-sufficient extreme* of personal particularity, while at the same time *bringing it back to substantial unity* and so preserving this unity in the principle of subjectivity itself' (§ 260).

The state thus includes the family and civic society, the latter also and especially as the world of particularity and the system of needs centred around the individual and his [or her] rights. But the family and civil society are not left to their own devices, organized only functionally and turned over to random circumstances devoid of any further orientation; rather, they appear as elements of an overarching order that points beyond the mere particularity and singularity of individual existence, which underlies them and forms the precondition for the capacity of subjectivity and particularity to develop without getting lost (in an anarchy of the spiritual-ethical world).[9]

4. That the concept of the state develops in this way and comes to realization is a process within history and belongs, as Hegel emphasizes, largely to the modern world. The state by no means always existed and was by no means always specified in this form. For Hegel, genuine progress in the unfolding of the spirit is at work here. It runs from the incomplete, merely substantive state of classical antiquity, in which universality *was* present, but as a still undifferentiated substantive unity, in which—as in the Platonic state—'subjective freedom is not yet recognized'; to the medieval state, in which the principle of universality does not find a sufficient form in reality; down to the 'modern' state, that is, the state of his day, whose essence is 'that the universal should be linked with the complete freedom of particularity [*Besonderheit*] and the well-being of individuals', such that 'the universality of the end cannot make further progress without the personal [*eigene*] knowledge and volition of the particular individuals [*der Besonderheit*], who must retain their rights.'[10] This, not least, is the achievement of modern state theory, its work on the concept of the state, which Hegel

[VI] Translator's note: Hereafter, parenthetical references to paragraphs within the text refer to *Philosophy of Right* if marked with an '§' and to *Philosophy of World History*, if marked with 'Hist.'.

[9] §256 Addition, §182 Addition.

[10] §260 Addition, §262 Addition, §273.

acknowledges, and to which he accords world-historical significance. At the same time, he wants to preserve it from petering out into mere subjectivity, which sees the universal of the state merely as (subjective) commonality, and in the process confuses the state with civil society.

b) What is the foundation of the state, seen and conceptualized in this way by Hegel? Does it rest in itself or does it owe its existence to a preceding force that carries and constitutes it?

1. To begin with, the state, in its presented structure and concrete shape, is not simply something present, a historical given, which exists thus in the positivity it has now achieved. In this achieved positivity it is more, namely the realization of reason-determined freedom, which has here found a valid shape and organization. Hegel says that the state, this state, 'is the *rational* and for itself' (§ 258), the 'actuality of the ethical Idea' (of freedom) (§ 257). That the state is this way is no accident, some lucky chance of history, which has simply turned out this way. Rather, the state in its actual conceptualization is the historical actualization of the spirit—i.e. truth of reason—in the world. 'The state is the world which the spirit has created for itself; it therefore follows a determinate course which has being in and for itself' (§ 272, Addition); 'The state is the spirit which is present in the world and which *consciously* realizes itself therein' (§ 258, Addition). The political order receives and has its rational form in the evolved state (which is developed in line with its destiny), it has become the shape of freedom. Out of this there arises for the state a principal legitimation, the character of something resting in itself, which requires no further legitimation from purposes lying beyond itself.

2. But the state in this way is not merely realization and a realm of reason; as such, as the realization of reason, it is for Hegel a thought of God and—concretely and historically—the product of religion. Reason-truth, which Hegel sees unfolding in history and taking shape in concrete forms of life, is not based on some kind of 'autonomous' reason deduced from self-established premises; it is a reason borne by the divine and determined by the spirit of God: 'The state consists in the march of God in the world, and its basis is the power of reason actualizing itself as will' (§ 258, Addition). This dictum, which, contrary to some misunderstanding, by no means entails an apotheosis of the state, finds a more detailed explanation in the *Lectures on the Philosophy of World History*. We read there: 'The state, then, shares a common principle with religion. Religion is not something introduced from outside in order to regulate the workings of the state and the conduct of individuals towards it from within; on the contrary, it is the original inner principle which determines and activates itself within the state ... as already pointed out, the true sense of this relationship is that the state has already grown out of a definite religion, that it shares the same principle with it, and that its entire political, artistic, and learned life are dependent upon it'(Hist., 108f.). Here the state is presented specifically as the product of religion. But it is not traced back directly to a creative or formative act on the part of God, and thereby posited as divinely legitimated and inviolable. Nor is it conceived, like all 'existing authorities' (Rom. 13.1), as established 'by an act of God'; instead, it is seen as the expression, the realization of religion in the

world. Religion determines and actuates its innerness, the spirit of (revealed) truth that lives and becomes conscious within it, through the fact that the state becomes real in the coexistence of humans; it inserts its content, which determines the thoughts and actions of humans, through these very thoughts and actions into the political sphere in such a way that attitudes and manners, goal orientations and ideas of order are called forth, which make possible the political organizing form of the 'state', indeed, which in a sense establish and then sustain it. 'Religion should accordingly be seen as necessarily inseparable from the political constitution, from secular governments, and from secular life. The universal principle is present in the world and must be realized within it, for the world is the object of its knowledge.' It 'permeates all the particular areas of national life, so that the latter becomes imbued with a practical religious consciousness of truth. Thus, the political constitution, the system of justice, ethical life in general, art, and science are all manifestations of truth in particular areas of national existence' [Hist., pp. 109, 110].

3. What Hegel formulates here is, first of all, a universal principle of the interconnection of state and religion and the generation of the state by religion. But that is only a part of the truth. This principle applies concretely and specifically to the developed state that Hegel was dealing with in his day. This state is not the creation of religion in general: rather, in its characteristic unity of universality and particularity (§ 261, Addition), in the recognition and development of subjectivity (§ 260), it is the product of the *Christian* religion. For it was only with the Christian religion that 'the principle of the *self-sufficient and inherently infinite personality* of the individual', the principle of subjective freedom, came into the world (§ 185 Addition). Out of and through the Christian religion, which contains within itself the principle of subjectivity through the divine revelation in Jesus Christ and brings it into the world as a principle, the state acquires its depth and concrete rationality, which sets it apart from earlier forms of political order and also relativizes the old differences in the forms of the state. Universality and particularity are combined within it, it allows 'the principle of subjectivity to attain fulfilment in the *self-sufficient extreme* of personal particularity', while at the same time bringing it back to 'substantial unity', in that this unity acquires existence in individuals (§§ 273, 260). The Christian religion, as the 'religion of freedom' (§ 270, Addition),[11] brings forth the state as the reality of freedom.

II.

For Hegel the question of how, on the basis of this connection between state and religion, the relation between the two is constituted is a priori not the abstract question about the relation between any state to any religion, but the

[11] The Christian religion of freedom is explicated in detail in his *Vorlesungen zur Philosophie der Religion*, vol. II, Glockner ed., 3rd ed. (Stuttgart, 1959). [English: *Lectures on the Philosophy of Religion*, translated by R. F. Brown, P. C. Hodgson, and M. Steward (Oxford, 2007)]; also in his *Vorlesungen über die Philosophie der Geschichte*, Glockner ed., 3rd ed. (Stuttgart, 1949), p. 427f. [English: *Lectures on the Philosophy of World History* (note 5)].

concrete question about the relation of the developed state to Christian religion. This is the central theme in the great Addition to § 270 of his *Philosophy of Right*, but also in § 552 of the *Philosophy of Mind*. In the process, the relationship of the (concrete) state to other religions, for example Judaism, and to Christian denominations like the Quakers, Mennonites, and other sects, is addressed along the way.

a) The basic nature of this relation as seen by Hegel can be summarized in three statements.

1. The relationship between the state and (Christian) religion is not that of a confrontation between two separate forces living out of their respective principles (and of the institutional-organizational formations that emerge from them), which are initially independent from each other, but then, exert authority over the same human beings and relate to them, enter into a relationship, demarcate spheres of action, and eliminate fields of conflict, and in so doing enter into some kind of relationship of equality or of supraordination and subordination. That perspective is suggested by today's relationship between state and religion, or state and church, but it already presupposes the neutral state detached from religion as its foundation. Hegel's perspective is different. To him, it is a relationship of *parallelism*. State and religion (church) are different forms of reality and actualization of the same, unitary substance. Religion in the broader sense, that is, the divine spirit in the world, differentiates itself into religion in the narrower sense (ritual, doctrine, church) and the state, with each actualizing itself in distinct forms in the world.

2. The actualized form of religion in the broader sense, which manifests itself in the state, is that of thinking consciousness, of the universality forming itself externally as law:[12] 'The state is the divine will as present spirit, *unfolding* as the actual shape and *organization of a world*' (§ 270). By contrast, the actualized form of religion in the narrower sense is '*in the form of feeling, representational thought, and faith*'(§ 270). This juxtaposition of (Christian) religion and the state as the actualized forms of the religious content is visibly influenced by the situation in which especially Protestant theology found itself under the influence and conditions of the Enlightenment.[13] [Protestant] theology, bowing to the demands of rationalism, had largely lost its faith content and set it aside. Translated into the praxis of life, this meant that everyday life stood devoid of faith content and that religion withdrew into subjectivity, the interiority of the believing subject, where it existed in the form of mere faith and emotion, without carrying out the transition to representational and then object-appropriating thought [*begreifendes Denken*] and to the idea.[14] The truth appears in it thus merely as something veiled in the subjectivity of feelings and imagining, a truth that lives

[12] *Philosophy of World History*, p. 100: 'But a state requires laws, which means that its ethicality is present not only in an immediate form, but also in a universal form as an object of knowledge. It is the fact that this universal is known which lends the state its spiritual quality.'

[13] See Emanuel Hirsch, *Geschichte der neueren evangelischen Theologie*, vol. 5.1 (Gütersloh, 1960), pp. 3–144.

[14] On this see also Hegel's remarks in *Philosophy of Mind*, §564.

merely in the sphere of the inner (§ 270). Against this, Hegel asserts the objective content of religion, here the Christian faith, its implementation in the world also as the reality of the latter. The fact that he sees this objectification and realization as taking place almost solely in the state reveals a specific perspective indebted to his age. In particular, this perspective touches insufficiently on the Catholic creed, whose theology had not become stripped of substance in the same way under the influence of the Enlightenment.[15] Unaffected by this, however, is the realization and observation that the objectification and actualization of the elements of the Christian faith take place also—and in a specific way—in the state. It happens in the 'momentous transition of the inner to the outer', the incorporation of the reason that is present in the divine spirit into reality, which is born by religion in the narrower sense as the interiority, but which is itself not the activity of religion, but of the state. For Hegel this is what 'the whole of world history has worked to achieve. Through this work, educated humanity has actualized and become conscious of rational existence [*Dasein*], political institutions, and laws' (§ 270).

3. The basic determination of the relationship between state and religion as given by Hegel presupposes the split between church and state, and thus the dissolution of the unitary religio-political world of the Middle Ages. According to Hegel, it was only via the particular churches, i.e. as a result of the religious schism, that the state acquired its spiritual independence, its universality that overarches the confessional conflicts, and the principle of its form (§ 270). In this Hegel sees the world-historical importance of the Reformation.[16] However, this does not amount to a kind of disconnecting of the state from religion, but its own form of realizing the religious content, as for example the right of the individual to freedom of religion and confession, something the contending religious parties were unable to bring to reality by themselves.[17] In the separated, divided existence of state and churches, Hegel nevertheless sees preserved the substantive unity of an internally differentiated *Reich* (understood as the order of the world) shaped by the truth of the Christian religion in the broader sense, namely at a higher level that overcomes forms of unfreedom.

b) This basic determination of the relation between state and religion leads Hegel to reject a number of notions about the relation between state and religion or state and church, notions that were discussed and postulated in his day,

[15] On this see Eduard Hegel, *Die katholische Kirche unter dem Einfluß der Aufklärung des 18. Jahrhunderts* (Opladen, 1975), pp. 25–31

[16] See *Philosophy of Mind* (note 5), § 552 Addition; Reinhard Maurer, 'Hegels politischer Protestantismus', *Der Staat* 10 (1971), pp. 455ff.

[17] The example of religious freedom as the external right of the individual, which the state had to push through against the opposition of the churches, most sustained by the Catholic Church, but which today is recognized by both Christian churches [Protestant and Catholic] as the correct and commanded Christian solution to the relationship between the religious claim to truth and freedom—see most recently the declaration *De libertate religiosa* by the Second Vatican Council—shows clearly how the state itself, especially in its universality that has become independent vis-à-vis the churches, has realized certain religious content of Christianity. See also Ernst-Wolfgang Böckenförde, 'Zum Verhältnis von Kirche und moderner Welt', in *Studien zum Beginn der modernen Welt*, ed. by R. Koselleck (Stuttgart, 1977), p. 155 (161f.).

not least under the banner of the progressive political restoration. His reflections in this regard are embedded in the intellectual-political debates of the time.

1. To begin with, he rejects the notion of seeing in religion chiefly 'comfort against injustice' and the hope for a substitute for the earthly loss against the background of public misery. For Hegel this is nothing other than the degradation of religion into a means of edification and inner consolation, and at the same time the proclamation of indifference towards the course and business of reality as a religious demand—precisely what Karl Marx several decades later would aptly describe as 'opium of the masses'. In the face of religion, the state and its business, that is, the worldly political order, seem like an undertaking of no serious purpose or like a matter of indifferent capriciousness. Religion understands itself and is sufficient unto itself as its own interiority. The result is that it either constitutes itself as the real apolitical realm of life, or claims for itself vis-à-vis the state—on the basis of its own interiority—to 'determine and hold what is right'. Both are for Hegel the thoughtless tearing apart of state and religion.

2. Hegel likewise condemns the polemical turn of religion against the state, which proceeds from the premise that religion already contains everything that matters, with the result that there is no need—at least for believers—of the law and of the particular distinctions and institutions established by the state. Hegel sees in this—he is talking here about Pietism and Schleiermacher, but also the religious subjectivism of Romanticism[18]—the foundation of religious fanaticism: the institutions of the state and the legal system are stripped of their obligatoriness as an inappropriate barrier to the infinitude of the religious feeling. However, since actions and decisions must still be taken in real life, that is done entirely out of the subjective notion, that is, in personal opinion and argument, though these step forward with the claim of absolute—because religious—certainty. Hegel's criticism is of biting incisiveness: 'Those who "seek the Lord" and assure themselves, in their uneducated opinion, that they possess everything *immediately* instead of undertaking the work of raising their

[18] In the addition to § 270, which contains numerous polemical arguments, Hegel does not name any names; the particular opponents must therefore be deduced from the context and from the characterization of the position articulated by Hegel. That the polemic (pp. 293–295) refers to the teachings of the Herrnhuter Brethren and to Schleiermacher is suggested by the formulations it employs ('To the righteous, no law is given', 'Be pious, and you may otherwise do as you please'—p. 293; 'Those who "seek the Lord" and assure themselves, in their uneducated opinion, that they possess everything *immediately*'—p. 294). The Herrnhuters found the value of religion largely in an inner community of the heart with the Lord and the inner experience of salvation; Schleiermacher, who had also gone through the school of the Herrnhuter Brethren, had, in his early period (e.g. in the *Reden über die Religion an die Gebildeten unter ihren Verächtern* [1799], trans: *On Religion: Speeches to its Cultured Despisers*, trans. John Oman (New York: Harper & Brothers (1958)), proclaimed the later amended statement: not he has religion who believes in a Sacred Scripture, but he who does not need one and could probably make one himself. On this see also Franz Schnabel, *Deutsche Geschichte im 19. Jahrhundert*, vol. 4: *Die religiösen Kräfte*, 2nd ed. (Berlin, 1951), pp. 302ff. The vehemence of the polemic against Schleiermacher can probably be explained in part also by the political situation in which Hegel found himself in the summer of 1820; on this see Hegel, *Vorlesungen und Rechtsphilosophie 1818–1831*, edited with commentary by K. H. Ilting, vol. I (Stuttgart, 1972), pp. 44f., 60f. Hegel is not directly attacking Friedrich von Schlegel and Novalis here. However, he refers to § 140, where he places them on the highest level of hypocrisy.

subjectivity to cognition of the truth and knowledge of objective right and duty, can produce nothing but folly, outrage, and the destruction of all ethical relations' (§ 270, p. 294).[19] What such religious zeal—which already contains within itself the whole world—accomplishes in reality is for Hegel nothing other than the exposure of the order of the state to the uncertainty and disruption fostered from within: 'For when piety adopts the role of the state, it cannot endure anything determinate, but simply destroys it' (§ 270, Addition, p. 304).

3. Hegel is further opposed to the spiritual hierocracy of religion or church vis-à-vis the state.[VII] What constitutes this hierocracy is that the church reinterprets the simple difference in the way state and religion manifest the realization of the same substance (religious content) into an antagonism, and, invoking the absolute content of religion that it contains within itself, regards the spiritual and the ethical as belonging solely to it. All that is left to the state is then the pursuit of merely external ends, such as the security of life and property and the guarantee of subjective freedom; it becomes a matter of need and a mere instrument, while the church—'forecourt' to the Kingdom of God—thinks it is an end in itself (§ 270, p. 297). Hegel's criticism here is directed against the position that empties the state of its own and autonomous spiritual-ethical substance in the name of a church and its doctrine claiming the truth about and for the world solely for itself. The opponents it addresses are probably contemporary but also fundamental manifestations of Catholic thinking about religion, church, and state.[20] This position can be derived, for one, from an external hierocratic thinking, which was widespread in older Catholicism. On the basis of a still presupposed unitary religio-political world, the Church is accorded the binding decision-making competency on all questions concerning ethics, and the autonomy of the state is reduced in this regard to implementation, to the indifferent, and to the socio-technical detail.[21] This position can also be

[19] *Philosophy of Right*, §270, p. 294. He goes on to say: 'Instead of mastering one's opinions by the labour of study and subjecting one's volition to discipline so as to elevate it to free obedience, the easiest course is to renounce cognition of objective truth, to nurse a sense of grievance and hence also of self-conceit, and to find in one's own godliness all that is required in order to see through the nature of the laws and of political institutions, to pass judgement on them, and to lay down what their character should and must be. And indeed, since these are the findings of a pious heart, they must be infallible and indisputable.' Any parallels in the present, not excluding politically engaged clergy and theologians, are purely coincidental.

[VII] Usually, hierocracy indicates a form of authority where state power is exercised by a priesthood, religiously legitimated in the wisdom of the priesthood (as distinguished from a God-given religious legitimation such as the divine right of kings). Note that here hierocracy is meant differently, as Böckenförde explains.

[20] Hegel probably had Joseph von Görres in mind as a contemporary representative. Although no direct reference to Görres can be identified in the polemics of § 270, a few passages could be talking about Görres. But the clues are more direct in the Addition to § 270. Here Hegel engages critically with the notion that the state needs sanctification, invigoration, and animation from religion or the Church, a notion that Görres had advocated as quintessential in his tract *Teutschland und die Revolution von 1819*; see Joseph Görres, *Ausgewählte Werke in zwei Bänden*, ed. by W. Frühwald, vol. I (Freiburg, 1978), pp. 438ff.

[21] This competency of the church follows from the qualification of the church as a *societa perfecta*, which, as such, disposes over all means to achieve its spiritual ends and to lead the faithful to eternal salvation. Since that also includes the ethical life, the preservation of the natural and divine law, the content of which must

derived in a modern way, where the state is justified as a mere state of need and reason: the state is stripped of its own positive competency in the ethical-substantive realm by invoking its neutrality and the principle of subsidiarity, and that competency is assigned to communities and institutions 'closer to the individual', like the churches.[22]

4. Finally, Hegel also rejects the organizational unity and linkage of state, religion, and church—in opposition to the alliance of throne and altar sought by some representatives of the Restoration. Such a unity does not allow the distinction that has emerged in the form of the consciousness between religion in the narrower sense and the state to come into being. To be sure, Hegel advocates a unity of the (developed) state and the Christian religion or church, which lies in the truth of the principles and disposition that govern them. But precisely for this truth it is essential within the Christian religion, which also has subjectivity as its content, that the distinction in the form of consciousness between church and state come into its particular existence.

c) Following this negative demarcation, we must now move to the positive determination of the relation between the state and the (Christian) religion. State and religion in the narrower sense stand side by side and in relation to one another as separate and distinct manifestations of the same content, that of revealed divine truth. For Hegel this leads to a reciprocal relationship of recognition, and beyond that, first, to a relationship of the affirmation of religion by the state, and, second, to a dependence of the state on religion as its sustaining foundation.

1. The state possesses its rationality and ethical substance[VIII] not only when it takes on religion (the church), but inherently, as an autonomous form of realization. In the process the state refers only to the external; what it pronounces as

be interpreted and concretized by the church, *it* possesses the binding decision-making competency; on this see now Ernst-Wolfgang Böckenförde, 'Staat-Gesellschaft-Kirche', Section I.i, in *Christlicher Glaube in moderner Gesellschaft*, vol. XV (Freiburg, 1982), pp. 18–26.

[22] The foundation for this is the link between a value-based personalism and the principle of subsidiarity, which was advanced especially in the Catholic post-war social doctrine (particularly in the 1950s and 1960s), and which played an important role in the dispute over the status of ecclesiastical educational institutions and the primacy of the church's youth and social welfare over that of the state. See, for example, the essays by A. F. Utz and H. E. Hengstenberg in the anthology *Das Subsidiaritätsprinzip*, ed. by A. F. Utz (Sammlung Politeia, vol. II) (1953), pp. 15f., 28f., 38f.; Ewald Link, *Das Subsidiaritätsprinzip. Sein Wesen und seine Bedeutung für die Sozialethik* (Freiburg, 1955); Joseph Höffner, 'Die Subsidiarität in der Jugendhilfe', *Die Kirche in der Welt* 10 (1958), pp. 77ff.; Anton Rauscher, 'Subsidiaritätsprinzip und berufsständische Ordnung', in *'Quadragesimo Anno': eine Untersuchung zur Problematik ihres gegenseitigen Verhältnisses* (Münster, 1958), esp. pp. 50–60; G. Wildmann, *Personalismus, Solidarismus und Gesellschaft* (Freiburg, 1961), pp. 121ff. For a critical response see Trutz Rendtorff, 'Kritische Erwägungen zum Subsidiaritätsprinzip', *Der Staat* 1 (1962), pp. 405 (418ff.); Roman Herzog, 'Subsidiaritätsprinzip und Staatsverfassung', *Der Staat* 2 (1963), pp. 399 (404ff.), and, as an anti-critic, A. Rauscher, 'Subsidiaritätsprinzip, Staat, Kirche', *Stimmen der Zeit* (1963), pp. 124ff. This position resounds also in the formula 'the church as the life principle of society' (Gustav Gundlach, *Die Ordnung der menschlichen Gesellschaft*, vol. I (Cologne, 1964), pp. 381ff).

[VIII] Note that *Sittlichkeit* is translated here as 'ethical substance'. The literature on Hegel is heterogeneous in this regard: sometimes *Sittlichkeit* is translated as ethical order, sometimes as ethical substance. To us the translation as 'order' appears less suitable in the given context.

content belongs to the determinate idea, and what it demands has the form of a legal obligation, it does not encroach upon the sphere of the inner, which as such does not constitute its domain (§ 270, pp. 296-97, 298; Addition p. 302).[23] At the same time, however, it is not simply separated from the inner realm, which is the domain of religion in the narrower sense. When a person takes action, the inner passes into the outer, and the Christian religion, which is not simply limited to ritual, necessarily affects the external, and thus the sphere of the state, via doctrine (i.e. church teachings), which is the point of mediation and transmission. Although this doctrine has its province first of all in conscience, which it shapes, it is 'not just an internal matter for the conscience; as doctrine, it is in fact an expression, indeed the expression of a content which is intimately connected, or even directly concerned, with ethical principles and the laws of the state' (§ 270, p. 297). Because state and church collide here, encounter each other, the crucial thing is the kind of relationship they enter into in the process. Since the state itself has the Christian religion—in its religious content—as its basis and root, it is a matter of religion in the narrower sense or of the church to recognize its competency to concretize and shape this truth in its domain and to acknowledge the form of certainty that corresponds to it. Because 'ethical principles and the organization of the state in general may be drawn into the province of religion', this gives the state, on the one hand, 'religious accreditation'; on the other hand, the state retains the right to assert these principles and organization against claims arising from subjective religious convictions, and to fend off interferences in this regard (§ 270, p. 299). The interiority, the faith, the sentiment of the ethical, and the elevation of the disposition that religion has and cultivates as its content in ritual and doctrine, should not be directed against the state, but towards it and underpin it. Even if the state displays defects and stands within the sphere of caprice, chance, and error, what matters is the affirmation of the state as form and idea, of the construction of its order (§ 258, Addition).

2. The state for its part is dependent on this affirmation, on being underpinned by religion, as the order of concrete freedom it is not autarchic and self-sustaining. It rests within the mores and ethos [*Sitte und Gesittung*] of the citizens who recognize and sustain the state. But mores and ethos have their source and strength in religion, in conscience shaped by religion. Hegel not only asserts this connection as a postulate or an observation from experience, but establishes it on reasoned grounds: 'Since religion is the consciousness *of absolute* truth, whatever is supposed to count as right and justice, as duty and law, i.e. as *true* in the world of the free will, can only count insofar as it has a *share* in the truth, is *subsumed* under that truth and *follows from* it' (*Philosophy of Mind*, § 552, p. 156). This general, universally applicable statement is then

[23] It deserves mention that Hegel, irrespective of his determination of the state as an ethical state and its limitation on the external, to an order manifesting itself in laws and regulated obligations, leaves the inner realm and the personal disposition untouched. It is precisely in this that the state is an institution of freedom.

reinforced and taken further with respect to the concrete problem of his day, the relationship of the developed state to the Christian religion.

> But if genuine ethics is to be a consequence of religion, then this requires that religion have the genuine content, i.e. that the Idea of God known in it be the genuine one. Ethical life is the divine spirit as indwelling in self-consciousness, in the actual presence of self-consciousness as a people and the individual members of that people; this self-consciousness retreating into itself out of its empirical actuality and bringing its truth to consciousness, has in its faith and in its conscience only what it has in the certainty of itself, in its spiritual actuality. The two are inseparable' (*Philosophy of Mind*, § 552).

If two kinds of conscience, a religious one and a moral one different in content, therefore cannot exist, the religious content, as the inherently highest truth, wields—as Hegel says explicitly—'a sanction over the ethical life standing in empirical actuality'. In this way, religion is 'the basis of ethical life and of the state' (*Philosophy of Mind*, § 552, p. 156).

For Hegel, this realization does not stand in isolation; he places it into the scale of his time: 'It has been the massive error of our times to want to regard these inseparables as separable from one another, in fact even as mutually indifferent.' Part of this 'massive error' is to see the relationship of religion to the state such that:

> the state already exists for itself in some other way and from some force and power, while religion is the subjective affair of individuals and had to be added, perhaps as something desirable only for strengthening the state, or is even a matter of indifference, since the ethical life of the state, i.e. rational law and constitution, stands firm for itself on its own ground (*Philosophy of Mind*, § 552).[24]

3. For Hegel the inseparability and connectedness of the state and the Christian religion has a number of consequences with respect to how the relationship between state and church is organized. While this need not be discussed in detail here, I will briefly mention three consequences that are particularly pertinent to our topic.

(1) The state must offer 'every assistance' to the ecclesiastical community in its religious goals and protect it externally, just as the latter is subject to state laws with respect to its property, its external actions that reach into the worldly realm, and its employees. By doing this, the state does not engage in something arbitrary and discretionary, but fulfils a duty.

[24] In the *Philosophy of Mind*, this is followed by a harsh polemic against the Catholic religion, which, Hegel maintained, was (still) an unfree religion and was unable to bring forth and sustain a state as the actuality of freedom. With respect to this polemic, one must ask—leaving aside Hegel's political Protestantism (see above note 18)—to what extent it is based on a distorted and inaccurate perception of the Catholic religion, and, furthermore, to what extent its points of contention were in fact part of the reality of the Catholic religion at the time, but do no longer pertain to the Catholic religion as it has manifested itself since then and especially in the wake of the Second Vatican Council.

(2) It is part and parcel of 'the nature of the case' that the state should require of its citizens that they belong to *a* church, not a specific one, but some kind of church, since religion—or more precisely: the Christian religion—'is the moment which integrates the state at the deepest level of the disposition [of its citizens]' (§ 270, p. 295). The neutrality exercised by the state concerns only the confessional divisions within Christianity, it does not exist towards Christian religion as such or towards religion as a whole.[25]

(3) When it comes to religious communities which, because of their understanding of religion, do not—or only partially—recognize the direct duties towards the state (Hegel had in mind the Quakers, Anabaptists, and other sects), the state exercises tolerance, that is, it overlooks the anomalies and does not make use of its right to exclude them from public activity. For Hegel, it is the strength of the state developed for its purposes that it can act in this regard more liberally since it can rely in doing so on the strength of mores and the inner rationality of its institutions. Although the members of such religious communities cannot be full members of the state, given the interconnectedness of rights and duties, they live within civil society as full members and under its laws. To Hegel, it is the very expression of the universality of the state that these individuals, as well as the Jews, are considered legal persons in civil society and are recognized as such.[26]

III.

If the developed state and the Christian religion are thus closely and inseparably interrelated, the question about the right of conscience within and towards the state takes on special importance. It contains the counter-question of how the recognition of the subjectivity and particularity of the individual within a state that has and finds its ground in the religious truth of Christianity manifests and proves itself concretely. The status of conscience—more specifically: of the divergent, non-conforming conscience—is the central issue here.

1. Conscience for Hegel is the expression and form of developed subjectivity. It expresses 'the absolute entitlement of subjective self-consciousness to know *in itself* and *from itself* what right and duty are, to recognize only what it thus knows as the good; it also consists in the assertion that what it thus knows and wills is *truly* right and duty' (§ 137, p. 164). This definition is concise and gets at

[25] It corresponded to the legal situation in Prussia at the time that while every citizen had the free 'choice of the religious party' to which he wished to belong, and was free to switch to a different religious party, he did not have the right to belong to no religious party at all, §§ 40, 41 II II ALR. Leaving the church was possible only in the form of joining another. Only the Prussian Constitution of 1850 (Article 12) guaranteed also the right to no religious affiliation, see Gerhard Anschütz, *Die Verfassungskurkunde für den preußischen Staat vom 31.1.1850* (Berlin, 1912), Commentary 4 on Article 12, p. 195f.

[26] Hegel's support for the emancipation of the Jews—here he was defending the governments against contemporary attempts at 'Christian' restoration—is clear and emphatic. The outcry against it 'overlooked the fact that the Jews are primarily human beings', and that humanity was 'not just a neutral and abstract quality' (§ 270, footnote, p. 295).

the heart of the matter. In conscience, the unfolding of the (divine) spirit in the human being becomes the formal element of his subjectivity.

The sacredness and inviolability that conscience asserts as its attribute is not something it possesses by virtue of its mere presence, however; rather it derives it from the idea of conscience, namely that it is the unity of subjective knowledge and objective content (what is good in and of itself) (§ 137). However, whether the individual particular conscience corresponds to this idea of conscience is initially an open question, and unless mere empirical subjectivity as such—irrespective of content—is to become the insurmountable authority, it must remain subject to a considered judgment. Here Hegel is addressing head-on the tension that lies in the concept of conscience and seeks to deal with it.[27] If conscience invokes merely its (empirical) Self, mere conviction and certainty, it goes against what it lays claim to being, namely the rule of a reasonable, inherently valid mode of conduct. That is why it must yield to the judgment of whether its content is truthful, that is, rational. On the other hand, it is precisely the peculiarity of conscience that already in its merely formal certainty it represents exactly the certainty of this subject and the only thing that is obligatory for it. This leads to the famous 'ambiguity' with respect to conscience, which Hegel articulated in classic succinctness: 'The ambiguity associated with conscience therefore consists in the fact that conscience is assumed in advance to signify the identity of subjective knowledge and volition with the true good, and is thus declared and acknowledged to be sacrosanct, while it also claims, as the purely subjective reflection of self-consciousness into itself, the authority [*Berechtigung*] which belongs only to that identity itself by virtue of its rational content which is valid in and for itself' (§ 137, p. 165).

2. For Hegel, the solution cannot be that the state must recognize every conscience as mere subjective knowledge, as obligatory for itself in its merely formal certainty. Since the state—as a developed state—in turn represents its objective content, is reason made concretely manifest in its configuration and laws that are presupposed as ethical-rational, there is no *right* of the divergent conscience towards it. In this position, Hegel not only picks up the right of reason and emphasizes truth that has become external actuality, but he also addresses the problem of the *formation* of conscience,[28] something that is largely neglected by the modern discussion of freedom of conscience, which focuses solely on subjective, formal conscience. Conscience is designed to form itself in relationship to and absorb within itself the content of religious truth and the surrounding world, which in Hegel is (still) a moral world shaped by morality [*Sitte*] and reason. In this way, to use Hegel's terminology, it turns from merely formal conscience into truthful conscience. It is merely the exception that conscience is driven to self-reflection, into its own inwardness, there to construct a better

[27] On this see *Philosophy of Right*, §§ 137 and 138, with notes; the following reflections are also based on these passages.

[28] Especially in *Philosophy of Right* § 138 and Addition.

world and set it up against the externally existing world. If that situation does in fact transpire, for example, to speak with Hegel, when 'the actual world is a hollow, spiritless, and unsettled existence' (§ 138 Addition), and reason-seeking can no longer find itself in the rights and duties that hold in it, the individual and his conscience cannot be prevented from withdrawing from the actual into the inner world. But that is the expression of a ruined actuality that has become pathological.

3. If the subjective, merely formal conscience can thus not lay claim, in the achieved normal constellation of the state, to a right of its own against the state, the relationship of the state to the divergent conscience is by no means an arbitrary one for Hegel. Rather, it is, as much as possible, a relationship of tolerance. This emerges clearly from Hegel's already-mentioned remarks on the status of sects and non-Christian religious communities in § 270 of the *Philosophy of Right*.[29] For it was precisely the consciences of the Quakers, Mennonites, Jews, and so on that were the relevant deviant consciences in Hegel's time, which—because of their religious conviction and ethical convictions shaped by it—opposed the valid state-legal order and its duties more or less comprehensively. Hegel recommended tolerance and turning a blind eye, as well as the acceptance of a merely passive fulfilment of existing duties, instead of the active fulfilment that is inherently called for (e.g. military service). In this regard the state should behave all the more liberally, the stronger it is in its own rationality and the power of the mores [*Sitten*] sustaining it, though without the necessity—therein lies the difference between right and tolerance—of allowing itself to be called into question by the deviating consciences.

Needless to say, and this needs to be emphasized again, all of these considerations that Hegel offers for the individual, subjective conscience in its relationship to the state presuppose the state that is grounded on and in the Christian religion. These considerations are not developed and do not apply to the emergency and rational state, which leaves out the substantive—especially religious—content, and does not act in relationship to this content as something that is obligatory for it. In this state the relationship can be a different one, and the subjective conscience can, if necessary, become also a refuge of rationality vis-à-vis a substantively empty actuality of the state.

IV.

This reflection already brings us to the realm of the concluding question. It concerns the significance that Hegel's determination of the relation between state and religion has for that relation today.

[29] Moving from *Philosophy of Right* §§ 137, 138 to § 270 in order to determine Hegel's position is justified because Hegel limited himself, in § 137, to the formal conscience, to the extent that it was part of morality, and refers to *Sittlichkeit* when it comes to questions of the moral and truthful conscience. It is only in § 270 that the problem of the deviating conscience (in terms of content) is elaborated on.

1. Hegel's determination is based on the *parallelism* of state and religion in the actualization of a uniform substance, namely the religious content that has come into the world in and with the Christian religion. As I have shown, this applies not only generally, but also in details. In its universality and its developed form, the state appears as an actualization and implementation of the content of the Christian religion in the form of a worldly-external reality; it has in this its ground and the substantive foundation of its order, from which it lives substantively and which it in turn holds fast. In this sense it is a Christian state, irrespective of or precisely in its worldly rational form.

In the nineteenth century it was the Prussian Constitution of 1850 which made an attempt to cling to and carry on this constellation, after it had already become problematic by virtue of the forward-moving development of the state's neutrality towards religion. On the one hand, Article 12 of the Constitution guaranteed the freedom to profess one's religion, the private and public exercise of religion, the association into religious organizations, and the independence of civil and citizenship rights and duties from religious belief. Following this, Article 14 then stipulated the following:[30]

> The Christian religion shall be taken as the basis of those state institutions which are connected with the exercise of religion without prejudice to the religious liberty guaranteed by Article 12.

Looking at the subsequent development, this attempt remained an attempt, and in its day it already raised as many problems as it resolved.[31] But the spirit of Hegel was present in it once more, even as it was already waning.[32]

2. The state today, also and especially the state of the Basic Law, has moved away from this in its disposition and substance. It is a state that is neutral towards religion and other worldviews,[33] a state in which religion has been set free, in two ways. It has been freed for the exercise by the individual and in the sphere of society, and thus also freed to take on societal-political efficacy and importance. At the same time, however, it is set free in the sense that the state itself no longer has or advocates a religion, does not act towards a particular religion as its foundation, which means that religion or a particular religion has no necessary institutional participation in the universality of the state. 'Religion is no longer the spirit of the state ... Religion has become the spirit of civil

[30] Ernst Rudolf Huber (ed.), *Dokumente zur deutschen Verfassungsgeschichte*, vol. I (Stuttgart, 1962), p. 402. English translation of the Constitution of 1850 (with an introduction and notes by James Harvey Robinson) in *The Annals of the American Academy of Political and Social Science*, vol. 5, Supplement 8 (Sep., 1894), pp. 1-54.

[31] On this see the detailed commentary in Anschütz (note 25), pp. 264–282.

[32] On the genesis of Article 14, which was found neither in the original Constitution of 1848 nor in the draft of the imposed constitution, but came about only in the plenary deliberations of the latter in the chambers of the Landtag, see Anschütz (note 25), pp. 260–264.

[33] See BverfGE 19,1 (8); 19, 206 (216); 24, 236 (246); Alexander Hollerbach, 'Die verfassungsrechtlichen Grundlagen des Staatskirchenrechts', in *Handbuch des Staatskirchenrechts der Bundesrepublik Deutschland*, vol. I (Berlin, 1974), pp. 250ff.

society... It is no longer the essence of community, but the essence of difference.'[34] The universality of the state, that which forms it in spirit and establishes what is jointly binding for the human beings united into a unity within it, is not determined by a particular religion, but, disconnected from it, by worldly political purposes that are autonomous vis-à-vis religion. Given the cultural heritage and the traditional societal and political culture, those purposes may converge in no small number of cases with notions that are grounded in (Christian) religion, but in terms of the principle of the state's construction, that convergence is accidental, not necessary. Religion, or a particular religion, has no normative status in and for the state.

3. This fundamental difference between the state of today and the state as Hegel saw and conceived it rules out the adoption of the individual determinations of the relation between state and religion furnished by Hegel. From this perspective, the modern state is now only a *rational state*, the organization of the subjective commonality (common needs and interests) on the basis of the recognition of subjectivity, but without binding maxims as to the content of that subjectivity. Defining and finding the content of subjectivity remains a matter of subjectivity itself, within the boundaries of the rights of others and the basic external needs of coexistence. The formative principle is the nature of needs and the (merely) subjective principle. The binding and obligatory element of the common order is pluralism, that is, the open competition among various offers to define such content and the possibility of choosing among them (or not chose any of them). Christian religion, too, appears as one of these offerings, though without any farther-reaching obligatoriness (except for those who accept it).

It seems, however, that this reduction of the state that is neutral with respect to religion and worldviews to the mere rational state is correct only as a model type, while in the actual state it can be headed off and limited by the guarantee in constitutional law of substantive principles or institutions. With respect to the Basic Law, one can point to the respect for and protection of human dignity (Article 1 Section 1) and the state protection of marriage and family (Article 6 Section 1). It is questionable, however, whether an obligatoriness of substantive content derived from religion has been or can be achieved in this way. For the stipulated guarantees such as 'human dignity' or 'marriage' are, in terms of their content, not self-evident but in need of interpretation. And within the framework of the state neutral as to religion and worldviews (and the pluralistic society associated with it), this interpretation, as an obligatory one, cannot be achieved on the basis of one of the competing religious or ideological offerings of meaning and obligatoriness—that would rightly be seen as a violation of state neutrality; it can be created only by the

[34] Karl Marx, *Zur Judenfrage* I, in his *Frühschriften*, ed. by S. Landshut (Stuttgart, 1953), p. 180. English translation: http://www.marxists.org/archive/marx/works/1844/jewish-question/

remaining universality of this state or a general consensus that exists within society. The Christian notion of human dignity, which proceeds from the transcendent-metaphysical determination of man, his likeness to the image of God and his calling to eternal salvation, is only one possible notion, but not the universally binding one. And the marriage that is under the protection of the state order is not the Christian marriage; it can only be a 'worldly' marriage (whatever that may be).[35]

4. If the necessary connection of the developed state and Christian religion as spelled out by Hegel is more than a merely subjective hypothesis, then the state unmoored from (Christian) religion, which exists without any connection to a preceding, inviolable content, finds itself in a precarious situation as far as its own basis is concerned. Although it can invoke the requirements of human needs and the guarantee of the formal subjective freedom, beyond that it is devoid of a spiritual principle, it stands—as Hegel says—'in the air'. To that extent it has a basis and support only in the prevailing consensus of the citizens. This consensus, however, is not an objective, normatively demanded consensus that refers to an objective principle binding upon both the state and the citizens, but a subjective consensus that is shaped by the actually existing, shared notions. But this consensus is sought in order to objectify it, to enshrine it in 'values' that are supposed to impart a 'value foundation' to the state. For such objectification, however, the 'values' are nothing more than a surrogate.[36] Since they have no inherent content and no specific determination, but merely a designatory function, which expresses an existing consensus, everything flows back again to the prevailing consensus of the shared notions. That consensus is a fluid element, is subject to the normative fluctuations, to the so-called 'changing values' of the time, in which a variety of forces are involved; but under the conditions of pluralism it is without objective orientation, which confronts the consensus as something obligatory and around which mores and ethics can take shape and attach themselves. If this consensus is no longer sustained by the existing legacy, but becomes precarious, it must eventually be newly created as the condition of survival—the necessary price for the subjectivity that was previously fully unleashed. This can be done by the state for its self-preservation, or by the new need for the creation within society of an obligatoriness with which individuals can identify. Of course, in both cases one enters onto the level of surrogates,

[35] This is in line with the established case law of the BVerfGE. According to this case law, the protective maxim of the constitution guarantees 'the institution of marriage not abstractly, but in the elaboration that accords with prevailing notions that have found substantial expression in the legal regulations' (BVerfGE 31, 58 [82f.] with reference to BVerfGE 6, 55 [82]; 9, 237 [242f.]; 15, 328 [332]). It is further stated: 'Accordingly, the constitution is based on the picture of the "secularized" [*verweltlichten*] civil-law marriage', a point of departure that returns also in the decision on the constitutionality of the 1976 law amending marriage law (introduction of the principle of irretrievable breakdown), see BVerfGE 53, 224 (245).

[36] On this see now Gerhard Luf, 'Zur Problematik des Wertbegriffs in der Rechtsphilosophie', in *Jus Humanitatis. Festschrift Verdroß* (Berlin, 1981), pp. 127–146; earlier already Carl Schmitt, 'Die Tyrannei der Werte', in *Säkularisation und Utopie. Ebracher Studien* (Stuttgart, 1967), pp. 37–62.

which are open to manipulation and to the strategy of the political steering of consciousness. In the process, we often witness—beyond the debates over basic values—recourse to a *religion civile* as a basic political ideology. Under this condition, too, a community can live and find an existential form of its own. But with respect to the reality of concrete freedom, this seems like a 'second' and perhaps no more than a third path.

VIII

The Secularized State

Its Character, Justification, and Problems in the Twenty-first Century [2007]

Talk of the secularized state, at times also of the post-secularized state, is very widespread today.[I] On the one hand, the secularized state, irrespective of an expected rise in the importance of the religious, continues to be regarded as an epochal cultural-political achievement, for it has allowed people of different religious beliefs and ideological convictions to live peaceably and freely within and under a shared regime. On the other hand, the question arises whether this state, by its very conception, is sufficiently up to the new challenges posed by a stronger return of the religious and the growth of fundamentalist currents—that is to say, whether there may not be a need for a restructuring of the secularized state, and possibly even a metamorphosis to a post-secularized one.

But what exactly does it mean to speak of the secularized state? What does the secularity of the state mean? Does it refer only to its secularity as distinct from a sacral order? Does it refer to distance to any religion and a constitutive independence from religion? Or does it refer to an encompassing neutrality towards religion and worldview [*Weltanschauung*], a neutrality that gives them space—including public space—though without identifying with them in any way? Thus, if we wish to examine the justification of the secularized state (section II) and with it the problems it confronts in the twenty-first century (section III), the first thing we must do is clarify its character, that is, what makes up its structure and substantive conception (section I). I will refrain from looking at the historical emergence of the secularized state, as interesting as this process is, for reasons of space and because I have discussed it at length before.[1]

[I] Editors' Note: The article is based on the prestigious 'Siemens-Lecture' of the Carl Friedrich von Siemens Foundation in Munich that Böckenförde gave in 2007. His task was to revisit the topic of his seminal article, 'The Rise of the State as a Process of Secularization' (Chapter V in this volume), which he had published exactly fifty years earlier.

[1] E.-W. Böckenförde, 'Die Entstehung des Staates als Vorgang der Säkularisation' [1967], in Böckenförde, *Recht, Staat, Freiheit*, 4th ed. (Frankfurt, 2006), pp. 92–114, Chapter V in this volume.

Religion, Law, and Democracy. Ernst-Wolfgang Böckenförde, Oxford University Press (2020). © E.W. Böckenförde, M. Künkler, and T. Stein 2020. DOI: 10.1093/oso/9780198818632.003.0011.

I.

The character of the secularized state can be described, first of all, by stating that in it, religion—or a specific religion—no longer constitutes the binding foundation and animating force of the state order. Instead, state and religion are fundamentally separated, the state as such has no religion and does not represent one. It has emancipated itself from the embrace of religion, which was long determinative for the political system in antiquity and the Middle Ages, and in that sense it has become secularized. In shaping the coexistence of people, the state pursues solely worldly purposes and derives its legitimacy from them; spiritual and religious purposes lie 'outside its sphere of competence'.[2] In this it realizes a principle that Michel de L'Hôpital, chancellor to the King of France, had already formulated in 1562, on the eve of the Huguenot wars, in words that anticipated the future development: it did not matter, he declared in the king's Council, which was the true religion, but how men could live together.[3]

But does this separation of religion and state not lead to a godless state, a state without God? It would be premature to say so. To be sure, the state loses the quality of a *societas perfecta*,[II] in the sense of a comprehensive polity that incorporates all spheres of human life within itself, a polity sufficient unto itself, as presented in the political theory of Aristotle.[4] But religion is by no means negated or set aside by the secularized state. The latter finds religion in existence and establishes a relationship to it. Two things characterize this relationship: first, religion is released by the state, is set free. Its acceptance, organization, and exercise are no longer a state matter, nor is religion guided and directed by the state. The secularized state—and this was a protracted process—foregoes any form of religious sovereignty, and it no longer lends its power to enforcing religion or religious demands. Second, however, the freedom and effectiveness of religion are constrained by the state and its legal order when it comes to the state's worldly tasks and purposes.

As far as the release of religion is concerned, it means that religion, as Karl Marx recognized so early,[5] is consigned, from the perspective of the state, to the social sphere. It ceases to determine the spirit of the state, which thus can no longer be a Christian or Muslim state, or one shaped in obligatory fashion by any religion. Rather, religion unfolds within civic society and its liberal order. From there, of course, depending on the prevailing political decision-making

[2] '*[A]ußerhalb seines Befugniskreises*' in the apt formulation of the liberal constitutional scholar Robert von Mohl: *Das Staatsrecht des Königreichs Württemberg*, vol. I (Tübingen, 1829), p. 9.

[3] Leopold von Ranke, *Französische Geschichte*, Andreas edition, vol. I (Wiesbaden, 1957), p. 157.

[II] The concept of the *societas perfecta* was originally developed by Aristotle, who characterizes the polis as the all-encompassing community which is able to achieve the telos of all human communities: happiness. In the Catholic Church's tradition *societas perfecta* was ascribed to both the Church and the state.

[4] Aristotle, *Politics*, III.9, 1280b, 29–34.

[5] Karl Marx, 'Zur Judenfrage I', in his *Die Frühschriften* (Stuttgart, 1953), p. 183.

processes and how strong religion is within the faithful as citizens, it can exert and acquire influence upon the state, in the direction of shaping and ordering human coexistence. Political advocacy for goals and demands derived from religious motivations is thus by no means ruled out.

This brings us to the boundaries that are drawn to the development and efficacy of religion in accordance with the character of the state and its legal system. The secularized state, which as such does not have or represent a religion, acts and understands itself as a religiously neutral state. First, it does not identify with any religion or religious community and its desires; second, through the guarantee of religious freedom it grants religion space for its own development; third, however, it denies religion access to state institutions and offices, and blocks the overthrow of the principle of the state's own religious neutrality through, for example, the formation of a majority-based political will. In this constellation, the first and third points are unproblematic. The crucial question lies with the scope and boundaries of the developmental space for religious liberty within the framework of the state's legal system.

In this respect, two different concepts of state neutrality have evolved. First, the concept of distancing neutrality, realized in exemplary fashion in the French *laïcité*—though not in Turkey's secularism, which is nothing other than a state-administered Islam.[6] Second, the concept of open, encompassing neutrality, as found above all in the Federal Republic of Germany, but by no means only there.[7] Distancing neutrality tends towards consigning and confining religion to the private and private-social sphere. Open, encompassing neutrality additionally accords it room to develop in the public sphere, for example in schools, educational institutions, and in what is summarily referred to as the public order—though, of course, it does so without any form of identification.

The difference between the two concepts is not only a formal one, but exerts its effect above all in spheres that have simultaneously a spiritual-religious and secular-political aspect (*res mixtae*).[III] Those spheres exist wherever a religion is not limited to the worship of God in the form of liturgy and ritual, but incorporates also life in the world and relevant precepts governing behaviour, as is

[6] In Turkey, questions of faith and religious ritual are within the purview of a state authority, the Office for Religious Affairs (Diyanet). Following its expansion in 2003, it has about 100,000 employees, among them prayer leaders, preachers, and muezzins, and it oversees close to 70,000 mosques. Under the aegis of this office, a kind of Sunni state Islam is laid out as the basis of religious instruction and education. See Günter Seufert, 'Laizismus in der Türkei–Trennung von Staat und Religion?' *Südosteuropa-Mitteilungen* 1 (2004), pp. 18–29.

[7] Michael Brenner, 'Staat und Religion', *Veröffentlichungen der Vereinigung der Deutschen Staatsrechtslehrer* 59 (2000) , pp. 270–275, and E.-W. Böckenförde, 'Diskussionsbeitrag', ibid., pp. 316–318; E.-W. Böckenförde, 'Bekenntnisfreiheit in einer pluralen Gesellschaft und die Neutralitätspflicht des Staates', in his *Kirche und christlicher Glaube in den Herausforderungen der Zeit*, 2nd ed. (Münster, 2007), pp. 446–448.

[III] *Res mixtae*, literally things of mixed character, here in matters of state and church, refer to those areas of German law that demand cooperation between church and state, such as in the realm of religious instruction in public schools, or the employment of chaplains in public hospitals or the armed forces. Opposite to the *res mixtae* are those affairs over which the churches have full rights of self-determination, such as those concerning religious doctrines and rituals.

the case in the Christian religion, but also in Islam and Judaism. In this respect, distancing neutrality shapes the legal system in a purely secular way and turns away religious aspects as irrelevant and private. By contrast, open neutrality seeks to create a balance, in that affirming and leading a life in accordance with religion, to the extent that it is compatible with the secular goals of the state, is permitted also within the public sphere by the legal system and is incorporated into the latter.

II.

Where, then, does the justification of the secularized state stand? From where does it derive this justification? After all, it is by no means self-evident that a political order that organizes and governs the coexistence of human beings does not include religion, but in a sense leaves it outside the door and takes a separation of religion and the political system as its point of departure. This was not so in the ancient polis, in the Roman Empire, and most certainly not in the unitary religio-political world of the Middle Ages. What, then, imparts legitimacy to the secularized state?

1. The traditional justification is quickly explained. It is closely interconnected with the formation of the state as an expression of the secularization of the political system.[8] That secularization grew out of the defence against ecclesiastico-religious claims to supremacy in the worldly realm, claims that were widespread not only in the Middle Ages on the basis of an existing, unitary religio-political world, but also in the early modern period. Especially in the wake of the religious schism of the Reformation, where these claims and their underlying positions led to the confessional civil wars, the political order, for the sake of creating and guaranteeing the public peace in the coexistence of humanity, had to attain its own justification independent of any particular religion. That was the only way it could achieve and assert political autonomy. This happened, and could only happen, through a principled distinction between a religious and a political level, the formulation of genuinely secular tasks and goals of the political system, and the assertion of its supremacy in these tasks and goals against ecclesiastical-religious claims—precisely the features that constitute the secularization of the political system.[9] Religious freedom was not the guiding principle in this process, but arose more as a consequence: for one as a defence against ecclesiastico-religious intolerance, for another as a political decision to make possible and realize the coexistence of people of different religions and denominations in a pacified order; religious freedom was gradually realized within the framework of secular tasks.[10]

[8] On this see Böckenförde (note 1).

[9] For a detailed account see Böckenförde (note 1), pp. 100–108; more recently also Christian Walter, *Religionsverfassungsrecht* (Tübingen, 2006), pp. 28–38.

[10] An overview of the various stages of religious freedom, which began with a narrowly circumscribed freedom of conscience and their recognition is provided in: Wilhelm Kahl: *Lehrsystem des Kirchenrechts und*

Is this kind of justification still sustainable, does it still possess legitimizing power now that the churches have entirely renounced the old claims to power, have accepted religious freedom as the external law, and have also made their peace with the fundamental separation of state and religion? One could ask whether it is time to dismantle the old defences. Yet this question should not only be related to the relatively peaceful present, but should also be projected into the future. If one does that, it does not seem far-fetched that this justification will retain or regain its legitimizing power as a barrier against a possible advance of religious movements with a more fundamentalist bent, also in the clash with Islam, which so far has seemed barely able to accept a fundamental separation of state and religion.

2. Independent of this, a new justification has by now accrued to the secularized state, namely from the direction of human rights. The idea and principle of human rights generally places the justification of the state on a new foundation. Human rights, as programmatically formulated in the Virginia Bill of Rights of 1776 and the French Declaration of the Rights of Man and the Citizen of 1789, aimed not only at proclaiming the rights of liberty of the individual against the power of the state, but also intended to furnish the state as such with a different and new kind of legitimation. Their claim, which gradually asserted itself, was to form the foundation of the entire human community; guaranteeing and securing them appears as the central task of all state power, its proper and new very purpose [*Umwillen*].[11] For Germany, in the wake of the experiences of the Nazi period, this prevailed once and for all in the Basic Law (Article 1 Section 2). The state exists for the sake of the individual, not the individual for the sake of the state, as the draft of the Constitutional Convention of Herrenchiemsee put it programmatically.[12] Those human rights included centrally the fundamental right of religious freedom, in origin the first fundamental right of the autonomous individual.[13] Fully recognized and realized, it leads the state to liberate religion for the individual, guaranteeing both freedom of religion and freedom from religion. The necessity and justification of a worldly—and therefore secularized—state that is itself no longer religiously bound, but is neutral towards religion, is grounded in religious freedom.

der Kirchenpolitik (Freiburg-Leipzig, 1894), pp. 204–236, 322–328; Gerhard Anschütz, 'Religionsfreiheit', in G. Anschütz and R. Thomas (eds.), *Handbuch des Deutschen Staatsrechts*, vol. II (Tübingen, 1932), pp. 575–580.

[11] Programmatic is the *Déclaration des droits de l'homme et du citoyen* of 26 August 1789, Article. 2: 'Le but de toute association politiques est la conservation des droits naturels et imprescriptibles de l'homme. Ces droits sont la liberté, la proprieté, la sûreté, et la résistance à l'oppression' [The aim of all political association is the preservation of the natural and imprescriptible rights of man. These rights are liberty, property, security, and resistance to oppression].

[12] *Bericht über den Verfassungskonvent von Herrenchiemsee* (Munich, 1948), 61.

[13] This much discussed thesis of Georg Jellinek, *Die Erklärung der Menschen- und Bürgerrechte*, 4th ed. (1927), still holds, for good reason: religious freedom in the form of the freedom of conscience for the first time brings to bear the direct relationship of the individual and the state, beyond the distinctions and bonds of social estates, as well as the fundamental prioritizing of the individual and the purposes of his life over the state.

Upon closer examination, this justification has some influence on the *nature* of the state's religious neutrality. After all, the human right of religious freedom, which encompasses the freedom of belief, the freedom to profess, and the free exercise of religion, aims at religious freedom not only in the private but also the public sphere, at the general possibility of living life in accordance with religion, though naturally within the framework of the basic demands of social coexistence.[14] The appropriate form of neutrality is therefore the open, encompassing neutrality of the state, which guarantees also this public sphere for the development of religion. The distancing neutrality of *läicité* thus appears as merely the lesser form of neutrality, which is subject to growing objections as the fundamental rights are being realized and is coming under pressure to justify itself.

3. Beyond this, a third justification of the secularized state is presently coming into view, and from a side from which it was not necessarily expected. I am talking about a theological justification, more specifically, one derived from political theology. It arises from the newly acquired position and doctrine of the Christian churches—among them above all the Catholic Church—regarding religious freedom. Here, and I am referring to the Catholic Church, the position on religious freedom has undergone a 'Copernican revolution'.[15] As late as the nineteenth century and into the twentieth, the Church, through pronouncements by its popes, had still strictly rejected religious freedom as an external right within the framework of the state's legal system. Later it declared it at most an evil to be tolerated, acceptable in certain situations for the sake of higher goods.[16] With the declaration on religious freedom by the Second Vatican Council, the Catholic Church made a positive and, in its justification, final about-turn. The external right to religious freedom is not merely accepted

[14] This explains the endeavour to draw the protective sphere of religious freedom as broadly as possible, as Christian Walter has recently posited (note 9), pp. 496–513. However, that does not rule out making a more precise differentiation of the partial guarantees of religious freedom, such as freedom of belief, freedom to profess, and the freedom to exercise one's religion.

[15] The expression from Josef Isensee, 'Die katholische Kritik an den Menschenrechten', in E.-W. Böckenförde (ed.), *Menschenrechte und Menschenwürde* (Stuttgart, 1987), p. 141.

[16] The condemnation or rejection of religious freedom is evident in the encyclical *Quanta cura* of Pope Pius IX of 1864, as well as the associated Syllabus (Nos. XV and LXXVII), the encylicals *Immortale Dei* and *Libertas praestantissimum* of Pope Leo XIII, and—to some extent embedded ethically—in the so-called Tolerance Address of Pope Pius XII in 1953. The references can be found in Denzinger, *Enchiridium Symbolorum*, 26th ed. (Freiburg, 1947), Nos. 1690, 1777/78, 1874, 1932, and, for Pius XII, in Utz-Groner, *Aufbau und Entfaltung des gesellschaftlichen Lebens. Soziale Summer Pius XII.*, vol. II, Nos. 3977 and 3978. On the interpretation and consequences of this doctrine see E.-W. Böckenförde, *Kirche und christlicher Glaube in den Herausforderungen der Zeit* (Münster, 2004), pp. 202–207. Cardinal Ottaviani, for many years the Pro-Prefect of the Vatican Congregation of the Doctrine of the Faith, defended it as follows at late as 1960: 'You might say that the Catholic Church thus needs two kinds of measure and weight. For where it itself governs, it wants to restrict the rights of those of other faiths, but where it constitutes a minority of citizens, it demands the same rights as the others. To this one should respond: in fact, two kinds of weights and measures must be employed, one for truth, the other for error' (Alfredo Ottaviani, *Institutiones iuris publici ecclesiastici*, vol. II: Ecclesia et Status, 4th ed. (Rome, 1960), pp. 72–73).

as a given that the Church encounters, but is explicitly justified positively as grounded in the dignity of the human person (*ipsa dignitate personae humanae*).[17] It therefore exists independent of the truth of the religious conviction and the responsible search for this truth;[18] it has the character of a right of freedom and a human right. With that the recognition of religious freedom turns from a concession into a commandment, a commandment that has its foundation in the Christian faith and its vision of the human being.

But if it is a commandment that follows from the content of the Christian faith and its truth, the recognition of religious freedom is a matter of political theology, political theology in the sense of the precise and clarifying definition of Heinrich Meier.[19] For it is the truth of divine revelation on which and for the sake of which the position of religious liberty is staked out and asserts a binding claim that demands obedience. This lends unexpected support to the secularized, open, and neutral state, far removed from and cutting across the post-secular expectations. Pope John Paul II, who had been substantially involved in pushing through the declaration on religious liberty in the Council Hall, drew very clear consequences from this by completely setting aside the traditional Catholic doctrine of the state as formulated by Pope Leo XIII. During his pastoral visit to Cuba in January 1998, he declared: 'A modern state cannot make atheism or religion one of its political ordinances. The state, while distancing itself from all extremes of fanaticism or secularism, should encourage a harmonious social climate and a suitable legislation that enables every person and every religious denomination to live their faith freely, to express that faith in the context of public life'.[20] This, even if indirectly expressed, is a clear repudiation of the religious state and an unequivocal affirmation of the open, encompassing, religious neutrality of the state. And it does this not simply by disregarding the Christian legacy, but as part of the Church's doctrine itself. What has occurred here is nothing more and nothing less than the result of the necessary, at times arduous, dialogue between faith and reason, which in this case had led to a purification of the faith through the reason of the Enlightenment. In this way, as Pope Benedict XVI put it not long ago, the faith newly realized its inner capaciousness and its own reason. For it was a task imposed upon Christians to 'welcome the true conquests of the Enlightenment, human rights and especially the freedom of faith and its practice, and recognize these also as being essential elements for the authenticity

[17] *Declaratio de libertate religiosa*, No. 2: 'Insuper declarant ius ad libertatem religiosam esse revera fundatum in ipsa dignitate personae humanae, qualis et verbo Dei revelato et ipsa ratione cogniscitur.'

[18] Ibid.

[19] Heinrich Meier, *Was ist Politische Theologie?* (Munich: C. F. v. Siemens Stiftung, Sonderdruck, 2006), p. 13. Political theology in his definition refers to 'a political theory, political doctrine, or political positioning, for which, according to the self-understanding of the political theologian, divine revelation constitutes the highest authority and final foundation'.

[20] John Paul II, sermon in Havana on 25 January 1998; English translation: http://www.ewtn.com/cuba/words.htm.

of religion'.[21] This has now happened. Some discussions in Germany create the impression that among believing Christians, as well, it is still quite a struggle to accept this and realize it in concrete conduct.

III.

Thus new and potent justifications have accrued to the secularized state, but this neither describes nor solves the problems it confronts in the twenty-first century. There are several of these problems. They relate to its character as a secularized state as well as a liberal and constitutional state that guarantees fundamental rights. Here I would like to single out two problems that seem particularly important. The first is this: from where and how does the liberal, secularized state acquire—currently and in the future—the measure of pre-legal togetherness and sustaining ethos that is indispensable for a thriving coexistence in a liberal system? The second, connected problem is this: to what extent can the state sustain its constitutive guarantee of religious freedom, religious neutrality, and the equality of all religious communities in the face of growing religious and worldview pluralism and increasing migration, seeing as it simultaneously depends on a living culture—which is not infrequently shaped by religious traditions (fermenting agents)—as the shared, binding foundation?

1. The first problem to which we shall turn is part of the larger context of pre-legal conditions on which a polity, especially a liberal one, depends for its viability. No state can be built solely on the concentration of power and the exercise of coercion, no matter how indispensable these are. It simultaneously needs services, which guarantee legitimacy, and the attitudes of the people, by dint of which they engage for the most part in voluntary acts of obedience.[22] Likewise it would be an illusion to believe that a state system could live entirely by guaranteeing self-related, individual freedom, without a unifying bond that conveys a certain us-feeling and precedes this freedom.[23]

This unifying bond, often described with the concept of relative homogeneity,[IV] controversial but for that reason not necessarily wrong, has numerous facets.

[21] Address by His Holiness Benedict XVI to the Members of the Roman Curia at the Traditional Exchange of Christmas Greetings, 22 December 2006. English text: http://www.vatican.va/holy_father/benedict_xvi/speeches/2006/december/documents/hf_ben_xvi_spe_20061222_curia-romana_en.html.

[22] Fundamental discussion by Hermann Heller, *Staatslehre* (Leiden, 1934), pp. 238f., 242ff.

[23] See E.-W. Böckenförde, 'Die Zukunft politischer Autonomie', in his *Staat, Nation, Europa*, 2nd ed. (Frankfurt, 2000), pp. 109–114. [included in volume I of this edition]

[IV] With 'relative homogeneity' Böckenförde refers to a term coined by Hermann Heller (1891–1933), constitutional scholar in the Weimar Republic (see H. Heller, *Staatslehre*, ed. G. Niemeyer, 3rd ed. (Leyden: Sijthoff, 1963), p. 230), pointing to a necessary sense of we-consciousness and a shared sense of belonging in the citizenry. The term homogeneity must not be understood in his work as denoting the opposite of pluralism or heterogeneity, but as a marker for societal cohesion (which he deems necessary to sustain democracy in the long term). In democratic politics, this cohesion needs to be created in society (through communication, participation in shared activities, exchange etc.) and cannot be imposed by the state as that would violate the democratic state's liberal principles.

It can be fed from various sources: socio-economic as well as biological-natural ones, although the latter are often overestimated, and not least cultural-mental ones. For our topic, the problems of the secularized state, the cultural-mental factors carry the greatest significance. Among them, religion plays an important, but by no means the only, role.

a) If the state encounters one or more religions that in turn accept religious freedom and the secularized state, something that is the case today with the Christian religion in its various denominations, this can certainly generate a unifying bond and a sustaining, stabilizing force. However, the precondition is that the religion is alive among its believers, the citizens, and exerts an effect on behaviour as a lived religion. But that is not something that the secularized state has in its control. Using the means at its disposal, it cannot guarantee the survival and vitality of a religion, nor can it declare a religion to be the obligatory foundation of the community's shared life. The religious freedoms it ensures guarantees only the *possibility* of religion and religious vitality, not the existence of religion as such. Of course, what the state can and should do is support and protect religion and religious vitality to the extent that they in fact exist—protect them also against hostility and denigration that go beyond free and open discussions and debates, including those critical of religion. This is entirely compatible with the necessary neutrality with regard to religion and other worldviews. My most frequently quoted statement, which is misinterpreted at times, also is not contrary to what I have just said.[24] [V]

If one takes stock in this regard, the outlook is not exactly encouraging, however. I am referring to Germany, for example. The share of baptized Christians in Germany as a whole is about 62.8%, in the new federal states only around 30%, among children and teenagers there only around 15%. But in Hamburg, as well, the number of baptized has been below 50% for years, and the situation in Bremen is likely to be similar. Even in Munich, the capital of Bavaria, a *Land* still regarded as Christian, the figure is no more than 53.7%, while in Frankfurt am Main it is merely 47.2%.[25] This is the statistical data of external membership. It says nothing yet about the inner vitality of the Christian faith, its practical exercise, and its transmission to the next generation. To that extent the circumstances seem rather degressive and highly precarious. They are being promoted by a social-communicative and audiovisual environment that is increasingly woven through by an areligious spirit, and in part also by a self-secularization within the churches. As a result, the state can build upon the Christian religion

[24] E.-W. Böckenförde, 'Der freiheitliche säkularisierte Staat … ', in S. Schmidt and M. Wedell (eds.), *'Um der Freiheit willen … ' Kirche und Staat im 21. Jahrhundert* (Freiburg, 2002), pp. 19–23. See also Karl Hemann, 'Säkularisierter Staat: Woher kommen das Ethos und die Grundwerte? Zur Interpretation einer bekannten These von Ernst-Wolfgang Böckenförde', ibid., pp. 24–30.

[V] *'The liberal, secular state is sustained by conditions it cannot itself guarantee. That is the great gamble it has made for the sake of liberty.'* See Chapter V in this volume, p. 167.

[25] For the figures (rounded off) for Germany as a whole: Statistisches Jahrbuch 2006: Kirchliche Verhältnisse (as of 2004); for Munich, the figures come from the City of Munich as of 2006. A comparison with the figures three years earlier shows the trend: Germany as a whole 64.5%, Munich 56.5%, Frankfurt/M. 48.7%.

as a force that binds all together and conveys a sustaining ethos only to a limited extent, and increasingly less so in the future. The problem with religions that have a tense relationship with the secularized state and religious freedom and reject both will be examined at a later point.

b) In addition to religion, the civil religion often invoked in recent years should be considered as a sustaining and ethos-conveying force. Of course, the first step is to clarify what this often multifaceted concept might mean in the final analysis.

On the one hand, the term civil religion refers to certain elements of religious culture that are de facto or also institutionally integrated into the political system.[26] Here one might think of the incorporation of religious phenomena and statements in public speech, social-political events, or representative political acts, such as the swearing in of the head of state and the government. In this way, a meaningful connection to the religion that is presupposed as existing is symbolically expressed, and the secular polity is thus indirectly legitimized religiously. In this form, however, civil religion can hardly fill a void created by the disappearance or weakening of lived religion. After all, to exert its effect, civil religion itself remains tied to a (still) existing religiosity, which it seeks to make amenable to secular use through symbolic acts and pronouncements. If that religiosity is missing, civil religion runs on empty, becoming an external ornament that is no longer taken seriously, or a piece of public hypocrisy.

Of course, civil religion can also have a different meaning, one that picks up on the 'religion civile' as developed by Rousseau in the next-to-last chapter of his *Contrat social*.[27] Civil religion now means a sustaining ideology that is intended to preserve the polity and is made obligatory as a foundation of values. It becomes in the literal sense a *civic* religion, secular in the real sense. It derives its content from presumed—and as such, posited—mental conditions fundamental for the coherence of the polity, 'sentiments de sociabilité', without which, as Rousseau asserts, one can be neither a good citizen nor a faithful subject.[28] If the secularized state resorts to such a form of self-protection, it dismantles a piece of its freedom, its characteristic liberal core. For such a civic religion, proclaimed as the value foundation of the state system, is inherently intolerant. It demands a positive affirmation, as a person must stand on its ground in terms of his or her positions and attitudes. It cannot tolerate deviations, and freedom exists only on its basis and within its framework. Already in Rousseau we read: the person who does not believe in the principles of the 'religion civile' but rejects them can be banished from the state,

[26] Hermann Lübbe, *Religion nach der Aufklärung* (Graz, 1986), pp. 308, 321. See also Eberhard Jüngel, 'Religion, Zivilreligion und christlicher Glaube', *Essener Gespräche zum Thema Staat und Kirche* 39 (2005), pp. 55–57.

[27] Jean-Jacques Rousseau, *Du contrat social*, Book IV, Chap. 8, ed. Bouchardy (Paris, 1946), pp. 205ff. English translation: http://www.constitution.org/jjr/socon.htm.

[28] Rousseau, ibid., p. 218; an apt characterization of the Rousseauan civil religion appears in Lübbe (note 26), p. 308f.

not because he does not believe its principles, but because he is 'insociable', incapable of living within society.[29]

This makes clear the terrain the secularized state enters upon if it establishes a civil religion of this kind for the purpose of stabilizing itself. The danger is not as remote as one might think. The constant appeal to the 'value system of the Basic Law' and the insistence that all who live here and wish to live here, be they Germans or foreigners, must profess it, is the entrance gate. Loyal adherence to the existing laws, with freedom of thought, is then no longer sufficient to live in the state as a fully equal citizen or *Schutzverwandter* (resident with limited rights), and to enjoy liberty. Instead, an affirmation, the proclamation of a certain disposition is demanded as the precondition, and freedom is thus restricted to the parameters drawn in this way. It is not difficult to fathom what consequences that entails.[30] Fundamentalism can also appear in the guise of a fundamentalism about the value system. The Federal Constitutional Court should be congratulated for its courage, not merely in general, but for having closed the entrance gate at one important point. In its ruling on the application of Jehovah's Witnesses for status as a corporation under public law, it stated that what mattered was not a positive closeness to the state and certain attitudes and dispositions, but conduct, faithfulness to the law in the sense of loyal adherence to existing law.[31] The faith-based belief of this religious community that the state is inherently pernicious and more like an instrument for the rule of evil remains unaffected—in a liberal system, ideas are free.

c) If a recourse to the civil religion thus seems hardly fruitful in its first version, and highly problematic in its second, this raises the question—an obvious one, in any case—about culture as a shared bond that also transmits a sustaining ethos. Spiritual forces, mental realities, and traditions interact within culture, forming into habitual attitudes and the attendant ethos. It goes without saying that such a culture is not a static, and above all not a fixed normative stock: it lives, especially in the secularized state, in freedom and from free as well as spontaneous impulses. As such it has no binding force; instead, in the form in which it exists and develops, it is something de facto given. Under the banner of the freedom of opinion, art, and *Weltanschauung*, it becomes—more strongly than before—a movable, even fluid element. Its shaping effect can dissolve into

[29] Rousseau (note 27): 'Sans pouvoir obliger personne à les croire, il peut banner de l'Etat quiconque ne les croit pas; il peut le bannit, non comme impie, mais comme insociable.'

[30] One consequence is the distinction and opposition of formal freedom and the legitimate use of freedom. The exercise of the rights of freedom, such as religious freedom, parental child-raising rights, or freedom of expression, are tied—beyond the boundaries laid down by law—to unwritten provisos concerning attitudes and the value system, into which much can be projected, depending on the Zeitgeist. As a result, the constitutional state's principle of freedom is impaired at its core. That was already the principled objection against the praxis of the so-called Radicals Decree concerning employment in the public sector. See E.-W. Böckenförde, 'Verhaltensgewähr oder Gesinnungstreue?', in his *Staat, Verfassung, Demokratie*, 2nd ed. (Frankfurt, 1992), pp. 277–286.

[31] BVerfGE 102,370 (394f.); on this and follow-up problems see Walter (note 9), pp. 560–565.

random multiplicity, nor is it immune, as a sustaining force, against medial dissolution.

Precisely for that reason, the secularized state depends on supporting and—as much as it is able—protecting the existing, lived culture. For its own sake, it must engage in the cultivation of culture, though of course not at the expense of, but within the framework of, its liberal order. The fields of activity for this are numerous. Above all the mandate of providing education and schooling comes into play, the exercise of which is today widely neglected. Likewise, to give only one more example, the maintenance and promotion of education and research in the humanities, which is in danger today of being overwhelmed by utilitarian thinking guided by economic considerations.

2. This brings us to the second problem area mentioned above. A dilemma becomes evident here. Today, and increasingly so in the future, the secularized state depends on an existing and lived culture as a core that conveys a relative sense of togetherness and gives rise to an ethos that sustains the state order. However, this culture was formed, not only marginally, but extensively out of certain religious roots, out of traditions and forms of behaviour shaped by them. Even as a secular culture, which is what it is today, those roots are still inherent in it, be it as sediments, be it as lived elements of tradition. If this culture—under the banner of a general pluralization, caused in part also by increasing, politically instantiated migration processes and rising international freedom of movement—now begins to reshape itself in the direction of a rather heterogeneous diversity (ethical, religious, cultural), is this state able to guarantee full religious freedom, religious neutrality, and equal status of all religions, without the cultural base on which it rests increasingly fragmenting, hollowing out, and losing its binding force? The unfortunate headscarf debate, which keeps moving from one round to the next not only in Germany, is a symptom of this dilemma. Can a solution be found?

a) To illustrate the problem, I would like to recount some correspondence I had two years ago with Cardinal Ratzinger, at the time the Prefect of the Sacred Congregation for the Doctrine of the Faith. In response to my plea against a general prohibition of headscarves for teachers,[VI] the Cardinal wrote that while he was in nearly complete agreement, his thinking was somewhat different on one point. In a state neutral with regard to religion and other worldviews, it is not necessary to treat all symbols appearing in public equally, meaning that either all or none may appear in public. After all, a state does have its own cultural and religious roots, which remain constitutive for it in a certain regard even if it knows itself to be obliged to exercise neutrality vis-à-vis religions.

[VI] Böckenförde took an active part in the German headscarf debate in several ways: he advised the parliamentary group of the Green Party in the state of Baden-Württemberg with regard to a legislative ban on teachers wearing a headscarf (which he criticized), and he wrote several articles and gave interviews in newspapers on the issue (see e.g. 'Bekenntnisfreiheit und die Neutralitätspflicht des Staates', in Sabine Berghahn and Petra Rostock (eds.), *Der Stoff aus dem Konflikte sind: Debatten um das Kopftuch in Deutschland, Österreich und der Schweiz* (Bielefeld: transcript, 2009), pp. 175–192; and 'Das Koptuch ist ein Stück Integration', *Süddeutsche Zeitung*, 17 July 2006).

Otherwise, according to the Cardinal, the privileges of Sunday would have to vanish, and the laws in matters of marriage and the family would have to take account equally of Muslim and Christian tradition. In conclusion, he states: 'A state cannot cut itself off completely from its own roots and elevate itself into a state of pure reason, so to speak. One that, without a culture and profile of its own, treats all traditions relevant for ethos and the law equally and classifies all public statements of religions as equal. What was addressed in the discussion in recent years fairly inadequately with the term *Leitkultur* [guiding culture] has a basis in reality.'[32] [VII]

In my response I wrote that the reservation he raised pointed to an important problem, one that was easily overlooked in the debate and which I, too, had not picked up on: 'You are right, every state order has its own cultural as well as religious roots, and that finds expression more or less in its institutions and its legal system, even (still) when the state is a secular state that is neutral towards religions and other worldviews. For the sake of treating religions equally, it must not deny them, and it can maintain its "ordre public" shaped by them.' However, given the recognition of religious freedom as a human right, which is grounded in the dignity of the human person (*Dignitas humanae*, c. 2), I argued that it was part of this ordre public that other religions and denominations are not excluded from or substantially constrained in this freedom of holding their faith and professing it privately and publicly; 'to that extent, religious freedom is not divisible, and an openness also for the religious symbols of other denominations and religions must take hold. Any existing "*Leitkultur*" (the term is indeed not a good one) must also absorb into itself such an openness without for that reason having to deny its own character'.[33] I also referred to two examples of how the two can be reconciled: the Ford plants in Cologne are said to have organized their workflow in such a way that the predominantly Muslim Turkish workers can observe their prayer times, and in the Prussian Gymnasien no tests were written on Saturdays to allow Jewish students to reconcile school attendance and the Sabbath commandment.

For me, the essence of this discussion is this: on the one hand, religious freedom as a human right cannot and must not be subject to a cultural reservation, and, on the other hand, religious freedom and the equality of religions cannot give rise to a claim to level the religiously determined imprinting of culture and way of life as part of the *ordre public*. With respect to this imprinting,

[32] Joseph Cardinal Ratzinger, letter to the author dated 30 April 2004; see also his *Werte in Zeiten des Umbruchs* (Freiburg i. B., 2005), p. 136f.

[VII] *Leitkultur* is a political concept that has been hotly debated in Germany for more than three decades. Originally, the term was introduced by the German-Syrian political scientist Bassam Tibi, presenting a normative idea of a common liberal culture in Europe which he felt should be more assertive in public life, and not tolerate rights violations in the name of cultural relativism. Later, however, the concept was re-ascribed, inter alia by CDU politician Friedrich Merz, to denote a majoritarian Christian notion of a leading culture, into which those of different cultural and religious heritage should assimilate.

[33] E.-W. Böckenförde, Letter to Cardinal Ratzinger dated 28 June 2004.

the members of other religions (mostly minority religions) live in a diaspora. Incidentally, when it comes to such a life in the diaspora, Islam and the Jewish religion contain explicit directives to honour the laws and customs of the land.

b) To what extent can one derive from this clues to a solution to the problem? In view of the growing and rather heterogeneous religious-cultural diversity, the transition to a strictly distancing neutrality of the state could suggest itself as the 'second choice', so to speak, in order to relegate such diversity into the private sphere and to disencumber public life of it. To win general acceptance, this path would have to steer towards an ideology of laicism, of the kind that is operative in France. But it does not provide a sustainable solution. People want to live according to their roots not only halfway and in private but wholly, they do not want to be cut off from them, and they have a right to this. The sought-after integration also has the goal of incorporating people into the shared order without demanding that they give up their identity, and it differs from pure assimilation precisely in this regard. Integration presupposes the ability to live according to one's own roots. We must therefore stick with an open, encompassing neutrality, which gives public space also to diversity without for that reason dissolving the fundamental structure of one's own order.

By contrast, the road to a solution lies in the stabilization of an open and secular liberal order. That requires freedom-related but also freedom-constraining laws, adherence to which is then strictly enforced. These laws must set out clear, inherently justified road markers and lines, which also contain circumscribed spheres of tolerance, but do not diverge into the complexity of permanent weighing and balancing.[34] This is indicated in a number of areas, two of which I will highlight: the mandatory nature of universal schooling, including the way students behave in school (including in co-educational settings) and present themselves, and the protection of religious beliefs—in those things that are sacred to them—against defamation and disparagement.[35] Such freedom-related laws, if they are consistently and impartially applied, are able to generate a new kind of unifying bond across a plural, partly centripetal cultural reality: the commonality of life in and under a legal order that is grounded in reason and inviolable. In this way, Montesquieu's important statement—'Liberty

[34] Of course, the trend of contemporary legislation, which increasingly provides only normative objectives and open concepts instead of substantively defined if-then-regulations, is going into a different direction. It is further promoted by a widespread direction in the doctrine of fundamental rights and the weighing decision-making adjudication of the constitutional court on fundamental rights. An example of the latter is BVerfGE 83, 130 (142f.)—Mutzenbacher. That decision prohibits the legislator from regulating the necessary balancing of artistic freedom (Article 5 Section 3) and youth protection (Article 5 Section 2), such that youth protection is generally accorded precedence with certain kinds of writings that pose a danger to the young. Instead, here, too, the decision must be made on a case-by-case basis. Fundamental critique in Bernhard Schlink, *Abwägung im Verfassungsrecht* (Berlin, 1975).

[35] In case this latter is not self-evident out of respect for the conviction of others, it is the task of the law and statutes to set down boundaries of what is permissible and to endow it with sanctions. With respect to the former, courts have gone too far in several cases with the recognition of claims to exemption on the basis of Article 4Basic Law, see the references in Starck, in von Mangoldt, Klein, and Starck, *Bonner Grundgesetz, Kommentar*, 4th ed., marginal note 94 with note 273 on Article 4 Section 1.2.

is a right of doing whatever the laws permit'[36]—acquires a new meaning and legitimating force: the law, not arbitrariness, is the coating of freedom, also and especially under the conditions of partial heterogeneity.

This brings us back to the question about the necessary commonality and the sustaining ethos in the secularized state. If the state proceeds in this way, it creates a kind of commonality that is able to overarch plurality and the partial heterogeneity: the shared life under liberty-related laws, the boundaries of which must be observed by all equally. Instead of expansive professions of values, loyalty to the law becomes the foundation of a shared life. The attendant ethos of lawfulness is able to help sustain and stabilize such an order.

3. However, can such a concept be implemented vis-à-vis religions and religious beliefs which themselves do not accept a fundamental separation of state and religion (thus rejecting the secular state), and believe they cannot do so for theological reasons? This question is important for the relationship to Islam and to the possibility of integrating people committed to the Islamic faith into the secularized state—quite apart from Islamist fundamentalism and terrorism. Specifically, the question is this: To what extent is it permissible—indeed, imperative—to demand from Islam and Muslims the recognition of the secular state and its order?

This question concerns not only the recognition of and adherence to the existing laws, including their impact on the freedom of religion of Muslims. In this regard it could be readily answered with reference to the Fundamental Declaration by the Central Council of Muslims in Germany in 2001. It stated: 'As a matter of principle, Islamic jurisprudence obliges Muslims in the diasporato respect, and abide by, the local legal order. Against this background, asking for, and accepting, a visa, a permit of residence or a foreign nationality are considered as contracts to be respected by the members of a Muslim minority.'[37]

The question also pertains to the fundamental attitude to the principle of the separation of religion and the state, in which the secularized state has its basis, and the consequences that arise from it. It is not yet answered with the above-mentioned Fundamental Declaration, for it relates only to the situation in the diaspora. But what holds if the situation of the diaspora no longer prevails? Does the rejection of a separation of religion and state gain the upper hand and become decisive? This question must not be excluded from an honest dialogue.

a) The secularized state makes Islam and its followers an offer that has two sides to it. On the one side, it expects and demands from them loyalty to the laws and in this sense fidelity to the law, whereby it leaves them with an 'internal reservation', the possibility, namely, of taking a distanced stance towards its order and rejecting it when it comes to fundamentals. By thus not tying the status as an equal citizen to a profession of the value system as its condition,

[36] Montesquieu, *De l'Esprit des lois*, Book XI, Chap. 3.

[37] Article 10 of the Fundamental Declaration of the Central Council of Muslims in Germany. English version: http://muhammad.islam.de/3037_print.php.

but remaining content with respect for and compliance with the laws, the state affirms its liberal nature.

Such a concept does not appear utopian from the outset. Under different scenarios it has passed the test. For this was the way in which Catholics could be integrated into the secularized state in the nineteenth century and later, as well. They did not have to affirm religious freedom (as a principle), which is something they could hardly do on the basis of their faith until the Second Vatican Council.[38] They were even allowed to advocate the 'Catholic state as a thesis', as had been laid down in the state doctrine of Pope Leo XIII, and declare the religiously neutral state of the modern age to be a 'national apostasy', as Klaus Mörsdorf still did as late as 1964;[39] all they had to do was respect religious freedom as a legal reality and to conduct themselves accordingly. They did that, and over time they dismantled their reservations.

On the other side, the secularized state cannot and must not give any religious conviction, no matter what support it might enjoy among the people, the opportunity, by making use of religious freedom and democratic possibilities, to undermine its liberal order from within and eventually do away with it.[40] Here is what follows from this proposition: Were one to posit that a religion, currently Islam, proves resistant to religious freedom over the long term, that is, seeks to dismantle it if it has the political possibilities for doing so, for example via the formation of a majority, the state would have to ensure that this religion—or its followers—remain in a minority position, and that the diaspora proviso therefore continues to apply. That might necessitate relevant political measures in the area of freedom of movement, migration, and naturalization.

b) What remains as the fundamental question, therefore, is to what extent Islam can be moved to embrace a fundamental separation of religion and the state. Here one must pay very close attention to the attitudes within Islam and must not rashly equate them with statements by Islamist groups. Such a move cannot be ruled out simply because Islam posits the truth and universal validity of its message. The Christian churches do the same, especially the Catholic Church, and yet they found their way—of course not without internal struggles—to an acceptance of religious freedom and the secularized state. The question is thus whether a parallel development, a kind of reenactment of the development that happened particularly within the Catholic Church, seems possibly for Islam without self-surrender. After all, in its history the Catholic Church has also advocated all the positions against religious freedom and the separation of religion and the state currently being advocated by Islam or the

[38] See the references to the traditional Catholic teachings on tolerance in note 16.

[39] This position followed as the essence from the state doctrine of Pope Leo XIII, especially in his encyclicals *Diuturnum illud* and *Libertas praestantissimum*, see the references in Peter Tischleder, *Die Staatslehre Leos XIII.* (Mönchengladback, 1923), pp. 187ff. Klaus Mörsdorf, *Lehrbuch des katholischen Kirchenrechts*, vol. I, 11th ed. (1964), p. 57. See also Albert Hartmann, *Toleranz und christlicher Glaube* (Frankfurt am Main, 1955).

[40] This can also give rise to concrete problems locally. See the interview with Stefanie Vogelsang, the *Baustadträtin* (Construction Councillor) of Berlin-Neukölln, 'Wir müssen die gemäßigten Muslime schützen', *FAZ*, 4 August 2006, p. 38.

Islamists.[41] It therefore deserves special attention when Pope Benedict XVI, reflecting the teachings and history of his own Church, points out that the Islamic world today, with great urgency, confronts a task very similar to what has been imposed upon Christians since the Enlightenment, and was brought to a concrete resolution for the Catholic Church by the Second Vatican Council as the fruit of a long struggle. What is at stake, according to the Pope, is the position of the community of believers in the face of the insights and demands that grew out of the Enlightenment.[42]

Of course, this does not yet answer the question I have posed. Doing so exceeds my competencies, as it would presuppose a precise knowledge of Islam and its currents. If the answer tends to be positive, there is no further fundamental problem, although vigilance, firmness, and patient openness to dialogue continue to be called for in order to underpin and promote the aforementioned development. If the answer is more sceptical, the state, irrespective of its liberality and openness, is obliged to erect barriers that prevent the followers of Islam from directly or indirectly emerging out of their minority position within the state. This would not constitute a self-contradiction, but merely the self-defence of the secularized state. At the same time, inherent within it would be the indication of an indispensable foundation of reason, or, if you like, the 'natural law' of the secularized state, which might possibly be connected to the antique-Judaeo-Christian cultural sphere as reflected against the horizon of the Enlightenment.

[41] See Böckenförde (note 16), pp. 202–207.

[42] Pope Benedict XVI (note 21), p. 8.

PART III

ON THE THEOLOGY OF LAW AND POLITICAL THEORY

Böckenförde on the Relationship Between Theology, Law, and Political Theory

Mirjam Künkler and Tine Stein

Part III comprises four articles dealing with the relation between theology, law, and political theory. Throughout all of these, Böckenförde clearly distinguishes between the demands on the individual that arise from religion, positive state law, and politics respectively. He also points out that religious legal concepts and state law need not be irreconcilably opposed to each other—there is the possibility of reconciliation between the truth-claims of revealed religion and the positivity of modern state law, as long as religious claims do not claim to be universally binding. Since the Second Vatican Council, the Catholic Church and the democratic constitutional state share common ground in the recognition of the freedom of the individual. The chapters reflect Böckenförde's personal belief and attitude, expressed in the motto *civis simul et christianus* [being a Citizen and at the same time a Christian]: being a devout Catholic is compatible with being a committed democratic citizen at the same time, seeking to withstand the possibly arising tensions.

The first chapter in this section, titled Political Theory and Political Theology: Remarks Regarding their Reciprocal Relationship (Chapter IX), was published in a volume that was widely acclaimed among scholars working in the field of politics and religion. Edited by religious philosopher Jacob Taubes in 1983, the volume was—somewhat cryptically—entitled *The Prince of this World. Carl Schmitt and the Consequences.*[1] In his contribution, Böckenförde takes up the relation between political theory and political theology by presenting his understanding of Carl Schmitt's political theology. Böckenförde characterizes Schmitt's dictum that all modern concepts of the state are secularized theological concepts as presenting primarily a conceptual sociological approach to state law concepts: as with sovereignty, the attributes of the almighty were transferred to the state and ultimately to the people, which now have both become

[1] Jacob Taubes (ed.): *Der Fürst dieser Welt. Carl Schmitt und die Folgen* (Munich: Wilhelm Fink, 1983). While the main title referred to Hobbes' Leviathan, the subtitle of the book indicates that it is Carl Schmitt who is assumed to stand in for the prince.

Religion, Law, and Democracy. Ernst-Wolfgang Böckenförde, Oxford University Press (2020). © E.W. Böckenförde, M. Künkler, and T. Stein 2020. DOI: 10.1093/oso/9780198818632.003.0012.

legal concepts. Schmitt's political theology is therefore primarily a juridical one, according to Böckenförde.

Böckenförde agrees with Schmitt's conclusion that political theory should acknowledge political theology as nothing external to it, but as an important aspect of political theory itself, which for centuries guided its underlying conceptions. But unlike Schmitt, Böckenförde embraces the dissolution of the medieval world and accepts the differentiation of religion and state as irreversible. This dissolution is also not normatively lamentable. By contrast, it made possible the modern concept of freedom, including freedom of conscience, which for Böckenförde is one of humanity's greatest achievements.

Böckenförde then explicitly distances himself from Schmitt's delimitation of political theology to its juridical aspects and suggests that in order to fully appreciate the meaning of political theology, one needs to study the institutional translation of theology into political action. He terms the latter programme *institutional political theology*, which explores what Christianity has to say about a state's status, legitimation, structure, and the relation between church and political authority. Classic examples are Augustine's concept of the Kingdom of God with its differentiation between *civitas terrena* and *civitas Dei*; Thomas Hobbes' idea of a Christian Commonwealth; or the political theology of the Second Vatican Council that embraced the principle of religious freedom, which Böckenförde considers a sea change in Catholic doctrine of the supremacy of truth towards the acknowledgement of potential error.

Institutional political theology in turn should be distinguished from *appellative political theology*, one primarily concerned with a call to action, as manifested inter alia in liberation theology or Pope John Paul II's political theology, which Böckenförde presents in a favourable light. By focusing on the words of Jesus and the Gospel that appear 'nonpolitical' at first glance, Pope John Paul II made a case for dignity, liberty, and the duty of man to take the side of the weak and to reject violence.[2] In Böckenförde's view, since politics is essentially concerned with relations between individuals and groups, religion cannot avoid being political in this sense and must put forward its own position. But *appellative political theology* must be careful not to be misused to arbitrarily justify any political end.

The thrust of the argument that Böckenförde pursues in the article takes issue with 'a barely concealed atheistic' as opposed to agnostic posture with which 'political science becomes in the true sense an atheistic science'.[3] According to Böckenförde, this posture stems from a wrongly drawn conclusion from what he calls 'the bracketing of the God question' in political theory,[4] caused by the

[2] Böckenförde has written in more detail about this in 'Das neue politische Engagement der Kirche. Zur "politischen Theologie" Johannes Pauls II', *Stimmen der Zeit* 198 (1980), pp. 219–234.

[3] Chapter IX in this volume, p. 249.

[4] With this formula Böckenförde is referring to the lawyer Arnold Brecht (1884–1977), who in his book *Political Theory. The Foundations of Twentieth-Century Political Thought* (Princeton, NJ: Princeton University Press, 1959, originally written in German), had included a chapter on political science and the belief in God in the twentieth century. Brecht had been representative of Prussia in the Weimar Republic's upper house (Reichsrat) and, after having defied Hitler during his inaugural speech in the Reichsrat in February 1933, was dismissed

impossibility of answering the question of God on scientific grounds. The right conclusion, Böckenförde holds, with which the 'bracketing [would adhere] to the premises on which it is based, [. . . would] not declare the God question as settled but as scientifically unanswerable. That is to say, the existence of God, divine revelation, and the truth of theological arguments can be neither confirmed nor refuted by science, which means these questions remain open in both directions.'[5] Hence, political theory should not only take into account the relation of political entities to religious attitudes, as is common practice in the social sciences. It should also be open to try to understand religion, religious convictions, and theological doctrines 'from within'.[6]

How can modern secular law be adequately understood from a theological perspective? The article 'Reflections on a Theology of Modern Secular Law' (Chapter X) is devoted to this question. It is based on Böckenförde's acceptance speech on the occasion of being awarded an honorary doctorate by the Faculty of Catholic Theology of the University of Bochum in 1999. Again, Böckenförde's intention is to decouple Catholicism from natural law reasoning and to reconcile it with the positivity of modern state law.[7] Thus, the speech goes to the heart of much Catholic legal thought with its natural law doctrine and what in Böckenförde's view is a misguided concept of law. He argues that the main problem of the classic Catholic conception of natural law is that it does not distinguish between morality and law, especially with respect to their different functions.[8] Thus, it increasingly diverged from political thought outside the Church since the sixteenth-century, when positive law began to be conceptualized as a means to enable the coexistence of people with different beliefs. This divergence has two problematic consequences: first, it generates an inner reservation against the binding nature of state law and second, religious truth claims take a totalitarian form in relation to state law: 'if this moral principle is transferred abruptly to the legal order, meaning that no distinction is drawn between the external right of the person, which must be recognized as such,

from the civil service. Brecht then emigrated to the United States, where he subsequently taught at the New School for Social Research in New York for two decades. He served as an advisor to the drafters of the West German Basic Law.

[5] Chapter IX, p. 249. [6] Chapter IX, p. 250.

[7] Christoph Möllers argues that Böckenförde is the only Catholic legal theorist who makes this attempt in a serious fashion. See Christoph Möllers, 'Römischer Konziliarismus und politische Reform. Ernst-Wolfgang Böckenförde zum 80. Geburtstag', *Zeitschrift für Ideengeschichte* 3(4) (2010), pp. 107–114.

[8] Böckenförde's endeavours to dispute and criticize Catholic natural law doctrine dates back to the early 1970s when he and Franz Böckle, a Catholic theologian at the University of Bonn, initiated a joint research programme that brought together theologians, constitutional lawyers, historians, and social scientists in order to scrutinize the pitfalls of Catholic natural law doctrine. The project resulted in a widely acclaimed volume, edited by Franz Böckle and Ernst-Wolfgang Böckenförde, *Naturrecht in der Kritik* (Freiburg: Herder, 1973). The sociologist Franz-Xaver Kaufmann, who was a member of the group, remembers that Böckenförde especially objected to the claim of the political bindingness of natural law as an undisputed guiding principle for state law. That claim was raised by Catholic theologians as well as Christian Democratic politicians. See Franz-Xaver Kaufmann, 'Ernst-Wolfgang Böckenförde—Porträt eines Zeitgenossen', in Hermann-Josef Große Kracht and Klaus Große Kracht (eds.): *Religion, Recht, Republik. Studien zu Ernst-Wolfgang Böckenförde*, Paderborn: Ferdinand Schöningh 2014, pp. 199–207.

and the ethical-moral exercise of the law, which is subject to the demands of truth, the consequences are freedom-destroying and totalitarian'.[9]

Building on Vatican II, when the congruence of morality and law in Catholic thought was ultimately broken, Böckenförde develops an argument in favour of secular law as comprehensible from a theological, Catholic perspective. He holds that an appropriate doctrine of natural law should differentiate between 'the part of natural law that is and can be related to external, state-supported and state-guaranteed law on the one hand, and the part that is obligatory only as an ethical-moral [*ethisch-sittlich*] commandment . . . on the other'.[10] Therefore, the question that his article seeks to answer is how one can 'derive from theological reflections a measure or points of orientation for disassembling the ethical-moral [*ethisch-sittlich*] natural law into the realm of external law that is aimed at being enforceable and guarantees public peace, and the realm of behaviour that is commanded only ethically and morally [*ethisch und sittlich*]?'[11] Crucial for such a project is the Christian understanding of human dignity and of the human condition as affected by sin and thus as ambivalent, neither totally prone to good nor to evil. Moreover, Böckenförde argues that the resurrection of the dead would imply that not all elements of injustice have to be dealt with in this world, but that God is the last judge—which amounts to a relief for the human legislator and judge. He also points to the historical contextuality of revelation, suggesting that Biblical mores must be understood as being historically embedded.

In a last step, Böckenförde identifies three demands that arise from these theological considerations for secular law. First and most crucially, he holds that every human being must be recognized as a dignified legal subject as enshrined in the principle of human dignity. Further, (in what may be regarded as a contribution to the debate on universalism versus particularism) Böckenförde argues that the concrete instantiation of human rights, including the balance struck between individual freedom and the common good in every society, depends on the underlying culture including specific customs, societal practices, and ideas of living together:

> One must therefore distinguish between the genuine rights of the human being as a person, rights that make it possible for him to walk upright, rights that constitute an absolute given, and those rights that shape the social environment in which humans interact, including their relationship to the political community—here several forms can exist which preserve man's status as a subject in different ways and forms.[12]

Böckenförde also adds that Catholics should not be self-righteous when judging other legal systems given the history of the Catholic Church, which denied and fought against the idea of individual freedom for centuries. Second, Böckenförde argues that a state legal system must keep clear of the Aristotelian goal of the

[9] Chapter X in this volume, p. 265. [10] Chapter X, pp. 266–267.

[11] Chapter X, p. 267. [12] Chapter X, p. 272.

good life, since secular law cannot guarantee more than a minimum of ethical social behaviour. Its focus must rather lie on securing rights and equal freedoms, and on ensuring that state law meets the requirements inevitably arising from the need for peaceful social coexistence. Third, and as a consequence, while taking sin seriously, the Church should recognize that law cannot demand from people actions that are not accomplishable. Böckenförde notes that Catholics in general have begun to move closer to the position of Luther, who held that positive law must occupy a middle ground between the ambitions of divine law and the realities of human nature.

Nevertheless, despite his critical stance on the traditional Catholic natural law doctrine and his insistence on differentiating between morality and law, Böckenförde does value the idea of natural law as an important pre-positive moral foundation of the state. As he lays out in particular in the last longer treatise he has written 'On the Ethos of Jurists' of 2010, natural law should be understood as a form of legal ethics with a legitimizing, directive, and corrective function for state law.[13] Thus, natural law reasoning of any kind, religious or otherwise, should be accepted as a legitimate voice in the public sphere. Böckenförde's careful distinction between legal ethics on the one hand and state law on the other becomes clear also in the next chapter, revealing a highly differentiated understanding of being a Christian while holding public office as a constitutional judge.

Chapter XI, 'A Christian in the Office of Constitutional Judge', is devoted to personal reflections on the dilemma he faced during his tenure as a constitutional judge: trying to bridge his Christian spirituality with his tenure as a high-ranking public servant in a secular state, committed to nothing but the letter of the law. This brings him to discuss his motto *civis simul et christianus* in more detail. Christian spirituality is defined here 'as the realization of God's devotion in baptism through the response to this devotion. It finds its forms of expression and its concretization not only in prayer and divine service, but precisely also in daily life; ... Christian spirituality knows no separation between the personal-private and the occupational spheres.'[14] The article goes back to a speech he delivered to a circle of Catholic intellectuals, initiated by himself and Hans F. Zacher, former president of the Max Planck Society. The idea behind the circle, which met twice a year during the 1990s, was to provide a platform for dialogue with the German Episcopate and offer the bishops advice from a lay point of view. The topics included in particular the (ineffective) reception of church norms by the local churches and the (unsatisfactory) position of women in the Church. However, the reform ideas developed in this circle were taken into account by only a few individual bishops.[15]

Böckenförde looks back on his struggle with the Catholic teachings before Vatican II, which then still defined the state as ideally Catholic. The Church

[13] Ernst-Wolfgang Böckenförde, *Vom Ethos der Juristen* (Berlin: Duncker & Humblot, 2010), pp. 44ff. For a detailed discussion of his approach to natural law, see: Judith Hahn, 'Ernst-Wolfgang Böckenförde's Approach to Natural Law as Normative Legal Ethics', *Oxford Journal of Law and Religion* 7 (2018), pp. 1–28.

[14] Chapter XI, p. 280.

[15] Franz-Xaver Kaufmann (note 8), p. 204f.

essentially demanded every believer in public office to act as a vanguard for Christian natural law. By making clear that as a judge he would be required to prioritize the public good over Catholic demands, Böckenförde disappointed certain Catholics who had hoped that he would judge in accordance with Church doctrines. Quite the contrary, Böckenförde fully embraced the democratic, religiously neutral political order and justified his position by insisting on the strict neutrality demanded from a judge. He came to this conclusion as a Christian, as which he felt bound to the common weal. If the common weal were to be understood not merely as an abstract ideal, but as a good to be realized within the framework of constitutional democracy, then Christians would have to accept the secular state and act religiously and ideologically neutral within its framework, without a 'reservation based on authoritative natural law ... and without having the "Catholic state" in the back of one's mind as the real goal'.[16] In his swearing-in as judge on the Federal Constitutional Court, Böckenförde took the oath with religious affirmation, thereby deviating from his previous oath-giving practice in the appointment procedure as professor-cum-civil servant. His reasoning was to appeal to the innermost attachments that can be mobilized while calling for divine assistance, in order to fulfil the duties of the office as constitutional judge in an appropriate way. In other words, he summoned the forces of his faith to help him rely solely on the positive legal order and interpret the law solely according to the standards of the constitution without regard to personal political and religious convictions.[17] Böckenförde also argues that the fact that constitutional court judges have the last word in many genuinely political conflicts requires a special scrupulousness in the interpretation of the constitution, which must be free of religious-metaphysical or partisan considerations in its justifications.

In preparation of joining the bench, Böckenförde relinquished his activity as a consultant for the Central Committee of Catholics and also suspended his membership of the Social Democratic Party, in order to circumvent any allegations that he would act as a judge on behalf of a specific constituency, be it of religious or political nature. In his view, Christian spirituality can manifest itself in faithfulness to one's office and in an integrity that is open to the world. If an unsolvable conflict should occur, the possibility of a public withdrawal always remained. In fact, an intense inner conflict did arise when a new law on abortion was brought to the Constitutional Court in 1992, and it seemed as if Böckenförde's opinion could become the decisive one in swaying the court's decision.[18] In this article and even more explicitly in the biographical interview,

[16] Chapter XI, p. 282.

[17] See Dieter Gosewinkel's comment in the Biographical Interview (Chapter XVI), which draws a connection to the dictum: 'According to this thesis, the liberal, secularized state is sustained by conditions it cannot itself guarantee. It follows from this that a state depends all the more on the fact that a person who joins it and assumes a special responsibility also brings along his inner powers of commitment.' (p. 388).

[18] In 'Portrait of a Contemporary' (note 8, p. 203), Kaufmann mentions that Böckenförde invited him and a few others to a confidential conversation in a small circle. Kaufmann recalls the extraordinary seriousness that Böckenförde employed in the struggle for a constitutionally, morally, and politically acceptable position.

Böckenförde insists that it was clear to him at the time that he had to decide the case exclusively in accordance with the Basic Law and that it would have amounted to an abuse of the office—for which he had sworn the oath with religious affirmation—had he taken advantage of his seat on the bench to advance Catholic positions.[19]

Like Chapter X, 'Reflections on a Theology of Modern Secular Law', Chapter XII, titled 'On the Authority of Papal Encyclicals: The Example of Pronouncements on Religious Freedom', is based on a speech. Böckenförde gave it on the occasion of being awarded another honorary doctorate in theology in 2005, this time from the Faculty of Catholic Theology at the University of Tübingen. Böckenförde took the opportunity to devote himself to connecting two of the most important concerns throughout his life: the freedom of man and the constitution of the Catholic Church. For Böckenförde, this closes a circle that began with his 1957 debut article 'The Ethos of Modern Democracy' and which he followed up with his work on the Catholic Church's stance on Hitler's seizure of power (1961) and his publications on religious freedom (1964, 1968, 1970, 1986, 1990).[20] Again, as in Chapter X, Böckenförde is interested here in determining the content of religious-ethical and religious-legal norms as well as the relation between religious norms and state law. He observes a certain tension in Church discussions between the magisterium on the one hand and the people's faith on the other, which should be resolved, he proposes, on the basis of theological, not legal, arguments.

Böckenförde's argument proceeds in four steps. First, Böckenförde states that an encyclical is not part of the infallible magisterium, for which the criteria are strict. Conversely, this means that encyclicals are inherently fallible: 'Papal encyclicals as a separate genre of papal doctrinal pronouncements are not infallible as such; or put differently, and to some ears perhaps shockingly, they are in principle fallible, error cannot be ruled out *a priori*.'[21] Second, historical evidence for this definition is given with reference to magisterial statements on religious freedom. In the nineteenth century, religious freedom was condemned as the right to say no to the true and only (Catholic) religion; freedom was thus exclusively understood as the freedom to take on the right faith. Liberal understandings of the right of religious freedom were dismissed as leading to the dissolution of the divinely given order of truth. As Böckenförde shows, this position is based on a perceived unity of morality and juridical law, which fails to distinguish their respective functions: 'And because of the presupposed necessary unity of law and morality, according to which the law—natural law as well

See 'Böckenförde on the Right to Life, Human Dignity, and its Meta-positive Foundations' (Introduction to Part IV in this volume) for the Federal Constitutional Court decision on abortion (1992) in which Böckenförde participated.

[19] 'I swore an oath on the constitution and that I would preserve it against everybody. If the constitution contains any shortcomings with respect to my convictions as a Catholic Christian, I must accept that. I may not attempt to undermine it, and to seek to become active as a Catholic vanguard, so to speak. If one has a problem with this and concerns of conscience, one may not in honesty assume such an office.' Chapter XVI, pp. 391–392.

[20] See Chapters I, II, and IV in this volume.

[21] Chapter XII, p. 293.

as positive law—is merely the external aspect of ethics related to the realm of human interactions, it cannot be differentiated.'[22] The Declaration on Religious Freedom of the Second Vatican Council is then presented by Böckenförde as embodying an epochal shift from the right of truth to the right of the person.[23] With this document, the freedom of conscience and religion, which is to be guaranteed by the state, is endorsed and provided with a theological legitimation, namely the dignity of the human person arising from the likeness of God. Böckenförde underlines this theological argument by stressing that religious freedom must be guaranteed by the state because 'God has created humans as free persons and because the path to truth presupposes freedom', a statement which can be seen as his credo in light of his identity as a Catholic thinker, as a legal scholar and as a political theorist.[24] This turn in the magisterial pronouncements also means that the assumption of a unity of morality and law is given up. While there is a duty to cling to the once revealed truth in the moral realm, the legal right of religious freedom is directed to ward off interventions by third parties and the state.[25] Thus, the magisterial pronouncement forms a decisive break with, or 'partial annulment' of, the old doctrine. This reversal in the Church's teaching may also occur in the future in other doctrinal areas, Böckenförde holds.

However, in the third step of the argument, Böckenförde proposes that the fact that encyclicals can in principle be fallible (and have proved to be fallible with regard to the statements on religious freedom, for example) does not mean that they are entirely noncommittal. Thus, he aims to provide a more precise theological determination of the authority of encyclicals. To this end, he characterizes the order of the Church as being shaped, on the one hand, by the authority and hierarchy of the ministries, and, on the other, the concept of the communio-ecclesiology elaborated in the Second Vatican Council. Although encyclicals are prescriptive and claim to be accurate, they must also be open to criticism, Böckenförde holds. On his account, such criticism does not signal a lack of faith,[26] but rather an important corrective that needs to be taken into account by the magisterium. Otherwise, there is the danger that the connection between traditio and receptio,[27] between the authority of the teaching

[22] Chapter XII, p. 296.

[23] See in detail Chapters IV and VII in this volume.

[24] Chapter XII, p. 298.

[25] See, in detail: Ernst-Wolfgang Böckenförde, 'Einleitung zur Textausgabe der "Erklärung über die Religionsfreiheit"', in Ernst-Wolfgang Böckenförde, *Kirche und christlicher Glaube in den Herausforderungen der Zeit. Beiträge zur politisch-theologischen Verfassungsgeschichte 1957–2002*, 2nd expanded edition in 2007 (Münster: LIT Publishing House, 2007), pp. 231–246

[26] See annotation XIV in Chapter XI for the theological concept of the *sensus fidelium*. Böckenförde relies here and in the following on the analyses of his older brother Werner Böckenförde, a theologian and canon lawyer who proposed the theological idea of a *sensus fidelium* (sense of the faithful) to open up a space of debate within the Catholic Church. For his writings, see Norbert Lüdecke and Georg Bier (eds.), *Freiheit und Gerechtigkeit in der Kirche. Gedenkschrift für Werner Böckenförde* (Würzburg: Echter, 2006). For a more detailed account of how Ernst-Wolfgang relies on Werner Böckenförde, see Hahn (note 13), p. 21f.

[27] By contrast, Böckenförde delimits the prevailing principle in the state, where the connection between authority and norm addressees is based on the relationship between law / command and obedience (loyalty).

staff, which traditionally provides meaningful orientation, and the faithful's willingness to follow, might be dissolved. Employing a dialectical formulation, Böckenförde presents the dogma of infallibility as a principle that may indeed serve to protect the Church from an exaggerated claim to authority: if it were to be reserved for exceptional situations that protect the central core of belief, teachings of comparatively lesser importance could be assumed to be revisable, thereby underpinning inner-church freedom.

Church political practice, however, is far from such an understanding. As Böckenförde shows in the fourth and last step of his argument, with the 1983 Codex Iuris Canonici (Code of Canon Law) reform, the demand of new canon 752 for an 'inner readiness to follow' is considerably more far-reaching than the old regulation of 1917.[28] The fact that, according to the new regulation, the faithful are only allowed to represent and express what corresponds with proclaimed doctrine leads to 'every public questioning and criticism, that is, in the form of a scholarly discussion' being ruled out.[29] Against this background, the concluding remarks of the article are dedicated to the character of canon law and its need for reform. Böckenförde views this special type of law as determined by theology, that is, the character of the Church as a sacramental institution of salvation. At the same time, however, in order to do justice to the concept of law, church law must contain the features 'that are the constituent qualities of law as a system related to personal freedom and communication' in order for it to earn the right to organize the coexistence of human beings under a condition of freedom. Thus, for canon law to be an order of law rather than an order of power, it must entertain certain fundamental principles, including the generality of legal rules, the impartiality of judges, the obligation to give reasons for decisions, and the right to be heard.

Since current Church law is nowhere near this, Böckenförde's argument may be read as an important contribution to today's debate on the need for reform of the institutional structure of the Catholic Church.[30] In one of his last ever published essays (published in the German daily *Süddeutsche Zeitung*), he sharpened his critique of the sclerotic constitution of the Church in light of the

[28] Can. 752: Although not an assent of faith, a religious submission of the intellect and will must be given to a doctrine which the Supreme Pontiff or the college of bishops declares concerning faith or morals when they exercise the authentic magisterium, even if they do not intend to proclaim it by definitive act; therefore, the Christian faithful are to take care to avoid those things which do not agree with it. (http://www.vatican.va/archive/ENG1104/__P2H.HTM)

[29] Chapter XII, p. 303. Note that Pope Francis advocated inter alia for a bold freedom of speech in his address on the eve of the conclave, see (in the German translation) 'Im Wortlaut: Was der Papst vor der Papstwahl sagte', *Die Presse*, 23 March 2013, https://diepresse.com/home/panorama/religion/1381892/Im-Wortlaut_Was-Bergoglio-vor-der-PapstWahl-sagte, see also 'Pope's Handwritten Notes of 2013 Speech to Cardinals now Published, *The Telegraph*, 17 March 2017, https://www.telegraph.co.uk/news/2017/03/17/popes-handwritten-notes-2013-speech-cardinals-now-published/

[30] Again, Böckenförde's brother Werner Böckenförde laid the ground for a critical analysis of the—according to both Böckenförde siblings: misguided—constitutional structure of the Catholic Church. See Werner Böckenförde, 'Zur gegenwärtigen Lage in der römisch-katholischen Kirche. Kirchenrechtliche Anmerkungen', in: Norbert Lüdecke and Georg Bier (eds.), *Freiheit und Gerechtigkeit in der Kirche. Gedenkschrift für Werner Böckenförde* (Würzburg: Echter, 2006), pp. 143–160.

sexual abuse scandals: in order to maintain its ostensible 'holiness', the Church shielded clerical perpetrators instead of helping the victims.[31] Böckenförde coined this an 'acting according to Church raison'—the well-being of the Church as an institution was placed *above* the well-being of the very believers whom the Church is meant to serve and protect. Böckenförde was clear that the Church would need to submit itself to criminal investigation and that it would need to aid rather than obstruct the judiciary's indictment of the perpetrators. Internally, the perpetrators as well as those who shielded them would have to acknowledge their guilt and sins, and the institutional structure of the Church would have to be reformed thoroughly. The guideline of such a Böckenfördean reform programme would be: do not be afraid of freedom![32]

[31] Ernst-Wolfgang Böckenförde, 'Das unselige Handeln nach Kirchenraison', *Süddeutsche Zeitung*, 29 April 2010.

[32] According to Pater Langendörfer, secretary of the German conference of Bishops, summarizing Böckenförde's advice towards the Church in a memorial speech. See Hans Langendörfer, 'Worte zum Abschied', *Der Staat* 58 (2019), pp. 457–459 (458).

IX

Political Theory and Political Theology

Comments on their Reciprocal Relationship [1981]

The following reflections cannot be exhaustive. They are intended merely as initial delineations and orientations that can help prepare for the systematic exploration of this topic. They limit themselves to political theology within the sphere of Christian religion, even though political theology exists also beyond it. Their point of departure is that political theology must no longer be something of which political theory and political sociology take no notice at all or only at the margins.

I. POLITICAL THEOLOGY AS AN ELEMENT OF POLITICAL THEORY

For thousands of years, thoughts and teachings about the political order among humans were tied to religious and—in the Christian period—also to theological notions. This is revealed by a look at Plato's *Politeia*, Cicero's *de legibus*, Eike von Repgow's *Sachsenspiegel*,[1] and Thomas Aquinas's section on 'de lege' in his *Summa theologiae*, to mention merely a few examples. It was only the political theorists of the late seventeenth and eighteenth centuries who, prompted not least by the religious civil wars, articulated a purely rational theory of political order, one that proceeded from the elementary natural needs of humans and the meeting of those needs, even if religio-theological topoi and arguments continued to strongly influence their thinking. For Karl

[1] Editors' Note: The *Sachsenspiegel* is a collection of legal norms as a record of existing customary law, written in 1220 by Eike von Repgow, administrator of Saxony. According to legal historian Karl Kroeschell, Eike evaluated the customary law he observed against the principles of reason and divine truth, thus merging the norms into an ideal rather than merely documenting them. Moreover, he included in the code the Christian doctrine of the two swords, which divided power between the pope and the emperor.

Religion, Law, and Democracy. Ernst-Wolfgang Böckenförde, Oxford University Press (2020). © E.W. Böckenförde, M. Künkler, and T. Stein 2020. DOI: 10.1093/oso/9780198818632.003.0013.

Marx, finally, part of the natural self-realization of the human being within the political system was the liberation from religion.[1] Independent of that, the scientific approach of the nineteenth and early twentieth centuries entailed leaving aside any religio-theological argument because it was not subject to scientific proof. The political and social sciences were to be strictly based on rational, empirically verifiable statements, and on that basis understand and explain the processes of social life and the structures of order. This, precisely, is what established them as a science.

Arnold Brecht has aptly characterized this problem of the 'bracketing of the God question' that occurred here, and which largely still shapes political theory to this day.[2] This bracketing can be done such that the God question is proclaimed to be (scientifically) settled and therefore obsolete. In that case we are dealing with a barely concealed atheistic posture, and political science becomes in the true sense an atheistic science. By contrast, if the bracketing adheres to the premises on which it is based, it does not declare the God question as settled but as scientifically unanswerable. That is to say, the existence of God, divine revelation, and the truth of theological arguments can be neither confirmed nor refuted by science, which means these questions remain open in both directions. But if the God question remains open in this way, it cannot in turn be left out of consideration. For if God exists, if a divine revelation has occurred, if theological statements contain truth, this carries far-reaching significance with respect to the tasks and epistemological object of the political sciences, and especially political theory. The argument that it is irrelevant whether God exists or not, whether (Christian) religion is the expression of divine revelation or a human invention, because certain other things matter when it comes to the political coexistence of human beings, is fundamentally ruled out, as it nullifies the openness of the God question.[3] Such a move does seem to make sense, precisely because the existence of God and a divine revelation is not an object of cognition by the political sciences, but of faith. But by choosing this option one follows a *virtual* atheism, perhaps without being aware of it. For from the perspective of (political) science, the existence of God and of a divine revelation do not matter; they remain—scientifically—inconsequential, which is why one can neglect them. Political theory remains within the realm of rational cognition

[1] Karl Marx, 'Zur Judenfrage' (1843), in his *Die Frühschriften*, ed. by Landshut (Stuttgart, 1953), pp. 171ff.

[2] Arnold Brecht, *Politische Theorie. Die Grundlagen des politischen Denkens im 20. Jahrhundert*, 2nd ed. (Tübingen, 1976)), Section XIII: Die politische Wissenschaft und der Glaube an Gott im 20. Jahrhundert, pp. 550ff., esp. 558ff. English: *Political Theory. The Foundations of Twentieth-Century Political Thought* (Princeton, NJ, 1959). [Brecht wrote the book originally in English, then translated it into German with Irmgard Kutscher].

[3] This formula shows a striking parallelism to the famous formulation of Hugo Grotius, which appeared already in Late Scholasticism: the commandments of natural law grounded in reason would hold even if—perish the thought—God did not exist. This formula served as the vehicle for uncoupling natural law from its theological-metaphysical foundation and for the transition to a purely intrinsic law of reason justified by guiding human ideas of purpose. E. Cassirer, *Die Philosophie der Aufklärung* (Tübingen, 1931), pp. 313ff.; H. Welzel, *Naturrecht und material Gerechtigkeit*, 4th ed. (Göttingen, 1962), pp. 108ff.

and what can be a part of it methodologically. It excludes what goes beyond, at first only methodologically, but as a consequence also substantively, while at the same time advancing the claim that it is a sufficient basis for a full understanding of political-social reality and the problems of political order.

To date, political theory has barely engaged this problem (which applies in the same way also to other sciences that deal with human activity), let alone discussed it thoroughly. But the problem returned to it in another form, and it is possible that this return makes it seem less urgent to deal with it. The return took place by way of the concept of sociology as the science of social behaviour, which underlies the grand sociology of Max Weber. In this sociology, the question about the motivations behind and inner driving forces of social action—and the ideas and convictions that sustain them—gained importance, and in connection with this also the question about the *belief* in legitimacy that guarantees the acceptance and stability of political authority. After all, Max Weber's well-known legitimacy types of political authority do not concern objective-substantive forms of legitimacy, but explicitly types of beliefs in legitimacy, that is to say, ideas within the consciousness of those subject to authority, ideas that bring forth a voluntary willingness to obey and accept, irrespective of the objective reality of authority.[4] Regardless of the classification of these types of legitimacy in Max Weber, which provides an instructive example for the virtual atheism of his sociology,[5] religion, religious convictions, and statements of theology thus found their way back into scientifically explicable politico-social reality. Ever since, they have been seen and accepted as a factor that shapes this reality by virtue of motivating behaviour, a factor which, irrespective of its 'irrational' origins and character, must not be ignored if one is to adequately grasp this reality and the problems of political order inherent in it. It is therefore no longer a cause for surprise if today a theory of political order and an understanding of the structure of politico-social entities and forms of behaviour seem incomplete or inadequate if they fail to take into account their relationship to and dependence on basic religious attitudes and beliefs, their mediation in theological doctrines and pronouncements. However, in order to fully grasp religion, religious convictions, and theological doctrines as shaping factors of politico-social reality, they must be understood and given expression 'from within', that is, on the basis of their own assertions and gestalt; a merely 'external' view reduced to the socio-functional aspect

[4] Max Weber, *Wirtschaft und Gesellschaft*. Studienausgabe (Cologne, 1964), Part 1, Chap. 3: Die Typen der Herrschaft, §§ 1 and 2, pp. 157–160. English text available at: http://www.archive.org/details/MaxWeberEconomyAndSociety

[5] This emerges above all with 'Charismatic Authority' (§ 10). The criterion of 'charisma' is 'a certain quality of an individual personality by virtue of which he is considered extraordinary... How the quality in question would be ultimately judged from any ethical, aesthetic, or other such point of view is naturally entirely indifferent for purposes of definition.' Specific instances include the (divinely sent) prophet, the berserker, the shaman, and the revolutionary Kurt Eisner. This conceptualization is as scientifically neutral as the classification of religion under the sociological concept of superstition.

would remain inadequate and would once again lead directly into the bracketing exclusion of the God question.

There was yet another factor. The analysis of the foundational legal-political concepts of modern state theory undertaken by Carl Schmitt at the beginning of the twentieth century laid bare their origin in the Christian theological tradition. 'All significant concepts of the modern theory of the state are secularized theological concepts'—this apt core thesis of Carl Schmitt's,[6] repeatedly confirmed since, not only made clear the translation process that had occurred from theology to jurisprudence, it also showed how little modern thinking about state theory, which regarded itself as entirely secular and scientific, had escaped theology, and instead lived off the latter in the form of the acquisition of concepts. One more reason not to see political theology as something lying outside political theory, something that confronts it without any connection, and to grasp it rather as a substantial element of political theory, not only of speculative theory but also, and precisely, of a theory focused on concrete experience.

II. THE SUBSTANTIVE CONTENT OF THE CONCEPT OF POLITICAL THEOLOGY: LEGAL, INSTITUTIONAL, APPELLATIVE POLITICAL THEOLOGY

If political theology is considered an element of political theory with respect to its epistemological aspects, the first order of business is to ascertain the various meanings of the concept of political theology. After all, in the contemporary discussion the term 'political theology' is not used in a standard way, but with a meaning that varies substantively and systematically.

1. Political theology refers, first of all, to the process of translating theological concepts to the state-juridical realm. It is in this sense that Carl Schmitt introduced the term 'political theology' into the scholarly discourse in 1922 and gave it its classic definition. Such a process of conceptual translation, which was simultaneously the adoption of a position, took place in exemplary fashion in the development of the concept of state sovereignty and in the theory of popular sovereignty. Attributes that served theologically to characterize God, his omnipotence, creative power, and the like (*potestas absoluta, creatio ex nihilo, norma normans, potestas constituens* ...), were transferred in part to state power and those who held it, in part to the people as the bearer of political authority [*Herrschaftsgewalt*],[7] who were thus endowed with positions and qualities which had formerly been accorded only to the God of Christian revelation.

[6] Carl Schmitt, *Political Theology: Four Chapters on the Concept of Sovereignty*, trans. by George Schwab (Cambridge, MA, 1985), p. 36.

[7] References in Carl Schmitt (see note 6), pp. 36–53, and in his *Die politische Diktatur*, 3rd ed. (Berlin, 1964), p. 141f.

With this form of political theology we are not really dealing with theological statements, but with a conceptual sociology, namely a sociology of legal—or more precisely: state-juridical—concepts. These are stripped of the autonomy they assert and are traced back to their sociological basis, which turns out to be a recasting of theological positions. In this context it is worth mentioning that the first three chapters of Carl Schmitt's treatise on Political Theology first appeared in a commemorative volume for Max Weber under the title 'Sociology of the Concept of Sovereignty and Political Theology'.[8] This form of political theology has been aptly referred to as *juristic* political theology.

2. Political theology is understood as the embodiment of the pronouncements of a belief in God (a divine revelation defined in more detail substantively) about the status, legitimation, task, and possible structure of the political order, including the relationship of the political order to religion. If the community of faith is organized as a church, these pronouncements include the relation between church and state. Political theology in this meaning is widespread not only, but very strongly in the realm of the Christian religion and its denominations. The Christian religion is not only the veneration of God in the form of rituals; beyond that, it encompasses a doctrine of life with normative accent that reaches into nearly all spheres of life, as well as an interpretation of the existential reality of human beings (the 'world'). This leads invariably to statements/teachings concerning the orders of political coexistence, their status (within the framework of the theological interpretation of the world), tasks, sphere of competency, and legitimation. Formulations of this kind of political theology are numerous within the history of Western Christendom: beginning with Augustine's notion of empire and God with the distinction between *Civitas Dei* and *Civitas terrena*, to what is known as the Gelasian doctrine of the two swords, the hierocratic system of Pope Innocent III,[II] the two-kingdom theory of Martin Luther, to Thomas Hobbes' 'Christian Commonwealth'[9] and Hegel's political Christology,[III] but extending also to the state doctrine of Pope Leo XIII[IV] and the new political theology of the Second Vatican Council. All of

[8] M. Palyi (ed.), *Hauptprobleme der Soziologie. Erinnerungsgabe für Max Weber*, vol. II (Munich and Leipzig, 1922).

[II] Pope Innocent III (pope 1198–1216) held that the pope as vicar of Christ and endowed with divine legitimacy is the sole power on earth. Every other worldly power derives its competence from the pope. This hierocratic theory stood in opposition to the dualistic doctrine of the two swords according to which there was a spiritual and a worldly sword. Yet even on the basis of the doctrine of the two swords, popes had claimed primacy over worldly rulers.

[9] On this—and against the still widespread rationalistic-atheistic interpretive approach—see K. Schilling, *Geschichte der sozialen Ideen*, 2nd ed. (Stuttgart, 1966), pp. 277–293; J. R. Hood, *The Divine Politics of Thomas Hobbes* (London, 1964); Carl Schmitt, 'Die vollendete Reformation', *Der Staat* 4 (1965), pp. 51–69; more recently J. Taubes, 'Leviathan als sterblicher Gott', in J. Taubes (ed.), *Der Fürst dieser Welt* (Paderborn, 1983), pp. 9–15, and the review of the literature in B. Willms, *Der Weg des Leviathan* (Berlin, 1979), pp. 114ff.

[III] On Hegel's political Christology, see Chapter VII in this volume, 'Remarks on the Relationship between State and Religion in Hegel'.

[IV] Pope Leo XIII (in office 1878–1903) held in encyclical 'Immortale Dei' (1886) that only a state based on the Christian faith was a truly legitimate state and that religious liberty and freedom of

these systems or blueprints revolve around the (theological) status, legitimation, and tasks of the political order and the relationship between ecclesiastical and political power or between ecclesiastical and political institutions. Political theology in this sense, in its concrete content, is an *institutional* political theology. In a narrower sense, this concept of political theology was employed by the theologian Erik Peterson in his famous essay 'Monotheism as a Political Problem'.[10] According to Peterson, political theology refers only to the theological justification of Caesaro-papist or any other kinds of rule by one person. Because of the doctrine of the Trinity of the Christian religion, Peterson declared this an impossibility in terms of Christian theology, and upon this he erects his thesis that the Trinitarian concept of the God of Christian revelation puts to rest all political theology. Even if Peterson's concrete reasoning were true, which is not something that can be examined here,[11] this would do away only with this special variant of political theology, but by no means with every (Christian) political theology. In the abstract generalization of a concrete question under discussion, Peterson's thesis is the expression of conceptual weakness,[12] and developments have long since left it behind.

3. Political theology means the interpretation of Christian revelation with respect to the commitment it demands from Christians and the Church to the political-social system (and its change) as the realization of Christian existence. This form of political theology arose initially out of a polemical differentiation from the long-prevailing 'privatistic' theology, for which the realization of a Christian life took place primarily through the individual realization of faith, an individual life in faith, and individual-personal perfection. In contrast to this, political theology places front and centre the appeals and impulses of Christian revelation for the socially and politically relevant conduct of Christians, the commitment to altruism, (social) justice, and liberation from oppression. From

conscience were illegitimate deviations from Christian natural law. The Second Vatican Council fundamentally altered the official doctrine in the declaration 'dignitatis humanae'. On this, see Chapter IV in this volume, 'Religious Freedom Between the Conflicting Demands of Church and State'.

[10] Erik Peterson, *Der Monotheismus als politisches Problem. Ein Beitrag zur Geschichte der politischen Theologie im Imperium Romanum* (Leipzig, 1935). English translation in Erik Peterson, *Theological Tractates*, ed. and trans. by Michael J. Hollerich (Stanford University Press, 2011).

[11] Detailed criticism in Carl Schmitt, *Politische Theologie* II (Berlin, 1970), esp. pp. 57–93. English translation: *Political Theology II: The Myth of the Closure of Any Political Theology*, trans. by Michael Hoelzl and Graham Ward (Polity Press, 2008), pp. 37–60.

[12] This applies also to the complete substantive adoption of Peterson's thesis by Hans Maier, 'Politische Theologie', *Stimmen der Zeit* 183 (1969), pp. 76ff. The valid engagement with Erik Peterson's thesis has now been undertaken by Peter Koslowski, 'Politischer Monotheismus oder Trinitätslehre', in Taubes (ed.), *Der Fürst dieser Welt* (note 9), pp. 26ff. As a result, the thesis was returned to its limited truth content concerning only the thought form of political religion, and refuted in its further-reaching claim aimed at political theology in the sense of a theology of politics and the political order. The formulations of the text, which was written back in 1980, thus require supplementation and correction drawing on Koslowski's reflections, see E. W. Böckenförde, 'Staat-Gesellschaft-Kirche', in *Christlicher Glaube in moderner Gesellschaft*, vol. XV (Freiburg, 1982), p. 106.

this, following the critique of prevailing social conditions, the theological legitimation of certain political initiatives or actions is derived more or less categorically. In this scenario, the danger of a transition from an argumentatively grounded theology to a merely activist (often Marxist-inspired) theologizing politics is close at hand.

Political theology in this sense includes, in Germany, chiefly the works of Johann Baptist Metz[13] and his school, as well as so-called revolution theology[14] and liberation theology,[15] which are widespread in South America and were in part adopted by the World Council of Churches in Geneva. It is not a theology of politics or political order, but provides a justification for and shape to the faith-motivated political-social activism of Christians; it is aimed directly at behaviour and action. From this perspective, it is an (ethically motivated) *appellative* political theology.

III. SUBSTANTIVE-SYSTEMATIC INTERCONNECTIONS OF THE VARIOUS MEANINGS OF THE CONCEPT OF POLITICAL THEOLOGY

The various meanings of political theology spelled out here are not discrete and unconnected: substantive-systematic connections exist between them.

1. Legal political theology as a process of a conceptual transfer from the realm of theology to that of state law and politics can be criticized as well as disqualified using the questions and pronouncements of institutional political theology. For the conceptual transfer practised by legal political theology is not the mere adoption of concepts, but simultaneously the adoption of positions. These adoptions—which take place for example in the formulation of the concepts of sovereignty, *majestas*, ominpotence of state power, *pouvoir constituant*, and so on—can be unquestionably (dis)qualified theologically, in the sense of institutional theology, as an apostasy from faith, in that humans accord themselves (popular sovereignty) and their political constructs divine attributes, and in so doing rebel against God and his divine revelation and put themselves in his place. The political theology of the counterrevolution (Bonald de Maistre, Donoso Cortes) has explicitly advanced this kind of critique.[16]

2. Between institutional and appellative political theology (to the extent that the latter is not merely theologizing politics) there exists a relation of reciprocal

[13] J. B. Metz, *Zur Theologie der Welt* (Mainz and Munich, 1968); *Glaube in Geschichte und Gesellschaft* (Mainz, 1977), §§ 3 and 4. Also the volume by H. Peukert (ed.), *Diskussion zur 'Politischen Theologie'* (Mainz and Munich, 1969).

[14] See the volume edited by E. Feil and R. Weth (eds.), *Diskussion zur 'Theologie der Revolution'* (Mainz and Munich, 1969), with an appendix of documents and a bibliography (as of 1969). Since then, among others, Ernesto Cardenal, *Kubanisches Tagebuch* (Gütersloh, 1977).

[15] An overview, combined with an internal theological discussion, is provided in the volume by K. Lehmann et al., *Theologie der Befreiung* (Einsiedeln, 1977). Also, G. Guitterez, *Theologie der Befreiung*, 2nd ed. (Mainz and Munich, 1967); J. M. Bonino, *Theologie im Kontext der Befreiung* (Göttingen, 1977).

[16] On this see Schmitt (note 6), pp. 53ff.

influence and kinship. The pronouncements of institutional political theology about the status, legitimation, task, and possible structure of the political system motivate and determine also the nature and content of the political behaviour and activism of the faithful. Here I only need to point to Luther's two-kingdom theory and his theological concept of worldly authority and its effects on the political behaviour of Protestant Christians and their readiness to obey; something similar can be said for Pope Leo XIII's doctrine of the state with respect to the political behaviour of countless Catholic Christians. On the other side, the theological statements about the political-social commitment of believers, which is inherent in and demanded by the Christian message of salvation, has inescapable repercussions for the status, legitimation, tasks, and possibly also the structure of the political order. The goals and impulses of action laid out in this message are involved in defining the status of that structure, they place it into a certain utilitarian relationship, and so on. One can say that a different approach to the question ends up looking at the same concrete problem, namely the (theologically motivated and defined) behaviour of Christians and of the Church in relationship to and within the political systems. In institutional political theology this happens institutionally and through institutional mediation, in appellative political theology with a direct orientation towards behaviour.

This parallelism within the differences is less surprising than it may seem at first glance. Institutions of political and social life, if we trace them back to their core, are social and in part also organizational consolidations of specific expectations of behaviour shaped by certain notions of order (ideas).[17] They confront individuals as 'objective' realities or constructs, who appropriate them (in their conduct) or accommodate themselves to them and thereby continue to sustain them. Institutions and thinking in terms of institutions thus aim at influencing and guiding behaviour, except they do so in a special way, one that is mediated through institutions and thus focused more on stability and continuity. It therefore makes perfect sense that in a time when political and social life was largely shaped by and found its order in institutions (which was true well into the nineteenth century), institutional political theology stood in the foreground, while in the contemporary democratic age, in which political and social life are strongly shaped by action and movement following a substantial dismantling of mediating institutions, appellative political theology is increasingly occupying the field.

3. Institutional political theology stands within a hermeneutic-theological tradition that reaches back into the classical polis religion and theology, the formative elements of which were long operative within it. However, at its core it is a genuine interpretation of divine revelation, is always referred back to it, and must always justify itself out of it. With appellative political theology it shares a theological starting point: both have the common denominator that they are *theologically* oriented forms of political theology; as such, they stand opposed

[17] M. Hauriou, *Die Theorie der Institution und zwei andere Aufsätze*, ed. by Roman Schnur (Berlin, 1965), pp. 27ff.

to legal political theology, which pursues different epistemic interests—namely, conceptual-sociological ones.

Given this theological starting point of political theology, it seems impossible that political theology could ever cease or 'be finished' as long as theology exists and Christian revelation is (and is understood) as a theology, the content of which encompasses also the behaviour of Christians oriented to the world. This statement concerns political theology as a theological-scholarly discipline. However, the question that remains, and which is the thrust of some of the contemporary discussion about political theology, is whether the correct *content* of political theology is or should be such that a precise demarcation is possible between the spheres of religion and politics, the spiritual and the worldly, and church and state. If that were the case, political theology would continue to exist (as a theological discipline), but the content of this political theology would be non-political, removed from entanglement in topical political conflicts; the relational field of religion and politics, church and state would be eliminated as an arena of political conflict.

IV. THE INDISSOLUBILITY OF THE POLITICAL CONTENT OF POLITICAL THEOLOGY: THE EXAMPLE OF JOHN PAUL II

Ever since the intellectual conflicts over the Investiture Controversy, attempts have been repeatedly made to demarcate the realms of religion and politics, of the spiritual and the secular, in order to subsequently define the spheres of competency of the Church and the political order.[18] The variable outcomes were influenced by the position of the persons and institutions involved, especially by the power of interpretation which the church(es) and its (their) theology, on the one side, and the bearers of the political order and their legal and later rationalistic theoreticians, on the other side, knew how to successfully assert and defend. These disputes revolved less around abstract concepts and more around the spheres of competency of authorities and institutions, which laid claim to the interpretation of what is spiritual (ecclesiastical) and what is secular (political).[19] The sense—for many, perhaps: the hope—that under the banner of the modern constitutional state, which guarantees religious freedom, and of the contemporary churches, which recognize and invoke this religious freedom, the old tension will be resolved and a problem-free coexistence of religion and politics will become possible, is deceiving. To be sure, it may be possible, on one side or the other, to separate out certain areas that are (have become) unproblematic, as today, for example, religious rituals and the awarding of church offices or cases

[18] On the beginning of these conflicts in the Investiture Controversy: E. Rosenstock, *Die europäischen Revolutionen und der Geist der Nationen*, 2nd ed. (Stuttgart, 1951), pp. 131ff., 143ff.; A. Mirgeler, *Rückblick auf das abendländische Christentum* (Mainz, 1961), pp. 109ff.

[19] Particularly striking is the theory of the *potestas indirecta* of the Church as developed by Cardinal Bellarmin at the end of the sixteenth century (on this see F. X. Arnold, *Die Staatslehre des Kardinals Bellarmin*, 1934), and the fundamental critique by Thomas Hobbes (*Leviathan*, cap. 42).

of mere state regulations. But what remains is the broad swath of *res mixtae*, which, as Carl Schmitt put it, 'constitute... the entire earthly existence of this spiritual-worldly, spiritual-temporal, double-creature called a *human* being'.[20] [V] Even a modern liberal constitutional state, for which spiritual purposes lie outside its sphere of competency, will claim for itself the authority to define where the political sphere subject to its authority begins and how far it extends. And a church that has not lost its self-assurance will (in exercising religious freedom) bring its doctrine and theology to bear (vis-à-vis as well as through its faithful) also where it intrinsically touches upon the political realm or intervenes in it. Thus, in the liberal constitutional state, as well, and given a religious freedom that is recognized and practised by the church and the state, religiously and politically, a general demarcation between religion and politics and their problem-free coexistence cannot be expected. The content of political theology will not become non-political; rather, it remains potentially and—as the case may be—also actively political. Why? The reason is simple, but because of the apparent difficulty of accepting and understanding it, it needs constant highlighting: the political is not a demarcatable field that stands alongside or below the religious sphere; rather, it constitutes a public relational field between humans and groups of humans, which is characterized by a specific degree of intensity of association or disassociation, and which can derive its 'material' from all areas and spheres of life (Carl Schmitt).[21] Depending on the situation, religion, too—or more precisely: beliefs, basic religious attitudes, religious-theological doctrines, and behavioural rules, can always be drawn into the relational and tension-filled sphere of the political. Religion and theology cannot desire to escape this by limiting themselves to 'purely' religious-theological statements and teachings; it would mean merely the transition to a curtailed, politically accommodated religion or theology. If religion and theology assert themselves uncurtailed without any considerations for current politics, obligated merely to their own mandate and content, they are not invariably also political factors and forces at all times, though they will be from time to time.

The clearest example of this is the 'political theology' of the current Pope, John Paul II, the content and effects of which we are experiencing as contemporaries.[22] Its starting point is entirely 'non-political' by basing itself solely on the proclamation of the Christian message of salvation, the Gospel. The Pope sees the real mission and deepest identity of the Church in the proclamation

[20] Carl Schmitt, *Politische Theologie* II (note 11), p. 107 (English: *The Concept of the Political*, trans. by George Schwab (Chicago, 1996), p. 115).

[V] *Res mixtae*, literally things of mixed character, here in matters of state and church, refer to those areas of German law that demand cooperation between church and state, such as in the realm of religious instruction in public schools, or the employment of chaplains in public hospitals or the armed forces. Opposite to the *res mixtae* are those affairs over which churches have full rights of self-determination, such as those concerning religious doctrines and rituals.

[21] Carl Schmitt, *Der Begriff des Politischen*, 3rd ed. (Berlin, 1963), p. 27. English: p. 26.

[22] In greater detail, see E. W. Böckenförde, 'Das neue politische Engagement der Kirche. Zur 'politischen Theologie' Johannes Pauls II', *Stimmen der Zeit* 198 (1980), pp. 219ff.

of the Gospel, the proclamation of Christ himself; its mandate is a religious-theological one, and *only* a religious-theological one, and it is not aimed at political goals and not at taking sides in political conflicts. In line with this is also the consistently theological-Christological argumentation that the Pope presents in his speeches, sermons, and addresses. He proclaims the truth of Christ, the mystery of his redemption and its repercussion for humanity. But precisely because he invokes and focuses on this without abbreviation and opportunistic considerations, his message (also) takes on a political character. For the truth of Christ, as the Pope says time and again, is also a truth for people and of people—of their dignity, the right to liberty, and the ultimate purpose of human beings.

Advocating this truth therefore means and simultaneously demands advocating for the dignity and rights of human beings, further standing up for the poor and the suffering, and rejecting the path of violence, as Christ lived in exemplary fashion. Such a message, delivered into various concrete situations, as is happening, and converted into practical action, has an eminently political effect and invariably assumes—depending on the situation—political character, though without ceasing to be a genuine proclamation of the Christian message of salvation.

X

Reflections on a Theology of Modern Secular Law [1999]

I. THE QUESTION AND OBJECTIONS TO IT

In what follows, I will present some reflections on a theology of modern secular law.[1] The goal is not to 'baptize' secular law—which has become autonomous—and appropriate it theologically. Rather, the intent is to prepare theology for a dialogue with modern secular law. But an initial objection is whether this is even the right issue to raise. After all, is modern secular law not something thoroughly *secular*? For one, it does not inherently advance a theological claim, in the sense, for example, of a theological legitimation or obligatoriness. For another, it seems entirely independent of theological judgment or condemnation with respect to its validity and normative guiding power. Today, law is derived largely from regulations enacted by the state's legislative body. Those regulations rest on the legislative authority granted or presupposed by a given constitution; through the practice of judicial rulings they are elaborated and, if necessary, supplemented. Beyond that, it would seem, there is no need for any additional—especially theological—legitimation. I shall leave open the question to what extent this is—from a secular perspective—an adequate answer.[1] For our question proceeds not from the perspective of secular law, but from the perspective of theology. The topic here does not concern claims and guidelines of secular law with respect to theology, but reflections and positions of theology with respect to secular law. Such positions and reflections are possible because Christian theology is not limited to the doctrine of God, ritual, and liturgy. It always places itself also in relation to the temporal world and its organization, examining and judging it from a theological perspective. It does so because divine revelation inherently encompasses also the conduct of the faithful, their behaviour in the world and for the world.

[1] Editors' Note: The article is based on Böckenförde's lecture given on the occasion of being awarded an Honorary Doctorate by the Faculty of Catholic Theology of the Ruhr University Bochum in 1999.

[1] From a secular perspective, too, the question that arises is what the citizens' loyalty and voluntary obedience to the law rest on, and to what extent importance also attaches to a legitimation of positive law as a system that must be obeyed because it has a religio-theological legitimation.

Religion, Law, and Democracy. Ernst-Wolfgang Böckenförde, Oxford University Press (2020). © E.W. Böckenförde, M. Künkler, and T. Stein 2020. DOI: 10.1093/oso/9780198818632.003.0014.

A second objection to my topic concerns specifically *Catholic* theology. Has Catholic theology not surrendered the question about legal claims and guidelines to natural law since time immemorial? Is it therefore its business at all to answer this question, or is it rather the business of a philosophical natural law doctrine that argues with the tools of natural rational cognition?

When it comes to this objection, it seems to me that the premise must be questioned. Does natural law as taught and advocated by the Catholic Church lack a theological dimension? Already talk of a 'Christian natural law' as distinct from classical natural law and the rational law of the Enlightenment should make us sit up and take notice.[2] The concept of nature that underlies the Catholic doctrine of natural law is not scientific but metaphysical; it conceives of nature as God's creation. It emanates from the hand of God, He preserves it, into it He has placed His thoughts, His plan of order. The latter can be discerned from the essence, the natural endowment, and propensity of all created things, and here especially of humans themselves. For this concept of nature, the ontological likeness of man to God is a 'fundamental fact', as Josef Fuchs S.J. has put it.[3] And a classic author of Christian natural law, Thomas Aquinas, states quite unself-consciously that humanity's natural destiny is its calling to eternal salvation in the contemplation of God, the *visio beatifica*.[4] The concepts of nature and of humanity's natural destiny can thus not be uncoupled from theological statements, which are part of divine revelation. Rather, they have these statements as their precondition and are shaped by them.[5] One cannot reply by saying that this kind of argumentation blends the natural and the supernatural, while the Church's doctrine of natural law carefully distinguishes the two and uses only a concept of nature abstracted from the supernatural as the foundation of natural law. It is true that this distinction between natural and supra-natural is made. However, it itself stands within the context of a specifically theological argumentation, as Josef Fuchs' fundamental study of the theology of natural law has shown.[6] This argumentation works with an abstraction of the total reality of human nature in order to use it to solve problems of the doctrine of salvation, the original state in paradise, and the consequences of the Fall, and to defend the rational knowability of natural law. But this does nothing to change the fact that the concept of the nature of man, as enshrined in God's creation and man's likeness to God, establishes—and in the final analysis wants to establish—a theonomy of natural law.[7]

[2] See Alexander Hollerbach, 'Das christliche Naturrecht im Zusammenhang des allgemeinen Naturrechtsdenkens', in Böckle and Böckenförde (eds.), *Naturrecht in der Kritik* (Mainz, 1973), pp. 9–38.

[3] Josef Fuchs S.J., *Lex Naturae. Zur Theologie des Naturrechts* (Düsseldorf, 1955), p. 57.

[4] Thomas Aquinas, *Summa Theologiae* I, II, qu. 3 art. 8.

[5] Rainer Specht, 'Über philosophische und theologische Voraussetzungen der scholastischen Naturrechtslehre', in Böckle and Böckenförde (note 2), pp. 39–60, esp. 45ff.

[6] Fuchs (note 3), pp. 43–50.

[7] Ibid., pp. 63ff.; see also Franz Böckle, *Fundamentalmoral* (Munich, 1977), pp. 80ff.

But did Vatican I not assert that the existence of God is securely knowable by way of natural reason? This statement is often understood to mean that it also declared that natural law, in presupposing the existence of God as the creator of nature, has a genuinely rational basis. Knowledge of the existence of this Creator-God, it is argued, *is* rationally knowable and not conditioned by a preceding act of faith. Two things should be said about this. First, the question is to what extent this 'natural reason' refers to reason as such, that is, to an (ideal-typical) abstraction and not to the cognitive force of the reason of concrete human beings. For Vatican I stated at the same time that reason in concrete human beings, which is often weakened, is elevated to the point where it can attain such knowledge by the aid of divine revelation.[8] Second, and this is of considerable importance, Vatican I defined its pronouncement as a tenant of faith. Robert Spaemann has pointed out the dialectic of this dogmatization.[9] It makes into an obligatory tenet of faith that faith is not necessary to realize the existence of God. Faith itself appears as the guarantor of the theological dimension of reason and its autonomy; faith describes reason as that which logically precedes faith; however, as Spaemann has said, it simultaneously shows itself as that which historically and existentially precedes reason. One can therefore say that Vatican I, from an objective perspective, at least left open the question it believed it could decide authoritatively.

II. CRITIQUE OF THE TRADITIONAL DOCTRINE OF NATURAL LAW

Accordingly, the Catholic doctrine of natural law certainly displays a theological reference and a theological foundation. It could therefore make sense to answer our question about a theology of modern secular law by pointing to the doctrine of natural law. Is this doctrine not the appropriate form, both of a theology of law as such, and of a theology of modern secular law? If we engage this answer heuristically, we arrive at the real problem: what is the nature of the concept of law that underlies the doctrine of natural law? Is it able to grasp modern law—which is crucially shaped by state laws—in its unique character, its task and goal, in order to formulate, on this basis, claims and guidelines with respect to this law?

1. The doctrine of natural law conceives of the law as part of the moral order of the world [*sittliche Weltordnung*]. Concretely, the law concerns the sphere of the moral order that deals with external actions and behaviours among human beings; with that, it excludes the relationship of man to God, to himself, and to external nature. It is precisely this, and this alone, that constitutes

[8] Heinrich Denzinger and Peter Hünermann, *Enchiridion Symbolorum definitionum et declarationum de rebus fidei et morum. Kompendium der Glaubensbekenntnisse und kirchlichen Lehrentscheidungen* (Freiburg, 1991), Nos. 3004, 3005.

[9] Robert Spaemann, *Der Ursprung der Soziologie aus dem Geist der Restauration* (Munich, 1959), p. 198.

the demarcation of the law from morality. Substantively, in material terms, it is identical with the moral order that arises and is derived from divine natural law. I not only learned this in my first semester from Professor Josef Höffner,[II] who had just been called to Münster, it is also in line with the proven teachings of the Church. Let me cite two *auctores probati* from the nineteenth and twentieth centuries. We read the following in Theodor Meyer S.J.:

> Conceived in its external relationship, the legal order is ... in its purpose and by its nature an inner component of the entire moral system. In truth, it is nothing other than the embodiment of the moral bonds by which the aforementioned social structure in accordance with God's intent is, on the one hand, infallibly realized, and, on the other hand, preserved at all costs in its realization.[10]

Or, to summarize it more briefly in the language of the Church: 'Ius ea est universi ordinis moralis provincia, quae obiectivas strictae iustitiae socialis normas comprehendit.' [The law is the realm of the universal moral order that encompasses the objective norms of strict social justice.][11] And Johannes B. Schuster formulated in 1950: 'Finis iuris praeceptivi est ordinare actiones sociales, ut homo moraliter vivat, non abstrahit a fine honesto, sicut Kant admittet.' [The aim of positive law is to arrange social actions such that man lives morally; the law cannot be separated, as Kant claims, from this worthy cause.][12] Pope Leo XIII erected his imposing doctrinal edifice entirely on this foundation and within this framework. The law of nature [*Naturgesetz*], which is the same as natural law when it relates to humans, is conceived as the eternal law (*lex aeterna*), which is imprinted (*insita*) into reasonable beings and guides them towards a specific goal and relevant action; it is a rule that determines our actions and restrains us from sin.[13] Logically, the essence of human laws—that is, positive law—must be 'that their origin from the eternal law is clearly illuminated and that they do not ordain anything that is not contained in the latter as the starting point of all law'.[14]

The concept of law which underlies the doctrine of natural law is thus a genuinely *moral* [*ethischer*] one.[III] Law appears to be part of the moral [*sittlich*]

[II] Josef Höffner (1906–1987) was Bishop of Münster (from 1962 onwards) and Archbishop of Cologne (1969–1987). A highly educated man, he held doctorates in theology, philosophy, and political science, as well as a habilitation in theology. Höffner was appointed professor of theology at the University of Münster in 1951, where he founded the Institute of Christian Social Sciences.

[10] Theodor Meyer, *Die Grundsätze der Sittlichkeit und des Rechts. Nach Maßgabe der im Syllabus § VII verzeichneten Irrtümer beleuchtet* (Freiburg, 1868), p. 129f.; see also Viktor Cathrein, *Recht, Naturrecht und positives Recht* (Freiburg, 1909), pp. 308ff.

[11] Theodor Meyer, *Institutiones iuris naturalis*, pars I (Freiburg, 1885), p. 394.

[12] Johannes B. Schuster, *Philosophia moralis* (Freiburg, 1950), p. 84.

[13] Encyclical 'Libertas praestantissimum' of 20 June 1888; in Helmut Schnatz (ed.), *Päpstliche Verlautbarungen zu Staat und Gesellschaft* (Darmstadt, 1973), p. 151.

[14] Ibid., p. 155.

[III] Böckenförde's use of the German concepts *ethisch*, *sittlich*, and *Sittlichkeit* have been translated here as moral, morals, and morality respectively, in line with the literature on law and morality.

law of nature; what does not become visible is the specific characteristic of the law which does not separate it from morality [*Sittlichkeit*], but distinguishes it in terms of its task. Put in a nutshell, in the Catholic doctrine of natural law, law and morality [*Ethik*] are thought of as one. At a time when law and morals were closely interwoven also in the order of positive law, this was not a special problem. But with the separation of law and morals that emerged in the secular realm in Europe from the sixteenth and seventeenth centuries onwards—not least as a result of the legal response to the religious schism and as an aspect of the history of European freedom—this did become a problem. What has changed since?

Established positive law increasingly assumed the character of a legal order aimed at securing the public peace, at implementation and enforcement. Its goal became secular, earthly purposes: regulation of the external coexistence of people of different faiths and different attitudes toward life; abstention from a legally binding guidance to the perfected, virtuous life (*eudaimonia*); an opening up to the guarantee of legal freedom as the fundamental task of the law through the recognition of rights of liberty towards the state and its power of governance; the fundamental freedom from non-state power, including that of the Church, which was less and less allowed to borrow the *bracchium saeculare*.[IV] The Church's teaching of natural law did not follow this separation of law and morals: it clung, and to this day clings, in principle to conceiving of law and morals as one.[15]

In so doing, however, it no longer grasps the reality of modern secular law, which is precisely that of a separation of morals and law as legal state law. As a result, the intended effect of natural law as a binding guideline for established positive law, its binding role of providing criticism and guidance, became—had to become—questionable. After all, to invoke a saying by Thomas Aquinas that will occupy us further later on, a measure must be homogeneous with that for which it is considered a measure.[16] However, a measure that thinks of law and morals as one is not homogeneous with a positive law that is based on the separation of morals and law.

2. What I have just spelled out is not merely a self-contained theoretical reflection far removed from reality. It has practical consequences in various respects.

[IV] *Brac(c)hium saeculare* ('worldly arm') is a concept that determines the relation between Church and state—the state lends the Church its worldly power for the Church to fulfil its purpose.

[15] Characteristic of this is the major work by Johannes Meßner, *Das Naturrecht*, 1st ed. (1950), 5th revised ed. (1966). All editions carried the subtitle that always confused me ever since I was a student: 'Handbuch der Gesellschaftsethik, Staatsethik und Wirtschaftsethik'; see also the 5th ed. (Innsbruck, Vienna, Munich, 1966), p. 312. [English: Johannes Messner: *Social Ethics: Natural Law in the Western World*. Trans. J. J. Doherty. (St. Louis: B. Herder Book Co.,1965)] Here the thinking of law and morals as one unity takes on a focal point towards morals; in this direction also Arthur F. Utz, 'Naturrecht als Sammelbegriff nichtpositivistischer Rechtstheorien', *Archiv für Rechts- und Sozialphilosophie (ARSP), Suppl. I: Zeitgenössische Rechtskonzeptionen* 4 (1979), p. 13.

[16] Thomas Aquinas, *Summa Theologiae* I, II, qu. 96 art. 2 cc.

a) For one, it is part of the doctrine of natural law that state laws are ethically and morally [*ethisch und sittlich*] binding only in so far as they accord with natural law. If there is a substantive deficit with respect to natural law, state laws lack such obligatoriness. In that case, observance of the laws is not binding upon the conscience. It can at best be commanded secondarily, if non-observance would cause considerably greater harm to the common good.[17] If the law contradicts natural law directly, it must not be observed. Given the conceptual unity of morals and law in the concept of natural law, parts of positive law are thereby deprived of ethical-moral obligation not only when we are dealing with the violation of elementary *legal* principles, but beyond that. To that extent the doctrine of natural law, in terms of its primarily moral criteria, controls the loyalty of the citizens to positive law, it intervenes *potestate indirecta*[V] in the realm of secular law that is the purview of the state.

b) Far more consequential is a second aspect: the Catholic doctrine of natural law has fallen into a difficult-to-resolve dilemma with respect to the cardinal points of secular law. Looking back, this dilemma has led to mistakes that are difficult to comprehend. By way of explanation, let me point to the principled rejection of the right of religious freedom by the Popes of the nineteenth century and extending all the way to Pope Pius XII's[VI] so-called tolerance address of 1953. The sorry history of these doctrinal pronouncements need not be repeated here—I have addressed it in several essays.[VII] Here it must be noted that it was precisely this unity of law and morals that produced these mistakes. For in moral terms, within the framework of a natural moral law [*natürliches Sittengesetz*] aimed at the perfection of man, and with respect to the moral responsibility of man to God, it is certainly true to say that error has no right against truth, and that rights are given only to be exercised in accordance with truth.[18] Ethically speaking there is neither arbitrariness nor neutrality towards truth or error, true and false, and good and evil cannot exist side by

[17] See, among others, Bernhard Häring, *Das Gesetz Christi*, vol. I, 6th ed. (Freiburg, 1961), pp. 307–312.

[V] The Catholic doctrine of a *potestas indirecta* (indirect power) implies the idea that the Church has the right and even the duty to intervene in worldly affairs for the sake of the salvation of the believers, while acknowledging in general the two realms of church and state as separate. The model of a *potestas spiritualis* and *temporalis directa* allocates to the Church supreme power in religious and worldly affairs. The *potestas indirecta* doctrine goes back to Cardinal Bellarmin (1542–1621), an Italian Jesuit and prominent figure of the Counter-Reformation.

[VI] Pope Pius XII (1939-1958) stated in a 1953 address on international understanding and tolerance delivered to Italian jurists that 'that which does not correspond to truth or to the norm of morality objectively has no right to exist, to be spread or to be activated'. The document can be found at http://www.ewtn.com/library/papaldoc/p12ciri.htm

[VII] Böckenförde has repeatedly analysed and criticized the pre-Vatican-II doctrine on religious freedom (for example, in his article 'Ethos of Modern Democracy and the Church' in this volume, Chapter I). The paradigm shift of Vatican II towards a full justification of religious freedom in human dignity was discussed by Böckenförde in his article 'Einleitung zur Textausgabe der "Erklärung über die Religionsfreiheit"' (1968), in Ernst-Wolfgang Böckenförde: *Kirche und christlicher Glaube in den Herausforderungen der Zeit*, 2nd ed. (Münster: LIT Verlag, 2007), pp. 231–246, parts of which were reprinted in his article 'Religious Freedom between the Conflicting Demands of Church and State', Chapter IV in this volume).

[18] See E.-W. Böckenförde, 'Religionsfreiheit als Aufgabe der Christen' (1965).

side. Wherever such arbitrary moral freedom was postulated, the Popes rightly opposed it. But if this moral principle is transferred abruptly to the legal order, meaning that no distinction is drawn between the external right of the person, which must be recognized as such, and the ethical-moral exercise of the law, which is subject to the demands of truth, the consequences are freedom-destroying and totalitarian. The right of truth and of those who believe they possess it takes the place—with the requisite power of enforcement—of the right and the freedom of the person.[19]

What we encounter here is thus a considerable deficiency in the power of discrimination. A doctrinal structure was perpetuated which was no longer able, given its premises, to adequately grasp the reality it sought to shape normatively (though doing so is an act of the virtue of prudence). This led the popes to teachings which—presented with a claim of natural law—condemned something (namely the right to freedom of religion) that the doctrine of the Second Vatican Council granted to humans *dignitate personae humanae*. And these teachings were not without practical consequences, because they caused a narrowing of perspective (to put it mildly). Here is one example, which is connected to the large-scale politico-ethnic religious persecutions that occurred between 1941 and 1943 in the authoritarian state of Croatia.[20] Without that event, the tragedy that has been taking place in the former Yugoslavia since 1991 can hardly be understood. Archbishop Stepinac of Zagreb, recently elevated to the honour of the altars,[VIII] recorded the following in his diary under 27 April 1941, about his meeting with the Poglavnik,[IX] soon to be the leader of Croatia:

> When the archbishop had finished, the Poglavnik responded that he wished to help the Catholic Church in every way. He also said that he would exterminate the sect of the Old Catholics, which he called nothing other than a Society for Divorce. He also added that he would not be tolerant towards the Serbian-Orthodox Church, because to him it did not represent a church, but a political organization. From all of this the archbishop got the impression that the Poglavnik was a sincere Catholic, and that the Church would have freedom in its actions.[21]

Archbishop Stepinac thus had no doubt that the Poglavnik—irrespective of the plans he laid out—was a 'sincere Catholic', and his plans drew no comments at all. This seems comprehensible only from the kind of position that Pope Pius

[19] Ibid.

[20] On this see Ladislau Hory and Martin Broszat, *Der kroatische Ustasha-Staat* (Stuttgart, 1964), pp. 94ff.; Edmond Paris, *Genocide in Satellite Croatia 1941–45* (Institute for Balkan Affairs, 1961), esp. Chap. 4: The Massacres Begin, pp. 59–87, and Chap. 5: Massacres and Forced Conversions, pp. 88–126.

[VIII] The 'honour of the altars' is a metaphor for the beatification of persons, by which the pope declares a deceased person a saint.

[IX] Ante Pavelić, leader of the fascist Croatian Revolutionary Movement Ustaše and later the Independent State of Croatia (1941–1945) used this title. The meaning had evolved from 'chief' into 'supreme leader', comparable to 'duce' or 'Führer'.

[21] Let me mention Carlo Falconi, *Das Schweigen des Papstes* (1966), pp. 328–329.

XII had still advocated in 1953: what did not accord with the truth had objectively no right to exist, engage in propaganda, or take action; not intervening against falsehood with coercive measures by the state could be justified under certain circumstances, but such restraint was not imperative.[22]

3. Against this background, the about-face that took place with the recognition of the right to religious freedom by the Church itself becomes clear. This recognition makes the differentiation between morals and law in Church doctrine unavoidable, indeed, it already has it as its prerequisite. The Second Vatican Council's declaration on religious freedom acknowledges an inalienable external right of the human being to religious freedom (*ius ad libertatem religiosam*). It does so independently of the objective truth of the religious conviction and independently of the subjective striving for this truth. This right, said the Council, is preserved also for those who do not fulfil their obligation (*obligatio*) to seek the truth and adhere to it.[23] With this the decisive step was taken: the previous conceptual unity of morals and law, the genuinely moral legal concept of the doctrine of natural law was broken up, and at the same time the premise on which Leo XIII's doctrine of the state was based was set aside. Perhaps that is exactly why the participants at the Council wrestled so long and intensively with the declaration on religious freedom.[24] When I was in Poland last year [1998] giving lectures, one of the participants at the seminars of Karol Wojtyla at the University of Lublin reported to me how the latter had told a college in reference to the declaration on religious freedom, which he had championed vigorously at the Council: 'That was a revolution.' He participated in this 'revolution' and did not step back one iota from it as Pope; instead, he affirmed it through his constant advocacy of full religious freedom.[25]

If Church doctrine has thus provided an impulse of its own not to continue to think of law and morals as a unity and to abandon a purely moral concept of the law, the task that needs to be accomplished can be discerned more clearly: the doctrine of natural law, insofar as we are talking about guidelines and criteria for modern secular law, would have to be broken down into the part of natural law that is and can be related to external, state-supported,

[22] Utz and Groner, *Aufbau und Entfaltung des gesellschaftlichen Lebens. Soziale Summe Pius XII*, vol. II, Nos. 3977 and 3978.

[23] *Declaratio de libertate religiosa*: AAS 58 (1966), pp. 929ff., No. 2; see on this E.-W. Böckenförde, 'Einleitung zur Textausgabe der Erklärung über Religionsfreiheit' (1968).

[24] See the reports by J. Hamer in J. Hamer and Y. Congar (eds.), *Die Erklärung über die Religionsfreiheit* (Paderborn, 1967), pp. 85ff., 104 ff., and P. Pavan, *Lexikon für Theologie und Kirche*, 2nd ed., vol. XIII (Freiburg, 1970), pp. 704–711.

[25] Thus most recently in his sermon in Havana during his pastoral visit to Cuba on 25 January 1998, see *L'Osservatore Romano* (5 February 1998). We read there: 'A modern state cannot make atheism or religion one of its political ordinances. The state, far from all fanaticism and extreme secularism, must promote a quiet social climate and adequate legislation, so that it will be possible for every person and every religious community to live their faith freely and exercise it also in public life.'

and state-guaranteed law on the one hand, and the part that is obligatory only as an ethical-moral [*ethisch-sittlich*] commandment, and is—of course—also valid as such, on the other. Is this possible, and if so, how? This question, then, is our topic.

III. THEOLOGICAL ASPECTS FOR DIFFERENTIATING AND OVERCOMING THE TRADITIONAL CONCEPT OF NATURAL LAW

It hardly seems possible to develop this distinction out of the concept of natural law that underlies the doctrine of natural law: after all, it rests precisely on the conceptual unity of law and morality. The differentiation that is called for thus requires a *preceding* starting point. Where can this starting point be found?

One could think of an empirical approach. After all, does the development of the law in recent centuries not show, not least in its ups and downs, where positive, state-guaranteed law must specify and cling to something inalienable? And is it not equally evident where the law, in shaping itself and in response to changing circumstances, commands possibilities to translate moral postulates into law, but also encounters limits in doing so? This kind of empiricism is undoubtedly useful, it provides an outlook on and stimuli for theoretical reflection. But by itself it is not yet sufficient. It may stimulate and render plausible pragmatic attributions and considerations, but it cannot go beyond that level. Such pragmatic attributions and considerations are certainly meaningful for solving the task at hand, but they require a meta-empirical foundation and reference point, lest they are left hanging and are surrendered to opinion and argument. This meta-empirical foundation, which provides the preceding starting point for the necessary differentiation of the doctrine of natural law, requires *theological* explication. This essay is an attempt to make a contribution to this explication. However, this is not about the theological justification of law as such, but about a more limited question: How can one derive from theological reflections a measure or points of orientation for disassembling the ethical-moral [*ethisch-sittlich*] natural law into the realm of external law that is aimed at being enforceable and guarantees public peace, and the realm of behaviour that is commanded only ethically and morally [*ethisch und sittlich*]? And what does this mean for determining the status of modern secular law, its tasks, goals, and limitations? Four points seem important to me in this regard: 1. The statement of Revelation about man; 2. The damaged state of man from the power of sin; 3. The promise of resurrection from the dead and the Last Judgment; 4. Divine revelation as a historical event.

1. Revelation states that man is created in the image of God. 'Let us make man in our image', we read in the first book of Genesis, 'So God created man in his own image; in the image of God he created him' (Gen. 1.27). From a theological

perspective this endows man with a unique dignity, existence for his own sake. This dignity, created by God, was 'wonderfully restored' through the incarnation of God in Jesus Christ, as expressed by the profound offertory prayer of the Holy Mass, which fell victim to Paul VI's reform of the liturgy. It means, translated into the worldly realm, the complete subject status of man, that he is *sui iuris*, his own master, as Kant put it,[26] or to use the image of Ernst Bloch, that he has the right to walk with his head held high.[27] And the creation story in Genesis says another thing about man: 'in the image of God he created him; male and female he created them' (Gen. 1.27). The individual human being does not live isolated and left to his own devices, but necessarily in companionship—not only sexual companionship—with his kind; between humans, dignity is not graduated, rather there is fellowship on the basis of equal dignity.

This substance of this theological statement is illustrated by the philosophical understanding of what constitutes the uniqueness and dignity of man.[28] Christian-guided philosophy has repeatedly reflected this. It found this uniqueness and dignity in the immortal soul as it relates to the body; in humanity's reason and its unique spiritual capacity, which elevates it above all animal life; finally, in the personhood of the human being, in his capacity to personal self-determination of his conduct—characteristics that always encompass also the relationship of human existence to community, as reflected in spiritual-ethical communication, language, division of labour, art, and dialogic thinking and cognition.

2. This first reflection must be immediately joined by a second one. Human beings, as they are and live, are *not undamaged*. Part of the theological conception of man is the power of sin. This power can be conceived of and interpreted in different ways: with Saint Augustine as the determination of man through a concupiscence that shapes his environment and is inherent in him;[29] with Thomas Aquinas as a subtle inclination contrary to reason, but not one that touches the core of human nature;[30] or with Martin Luther as a damage or sinfulness that reaches into the nature of man.[31] But in any case, it attests

[26] Immanuel Kant, *Metaphysik der Sitten: Einleitung in die Rechtslehre*, §8.

[27] See, for example, Ernst Bloch, *Das Prinzip Hoffnung*, Gesamtausgabe, vol. 5, pp. 274 and 1618. From the expressive pictorial metaphor one must distinguish the concrete interpretation that Bloch—bound to Marxist-Utopian thinking—gives it; see also Christof Gramm, *Zur Rechtsphilosophie Ernst Blochs* (Pfaffenweiler, 1987), pp. 48ff.

[28] Here we see the dependence of theology on philosophy, so that its own statements become adequately understandable and thus also open to discussion; on this see also the most recent encyclical of John Paul II, *Fides et Ratio*.

[29] See, for example, Aurelius Augustinus, *Confessiones* V, c. 10 and 18; *De civitate Dei*, XIII, c. 14–15; *De peccatorum merities*, II, c. 4.

[30] Thomas Aquinas, *Summa Theologiae* I, II, qu. 71 art. 2; qu. 91 art. 6.

[31] One passage to stand for others: Martin Luther, 'Römerbrief-Vorlesung', WA 56, 361, lines 18–21: 'Haec curvitas et pravitas et iniquitas in Scripturis multipliciter arguitur sub nomine fornicationis et idolatriae, et est ... profundissima in nature, immo est ipsa vulnerata et per totum fermentata natura.' Also, Gerhard Ebeling, *Disputatio de Homine*, Part 3: Die theologische Definition des Menschen, *Lutherstudien*, vol. II (Tübingen, 1989), § 39.

to the presence of an inner dichotomy within man, namely a dichotomy that contains within itself not only the possibility, but also the concrete reality of 'good' and 'evil' and corresponding behaviour. Of course, this statement is simultaneously embedded in the faith horizon of God's obliging and justifying grace. The contrast to today's widely accepted truism 'we are all OK' is thus clear.

There is no need to engage here the theological dispute about the extent and intensity of this damaged state of man—as keywords I shall mention only the concepts *intentio corrupta* and *natura corrupta*—or to clarify the question about its origin, one keyword: original sin. We can also leave open the question of whether a bridge exists between the positions of Augustine, Thomas Aquinas, and Martin Luther, and where it may be found. Put in philosophical terms, the statement of faith can be understood to mean that the human being is ambivalent in his habitus; he is not necessarily good and not necessarily evil, but instead carries both possibilities within himself. Experience also confirms this. Nobody who does not close his eyes to experiential reality can deny this ambivalence. All it takes is a look at the twentieth century, its wars, crimes, persecutions, genocides, and especially the Holocaust. They all reveal what humans can do—and have done—to one another, and they show the depths of depravity that are also hidden in man.

3. The third consideration connects to the resurrection from the dead promised to man, to eternal life as a life after death, and to the Last Judgment.[32] This kind of connection may seem far-fetched, but it is no less significant. It entails, with reference to our topic, relief from the necessity of a complete equalization of right and wrong in this world, the total worldly restoration of justice. Although in theological terms the secular striving for justice is of great importance to the orderly coexistence of human beings, at the same time it remains something provisional and incomplete. Where this striving is not fully successful, where it remains more or less stuck in worldly sinful entanglements, this need not be the cause for bitter resignation or despair, nor does it give rise to an irresolvable tragedy. In the final analysis, *God* is the judge of man's actions, full justice emanates from Him—as does His mercy towards humankind. In their relationship to one another, human beings need not and must not represent God's judicial power; God Himself received satisfaction once and for all through the redemptive act of Christ, to the extent that it is even needed.[33] That is why Augustine points out that the law that is given to guide the polity leaves much permitted and unpunished that will be sanctioned by divine providence, without therefore blaming this law for not accomplishing everything.[34]

[32] All of these are part of the Nicene-Constantinopolitan Creed.

[33] On this see most recently the thoughtful reflections by Eugen Biser, 'Umstrittenes Kruzifix. Vom Zweck und Sinn des Kreuzes', in Thomas Brose (ed.), *Deutsches Neuland. Beiträge aus Religion und Gesellschaft* (Leipzig, 1996), pp. 283–291.

[34] Augustine, *De libero arbitrio*, I.14.

4. Another point needs to be considered. God's revelation reached humankind by way of a *historical event*. It took place at a specific time and within history, namely in God's revelation through the covenant with His people (Israel) and the revelation through his incarnate son Jesus Christ. In that sense it 'irrupted' into history and radically altered the horizon of reality at a specific time. It made manifest within history certain truths which had hitherto been known only partially or not at all. I consider it an entirely permissible interpretation to see in this simultaneously a process that lifted up a reason that was mentally bound up in a certain way and thus 'weakened' or overlaid with myths; it was freed up for new understanding and insights that were regarded as true and immune from being lost (again). But this also means that there can be insights and demands, also with a view towards the law, that cannot be shown to have been 'always true' and always universally recognized, but which are nevertheless inherently valid once they have been attained. The attempts by Neo-Scholastic natural law thinkers to show scientifically, for example, that there had always been a recognition of monogamy and its indissolubility were touching, but nothing more. It was only by His revelation that God removed the cataract, so to speak, from human thought and cognition, making it possible for truths that had previously been hidden or covered up to be fully recognized and grasped as 'natural' truths. There is much to suggest that the recognition of human dignity and its inviolability represents such a case.[35] That holds irrespective of all the violations of human dignity perpetrated also by organs of the church and legitimized by theologians.[36] One must bear this in mind also when evaluating and dealing with legal systems that have not yet been touched by this kind of liberation into understanding.

IV. CONSEQUENCES WITH A VIEW TOWARDS A THEOLOGY OF MODERN SECULAR LAW

What, then, follows from these reflections? They do not give rise to any system of a theologically grounded secular legal order, nor to an arsenal of supreme principles from which, through scholastic methodology by way of deduction, all necessary things could be derived. What these reflections indicate are, as I have said, theological points of orientation. They mark out gauges for the demands upon secular law, for the assessment of the possibilities and limitations inherent within in. Of course, these gauges cannot be derived so much from

[35] On the emergence of the notion of human dignity with Christianity and its further conceptual development see Christoph Enders, *Die Menschenwürde in der Verfassungsordnung* (Tübingen, 1997), pp. 176ff.

[36] A striking—but by no means the worst—example is the condemnation and execution at the stake of Jan Hus by the Council of Constance in 1415. This occurred with the breach of the safe conduct from Emperor Sigismund. Theologians argued that a promise of safe conduct need not be honoured in the case of recalcitrant heretics. See also H. Jedin (ed.), *Handbuch der Kirchengeschichte, vol. III.2: Vom kirchlichen Hochmittelalter bis zum Vorabend der Reformation* (Freiburg, 1985), pp. 556ff.

each individual consideration and side by side; rather, the considerations must be pondered in concert and seen in their mutual complementariness. Moreover, we are not talking about a conclusive answer, but about impulses for further reflection.

1. Indispensable as a theological guideline for the secular legal order is the recognition of every human being as a legal subject and a legal person. To that extent, this is nothing other than a realization of the human dignity that is fundamental to the notion that every person is created in the image of God. Through all social relationships and in all power relations, secular law must guarantee the right to walk upright—incidentally, this inalienable demand grounded in revelation is also made against the Church and church law. This includes material legal positions, but also positions in procedural law, because it is especially in the latter that the recognition of the other as a subject finds expression.[X] In addition, it includes legal protection by judges whose impartiality is guaranteed.

(a) It might seem to make perfect sense to include in this theological guideline the recognition of human rights as they are discussed today. In this case, however, restraint and differentiation are called for, even if it goes against the zeitgeist, including today's theological zeitgeist. In the declarations of human rights that underlie the demands for the recognition of human rights—they are chiefly the French Declaration of the Rights and Man and Citizen of 1789 and the Universal Declaration of Human Rights by the UN in 1948—two layers intersect: one layer relates to the immediate legal sphere of the human being as a person, and another layer concerns the social relationships among humans. That second layer is shaped by a specific conception of social and political order. It proceeds from individuals who are on their own and largely liberated from social and legal bonds, a notion that underlies the Enlightenment ideas as a law of reason. It is the basis for the formulation of a number of human rights—one need recall only Articles 4, 6, and 17 of the French Declaration.[37] They establish the normative foundation for a specific social order, namely that of a capitalist industrial economy shaped by emancipation and built upon the security and freedom of private property. This emancipatory-individualistic shaping of human rights is undoubtedly one

[X] The German legal tradition distinguishes between 'formal' (procedural) and 'material' (substantive) rule of law. The former is a commitment to ruling qua formal procedures without a normative commitment to human rights, while the concept of 'material rule of law' refers to a constitutional state with human rights and other liberal commitments.

[37] **4.** Liberty consists in the freedom to do everything which injures no one else; hence the exercise of the natural rights of each man has no limits except those which assure to the other members of the society the enjoyment of the same rights. These limits can only be determined by law. **6.** Law is the expression of the general will. Every citizen has a right to participate personally, or through his representative, in its foundation. It must be the same for all, whether it protects or punishes... **17.** Since property is an inviolable and sacred right, no one shall be deprived thereof except where public necessity, legally determined, shall clearly demand it, and then only on condition that the owner shall have been previously and equitably indemnified.

possible concretization of the human rights idea, but it is contingent and culturally determined, and by no means the only possible and valid one. Other concretizations are conceivable. The idea that the human being has dignity and rights, that he is destined to walk upright, is capable of different manifestations, including one that differs according to cultural spheres and has a stronger communal orientation. One must therefore distinguish between the genuine rights of the human being as a person, rights that make it possible for him to walk upright, rights that constitute an absolute given, and those rights that shape the social environment in which humans interact, including their relationship to the political community—here several forms can exist that preserve man's status as a subject in different ways and forms. This is something that must be kept in mind also in the dialogue about human rights with Asian, emphatically community-oriented cultures.

(b) Recognizing man's status as a subject, respecting and protecting his human dignity, does not demand the elimination of all relationships of dependency and status-specific legal relationships among humans. Man lives necessarily in relationships, his 'I' develops only on the ground of the 'We', and this 'We' is in no way merely subsidiary, but has a part in constituting the individual. A priori contained therein are ties, dependencies, as well as reciprocal dependencies, in which one person becomes the means for the purposes of others or for the fulfilment of general purposes. These can be formed in different ways. What is crucial for humans to remain 'a purpose unto themselves', for their status as subjects to be recognized, and for their freedom to be preserved is not—as Cardinal Ratzinger has rightly noted[38]—that relationships of this kind do not exist, but that they are justly arranged. This just order shows itself for example in the relationship between a service and consideration in return, in obligatory duties and legal entitlements, in dependency and protection. This order is most readily realized if the reciprocal roles or positions are nearly symmetrical, if there is not only one position that is in each instance objectively desirable.

2. Another consequence: there is reason to move away some distance from the 'good life' in the sense of the Aristotelian eudaimonia as the obligatory goal for the state order and the legal system that sustains it. The point here is not to question eudaimonia as the ethical-moral goal for the life of the individual, which then also radiates its effects into society. But the question that must be asked is the extent to which this goal is to be achieved—given the theologically grounded personal freedom that characterizes man—by the law itself, which is focused on actual implementation secured by the threat of coercion. To be sure, the legal system is supposed to secure the sphere of freedom for ethical-moral conduct. But to what extent, beyond this, is it supposed to bring about such conduct and behaviour—indeed, the perfected life—with its characteristic

[38] Josef Kardinal Ratzinger, 'Freiheit und Befreiung. Die anthropologische Vision der Instruktion 'Libertas conscientia', *Internationale Katholische Zeitschrift Communio* (1986), p. 414.

instruments of authoritative commands, with the result that the act of freedom ceases to matter?

What is incontrovertible is the boundaries drawn by the law to secure the rights and the equal freedom of others, as well as the integration into the indispensable demands of social coexistence (social compatibility) emanating from the law. Beyond this a wide field opens up. Within it, shared traditions and goals of coexistence can and will be consolidated into legal rules, but these must then be carried by consensus in the general consciousness and must not impair the rights of freedom of the person. I will illustrate the problem in greater detail using two examples.

The first example is once again the freedom of religion. Divergent religious convictions also entail divergent notions about the goal and meaning of life, and what is good and perfect in relationship to them. The law must give space for realizing them, within the framework of the demands of fundamental social compatibility. It is the task of law to create for humans the possibility to become free, free also in the sense of such divergent notions, the ability to be true to oneself, but not to prescribe any one of these notions as obligatory. Such a possibility cannot be questioned even by invoking an objective order with a Christian imprint. Quarrels over minarets for Islamic mosques and over the wearing of headscarves by teachers, if they are not indoctrinating their students in the classroom, are devoid of any theological legitimation; they are also rather absurd in a secular legal system. The personal rights of liberty of the individual are his clothes, which must not be stripped from him under pretexts that invoke the community; in fact, community relationships are built upon them.

The second example is the widely discussed statement by Georg Jellinek about law as the ethical minimum.[39] It states not only that the legal system does not and cannot make all ethical-moral demands obligatory. It also asserts that the virtuous life can be prescribed to the individual with only limited legal obligatoriness (relative to the demands of social compatibility), while the rest must be placed into his ethical-moral responsibility as an act of freedom. The law does not judge the exercise of this responsibility, nor does it legitimize irresponsibility. Theologically this must not be condemned, but must in fact be acknowledged, if one proceeds from the assumption—as I have spelled out—that the state and the state's law do not stand in for God's judicial power.

3. A very important third consequence lies in the fact that the legal order is and must be open to taking into account, in pursuit of its goals and their more detailed elaboration, the circumstances of the *conditio humana*, concretely, the already-mentioned damaged state of human nature. This entails a variety of repercussions:

[39] Georg Jellinek, *Die sozialethische Bedeutung von Recht, Unrecht, und Strafe* (Vienna, 1878; reprint: Hildesheim, 1967), pp. 42ff.

(a) For one, an element of 'authority' is and remains characteristic of the legal system. That is to say, it has and requires its own authority derived from its goal in the interest of and for the welfare of humanity. The criterion it establishes, and the commandments and prohibitions derived from it, cannot be dependent solely on the empirical consensus in society or among social groups and its continuation. The authority-free discourse also cannot be *the* principle on which the law is based, no matter how important discursive elements are for it.[40] For if it is true that the human being is ambivalent in his habitus, this demands—especially also for an orderly coexistence—guideposts and supports for the individual, as well as commandments and prohibitions backed by sanctions, which result not merely from the consensus of human beings. In that sense there is a parallel to education. For education to be true education, it also works with guidelines towards which humans are educated; it does not give free rein to any and every inclination.

(b) For another, the legal system can and must take into consideration that its prescriptions and commandments can be met by human beings as they are, that is to say, under the conditions of their sinfulness as described above. That alone creates the possibility that these prescriptions and commandments will be translated into social validity, that is, the possibility of their actual observance on which secular law depends for the sake of its society-ordering function.[41] Reflections and considerations that arise from this therefore have theological backing, even if in the process a difference to the order of moral natural law [*sittliches Naturgesetz*] emerges. From the perspective of natural law, these may be second-best or deficient solutions. But they can be contemplated insofar as they alone give reason to expect validity and enforceability. This does not advocate a relativism that merely chases the conditions prevailing at a given time. For it remains true, and one must not overlook this, that no legal provision can positively ordain behaviour that fundamentally contradicts the moral natural law, turning it into a legal commandment—and that is no small thing. Thus, the goal orientation—and the guiding criterion arising from it—also remains in force. But its realization takes place gradually and with limited scope, and accepts limitations resulting from the entanglement of the law in the conditions that render it effective, which are also shaped by the *conditio humana*. Those conditions of efficacy include, among other things, that the demands and commandments of the law must find support within the *actually existing* ethical-moral consciousness of humans, which helps to sustain them. We must add that the societal and political starting conditions for legal regulations and decisions can be strongly predetermined by prevailing conditions and patterns of

[40] This in response to Jürgen Habermas, *Faktizität und Geltung. Beiträge zur Diskurstheorie des Rechts und des demokratischen Rechtsstaates* (Frankfurt, 1992), pp. 151ff., 187ff. See also Robert Spaemann, 'Die Utopie der Herrschaftsfreiheit', in his *Zur Kritik der politischen Utopie* (Stuttgart, 1977), pp. 104–126.

[41] E.-W. Böckenförde, 'Staatliches Recht und sittliche Ordnung', in Fechtrup, Schulze, and Sternberg (eds.), *Aufklärung durch Tradition. Symposion der Josef Pieper Stiftung zum 90. Geburtstag von Josef Pieper* (Münster, 1995), pp. 92ff.

behaviour that are owed to the damage state and sinfulness of humanity—Pope John Paul II speaks variously of 'structural sin' in his speeches and encyclicals.[42] That being so, the only solutions that seem possible a priori or at least initially are those in the sense of a makeshift order or lesser evil.

If all this is taken into consideration, there is no prohibitive barrier to engaging with a moral basis for secular law and its regulatory concepts, which is quite a reduced basis relative to ethical-moral natural law. One can participate in 'second tier' regulations, irrespective of existing shortcomings vis-à-vis the moral natural law. The goal in all of this remains the achievement of a relative optimum with regard to the realization of ethical-moral contents, yet what opens up—theologically legitimated—is a field of responsible weighing on the basis of an adequate understanding of reality, as conveyed by the virtue of wisdom.

This problem, too, I would like to illustrate with an example. Since the beginning of the 1970s, when the discussion over changes to the penal law against abortion began, German Catholic bishops consistently advocated the position that abortion could never be a solution to an unwanted pregnancy, because it constituted the killing of an innocent human being. This is clear and unequivocal Church doctrine. Moreover, they rejected in principle any legal regulations that sought to depart in any way from the comprehensive criminalization of every termination of a pregnancy (with the sole exception of a threat to the health and life of the mother), and declared that they could never accept such regulations. In the process, the question was never raised to what extent this comprehensive criminalization, when it existed formally, was practically carried out and enforced, and to what degree it actually exercised a protective function. The position taken by the bishops may be entirely justifiable morally. But to the extent that it closes itself off fundamentally from the real development of the law, it invariably relinquishes a shaping influence on this law.

This was evident not only in a statement by Cardinal Höffner in an official interview in 1972. Placed into context, it asserted that no Catholic could give his vote in the election to a candidate who advocated a meaningful loosening of what was at the time a strict criminalization of abortion.[43] [XI] After that, the only choice left to the voter loyal to the Church for his second vote,[XII] as he looked at the different parties, was to abstain or cast it for the [far-right ultranationalist] National Democratic Party (NPD). We see the same thing currently in the upcoming issue about the general introduction of the abortion drug RU 486. A very weighty argument against it arises on the ground of

[42] Already in his inaugural encyclical 'Redemptor Hominis', No. 16; also his address at the Third General Assembly of the Latin American Bishops in Puebla on 1.28.1979, No. III.2 and 3, in *Osservatore Romano*, 2.2.1979, p. 10.

[43] Interview with the Catholic news agency KNA on 2.22.1972, p. 4/5; excerpts printed in *Kirchenzeitung für das Erzbistum Köln*, No. 8 (2.25.1972).

[XI] See on the debate on a reform of abortion law, annotations XIX and XX in Chapter XVI of this volume.

[XII] In the German mixed member proportional representation system, the voter has two votes with distinct functions. The first vote is given to a candidate representing a one-member district, the

current law, if it is taken seriously. According to medical understanding, the efficacy of the drug is ensured only up to the eighth week of pregnancy, after which it drops very quickly to barely 50% as early as the eleventh week of pregnancy.[44] With that, the concept of counselling as a protective instrument for the unborn child as provided for in the law is seriously threatened. The counselling period is reduced—once a pregnancy is established—to between one and one-and-a-half weeks.[XIII] In the vast majority of cases this time is much too brief to work through the existing pregnancy conflict in personal counselling, to present a woman with perspectives on a life with the child, and to provide possible assistance. For the bishops, however, it is now difficult to argue on the grounds of a regulation they reject in principle, and which they say they can never accept.

To avoid any misunderstanding: this is a not a plea to declare the existing law as a whole morally and legally defensible. When it comes to its factual determination of medical indication, which has got out of hand substantively and in its temporal scope, I consider it indefensible not only morally, but also legally, because it almost entirely drops in this regard the necessary focus on protection also for the unborn child. The issue here is only to show a fundamental problem, using this law as an example.

4. The fourth and final consequence is that a certain restraint is called for when assessing or possibly condemning earlier or foreign legal systems, which did not or do not conform to the demands arising from the theological determination of the status of the human being. These kinds of demand became known historically in divine revelation; they were not evident at all times, even as they were then revealed as something that had always been true and valid. This realization of historicity does not justify abandoning these demands on the law or relativizing them; advocating for them, also for their general diffusion into other cultures, is called for. But this should be combined with restraint when it comes to the blanket condemnation—ex post and from the outside—of such legal systems and of the people acting within them, on the grounds that they were or are caught in mythical or ideological entanglements and

second to a party list, which in each Land is established by the respective party. Half of the seats in the Bundestag are reserved for the candidates who won their electoral district (based on a majority of votes), and half are distributed to the candidates on the party lists (based on proportional representation). In the end, complex mathematical procedures are applied to ensure through overhang seats that the distribution of seats in the Bundestag represents quite closely the overall proportion of votes.

[44] Interview with the president of the German Society for Gynecology and Obstetrics, Prof. Dr. G. Kindermann, *Badische Zeitung* (23 January 1999).

[XIII] In Germany, the law on abortion is twofold. Within the first three months of a pregnancy an abortion is not criminally prosecuted on condition that ethical counselling has taken place. However, as the Federal Constitutional Court has ruled, an abortion is still seen in this case as unlawful because the protections of Articles 1 and 2 Basic Law are seen as extending also to unborn life. After the first trimester, an abortion may only be undertaken if a medical indication exists, i.e. the health of the mother or child is severely at risk.

are shaped by a belief in natural religion or some other mindset. Perhaps the Biblical parable of the grain of wheat can help us here: it is put into the earth, where it initially dies, but eventually bears a rich harvest (John 12.24). It has meaning not only with respect to the relationship of Christian revelation to the world into which it came, but also with respect to revelation itself. Let me refer back to freedom of religion once again. Beginning with Saint Augustine,[XIV] it took more than 1,500 years before the seed of the statement of revelation about humanity that had been implanted into the history of Christianity had flourished into the law's recognition of religious liberty. And it succeeded only across many obstacles and required bitter impulses from the outside. This should not only keep us from feeling self-righteous, it also creates an openness for transitional solutions that lead gradually to a goal, and for the need for intellectual and personal persuasion.

V. THE THEOLOGICAL STATUS OF MODERN SECULAR LAW

I am coming to my conclusion. How can the theological considerations I have laid out, and the conclusions drawn from them about the characteristic nature, possibilities, and limitations of secular law, be summarized into a concluding final verdict?

1. Secular positive law is not simply uncoupled from the natural ethical-moral principle [*ethisches-sittliches Naturgesetz*], from natural law [*Naturrecht*], and devoid of any connection to it. But it has and is given its own, theologically justifiable status distinct from the ethical-moral order of natural law. This status can be described as the (external) system of preservation for human beings who live in and under a *conditio humana*, which is characterized, on the one hand, by dignity and personal liberty, and, on the other hand, the damaged state of humanity [*Versehrtheit des Menschen*] and what flows from it. This status as a system of preservation is not an empty, deficient status, it is one that must be positively specified and filled out; it has its own criteria. However, as we have seen, it remains distinct from the moral natural law [*sittliches Naturgesetz*] that underpins the Catholic doctrine of natural law [*Naturrecht*].

2. That this argument involves a pronounced approximation to Martin Luther's doctrine of law, is for Catholic theology today—thank God—no longer an argument against it. For it was precisely Luther who accorded the law, the *usus legis politicus*, the character of a system of preservation, a kind of intermediate status between the *lex divina* as the law of divine love and the realities of human nature turned in upon itself by sin.[45] And Luther also speaks of natural

[XIV] The young St. Augustine held that nobody could be coerced into believing, arguing for an early form of religious tolerance. Later in his life, while struggling as a bishop with heretical movements and trying to uphold unity in the Church, he justified compulsion in religious matters.

[45] Johannes Heckel, *Lex Charitatis*, 2nd ed. (Munich, 1973), pp. 100ff., 136ff.

law, but not in the sense of a derivation from *lex naturalis*, but in the sense of a human natural law, which is an expression of a reason focused on this world, an 'external justice of the flesh' and only a shadow of the divine law, but still a good work of reason for human beings.[46]

3. Yet the thesis of the law as a system of preservation in a broad sense can also invoke a tradition of Catholic theology, namely a major figure within it, Thomas Aquinas. One only has to open up the right page in his writings. Theologians mostly refer to his remarks about *lex naturalis*, and they find there what they are looking for with a view towards the concept of natural law. But his theology of positive law is found in the *Quaestio de lege humana* (I, II, qu. 96). Although for Thomas, following Aristotle, it is the task and intention of human law to lead to virtue, the question he asks himself in the process reveals his specific perspective: is it the task of human law to repress all vices (*omnia vitia*)? What he, as a theologian, has to say in justifying his answer in the negative deserves, across seven centuries, to be retained and brought to awareness. Allow me, therefore, to quote some passages:[47]

> law is framed as a rule or measure of human acts. Now a measure should be homogeneous with that which it measures, . . . since different things are measured by different measures. Wherefore laws imposed on men should also be in keeping with their condition, for, as Isidore says (Etym. v. 21), law should be 'possible both according to nature, and according to the customs of the country' . . .
>
> Now human law is framed for a number of human beings, the majority of whom are not perfect in virtue. Wherefore human laws do not forbid all vices, from which the virtuous abstain, but only the more grievous vices, from which it is possible for the majority to abstain; and chiefly those that are to the hurt of others, without the prohibition of which human society could not be maintained . . .
>
> The purpose of human law is to lead men to virtue, not suddenly, but gradually. Wherefore it does not lay upon the multitude of imperfect men the burdens of those who are already virtuous, viz. that they should abstain from all evil. Otherwise these imperfect ones, being unable to bear such precepts, would break out into yet greater evils.

The article closes with the statement: 'Wherefore, too, human law does not prohibit everything that is forbidden by the natural law.'

With that, the sphere of its own weighing and decision-making is freed up for positive law. And here begins the work—by no means arbitrary, but also guided theologically—on positive law and for positive law.

With this reference back to Thomas Aquinas the circle closes, substantively and biographically. My first encounter with Aquinas dates back to 1952. As a student of jurisprudence I decided, without any ulterior motive and with no thought to the practical utility for future exams, to enroll in Professor Hans

[46] See also Martin Heckel, 'Rechtstheologie Luthers', in *Evangelisches Staatslexikon*, 3rd, rev. ed. (1987), vol. II, Section II, 10–16, cols. 2833–38.

[47] *Summa Theologiae*, I, II, qu. 96, art. 2. English translation: http://www.ccel.org/ccel/aquinas/summa.html.

J. Wolff's seminar on the philosophy of law, and took on a paper about the concept of justice in Thomas Aquinas. As a result of this paper, my teacher, Hans J. Wolff, encouraged me to pursue a scholarly career. Ever since, for more than forty years, Thomas Aquinas has stimulated me as a teacher and accompanied me on the search for what is right and true for the law, for positive law, not least in friendly—and sometimes contentious—disputes with theologians and the pronouncements of the Church's magisterium. It is thus not without its inner logic that my invoking him forms the conclusion to my expression of gratitude to the Bochum faculty for the honour it has shown me by conferring upon me the doctor theologiae.

XI

A Christian in the Office of Constitutional Judge [1999]

I. PROFESSIONAL LIFE AND CHRISTIAN SPIRITUALITY

As a Christian, one seeks to live Christian spirituality. But what exactly does Christian spirituality mean? In his essay, Abbot Ansgar gave a concise, and perhaps accurate, definition: 'Spirituality is the integration of all of life into a way of life borne by and reflective of faith.'[1] These words can be supplemented by those of Monsignore Ducke: Christian spirituality is the life-shaping power of faith that is drawn from the heart. In theological terms, Christian spirituality appears thus as the realization of God's devotion in baptism through the response to this devotion. It finds its forms of expression and its concretization not only in prayer and divine service, but precisely also in daily life; it is a holistic way of life.

Two things follow from this. First, Christian spirituality knows no separation between the personal-private and the occupational spheres: it realizes itself in both, it relates to all of life, it is undivided. Christ's call applies also to one's profession, which is usually work in the worldly realm: 'You shall be my witnesses, you are the salt of the earth, the leaven that permeates the world.' But how can this be put into practice? What does 'doing the words of Jesus' mean for being active in one's profession and society?

Second, this realization of Christian spirituality has a special quality if the profession is a public office, especially an office of the state. Here Christian spirituality specifically encounters pluralistic normality. The state in which we live is no longer a 'Christian state', it itself does not have or profess a religion, it does not have its centre in the truth of the Christian faith. Its guiding idea is not that truth, but neutrality with respect to religion and other worldviews. It is a house, a

[1] Editors' Note: Abott Ansgar (801–865), also called the "Apostle of the North", was Archbishop of Hamburg-Bremen and a key figure in the Christianisation of Northern Europe. Monsignore (Karlheinz) Ducke (1941–2011) was a Catholic priest in the former GDR, who played an important role in the months after the fall of the Berlin Wall. Together with Protestant pastors he moderated the 'Round Table Talks' in which the citizens' movements and government representatives of the GDR met to collectively frame a consensual transition to democracy, including a new GDR constitution (the latter project was superseded by the quick accession of the GDR to the FRG and its Basic Law in October 1990).The Round Table was an institution invented in Poland several months earlier, where a pact was concluded between the trade union *Solidarność* and the communist government to introduce desired political and economic change without immediately deposing the regime.

Religion, Law, and Democracy. Ernst-Wolfgang Böckenförde, Oxford University Press (2020). © E.W. Böckenförde, M. Künkler, and T. Stein 2020. DOI: 10.1093/oso/9780198818632.003.0015.

common house, in which Christians and non-Christians live together as equal citizens and bearers of rights. The guarantee of religious freedom ensures that Christian faith can be realized by Christians *in* this state, but the state itself does not realize it.

How, then, does Christian spirituality manifest itself as a faith-based way of life in an office that is part of this state order and plays its part in realizing it? To put it differently: How, in such an office, can the professional life be brought before God?

II. HISTORICAL-BIOGRAPHICAL FLASHBACK

At this point a historical-biographical flashback is necessary to allow the full scope of the question and the problem to become clear. Arising from a strong interest in politics, which was born out of my conscious experience of the final years and end of the Third Reich, the question of how to be *civis simul et christianus* [citizen and Christian at the same time] was already preoccupying me in secondary school and then at university, and it has accompanied me throughout my life ever since. What guidance on this question was offered by Church teachings—indeed, by official church doctrine—after the war and well into the 1950s?

The relationship of Christians to politics and to the holding of political office was shaped decisively in the application and elaboration of Pope Leo XIII's doctrine of the state.[II] The latter has its foundation in a binding *ordo* of Christian natural law. It gave rise to objective claims of validity and absoluteness, which had to clash with the construct and rules of a democratic system resting on the equal political rights of all citizens and the freedom of political decision-making.[1] To illustrate with an example: during the deliberations of the Parliamentary Council in the spring of 1949, the Catholic bishops were determined to reject the Basic Law as a whole because it did not contain the recognition of the confessional right of parents, that is, the right of parents to determine the confessional character of public schools (with respect to the *Volksschule* [compulsory elementary and lower secondary education]). A pastoral letter to that effect had already been prepared, but Adenauer (at the time the president of the Parliamentary Council) was able to prevent this in internal negotiations. In the eyes of the Church, democratic majority decisions could exist only below and above what was regarded as inalienable natural law within the framework of the presupposed *ordo*. The criterion for whether a political

[II] Pope Leo XIII (pope 1878–1903) addressed in his magisterium pressing contemporary issues of early industrial capitalism and argued for social justice in his famous encyclical *Rerum Novarum*. However, with regard to state doctrine, he retained medieval Thomistic ideas of a natural order with God as Creator of the world and its ruler. He considered it unlawful to grant an unconditional right to freedom of thought, speech, or worship.

[1] See on this E.-W. Böckenförde, *Der deutsche Katholizismus im Jahre 1933. Kirche und demokratisches Ethos* (Freiburg, Basel, and Vienna, 1988), Introduction, p. 10f. (included in this volume as Chapter II).

party was electable for Christians was its (at least) practical recognition of natural law,[2] with the Church claiming for itself the authority to interpret this natural law and thus determine its scope. Moreover, on the basis of Leo XIII's state doctrine, the position of the 'Catholic state as thesis' held. It maintained that the state as such should be a Christian (Catholic) state. However, if the concrete circumstances did not permit the realization of this goal, because it would create discord or civil war, the state could grant religious tolerance and temporarily dispense with the complete realization of the Christian *ordo*. Religious tolerance arose as a concession, not from a right of the person to religious freedom.[3]

The upshot of these positions was that Christians in political offices should act as the phalanx or vanguard for the realization of (Christian) natural law. Divergent views among Christians could legitimately exist only on purely factual matters unaffected by natural law; only to this extent were compromises and coalitions with other political forces possible.

As time went on, I developed growing doubts about the sustainability of this concept for the realization of the *civis simul et christianus*, namely precisely with regard to the foundations and functional conditions of a democratically organized state. In the process, the concept of the common weal, which is indigenous to both the Christian and the secular *ordo*, became the bridge concept for my reflections in order to reconcile them with the traditional Christian state doctrine and not simply set the latter aside. To my mind, if one understood this common weal not as a normative-abstract ideal, but as something related to the reality of a democratic and liberal state, this raised two positions that Christians, too, should not only accept but actively and positively advocate.

The first is the possibility for Christians to place themselves fully into the democratic order, to work within its framework and under its conditions for the realization of the common weal without a permanent reservation based on authoritative natural law. The second is the possibility to fully recognize the religious-ideological neutral state, which guarantees religious freedom as a basic right, without having the 'Catholic state' in the back of one's mind as the real goal. This amounted to turning one's back on the position of Pius XII's toleration address of 1953, which maintained that error as such had no 'right to exist, engage in propaganda, and take action [against the truth]' not only morally, but also within the external sphere of the law, though special circumstances could justify(!) not interfering in this regard with prohibitions.[4] By contrast, for me, especially in my capacity as a jurist, the right of the individual to religious freedom, independent of the content of faith, was obligatory. The step towards

[2] Thus explicitly Bishop Michael Keller of Münster in what would become his famous address at the convention of the Catholic Workers' Movement [Katholische Arbeitnehmer Bewegung, KAB] in Rheinhausen, see Michael Keller, *Iter para tutuem*, 2nd ed. (Münster, 1961), pp. 459ff. (465).

[3] See Peter Tischleder, *Die Staatslehre Leos XIII* (Mönchengladbach, 1923), pp. 187ff.; an updating, also by developing Pius XII's so-called Toleration Address, was offered by Albert Hartmann, S.J., *Toleranz und christlicher Glaube* (Frankfurt, 1955).

[4] Text by Utz and Groner, *Aufbau und Entfaltung des gellschaftlichen Lebens. Soziale Summe Pius XII*, vol. II Nos. 3977 and 3978. (English translation see http://www.ewtn.com/library/papaldoc/p12ciri.htm).

the acceptance of this right that Pope John XXIII made in his encyclical 'Pacem in terris' (1963) was for me a stroke of liberation.

My early essays arose out of this context: 'The Ethos of Modern Democracy and the Church' (1957), 'German Catholicism in 1933' (1961/62), and 'Religious Freedom as a Task of Christians' (1965).[5] They were a reflection of the engagement with the prevailing church teachings and at the same time an attempt to reorient this church doctrine and practice through criticism from the inside, to change it from a personal struggle for Christian spirituality. The goal was to achieve credibility of the *civis simul et christianus*.

III. THE OFFICE OF CONSTITUTIONAL JUDGE AND CHRISTIAN SPIRITUALITY

Now on to the real topic: the office of constitutional judge and Christian spirituality.

1. The starting point for me was that it is—and must be—part of Christian spirituality to take on such an office as intended in the constitution: as an office in a democratic and religiously and ideologically neutral state. It seems to me that it is a part of and an imperative especially of Christian conduct in the world to fully embrace this office, its task as well as its commitments.

This office is not one that is politically formative in an active and deliberate way, as is the case for members of parliament or the government. It is a *judicial* office: it is charged with preserving and guaranteeing the constitution in the way it is fixed as a legal system and articulated as to content. That means right away that it is not a sphere of activity in which one could act as an agent for the Catholic cause, as an advocate for the realization of a Christian natural law, or as a representative of the Church's concerns. Precisely such an approach would invert the meaning and function of the office as envisaged by the constitution, for it demands strict independence also towards one's own politically or religiously motivated views and priorities. What matters is the commitment solely to the constitution as the order created for and applicable to the political community.

This takes on special importance because of the power of interpretation that a constitutional court commands. Such a court is mandated to come up with the final, non-appealable and therefore authentic interpretation of the constitution. In the process it often confronts the task of defining in greater detail more or less open normative principles, many of which are contained in the constitution as a framework, not least in the fundamental rights. However,

[5] See E.-W. Böckenförde, 'Das Ethos der modernen Demokratie und die Kirche', *Hochland* 50 (1957/58), pp. 4–19 (included in this volume as Chapter I); 'Der deutsche Katholizismus im Jahre 1933. Eine kritische Betrachtung', *Hochland* 53 (1961), pp. 215–239 (included in this volume as Chapter II); 'Der deutsche Katholizismus im Jahre 1933. Stellungnahme zu einer Diskussion', *Hochland* 54 (1962), pp. 215–245; 'Religionsfreiheit als Aufgabe der Christen?', *Stimmen der Zeit* 176 (1965), pp. 199–213, (most parts of which are included in this volume as Chapter IV).

this kind of closer definition, which goes well beyond mere application or strict deduction, must not be used as a 'loophole' for clandestinely smuggling certain positions into the constitution, positions that are not already contained in the constitution itself, its regulatory context, and its idea of order. When it does happen, the court engages in the articulation of (legal) policy, which is not its task but that of the legislature. No office in the democratic state is invested with as much trust as that of the constitutional judge; not only is it free from oversight, it is also exempt from justification and endowed with the authority of the 'last word'.

How did my intention of immersing myself fully into this office and to internally accept its commitments and obligations find concrete expression?

- The judge's oath that I swore at my appointment was the first and only oath of office I performed with a religious affirmation. A religious oath mobilizes the internal powers of commitment of someone who swears it consciously. I wanted to mobilize those powers on behalf of the obligation to this office.
- I told my party, the SPD, that I would not exercise the rights of my party membership for the duration of my judicial office. This pronouncement arose from the fact that the party bylaws do not envisage putting membership on hold, which is what I considered the appropriate step.
- Finally, I terminated my work in the Executive Committee of German Catholics because the Executive Committee undertakes activities—legitimately so—in the pre-political realm and targeted at politics.[III]

From the outset, the goal was to avoid any appearance that I was in any way an 'advocate' in this judicial office—either of a political party or of organized Catholicism.

2. The question of how Christian spirituality could be realized in the exercise of such a judicial office did not arise sporadically, but continuously. The problems emerged with particular clarity in two areas, which I want to address in greater detail: in the area of state-church law [*Staatskirchenrecht*], and concerning the law on abortion.

a) The state-church law of the Basic Law rests essentially on the adoption of what is known as the Weimar Church Compromise (Articles 136–141 WRV). Time and again there have been efforts to dissolve this compromise—described in the Weimar period as a 'separation of its own kind'[6]—towards one side or the other: either in favour of a more extensive autonomy of the churches, or in favour of a strict separation of state and Church and a levelling of the special

[III] The executive committee of German Catholics is elected by an assembly of Catholics representing the different groups and branches of lay German Catholicism. Its tasks include organizing the biennial Catholic *Kirchentag* (Church Day), discussing pending issues with the German Conference of Bishops, and representing lay Catholicism in public. Böckenförde served as an advisor to the committee for many years.

[6] Godehard Joseph Ebers, *Staat und Kirche im neuen Deutschland* (Munich, 1930), p. 133.

status of the churches. In this area my goal was to preserve and continue this compromise rather than dissolving it in constellations favouring one side—that of the Church. I opposed such tendencies that were evident in existing case law.[7] For me it would have been a transgression against the mandate of the office I had assumed—and thus a renunciation of Christian spirituality—had I tried to act on these questions as a representative of church interests, according to the motto 'our man on the Federal Constitutional Court'.

b) The constitutional dispute over the law on abortion brought a dramatic intensification of the problem in some respects. According to my personal conviction, which is supported by my faith, an abortion is not only a very terrible thing, it is also the killing of a (still unborn) human being, a human being who is entirely defenceless and in extreme need of protection. I share all essential positions in the encyclical 'Evangelium vitae'—not always their justifications, but their conclusions. In *Christian* terms, one can hardly discern a reason that would make an abortion appear permissible and justifiable. After all, living a Christian life also entails the willingness to make major, life-constraining sacrifices. The situation is different on the legal level, also the natural law level. Here one can certainly identify limits to a mother's sacrifice, limits where the *legal* obligation to bring a pregnancy to term, enforceable with coercive or punitive actions, ends.[8]

During the proceedings before the Federal Constitutional Court, the public discussion became at times highly political and emotional; for a while it was focused on me, because it was assumed that I would play a key role in the vote: four judges were supposedly against the law, three considered it constitutional, which is why the decision depended on my vote (a 4:4 split decision means that no unconstitutionality can be determined). A well-known journalist spoke of the 'three souls' in my breast: that of the Catholic, of the jurist, and of the Social Democrat.[9] Which would carry the day? Alice Schwarzer[10] showered malicious gleefulness on the Social Democrats: they would have only themselves to blame if the law failed, for how could they have sent a practising Catholic to the constitutional court?[IV] On the other side, so I was told, novenas were held in religious houses to keep judge Böckenförde from 'giving in'.

[7] See, for example, BVerfGE 42, 312 (334), thinning out of the 'law that applies to all' as a barrier to the church's self-determination in accordance with Article 140 Basic Law, and Article 137 Section 3 Weimarer Reichsverfassung.

[8] The clearest example is a pregnancy resulting from rape.

[9] Hanno Kühnert, *Die Zeit* (12 April 1992), p. 3.

[10] See *Emma* (Jan./Feb. 1993), pp. 68–69.

[IV] Alice Schwarzer (1947–) is one of Germany's most outspoken feminists. She founded the feminist monthly magazine *Emma* in the 1970s (still in print) and was at the forefront of the campaign to decriminalize abortion. Böckenförde, a member of the Social Democratic Party since 1967, had been nominated to the Federal Constitutional Court by the Social Democrats in 1983. Throughout his life his position on abortion remained closer to that of the rival party, the Christian Democrats (CDU).

What to do? Take advantage of the office of judge to help one option prevail against the 'culture of death', deploy the court's powers of assertion—by virtue of its authoritative powers of interpretation—for a core position of Christian truth? Seize the opportunity to act as a 'vanguard'? The only thing that was relevant to me in the entire process was the 'soul of the judge', which was, revealingly enough, not introduced into the public discussion. Anything else, including the option for the Catholic in me, would have amounted in my mind to a violation of my official duty and of the oath of office I had sworn with religious affirmation. The question could and had to be decided solely according to the guarantee in the constitution, on the basis of its content and scope, independent of the extent to which it is aligned with Christian-ecclesiastical positions or falls short of them.

I emphatically defended and supported the fundamental approach of the decision: that unborn human life, by virtue of its participation in human dignity, has a right to life from the beginning of pregnancy, and that every abortion during the entire duration of the pregnancy is fundamentally wrong.[11] This is so because—and the senate informed itself thoroughly on this point—it is one of the definite insights of modern medical anthropology (and not simply part of a faith-based position) that the development of human life experiences no further rupture or qualitative leap once the sperm and egg have fused. It follows from this that the embryo develops *as* a human being rather than into a human being. Added to this are specific considerations of constitutional law: Which basic rights and rights of the woman (mother) must be considered? How far does the guarantee especially of the constitution extend vis-à-vis the legislature? To what extent does the legislature have an evaluative prerogative which the constitutional court must respect? To what extent does the legal duty to protect unborn human life depend primarily on the actual efficacy of the law or on an internally coherent normative concept?

I am aware that the outcome of the decision[V] must be seen as highly unsatisfactory from a Christian point of view, and that there are good reasons for seeing the new law passed three years after the court's decision as an 'unjust law' in the sense of Catholic moral theory.[VI] This law could not even make up its mind to explicitly qualify an abortion carried out during the first twelve weeks following counselling as wrong—even if it went unpunished—as the court had stipulated.[12]

[11] BVerfGE 88, 203 (251ff.).

[V] The 1993 FCC decision reaffirmed the 1975 ("first") FCC abortion decision, according to which "abortions performed at any point during a pregnancy must be fundamentally considered a wrong and thus unlawful." The court also ruled, however, that medical or criminal indications would justify an exception to this principle and in such cases abortion would be lawful. Further, if an abortion was undertaken in the first trimester and the woman had undergone mandatory ethical counselling, abortion would remain 'illegal but exempt from punishment'. The 'illegal but exempt from punishment' formula has become famous for the case and is commonly regarded as a legal innovation in penal law, and very likely goes back to Böckenförde (see p. 311–12). Notably, although Böckenförde joined the majority decision on the case, he did pen a dissenting opinion on the question of whether there are constitutional grounds for the prohibition of public funding for abortions.

[VI] Contrary to the Court's decision, the changed law of 1995 did not explicitly qualify abortion as unlawful.

[12] BVerfGE 88, 203 (255, 279).

IV. WHAT REMAINS?

In conclusion and looking back, however, the question that remains is this: Where does all of this leave us? Does this kind of behaviour, which seems right and necessary to me, not lead to the disappearance of Christian spirituality? Does it not lead to a complete assimilation to the 'world' and its ways? Could not anyone else do the same, and is there anything specifically Christian still visible here? Does Christian spirituality not turn into an atrophied entity, in which only fidelity to the office and personal credibility are left?

Yet the question can also be asked the other way around: Does Christian spirituality, precisely in fidelity to office and personal credibility, not demonstrate its openness to the world and its service to the world, unselfishly, in the embrace of all rather than any specific group or one's own? Moreover, what options are there? One option could be missionary work. But is that possible by infiltrating or instrumentalizing the institution? After all, missionary activity is neither credible nor Christian if a Christian—to that end—acts in a partisan fashion in institutions like a court, seeking his own advantage at the expense of what has been laid down as obligatory for all. Another option would be withdrawal from engagement into inner emigration. Although the Christian does not assimilate to the world by doing so, he remains entirely within himself and seeks to remain 'pure'. But can anything emanate from Christian spirituality with this kind of self-referentiality? It then leaves the world to itself and does not contribute to sustaining it.

To be sure, Christian spirituality must also be able to become a sign of dissent within and towards a secular world, which is compliant with respect to the culture of death or entirely under its spell. The crucial thing is how this can be done. It seems to me, at any rate, that it can be done only by preserving sincerity and the credibility of one's actions, not by setting them aside. Should there be situations of conflict that call for a sign of dissent because loyalty would lead to the renunciation of Christian spirituality, the option that remains is public resignation from the relevant offices—that, too, is a visible sign. What is not an option is their (disloyal) instrumentalization. The example of King Baudoin of Belgium, who had himself declared incapable of exercising his office for one day so he would not have to sign the Belgian abortion law, but who did not abdicate the throne, strikes me as only half-successful.

Was the manner in which I sought to exercise the office of judge entrusted to me—taken typologically and with reference to this office—the right way to realize Christian spirituality within pluralistic normality? I am open to argument, but I believe the answer is yes. At any rate, there is something that has not happened to date and which I would rather see as an affirmation of my position: I have not been awarded a Catholic medal for my work as a judge.[VII]

[VII] Böckenförde was appointed Knight Commander of the Pontifical Equestrian Order of St. Gregory by Pope John Paul II and he received honorary doctorates from the Faculties of Catholic Theology at the University of Bochum and the University of Tübingen, but it apparently is important for him to emphasize here that he did not receive any honors for representing Catholic interests on the court.

XII

On the Authority of Papal Encyclicals

The Example of Pronouncements on Religious Freedom [2006]

I would like to express my deep and sincere gratitude for the honour bestowed upon me by the High Catholic Faculty of Theology.[I] The honorary doctorate is the highest scholarly distinction a faculty can grant, and I am conscious of its magnitude. I see it as a recognition—indeed, in some sense as the crowning—of my efforts, soon five decades old, to ask questions, from the vantage point and the profession of a jurist, about church doctrine and practice, the relationship between church and state, church and politics, and the relationship of the laity to the ecclesiastical office—questions about their content, sustainability, and theological validity. It was an undertaking that was initially accompanied more by criticism than approval—let me recall merely the medium-sized earthquake that my essay about German Catholicism in 1933 caused among the Catholic-ecclesiastical public.[1] A change in the direction towards respect and partial—though at first still hesitant—approval came with the various contributions on religious freedom, the first of which was written during the debates of the Vatican Council,[2] and those dealing with the political mandate of the Church.[3] Eventually there were discussions as between equals, coupled with growing recognition by the discipline of theology. With the bestowal of the honorary doctorate by the faculty of Tübingen, following that by the Bochum Faculty of Theology, this recognition now receives its second underpinning and thus

[I] Editors' Note: The article is based on Böckenförde's lecture given on the occasion of being awarded an Honorary Doctorate by the Faculty of Catholic Theology of the University of Tübingen in 2005. By that time, Böckenförde had already received honorary doctorates in law from the Universities of Basel (1987), Bielefeld (1999), and Münster (2001), and in Catholic Theology from the University of Bochum (1999).

[1] See E.-W. Böckenförde, 'Der deutsche Katholizismus im Jahre 1933. Stellungnahme zu einer Diskussion', *Hochland* 61 (1962), pp. 217ff., with the statements referenced there in note 1. (Article included in this volume as Chapter II).

[2] E.-W. Böckenförde, 'Religionsfreiheit als Aufgabe der Christen', *Stimmen der Zeit* 176 (1965), pp. 199–213. (Most parts of this article are included in this volume as Chapter IV).

[3] E.-W. Böckenförde, 'Politisches Mandat der Kirche?' *Stimmen der Zeit* 184 (1969), pp. 361–373.

Religion, Law, and Democracy. Ernst-Wolfgang Böckenförde, Oxford University Press (2020). © E.W. Böckenförde, M. Künkler, and T. Stein 2020. DOI: 10.1093/oso/9780198818632.003.0016.

ultimate affirmation. This is truly a good experience and for me a special occasion for gratitude and joy.

I. WHY THIS TOPIC?

Why did I choose for my lecture the topic listed in the invitation and the programme? Perhaps some had expected a different one, focused more on today's challenges of bio-ethics. But I have spoken about that repeatedly and, as I believe, clearly,[4] so there is no need to elaborate on it again. The chosen topic has a biographical connection, and it may become apparent that it is not without current interest. While working on an introduction to the edition of the text of the conciliar declaration on religious freedom (as late as 2000, Arthur Fridolin Utz, OP,[II] called it scandalous that my introduction was attached to a translation of the declaration commissioned by the German bishops[5]), I came across the statements of the popes in the nineteenth century concerning freedom of conscience and religion—especially those by Pius IX and Leo XIII. I could not agree with the thesis that the declaration was merely a development of those statements in the face of new circumstances and did not challenge the continuity of Church doctrine. Rather, I found incompatible positions, each put forth with a claim to natural law validity and with the relevant justification.[6] Faithful to the maxim 'stay with what you know', I passed the problem this posed to the theologians for an interpretation. They would have to clarify whether the relevant papal pronouncements of the nineteenth century had articulated prohibitions contrary to natural law, or whether Christian natural law contained such a breadth of variability that within one century two contrary, mutually exclusive, statements are possible on the very same question.

As far as I can see, there is still no adequate answer. In his 1987 Academy lecture titled 'Truth and Freedom', Walter Kasper tried to demonstrate with a series of arguments that the conciliar declaration fully preserved the substance of the existing tradition, if one posited a hermeneutically reflected historical

[4] E.-W. Böckenförde: 'Das Tor zur Selektion is geöffnet', *Süddeutsche Zeitung* No. 12 (16 May 2001), p. 11 (also in Christian Geyer, ed., *Biopolitik. Die Positionen* (Frankfurt am Main, 2001), pp. 112–115); 'Die Frucht einer verbotenen Tat. Wie weit reicht der Achtungsanspruch der Menschenwürde?' *Süddeutsche Zeitung* (28 January 2002), p. 9; 'Menschenwürde als normatives Prinzip. Die Grundrecht in der bioethischen Debatte', *Juristenzeitung* (2003), pp. 809–815 (included in this volume as Chapter XIV).

[II] Arthur F. Utz (1908–2001) was a Swiss Dominican, and a social philosopher specialized in Thomas Aquinas; beside Oswald von Nell-Breuning, he is deemed the doyen of Catholic social ethics. He held the chair for ethics and social philosophy at the University of Fribourg (Switzerland) and founded there the International Institute for Social Sciences and Politics (later 'Union de Fribourg—International Institute for Social and Political Sciences').

[5] Arthur F. Utz OP, *Sozialethik Part V: Politische Ethik* (Bonn, 2000), p. 146, note 1.

[6] E.-W. Böckenförde, 'Einleitung zur Textausgabe der Erklärung über die Religionsfreiheit', in *Erklärung über die Religionsfreiheit* [Latin and German] (Münster/W., 1968), p. 18 (= his *Kirche und christlicher Glaube in den Herausforderungen der Zeit* (Münster, 2004)), (parts of which are included in this volume as Chapter IV).

understanding of tradition, not least by reaching back before the long-lasting Constantinian epoch 'to the older and original Christian tradition'.[7] But he does not address the problem of the concrete existence of contrary statements within a century. Arthur Fridolin Utz takes a different approach.[8] He defends the statements of the nineteenth-century popes and declares categorically that no divergence exists, let alone a contradiction. After I had challenged his view,[9] he explained the background to his argument as follows in a personal letter in 1990: 'A Catholic is (and must be) convinced on the basis of his faith that no essential divergences are possible in conciliar decisions. He is therefore compelled by his faith to search for an interpretation that meets this demand.'[10] This does seem very much like circular reasoning, and it cannot suffice as a theological-scholarly argumentation.

And so, encouraged by my promotion to an honorary theologian by the High Faculty, I would like to venture onto this field myself and search for an answer. I will do so by situating the question simultaneously within a general framework, namely that of the authority of papal encyclicals as such. The points I will address are as follows: (1) What is the general status of papal encyclicals; (2) To what extent is there a substantive contradiction or merely a secondary difference between the pronouncement on religious freedom in papal encyclicals of the nineteenth century and the statements of the conciliar declaration *de libertate religiosa*?; (3) What does the result of this inquiry imply for the authority and binding nature of papal encyclicals?; (4) To what extent does this raise questions about the doctrinal normativity of the CIC [Codex Iuris Canonici] of 1983?

II. THE AUTHORITY OF PAPAL ENCYCLICALS IN GENERAL

Let us turn to the first issue. In formal terms, encyclicals represent, first of all, a specific literary form of papal pronouncement, namely a circular letter by the pope to the entire episcopacy of the Church or a part of it, and by way of the bishops also to the faithful.[11] Customary since Pope Benedict XIV (1740–1758), they have been used with growing frequency since Gregory XVI as a means of guiding the Church: we have about ten from Gregory XVI, thirty-three from Pius IX, forty-eight from Leo XIII, twelve from Benedict XV,

[7] Walter Kasper, *Wahrheit und Freiheit. Die 'Erklärung über die Religionsfreiheit' des II. Vatikanischen Konzils* [Sitzungsbericht der Heidelberger Akademie der Wissenschaften, Phil.-hist. Kl., 1988, Bericht 4] (Heidelberg, 1988), passim, especially pp. 36–37.

[8] Arthur F. Utz OP, 'Religionsfreiheit aus katholischer Sicht', *Internationale Katholische Zeitschrift—Communio* 23 (1990), pp. 155–157; see also note 5, pp. 145–147.

[9] E.-W. Böckenförde, *Schriften zu Staat, Gesellschaft, Kirche*, vol. III: *Religionsfreiheit. Die Kirche in der modernen Welt* (Freiburg, 1990), Introduction, p. 9f.

[10] Letter of 6 December 1990 to the author.

[11] Article 'Enzyklika' in *Lexikon für Theologie und Kirche*, 3rd ed., vol. III, col. 698; 2nd ed., vol. III, col. 910.

thirty from Pius XI, and twenty-three from Pius XII. While their content may vary, for the most part they are doctrinal encyclicals that can and do refer to matters of doctrine and ethics in the broader sense, as well as teachings relating to society, the state, and the economy. It is only these doctrinal encyclicals that will concern us here.

In doctrinal encyclicals, the pope acts as the chief teacher of the Church on questions of faith and ethics. What status do these encyclicals have in terms of their authority? To be sure, as statements from the chief shepherd and teacher of the Church, they surely have a special authority, in accordance with the hierarchical structure of the Church. But exactly what kind of authority? Speeches, sermons, and messages from the pope are also statements from the chief teacher and are distinct from encyclicals. On the other hand, encyclicals are not explicitly mentioned in the CIC of 1983.[III] Their locus should thus be determined—in the language of the 1983 CIC—by differentiating them from the infallible and the non-infallible papal magisterium. On the occasion of the encyclical *Humana vitae*, Hans Küng,[IV] in an effort to relativize its putative or real claim to validity, directed his criticism at the infallible papal magisterium itself and at substantive infallibility tendencies in official Roman theology.[12] Because he was thereby also referring to formal positions *de fide*,[V] this evoked defensive reactions rather than sparking further discussion.

To me it seems more correct as well as more fruitful to engage in the discussion the other way around: by taking the infallible magisterium of the pope as the starting point and determining the status of papal encyclicals by demarcating them in relationship to him, that is, upwards. After all, the infallible magisterium of the pope is precisely and restrictively circumscribed in terms of form and conditions. It stands as an extraordinary magisterium alongside the infallible regular and universal magisterium of the Church as a whole, that is to say, the College of Bishops[VI] jointly among themselves and with the pope[VII]

[III] The Codex Iuris Canonici of 1983 is, in the words of its promulgator Pope John Paul II, the 'fundamental body of ecclesiastical laws for the Latin Church'. The 1983 codex replaced the 1917 Code of Canon Law and was intended to be a reform law, transforming the ecclesiology of Vatican II into church law. It is hotly debated whether this intention succeeded.

[IV] Hans Küng (b. 1928) is a Swiss Catholic priest and a theologian whose licence to teach as a Roman Catholic theologian at a German university was withdrawn by the Vatican after Küng's rejection of the doctrine of papal infallibility. He remained a professor at the University of Tübingen, henceforth teaching ecumenical theology instead of Catholic theology. Küng founded in 1995 the Global Ethic Foundation that seeks to underline the common ground in world religions and philosophy.

[12] Hans Küng, *Unfehlbar? Eine Anfrage* (Zurich, 1970), esp. pp. 41–100.

[V] *De fide* stands for those truths of faith which the Church's official doctrine (magisterium) has pronounced as truths with the highest degree of certainty.

[VI] The college of bishops, whose head is the Supreme Pontiff and whose members are bishops by virtue of sacramental consecration and hierarchical communion, 'together with its head and never without this head, is also the subject of supreme and full power over the universal Church'. See can. 336.

[VII] 'The college of bishops also possesses infallibility in teaching when the bishops gathered together in an ecumenical council exercise the magisterium as teachers and judges of faith and morals who

(can. 749 § 2 CIC/1983).[13] As such, it is bound to the fact that the pope acts as the supreme shepherd and teacher of all faithful (*ex cathedra*[VIII]) and in that capacity proclaims a doctrine of faith or ethics as one that must be definitively adhered to (*tenendum*). And the rule is, as stated by can. 749 § 3 CIC (picking up on and specifying Vatican I), that the infallibility of doctrine exists only when it is patently obvious (*manifesto*) that it has been pronounced as infallible;[14] a presumption of infallibility therefore simply does not exist.

It follows from this that encyclicals as such have no part in the infallible magisterium. They do not meet the described objective and formal criteria and therefore remain pronouncements of the pope's magisterium ordinarium. But what holds in that case is a maxim that is familiar to the jurist and for which he has a special eye: *enumerative ergo limitative*. If it is explicitly specified—as was done by Vatican I—that a papal doctrine acquires infallibility under certain conditions, this simultaneously determines that everything that is taught without or beyond these conditions does not participate in infallibility. And this limitation is not an interpretational addendum, but was deliberate in Vatican I and as such intentional. Bishop Gasser, the spokesman for the Deputation on Faith, which deliberated the draft on infallibility, explained the case of the pope speaking *ex cathedra*: the pope is infallible only when he is defining matters of faith and morals for the entire Church through a solemn judgment; 'not just any manner of presenting a doctrine is sufficient, what is required is the manifest intention (*intentio manifesta*) of defining doctrine or putting an end to uncertainty concerning a doctrine by making the definitive decision and presenting the doctrine as one that must be observed by the entire Church'.[15]

Incompatible with this clear and formal limitation are purely material theories of infallibility that also seek to make the unambiguousness and continuity of papal teachings into a criterion of infallibility. They may well have had their validity before Vatican I, when the question of infallibility was still open; afterwards, however, they are mere opinions that no longer have theological-doctrinal backing, even though they continue to be propounded—perhaps with calculated intent.[16]

declare for the universal Church that a doctrine of faith and morals is to be held definitively; or when dispersed throughout the world but preserving the bond of communion among themselves and with the successor of Peter and teaching authentically together with the Roman Pontiff matters of faith or morals, they agree that a particular proposition is to be held definitively' (can. 749 § 2 CIC/1983).

[13] Norbert Lüdecke, *Die Grundnormen des katholischen Lehrrechts in den päpstlichen Gesetzbüchern und neueren Äußerungen in päpstlicher Autorität* (Würzburg, 1997), pp. 264–269.

[VIII] *Ex cathedra*, literally 'from the chair', is the Latin expression for the pope's right to be the final arbiter in questions of faith and morals.

[14] On this in greater detail see Lüdecke (note 13), pp. 246ff.

[15] See Bernhard Brinkmann, 'Gibt es unfehlbare Äußerungen des 'Magisterium Ordinarium' des Papstes?' *Scholastik* 28 (1953), pp. 202–221 (205).

[16] References in Lüdecke (note 13), p. 269, note 171.

The result can be expressed in two ways. Papal encyclicals as a separate genre of papal doctrinal pronouncements are not infallible as such;[17] or put differently, and to some ears perhaps shockingly, they are in principle fallible, error cannot be ruled out a priori. When Church documents or the literature speak of the non-infallible papal magisterium or the non-infallible exercise of the ordinary magisterium,[18] this says in essence the same thing, except that it is wrapped in semantically inconspicuous garb.

What remains, however, is the question of whether this theoretical possibility of error is more than merely an abstract hypothesis, comparable to the late-Scholastic disputation thesis, *etsi per impossibile daremus non esse Deum*,[19] [IX] or whether one should also consider it a practical possibility, which should thus come into play when determining the authority of papal encyclicals. This brings us to the above-mentioned encyclicals of the nineteenth-century popes with respect to their statements about religious freedom. We have now come to the second main point.

III. THE STATEMENTS OF PAPAL ENCYCLICALS ON RELIGIOUS FREEDOM

It pays to take a very close look at these encyclicals, as they represent a striking case study. What they promulgated and taught did not concern a rather trivial marginal issue that one could ignore, but a central facet of the attitude and behaviour of the Church and its faithful with respect to the world in which humans live and how they organize it.

a) What is, in this regard, the relevant content of these encyclicals? I am drawing on Gregory XVI's *Mirari vos* (1832), Pius IX's *Quanta cura* with the appended *Syllabus errorum* (1864), and Leo XIII's *Libertas praestantissimum*.[X] *Mirari vos*

[17] This applies only to encyclicals in their own right. If doctrines that are already fixed as infallible are newly presented or accentuated in an encyclical, they do not lose their character of infallibility as a result. Moreover, the pope can also announce an *ex cathedra* decision in an encyclical, provided the decision meets the requisite criteria for being *ex cathedra*. See also Otto Hermann Pesch, 'Über die Verbindlichkeit päpstlicher Enzykliken', in A. Görres (ed.), *Ehe in Gewissensfreiheit* (Main, 1969), p. 23 (26ff.).

[18] Thus Lüdecke (note 13), p. 304.

[19] On the genesis and character of this formula see E.-W. Böckenförde, *Geschichte der Rechts- und Staatsphilosophie. Antike und Mittelalter* (Tübingen, 2002), p. 314 with note 4.

[IX] The formula 'to assume the unthinkable that God does not exist' was already introduced by Gregor von Rimini in the first half of the fourteenth century, but became more widely known as a formula of early secular political thought in the seventeenth century with natural law thinker Hugo Grotius.

[X] *Miraris vos*, literally 'you wonder', takes up the first sentence of the encyclical: 'We think that you wonder why, from the time of Our assuming the pontificate, We have not yet sent a letter to you as is customary and as Our benevolence for you demanded.' The subtitle denotes more clearly the topic: 'On Liberalism and Religious Indifferentism', which are seen as causes for the 'absurd and erroneous proposition which claims that liberty of conscience must be maintained for everyone' (http://www.papalencyclicals.net/Greg16/g16mirar.htm). *Quanta cura* means literally 'great care' or 'concern' (see first sentence 'With how great care and pastoral vigilance the Roman Pontiffs, our predecessors, fulfilling the duty and office committed to them by the Lord Christ Himself ...', again the subtitle makes clear what the encyclical is about: 'Condemning Current Errors' and so condemned the indifferentism which 'gives rise to that absurd and erroneous proposition which claims that liberty of conscience [*libertatem conscientiae*] must be maintained for everyone'.[20] This pestilential error, we read further, prepared the way for the full and immoderate freedom of opinion that was spreading widely in the ecclesiastical and civil realms.[21] The encyclical *Quanta cura*, conscious of the apostolic duty, rejected, prohibited, and condemned a great many erroneous opinions and doctrines.[22] Among those it included, with reference to Gregory XVI, the erroneous notion that 'liberty of conscience and worship is each man's personal right, which ought to be legally proclaimed and asserted in every rightly constituted society';[23] furthermore, the Syllabus lists as erroneous views worthy of condemnation that '[E]very man is free to embrace and profess that religion which, guided by the light of reason, he shall consider true',[24] and that '[I]n the present day it is no longer expedient that the Catholic religion should be held as the only religion of the State, to the exclusion of all other forms of worship.'[25]

Libertas praestantissimum, finally, one of Leo XIII's influential encyclicals, deals, among other things, critically with freedom of worship. Since it is God who has created humans for society and placed them within the company of others like them, society—according to the encyclical—must recognize God as its 'founder and parent', and to serve Him in reverence as its Lord and Master. 'Justice therefore forbids, and reason itself forbids, the State to be godless; or to adopt a line of action which would end in godlessness—namely, to treat the various religions (as they call them) alike, and to bestow upon them promiscuously equal rights and privileges.' Rather, since the profession of a religion is necessary in a state, the latter must profess the only true religion.[26] This is the style that leads to the core statement in the conclusion: 'From what has been said it follows that it is quite unlawful to demand, to defend, or to grant unconditional freedom of thought, of speech, or writing, or of worship, as if these were so many rights given by nature to man. For, if nature had really granted them, it would be lawful to refuse obedience to God.'[27]

the appended *syllabus errorum* (directory of errors) consists of a list of eighty 'errors', ranging from rationalism to socialism and liberalism. (http://www.papalencyclicals.net/pius09/p9quanta.htm)

[20] Arthur F. Utz and Br. von Galen (eds.), *Die katholische Sozialdoktrin in ihrer geschichtlichen* Entfaltung, vol. I (Aachen, 1976), II, pp. 148–149. English text: http://www.papalencyclicals.net/Greg16/g16mirar.htm

[21] Ibid.

[22] Utz and von Galen (note 20), vol. 1, II, pp. 172–173. English text: http://www.papalencyclicals.net/Pius09/p9quanta.htm

[23] Utz and von Galen (note 20), vol. 1, II, pp. 166–167.

[24] Utz and von Galen (note 20), vol. 1, II, pp. 38–39. No. 15 of the Syllabus: http://www.papalencyclicals.net/Pius09/p9syll.htm

[25] No. 77 of the Syllabus. See Utz and von Galen (note 20), vol. 1, II, pp. 52–53.

[26] Utz and von Galen (note 20), vol. 1, II, pp. 202–203. English text: http://www.vatican.va/holy_father/leo_xiii/encyclicals/documents/hf_l-xiii_enc_20061888_libertas_en.html. Quote in No. 22.

[27] Utz and v. Galen (Note 20), vol. 1, II, p. 208/09. English text: http://www.vatican.va/holy_father/leo_xiii/encyclicals/documents/hf_l-xiii_enc_20061888_libertas_en.html. Quote in No. 42.

If one wants to appreciate and interpret these pronouncements without bias, it is of course necessary to place them within their time and context. The papal condemnations and doctrines were prompted by the struggle, on the one hand, with agnostic liberalism and indifferentism as a worldview, which was linked to a rising anti-clericalism especially in the Romance countries; and, on the other hand, with the ideas of political order of the Enlightenment and the French Revolution, which not least contained the liberal and in tendency also the democratic conception of liberty,[28] which in their initial practical application, of course, by no means avoided totalitarian excesses.

The popes opposed this development in defence of the Catholic religion as the true religion and of the divine order given by it. On the basis of a theonomic worldview, they held up against the liberal concept of freedom a self-contained ordo resting on the true religion and a corresponding legal-political system, which was obligated to the truth—defined as the understanding of man's religious and moral calling provided by reason and revelation; it was an order commanded by God and the only legitimate one.[29] A core element of this order was—also and especially in its justification on the basis of natural law, already evident in Pius IX and elaborated into a doctrinal system by Leo XIII—the unity of law and morality, namely on the basis of the rational cognition guided and controlled by the Church. Rudolf Uertz recently laid this out in an impressive study.[30] There was no place in this cognition for external rights—especially rights of freedom—that made possible, and perhaps protected, a deviation from the order of truth. Freedom was conceivable only as freedom for something, for a given goal, as freedom to embrace the true faith and to attain man's religious and moral destiny.

This explains the fundamental—indeed, the categorical—rejection of a right to religious freedom, especially as a natural right or the right of every human; such a right amounted to the dissolution of the given (divine) order of truth. And this rejection concerns not only the moral sphere, where it indeed has every right,[31] but at the same time also the external sphere of the law, the juridical law; the former is not differentiated in any way from the latter and acknowledged as having a separate task and function. And because of the presupposed necessary

[28] See Josef Isensee, 'Die katholische Kritik an den Menschenrechten. Der liberale Freiheitsentwurf in der Sicht der Päpste des 19. Jahrhunderts', in E.-W. Böckenförde and R. Spaemann, eds., *Menschenrechte und Menschenwürde* (Stuttgart, 1987), pp. 143–147.

[29] Isensee (note 28), pp. 148–156.

[30] Rudolf Uertz, *Vom Gottesrecht zum Menschenrecht. Das katholische Staatsdenken in Deutschland von der Französischen Revolution bis zum II. Vatikanischen Konzil (1789–1965)* (Paderborn, 2005), pp. 198ff., 236ff. The young theology professor Joseph Ratzinger characterized this concept of order in 1964 as follows: ' "Natural law" was supposed to cover the positive law of the Church, but was in turn sustained by the positive law of the Church. In this peculiar intermixing of natural law and positive law of faith lies the problem of the Church's situation in the modern age, a time of transition from a purely ecclesiastical society to one with mixed worldviews.' Joseph Ratzinger, 'Naturrecht, Evangelium und Ideologie in der katholischen Soziallehre', in K. von Bismarck and W. Dirks (eds.), *Christlicher Glaube und Ideologie* (Mainz, 1964), p. 28f.

[31] This is uncontested, and to this extent one must agree completely with A. F. Utz (note 5), pp. 145ff.; see also E.-W. Böckenförde (note 6), pp. 12ff.

unity of law and morality, according to which the law—as natural law as well as positive law—is merely the external aspect of ethics related to the realm of human interactions, it cannot be differentiated. To formulate it in terms of controversial theology, or today ecumenically, we see the absence of any approach to a theologically grounded doctrine of the two kingdoms.[32]

b) The clash between the papal pronouncements and the *Declaratio de libertate religiosa* is thus evident. For the latter states explicitly that the human person has the right to religious freedom, understood as the freedom from any coercion, privately and publically, as an individual or in conjunction with others.[33] And this right is not grounded in a specific subjective constitution of the person—such as his standing within religious truth or entanglement in an *error invincibilis*[XI]—which must be tolerated, but in the dignity of the human being, *ipsa dignitate personae humanae*. That is why religious freedom, as the Declaration states explicitly, remains intact also for those who do not fulfil their duty to seek the truth and adhere to it.[34] With this, the Declaration takes the epochal step from the right of truth to the right of the person.[35]

Does this contrariness constitute a genuine contradiction, one that renders the papal pronouncements and the declaration on religious freedom substantively incompatible, and therefore either the teachings of these encyclicals or the conciliar declaration erroneous? Or can the contrariness be resolved in the sense that it represents a further development and detailing of the papal teachings by the council or their application to a fundamentally altered situation?

Two arguments for resolving the contrariness and avoiding a contradiction deserve serious consideration. The first argument invokes a differentiation and further development of the previous doctrine. In the face of altered circumstances, the conciliar declaration is now said to arrive at a distinction between the realm of external law and the realm of morality: it fully maintains and affirms the previous principles for the moral realm, but restricts their validity to this sphere, no longer extending to the realm of external law.[36] This, so the argument goes, is the important developmental step.

[32] Of course, such an approach can already be found in Thomas Aquinas, if one searches the *Summa theologiae* not only for the *quaestiones* about *lex naturalis*, but also and especially those about the *lex humana* (I, II, qu. 96). See E.-W. Böckenförde, 'Überlegungen zu einer Theologie des modernen säkularen Rechts', in E.-W. Böckenförde, note 1, p. 413f (Chapter X in this volume, p. 263).

[33] *Dignitatis humanae*, No. 2. English text: http://www.vatican.va/archive/hist_councils/ii_vatican_council/documents/vat-ii_decl_19651207_dignitatis-humanae_en.html

[XI] *Error inconvincibilis* is a term of moral theology. An error is insurmountable if it cannot be avoided or averted, no matter what. When a decision is made under the influence of such an error, it is made unwillingly, and therefore the bearer cannot be held accountable for it.

[34] Ibid.

[35] This characterization first in E.-W. Böckenförde (note 6), p. 9. See also Max Seckler, 'Ein revolutionärer Umbruch mit Fragezeichen', in M. Kessler, W. Graf Vitzthum, and J. Wertheimer (eds.), *Konfliktherd Toleranz?* (Tübingen, 2002), p. 151 (164–166).

[36] Representative of this, Utz (note 5), p. 146f.; Utz (note 8), pp. 166ff; see also Pietro Pavan, 'Erklärung über die Religionsfreiheit. Einleitung und Kommentar', *Lexikon für Theologie und Kirche*, 2nd ed., vol. XIII (Freiburg, 1967), cols. 714ff.

This is correct in terms of the objective state of affairs. But what does it mean? One may see it as a further development and differentiation, but this further development contains a partial renunciation of the previous doctrine and to that extent disrupts the continuity. There is no way around this. What the nineteenth-century encyclicals taught referred without distinction to the moral realm and the realm of external law; it was grounded in this *nondistinction* as a demand of right reason and the divine order, and that is also how it was understood. By contrast, the conciliar declaration asserts the exact opposite for the realm of external law, namely the right of the person to religious freedom independent of the objective truth of his own convictions, that is, also in cases of error and independent of the striving for this truth. And it justifies this right in terms of natural law and grounded in the essence of the human person, his nature of freedom.[37] With that, the old doctrine was itself declared contrary to natural law as far as it concerned the realm of external law.[38] With respect to the relationship of the Declaration on Religious Freedom to the enumerated encyclicals, there is clearly a partial contradiction and a partial revocation of the latter by the former. Even if it is only a partial contradiction and a partial revocation, this does not abrogate the erroneousness and the error. *Bonum ex integra causa, malum ex quolibet defectum*,[XII] we read in Thomas Aquinas. There was good reason why Karol Wojtyla, the Archbishop of Krakow, upon his return from Vatican II, said to his colleague Myskow of Lublin: 'This was a revolution'[39]—one, incidentally, in which he had participated significantly in the conciliar deliberations.

The second argument can point out that the older teaching had always been linked—and since Leo XIII, explicitly so—with a reservation that its full application depended on a given situation. And, in fact, we read the following in Leo XIII's encyclical *Immortale Dei*: 'The Church, indeed, deems it unlawful to place the various forms of divine worship on the same footing as the true religion, but does not, on that account, condemn those rulers who, for the sake of securing some great good or of hindering some great evil, allow patiently custom or usage to be a kind of sanction for each kind of religion having its place in the State.'[40] A distinction is thus drawn between the thesis (what should inherently be so and is internally justified) and the hypothesis (all that can be realized under a particular reality), and an evil is tolerated depending on the circumstances. This is particularly evident in Pius XII's toleration address of 1953,

[37] *Dignitatis humanae*, No. 2: 'Ius ad libertatem religiosam esse revera fundatum in ipsa dignitate personae humanae, qualis et verbo Dei revelato et ipsa ratione cognoscetur.'

[38] See E.-W. Böckenförde, 'Einleitung', No. 5 e (note 6), p. 18.

[XII] This Scholastica principle suggests that three requirements need to be met for an action to be classified as 'good': the action must be good in itself, the intention must be good, and the circumstances must be good.

[39] References in Böckenförde (note 1).

[40] *Immortale Dei*, Nr. 41 (*Haec quidem*), see Utz and von Galen (note 20), vol. 3, XXII, pp. 2142–2143. English text: http://www.vatican.va/holy_father/leo_xiii/encyclicals/documents/hf_l-xiii_enc_01111885_immortale-dei_en.html, No. 36.

which in its approach followed the old doctrine.[41] The argument in the sense of the old doctrine could thus be as follows: in the face of yet another changed situation, the conciliar declaration decided to forego a complete application to the realm of external law, though without giving up the thesis as such.[42] This argument presents itself as a way of achieving a mediation, but it is neither conclusive nor viable. For the conciliar declaration does not proclaim the general acceptance of an evil in the realm of external law. Rather, there is a transmutation into something positive, into a natural law: the external right to religious freedom is no longer justified by the general acceptance of an evil, but by the dignity and nature of the human person.

It looks no different from a theological perspective. One could certainly ask from a theological vantage point what God, as He looks upon the world, should do other than approve and reiterate the central thesis of Pius XII's toleration address. But if one accepts this perspective, it surely applies only to the first statement, but not to the second. Theologically, error can indeed be characterized as an evil with respect to the truth as revealed by God, an evil that inherently does not possess a right to exist, engage in propaganda, and take action against the truth. But following the sense of the conciliar declaration, the second sentence would have to state: not intervening with state laws and coercive measures with respect to the exercise of religion is commanded because God has created humans as free persons and because the path to truth presupposes freedom.

Both arguments for dissolving the contrariness and avoiding a partial contradiction therefore do not produce the desired result. A final way out would be to question the rank and validity of conciliar decisions as against papal encyclicals. It is, however, futile. The College of Bishops together with the pope is, like the pope himself, the bearer of the supreme and complete authority (*supremae et plenae potestatis*) with respect to the Church as a whole (can. 336 CIC); it acts as such a bearer in the Ecumenical Council; even if it does not definitively proclaim a doctrine of faith or morality as binding upon the entire Church, but, independent of the Church, makes decisions that take effect only with the approbation of the pope, the Council exercises an authentic, proper magisterium of the Church (can. 749 § 2, 752 CIC). This is not subordinate to the regular magisterium of the pope, but surely of equal rank.

[41] A. F. Utz and F. Groner, *Aufbau und Entfaltung des gesellschaftlichen Lebens. Soziale Summe Pius XII*, vol. II, Nos. 3977 and 3978. English text: http://www.ewtn.com/library/papaldoc/p12ciri.htm, paragraph V: 'Thus the two principles are clarified to which recourse must be had in concrete cases for the answer to the serious question concerning the attitude which the jurist, the statesman and the sovereign Catholic state is to adopt in consideration of the community of nations in regard to a formula of religious and moral toleration as described above. First: that which does not correspond to truth or to the norm of morality objectively has no right to exist, to be spread or to be activated. Secondly: failure to impede this with civil laws and coercive measures can nevertheless be justified in the interests of a higher and more general good.'

[42] In this direction Utz (note 5), p. 146f., for example.

IV. CONSEQUENCES FOR THE AUTHORITATIVE AND OBLIGATORY STATUS OF PAPAL ENCYCLICALS

This, then, is our third question: What are the consequences for the authority and obligatoriness of papal encyclicals from what I have laid out?

My conclusions have demonstrated not only that such encyclicals can be theoretically and abstractly fallible, but that some have also been concretely and genuinely fallible, having succumbed to an error. This cannot be set aside as irrelevant.[43] Something that happened and became real, not in a marginal, but in an important case, can thus happen also in other cases. It therefore cannot be said that the assistance of the Holy Spirit, of which the pope is assured as the bearer of the highest magisterium of the Church, practically rules out the theoretical possibility that encyclicals could be fallible.

a) Of course, it would be wrong to deduce from this the general non-obligatoriness of encyclicals, according to the dictum: once in error, perhaps always in error. Even in science this is not how it is. A recognized author of high scholarly authority does not lose all of his authority from a demonstrable error in his field of work. But what he says will no longer be generally accepted virtually unquestioned, but will be subjected—also in other fields of work—to verification and, as the case may be, called into question with sound arguments.

However, this cannot be readily transferred to the authority of papal encyclicals. The issue in the Church is the authority of hierarchical offices and office holders, not that of individual authors. Nevertheless, it may be a helpful guide in the effort to define the authority and obligatoriness of encyclicals with greater theological precision. The authority of Church offices is grounded in the order of the Church. This order is not without hierarchical character, but its fundamental structural concept is not that of an institution of salvation administered from the top, but that of a communion, as the Second Vatican Council worked out.[XIII] As Walter Kasper has shown,[44] this communion means first and foremost the shared participation in the gifts of salvation, that is, the Holy Spirit, the Gospel, the sacraments, which binds together all members of the Church in a

[43] Rather, the actual, real-life experience provides a confirmation of the thesis that Archbishop Levada, not the Prefect of the Congregation of Faith, developed in his 1971 dissertation on the relationship between the infallible ecclesiastical magisterium and natural law (Natural Moral Law). Its thrust is that formulations of natural law are unsuitable as the secondary object of an infallible definition. This is because 'the human process of formulating moral norms is marked by an essential dependence upon the data of human experience', which is why formulations 'must remain essentially open to modification and reformulation based upon moral values as they are perceived in relation to the data and the experience which mark man's understanding of himself' (William J. Levada, *Infallible Church Magisterium and the Natural Moral Law. Excerpta ex dissertatione ad Lauream in Facultate Theologiae Pontificae Universitatis Gregoriana* (Rome, 1971), p. 77f.).

[XIII] The theology of 'Communio' was developed in the Second Vatican Council's text *Lumen Gentium*. For the first time, a comprehensive ecclesiological self-understanding was developed, including, among other elements, the idea of the collegiality of bishops, the Church as God's people, and the meaning of the laity for bearing witness of Christ in worldly affairs. The guiding principle is the idea of shared participation and shared responsibility of all members of the Church as equals.

[44] Walter Kasper, 'Kirche III', in *Lexikon für Theologie und Kirche*, 3rd ed., vol. V, col. 1467.

fundamental equality and brotherliness; it realizes itself in this shared participation, which happens in and out of shared responsibility and in the process is carried by different gifts of the spirit, offices, and services. The offices in the Church, like those of the bishops and not least the office of the pope, have the task of strengthening Christians as participants in the communion in faith, to be pastors to them in the true sense of that word, who—and here I refer to Benedict XVI's enthronement sermon—set out to lead mankind out of the deserts, both external and internal, to the places of life, to friendship with the Son of God, who gives us life.[45] The pastor who looks after the well-being of this flock in this way not only stands shoulder to shoulder with them, but like Christ in relationship to the saved, he also faces them with a power of his own. This is the basis and origin of his authority, though it does not separate him from the community of the communion. In and with this authority he is the servant of the faithful, not the bearer of a separate dominion, but rather the trustee of the Spirit that lives in the Church and preserves it. To the members of the Church he provides orientation and help in strengthening the faith, he strives—to invoke Benedict XVI once again—to save them from sliding into the salt waters of suffering and death.[46]

b) Can we deduce from this something about the authority and obligatoriness of papal encyclicals? I believe we can. And how can this insight be conceptualized to prevent it from remaining stuck in edification?

Since these encyclicals, ex definitione Vat. I, do not share in the infallibility that is supposed to secure the Church's identity of faith, they are not closed but open to dialogue within the communion of the Church. And this is all the more true as the flock that stands face-to-face with the shepherd are personal beings, capable of rational moral-ethical understanding and by no means excluded from the gift of the Spirit.[47] Of course, this requires concretization in a tangible way. The jurist may make a contribution to this with the categories at his disposal. That contribution looks as follows.[48]

By virtue of the authority of the papal pastorate and magisterium, papal encyclicals certainly have obligatoriness. They represent a guideline and above all possess the presumption of rightness. Of course, this presumption of rightness is not absolute and therefore irrefutable, but refutable. However, the burden of proof is reversed when it comes to such a refutation. It is not the papal magisterium that must prove the correctness of the doctrine asserted in an encyclical in order to lay claim to obligatoriness; rather, the faithful and the

[45] Benedikt XVI, 'Aus dem Salzmeer der Entfremdungen ans Land des Lebens', *FAZ*, No. 95, 25 April 2005, p. 2; see also *Osservatore Romano* (German), No. 17, 29 April 2005, p. 2f. English text: www.vatican.va/holy_father/benedict_xvi/homilies/2005/documents/hf_ben-xvi_hom_20050424_inizio-pontificato_en.html

[46] *Osservatore Romano* (note 45), p. 3.

[47] See E.-W. Böckenförde, 'Autorität – Gewissen – Normfindung. Thesen zur weiteren Diskussion', in his *Kirche und christlicher Glaube in den Herausforderungen der Zeit* (Münster, 2004), pp. 383ff.

[48] This can also be understood as specifying and possibly also corrective continuation of the approach of Otto H. Pesch (Note 17), pp. 31-33, which is geared toward loyalty through engagement as the conduct that Catholic Christians owe the encyclicals.

members of the Church, if they wish to question its obligatoriness and orientational force (for them), must have conclusive, compelling reasons against the rightness of the encyclical, derived from their own efforts at cognition. As long as such an internal and external proof has not been carried out, obligatoriness remains intact. This neither abrogates the authority of an encyclical nor reduces it to a mere offering with which each person can do as he sees fit. But it is brought into a necessary balance, such that it is not completely exempted from proving itself in the reception by the sensus fidelium.[XIV]

I believe that it is precisely this that also corresponds to the life principle of the Church as a living community of faith, a principle that differs substantially from that of a worldly political organization like the state. The former life principle, unlike the latter, rests not on the relationship of law/commandment and external obedience (loyalty), but—in keeping with the communion structure—on the relationship of tradition and reception.[49] The magisterium, including also the supreme magisterium, presents doctrine with the authority bestowed upon it, it draws on tradition and its own (faith) knowledge, and from this offers orientation and guidance; as such it addresses itself to other office holders and to the faithful as living members of the Church who are endowed with reason and bound in faith. The nexus created here is that of authority and trust, on the one hand, and inner readiness to follow, on the other hand; a readiness, to be sure, that does not eliminate but absorbs independent thinking and the understanding conveyed by it.[50] This sets it apart from unconditional subordination, which is contrary to the life principle of the Church, indeed, ends up destroying it. That is why justified criticism is by no means excluded; it is possible also publicly and is not a lack of a sense of faith or of a *sentire cum ecclesia*,[XV] but rather the contrary.

However, this can lead not only to critical questioning, but also to the refusal of reception. Should such criticism or refusal of reception happen more frequently, it proves to be—if it is understood based on the life principle of the Church—an appeal and sign for the magisterium itself: an appeal and sign to

XIV The concept of *sensus fidelium* indicates the instinct of faith of all Christians. See *Lumen Gentium*, 12: The entire body of the faithful, anointed as they are by the Holy One (1 John 2, 20.27) cannot err in matters of belief. They manifest this special quality by means of the entire people's supernatural discernment in matters of faith when 'from the Bishops down to the last of the lay faithful' they show universal agreement in matters of faith and morals. That discernment in matters of faith is aroused and sustained by the Spirit of truth. (http://www.vatican.va/archive/hist_councils/ii_vatican_council/documents/vat-ii_const_19641121_lumen-gentium_en.html)

49 See, for example, *Lumen gentium* c. 7, also Joseph Ratzinger, 'Kirche III', 3, in *Lexikon für Theologie und Kirche*, 2nd ed., vol. VI, cols. 176ff.; Joseph Ratzinger, *Ökumene und Politik* (Einsiedlen, 1987), pp. 16ff.; Walter Kasper, 'Kirche III', in *Lexikon für Theologie und Kirche*, 3rd ed., vol. V, col. 1467f. Winfried Aymans, in *Handbuch des katholischen Kirchenrechts*, 2nd ed. (Regensburg, 1999), §63B: 'Die Communio-Struktur des Glaubenslebens der Kirche', pp. 667–669.

50 This should simultaneously be noted critically vis-à-vis the instruction about the ecclesiastical calling of the theologian by the Vatican Congregation for the Doctrine of Faith of 1990, especially No. 23.

XV The appeal to 'feel with the Church' goes back to Jesuit founder Ignatius of Loyola's Spiritual Exercises, including his eighteen rules to have the true sentiment towards the Church. These rules demand praising and obeying the Church.

listen to the *sensus fidelium*. In his Apostolic Letter at the beginning of the new millennium, the aging John Paul II pointed explicitly to the 'pastoral truth' that the shepherds had to make their own: namely, to listen to the entire people of God as much as possible. He did so by quoting the admonition of Saint Paulinus of Nola, to listen to all believers, because the Spirit of God breathes in everyone.[51] If that listening takes place, it can be the occasion for the magisterium to question its own doctrine and to rethink it, perhaps to justify it differently and more convincingly, or to modify and even correct it. As we have seen, encyclicals, irrespective of their authority and authenticity, are also open to revision.

c) Against this background, the dogma of infallibility also reveals a side that has hitherto received little attention. From the outside, especially from a historico-sociological perspective, it may appear as the dogmatic protection of an absolutism in the constitution of the Church; though in this case, attention would have to be directed more strongly at the—equally dogmatized—primacy of jurisdiction (*Jurisdiktionsprimat*).[XVI] By contrast, seen internally, and theologically, the dogma can take on a different meaning, precisely because of its formalizing and limiting function, of which I have already spoken. It then reveals itself as the guarantee, given with the assistance of the Holy Spirit, that the Church of Jesus Christ, for all the humanity that is also at work within it, does not lose the revealed core of the faith and the sense of faith over the course of time, that is, that the gates of hell will not overwhelm it. From this perspective, it relates to the exceptional situations, to the defence against serious threats and errors in questions of faith, but it is not a call for the development of a comprehensive edifice of faith. In that the dogma of infallibility, in its limiting and in this limitation binding definition, simultaneously defines also the potential fallibility of all other doctrinal statements, it preserves the Church and its magisterium also from destructive exaggerations of its own claim to authority and in so doing undergirds freedom within the Church. Seen in this way, the conciliar declaration *De liberate religiosa*, beyond its immediate content, has sent a signal—surely not in opposition to the assistance of the Holy Spirit—that papal doctrinal statements are subject to revision, on the basis of the doctrine of infallibility, on a far broader scale than previously assumed, and that the truth claim of the Catholic faith is not touched by this. Does this not entail a clarifying and liberating effect on the Church?

[51] John Paul II, 'Apostolic Letter Novo Millenio Ineunte' of 6 January 2001: www.vatican.va/holy_father/john_paul_ii/apost_letters/documents/hf_jp-ii_apl_20010106_novo-millennio-ineunte_en.html

[XVI] The papal primacy of jurisdiction is regulated in can. 331: 'The bishop of the Roman Church, in whom continues the office given by the Lord uniquely to Peter, the first of the Apostles, and to be transmitted to his successors, is the head of the college of bishops, the Vicar of Christ, and the pastor of the universal Church on earth. By virtue of his office he possesses supreme, full, immediate, and universal ordinary power in the Church, which he may always exercise freely.'

V. QUESTIONS TO CANON LAW, ESPECIALLY CAN. 752 CIC 1983

We have really come to the end now. But in conclusion there still remains one question that must be asked: namely, to what extent does the concept laid out here stand in a relationship of tension, indeed, discrepancy, to valid canon law, specifically, the teaching law of CIC 1983 and its notion of authority, and if that is the case, how should one respond to it?

a) According to can. 752, a 'religious submission of the intellect and will' [*intellectus et voluntatis obseqium*] must be given to a doctrine proclaimed by the pope or the College of Bishops concerning matters of faith and morals. What does that mean? What is demanded is an obedience which, in its entirety, displays two inseparable sides: intellectually: inner consent; volitionally: external adherence. The expectation is that a possible lack of insight or understanding is bridged with the help of an act of will and in this way guided after all to an inner consent, in the sense of a religiously motivated obedience in the recognition of the Church's authority.[52] This duty of obedience was newly introduced in CIC 1983. The CIC 1917 noted in this regard only the duty to avoid, apart from heresy, above all those errors that come close to heresy, and for that reason to follow all constitutions and decrees by which such erroneous notions were rejected or dismissed by the Holy See.[53] This was a negative-exclusionary obligation, namely to avoid heresies and explicitly condemned errors, not a duty of positive agreement with all articulated doctrines without further differentiation. The duty of agreement that is now demanded is given a further special emphasis in that the faithful now have imposed upon them a duty of omission, namely, that 'the Christian faithful are to take care to avoid those things which do not agree with it [i.e., a proclaimed doctrine]' (can. 752, second part of the sentence). Whereas only *contrary* doctrines of every kind must be avoided when it comes to pronouncements of faith (can. 750 §1, second half of the sentence), here everything that is simply not in agreement must be avoided. The double negation to 'avoid those things which do not agree' means positively the duty to advocate and express only those things that are in agreement.[54] If this norm is taken seriously as a Church law in keeping with its claim, a person's own contrary understanding is utterly irrelevant. Even a carefully verified, seemingly conclusive understanding can lead merely to the exceptional internal suspension of assent, the so-called silent obedience;[55] every public questioning and criticism, also in the form of scholarly discussion, is ruled out.

52 Lüdecke (note 13), p. 329.

53 CIC 1917, can. 1324: Satis non est haereticam pravitatem devitare, sed oportet illos quoque errores diligenter fugere, qui ad illam plus minusque accedunt; quare omnes debent etiam constitutiones et decreta servare quibus praevae huiusmodi opiniones a Santa Sede proscriptae et prohibitae sunt.

54 This has been correctly brought out also by Norbert Lüdecke (note 13), p. 329.

55 Thus also Lüdecke (note 13), p. 330.

What is evident here is a clear tendency to elevate, as much as possible, the authority and obligatoriness of pronouncements by the ordinary papal magisterium; and while formally distinguishing it from the infallible magisterium, to strongly assimilate it substantively to the latter. The ordinary papal magisterium is supposed to be shielded from any public questioning and criticism, to act in a quasi-sovereign fashion, without in the process being exposed to any challenges from the outside. This is surely a disciplinary over-exertion of papal authority, one that is not in accord with the inner life principle of the Church as laid out, and does not serve it. Must every believer and theologian in fact watch and wait silently, without becoming personally engaged, until the magisterium itself might arrive at a better understanding? To expect everything from the Holy Spirit and to pass the responsibility to it alone without personal effort and action can also be a kind of presumptuousness. To take only the development towards the recognition of religious freedom by the Church: how could that recognition have spread and come about unless there had been critical, including public, questioning by theologians and committed laypeople, like the representatives of Christian Personalism[XVII] at the beginning of the twentieth century.[56]

Of course, on behalf of can. 752 CIC one must not overlook that the formula of the 'submission of the intellect and will', which must be accorded to the non-infallible magisterium of the pope, has been taken over from *Lumen gentium*, cap. 25;[57] it had received the prevailing Canonistic doctrine that had taken shape since Vatican I.[58] Of course, *Lumen gentium* understands this obedience in the sense that the supreme magisterium of the pope must be 'acknowledged with reverence' (*reverenter agnoscatur*) and its judgments must be 'sincerely adhered to' (*sincere adhaereatur*), in line with the understanding and intent proclaimed by it. The case of dissent, whether from theologians or believers, and how one should proceed if that happens, is not dealt with at all, even though there were also canonistic doctrines about it; it was thus kept open in conciliar terms.

XVII Jacques Maritain (1882–1972) was a Catholic French philosopher, with an extensive oeuvre that contributed to a renaissance of Thomism as well as to a Christian ethics grounded in the human being as a person with individual rights. He was one of the main drafters of the Universal Declaration of Human Rights and very influential in outlining an agenda for the reform of the Church to be discussed during the Second Vatican Council.

56 On this process and the difficulties to which actors are exposed along the way, see the detailed discussion by Rudolf Uertz (note 30), pp. 323ff., 370–381, 419–433, 439ff.

57 *Lumen gentium*, c. 25: '(F)ideles autem in sui Episcopi sententiam de fide et moribus nomine Christi prolatam concurrere, eique religioso animi obsequio adhaerere debent. Hoc vero religiosum voluntatis et intellectus obsequium singulare ratione praestandum est Romano Pontificis authentico magisterio etiam cum non ex cathedra loquitur.' English text: 'In matters of faith and morals, the bishops speak in the name of Christ and the faithful are to accept their teaching and adhere to it with a religious assent. This religious submission of mind and will must be shown in a special way to the authentic magisterium of the Roman Pontiff, even when he is not speaking ex cathedra; that is, it must be shown in such a way that his supreme magisterium is acknowledged with reverence, the judgments made by him are sincerely adhered to, according to his manifest mind and will.' (www.vatican.va/archive/hist_councils/ii_vatican_council/documents/vat-ii_const_19641121_lumen-gentium_en.html)

58 Discussed in detail in Lüdecke (note 13), pp. 312–324.

This open field is now closed by can. 752 with the intensifying second half of the sentence quoted above, which was consciously formulated—also on the basis of post-conciliar experiences—with its prohibition of any public dissent;[59] on the basis of *Lumen gentium* there was no need for this.

b) This gives rise to a concluding query to canon law. According to the view asserted by the Munich School under Klaus Mörsdorf,[XVIII] which I consider correct, canon law is *theologically* underpinned; it is grounded in the visible and sacramental character of the Church as a salvific community;[60] in like manner, the science of canon law is a discipline grounded in theology. At the same time, however, canon law, if it bears its name deservedly, is a sphere of the law and therefore constitutively bound to what makes law, by its nature, a cultural manifestation that is related to the coexistence of human beings in freedom.[61] It cannot free itself from this by invoking a theological foundation, lest it end up contradicting itself and being perverted into an ecclesiological system of power. Both aspects, the theological foundation and the essential characteristics of a system of law, must be united and integrated.[62] Much the same holds for the discipline of canon law as the science of Church law.

But if that is the case, it gives rise to consequences in two directions. For one, it is not canon law that determines theology, but, inversely, theology determines canon law; the scope, reach, and peculiar nature of canon law must be theologically derived and legitimated, and because they belong to law they are not autonomous. For another, inherent in the elaboration of canon law must be the very principles that are part of the constitutive qualities of law as a system related to personal freedom and communication: such as the recognition of every individual as a personal subject with autonomy and a claim to being heard, and the processes for resolving conflicts based on this; the universality of legal rules, the fact that they work both for and against me; the principle of *audiatur et altera pars*,[XIX] the settling of disputes by uninvolved and independent judges; and, finally, the obligation to justify legal and administrative decisions.[63]

[59] On this see Norbert Lüdecke (note 13), pp. 341–349.

[XVIII] Klaus Mörsdorf (1908–1989) was a Roman Catholic priest and professor for canon law who headed the Institute of Canon Law at Ludwig-Maximiliam-University Munich. Mörsdorf was also a peritus (counsellor) of the Second Vatican Council and was involved as an advisor in the 1983 reform of the Code of Canon Law.

[60] Klaus Mörsdorf, 'Zur Grundlegung des Rechts der Kirche', *Münchener Theologische Zeitschrift* 3 (1952), pp. 329–332; Eichmann and Mörsdorf, *Lehrbuch des Kirchenrechts*, vol. I, 11th ed. (1964), pp. 13–21. See also Antonio M. Rouco-Varela, 'Allgemeine Rechtslehre oder Theologie des kanonischen Rechts', *Archiv Für Katholisches Kirchenrecht* 138 (1969), pp. 95–113; Peter Krämer, *Theologische Grundlegung des kirchlichen Rechts* (Trier, 1977).

[61] For detailed discussion of this problem see Gerhard Luf, 'Rechtsphilosophische Grundlagen des Kirchenrechts', *Handbuch des katholischen Kirchenrechts*, 2nd ed. (Regensburg, 1999), ∞ 4, 33–48, esp. pp. 37ff.

[62] See Luf (note 61), p. 46f.

[XIX] *Audiatur et altera pars* is a legal and moral principle already extant in Roman law, according to which one should always listen to the other side and that in a trial or in any kind of conflict no one should be judged without a fair procedure in which he or she can respond to the accusations.

[63] On such legal principles, which make a system of law into a legal system in the first place, see most recently the impressive work of Werner Offenloch, *Erinnerung an das Recht* (Tübingen, 2005), pp. 67–80.

The ecclesiastical legislator, as well, no matter how much he might consider himself legally free and sovereign, does not stand outside these contextual relationships. Canon law must be in accord with its pre-canonical prerequisites if it does not want to lose its sustaining ground, and it must contain the abovementioned legal principles within itself to prove itself a system of law instead of a mere system of power.

If one proceeds from this, then the communio structure of the Church, which has theological and legal valence, must be reflected also in canon law and have concrete effect. That is certainly not the case in the attempt of can. 752 (an attempt that is likely to be ineffectual in practice) to eliminate every kind of public criticism of pronouncements by the non-infallible papal magisterium and thereby eliminate discourse itself; it is in fact contrary to that requirement. And since this norm of canon law is itself not a statement of the papal magisterium, but an act of the papal legislator, it may be publicly criticized also under the validity of can. 752.

PART IV

BASIC NORMS AND THE PRINCIPLE OF HUMAN DIGNITY

Böckenförde on the Right to Life, Human Dignity, and its Meta-positive Foundations

Mirjam Künkler and Tine Stein

Part IV contains three articles that reflect Böckenförde's stance on the right to life, human dignity, and the meta-positive foundations of constitutional law. Over a period of four decades, he repeatedly dealt with the issues of protecting the unborn child on the one hand and women's right to self-determination on the other. He did so in the context of both abortion law and bioethics against the backdrop of new medical-technological developments, such as pre-implantation genetic diagnosis. As in the articles contained in Part III of this volume (dealing with the relationship between theology, law and political theory), the determination of the relation between ethical and legal reasoning is once again a major concern for Böckenförde. The considerations presented here gain in relevance when we reflect on the fact that as a judge on the Federal Constitutional Court Böckenförde was involved in the seminal second abortion decision of 1993. And even after his retirement from the bench, his bioethical positions continued to play a major role in public debates.

The article 'Abolition of Section 218' was written in 1971, long before Böckenförde joined the court and in the midst of one of the most intense socio-political conflicts of the Bonn Republic in the 1970s. The bone of contention was the question of how the nearly 100-year-old Section 218 of the German Penal Code, which criminalized a termination of pregnancy under almost all circumstances, should be reformed. Two models dominated the discussion: While the 'term solution' *(Fristenlösung)* would legalize abortion in the first trimester of pregnancy, the 'indication solution' *(Indikationslösung)* would allow abortion for medical and criminal reasons only (e.g. if the mother's life was in jeopardy, or if the pregnancy was a result of rape). In the end, the parliament adopted the term solution in 1974 and legalized abortion in the first twelve weeks of a pregnancy, if undertaken with the consent of the pregnant woman and after medical counselling.

At this time, Böckenförde served as a legal advisor to the ruling Social Democratic Party, of which he had become a member in 1967. He had convinced the party's committee on legal policy of his own position in favour of

Religion, Law, and Democracy. Ernst-Wolfgang Böckenförde, Oxford University Press (2020). © E.W. Böckenförde, M. Künkler, and T. Stein 2020. DOI: 10.1093/oso/9780198818632.003.0017.

the indication solution laid out in this article. In addition, he drafted the discussion points for the Minister of Justice's speech in the decisive debate in the *Bundestag*.[1] When the vote took place, however, the requirement to vote along party lines was lifted, so that MPs were able to vote following their conscience. In the end, as mentioned, the majority opted for the term solution.

This particular article was addressed not only to the voting MPs,[2] but also to a religious audience. Böckenförde proved himself an inner-Catholic critic also in this matter, for he took a position that is in accordance with the Christian doctrine for the protection of unborn life, while at the same time criticizing some clerics' overly emotional engagement in the debate. Given the acknowledgement by the Catholic Magisterium that Christian moral teachings could not be the basis of state law (hard won in Vatican II), it appeared inappropriate to Böckenförde that clerics would exert pressure on Catholic citizens in this debate.[3]

The starting point of his investigation is the premise that the protection of human life is indispensable for any legal and political order that 'seeks to be a genuine legal order and not a kind of operative social engineering' and that this holds true beyond religious convictions.[4] Correspondingly, Article 2 of the Basic Law recognizes a right to life as a fundamental right. In the eyes of Böckenförde, this constitutional recognition must also include unborn human life, since there is otherwise no non-arbitrary criterion for determining the point in time at which human life begins to be worthy of protection: 'Fundamentally, such decisionistic specifications dispose over human life; by separating and differentiating human life worthy of protection from human life not (yet) worthy of protection, they turn themselves into masters over human life, instead of its servants.'[5]

In this respect, Böckenförde essentially supports the unlawfulness of abortion. He also shows that, despite Section 218, there had been many undocumented cases of abortion in West Germany, even after the introduction of

[1] See 'Biographisches Interview', in Ernst-Wolfgang Böckenförde, *Wissenschaft, Politik, Verfassungsgericht. Aufsätze von Ernst-Wolfgang Böckenförde* (Berlin: Suhrkamp, 2011), p. 409f. (this part of the interview is not included in the excerpts presented in this volume).

[2] This particular article was distributed among the members of the Christian Democrats' parliamentary group (CDU). This is particularly noteworthy in light of the fact that Böckenförde was a legal advisor to the SPD, not the CDU. See Ernst-Wolfgang Böckenförde, 'Vorbemerkung', in *Kirche und christlicher Glaube in den Herausforderungen der Zeit*, 2nd ed. (Münster: LIT Publishing House, 2007), p. 331.

[3] See the joint opinion of both Christian Churches 'Das Gesetz des Staates und die sittliche Ordnung', edited with a preface by Julius Cardinale Döpfner and Bishop D. Hermann Dietzfelbinger (Gütersloh: Publishing House Gerd Mohn, 1970), preface.

[4] Chapter XIII, p. 320.

[5] Chapter XIII, p. 322. Note that Böckenförde agrees in this article with the (at this time common) position that pregnancy effectively begins with nidation (rather than with the prior fertilization, as the Catholic Church has it) and that the unborn life should be protected from this point onwards. The argument is that only with nidation the criteria are met that justify viewing an embryo as an individual requiring protection. However, in his later writings Böckenförde changed his position and came to regard fertilization as the beginning of human life. See Chapters XIV and XV in this volume.

new contraceptives, and with disastrous social consequences. Böckenförde argues that unlike with moral norms, where a discrepancy between claim and reality does not affect the validity of the norm, a lack of social validity of legal norms has a negative effect on the legal system as a whole—the legal loyalty of citizens is threatened to diminish. In the realm of criminal law, Böckenförde argues, the moral consciousness of the population must be approximately reflected in the criminal norm: 'Speaking generally and especially with reference to a democratic state, the law is not an instrument to stabilize or revive ethical-moral postures and views whose presence have become fundamentally questionable in the conviction and stance of the legal subjects'.[6]

In a situation of low social acceptance of a criminal norm, which Böckenförde characterizes as a dilemma for which there can be no good solution, but only a least unsatisfactory one, he proposes a compromise. While he rejects the term solution, favoured by many Social Democrats, he proposes the prohibition of abortion for the reasons outlined above (i.e. to determine that life only begins after the first trimester is arbitrary) combined with an exemption for punishment if certain indications apply (rape, medical risks to the life of mother or child, and situations of 'extreme helplessness' such as severe existential insecurity). In other words, Böckenförde advocated for a legal policy reform according to which abortion would continue to be unlawful, although in specific cases of conflict (so-called 'indications'), it would not lead to criminal sentencing. In Böckenförde's view, this regulation could bring the criminal law more in line with social reality.

After the 1974 legal reform decriminalized abortion, the defeated political opposition (the Christian Democrats) brought the issue to the Federal Constitutional Court, which in 1975 struck down the law as violating Article 2 of the Basic Law (the right to life). In its decision (the so-called 'first abortion decision'), the court developed an argument very similar to Böckenförde's point of view, and suggested to the legislator the introduction of an emergency indication.[7] The parliament subsequently changed the law in 1976 to an indication solution with the effect that abortion was not punishable until the end of the twenty-second week of a pregnancy in case of (1) a severe danger to the health of the mother, or (2) a hereditary disease of the unborn child or harmful effects for the child during the pregnancy. Further, abortion was not punishable until the end of the twelfth week in cases where (3) the pregnancy was a result of rape or abuse, or (4) of social emergency (for example, in the case of a teenager's pregnancy). The two latter indications required counselling by a third party at least three days before the abortion was undertaken.

[6] Chapter XIII, p. 327.

[7] See for a summary, interpretation, and an English translation of the main passages of the decision, Donald P. Kommers and Russel A. Miller: *The Constitutional Jurisprudence of the Federal Republic of Germany* (Durham, NC: Duke University Press, 2012), pp. 373–386

Böckenförde returned to the abortion issue in the article 'The State as an Ethical State' (1978)[8] with a view to the legal development that had taken place in the meantime. He took up one aspect that he had already touched upon in the 1971 article. There, he had differentiated between a legal option on the one hand where indications are formulated as justificatory or exculpatory grounds, and an option on the other where indications are formulated 'entirely or in part as [...] an impediment to prosecution', which would leave the question of guilt to the individual.[9] He criticized that the position in favour of immunity from criminal punishment, for which there may be political reasons, was juxtaposed in the debate with an argument in favour of abortion's legality. In his view, the two ought to be dealt with independently from one another. In 'The State as an Ethical State', Böckenförde built on this differentiation and criticized the abortion debate for almost ignoring the important question of 'to what extent a potential immunity from criminal punishment ... need not simultaneously mean abortion's legalization, that is, a declaration of its legality. The widely defined indications of the law that is currently in effect function not only as reasons for criminal impunity, but simultaneously as general reasons of justification for all areas of the law.'[10] The reference to 'all areas of the law' is remarkable insofar as one may already recognize here the line of argumentation that the Federal Constitutional Court pursued in its second abortion decision in 1993, in which Böckenförde participated as a judge. With 'all areas of the law' Böckenförde is implicitly pointing to the argument that not only criminal law but also social law is affected by this question, as it had to be decided whether public health insurance (which is mandatory in Germany) would cover abortions.

German unification in 1990 required a new law harmonizing the different abortion regulations in East and West Germany. In the GDR, abortion had been legal in the first trimester, while in West Germany, as mentioned, this was only the case if criminal or medical or social indications applied. A 1992 reform legalized abortion in the first trimester after obligatory ethical counselling. No special indications were required. The law combined two efforts to protect unborn life: it withdrew the threat of legal punishment and introduced mandatory ethical counselling and new social support mechanisms for pregnant mothers and their families, such as state-funded day care and financial assistance.

In 1993, the Federal Constitutional Court had to decide on the 1992 abortion law reform. The majority decision, which Böckenförde joined, reaffirmed but qualified the Court's first abortion judgment of 1975 by ruling that '(a)bortions

[8] Included as Chapter III in volume I of this edition: 'The State as an Ethical State', in Ernst-Wolfgang Böckenförde, *Constitutional and Political Theory: Selected Articles*, edited and annotated by Mirjam Künkler and Tine Stein (Oxford: Oxford University Press, 2017). See also Ernst-Wolfgang Böckenförde, 'Keine Chance für eine gemeinsame Regelung? Gedanken zur abschließenden Beratung der Reform des Abtreibungsstrafrechts', *Stuttgarter Zeitung*, 12 February 1976, p. 6.

[9] Chapter XIII, p. 334.

[10] Footnote 22 in 'The State as an Ethical State' (Chapter III in volume I of this edition).

performed at any point during a pregnancy must be fundamentally considered a wrong and thus unlawful'.[11] The court put forth two qualifications, however: medical or criminal indications would justify an exception from this general principle and in such cases abortion would be lawful. Second, if an abortion was undertaken in the first trimester and the woman had undergone mandatory ethical counselling, abortion would remain unlawful but none of those involved (mothers and medical personnel) would be criminally prosecuted.[12]

The 'illegal but exempt from punishment' formula has become famous for the case and is commonly regarded as a legal innovation in penal law. Given the confidentiality of deliberation in the Federal Constitutional Court, Böckenförde refrained from commenting on how the formula entered the Court's consultation and how it eventually made its way into the majority decision. But in light of the fact that Böckenförde had already pointed to this option in several of his writings in the 1970s, it is very likely that he introduced it.

Although Böckenförde joined the majority decision on the court, he did write a dissenting opinion. The opinion deals specifically with the question of whether an abortion undertaken in the first trimester after ethical counselling must be covered by medical insurance. The Senate majority denied this due to the fundamental unlawfulness of the abortion. Böckenförde criticized that, '(t)he point is not that such services are required by constitutional law—they certainly are not—but only whether such services are prohibited from the outset by constitutional law'.[13] Böckenförde objected to the idea that term abortions were viewed in general as unlawful, as some of the term abortions might also fulfil the requirements for an indicated abortion, and in that case coverage by medical insurance should not be ruled out from the outset.[14] Therefore, he saw a need for the legislator to regulate the question of medical insurance coverage.

In his biographical interview, Böckenförde also emphasized the importance of compulsory ethical counselling as a way to protect unborn life. He argued that counselling was only credible if carried out purposefully for the protection of unborn life, while being open-ended and without criminal sanctioning.[15]

In 1999, the German Bishops Conference, under pressure from the Vatican, decided to discontinue its participation in the state's pre-abortion ethical consultation system, a situation which Pope Johannes Paul II regarded as implicating the Church in the conduct of abortions.[16] Böckenförde and other lay Catholics from the ranks of the Central Committee of German Catholics then

[11] Head Note 4, BVerfGE 203, Engl. transl. in Kommers and Miller (note 7), p. 387.

[12] Head Note 11, BVerfGE 388.

[13] BVerfGE, 88, 203 (359)

[14] As Justin Collings has observed: 'By placing all non-indicated abortions on the same (im)moral plane, Böckenförde wrote, the Court was operating at cross purposes with the rest of its opinion.' Justin Collings, 'Ernst-Wolfgang Böckenförde on the Federal Constitutional Court' in Mirjam Künkler and Tine Stein (eds.), *Understanding Böckenförde* (forthcoming), p. 21 of manuscript.

[15] See Biographical Interview (note 1), p. 448f (this part of the interview is not included in the excerpts presented in this volume).

[16] See ibid., p. 450.

founded the Catholic lay organization 'Donum Vitae' to offer that very service. The founders of Donum Vitae argued that the withdrawal of church institutions from the ethical consultation system would only diminish the chance of a wholehearted consultation encouraging women towards a decision in favour of life, and thereby contribute to an increase in abortions. Only after a long period of harsh criticism by Catholic bishops and even the prohibition of church staff to be associated with Donum Vitae,[17] the German Bishops Conference acknowledged in 2018 that the counselling offered by Donum Vitae had led to decisions in favour of not terminating pregnancies.[18]

After the turn of the century, Böckenförde continued his political engagement in this regard with a series of public essays against the backdrop of the burgeoning bioethics debate in Germany. Responding to new developments in biomedicine and biotechnology, politicians, philosophers, theologians, medical professionals, and others debated questions such as whether or not human stem cell research should be legalized, whether there were any circumstances at all that justified consumptive embryo research, whether pre-implantation genetic diagnosis should be limited to parents suffering from genetic diseases, and the like. This debate took place not only in academic circles but also in the wider public sphere, including in the country's main newspapers, weekly journals, and educational institutions with high outreach. Böckenförde intervened with some widely disseminated articles, two of which are included in this collection as Chapters XIV and XV.

'Human Dignity as a Normative Principle: Fundamental Rights in the Bioethics Debate' (Chapter XIV) was originally published in the *Deutsche Ärzteblatt* (German Doctors' Magazine), which is addressed to medical practitioners as well as a non-specialist public. In the article, Böckenförde argues that the legal principle of human dignity, enshrined in Article 1 of the Basic Law, not only suggests but indeed *requires* the prohibition of these techniques in Germany.

First, Böckenförde explains the history, status, and intent of Article 1. Drawing on the records of the Parliamentary Council (the constituent assembly which drafted the Basic Law), he shows that the drafters sought to set a counterpoint to Germany's total negation of human dignity under the Nazi regime. Following Article 1, the preservation of human dignity ought to be the first and foremost aim of the state, which should not only respect each human being's dignity but also protect it:

> It means that the recognition of and respect for every person as a subject, as the bearer of fundamental rights and the freedom to engage in responsible actions,

[17] A declaration by the German bishops of 20 June 2006 assessed that Donum Vitae is 'an association outside the Catholic Church', neither recognized by local bishops nor by the German Bishops' Conference. Church staff were prohibited from participating in Donum Vitae, and all other Catholics involved in ecclesiastical councils, committees, associations, and organizations were requested to renounce any senior cooperation with the association. See https://www.bistum-trier.de/bistum-bischof/bistumsverwaltung/kirchliches-amtsblatt/details/amtsblatt/erklaerung-der-deutschen-bischoefe-zu-donum-vitae-e-v/

[18] To underscore how close the issue was to his heart, Böckenförde decided shortly before his death that his obituary should request donations to Donum Vitae in lieu of flowers.

> is a given and not up for discussion. The recognition of and respect for human dignity appears as the foundation of the fundamental rights, not least of the right to life; it is supposed to guide also the application and interpretation of the fundamental rights.[19]

The Federal Constitutional Court, according to Böckenförde, adopted in its jurisprudence on Article 1 of the Basic Law the Kantian view that human dignity means every human being is an end in itself. 'Encompassed therein are a human being's status and recognition as an autonomous subject, the freedom to self-realization, the exclusion of instrumentalization as an object that can simply be disposed over—in positive terms: the right to rights that must be respected and protected.'[20]

But to whom does human dignity as the right to have rights belong? Böckenförde states, that '(i)t belongs to the human being independent of particular qualities, characteristics, or actual capacities; all that matters is being human, independent of the stages of this being'.[21] Thus, the unborn child, too, must be seen as a bearer of human dignity and the right to life following from it; thus unborn life must be protected by the state from the very beginning, that is, from the point of fertilization. He argues that other points in human development, such as the implantation of the embryo in the uterus, or the development of the central nervous system would be arbitrary criteria for designating eligibility as bearers of human dignity. If one were to reduce the life span at the beginning of human life, this would also open the gates to relativize the endpoint of life, as Böckenförde argued in another article.[22]

If unborn human life is included in the scope of protection of the principle of human dignity, what follows from this with regard to new biomedical possibilities? Böckenförde examines this question in a second step of the article. He differentiates between, on the one hand, embryos that are produced solely for the purpose of obtaining stem cells for research purposes, and on the other, embryos that are the surplus remaining after in vitro fertilization treatment.

In the former case, a complete instrumentalization takes place, which clearly amounts to a violation of human dignity. (The same holds true, he states, with regard to embryos produced for so-called therapeutic cloning, elaborated on later in the chapter). In the latter case, although these embryos are not created with instrumental intent, thus not harming the principle of human dignity, Böckenförde argues that the right to life would be violated were these embryos used for research purposes. While this right may be interfered with under certain—severe—conditions, these are not met here, particularly since the hoped-for therapeutic outcome of such research is highly uncertain.

As a consequence of these positions, Böckenförde also does not consider it permissible for embryonic stem cell lines to be imported into Germany from other

[19] Chapter XIV, p. 341. [20] Chapter XIV, p. 345. [21] Chapter XIV, p. 344.

[22] Ernst-Wolfgang Böckenförde, 'Menschenwürde und Lebensrecht am Anfang und Ende des Lebens. Aufriß der Probleme', *Stimmen der Zeit* 4 (2008), pp. 245–258.

countries with less restrictive legal standards. In this regard, the Bundestag issued what is known as a cut-off date regulation in 2002, according to which stem cell lines produced on the medical market up to a certain date may be imported for research purposes.[23] However, since the Bundestag had already altered the specific date once, Böckenförde warned of the bursting of a dam: 'If there is a second one, the third one will come.'[24]

Another bioethical issue Böckenförde intensively discussed concerned the permissibility of pre-implantation genetic diagnosis, resulting in a 2011 reform of the Embryo Protection Law.[25] Böckenförde makes out a clear violation of human dignity in this regard:

> The embryo created in vitro is not acknowledged and wanted as such, as a subject and 'purpose unto itself', but is dependent on specific characteristics and qualities it does or does not possess. It is only under these preconditions that it is accorded the chance to continue living and to develop as a human being. There can be no clearer expression that it does not share in human dignity, but only has value that is tied to certain characteristics.[26]

Whereas Chapter XIV provides a detailed discussion of the new biomedical developments in light of the Basic Law's principle of human dignity and the right to life, the article 'Will Human Dignity Remain Inviolable?' (Chapter XV) builds a bridge between these bioethical reflections and Böckenförde's constitutional theory. Originally published in a shorter version in the daily *Frankfurter Allgemeine Zeitung*, provocatively titled 'Human Dignity Was Inviolable. Farewell to the Drafters of the Constitution: The New Commentary on Article 1 Basic Law Marks a Paradigm Shift', the article was widely acclaimed and marked a cornerstone in the bioethics debate, especially with regard to constitutional reasoning and the meaning of meta-positive law.

The occasion of Böckenförde's public intervention was a new interpretation of Article 1 in the influential Basic Law commentary 'Maunz-Dürig'. For decades, Article 1 of the German Basic Law had been interpreted in accordance with the view that human dignity belongs to human beings as such and that Article 1 guarantees respect for the dignity of human beings and thus every individual. Böckenförde argued that the new commentary written by legal scholar Matthias Herdegen regarded the protective shield granted by Article 1 as dependent on circumstances: in the case of the question about the protection of prenatal dignity, for example, those circumstances lie in the developmental stages of the foetus and its developmental prospects in the mother's womb.[27] Böckenförde criticized that Herdegen's approach would result in a weighing of human dignity with fundamental rights. Yet, Herdegen's position

[23] See in more detail annotation III in Chapter XIV.

[24] See, Biographical Interview (note 1), p. 466.

[25] See in detail annotation IV of Chapter XIV.

[26] Chapter XIV, p. 351.

[27] Matthias Herdegen, 'Art. 1 Abs. 1 GG', in Theodor Maunz and Günter Dürig (eds.), *Grundgesetz, Kommentar* (Munich: Beck, 2003), pp. 1–58, para. 50.

was not singluar, as Böckenförde showed in a further step—since the 1980s several legal scholars and politicians had begun to disconnect being human, personhood, and the protection granted by Article 1 and argued that in order to be seen as endowed with human dignity, certain preconditions had to be fulfilled (dignity-defining skills, such as the ability of self-determination).

Böckenförde interprets this change in the commentary as both a shock to the foundation of the constitution and as a disregard for the intent of the constitutional framers. In his view, Herdegen's commentary misunderstands the principle of human dignity as a legal concept. While Herdegen did accord 'considerable suggestive power' to the notion of the Parliamentary Council that the clause on human dignity had incorporated a pre-legal claim into positive law, he maintained that it could not be used to determine the content of the positive law concept.[28] The only thing that Herdegen considered relevant in that regard was the fact that human dignity was enshrined in the constitutional text, and he determined its interpretation on the basis of the consensus of its commentators. For Böckenförde, human dignity would then be:

> left entirely to its own devices, detached (and cut off) from the linkage to the prior ethical content, which was present in the minds of the Parliamentary Council and so important for Dürig. Whatever can be said in this regard drifts into the 'background of intellectual history', which is learnedly discussed, but has no normative relevance. The fundamental norm of the Basic Law loses its supporting axis.[29]

Böckenförde relies on the widely accepted assumption that human dignity is an ethical concept derived from the Enlightenment, particularly from the Kantian notion of human beings as ends in themselves, as well as from the Christian tradition. However, as Böckenförde argues, the Parliamentary Council was motivated precisely by the idea of building upon these traditions and integrating the concept 'into constitutional law as a legal concept, in order to make it binding as a fundamental normative principle of state action. Something that existed prepositively was thereby incorporated into positive law' and the deliberations in the Parliamentary Council clearly show this intent.[30]

Böckenförde does not deny that the interpretation of the constitution as living law cannot be disconnected from historical developments and that it must be adequately equipped to meet new challenges. However, he argues that the principle of human dignity constitutes a fundamental norm which cannot be 'a variable of changing ideas of the prevailing zeitgeist'.[31] His concluding remarks in the *Frankfurter Allgemeine Zeitung* version sound almost melancholic when he asks how long the original constitution can bind generations, which no longer

[28] Ibid., para. 17, in the revised version of 2009 para. 19.

[29] Chapter XV, p. 356.

[30] Ibid. See in more detail: Tine Stein, 'Böckenförde und der Streit über die Interpretation der Menschenwürde zwischen geistesgeschichtlicher Herkunft und säkularer Verfassungsordnung', in Klaus Große Kracht and Hermann-Josef Große Kracht (eds.), *Religion-Recht-Republik. Studien zu Ernst-Wolfgang Böckenförd* (Paderborn: Schöningh, 2014), pp. 137–154.

[31] Chapter XV, p. 364.

have recourse to the experience of massive injustices and the mockery of human dignity under the 'Third Reich'. If these experiences are no longer present in the public consciousness, then the eternity guarantee of Article 79 Section 3, which establishes the immutability of Articles 1 and 20 of the Basic Law with the intent of enshrining the normative core of the constitution is powerless—the constitution would change its foundation through interpretation.

But Böckenförde did not despair in light of this development and fall silent. To the contrary, he forcefully set his positions and arguments against it.[32] After all, as he summed up the debate in the biographical interview, with its decision in aviation security law (which took place after Böckenförde's time on the court), the Federal Constitutional Court's jurisdiction rejected the relativization of the human dignity guarantee put forward by Herdegen and other voices in constitutional jurisprudence.[33]

In sum, Böckenförde's interventions in the bioethics debate might be regarded as an endeavour to protect the ethical foundation of law including its core principle of human dignity.[34] The constitutional state itself cannot guarantee specific interpretations. Thus, we encounter once more Böckenförde's dictum that *the liberal, secularized state is sustained by conditions it cannot itself guarantee.*

[32] Nevertheless, although invited, he declined to become a member of the German National Ethics Council where these issues are debated with a view towards influencing policy. Böckenförde suspected that instead of advising the parliament on these crucial issues, the council was primarily set up to deliver bioethical reasoning undergirding or even legitimating Chancellor Schröder's plans for comparably less restrictive policies. See Biographisches Interview (note 1), p. 469.

[33] Ibid., p. 468.

[34] See on this Judith Hahn, 'Ernst-Wolfgang Böckenförde's Approach to Natural Law as Normative Legal Ethics', *Oxford Journal of Law and Religion* 7 (2018), pp. 1–28, here p. 21.

XIII

Abolition of Section 218 of the Criminal Code?

Reflections on the Current Debate about the Prohibition of Abortion in German Criminal Law [1971]

The question of whether the current, general prohibition of abortion in Section 218 of the Criminal Code should be amended or abolished as part of the reform of criminal law has not only been the topic of controversial discussions of legal policy, but has also become the subject of media campaigns.[1] [1] The aim of these campaigns is more to generate or solidify a specific opinion or sentiment against the current Section 218 than to advance the discussion—which is certainly not an easy one in terms of the concrete issue at stake—with new arguments. One might be inclined to try and erect a counterposition that

[1] Editors' Note: The early 1970s saw vigorous debate about a reform or repeal of Section 218 (prohibition of abortion) of the German Criminal Code. Whereas the CDU generally favoured an 'indication solution', which would allow abortion for medical and criminal reasons (if the mother's life was in jeopardy, or if the pregnancy was a result of rape, for example), the governing coalition of SPD and FDP propagated a 'term solution', according to which abortion would generally be legal within the first trimester. Böckenförde was consulted on the matter by the parliament's judicial committee and the SPD Minister of Justice (see 'Biographisches Interview', in Ernst-Wolfgang Böckenförde, *Wissenschaft, Politik, Verfassungsgericht. Aufsätze von Ernst-Wolfgang Böckenförde* (Berlin: Suhrkamp, 2011), p. 409f.), advocating (like the CDU) an indication solution. The term solution was adopted in 1974 as new Section 218a. The defeated opposition brought the issue to the Federal Constitutional Court, which in 1975 struck down the law as violating Article 2 of the Basic Law (right to life and physical integrity). Parliament subsequently changed the law in 1976 to an indication solution with the effect that abortion would not be criminally prosecuted if undertaken after a doctor certified the necessity for medical, social, or criminal reasons. After German reunification in 1990, the abortion law was again reformed to bring the East and West German law in line and once again the law came to the Federal Constitutional Court, this time during Böckenförde's tenure there. The court in 1992 in general reaffirmed the 1975 court decision to the effect that abortion violated Article 2 of the Basic Law and was therefore unlawful except when criminal or medical indications applied. But the court also ruled that, even though generally unlawful, abortion would be exempt from criminal prosecution if it was undertaken in the first trimester and after the woman had undergone mandatory ethical counselling. The formula 'unlawful but exempt from punishment' has become famous for the case and is commonly regarded as a legal innovation in penal law. Due to the confidentiality rule of the court, it is not known which one of the judges introduced the formula, but in light of the fact that Böckenförde had already pointed to it in several of his writings in the 1970s (including in this essay), it is very likely that he did. See on this in more detail annotations XIX and XX in Chapter XVI and the introduction to part IV, p. 312f in this volume.

[1] See, for example, the magazine *Stern*, No. 24 (1971), the news magazine *Der Spiegel*, No. 23 (1971), pp. 134ff., the petition 'Aktion 218', as well as other reports in the press and on television.

Religion, Law, and Democracy. Ernst-Wolfgang Böckenförde, Oxford University Press (2020). © E.W. Böckenförde, M. Künkler, and T. Stein 2020. DOI: 10.1093/oso/9780198818632.003.0018.

is likewise (only) opinion-based as a way of warding off what is believed to be the imminent bursting of the dam.[2] But this kind of emotionalization does little for the issue. The question about the reform of the criminal prohibition of abortion is not an artificially generated but a genuinely existing problem, which simultaneously touches on basic questions of the legal order and of the ethical-moral foundation of our state. The problem can be brought to an intrinsically grounded and universally acceptable solution not through directed spontaneous actions and protests, but only—if at all—through a debate that is pertinent and based on arguments. This requires that each side, however well-founded or inalienable its own position may be or seem, is willing to engage in a discussion and in so doing open itself to a questioning of its own position with regard to its justification.

I. THE STARTING POINT OF THE DISCUSSION

Let us ask first about the *starting point* from which a discussion about the necessity or justification of the penal prohibition against abortion can and must be conducted in a state that is neutral with respect to religion and worldviews.

1. This starting point cannot be the Christian moral and ethical system as such. Today, in contrast to earlier times, this is acknowledged also among Christians and especially Catholics.[3] The state legal system and the Christian moral and ethical order lie on different levels; they are not separated from each other without a connection, but they are differentiated in terms of their goal and function. A popular image to illustrate their relationship is that of two intersecting circles with a shared vector. However, that comparison does not adequately express the specific relationship between the legal and the ethical-moral systems. The crucial thing is not so much that a shared realm exists between the legal and the ethical systems, that certain ethical-moral questions are thus simultaneously legal questions, and vice versa—that is surely correct, and the protection of human life is a classic example of this. What matters, instead, is that ethical-moral questions and problems are regulated and must be regulated by the legal system, using a particular framing of the question that arises from the task and function of the law, and precisely this framing is distinct from the ethical-moral

[2] As evident already last year in the Passau diocese newsletter, when, in the face of deliberations about reforming Section 218, the substance of which was by no means known yet, it said that the Federal Justice Minister wanted to give free reign to 'murder'. Most recently, the Episcopal General Vicariate of Essen distributed a leaflet against the abolition of Section 218, which is obviously aimed more at stimulating opinion than at objective discussion and persuasion; see *Frankfurter Allgemeine Zeitung*, 21 July 1971, p. 3.

[3] See on this the memorandum published by the chairman of the Conference of German Bishops, Cardinal Döpfner, and the chairman of the Council of the Evangelical Church in Germany, Bishop Dietzfelbinger, 'Das Gesetz des Staates und die sittliche Ordnung' (Gütersloh and Trier, 1970), p. 11f.: 'It is today universally recognized that neither the specifically Christian value conceptions nor the value conceptions of groups with other worldviews can be realized by the state-established legal system... Religions and worldviews must not succumb to the temptation to assert themselves as having sole authority by means of the state's legal system.'

order. Also in the realm in which law and the ethical order 'overlap', it is not for the state legal system to simply adopt ethical-moral commandments and prohibitions in terms of their content and scope, that is, to enact and sanction them as legal prescriptions and prohibitions; rather, it does so only to the extent that the specific tasks of the legal system demand or suggest as much. What is thus needed also in this sphere is a specifically legal justification—i.e., one derived from the contexts of the law—to prove or postulate that ethical-moral norms are also necessary legal norms.

2. The task of the law in modern society can be described, in brief, as the binding regulation (aimed at its validity in social life) of external human coexistence, in a way that secures or guarantees external peace, personal freedom, and security for all and every individual, as well as the possibility of suitable welfare. This description should be independent of specific religious or ideological goals; it is not oriented towards a perfected condition, but towards goals that represent necessary elements of the social coexistence in a society, elements that proceed from the subject status of the human being, [her or] his personal freedom and dignity as the essential point of orientation for shaping society's structure. From this perspective, the legal system is not primarily a system of virtue and truth, but of peace and freedom.[4] For the sake of the freedom of the individual, it limits itself to stipulating as legally binding only the minimum conditions of an orderly social coexistence, not the possibly desirable maximum conditions; it is, to use the phrase of Georg Jellinek, the 'ethical minimum'.[II] This is reflected also in the criteria that determine whether human social behaviour is punishable. The principle here is not to sanction ethical-moral misconduct as such, but to punish the kind of behaviour that upsets the foundation of orderly social coexistence to a considerable degree (principle of social harmfulness), and which cannot be warded off by other, less invasive means.

Also and precisely from this basis as well, which is not specifically determined by religion or other worldviews, the protection of human life appears as an indispensable principle of every legal system that seeks to be a genuine *legal order* and not a kind of operative social engineering. The Basic Law of the Federal Republic of Germany has explicitly recognized and positively formulated this universal principle. In Article 2 Section 2 it establishes the 'right to life' as a basic right for everyone. The explicit adoption of this right to life in the catalogue of basic rights—alongside the right to personal freedom and

[4] E.-W. Böckenförde, 'Religionsfreiheit als Aufgabe der Christen', *Stimmen der Zeit* 176 (1964/65), p. 209f, (most parts of which are included in this volume as Chapter IV).

[II] Georg Jellinek (1851–1911) was one of the most influential public law scholars in the Kaiserreich. Among his many important contributions to legal theory are his rights theory and his concept of the modern state (a doctrine of three elements: a state is made up of a territory, a people, and power). The 'ethical minimum' refers to the idea of law as embodying essential moral principles without which a society cannot exist.

physical integrity, which are part of the traditional stock of constitutions of constitutionally governed states—is without precedent in pan-German constitutional law.[5] It is not groundless to speculate that the authors [*Väter*][III] of the Basic Law were deliberately responding to the contempt for life demonstrated by the Nazi regime, and seeking to establish a special protection of human life by the state.[6]

3. Does this constitutional recognition of the right to life guarantee also the protection of unborn or developing human life? This question cannot be answered by pointing out that according to the Civil Code (BGB), the 'legal capacity of a person begins with the completion of birth' (§1 BGB). The constitution cannot be interpreted on the basis of the BGB (civil code). Instead, it must be interpreted on its own, in this case in terms of the principle laid down in Article 2 Section 2 of the Basic Law. The text of the Basic Law does not provide an explicit reference, and the deliberations in the Parliamentary Council, which recognized the problem, offer no secure clue whether developing human life ought to be seen as the bearer of the right to life or whether it ought to be seen as excluded from it.[7] If one goes back to the principle set down in Article 2 Section 2 of the Basic Law, what matters is whether the difference between unborn or developing human life and born human life is so weighty and essential as to provide a justification for having the protection established in Article 2 Section 2 begin only with—or limit it to—life following birth. That, however, is not the case. Medical and anthropological research are today in agreement that the transition from developing human life to the living human being is not a caesura that occurs at a specific point in time. Rather, it is a continuous development unfolding in accordance with its own telos, the biological-physiological preconditions for which are already in place at a very early moment, whether immediately upon fertilization, or with the completion of implantation.[8] It is at most for this very early moment that one can speak of a qualitative transition, the transition from (mere biological) life to (developing) *human* life. It would

[5] See Dürig in Maunz, Dürig, and Herzog, *Grundgesetz*, Note 8 on Article 2 Section 2.

[III] The Parliamentary Council consisted of sixty-five delegates selected by the parliaments of the newly founded *Bundesländer* (states) and five non-voting representatives of West Berlin. Four of the delegates were women: Elisabeth Selbert, Frederike Nadig, Helene Weber, and Helene Wessel. Only in the 1990s did it become common to refer not only to the 'fathers' but also the 'mothers' of the Basic Law.

[6] The effort to create solid bulwarks against the abuse of the law during the Nazi period emerges as a guiding principle at various points in the deliberations of the Parliamentary Council on the fundamental rights; see on this H. von Mangoldt, *Das Bonner Grundgesetz. Kommentar*, 1st ed. (Frankfurt and Berlin, 1953), introduction to the section on fundamental rights, p. 34. Mangoldt himself was a member of the Parliamentary Council and chairman of the Committee on Fundamental Rights, which deliberated on the section on fundamental rights in the Basic Law.

[7] See on this the report about the relevant deliberations in von Doemming, Füßlein, and Matz, 'Die Entstehungsgeschichte des Grundgesetzes', *Jahrbuch des öffentlichen Rechts*, NF vol. 1 (1951), p. 61.

[8] See the following among the newer literature: Blechschmidt, *Vom Ei zum Embryo* (1968); Kirchhoff, 'Der Beginn des Lebens aus biologischer Sicht', *Beiträge zur gerichtlichen Medizin* 27 (1970); Zimmer, 'Der Beginn

thus amount to an act of pure legal decisionism to have the special protection to the right of life, without consideration of the objective problem, begin only with birth (unborn children are generally viable outside the womb after the seventh month of pregnancy, and with special assistance even after the sixth month), or only with the seventh, sixth, or fourth month of pregnancy (at this point it is merely a matter of time on which the autonomous possibility of life depends). Fundamentally, such decisionistic specifications dispose over human life; by separating and differentiating human life worthy of protection from human life not (yet) worthy of protection, they turn themselves into masters over human life, instead of its servants.[9] [IV]

There are thus both general reasons, derived from the basic character of the modern legal system oriented towards the status of the individual as a subject, and reasons of positive constitutional law why the protection of human life that the legal system must guarantee embraces born human life as well as unborn, developing human life.[10] In principle, born as well as (still) unborn human life represent in equal measure a legal good to be protected.[11] This does not rule out that the legal system makes different regulations for the protection of both forms of human life. Unborn, developing human life is characterized by a unique biological and existential link with the life of the mother. This can give rise to specific situations of conflict that raise difficult problems of weighing-and-balancing, for which the legal system must find solutions that take into account the mother's right to life as well as the developing life's right to life.

des Lebens', *Deutsches Ärzteblatt* (1968); also, H. W. Lay, 'Zum Begriff der Leibesfrucht in §218', *Juristenzeitung* (1970), pp. 465ff.

[9] If the concrete human being is to truly be a subject, 'purpose in and of itself' for the order of the state and society, this must logically lead to a kind of 'prohibition' against defining the human being; for every definition turns what it defines into its object, disposes over it through inclusion and exclusion. I am grateful to Prof. Robert Spaemann (Stuttgart) for pointing this out. When it comes to the sphere of the law, this principle cannot be directly realized, because the legal system cannot do without definition, including with respect to the human being. But its application lies in the fact that all definitions about the human being can only be declaratory, the expression of something antecedent to the law, but they cannot be constitutive definitions, the expression of a legal decision.

[IV] Robert Spaemann (1927–2018), professor of philosophy in Stuttgart, Heidelberg and Munich, was a frequent interlocutor and occasional co-author of Böckenförde's. The two met in the famous Collegium Philosophicum of Joachim Ritter's in Münster, a colloquium that is generally considered one of the intellectual circles of key importance for the liberal-conservative grounding of the Federal Republic, and out of which grew the 'Historisches Wörterbuch', one of the leading humanities research projects in post-war West Germany.

[10] In the sphere of constitutional law, this is recognized by the prevailing opinion. See v. von Mangoldt and Klein, *Das Bonner Grundgesetz*, 2nd ed. (1956), Note V 2 on Article 2 Section 2, p. 186; Dürig in Maunz, Dürig, and Herzog, *Grundgesetz*, Note 21 on Article 2 Section 2; Herzog in *Juristische Rundschau* (1969), p. 442; Stein, *Lehrbuch des Staatsrechts*, 2nd ed. (1971), p. 203; probably also Maunz, *Deutsches Staatsrecht*, 17th ed. (1969), p. 115; without a position, Hesse, *Grundzüge des Verfassungsrechts der Bundesrepublik*, 4th ed. (1970), p. 150.

[11] With clarity and a sense for human dignity, this principle was already formulated in the General State Law for the Prussian Lands of 1794, a work of enlightened Absolutism (Article 10 Section I.1): 'The general rights of mankind belong also to the still unborn children, already from the time of conception.'

4. One can raise the question whether it does not follow from the reflections so far that one should regard not only the general protection of developing human life by the legal system as indispensable, but also its protection under *criminal law*. Dürig has advocated this thesis from the perspective of valid constitutional law: if Section 218 of the Criminal Code did not exist, the legislature would be constrained to insert it by virtue of the constitutional duty to protect also developing human life.[12] Herzog, like Dürig a commentator on the Basic Law, has countered this by pointing out that it is left to the political decision of the legislature how to realize the protection of developing human life commanded in Article 2 Section 2 of the Basic Law.[13] I believe that the alternative laid out here does not get at the core of the problem. The principle that has emerged from general reflections and is sanctioned by the constitution in terms of positive law is the effective protection of human life inclusive of developing life by the state's legal system. Since this is a legal good that must be unconditionally protected, the state is fundamentally obliged to employ also the strongest and most invasive means of protection and defence at its disposal: the threat and imposition of punishment. But this punitive sanction in turn is not an end in itself—the modern state does not take the place of God's judicial power. Rather, it stands within an intentional context: if it fails in every way to achieve its goal of protecting developing life in concrete reality, and instead creates considerable harm for social coexistence, or if its purpose is merely to avoid other possible and more effective protective measures, which would be more expensive, the necessity and justification for this punitive sanction becomes questionable; it then loses in every sense its connection to the common good.[14]

II. THE NEED FOR REFORM

If my reflections thus far are accepted as the starting point of the discussion over Section 218, I believe they could form the shared basis on which all citizens of our state could agree, regardless of their divergent, fundamental positions based on religion or worldviews—this would raise the initial question of whether a reform of the prohibition on abortion is in fact necessary. Is it not precisely a general criminal prohibition, as provided by current law, that appears as the necessary consequence of the state's duty of protection towards developing human life? This impression can—and must—arise if one looks only at the side of the norm. The punitive norm of Section 218, seen abstractly and by itself, is justified; its purpose is the protection of a legal good that does not exist for the sake of other, higher purposes and goals, but for its own sake.

[12] Dürig in Maunz, Dürig, and Herzog, Note 22 on Article 2 Section 2.

[13] *Juristische Rundschau* (1969), p. 445.

[14] This context is overlooked in the 'Stellungnahme der Bischofskonferenz zur Strafrechtsreform' of 25 September 1970.

But what is its effect, and what is the reality that has emerged under its validity and the practice of its implementation? The jurist who deals not only with inherently justified principles, but with a system aimed at and dependent upon realization, upon effective social validity, cannot ignore this side and must incorporate it into his considerations.

1. Estimates about the *annual number of illegal abortions* in the Federal Republic vary widely, because precise statistical data is, naturally, not available.[15] If one uses the estimates in the medical literature, which take as their starting point the abortion cases treated in certain clinics and thus have a certain objective point of reference, a deliberately cautious estimate yields a number of 200,000 to 400,000.[16] That amounts to about 25–40% of live births. (The number of live births was as follows: 1968: 969,825; 1969: 903,458; 1970: 810,000.)[17] By contrast, the number of abortions known to the police in the last ten years stood between 3,842 for 1961 and 1,005 for 1969, whereby a continuous downtrend is evident, with the exception of one year.[18] Since, in the view of the medical literature, the number of illegal abortions has been in decline in the last fifteen years, a result of the growing use of contraceptives, which means that an estimate of 400,000 illegal abortions for 1961 is not likely to be too high, we come up with a percentage of known cases of about 0.5–1%—or, to put it differently, a dark figure of 99–99.5%. It should be noted that these figures refer to cases *known* to the police, not to cases subsequently resolved, the number of which is lower still.

If one surveys the number of court convictions for abortion offences, it too—because of the dark figure—is exceedingly small. It fluctuates—again, with a continuous downtrend—between 1,865 for 1961, 947 for 1965, 605 for 1966, and 626 for 1967.[19] More important still than this number is the nature of the punishment carried out. In nearly 90% of all cases, pregnant women who performed the abortion (self-abortion) or had it performed were punished merely with a fine or with a suspended sentence of less than three months. The detailed breakdown for 1967 yields the following picture: total number of convicted adults, 301; punished with a fine, 116; with imprisonment up to one month, 63 (suspended sentence, 62); with imprisonment between 1 and 3 months, 96

[15] Detailed information on this is contained within the response by the Federal Minister of Justice to the inquiry by Representative Dr. Vogel and the CDU/CSU parliamentary group regarding the problem of abortion: Deutscher Bundestag Drucksache VI/2025, pp. 2–3.

[16] Uncertainty factors exist also with this basis for an estimate, see the discussion in the source referenced in note 15, Drucksache VI/2025, p. 3. Consequently, in order to argue on a reasonably reliable basis, I am using the lower range of the estimates.

[17] Drucksache VI/2025, pp. 2–3.

[18] The figures for each specific year can be found in the response by the Federal Minister of Justice cited in note 15, Drucksache VI/2025, p. 4.

[19] The figures for the years 1961 to 1966 in H.-J. Rudolphi, 'Straftaten gegen das werdende Leben', *Zeitschrift für die gesamte Strafrechtswissenschaft* 83 (1971), p. 105, Note 1; for 1967 from *Bevölkerung und Kultur*, published by the Federal Statistical Office, No. 9, *Die Rechtspflege* (1968), pp. 110–111 and 258–259 (the figure 626 includes convictions on the basis of juvenile criminal law).

(suspended, 90); between 3 and 6 months, 22 (suspended, 22); between 6 and 9 months, 3 (suspended, 2).[20]

This data speaks for itself. It more or less justifies the question of whether and to what extent the current state of the law still represents protection for developing human life, or whether—to put it pointedly—Section 218 is in force by being fundamentally not enforced. Likewise, the question arises as to what the criminal protection of developing life amounts to if it punishes the killing of that life in more than one third of the cases with merely a fine, and in another 50% with suspended prison terms of no more than three months—thus classifying it among misdemeanours and petty offences. Does such an assessment not contain a worse devaluation of developing human life than if there were no punishment at all?

However, this is only one side of the issue. We must add the *negative effects* produced by the current state of the law in view of the facts I have laid out. These effects are found, first of all, in the fact that a law whose social validity is so problematic and weak that it can be continuously violated on the scale described without punitive consequences, must be highly damaging to the principle of the validity of the law as such, an important factor for the common good, especially in a liberal democratic state. Laws that are not applied, that are not rendered socially effective, are a detriment to the legal system as a whole; beyond the concrete case, they contribute to diminishing the citizen's loyalty to the law. Moreover, it is inevitable, especially in our information-saturated age, that word quickly gets out that in this case a law exists whose practical validity and vigorous enforcement are highly deficient, thus triggering the harmful consequences mentioned above. The public self-reporting in recent months proves as much.[V]

For another, the negative repercussions include, and this seems even more serious, the emergence of a de facto 'accidental criminal law'. Given that 0.5–1% of cases are known (or a dark figure of 99–99.5%), anyone who eventually ends up before a judge and is punished no longer owes that circumstance to the general validity and enforcement of the law, but to some kind of 'accident'; [she or] he has been unlucky in the true sense of the word. The justice system, called upon to preserve and apply the prevailing law in an equal and uniform manner, becomes in part the instrument for the settling of private quarrels and acts of revenge, for it is largely these that bring the offence to light against the backdrop of the dark figure; and in part it becomes the enforcement organ for lucky strikes on the part of the police. And it is precisely this that prompts the courts to impose minimal sentences on a large scale, because they—rightly—seek to

[20] *Bevölkerung und Kultur* (note 19), pp. 110–111. The punishments for those convicted on the basis of juvenile criminal law are not included in this breakdown.

[V] In issue No. 24 of 6 June 1971, the magazine *Stern* featured 374 women, many of whom were prominent public figures, such as actresses Senta Berger and Romy Schneider, who conceded to have undertaken an abortion. See also note 1.

avoid this kind of redefinition of their function, and because it is hard to see the justice in a 'maximum' punishment based on happenstance.

A third negative effect is twofold: first, that Section 218 is no longer able to prevent the countless abortions. Second, because of the formal illegality that is maintained, it drives those seeking an abortion into isolation: 'officially' they cannot confide in anyone and thus also lack supportive encouragement. As a result, the abortion—if it happens—is forced to take place in the 'dark', that is to say, to be performed mostly by quacks, back-alley abortionists, and the like, which often entails additional, serious harm to the health of the pregnant women.[21]

2. What conclusion is to be drawn from this situation? First of all: the state of affairs described here cannot be weakened—and thus stripped of the challenge it poses—simply by pointing to the dark figures for other offences, and to the divergence between norm and reality in other areas of social life. It is certainly true that a mere discrepancy between norm and social reality is not inherently a cause for concern, nor does it necessitate the adjustment of the norm to reality. Rather, within certain limits such a divergence is a common feature of social life. Every norm, including a legal norm, exerts its behaviour-motivating force and its normative claim precisely by virtue of the fact that it is not coextensive with the social reality it governs, but stands in divergence to it, confronting it imperatively. That is also why it is fundamentally wrong, by invoking a sociological understanding of the law, to declare the abolition of the gap between legal norm and legal reality a maxim for the shaping of the law.

However, the situation changes when the relationship between norm and reality exceeds a certain measure. At this point there arises a systematic and unavoidable problem for the legal system, one that does not exist in the same way for ethics and the moral order. As a normative system, which is conceived in reference to and also dependent on social validity for the sake of its social regulatory (common weal) function, the legal system must be set up in such a way that the individual legal norm is in some form appropriate to the social reality it seeks to regulate and arrange and to the moral views of those to whom it is addressed. It can (and perhaps must) assume a relationship of tension to social reality and the existing social morality, precisely to support certain forms of behaviour commanded by legal principles or to bring them about in the first place. However, this relationship of tension must not become absolute, so to speak. Should that happen, the result is that the legal norm bypasses social reality, that it no longer 'grips', that the regular voluntary adherence to the legal norm by the subjects of the law is lost—an adherence that is a condition for the efficacy and enforceability of the state's guarantee of coercion against

[21] The number of several thousand deaths (indeed, 15,000 deaths) resulting from illegal abortions, which is occasionally floated in the public discussion, belongs in the realm of fantasy—the *total* number of women who died from any cause between the ages of 15 and 45 was 12,957 in 1967, for example (see Drucksache VI/ 2025, p. 5). Still, there is no cause to trivialize the deleterious health effects, or to dismiss them with the—pharisaical—reference that it is the pregnant women's 'own fault'.

law-breakers.[22] The legal norm then ceases to protect and secure where it is supposed to provide protection and security; instead, it tends to contribute to the corruption of the state's administration of justice (a criminal charge as an 'accident', the judiciary as a means of engaging in private feuds, punishment with minimal penalties, and so on.)

The legal system cannot avoid this dilemma, if that is what we want to call it. Every legal normatization [*Normierung*][VI] must show consideration for the standards of social morality and for social consciousness, it must be somehow related to them lest it deprive itself from the outset of its social efficacy. That holds even if these standards, when measured against ethical-moral principles, seem 'brittle'. Also—and perhaps especially—in this case, 'less' in terms of legal imperative, but with resonance within the legal community and truly enforceable, means 'more' in terms of normative and social effect. For the positive, consciousness-forming and motivating force of the law also depends on not demanding something unattainable for average human behaviour, relative to the given de facto standards. Speaking generally and especially with reference to a democratic state, the law is not an instrument to stabilize or revive ethical-moral postures and views whose presence have become fundamentally questionable in the conviction and stance of the legal subjects, no matter the cost. Especially commands and prohibitions under criminal law face the necessity, when it comes to the normative regulation of difficult and sometimes extreme situations of conflict (and no one denies that Section 218 is such an instance), of being guided by what can be objectively asked of the average citizen within the prevailing, overarching mental-social state of affairs—whereby the question of what can be asked may be determined independent of the individual case, but not independent of the general, subjective constitutions of these human beings.[23] Incidentally, as far as the principled aspect of the problem is concerned, all of this was already seen and spelled out by a classic Christian legal thinker.[24]

[22] The observance of a legal norm, to which the associates under the law respond with mass disobedience can also not be 'compelled' by the state organs, unless by means of terror. The condition for the efficacy of the state's guarantee of coercion is that it needs to be deployed only against 'outsiders'. A legal system that is only 'valid' when—to speak metaphorically—a police officer stands behind every citizen, loses its character as a legal order.

[VI] With normatization (*Normierung*), Böckenförde refers to the legal act of writing rules or provisions and rendering them positive law.

[23] One should consider the difference, for example, that exists between a believing Christian, who on the basis of his faith sees in every human being the image of God, and a non-Christian, to whom such a view is closed, when it comes to the (objectively) possible 'response' to a pregnancy that results from a rape.

[24] See Thomas Aquinas, *Summa Theologica* I.II, qu. 96 an. 2. This article responds to the question of whether human law should suppress all vices (*omnia vitia*). The answer is characterized by such sensitivity to the issue that I will quote it in full: 'Law is framed as a rule or measure of human acts. Now a measure should be homogeneous with that which it measures ..., since different things are measured by different measures. Wherefore laws imposed on men should also be in keeping with their condition, for, as Isidore says (Etym. v. 21), law should be "possible both according to nature, and according to the customs of the country". Now possibility or faculty of action is due to an interior habit or disposition: since the same thing is not possible to one who has not a virtuous habit, as is possible to one who has. . . Now human law is framed for a number of human beings, the majority of whom are not perfect in virtue. Wherefore human laws do not forbid all vices, from which the virtuous abstain, but only the more grievous vices, from which it is possible for the majority

3. Of course, this does not 'fundamentally' solve the problem posed by the present reality of Section 218. For the situation becomes especially precarious when the norms or principles that end up in a relationship of tension to social reality are not only those open to discussion (though they certainly hold a rank), but also a fundamental legal principle such as the inviolability of human life, which, in the final analysis, is indispensable to a legal system. This is precisely what characterizes the situation with the prohibition on abortion. In the first case, pragmatic considerations and solutions are entirely possible and perhaps appropriate. In the second case, there is a distinct risk that for the sake of a relative approximation of a norm to reality (entirely understandable in its necessity), the goal of which is to restore greater efficacy to the norm, a principle that must be unconditionally defended also and especially by a modern legal system is abandoned or at least fundamentally breached.

But is this undeniable danger enough to justify leaving the current state of the law untouched? Certainly not. For precisely this state of the law means—assuming one does not close one's eyes to the legal reality it has brought forth—that the protection of developing human life is barely effective any longer. Anyone who nevertheless considers that reality good or acceptable because a perfect world still exists in the normative sphere in the form of a general prohibition, and who is not challenged by the fact that this normative sphere captures reality so little, fails to grasp the real problem. He provides himself with a 'clean conscience' faithful to principle in a very easy way, one that neglects the responsibility for the countless victims of abortion. Consequently, the vantage point from which the various reform efforts should be assessed cannot be reduced to the question to what extent they abandon the previous principle of the general prohibition of abortion. Rather, it must focus on the question to what degree they seem suited to improving the present, *bad situation* with a view towards the protection of developing human life and the life of the mother without making it even worse. Moreover, one must not skirt the question of which societal causes have played a part in bringing about the current discrepancy between norm and reality and how they can be addressed, and to what extent the existing regulation has become so broadly ineffectual maybe because it transcended the bounds of what was reasonable with respect to certain situations of conflict.[25] That this principle of reasonableness can lay claim to validity for the state legal system in determining penal provisions was recognized also by the declaration of the Commissariat of the German Bishops: it respected in the case of state law the current exception to the prohibition against abortion (the so-called medical indication), which

to abstain; and chiefly those that are to the hurt of others, without the prohibition of which human society could not be maintained' (English translation: http://www.newadvent.org/summa/2096.htm#article2). To the objection that ethical errors are already forbidden by natural law, Thomas, invoking Augustine, responds that the *lex humana 'deficit a lege naturali'* (ibid. an. 2 ad 4).

[25] In this sense explicitly, see Albin Eser, 'Reform der Schwangerschaftsunterbrechung', *Die Medizinische Welt* 22 (1971), p. 726.

contradicts canon law prescriptions that are valid for Catholics.[26] [VII] Of course, the question is whether this already does adequate justice to the principle of reasonableness in the present situation.

At the same time, one must fully realize the following: given the social reality of abortion as it currently prevails, on the one hand, and the principle that human life is worthy of unconditional protection, on the other, every solution that seeks a way out of the present divergence of norm and reality remains somehow unsatisfactory. An ideal solution that satisfies everyone is, in principle, impossible here. One needs to say as much and admit that the true subject of the discussion and controversy is to find the least unsatisfactory solution.

III. PROPOSALS FOR A TIME-RESTRICTED EXEMPTION FROM PUNISHMENT

The reform ideas that are currently being most strongly propagated in the public sphere have as their goal, in one way or another, to leave abortion unpunished during the *first trimester of pregnancy*, under certain conditions.[27] [VIII] These proposals cannot be disqualified a priori. Rather, one must ask objectively and sobrely whether they achieve the goal pursued, if not by all, at least by most of their champions, namely to protect the developing human life as well as the life of the mother more effectively than before.[28] The thinking of the advocates goes something like this: since a general ban on abortions does not prevent a great many abortions and, moreover, entails the mentioned negative side effects, it seems more reasonable to let an abortion go unpunished for a restricted period of time, under the condition that the pregnant woman seek out a counselling centre ahead of time and/or has the procedure performed by a specialist. This

[26] According to c. 2350, §1 CIC, every deliberate killing of developing human life is prohibited, even if the developing life, because of special complications, threatens the life of the mother with death or if mother *and* child will die according to medical prognosis.

[VII] The document states that in general not all moral misconduct requires criminal prosecution. As a main ethical principle, however, the prohibition of taking a life should be anchored in state law. The text goes on to concede that there may be exceptional cases where the strict application of the law may cause serious moral conflict, such as when the pregnancy induces danger to the health and the life of the mother. Already the *Reichsgericht* of the Weimar Republic had acknowledged this conflict, the text notes, and ruled that an abortion undertaken in such situations can go without punishment. See Sekretariat der Deutschen Bischöfe, *Das Gesetz des Staates und die öffentliche Ordnung* (Gütersloher Verlagshaus, 1970), p. 29.

[27] These include the majority proposal of the *Alternativentwurf* [alternative draft] of a Criminal Code, the proposal from the Woman Lawyers' Association, proposals from suborganizations within the SPD, and the proposal from the FDP.

[VIII] Note that Böckenförde reports here on the term solution, including some conditions to be met (counselling, doctor), but not the conditions of specified indications (such as medical or criminal ones).

[28] This applies especially to the advocates of the majority proposal for an alternative draft of the Criminal Code, see *Alternativentwurf eines Strafgesetzbuches. Besonderer Teil, Straftaten gegen die Person*, 1. Halbband (Tübingen, 1970), p. 26.

makes it possible to counteract the decision of the pregnant woman to have an abortion—in the counselling sessions or through a trusted person, medical or otherwise.[29] Furthermore, this solution prevents harm being inflicted on pregnant women by quacks and so on, and it is possible to enforce the general prohibition (with the exception of specific indications) vigorously and effectively during the period after the cut-off point.

If one ponders this line of reasoning in detail, it does not appear to be cogent. Rather, there is reason to fear that it will not achieve the hoped-for reduction in the number of abortions, while the principle of the unconditional protection of human life is abandoned. These concerns are grounded in the following considerations:

1. If the termination of pregnancy goes unpunished within the first three months under the mentioned preconditions, it cannot be assumed that doctors, for example, will perform such a termination only in the case of a genuine indication, that is, a serious threat to the life or health of the mother. There will be countless doctors who would act this way and counsel pregnant women or girls accordingly, but from a sociological perspective there is insufficient reason to assume that this would be the general stance of the medical profession. Moreover, one can neither expect nor demand of physicians to uphold and maintain as effective, by their own volition and ethos, a principle that the legislature has been unable to establish or retain as a legal norm. In terms of its legal effect, this proposal thus amounts to leaving the decision of whether or not to keep a child with the pregnant women within the first trimester: in other words, the woman is granted the authority to dispose over the continued existence of developing human life. This is also how it would be seen within society. No formulations of the factual situation, however artful, can get around this.[30] Consequently, the principle that human life, including developing human life, is a legal good with an inherent value of its own, and is therefore fundamentally inviolable and must be unconditionally protected by the community of law, is breached or abandoned.

2. The expectation that such a regulation would nevertheless lead to a more effective protection of developing human life and the life of the mother (so-called containment effect) than was the case previously, is based on assumptions the cogency of which in my estimation runs into serious doubts. To begin with, this expectation presupposes that the current, general criminal prohibition for all intents and purposes no longer exerts *any kind of* behaviour-guiding force—in other words, that it keeps no or hardly any pregnant woman from having an abortion or (and this is often overlooked) provides protection for her against

[29] In this sense especially the justification of the *Alternativentwurf* (see note 28), p. 27.

[30] It has to strike one as astonishing when the advocates of the '*Mehrheitsvorschlag des Alternativentwurfs*' believe that the technical legal framing of the exemption from punishment as an exception could serve to *not* understand the regulation as the deliberate release of the destruction of developing life, see *Alternativentwurf* (note 28), p. 31. One would not really think that these reformers have so little sociological grasp of and experience with the 'parallel evaluation in the lay world'.

the desire for an abortion by third parties (unmarried father, relatives). To date that has not been proved; and in the absence of relevant empirical studies it is likely to be unprovable (of course, that applies also to the reverse argument). As a result one must fall back on justifiable suppositions. In this circumstance, however, the better arguments are on the side of the assumption that while the penal norm of Section 218 exerts a behaviour-guiding effect that is certainly weaker compared to other penal norms, that effect must be taken into account.[31] This applies especially to the protection of pregnant women against the desire for an abortion by third parties.[32]

This expectation posits, secondly, that in the case of a repeal of the general criminal prohibition the great number of illegal abortions will decline in favour of legal abortions, which will allow, first, positive counselling aimed at preventing the abortion, and, second, the protection of a pregnant woman against the harmful consequences of unqualified procedures. This, too, remains a vague supposition. The experience of Sweden with the first great step towards liberalization by no means confirms this assumption.[33] And the development in Great Britain, with its now two-and-a-half year-old regulation of abortion, would tend to lead one to the opposite conclusion. There, the number of clinical treatments following so-called artificial abortions (the starting point for the estimate of illegal abortions) has not declined, while numerous legal abortions have been added.[34]

3. All of this confronts, on the other side, the fundamental negative repercussions that must invariably arise because the principle of the inviolability of human life, including developing human life, is breached.

It seems impossible, given this breach, to still find a principled argument that would render so-called euthanasia impermissible a priori. The argument that developing human life begins only after the first trimester, meaning that it is only from this point on that the inviolability of human life can be dated, is untenable on the basis of our current medical and anthropological understanding: here the scientific debate revolves at most around whether life begins with fertilization or implantation. The proposal thus deliberately disposes, by means of a legal decision, over the moment from which human life becomes worthy of protection.[35] But if that can be done about the beginning, on what grounds should it then be ruled out that the same is possible about the end of human life, indeed, about the criteria that render life worthy of

[31] Even the advocates of the change themselves do not assume that society has moved on to the business of the day beyond Section 218; for if that were the case, it would make little sense to be pushing so emphatically for this change.

[32] This is also pointed out by H.-J. Rudolphi, 'Straftaten gegen das werdende Leben' (note 19), p. 118.

[33] See Lang-Hinrichsen, *Juristenzeitung* (1963), p. 725.

[34] See the results of a survey of 570 gynaecologists conducted by the British Medical Association, referenced in a report in the *Schweizer Ärztezeitung* 51 (1970), pp. 1315ff.

[35] This cannot be justified even by pointing to similar notions within the early Church, which (as, for example, in Augustine) posited the 'ensoulment' of the embryo only after forty days or three months.

(unconditional) protection? However much this may go against the intentions of the advocates of this proposal, this puts us on the road to human beings making the sovereign decision about the worth of human life.[36] It is also impossible to come up with a compelling argument that the right to life of unborn human life should be so fundamentally different from that of born life that in one case the authority of one person, the mother, to dispose over this right to life should be possible in principle, while it is ruled out a priori in the other case. The special biological and existential bond between developing human life and the life of the mother, which can lead to specific situations of conflict difficult to grasp for outsiders, does justify and require special regulations (e.g., a different scale of punishment, permission of certain indications, the recognition of special reasons for ruling out guilt or punishment), but it cannot justify the mother's freedom to decide over the continued existence of the still unborn human life.[37]

Contrary to all expectations, an effective sanctioning of abortion *after* the three-months cut-off point will hardly be achievable. Since the principled inviolability also of developing human life is breached, the line of separation bears the element of arbitrariness especially at this point, and it must invariably cast into question whether abortion as such is deserving of punishment. After all, what exactly is being punished here? The criterion of punishability is no longer the assault on developing human life as such—in this context it has been removed from the circle of legal goods worthy of consideration—but the specific point in time when this assault takes place.[38] But what is the reason why the same act, committed a week earlier free of punishment, should constitute a criminal injustice worthy of punishment if committed a week later? The only discernible argument, that the risk to the health of the pregnant woman is considerably greater after the third month, does not provide a sufficient reason. As of yet, our legal system does not recognize a general obligation—capable of penal sanction—to avoid threats to one's *own* health and to engage in healthful behaviour. Penal law is here being rethought into police law. One can therefore predict with a fair degree of certainty that judicial praxis will stick with minimal punishments when it comes to penalizing prohibited abortions after the first trimester.

[36] The reference to euthanasia in the Third Reich, which is not infrequently introduced into the public discussion in this context, therefore does not have the character of a malicious denunciation, but points to the (unfortunate) existence of a factual connection.

[37] However, most recently the Heidelberg criminal law jurist Bemmann has arrived at that conclusion for the period up to the sixth month of pregnancy. He posits for the pregnant woman a permanent defensive emergency situation vis-à-vis the impairment of the possibility of self-realization posed by the developing human life (the developing child appears as the unlawful attacker on the mother's legal rights), and goes on to deny that the pregnant woman has a general duty to tolerate even the normal constraints arising from pregnancy. See G. Bemmann, 'Zur Frage der Strafwürdigkeit der Abtreibung', *Zeitschrift für die gesamte Strafrechtswissenschaft* 83 (1971), pp. 91ff. Here individualism is taken to its extreme, a point that leads to its own collapse; already the notion of *social acceptability* [*Sozialadäquanz*], in this case as it relates to the behaviour of developing life, is entirely left out of the picture.

[38] Very forcefully spelled out by Rudolphi (note 19), pp. 124ff.

IV. POSSIBLE PATHS OF REFORM

The critical concerns that have been articulated against the so-called trimester proposals at the same time points in the direction where one must look for a reform solution that seeks to improve the protection of developing human life and the life of the mother over the existing, highly unsatisfactory situation, without ending up abandoning the principled inviolability also of developing human life.

1. Even if one takes seriously the social facts of abortion as they exist today and accepts that the current criminal norm is largely ineffective, the starting point for the penal regulation can be none other than a *general prohibition of abortion*. Any other solution, no matter how sensible it may seem from considerations of pure criminal policy,[39] abandons something a legal system that puts the (concrete) human being and his dignity at its centre must not relinquish. Even the high dark figure of illegal abortions is not a persuasive objection. After all, that figure is based to a considerable degree on the utter inability of developing life to protect itself, a life that usually has no one to assist it, prevent its destruction, or bring it to the attention of the prosecuting authorities.[40] But this special inability of developing human life to protect itself can be the least cause for depriving it also of the protection from a criminal norm.

However, more *de facto indications* can and must be added to the existing legal situation, indications that must be precisely circumscribed. This would eliminate what are, measured against the current state of consciousness of human beings and their ethical-moral capacity, objectively unreasonable demands of the current law, and thus render the criminal norm more humane and capable of being complied with, because it would no longer demand ethical-moral extremes without regard for extreme situations of conflict. At the same time, it would create the possibility (but, of course, no certainty) that the prohibition, in its new circumscription, would become more effective and be more vigorously applied in legal praxis.

But that is only one side of the issue. Of equal—if not greater—importance are *social policy measures* which, as much as possible, eliminate the social conditions from which the decision to seek an illegal abortion frequently arises. After all, the majority of abortions are not grounded in convenience or the desire for the unimpeded enjoyment of life or an unimpeded career (though there is no small number of such cases), but in dire material, social, familial, and psychological situations that women are trying to escape. With respect to changes and improvements in this regard, criminal law may essentially have only a 'subsidiary' character. Moreover, it is not only for the state, but equally so for society itself to become active in this area, especially through a demonstration of solidarity. Here is one example from the realm of the church:

[39] I must admit these considerations made even me waver for some time whether the trimester solution might not be acceptable in one form or another.

[40] See Rudolphi (note 19), p. 120.

How many illegal abortions may have been caused in part by the disdain that an illegitimate child and a single mother have encountered for a long time (and to some extent still do), especially from within the Church and in so-called good Catholic homes?

2. The de facto indications that should be put in place must not have the function of achieving, by a different way, the same result as the first trimester exemption. The basis for possible indications must be their *exceptional character* and the presence of an objective *emergency situation*. Such an emergency situation exists, first, if two equal legal rights conflict (e.g., the life and health of the mother against the life and health of the unborn child), and, second, when the duty of bringing the pregnancy to term seems unreasonable according to objective criteria, and not simply on the basis of the subjective ideas of the pregnant woman. And criteria of unreasonableness cannot be determined according to specific religious-ethical beliefs, but must be defined according to benchmarks of a secular legal system.[41] In such situations of conflict, the legal system can refrain from rendering a criminal value judgment without abandoning the principle that human life is inviolable. However, to keep things from getting out of hand, this should not be done by way of a general clause elucidated only with an example, as envisaged, for example, by the minority proposal of the alternative draft [*Alternativentwurf*].[42] Instead, it should be done by enumerating and circumscribing individual de facto indications. Moreover, August Wimmer has formulated a question which cannot be explored further here but is deserving of closer examination:[43] namely, whether such de facto indications should be formulated as justificatory or exculpatory grounds, or entirely or in part as a kind of impediment to prosecution, as a way of expressing that the legal system in this regard leaves the assessment of injustice and guilt to the judgment of the individual.

In terms of specific de facto indications, in addition to the existing medical indication one should, first of all, consider the so-called *ethical indication* (more precisely: rape indication). In this extreme situation of conflict, where developing human life has been created through a crime committed against the mother, with all the consequences for her emotional state, it seems possible that the legal system refrains from forcing the pregnant woman with criminal sanctions to bring the pregnancy to term. Of course, it would do so only from the perspective of unreasonableness, not because the developing human life that was created in this way has a lesser right to life.

One can and should also add an indication that is best labelled, drawing on A. Wimmer,[44] as an '*indication of extreme helplessness*'. Here the factual circumstance should be limited to the existence of an irreparable situation of human and/or social abandonment, which leads to a kind of emotional despair in the

[41] Thus rightly Eser (note 25), p. 725.

[42] See *Alternativentwurf* (note 28), p. 40.

[43] August Wimmer, 'Schutz des werdenden Lebens im kommenden Strafrecht', *Der Katholische Gedanke* (1970), p. 93.

[44] Ibid., p. 95.

pregnant woman or gives every reason to expect serious mental harm.[45] The exact formulation would have to be considered in detail.[IX] One could incorporate this indication also within an expanded concept of medical indication, since human health is not only a biological but also a mental phenomenon. However, preference should be given to a special formulation to make clear that this indication usually represents a failure by close relatives or society, who are unwilling or unable to guarantee the pregnant woman the necessary human-personal and social support to make her reasonably capable of dealing with the tasks and demands of motherhood and prevent her from falling into a situation of despair. This de facto indication would simultaneously represent a permanent challenge to society and the state's social policy to remedy it by seeing to the elimination of its causes.

A difficult problem is the so-called *eugenic indication*. That there could be any claims made on the basis of a state's alleged racial welfare is ruled out a priori. But the aspect of the 'life worth' of a child that is seriously malformed or not capable of developing cannot provide a justification, lest one open the door to the free disposability over human life. Here, too, we are left with the question of the (objective) reasonableness of expecting the mother to bring to term and give birth to a child that is, with moral certainty, seriously and irreparably impaired. At the same time, the problem here is different from the other indications: the starting point is not, as usually, an immediate, serious threat to the health or emotional-social situation of the mother, but a prospective threat. If, in the face of this situation of conflict, it may eventually seem tolerable from the point of punishment for someone to avoid this suffering and heavy fate, are there compelling reasons to limit this to the period before birth? And what if there are no reasons?

One must also point to the important and difficult procedural problems that come with every indication solution. Examining them in detail would require a separate essay. The effectiveness of any reform depends substantially on whether a solution is found in this respect that is meaningful and secures access to counselling centres or fiduciary doctors.

3. If the general prohibition against the termination of a pregnancy is fundamentally retained, the question arises as to the *point in time* from which the prohibition takes effect or must take effect. For the present state of the law, the predominant—if not the reigning—view of the legal literature for some years has been that one can speak of the interruption of a pregnancy (which, precisely speaking, represents the *termination* of a pregnancy) only from the moment of nidation, the implantation of the fertilized egg into the lining of the uterus, whereas measures and interventions before this time involve a *prevention*

[45] In this de facto situation, the justified core of the so-called social indication is embedded; in my view, a recognition that goes beyond this, e.g. one that would consider material and/or social difficulties as such sufficient for terminating a pregnancy, cannot be justified.

[IX] The conditions described here resemble what in the later 1976 abortion law were referred to as 'social indications'.

of pregnancy.[46] This view is justified with the argument that only implantation of the fertilized egg establishes the firm connection with the maternal tissue, fundamentally separable only through an external intervention, and triggers in the woman the complete shift in the relevant functional processes which, in biological-medical terms, constitute de facto pregnancy or the presence of a foetus.[47] There is much to suggest that this interpretation of what establishes an abortion in legal terms will very soon prevail, unless the legislature makes an explicit correction.

One must therefore ask whether such a correction seems necessary if one holds to the principle of the fundamental, unconditional protection also of developing human life. In my estimation, neither reasons of principle nor reasons of criminal policy demand this.

The opponents of the factual circumscription of abortion as spelled out insist that developing human life is created already by the act of fertilization. It is certainly true that the joining of sperm and egg creates new life, just as the sperm and the egg each have life already. However, the question is whether this life is already specifically human life, whether it is individuated and structured such that personhood and mental capacity, which separate the human being qualitatively from the being of other life forms, are already foundationally given here. With respect to the development of the embryo, both the ecclesiastical-theological and the philosophical tradition distinguished—into the eighteenth and in part into the nineteenth century—between 'souled' and 'unsouled' life, or between a 'developed' and an 'undeveloped' stage, and posited the quality of being human only for souled life or the developed stage.[48] When this distinction, which was carried by the notion of a gradual ensoulment, lost its scientific basis with the progress of biological-medical understanding about the continuity and development of the human organism, it was abandoned and the creation of *human* life was moved back to the moment of fertilization. In and of itself that is not yet an anthropological or philosophical-theological proof, but for now merely a new hypothesis, which—like the earlier hypotheses that are today recognized as untenable—is open to having its biological-scientific basis questioned. Today, biological-medical research knows that until nidation, the new life created by fertilization exists only as a possibility, a potentiality. About half of fertilized eggs never make it to implantation, but are abandoned by nature herself in a 'profligate selection'.[49] Only with implantation is the 'germinal material' that is previously and inherently 'condemned

[46] On this see the detailed account by Hans Werner Lay, which takes into account also the recent medical literature: 'Zum Begriff der Leibesfrucht in §218' (note 8), pp. 465ff.

[47] Ibid., pp. 466–467.

[48] On this see Dölger, 'Das Lebensrecht des neugeborenen Kindes und die Bewertung der Fruchtabtreibung in der Bewertung der heidnischen und christlichen Antike', *Antike und Christentum* 4 (1934), pp. 1ff.; Schmittlein, *Die Natur der menschlichen Leibesfrucht*, dissertation (Munich, 1966), and the brief, but very informative overview, including the legal-historical development, in H.-W. Lay (note 8), pp. 467–468.

[49] See Döring, *Empfängnisverhütung*, 4th ed. (1969), p. 41; Zimmer, 'Der Beginn des Lebens', *Deutsches Ärzteblatt* (1968), p. 452.

to biological loss'[50] maternally accepted. Only now does there arise the fixed connection and protective reciprocal relationship with the maternal organism, which now drives towards birth and the development of personhood out of its own intentionality, one that is no longer dependent in its realization on the uncertainty of an additional event.[51] Given these natural-biological circumstances, is it not the case that the far better and weightier, if not compelling, reasons suggest that the genesis of developing *human* life—meaning, a personal life constituted by the I–You relationship—takes place only with successful implantation?[52] This position is also taken by no small number of theologians, among them a proven author like Cardinal Mercier.[53]

The jurist has no competency to decide the question under discussion. What is at stake here is finding grounds for ensuring that the compelling reasons of criminal policy that argue against extending the threat of punishment—not against other kinds of legal protection, for example, vis-à-vis gene manipulation and the like—to the moment of fertilization are not eliminated a priori by compelling anthropological-ethical reasons. In terms of criminal policy, this extension would create a norm that would lack any chance at implementation from the outset. Whatever possible measures are taken between fertilization and implantation to prevent pregnancy is almost entirely beyond proof, as well as mere 'discovery', unless the state wishes to subject also the intimate sphere of its citizens to permanent control, surveillance, and so forth, following the Orwellian model. The criminal jurist A. Eser has noted, probably rightly so, that in this regard there is already a lack of capacity for punishment, irrespective of a potential guilt deserving of punishment.[54] From this side, too, there are *limits to the law*, and one should respect them for the sake of the validity and efficacy of the legal system. Added to this is the absence of a general consciousness and the real-life notion that something is 'aborted' or 'killed off' in interventions aimed at preventing implantation. What happens here lies in the realm of contraceptive and birth control measures in terms of consciousness and implementation.[55] From the other side, this points back to the fundamental question.

[50] Thus Zimmer-Brusis, 'Eine biologische Definition der Schwangerschaft', *Deutsches Ärzteblatt* (1970), p. 839, cited by H.-W. Lay (note 8), p. 467.

[51] On this, see Döring (note 49), p. 41; Sauser-Vodopivec, 'Medico-theologische Anmerkungen zur Humanontogenese', in *Gott und Welt. Festgabe für Karl Rahner*, vol. II, p. 857, says that before implantation, the zygote was still 'actually and prospectively utterly at the mercy of the maternal neuro-vegetative guiding forces' (quoted in Lay (note 8), p. 470).

[52] Are the 50% of naturally aborted fertilized eggs really supposed to be 'deaths' of human-personal beings destined—theologically speaking—for eternal salvation? What does that say about how God as the creator is dealing here through his creation with the image of himself he has created?—Incidentally, the teachings and practice of the Church to date—under the banner of the old (now probably modified) understanding of baptism—display a remarkable inconsistency in their stance on the embryo's capacity for being baptized and the non-performance of baptism for miscarriages or other complications during pregnancy.

[53] See the references in F. Böckle, in *Arzt und Christ* (1968), p. 69.

[54] Eser (note 25), p. 729.

[55] E. W. Hanack, *Der Nervenarzt* (1969), p. 506, points out that it is 'an entirely formal distinction' whether one intervenes in the complicated processes in a fertile woman, following ejaculation, one minute before or one minute after fertilization; given the general legal permissibility of contraception, this surely captures the state of the general consciousness.

For some the conclusions at which my reflections have arrived might seem not far-reaching enough and closed to a decisive reform of Section 218, while for others they have already exceeded the permissible bounds of a possible reform. But perhaps the attempt I have made here to walk the fine line between principles that are indispensable for our legal community, on the one hand, and the existing social reality of life that must be regulated, on the other, has rendered some of the questions under discussion clearer and some of the difficult legal problems more lucid, and has freed the necessary discussion itself from useless emotional polemic.

XIV

Human Dignity as a Normative Principle

Fundamental Rights in the Bioethics Debate [2003]

The debate in bioethics[1] over whether stem cell research, stem cell importation, pre-implantation diagnosis, and therapeutic cloning are permissible and justifiable remains in flux. Contrary positions clash. Is it possible to derive normative guidelines for this debate from the guarantee of human dignity in the Basic Law, in terms of its scope and content, and if so what do these guidelines look like in detail?

I. THE PROBLEM

The advances in biomedicine and biotechnology within the span of one generation are almost breathtaking. What was taught and researched in biology at schools and university when we were secondary students, and perhaps encountered later at university, and what is happening today? What prospects and possibilities have opened up? Let me pick out only a few examples: the fertilization and early embryonic development in humans can now take place outside the body, and gene technology allows for interventions in the nucleus of an embryo. It is no longer utopia but a real possibility to engage in selection with respect to offspring: negative selection oriented towards genetic defects, as well as positive selection aimed at desirable characteristics. Even germ line therapy, the alteration of human genetic endowment, and what is known as therapeutic cloning (i.e. the creation of pluripotent stem cells to create the potential for cures) are now by no means out of the question. What Aldous Huxley described in his brave new world as an obvious dystopia, namely the potential to create—indeed, fabricate—humans with predetermined characteristics, is no longer an unrealistic utopia. Terms like 'virtual child' or 'designer baby' no longer seem absurd. 'In the future, anyone who

[1] Editors' Note: This article is an expanded version with added footnotes of the essay 'Menschenwürde—"Dasein um seiner selbst willen"', published in *Deutsches Ärzteblatt* 19 (2003), pp. 1246–1249.

Religion, Law, and Democracy. Ernst-Wolfgang Böckenförde, Oxford University Press (2020). © E.W. Böckenförde, M. Künkler, and T. Stein 2020. DOI: 10.1093/oso/9780198818632.003.0019.

wants to have offspring will be able to select children based on their hair colour or IQ', Professor Judith Mackay, a prominent member of the World Health Organization, explained recently.

These nearly limitless possibilities created by the advances in biomedicine, biotechnology, and gene technology raise the urgent question about fixed markers and guidelines for how we humans should deal with one another and shape our shared lives. This is all the more true as these new possibilities not only concern economic interests, but are also linked to great expectations about medical progress and the chances to cure previously incurable diseases. Where can one find such fixed markers and guidelines?

II. THE GUARANTEE OF HUMAN DIGNITY AS A NORMATIVE MARKER

The Basic Law in Germany proclaims and ensures the basic right to life and the inviolability of human dignity. It comes as no surprise that these guarantees are present in the constitution as legally binding. It was the bitter experiences of the Nazi period that caused the inviolability of human dignity and the imperative to respect it to be incorporated into the Basic Law, along with the fundamental right to life, which previous constitutions did not know in this form. The deliberations in the [constitution-drafting] Parliamentary Council confirm this every step along the way.[1] Already some of the state constitutions created after 1945 had proclaimed the recognition or inviolability of the dignity of the person,[2] and the Parliamentary Council was familiar with the draft of the UN's Universal Declaration of Human Rights, which was adopted at the end of 1948; the Preamble to that Declaration spoke of the respect for the dignity inherent in all members of the human family.[3] But what transpired in the Parliamentary Council was more than the adoption and development of these ideas and formulations. Recognition and respect for the dignity of the human being was deliberately placed at the beginning of the Basic Law. The intent was to clearly show the (normative) foundation of the state order that was being newly established, and the very purpose [*Um-Willen*] of this order—so that the

[1] Especially relevant are the deliberations in the Committee for Fundamental Issues, see *Der Parlamentarische Rat 1948–1949. Akten und Protokolle*, vols. 5.1 and 5.2, edited by Eberhard Pikart and Wolfram Werner (1993), specifically the Third Session on 21 September 1948, ibid, pp. 38–50; Fourth Session on 23 September 1948, ibid., pp. 62–82; Twenty-Second Session on 18 November 1948, ibid., pp. 584–603; Twenty-Third Session on 19 November 1948, ibid., pp. 603–609; Thirty-Second Session on 11 January 1949, ibid., pp. 910–927. See also the summary in Doemming, Füßlein, and Matz, 'Entstehungsgeschichte der Artikel des Grundgesetzes', in *Jahrbuch des öffentlichen Rechts der Gegenwart*, Neue Folge, vol. I (1951), pp. 41ff., 48–53 (Article 1), 54–66 (Article 2).

[2] Thus Article 100 of the Bavarian Constitution of 2 December 1946; Article 5 of the Constitution of Bremen of 21 October 1947; Article 3 of the Constitution of Hesse of 1 December 1946; Articles 1 and 2 of the Constitution of Baden-Württemberg of 28 November 1946.

[3] See *Der Parlamentarische Rat* (note 1), vol. 5.1, Doc. 10, p. 220.

kind of degradation of human beings, the violation of their rights, liberty, and dignity that had occurred during the Nazi rule could not be repeated.[4] And the framers of the Basic Law were not content to merely proclaim the inviolability of human dignity; rather, they added to this pronouncement the following sentence: 'To respect and protect it shall be the duty of all state authority.' With this, recognition of and respect for human dignity was established as the binding normative principle for all state action and for how people live together within society. It means that the recognition of and respect for every person as a subject, as the bearer of fundamental rights and the freedom to engage in responsible actions, is a given and not up for discussion. The recognition of and respect for human dignity appears as the foundation of the fundamental rights, not least of the right to life; it is supposed to guide also the application and interpretation of the fundamental rights.[5]

III. SCOPE AND CONTENT OF THE GUARANTEE OF HUMAN DIGNITY

There thus exists a fixed point of orientation that is not merely an ethical-moral proposal one can accept or reject, but which, as part of the constitution, constitutes a binding normative principle. The question is to what extent this point endures in the face of the current debate over biomedicine and biotechnology. What is the more specific content of this guarantee of human dignity, and to whom does the guarantee refer?

Of crucial importance, to begin with, is the question of whether this guarantee, and the recognition and respect laid down in it, encompasses only born humans or also the embryo as autonomous subject. This concerns the legal status of the embryo. Is it also the bearer of human dignity, of its claim to respect, and of the right to life that flows from it, and if so, at what point? This question cannot be answered directly from the wording of Article 1 of the Basic Law. It is a matter of interpreting this text with respect to its scope, and this interpretation is clearly contested in the contemporary debate.

[4] See specifically the deliberations in the Committee on Basic Issues, Third Session of 21 September 1948, *Der Parlamentarische Rat* (note 1), pp. 40–44, 56–57; Fourth Session of 23 September 1948, ibid., pp. 64–66, 70/71; Twenty-Second Session of 18 November 1948; ibid., 598–601; Twenty-Third Session of 19 November 1948, ibid., 606–607.

[5] See, for example, the statement by the parliamentarian Dr. Bergsträsser on Article 1 of the Basic Law in the Fourth Session of the Committee on Basic Issues, *Der Parlamentarische Rat* (note 1), vol. 5.1, p. 63: 'that it would be the right thing to place at the front of the fundamental rights a few sentences that make clear very concisely the intent, meaning, and foundation of the fundamental rights'. The delegate Dr. Schmidt said the following about Article 1 (ibid., p. 84): 'It represents in a sense the general clause for the entire catalogue of fundamental rights. In its systemic importance it is the real key to the whole thing.' Similarly, in the Twenty-Second Session of the Committee, Dr. von Mangoldt (ibid., p. 594): 'From the general remarks on Article 1, which we had actually intended to be more like a preamble to all of the fundamental rights—this is how we had conceived Article 1 from the beginning ... '

The principal objection that is raised—and not only by scientists—is how an embryo of eight or sixteen cells can already be the bearer of human dignity. In view of the biological reality, the argument goes, such attributions are entirely unrealistic, in fact, they are virtually absurd. As a result, not a few focus on a later stage in the embryo's development and seek to justify it: implantation, the development of the brain, birth, the effective capacity for reason. The question is, can one proceed in this way?

1. *The correct method for approaching the question*

Whether these arguments are plausible and sustainable, and if so, to what extent, is an open question. What is important for now is the method on which they are based: normative qualities and consequences are derived from certain demonstrable scientific findings. What is the justification for doing so? Deducing normative qualities and postulates (Ought) from demonstrable scientific facts (Is) is generally considered a 'naturalistic fallacy', and such an argumentation is always sharply criticized in other contexts. Should that not apply also in this case?

Criteria for how people interact with one another, commandments and prohibitions regarding their behaviour, cannot be derived and justified as the result of scientific understanding, for they exceed the questions and horizon of science. Formulating and establishing these criteria is a matter for philosophy, ethics, and—not least—the law. Of course, scientific realities must be taken into account as a substantive point of reference, and they are starting points when it comes to the application of certain normative commandments. But they are not the source of these commandments or the basis of their validity. The commandments arise solely out of autonomous philosophical, ethical, and legal argumentation, out of its coherence and power of persuasion. To pick up two statements by Jutta Limbach, the former president of the Federal Constitutional Court: 'Jurisprudence is not competent to answer the question when human life begins'; 'natural science is not capable, on the basis of its insights, to answer the question from which point human life should be placed under the protection of the constitution'.[6] The latter, in particular, is also attested by the arbitrariness that characterizes the various trigger points for the attribution of human dignity put forth by those arguing on the side of natural science. The necessity why one trigger point rather than another establishes the ownership of human dignity is not demonstrated, nor can it be demonstrated scientifically-empirically. We are left with an imputed plausibility or a pragmatism that is sometimes interest driven.

It is also of little help to relate positions about the ontological and moral status of the embryo and their justification to scientific findings, and then

[6] Jutta Limbach, 'Mensch ohne Makel', *Frankfurter Allgemeine Zeitung* No. 47, 25 February 2002, p. 51.

ask about the extent to which these positions can be sustained on scientific grounds or are open to scientific criticism with respect to their consistency. This does avoid the naturalistic fallacies mentioned above and is to that extent attractive; moreover, one can proceed very lucidly with this approach.[7] But it means, conversely, that the philosophical/ethical/legal argumentation about the status of the embryo is, in the final analysis, placed on a par with the scientific debate, indeed, it is implicitly subjected to the control of the latter, even though the epistemological objects and methods—and consequently the possibilities of cognition—of the two realms are entirely different. This approach can hardly clarify whether one argumentation or the other is internally consistent and sustainable.

Likewise, enlisting and employing the concept of the person imperils the discussion rather than helping it. This move is made by philosophers as well as theologians and scholars of cultural studies. To be sure, the concept of the person has a venerable philosophical tradition that goes back to Boethius; within this tradition it was intended to give expression to the peculiar nature of the human being as the individual substance of rational nature, a substance that belongs as much to the natural and sensory world as to the intelligible world.[8] But the modern concept of the person has uncoupled itself from this. It now has the function of introducing a differentiation between human and personal life, and to conceptualize personhood (being-a-person) as a narrower concept vis-à-vis being-a-human.[9] Not every human life has personhood, thus rendering its bearer a person, only a life that is marked by certain characteristics and qualities. However, what personhood should be tied to is determined in different ways. Sometimes it is linked to the reciprocal relationship with the maternal organism after implantation, sometimes to viability outside the mother's body, sometimes primarily to self-consciousness or the capacity for self-determined action, whereby in the latter case the focus is on the actual presence of these qualities, not on their potentiality. Because the dignity of the human being is seen as grounded in a personhood defined in this way, it follows that human dignity does not belong to every human life form, but only to human life that constitutes a person. The concept of the person thus serves to demarcate the protective sphere of the commandment to respect human dignity; not all human beings or not all phases of human life share in human dignity.

[7] Thus especially Nikolaus Knoepfler, *Forschung an menschlichen Embryonen* (1999); 'Was definiert den Anfang des Menschen?' in Schweidler, Neumann, and Brysch (eds.), *Menschenleben-Menschenwürde* (2003), pp. 243–255.

[8] The definition in Boethius (*Contra Eutychem et Nestorium*, 5) is as follows: 'persona est natural rationalis individua substantia'. See M. Fuhrmann, 'Person I. Von der Antike bis zum Mittelalter', *Historisches Wörterbuch der Philosophie*, vol. 7, cols. 270–283.

[9] Dieter Birnbacher, 'Hilft der Personenbegriff bei der Lösung bioethischer Fragestellungen?', in Schweidler, Neumann, and Brysch (note 7), pp. 31–44; 'Das Dilemma des Personbegriffs', in Strasser and Starz (eds.), *Personsein aus bioethischer Sicht* (1997) (Archiv für Rechts- und Sozialphilosophie ARSP-Beiheft 73), pp. 9–25.

2. *The necessary extension to include the embryo*

However, such attempts at differentiation, which are at times undoubtedly undertaken with a focus on concrete results, cannot be conclusive. If the issue is the reach of human dignity and its protection, as the German constitution spells out, the starting point has to be what Article 1 Section 1 of the Basic Law declares: 'Human dignity shall be inviolable. To respect and protect it shall be the duty of all state authority.' This passage does not speak of the dignity of the person that must be respected and protected, but of the dignity of the *human being*. It belongs to the human being independent of particular qualities, characteristics, or actual capacities; all that matters is being human, independent of the stages of this being. Article 1 of the Basic Law does not know any differentiation according to such stages.[10] And the acknowledged dignity applies to every individual human being as well as to humans in general—the formulation 'human dignity' covers both, including the reference to humans as a species. What is being proclaimed is what belongs to every individual human and to the human being as such, namely an inviolable dignity, and how we humans should treat one another on the basis of this dignity and how the state should treat human beings, namely by acknowledging and respecting this dignity.

There may be disagreements about the substantive meaning of this dignity and its associated commandment of respect when it comes to specifics. In this regard there is good reason for the warning not to fragment the respect for human dignity into ever smaller manifestations, because that would only end up questioning the fundamental claim of human dignity and its inviolability. But what constitutes the core content of this statement, what makes up its normative essence, is less controversial than might appear. However, in the deliberations of the Parliamentary Council, Theodor Heuss regarded human dignity as a 'non-interpreted thesis',[11] and his words are today often quoted in the debates.[12] But he was by no means asserting that the statement was devoid of substance; rather, he was merely opposing its explicit justification on the basis of natural law, which could result in the adoption of deductions from natural law. Irrespective of the various attempts to determine the content of human dignity, a commonly accepted core is already evident in the Parliamentary

[10] Thus, a restriction of the commandment of respect and protection of Article 1 of the Basic Law to born humans or human beings who already display certain qualities and characteristics can be justified against the normative text of Article 1 only if unborn children or developing human beings without the qualities or characteristics in question are stripped of their humanness or membership in the human species. Consistent in this regard is the biologist Hubert Markl, the former president of the Max Planck Society, who declared that the concept of the human being was a culture-specific ascription that rested on an assertion and could be done in various ways, see H. Markl, 'Freiheit, Verantwortung, Menschenwürde', in Christian Geyer (ed.), *Biopolitik* (2001), p. 177 (180–183).

[11] *Der Parlamentarische Rat* (note 1), vol. 5.1, p. 72.

[12] A misquotation can be found in Jutta Limbach (note 6), where we read 'uninterpretable thesis'. If that were true, however, it would be evidence for a lack of normative content.

Council and later, as well.[13] It can be circumscribed with the formula (borrowed from Kant) of 'an end in itself' or with the interpretation given by the Federal Constitutional Court: 'existence as an end in itself'.[14] Encompassed therein are a human being's status and recognition as an autonomous subject, the freedom to self-realization, the exclusion of instrumentalization as an object that can simply be disposed over—in positive terms: the right to rights that must be respected and protected.

It is indeed uncontested that dignity in this sense belongs to every individual human, to all of us who confront one another, to the human beings with whom we negotiate, or quarrel, or whom we are raising—and that it finds expression in the recognition of this dignity. This dignity of living human beings is also what the Parliamentary Council had in mind. The necessary and contested question that invariably follows is how far this recognition of human dignity must extend into the life process of every human for it to remain true. Is it sufficient, as some argue, if this recognition of and respect for dignity begins only at a specific point in the life process of the human being, while the preceding life process remains disposable?[15] Or must this recognition and respect exist from the very outset, the very first beginning of this human life?[16] Only the latter can be the case if existence for its own sake or the purpose as such shall remain true and not turn into an empty declaration. The dignity that characterizes a

[13] From the deliberations of the Parliamentary Council, especially the 22nd and 23rd sessions of the Committee for Fundamental Questions on 18 and 19 November 1948, *Der Parlamentarische Rat* (note 1), vol. 5.2, pp. 585f., 590, 598, 606f.

[14] See Immanuel Kant, *Metaphysik der Sitten*, Tugendlehre §38; Kant, *Grundlegung zur Metaphysik der Sitten*, Vorländer ed. (1947), pp. 52, 60f.; *BVerfGE* 88, 203 (252).

[15] Thus, among others, Horst Dreier, in Dreier (ed.), *Grundgesetz*, Article 1 Section 1, notes 47, 50; Dreier, 'Lebensschutz und Menschenwürde in der bioethischen Diskussion', in H. Dreier and W. Huber, *Bioethik und Menschenwürde* (2002), pp. 39ff.; Hasso Hofmann, 'Die versprochene Menschenwürde', *AöR* 118 (1993), pp. 353 (361f., 375f.), because he sees Article 1 Section 1 of the Basic Law as the reciprocal promise of recognition by the individuals as bearers of the constitutive power; Adalbert Podlech, in *Alternativkommentar zum Grundgesetz*, Article 1 Section 1, notes 57f.; doubtful, but in agreement, Zippelius, in *Bonner Kommentar*, Article 1 Section 1 and 2, note 51. It does not lead to any other result if, in order to avoid artificial dividing lines with respect to the 'Whether' of the protection of dignity, one assumes a 'procedural view of the protection of dignity with the intensity of an existing claim to respect and protection that is dependent on developments', as is done by Matthias Herdegen in Maunz and Dürig, *Grundgesetz*, Article 1 Section 1, notes 56, 65–66 (as of February 2003). The development-dependent, varying quality of the claim to dignity derived from this view brings a fluid element to bear that opens up all kinds of leeways and dispositions, depending on the position taken, and eliminates the absoluteness that is inherent in human dignity and the respect accorded to it, without explicitly saying as much. The notion that human dignity and the respect for it mean different things in different life phases and situations is advocated by Bernhard Schlink, *Aktuelle Fragen des pränatalen Lebensschutzes* (2002), pp. 10–13. In the process, he takes account of, among other things, the difference between human life in its potentiality and its actuality, and of what is or is not capable of being relived and re-felt.

[16] Thus *BVerfGE* 39,1 (41); 88, 203 (251); also Günter Dürig in Maunz and Dürig, *Grundgesetz*, Article 1 Section 1, note 24; Wolfram Höfling, in Sachs (ed.), *Grundgesetz. Kommentar*, 2nd ed., Article 1, notes 46 and 47; Höfling, 'Gutachten für die Enquêtekommission des Dt. Bundestages "Recht und Ethik der modernen Medizin"', May 2001, pp. 34ff., 52ff., 197ff.; Christian Starck, in von Mangoldt, Klein, and Starck, *Grundgesetz*, vol. 1, 4th ed., Article 1 Section 1, note 18; Adolf Laufs, 'Fortpflanzungsmedizin und Menschenwürde', *NJW* (2000), pp. 2716ff.; Dieter Lorenz, 'Die verfassungsrechtliche Garantie der Menschenwürde und ihre Bedeutung für den Schutz menschlichen Lebens vor der Geburt', *Zeitschrift für Lebensrecht* (2001), pp. 38ff.

complete being cannot be separated and split off from its own history, but must instead encompass it.

For if one seeks to exclude a particular phase of the life process from the recognition and respect that is due to the human by virtue of his dignity, or to graduate this respect, on the grounds, say, that it is only a clump of eight or sixteen cells, or no implantation has taken place (which is uncertain, anyway), one tears a hole in the development of the individual human being. Should the respect for his [or her] dignity hold for every human being as such, it must belong to him [or her] from the *first* beginning of *his* [or *her*] life and extend to encompass it, not only after an interval which he [or she]—unprotected against instrumentalization and arbitrariness—must first have been fortunate enough to survive. At this point, then, scientific insights and facts become relevant, not as a source and foundation, to be sure, but as the substrate for the application of legal-normative argumentation and valuation.

However, this first beginning of the distinct life of the forming and developing human lies in fertilization, not later. Compared to the sperm and the egg, which are also forms of human life, fertilization creates a new and autonomous *human being*. It is characterized as unmistakably individual by the combination of a set of chromosomes specified in this particular way and none other. This is—scientifically uncontroversial—the biological foundation of the individual human. The later mental and psychological development is already laid down here; the human being is a body-mind-soul unity. For once the individual set of chromosomes has been fixed, there is no incision into the quality of what is developing.[17] The genetic program of development is completely present, requires no further completion, and unfolds in the course of the life process from an internal impulse, according to the criterion of its own organization. And this, precisely, is the characteristic that constitutes a human organism: a determined form that develops alive.[18] Of course, none of this can happen without all kinds of help from the outside, which also has a shaping influence: such as the supply of nutrition, contact and exchange with the maternal organism, and much more. But these things are nothing more than the necessary conditions for the possibility of independent development driven by an internal impulse. They are not that development itself, and they exist not only before but in part also after birth for some time. That nature can continue to influence the unfolding life process, that it can also—for example on the way to implantation—end it abruptly, is a fact, but it does not change its beginning with fertilization. This makes perfect sense also from a lifeworldly perspective. After all, it is not rare for parents to know exactly from which union their daughter or son sprang. It is from that point, the accomplished fertilization, and not the later implantation or formation of the

[17] Josef Wisser, 'Einzigartig und Komplett', in Christian Geyer (ed.), *Biopolitik* (2001), p. 221; Christian Starck, 'Verfassungsrechtliche Grenzen der Biowissenschaft und Fortpflanzungsmedizin', *JZ* (2002), pp. 1065 (1068f.). The formation of identical twins also does not constitute such a rupture. Rather, the division merely creates a second individual with the same set of chromosomes, thus the same genetic program and possibly the same chromosomal anomaly.

[18] On this see Gerold Prauss, 'Geprägte Form, doch zweckbewußt zerstückelt', *FAZ* No. 277, 28 November 2001, p. 50, a clear criticism of the theses of Christiane Nüsslein-Volhard, *FAZ*, 2 October 2001.

cerebral cortex, that they date the beginning of their child's life. The beginning of human life with fertilization is thus by no means counterintuitive.

Whether the human embryo enjoys the protection of human dignity and therefore also the right to life is thus not dependent on a kind of ontological fundamentalism, nor on whether a foetus of eight or sixteen cells can be empirically qualified as a person. Rather, what is decisive is that the recognition of human dignity as expressed by the Basic Law encompasses in its normative content—if it is not arbitrarily curtailed—also the first beginnings of the life of every human being and must be extended to include them. The human embryo is embraced by the protection of human dignity also in its early and earliest life phase, it must be respected and treated like a bearer of human dignity and the right to life.

IV. CURRENT APPLICATIONS

What, then, follows from this reach of the normative principle of human dignity for the problems that arise in the current bioethical debate? I will single out a few of these problems.

1. *Embryo-consuming research*

It is obvious that the (artificial) creation of embryos for research purposes, to derive from their use (which means: killing) stem cells that can be used for research, constitutes a profound violation of the protection of human dignity. Here the embryo is fully instrumentalized from the outset: it is produced only to be subsequently used to extract stem cells, not one iota of an existence for its own sake is still evident. As long as the guarantee of human dignity of the Basic Law holds, embryo-consuming research must remain prohibited, even if other states, such as Great Britain and in part also the United States, see the situation differently.[19] [II]

Another question concerns the production of stem cells when embryos are not produced for this purpose, but for other reasons, for example, to bring about

[19] Against a violation of human dignity Horst Dreier, in Dreier (ed.), *Grundgesetz*, Article 1 Section 1, note 59; likewise Hasso Hofmann, 'Biotechnik, Gentherapie, Genmanipulation—Wissenschaft im rechtsfreien Raum?' *JZ* (1986), pp. 253 (258). Questioning of the evident nature of a violation decision M. Herdegen (note 15), note 96; as here Ch. Starck (note 17), note 89 on Article 1 Section 1; W. Höfling, in Sachs (ed.), *Grundgesetz*, 2nd ed., Article 1, note 21.

[II] The German Embryo Protection Law is one of the strictest in the world. Introduced in 1990 and amended several times since then, it forbids the improper use of reproductive technology (prohibition of surrogate maternity and egg donation) and any improper use of human embryos for non-preserving purposes (such as research purposes with embryonic stem cells); it forbids the selection of sexes and in general the pre-implantation diagnosis of in-vitro-fertilized embryos (except in cases of serious genetic illness of the parents); it forbids insemination after the death of the sperm-giver; and it prohibits artificial alteration of human germ line cells, human cloning, and the creation of chimeras and hybrids. The embryo is defined as 'the human egg cell, fertilized and capable of developing, from the time of fusion of the nuclei, and further, each totipotent cell removed from an embryo that is assumed to be able to divide and to develop into an individual under the

a pregnancy (in vitro fertilization), and are no longer (can no longer be) used for this purpose. These are the so-called excess embryos. Here, too, the extraction of stem cells presupposes the use (i.e. killing) of embryos. Is this permissible?

Since these embryos were created to bring about a pregnancy, that is, their creation did not arise from an instrumentalizing intent, what is decisive here is not primarily the respect for human dignity, but the embryo's right to life (borne by human dignity), which serves to protect its biological-physical existence.[20] Now, the human right to life, which is grounded in human dignity, is not absolute and inviolable like the respect for human dignity itself. Under certain circumstances, it is possible to intervene in this right, as Article 2 Section 2 of the Basic Law explicitly states. The same holds also for an embryo's right to life. However, to be justified, such interventions presuppose extraordinary situations of conflict (examples are self-defence, a deliberate killshot, war to defend the country, dangerous police action). Since such interventions concern not specific restrictions, but in most cases all or nothing (i.e. life and death), they can be considered only if other, gentler means of conflict resolution are not available.

There is nothing to suggest that these stringent preconditions are currently fulfilled with a view to the interest in stem cell research. The interest of scientists is certainly legitimate, and also supported by the fundamental right of freedom of research. But just as it cannot justify the killing of a human being, it cannot legitimize the use or killing of an embryo, which is a human being *in nuce*. And neither can the right to health serve that purpose. After all, the interest in research does not concern existing life or the current health of one or more person, but quite uncertain expectations, expectations that stem cell research may one day give rise to cures for diseases that are presently incurable. And it is quite uncertain and disputed among scientists whether the expected results might not be achieved also with research on adult stem cells or stem cells from umbilical cord blood—that research on embryonic stem cells is not the only suitable means. Scientific advances in this field are very rapid.

Deriving stem cells from the killing of embryos can therefore not be justified. Initially this might seem like a rather abstract deduction, but it can be made quite understandable also in real-life terms. For example, how can one explain to a cystic fibrosis patient that destroying an embryo to obtain stem cells is not possible in the interest of research for a cure? The argument would be as

appropriate conditions' (section 8). For an English translation of the Act see: https://www.bundesgesundheitsministerium.de/fileadmin/Dateien/3_Downloads/Gesetze_und_Verordnungen/GuV/E/ESchG_EN_Fassung_Stand_10Dez2014_01.pdf

[20] For the beginning of the constitutional protection of life with fertilization and not later, see above all Christian Starck (note 17), Article 1, note 176; Dietrich Murswiek, in Sachs (ed.), *Grundgesetz-Kommentar*, Article 2, note 145; Günter Dürig, in Maunz and Dürig, *Grundgesetz*, Article 2 Section 2, note 21; Helmut Schulze-Fielitz, in Dreier (ed.), *Grundgesetz-Kommentar*, Article 2 Section 2, note 24; Philip Kunig, in von Münch and Kunig (eds.), *Grundgesetz-Kommentar*, vol. I, 4th ed., Article 2, note 49; Klaus Stern, *Das Staatsrecht der Bundesrepublik Deutschland*, vol. III.1 (1988), p. 1061f.; J. Spiekerkötter, *Verfassungsfragen der Humangenetik* (1989), pp. 46ff. For a detailed engagement with contrary opinions see Barbara Böckenförde-Wunderlich, *Präimplantationsdiagnostik als Rechtsproblem* (2002), pp. 169–179.

follows: Of course everything should and must be done to find ways to cure your serious illness. But you yourself were once a tiny embryo, both before and after implantation. And it cannot possibly be that you could have been eliminated, indeed, that there is a right to eliminate you, in order to possibly discover in this way some kind of remedy. Surely, the patient will understand this.

2. *Importation of stem cells*

The conclusion thus arrived at also provides a basis for evaluating the much-discussed importation of stem cells. We are talking about the importation of stem cells that were obtained elsewhere—(perhaps) legally according to local law—through the killing of embryos that were created for that purpose or were excess. If, as has been demonstrated, the destructive research on embryos produced for this very purpose violates the respect for human dignity, and the extraction of stem cells from so-called excess embryos can in no way be justified over the prohibition against killing, refraining from the importation of stem cells derived in this manner is simply a question of consistency and credibility. According to our system, these stem cells are the fruit of a forbidden act; their importation circumvents the existing ethically and legally grounded prohibition and cancels it out. Even well-intentioned, strict restrictions cannot alter this. The receiver of stolen goods is no better than the thief. Moreover, the repercussions of this irruption must not be overlooked: if stem cells obtained from destroying embryos somewhere else can be used here, why cannot these stem cells also be produced here—it is more cost-effective, efficacious, and avoids a lack of credibility. Such a corollary is irrefutable, and importation will become, by its own inherent logic, also the first step to domestic production. Jutta Limbach has rightly pointed out that the way out adopted by the Bundestag is not free of contradiction.[21] [III]

[21] (note 6), p. 51.

[III] Jutta Limbach (1934–2016) was a Federal Constitutional Court Judge and the Court's president (1994–2002). As outgoing president (i.e. at a time when there was no chance she would face this case as a judge if it ever came to the court) she had criticized the Bundestag's stance on this question. The Bundestag had discussed intensively the question of whether or not the import for research purposes of cell lines produced from embryonic stem cells abroad should be permitted. The Stem Cell Act of January 2002 consisted of a compromise between a strict prohibition of any import and a more liberal regulation: only those stem cell lines extracted from embryos prior to a given deadline (1 January 2002) could be imported. In 2008, the key date regulation was deferred from January 2002 to May 2007. This postponement was intended to be non-recurring. In the biographical interview (in a section not included in the English editions), Böckenförde commented: 'The first cut-off date was not satisfactory from my position, but it was an attempt to make a fresh start. Embryos that already existed before the deadline of 1 January 2002 could be used, but not those from a later date. Although this decision was a compromise, it also bore the possibility to distance oneself from it in the future. The matter was of course lost when the second cut-off date came. If there is a second one, the third one will come. That was the oath of disclosure.' See 'Biographisches Interview', in Ernst-Wolfgang Böckenförde, *Wissenschaft, Politik, Verfassungsgericht. Aufsätze von Ernst- Wolfgang Böckenförde* (Berlin: Suhrkamp, 2011), p. 466..

3. *Pre-implantation diagnosis*

Hardly any less topical and explosive is the question of the permissibility of pre-implantation genetic diagnosis (PGD). On the basis of the prevailing Embryo Protection Act, it is currently forbidden in line with the dominant and correct view, and the same is true in Switzerland and Austria; in Great Britain and France it is permissible within restricted parameters, and in Italy and Belgium—in the absence of a legal regulation—it is practised.[22] [IV] Some, among them the Deutsche Forschungsgemeinschaft (German Research Foundation) and a discussion draft by the German Medical Association, recommend a limited approval of PGD,[23] while the Final Report of the Bundestag's Commission of Inquiry on Ethics and the Law rejects it by a large majority, though the majority of the National Ethics Council[V] is in favour.[24]

What is PGD? Pre-implantation genetic diagnosis takes place within the framework of artificial fertilization outside the body. It is a diagnostic measure 'whereby one or several cells are taken from an embryo created in vitro following the first cell divisions in order to test them for genetic defects or

[22] See Barbara Böckenförde-Wunderlich (note 20), pp. 35–45.

[IV] At the time Böckenförde wrote this article, the Embryo Protection Law only regulated pre-implantation diagnostics in the case of sex selection and the Duchenne disease. Section 3 of the law reads: 'Whosoever undertakes to fertilize artificially a human egg cell with a sperm cell that is selected for the sex chromosome contained in it, shall be punished with up to one year's imprisonment or a fine. This shall not apply when the selection of a sperm cell is made by a physician in order to preserve the child from developing Duchenne-type muscular dystrophy or a similarly severe sex-linked genetic illness, and the illness threatening the child is recognized as being of appropriate severity by the body responsible according to Land legislation.' In 2011, a new clause was added (Section 3a), stating in its first paragraph: 'Whosoever subjects the cells of an embryo to *in vitro* genetic screening prior to its intrauterine transfer (pre-implantation genetic diagnosis) shall be punished with up to one year's imprisonment or a fine.' The following paragraphs regulate the exception, namely the legality of PGD in the case of the risk of serious genetic diseases and the procedural conditions under which an exception can be determined (through ethics committees and the like). The amendment was adopted after a year-long public debate, with contributions by the German Ethics Council and hearings in the Bundestag.

[23] Of course, in 2002 the Meeting of the German Medical Association came out overwhelmingly against such an authorization, see the press briefing by the German Medical Association, http://www.bundesaerztekammer.de.

[V] In 2001, Chancellor Gerhard Schröder established a national ethics council to advise the executive branch on biomedical and other issues. Böckenförde had been asked to join the council, but declined, partly for personal reasons, partly because he doubted the legitimacy of a council that was appointed by the chancellor instead of the parliament or the president of the Federal Republic (see Biographisches Interview (annotation III), p. 468f). In 2007 the National Ethics Council was transformed into the German Ethics Council, half of whose members are proposed by the Bundestag, and half by the government. All members are ultimately appointed by the president of the Bundestag.

[24] 'Schlußbericht der Enquêtekommission "Recht und Ethik der modernen Medizin"', BT. Drs. 14/9020 (14 May 2002), pp. 107–115. Of the nineteen members present at the time of the vote, 16 voted against any authorization of PGD or in favour of a restricted authorization. In the Nationaler Ethikrat (National Ethics Council), 15 of 24 members came out in favour of a limited authorization of PDG, 7 rejected it outright and 2 with qualification, but without criminal sanctions if the prohibition was ignored. See Nationaler Ethikrat, 'Genetische Diagnostik vor und während der Schwangerschaft', Umdruck, pp. 53, 54, and 75.

predispositions'.[25] It is currently used to select out those embryos in which a serious genetic disease, or the predisposition for such a disease, is found, and not implant them in the woman. The possibility of curing such defects, if found, does not exist on the basis of current medical knowledge and technology. The goal of PGD is thus a selection, not of defective sperm or egg cells, but of defective embryos, that is, of human beings in the earliest stage of their existence. If they show certain defects they are allowed to die off, instead of being transferred to the woman to make possible their further development.

There can be little doubt that PGD used in this way is an instrument of selection and that its use violates the respect for human dignity in the embryo.[26] It is not undertaken to fulfil the wish for a child: in vitro fertilization (IVF) as such is sufficient for that; it is undertaken to fulfil the wish for a genetically healthy child. The embryo created in vitro is not acknowledged and wanted as such, as a subject and 'purpose unto itself', but is dependent on specific characteristics and qualities it does or does not possess. It is only under these preconditions that it is accorded the chance to continue living and to develop as a human being. There can be no clearer expression that it does not share in human dignity, but only has value that is tied to certain characteristics.[27]

However, would a prohibition against PGD not clash with the human dignity and right to self-determination of the parents and especially the woman? Do human dignity and the right to self-determination not in turn prohibit coercing a woman into giving birth to a child without knowing whether or not it might be afflicted with serious illnesses? If we look at this issue more closely, we see that this is not the case. For the prohibition of PGD does not objectify or instrumentalize the parents or the woman, nor does it violate their right to self-determination. Their decision whether and when to fulfil their wish for a child, and how (possibly by way of IVF), is free and self-determined—except that they are required, if they want a child, to want the child as such and not merely a child with certain characteristics.[28] The path is blocked to the selection of embryos, which are, after all, human beings *in nuce*, and should not become a kind of disposable commodity in the hands of the parents or third parties. That is all.

The renunciation of PGD is also reasonable. If people regard it as unreasonable to have sick or genetically impaired children, either because of their own

[25] Barbara Böckenförde-Wunderlich (note 20), p. 11.

[26] Likewise Ute Sacksofsky, 'Der verfassungsrechtliche Status des Embryos in vitro. Gutachten für die Enquêtekommission des Dt. Bundestages "Recht und Ethik der modernen Medizin" ', September 2001, typescript, pp. 68–70; Chr. Starck (note 17), p. 1068f. A contrary position by M. Herdegen (note 15), Note 106; B. Schlink (note 15), p. 20. A rather doubtful view by W. Höfling (note 19), Article 1, note 21.

[27] See Immanuel Kant, *Grundlegung zur Metaphysik der Sitten*, Vorländer edition (1947), p. 52: 'der Mensch und überhaupt jedes vernünftige Wesen existiert als Zweck an sich selbst, nicht bloß als Mittel zum Gebrauch für diesen oder jenen Willen' *Metaphysik der Sitten*, Part 2, Metaphysische Anfangsgründe der Tugendlehre, §38.

[28] See Ute Sacksofsky (note 26).

genetic disposition or in general, they are free to refrain from biological parenthood.[29] That may be very painful in any individual case. But such a renunciation is reasonable if the alternative is to treat humans in the embryonal stage like objects over which one can freely dispose on the basis of changing criteria.

One must not overlook how wide a gate is opened if PGD is allowed, as has happened in a few countries.[30] To be sure, supporters of PGD currently call for its use only in cases of certain grave hereditary illnesses, provided that a large genetic risk exists. However, this already amounts to a severe discrimination against the human beings so handicapped or burdened with a genetic illness; they are the ones who really should not be here, whose life does not seem worth living, and whom a woman who is acting responsibly—also because of the burdens it would create—should not bear. This discrimination is further intensified if the illnesses in question are explicitly listed in a catalogue. And why should such a catalogue not be expanded further? In addition to the examples listed, there is a host of similarly serious cases, and by what right are they excluded? What is more: Are we talking only about illnesses that occur immediately or also about some that might emerge later, from the age of forty, for example? There is a lively debate about this, and in some other countries PGD is already being done with this in mind. Finally: Why only the defence against serious genetic illnesses, and not also a positive eugenics, the use of this tool for the sake of desired physical or mental characteristics, as for example gender, body type, or intelligence? What is objectionable about this once the possibility of diagnosis and disposition has been opened up in principle? Humans are merely making use of the possibilities their own research has created. But what are they turning themselves into in the process?

4. *Therapeutic cloning*

In conclusion a few remarks about so-called therapeutic cloning, for which the road has already been paved in Great Britain. There are various relevant projects in this field that must be distinguished. For one, research on embryonal stem cells is called for as basic research with a view towards therapeutic cloning. This work is supposed to discover how the development of pluripotent stem cells can be guided so they can be turned into nerve cells, liver cells, heart cells, or some other more closely defined cells (possibly as effective cures). For another, on the basis of this the issue revolves around two paths for a possible therapeutic use: either embryonal stem cells guided in a certain way are developed, or the nucleus of an adult cell from a patient is implanted into a enucleated egg cell (which serves as the shell) and released to develop further in the manner of an embryo. If one or the other development has reached a certain stage, the created cell formations are used with the goal that—depending on their characteristics—they are able to trigger curative responses in a person

[29] Ibid., p. 70.

[30] Regine Kollek, *Präimplantationsdiagnostik* (2000), pp. 75ff.

afflicted with certain diseases. The use of adult cell nuclei, which are taken from the person who is to be cured, represent therapeutic cloning in the narrower sense. Compared to the use of foreign stem cells, which can serve as a kind of spare parts depot, this approach has the advantage that there is no danger of rejection, something that is a concern with the other path (similar to organ transplantation).

When it comes to an assessment, one must distinguish between the therapeutic use of embryonal stem cells and adult cell nuclei. The use of embryonal stem cells does not differ from the destructive embryonic research with respect to the principle of human dignity and the prohibition against killing. Embryos created specifically for this purpose or obtained from elsewhere are used and in the process killed as means for external ends—in one case for research, in another for medical treatment. As shown above, the respect for human dignity and the prohibition against killing stand against this.

When it comes to the use of adult cell nuclei, therapeutic cloning in the narrower sense, the use and destruction of these cells does not constitute an act of killing. The adult cells, which are taken from a living and usually adult human being, are not embryos, not individual human beings, but merely cells. As such they can be used up for curative purposes. The peculiar characteristic and challenge is the manner of use. This is done in such a way that the cell nucleus is implanted in a previously enucleated egg cell, which artificially creates a new being without the fusion of sperm and egg cell. If this being were allowed to develop fully, without interruption, it would be genetically identical with the human being from which the cell was taken. This is hardly compatible with the respect for human dignity.[31]

[31] A different position again by M. Herdegen (note 15), note 107 (at the end); and B. Schlink (note 15), p. 20, with a view towards excess embryos and their potential to cure; in line with my views here is Chr. Starck (note 17), note 90 on Article 1 Section 1.

XV

Will Human Dignity Remain Inviolable? [2004]

In recent years the content of the guarantee of human dignity in the Basic Law has become the topic of a lively discussion.[1] That discussion was triggered not least by the tremendous advances in biomedicine and biotechnology, especially over the past decade. Symptomatic for the process that is taking place in the legal discourse is Matthias Herdegen's new commentary on Article 1 Section 1 of the Basic Law in the extensive and for a long time leading Commentary by Maunz and Dürig.[1] It is not an amendment to and updating of Dürig's commentary to reflect new problems and challenges, but an entirely new commentary—a farewell to Günter Dürig.

This process is also symptomatic because the first commentary by Dürig, published in 1958, remained untouched in the Commentary for nearly forty-five years, even though nearly all other articles of the Basic Law saw second and even third commentaries during this time. There was a good reason for this persistence. Dürig's commentary on Articles 1 and 2 was in a sense the ideational and normative scaffolding upon which the Commentary as a whole was erected, it gave it its profile and was part of its identity. There was a desire to retain it as long as possible, even if a supplement or reworking was long since due, given the developments in jurisprudence and the legal literature and newly emerging problems.

I. WHAT WAS DÜRIG'S COMMENTARY?

Dürig's commentary arose out of the founding situation of the Federal Republic as a contribution to the development of a new order, an order the Basic Law was seeking to erect following the experiences with the abuse of power and the

[1] Editors' Note: This article is an edited version of a lecture given at an event jointly convened by the Heinrich Böll Foundation and the Institut Mensch, Ethik, Wissenschaft in Berlin on 11 June 2004. The lecture is based on a widely discussed essay published in the *Frankfurter Allgemeine Zeitung* (9 March 2003, p. 33), titled 'Die Würde des Menschen war unantastbar. Abschied von den Verfassungsvätern: Die Neukommentierung von Artikel 1 des Grundgesetzes markiert einen Epochenbruch' (Human dignity was inviolable. Farewell to the drafters of the constitution: The new commentary on Article 1 Basic Law marks a paradigm shift).

[1] Matthias Herdegen, in Maunz and Dürig, *Grundgesetz. Kommentar*, Article 1 Section 1, as of 2003.

Religion, Law, and Democracy. Ernst-Wolfgang Böckenförde, Oxford University Press (2020). © E.W. Böckenförde, M. Künkler, and T. Stein 2020. DOI: 10.1093/oso/9780198818632.003.0020.

staggering contempt for human dignity in the Third Reich. Dürig, backed by the deliberations in the [constitution-drafting] Parliamentary Council, saw human dignity as the integration of a fundamental 'ethical value'[2] that had emerged in European history into positive constitutional law, which was thereby consciously and deliberately incorporating a pre-positive foundation. Moreover, he maintained that this guarantee was valid for the entire legal system, and not limited to the relationship of the citizen to the state, the traditional area in which fundamental rights applied. In keeping with this was the qualification of Article 1 Section 1 as an objective-legal norm, namely a fundamental norm, 'the supreme constitutive principle of all law'. That norm was then gradually developed in the system of values and entitlements of the fundamental rights section of the Basic Law, though without—in Dürig's eyes—being a subjective fundamental right itself.[3] For a subjective fundamental right to endure, it must be subject to necessary limitations and balancing within the context of the legal system, whereas the duty to respect and protect human dignity is meant to be—by the intent and wording of the text—universal and 'inviolable', immune to modifications even by constitutional amendments (Article 79 Section 3 Basic Law).

The practical positive-legal meaning of the guarantee of human dignity thus lies in the fact that it establishes a binding measure for all state action, defining the purpose and task of the state while also limiting it. It imposes the obligation not only to respect and protect human dignity within the relationship between the state and the citizen, but also to shape the overall legal system in such a way that human dignity cannot be legally violated by non-state forces, that is, by society and the relationship among individuals.

Dürig's articulation of the substance of human dignity clearly expressed the pre-positive foundation that Article 1 Section 1 transported into positive law (the *communis opinio* at the time): 'Every human being is a human being by virtue of his mind [*Geist*], which sets him apart from impersonal nature, and empowers him by its own decision to become self-aware, to be self-determining, and to shape himself and his environment.'[4] This freedom to shape oneself and one's environment is conceived as equal for all humans, it is inherent in a human being; what matters is not the specific realization within the concrete human being, but the 'equal abstract possibility', that is, the potential capacity for its realization.

Human dignity and the rights that spring from it belong also to unborn life, the *nasciturus*: 'At the moment of conception there is created a new nucleus of being and personality, which henceforth is no longer altered. Within it everything that is essential and particular to this human being is determined. It drives towards the development of what lies within it as a seed, and brings about that the person, whether growing or passing away, always remains himself.'[5]

[2] Günter Dürig, in Maunz and Dürig, *Grundgesetz. Kommentar*, Article 1 Section 1, margin note 1.

[3] Ibid., margin notes 4–10. [4] Ibid., margin note 18. [5] Ibid., margin note 24.

The *nasciturus* is thus the possessor of the fundamental right to life in the sense of Article 2 Section 2 of the Basic Law by virtue of his human dignity.

Dürig sought to specify the further content of the guarantee of human dignity as a fundamental objective-legal norm by looking at acts that violate it. His analysis was guided by the concept of the 'object formula' [*Objektformel*], which has been widely influential, reaching all the way into the adjudication by the constitutional court.[II] This *Objektformel* was intended to be the guiding principle, not a subsumption formula [*Subsumptionsformel*].

II. HERDEGEN'S FUNDAMENTALLY DIFFERENT APPROACH

Although the new commentary by Herdegen agrees with the conclusions of Dürig's commentary on a number of specific issues, what matters here is that it follows a fundamentally different approach. The guarantee of human dignity becomes flexible and adaptable, losing a good deal of its character as a pillar of strength. The renunciation of the guarantee of human dignity as the conscious adoption of a pre-positive, ethical [*geistig-ethisch*] content into positive law, to which it remains bound, is critical. The renunciation is clear:

> The notion prevailing in the Parliamentary Council that the Basic Law, through the human dignity clause, 'declaratorily' adopts into positive law an entitlement that supersedes the state and the constitution still has considerable suggestive power... However, when it comes to the assessment in terms of state law, the only things that matter are the (inviolable) anchoring within the text of the constitution and the exegesis of human dignity as a concept of positive law.[6]

Human dignity as a legal concept is thus left entirely to its own devices, detached (and cut off) from the linkage to the prior ethical content, which was present in the minds of the Parliamentary Council and so important for Dürig. Whatever can be said in this regard drifts into the 'background of intellectual history', which is learnedly discussed, but has no normative relevance. The fundamental norm of the Basic Law loses its supporting axis.

What becomes the guideline of interpretation is the adoption and communication of interpretive diversity, a focus on what emerges as the consensus in the process, and the restrained-sceptical search for evidentiary decisions. The decision to see the guarantee of human dignity as having the character of a

[II] In German constitutional jurisprudence, the object formula goes back to Günter Dürig's 1958 Basic Law commentary and, drawing on Kant, holds that human dignity protects each individual from being treated as a means to an end. The infringement on Article 1 Basic Law is thus to be determined from the act of violation: In accordance with Kant's prohibition of human instrumentalization or exploitation, a person's human dignity is disregarded if he or she is treated as an object rather than an end in itself. Böckenförde underlines with Dürig that the object formula should be understood as a guiding principle but not as a legal concept with which an individual case can be considered. Herdegen's approach, however, would result in a weighing of human dignity with fundamental rights, and thus ultimately in the relativization of human dignity.

[6] Herdegen, in Maunz and Dürig, *Grundgesetz. Kommentar*, Article 1 Section 1, margin note 17.

fundamental right, and the claim to dignity as being a subjective legal claim (unlike in Dürig more a problem of details rather than a fundamental structural alternative to seeing it as a fundamental objective legal norm), opens the door to the kind of weighing and balancing that is inevitable when fundamental rights claims collide, and to a flexible handling of the guarantee. The following statement can be seen as the key sentence in the commentary: 'In spite of the categorical claims to dignity by all people, the nature and scope of the protection of dignity are certainly open to differentiations that do justice to concrete circumstances.'[7]

What can one say about this sentence? Is it not inherently self-evident? Yes and no. On the one hand, it entails meaningful distinctions if one talks about the nature of the protection of dignity; on the other hand, it likewise entails the separation of the claim to dignity and the protection of dignity when it focuses on the scope of the latter.

This becomes abundantly evident in the contrast between protection for the dignity of born humans and that of prenatal life. While for every born person the full ownership of human dignity by virtue of membership in the human species is beyond question, independent of social characteristics or the capacity for a meaningful life, a sliding scale of disposability comes into play in dealing with the prenatal protection of dignity. The commentary bids deliberate farewell to the traditional discourse and takes refuge in a 'processual view of the protection of dignity, with the force of an existing claim to respect or protection dependent on evolving notions'.[8] The goal, on the one hand, is to avoid artificial lines of separation when it comes to the 'whether' of the protection of dignity, that is, to extend human dignity back to the earliest stage of human life; and, on the other hand, to achieve broad flexibility when it comes to the 'how' of the protection of dignity with respect to its force.

This can hardly add up. A protection of dignity seen in this light leads by its relativization invariably also to the relativization of the absoluteness and inviolability of human dignity itself, even though the appearance is created that the latter continues to exist. The justification occurs through reference to the already-mentioned key sentence: 'If the claim to dignity, in its scope, may be tailored at all to the concrete circumstances, this must hold in a special way for the developmental stages of human life.'[9] In the final analysis, this is about the doctrinal establishment of leeway for granting and dismantling the protection of dignity based on the interpreter's notions of what is appropriate.[10] This is actualized not least with a view to the current problems of biomedicine and human genetics, as can be demonstrated by a number of statements about the more detailed manifestations of the guarantee of human dignity, which do not reveal any solid ground.

[7] Ibid., margin note 50.

[8] Ibid., margin note 56.

[9] Ibid., margin note 65.

[10] See ibid., margin note 67.

III. PRECURSORS TO THE NEW COMMENTARY

Matthias Herdegen's new commentary on Article 1(1) of the Basic Law, and the rupture with tradition it documents, did not come out of the blue. It had its precursors and it does not stand alone at this time. I shall pick out a few aspects.

Already in 1985, prompted by the emerging problems of human genetics, Peter Lerche advocated a fairly restrictive rather than expansive understanding of human dignity.[11] He did so not least to preserve the unconditionality of the guarantee of human dignity and—to use modern terminology—its resistance to weighing and balancing. To that extent there can be no objection, as every expansion or further development of such a guarantee—even if there are good reasons in the face of new problems—simultaneously bears the danger of relativization, since both categorical prohibitions *and* certain exceptions to them are postulated.

What is important, however, is the argumentative approach that Lerche chose. Lerche maintained that human dignity, as a value to be unconditionally protected, can 'defend its contours only if it is fixed on that sphere—which tends to be narrow—in which the assent from members of the legal community occurs as something self-evident, a protective sphere that would have to apply 'self-evidently', and unconditionally, also if an Article 1 Section 1 did not explicitly exist'.[12] And Lerche adds: 'In important areas of human genetics, this self-evident nature becomes questionable, however.' If one takes a close look at what he is saying, this means that the definition of the content of human dignity is focused on the principle of consensus, the generally existing consensus, not one that exists once at a specific moment. According to Lerche, it makes very good sense to keep the protective sphere of human dignity to the narrow sphere that is able to rely on self-evident agreement.[13] This approach entails an uncoupling from a foundational, intellectual-ethical content to which the guarantee remains connected.

A comparable uncoupling is found a little later in Hasso Hofmann.[14] He turns away from the 'dowry theory' (*Mitgifttheorie*), which sees human dignity as grounded in the self-existence and rational nature of the human being, which are both regarded as qualities inherent in human beings (in his view this theory also shaped the large majority of the members of the Parliamentary Council in one way or another in the creation of the Basic Law), and from Niklas Luhmann's theory of performance.[15] [III] In their place he puts a social recognition

[11] Peter Lerche, 'Verfassungsrechtliche Aspekte der Gentechnologie', in Rudolf Lukes and Rupert Schols (eds.), *Rechtsfragen der Gentechnologie* (Cologne, Berlin, Bonn, and Munich, 1986), pp. 99ff.

[12] Ibid., p. 100. [13] Ibid., p. 110.

[14] Hasso Hofmann, 'Die versprochene Menschenwürde', *Archiv des öffentlichen Rechts* 118 (1993), pp. 353–377.

[15] Niklas Luhmann, *Grundrechte als Institution* (Berlin, 1965), pp. 68ff., 73f. with notes 54 and 56.

[III] The 'dowry theory' proposes that human beings are endowed with human dignity in the same way a bride is endowed with a dowry. The origin of this gift is either attributed to nature or to God; the latter perspective is conceived as the 'Christian dowry theory' mentioned below. The 'theory of performance', by contrast, suggests that human dignity is founded on certain human abilities.

theory of human dignity. The dignity of the human being, according to this theory, is constituted by social recognition, through the positive assessment of social claims to respect; in the legal sense it is not a concept of substance, quality, or performance, but a concept of relationship and communication, and cannot be conceived separately from a concrete community of recognition.[16] In this way, the constitutional guarantee of human dignity as a fundamental norm of the state reveals itself as a reciprocal promise by those sharing in the constitutive power to ground this state—for the sake of the dignity of the human being—on the mutual recognition as members of the community who are, in principle, equally free and worthy.[17] The idea of universal human dignity provides the motivation for doing this, but it is itself not the content or object of the guarantee.

This conception of the guarantee of dignity reduces the commandment to respect and protect human dignity from the outset to the members of this community of recognition; it does not, as Hofmann himself emphasized,[18] say anything about prenatal or expired human life. The embryo as such, again according to Hofmann, is not a possible subject of a social claim to recognition, though it can be the protected object of a legal obligation that living human beings impose upon themselves in relationship to it willingly and out of self-respect.

How far the guarantee of human dignity extends also preoccupied Horst Dreier in 1996 in greater detail in his extensive commentary on Article 1(1) of the Basic Law.[19] And he did this not least against the background of what were by then the increasingly obvious challenges of human genetics and reproductive medicine. On the one hand, Dreier adheres to the notion that the guarantee of human dignity is unconditional and immune to being weighed up; on the other hand, he argues that unborn human life should be excluded from its reach. The embryo has no human dignity status. 'The embryo lacks all preconditions (self-consciousness, reason, capacity for self-determination) that are constitutive for human dignity.'[20] It is only the 'dowry theory' in its Christian variant that could argumentatively justify the incorporation of unconscious and unborn human life into the guarantee of Article 1 Section 1, but its capacity to sustain such an argument is very limited in a state that is neutral with respect to religion or worldview. Dreier recommends shifting its protection from Article 1 Section 1 to Article 2 Section 2, where, because of the statutory reservation, graduated solutions in accordance with the different developmental stages of

By implication, individuals must each feature certain dignity-defining skills (such as the ability to self-determination) for them to be accorded human dignity.

[16] Hofmann, 'Versprochene Menschenwürde', p. 364. [17] Ibid., p. 369. [18] Ibid., p. 375.

[19] Horst Dreier in Dreier (ed.), *Grundgesetz. Kommentar*, vol. I (1996), Article 1 Section 1.

[20] Ibid., margin note 50. This statement is missing in the new edition (2nd ed., 2004). However, what is retained is that even the existence of a personal bearer (which needs to be identified in the first place), which human dignity requires, does not automatically lead to the applicability of the maxim of human dignity (as in the first edition), and that a shift of the legal evaluation of the protection of unborn life from human dignity to the protection of life is advisable, from Article 1 Section 1 of the Basic Law to Article 2 Section 2, 1 of the Basic Law; see ibid., Article 1 Section 1, margin notes 67 and 70.

human life are possible.[21] Through a different path of justification, this achieves the same—if not a greater—measure of flexibility and scope for weighing and balancing in dealing with embryos as Herdegen's processual view of the protection of dignity.

The thrust of the theses articulated by Brigitte Zypries, the current Federal Minister of Justice [2002–2009], is very much the same. She, too, does not see the embryo—at least until implantation—as the bearer of human dignity, for before implantation and the symbiosis with the mother, it cannot develop out of its own inherent power into a human being and as a human being.[22] To that extent it is devoid of human dignity, especially as an embryo in vitro, which is what matters particularly in view of the problems of human genetics and biomedicine. Of course, even Minister of Justice Zypries accords it a protection of life—again graduated—according to Article 2 Section 2 of the Basic Law.[23] This makes protective measures possible, for example in the relationship to freedom of scientific research, but these measures are not categorical in nature. This achieves mobility and flexibility in weighing and balancing with a view towards emerging or necessary parliamentary bills, not least the change to the Embryo Protection Act.[IV]

However, this approach, like that of Horst Dreier (not to mention others), is open to a fundamental objection in terms of legal doctrine. If Article 1 Section 1 of the Basic Law guarantees the respect for human dignity and thus for every human being, not only for certain humans or only those with specific qualities and capacities, thus linking it solely to being human, how can a being or entity that is not a human being in this sense, and has no share in being human, nevertheless be the bearer of the fundamental right to life according to Article 2 Section 2 of the Basic Law? That right concerns the protection of *human* life, not the protection of living mammals or of life as such, and thus it can belong only to human beings. Conversely: whoever is the bearer of the fundamental right to life invariably also shares in human dignity and its protection, because only a human being can possess that right. This reveals the decisionistic

[21] Ibid., margin note 51.

[22] Brigitte Zypries, 'Vom Zeugen zum Erzeugen? Verfassungsrechtliche und rechtspolitische Fragen der Bioethik. Rede beim Humboldt-Forum der Humboldt-Universität Berlin am 29.10.2003', typescript.

[23] Ibid., p. 4f.

[IV] The German Embryo Protection Law is one of the strictest in the world. Added to the criminal code in 1990 and amended several times since, it forbids the improper use of reproductive technology (prohibition of surrogate maternity and egg donation) and any improper use of human embryos for non-preserving purposes (such as for research purposes with embryonic stem cells); it forbids the selection of sexes and in general the pre-implantation diagnosis of in-vitro-fertilized embryos (except in cases of serious genetic illness of the parents); it forbids insemination after the death of the sperm donor; and it prohibits artificial alteration of human germ line cells, human cloning, and the creation of chimeras and hybrids. The embryo is defined as 'the human egg cell, fertilized and capable of developing, from the time of fusion of the nuclei, and further, each totipotent cell removed from an embryo that is assumed to be able to divide and to develop into an individual under the appropriate conditions' (Section 8). For an English translation of the law see: https://www.bundesgesundheitsministerium.de/fileadmin/Dateien/3_Downloads/Gesetze_und_Verordnungen/GuV/E/ESchG_EN_Fassung_Stand_10Dez2014_01.pdf

character—hardly tenable in terms of legal doctrinal theory—of the shift of the protection of unborn human life from Article 1 Section 1 solely to Article 2 Section 2 of the Basic Law; this is an outcome-determined functional construct to escape the absoluteness character of the guarantee of human dignity.

IV. 'SHAKING THE FOUNDATION' OR A LIVING DEVELOPMENT OF THE LAW?

The changes in the understanding of the content and scope of the guarantee of human dignity that we have noted raise some questions. Are they 'shaking the foundation' upon which our system of basic law rests, or are they an expression of the living development of the law in the face of new problems and challenges, which affects (must affect) also fundamental legal guarantees? Further, is it not necessary to detach the guarantee of human dignity from its pre-positive foundation, its conception as a 'pure concept of state law', as Herdegen has said, to liberate it into positive law from the fetters of an objective, natural-law-based argument about a value system that is no longer able to achieve a consensus? I will address the last question first.

Reference to the pre-positive foundation of the guarantee of human dignity, which I made in my FAZ essay,[24] has been repeatedly interpreted as a recourse to natural law, most emphatically by Hubert Markl.[25] [V] He finds it astonishing that a former justice of the Constitutional Court can still approach the concept of the human being or human dignity in a way that is deeply grounded in natural law and ontology, as though these things were not human cultural creations, but Platonic ideas resistant to any change in human thought and understanding, immune to a change in human decisions about the meaning of concepts.[26] That the dignity of the person should be given pre-positively by natural law strikes Markl as a veritable claim of interpretive sovereignty from the judicial ivory tower, a claim that must be rejected.[27] I can in fact agree with that. Böckenförde, who always advocated that positive law be taken completely seriously but should not be isolated from its historical-political context, has not become, as a jurist, a natural law champion in his old age. I deeply appreciate natural law and natural-law thinking, but it is not inherently a part of and the content of prevailing positive law; rather, it belongs into the sphere of legal ethics, the sphere in

[24] Ernst-Wolfgang Böckenförde, 'Die Würde des Menschen war unantastbar', *Frankfurter Allgemeine Zeitung* (9 March 2003), p. 33. [See editors' note I.]

[25] Hubert Markl, *Wer bestimmt, wann das Leben beginnt? Zur Frage der Deutungshoheit über den Lebensbeginn* (Berlin-Brandenburgische Akademie der Wissenschaften, 2003).

[V] Hubert Markl (1938–2015) was a German biologist and highly influential research manager. He led the German Research Foundation from 1977 to 1983 as Vice President and from 1986 to 1991 as President. In 1993 he became President of the newly founded Berlin-Brandenburg Academy of Sciences and Humanities (Berlin-Brandenburgische Akademie der Wissenschaften) and later President of the Max Planck Society (1996–2002).

[26] Markl (note 25), p. 11.

[27] Ibid., p. 13.

which positive law is criticized and possibly stripped of legitimacy, a sphere that generates impulses for changing and improving this law.

Reference to the pre-positive foundation of the guarantee of human dignity is nothing other than a necessary part of determining the content of Article 1 Section 1 of the Basic Law as positive law. What is at stake is probing into and determining what the Parliamentary Council, as the constitutional legislator, intended and desired by laying down this commandment of respect and protection as a fundamental constitutional norm.

What motivated the Parliamentary Council was the adoption of an intellectual and philosophical concept—the contours of which were derived from its roots in Christian tradition and the ideas of the Enlightenment, especially those of Immanuel Kant—into constitutional law as a legal concept, in order to make it binding as a fundamental normative principle of state action. Something that existed pre-positively was thereby incorporated into positive law. This is clearly revealed by the deliberations in the Parliamentary Council as well as by the temporal framework.[28] If that is so, it is not possible, when it comes to legally interpreting the concept of human dignity, to simply draw abstract conclusions or deviate from what this concept meant to the founding fathers and mothers of the constitution. That is even more true if one considers that the adoption of the guarantee of human dignity was a conscious founding act with a view towards the constitutional order that was to be newly erected. The Parliamentary Council did not intend to make a more or less empty shell—the content of which was to be filled anew time and again and in an interdisciplinary fashion—obligatory as a normative principle and endow it with inviolability (Article 79 Section 3 of the Basic Law); instead, it wanted to lay down a foundation that was then specified in greater detail. Maintaining this foundation and its inviolability against possible developments of the zeitgeist accords with the Council's positive will to establish a norm; it is not an interpretive excess arising from the usurped interpretive sovereignty of jurists. Abandoning this foundation in its binding force and historicizing it through the label 'dowry theory' is tantamount to renouncing the intent of the constitutional legislator.

This brings us to the first question, the living development and thus change that is characteristic of the law. Friedhelm Hufen has formulated his thesis in this regard very cogently. In the present, he argues, it is ever more clearly evident that 'the guarantee of human dignity formulated within a specific situation cannot be fixed within the national and international context at the level of 1949; like all constitutional law, it must develop further because of new challenges'.[29]

[28] Especially relevant are the deliberations in the Committee for Fundamental Issues, see Eberhard Pikart and Wolfram Werner (eds.), *Der Parlamentarische Rat 1948–1949. Akten und Protokolle*, vol. V, 1 and 2 (Boppard am Rhein, 1993). Here: Third Session of 21 September 1948, pp. 38–50; Fourth Session of 23 September 1948, pp. 62–82; Twenty-Second Session of 18 November 1948, pp. 584–602; Twenty-third Session of 19 November 1948, pp. 603–609; Thirty-second Session of 11 January 1949, pp. 910–927. For a summary, see Doemming, Füßlein, and Matz, 'Entstehungsgeschichte der Artikel des Grundgesetzes', *Jahrbuch des öffentlichen Rechts der Gegenwart*, Neue Folge, vol. 1 (1951), pp. 41ff., pp. 48–53 (Article 1), pp. 54–66 (Article 2).

[29] Friedhelm Hufen, 'Erosion der Menschenwürde?' *Juristen Zeitung* (2004), p. 313.

Further: 'It is being increasingly recognized that human dignity as an abstract principle can be directed against the human being himself, if it is used to block research and medicine, or is deployed against the self-determination of the human being.'[30] Brigitte Zypries argues on the basis of comparable methodological premises.

What is to be said about this? To be sure, the law as living law cannot disconnect itself from the progression of time and from new challenges, and its normative content cannot be frozen in place at the time of its creation. To avoid losing its ordering function, the law must normatively overarch the changing social as well as mental reality, it must not isolate itself and become disconnected from this reality. For that reason, the legal system knows more than a few open-ended concepts whose concrete content, starting from a solid core, can develop further and change. In fact, there are even —and this could further strengthen the argument—normative legal concepts that refer to specific social and ethical views and incorporate their respective content into the law and sanction it legally. One can speak here of gateway concepts [*Schleusenbegriffe*].[VI] The best known of these concepts is that of public order in police law. Gateway concepts mean those social norms—not legal norms—whose observance, in the view of the groups involved, is among the indispensable preconditions if human beings wish to coexist in a beneficial way.[31] These social norms, with their changing content, are incorporated into the law.

Might it thus be appropriate to regard human dignity also as such a gateway concept? A concept that incorporates, into its normative content, what society—in its ethical and interdisciplinary discourses—defines as human dignity, and which is in this sense sustained by a general consensus? Moreover, might this be an appropriate move also because the concept of human dignity is originally not a legal concept that grew out of a long legal tradition, but an intellectual-philosophical one? This approach may strike some as a way out of this whole dilemma, and it would also be a convenient way out. But it is a wrong way.

To be sure, the concept of human dignity is certainly an open-ended one, whose concrete implications are not fixed once and for all; rather, it displays a certain range of variation and accordingly can—and must—react to new challenges. But these concrete implications flow out of a solid core, the basic normative content. And this basic content cannot be understood in the sense of a gateway concept, for that goes against its normative meaning. Gateway concepts possess their functionality—which is focused on pragmatism and

[30] Ibid.

[VI] 'Gateway concepts are those which refer to existing ethical and social views and assign legally binding meaning to them in their changing content and sanction them legally, thereby channelling [*einschleusen*] them into positive law.' Ernst-Wolfgang Böckenförde: *Vom Ethos der Juristen*, 2nd ed. (Berlin: Duncker & Humblot, 2011), p. 28, note 47.

[31] Bill Drews, Gerhard Wacke, Klaus Vogel, and Wolfgang Martens, *Gefahrenabwehr. Allgemeines Polizeirecht (Ordnungsrecht) des Bundes und der Länder*, vol. II, 8th ed. (Cologne, Berlin, Bonn, and Munich, 1977), p. 130.

practicability—always and only within the framework of the foundations and principles laid down by the legal system. This functionality cannot be transferred to the foundations and principles themselves without dissolving their normative quality. Human dignity as a gateway concept: this turns the fundamental norm of the order of the Basic Law, which is supposed to be valid steadfastly and inviolably, into a variable of changing ideas of the prevailing zeitgeist. This would transform Article 1 Section 1 of the Basic Law into something that merely enhances changing notions, elevating them in their variability to inviolability and immutability. This cannot be its normative meaning, and this was definitely not intended by the Parliamentary Council.

V. BASIC CONTENT OF THE GUARANTEE OF HUMAN DIGNITY

But what, then, does the guarantee of human dignity contain, if it wishes to retain its integrity and not be given over to changing needs and zeitgeist ideas?

It seems to me that the basic content of this guarantee—with respect to its solid core, and irrespective of a certain openness—is less controversial than may appear at the moment. In a variety of approaches to determine the content of human dignity, this core substance can be circumscribed with the formula 'an end in itself' borrowed from Kant, or with the definition 'existence for its own sake' offered up by the Federal Constitutional Court. Incorporated in these definitions are the status and recognition of the human being as an autonomous subject, the freedom for personal development, the preclusion of being humiliated and instrumentalized like an object over which one can simply dispose—in positive terms, the right to rights that must be respected and protected.

The real point of contention and the crux in the dispute over the relativization and inviolability of human dignity is not so much what I have just said, but the question of whether and to what extent this guarantee belongs also to unborn human life in addition to born humans. This question arises from the development of human genetics, biotechnology, and reproductive medicine. To answer this question based on the normative content of Article 1 Section 1, it is advisable not to seek to ascribe certain qualities to zygotes of four or sixteen cells, but to proceed from the dignity of living, born humans. After all, there is no disagreement that they are the bearers of human dignity. The question is then how far this recognition of human dignity must extend into the life process of every human for it to remain true. Is it sufficient, as some argue, for the recognition of and respect for dignity to commence only at a specific point in the life process of the human being, while the earlier life process remains disposable? Or must this recognition and respect exist from the very origins, the first beginning of this human life? Only the latter can be the case if existence for its own sake or as an end in itself shall remain true and not turn into a pronouncement devoid of substance. The dignity that characterizes a finished human being cannot be separated from his own history, but must encompass it.

For if one seeks to exclude a certain phase in the life process from the recognition and respect that is owed the human being by virtue of his dignity, or to graduate this respect in a process-oriented way, for example, because it is only an embryo of eight or sixteen cells or because implantation (always uncertain) has not yet taken place, one tears a hole in the development of the individual human being himself. If respect for his dignity is to be valid for every person as such, it must be accorded to him from the outset, from the first beginning of *his* life, not only after an interval which he—unprotected against instrumentalization and arbitrariness—must first pass through successfully.

But this first beginning of the distinct life of the emerging and developing human being lies in fertilization, not at some later point. Compared to sperm and egg cell, which are also forms of human life, fertilization creates a new and independent *human life form*. It is characterized as unmistakably individual through the assembly of a particular genome in this specific form and none other. This is—scientifically uncontested—the biological foundation of the individual human being. The subsequent mental and psychological development is already laid out in it; the human being is a unity of body-spirit-soul. Once the individual set of chromosomes is fixed, there is no longer a rupture in the quality of what develops. The genetic program of development is completely present, requires no further completion, and unfolds within the course of the life process by itself, in accordance with its own organization. Of course, none of this can happen without manifold and indispensable help and support from the outside, which in turn has a shaping effect, such as the supply of nutrition, contact and exchange with the maternal organism, and much more. These are indisputably necessary conditions for the possibility of an autonomous development, but they are not this development itself; and they exist not only before birth, but to some extent also after birth for some time. That nature can continue to influence the unfolding life process, and can also end it abruptly (i.e. on the way to implantation), is a fact, but that does not nullify its beginning with fertilization. This makes perfect sense also from the way real life is experienced. It is not unusual for parents to know exactly from which union their son or daughter was created. Parents date the beginning of their child's life from this moment of fertilization, and not the later implantation, say, or the development of the cortex. To have human life begin with fertilization is thus by no means counter-intuitive.

The question of whether the human embryo enjoys the protection of human dignity and thus also the right to life is therefore not the product of an ontological fundamentalism, and dependent on it, nor is it dependent on whether an embryo of eight or sixteen cells can be empirically qualified as a person. Rather, what is crucial is that the recognition of the dignity of the human being as articulated by the Basic Law in terms of its normative content must also encompass—if it is not to be arbitrarily curtailed—the first beginnings of the life of every human being.

PART V

BÖCKENFÖRDE IN CONTEXT

XVI

Biographical Interview with Ernst-Wolfgang Böckenförde [2011]

Dieter Gosewinkel, a historian and legal scholar, conducted a series of extensive interviews with Ernst-Wolfgang Böckenförde in 2009–2010. The interviews cover Böckenförde's personal and intellectual biography, Böckenförde's academic and political writings, his religious convictions, and his tenure as a constitutional judge. This section contains selected excerpts from these interviews, with annotations by the editors to provide the reader with crucial background information. Additional excerpts are included in volume I of this edition.

CATHOLICISM AND THE ETHOS OF MODERN DEMOCRACY

G (Gosewinkel): Let us delve more deeply into a new set of issues, which we have already addressed in part: the question of Catholicism, Catholic thinking, and the ethos of modern democracy—in general, the relationship between the Catholic Church and a secular democratic order. First, I would like to look at a publication that made you a household name and public figure in 1957 overnight, the previously mentioned essay about the ethos of modern democracy and the Church. It appeared in the journal *Hochland*.[1] You published a number of important and well-known essays in this journal, and it has been your companion, as it were, since your youth. Could you say something about it and about Franz Josef Schöningh, its editor.

B (Böckenförde): My encounter with *Hochland* began after the war. The journal had been founded in 1903 by Carl Muth.[I] This was part of Catholics turning to

[1] Ernst-Wolfgang Böckenförde, 'Das Ethos der modernen Demokratie und die Kirche', *Hochland* 50 (1957), pp. 4–19. Included in this volume as Chapter I.

[I] Editors' Note: Carl Muth (1867–1944) was a journalist, editor, and Catholic thinker. An advocate of normative pluralism, he strove to overcome Christian denominational conflicts in the post-*Kulturkampf* period. Muth succeeded in making the magazine *Hochland* the leading publication of Catholic spiritual and intellectual life, being independent of (and critically regarded by) the Church. *Hochland* was published from 1903 to 1941, was then banned by the Nazi regime, but thereafter continued publishing from 1946 to 1971. Its articles were written not only from Catholic points of view, but also interdenominational and secular perspectives, and dealt with topics in various areas of knowledge, literature, and art.

Religion, Law, and Democracy. Ernst-Wolfgang Böckenförde, Oxford University Press (2020). © E.W. Böckenförde, M. Künkler, and T. Stein 2020. DOI: 10.1093/oso/9780198818632.003.0021.

the world intellectually, that is, getting out of a ghetto, in contact with modern culture and participating in it. The journal brought together Catholic intellectuals and offered them a forum. Above all, it did not just want to disseminate what came from the Church's magisterium, but to publish independently on the basis of a fundamental Catholic stance that was open to the world. Franz Josef Schöningh, the editor, inspired and cultivated precisely this openness and embrace of the world.[II] His main job was as the editor of the *Süddeutsche Zeitung*, and that is also where he earned his living. He oversaw *Hochland* on the side. He did so with circumspection, recruiting a whole host of younger authors and keeping on older ones. When I sent him my text [Ethos of Democracy], in June 1957, he said that I shouldn't write so modestly, but go at it a little more boldly. I then expanded and revised the text. After that he apparently liked it so much that he turned it into a special edition, along with his foreword, on the journal's fiftieth anniversary.[III] The edition was widely disseminated, and it invariably drew divided reactions.

G: About the historical background to this article: the Adenauer government was essentially at the height of its power, the fall of 1957 was the only time a single party achieved an absolute majority. For Adenauer's critics, the clericalism in power had in a sense reached its peak. Such charges came from the left-socialist camp and also from the liberal camp. The Federal Republic was in an obvious economic upswing, things were quiet domestically, the engagement with the National Socialist past was only slowly getting under way. Basically a high point of self-satisfaction had almost been reached, and the article arrived into this state of affairs; it expressed dissatisfaction, even

[II] Franz Josef Schöningh (1902–1960) was a German writer and editor. He joined the *Hochland* journal as an editor in 1935. After World War II, he co-founded the *Süddeutsche Zeitung*, one of Germany's leading dailies. In 1946, he re-established *Hochland* which had ceased circulation in 1941. Schöningh was a deputy civil administrator in East-Galicia from 1942 to 1944, from which the deportation of the Jewish population to forced labour and extermination camps took place. Recent historical research makes clear that Schöningh must have been aware in their entirety of the purposes of the so-called 'resettlement schemes' of which he was in charge from the civilian side of the administration, even though research also documents that he saved some Jewish families and individuals. All in all, there is a sense that Schöningh was not forthright after the war about his responsibilities in Sambor and Tarnopol between1942 and 1944. See Knud von Harbou, *Wege und Abwege—Franz Josef Schöningh* (Munich: Allitera, 2013).

[III] In the preface, Schöningh speaks of a '*Beunruhigung*', a sense of disquiet among leading Catholic intellectuals over the failure of the official Church to confront its role in the Nazi past. The strength and influence of Catholics in post-war West German democracy was epitomized by Adenauer and the absolute electoral majority gained by the Christian Democrats in 1957. This situation, Schöningh went on to say, carried the risk that the Catholic Church and Catholic organizations became all too self-contended, not scrutinizing their own failures prior to 1945. 'We behave as if the catastrophe of National Socialism had been an intermezzo only, and the clear proof that we were on the right path until 1933, on which we should now continue.' That would amount to missing all the painful lessons of the Nazi experience. He also warned against tying Catholicism to one particular political outlook or party. 'My father's house has many rooms' (John 14.2), he reminded readers. Although *Hochland* was far from being a left-leaning or even socialist publication, Schöningh reminded readers that Catholics can be socialists too. *Hochland* was to stand for normative pluralism, he insisted.

if it was carefully packaged and precisely reasoned. It revolved around a dissatisfaction with the way certain segments of the Catholic Church and the Catholic hierarchy were dealing with questions of the democratic order. This protest, which in a sense questioned the feeling of contentment, to me seemed to be the first impulse behind this article.

B: Yes, it was indeed an inner dissatisfaction, namely above all with the conduct of the Church hierarchy and of Catholicism in general, its stance towards democracy. I felt that democracy was not yet accepted in its structure. I tried to work through this and to make clear in the process what democracy was based on, that it is not simply majority dictatorship against which one had to draw sharp boundaries. The thesis was that one cannot simply posit natural law against democracy and insist rigidly that democracy can begin only beyond natural law. I argued against this and sought to demonstrate that there is such a thing as the ethos of democracy, and that the Church and Catholics really could and should engage with it. The Church could not, on the one hand, seek to participate in the democratic process through pastoral letters that addressed elections and instructed the faithful, and then, if it did not get its way, fall back on an incommensurable position as guardian. That naturally stirred up a hornets' nest.

G: Of course you were aware of that when you wrote this.

B: Yes, of course, after all I wrote it out of this feeling of unease and anger about the situation. But I tried not only to rake Church officials over the coals to some extent, but also to show how Catholic thinking should be reoriented *in politicis*, to lead to an acceptance of democracy on the basis of its structure.

G: In your own experiences within the life of the Church, did you often encounter voices in which this distance to democracy was clearly expressed? And in response, did you also feel misgivings or worries?

B: Yes, certainly, especially about the fairly widespread attitude that while there could be majority decisions in democracy, whatever belonged to the realm of natural law was valid a priori and cannot be subject to a majority decision. When it comes to that realm, even democratic principles, that is, especially the majority principle, could not be valid. In the process the scope of natural law was determined by the Church itself, based on its interpretation of the order of creation. The Church's magisterium revealed what followed in the realm of natural law from human nature itself, what has been placed into it by God.

G: This move by the Church to grant itself the power of definition did place secular law under reservation. With whom did you discuss this issue?

B: I don't remember exactly. The article came about when I was in Munich the second time, 1956/57, after finishing my legal studies and my legal dissertation. The impetus for its writing came from a lecture by Adolf Arndt at the Technische Hochschule in Munich, at the invitation of Hans-Jochen Vogel as the chairman of the Working Group of Social Democratic Academics.[IV] I felt validated by what he said and decided to write the article. After 1945, the situation for the Catholic Church was similar to the situation in Poland after 1989. Following the end of communism, that country also wanted to return to the previous state of affairs, without engaging with the realities of democracy. That created problems, and the originally strong influence of the Church was largely squandered. This was the very question in 1949 as in 1989, how democracy could be acknowledged without brushing aside the problems in the process. How does one create a democracy which, as a system of majority decision, which is what it is, also presupposes agreement about what is not subject to a vote, as Adolf Arndt put it?

G: Arndt's lecture was thus one of the triggers for you, the confirmation of a line of thinking that already existed?

B: Yes.

G: If one thinks about the political implications of this text, the KPD decision had been issued shortly before.[V] You say that the necessary formulation of a core area of democracy was carried out in this decision. You also relate positively to it: as you put it, it embodies the ethos of democracy. In the essay you also refer to the battles over schools in Germany.[VI]

[IV] Adolf Arndt (1904–1974) was one of the leading SPD politicians in the 1950s and 1960s as far as legal policy was concerned. He played a major role in the process of transforming the SPD from an ideological party deeply rooted in a socialist worldview to a reform-oriented Volkspartei (catch-all-party). This transformation opened up the opportunity for Böckenförde to later join the SPD, which was a rather unusual step at that time given his Catholic family background. Hans-Jochen Vogel (b. 1926) was one of Germany's leading social-democrat politicians from the 1960s to the 1980s. From 1960 to 1972 he served as mayor of Munich, and thereafter entered the federal government as a cabinet minister. In 1983, he ran against Helmuth Kohl for the chancellorship. From 1983 to 1991 he led the social democratic caucus in the *Bundestag*, and from 1987 to 1991 acted as Willy Brandt's successor as party chairman.

[V] In 1956, the Federal Constitutional Court ruled that the former Communist Party (KPD) was unconstitutional. According to Article 21 Section 2 of the Basic Law 'parties that, by reason of their aims or the behaviour of their adherents, seek to undermine or abolish the free democratic basic order or to endanger the existence of the Federal Republic of Germany shall be unconstitutional'. In 1952, the Socialist Reich Party (SRP), an openly neo-national-socialist party, had already been judged unconstitutional. See for a summary, interpretation, and translation of the main passages of both cases Donald P. Kommers and Russell A. Miller, *The Constitutional Jurisprudence of the Federal Republic of Germany*, 3rd ed. (Durham, NC: Duke University Press 2012), pp. 286–292.

[VI] From the beginning of the Federal Republic, the Christian churches lobbied for an 'Elternrecht', widely understood in this context as parents' natural (or God-given) right to decide on the education of their children. This would allow them to choose between denominational (or 'confessional') schools, inter-confessional ones (known as 'community' or 'joint' schools), non-confessional schools, or schools that propound a different, non-church worldview. In the end, the Parliamentary Council did not decide in favour of such a parental right. However, religious instruction was instituted as a regular (nondevotional) school subject in public schools (usually two hours a week).

B: Yes, they were also a trigger. These battles were always waged via natural law, in this case the right of parents to determine the confessional character of the school, and they protested against a law that did not reflect that.

G: You argue in favour of the affirmation of a pluralistic society.

B: Yes.

G: And unequivocally against all notions of a Christian state. You are quite clear in the criticism of such positions by the Catholic Church, which you label nonpolitical.

B: I polemicized against the Christian state in the essay on secularization ten years later.[2] In 1957 the issue was to achieve recognition for the ethos of freedom and equality, which is part of democracy, and to oppose removing the realms of natural law from the democratic principle, and from political decision-making and the decision-making authority sustained by it.

G: You also oppose autocratic thinking. You argue against the absoluteness of objectivity claims, and you call for a more pronounced historical thinking, or for historicity in general. To me this is an emphatic plea for a historicization of Catholic thinking itself, one in which natural law is *not* understood as absolute and supratemporal.

B: Yes.

G: When you look back on the impact of the text, where did you yourself venture forward most boldly with your theses?

B: For one with the criticism of reducing democracy to a mere majority decision, then by emphasizing the positive basic content of democracy and criticizing the natural-law order thinking, which had to be abandoned. Equally important to me was the issue of personal freedom, of tolerance, and that tolerance presupposes mutuality.

G: You use the word 'challenge'. You write about the pleasure of dispute. You trigger a dispute. You go against autocratic thinking. These are very stark words, for some at the time probably too stark. You earned dissent on the substance of your argument; Hermann Josef Spital's response was reprinted also in the anthology of your essays. But beyond that you surely received a great many responses, many of which were no doubt critical.

B: Yes, they were mostly critical, though some were also very approving. The responses by those in the establishment tended to be distanced and negative. I was then pushed to the Left or wherever else.

[2] Ernst-Wolfgang Böckenförde, 'Die Entstehung des Staates als Vorgang der Säkularisation', in *Säkularisation und Utopie. Ebracher Studien. Ernst Forsthoff zum 65. Geburtstag* (Stuttgart, 1967), pp. 75–94. [Included in this volume as Chapter V.]

THE CATHOLIC CHURCH AND 1933

G: Let us turn now to the *Hochland* articles about the role of German Catholicism in the year 1933. You published these two articles in 1961 and 1962.[3] Perhaps you could describe their historical background.

B: The occasion was twofold. For one, there was the polemic of Thomas Dehler, a committed liberal and former Federal Minister of Justice, who said that the *Reichskonkordat* had been a dirty business, in response to which Bishop Keller of Münster immediately went on the warpath and spoke of a 'defamation of the pope' and the like. For another, Morsey's great work *Das Ende der Zentrumspartei* [The End of the Centre Party] was a starting point for me.[4] I thought: 'What happened back then, you really ought to look into it sometime.' Morsey's very well-documented account was a kind of revelation for me. That is how I found my way to the pastoral letters and the pronouncements by Catholic organizations. I sat in the archive of Freiherr von Twickel. It had the Swiss Catholic journal *Ecclesiastica*, which always contained extensive documentation. There I came across some things. At first, I couldn't believe what I was seeing. It became surprisingly clear to me that these were exactly the positions that I had fundamentally criticized in my essay ['Ethos of Modern Democracy', of 1957]. That is also why I structured the essay ['The Catholic Church', of 1961] as a case study, in order to spell out and reinforce that the traditional theory of the Church was untenable. It was not supposed to be only a historical account, but a case study in order to demonstrate something theoretically and systematically by way of historical events. This is what gave rise to the grumbling. Not about the depiction of the events, but the second part of the essay, the theoretical conclusions, which was supposedly the worst part.

G: You see a connection between the article of 1957 and that of 1961?

B: Yes, for me the kind of material that was revealed was a confirmation of the path I had laid down in 1957. I now had illustrative material. During my research I came across a lot of things that astonished me, not least the almost eulogistic letters that cardinals Bertram and Faulhaber wrote about the signing of the Reich Concordat [see pp. 85–86 of Chapter II, this volume]. That is why I sat down and wrote and told Franz-Joseph Schöningh that I needed to have the freedom to quote *Hochland* authors too. Schöningh read the manuscript and wanted certain revisions. He was already ill, but shortly before his death he personally approved the article for publication. It appeared in February 1961, after Schöningh had already died. Of course, the essential point was that it was

[3] Ernst-Wolfgang Böckenförde, 'Der deutsche Katholizismus im Jahre 1933. Eine kritische Betrachtung', *Hochland* 53(3) (1961), pp. 215–239 [Included in this volume as Chapter II]; 'Der deutsche Katholizismus im Jahre 1933. Stellungnahme zu einer Diskussion', *Hochland* 54(3) (1962), pp. 217–245.

[4] Rudolf Morsey, 'Die Zentrumspartei', in Erich Matthias and Rudolf Morsey (eds.), *Das Ende der Parteien 1933* (Düsseldorf, 1960), pp. 281–453.

published in *Hochland*. In other journals, in the election year 1961, this would have immediately seemed like electoral support for the SPD. The article caused a medium-sized earthquake within German Catholicism.

G: If one looks only at the formulations, one can understand that reaction. Among other things, you describe German Catholicism as an influential enabler of the fascist revolt against society.

B: Yes, that had to do, among other things, with its rootedness in the so-called organic theory of the state. Of course, the Catholic leadership did not do this knowingly. It did not know that it was an enabler, but objectively looked at within the context of the time, that is what it was, even if it believed that it was defending the noble values of natural law.

G: You also write that the sense of historical and political legitimacy and continuity was being lost, and with it also 'the capacity to engage in political action related to history'.[5]

B: The text does not say historical and political, but historico-political action, that is, the adjective is important here. The capacity for political action related to history is what matters, not the capacity for political action as such.

G: From my perspective this is an article that takes the capacity for scholarly criticism right up to the pain threshold of the discourse within Catholicism, and it is also borne by a basic grass-roots democratic impetus that is related to the Church itself. Is it also a critique of your own Church leadership?

B: Yes, certainly, though not in terms of grass-roots democracy, but alluding to the Church's political inexperience and lack of competency. But that has nothing to do with 'church from below' or the like.[VII] That is not a track I took, neither then nor later.

G: Is that also something from which you would distance yourself?

B: Yes, even though I recognize that the consent of the faithful has great importance in the life of the Church; but the Church is not constituted on that basis.

[5] Ernst-Wolfgang Böckenförde, 'Der deutsche Katholizismus im Jahre 1933. Eine kritische Betrachtung', in *Hochland* 53(3) (1961), pp. 215–239 [Included in this volume as Chapter II].

[VII] The 'initiative church from below' was originally a Catholic network of lay groups, founded in the aftermath of the 1978 Catholic Church Day (*Katholikentag*), where disagreements regarding reform perspectives and political issues came to the fore. The initative was formed as distinct from the Central Committee of German Catholics, the official representation of lay Catholicism in Germany, which members of the initiative regarded as too close to the Church itself. In the past, the activities of the 'initiative church from below' included a critical dialogue with official ecclesiastical institutions as well as political activism relating to fair trade relations between the global North and the global South, and to the wider German peace movement. Nowadays, the importance of this network (which has become more and more ecumenical) has decreased, since the Central Committee of German Catholics has become much more diverse in its composition, more pluralistic with regard to its political outlook, and fully committed to a thorough institutional reform of the Catholic Church. On the committee, see also annotation XVIII.

G: But it is simultaneously also a principled statement for unequivocally more participation by laymen in the Church, is it not?

B: Yes, of course. Church officials as such should not assume any political responsibility and should not involve themselves actively in politics. But nothing precludes them from encouraging laypeople from taking on these tasks, and from offering guidance to that end. But the concrete expression is something they must leave to them. As Pope John Paul II put it: the Church is present in the world through the laity.

G: But it was in part an effort to save the reputation of liberalism and to protect it against the charge that it was the frightening counter-image of modernity.

B: To some extent it was definitely an attempt to save the reputation of political liberalism and a plea against the complete distancing from the modern world, following the motto: it's been all downhill since Thomas Aquinas . . .

G: And within the debates in the Church, is it also staking out a position for liberalism?

B: Yes, for a politically liberal, not an ideologically liberal way of thinking and against the dominance of the evaluation of all political activity from the standpoint of a self-contained, abstract natural law.

G: In the early Federal Republic there already existed, in the creation of the constitution and subsequently, a strong natural law tradition, whose revitalization reached to the very top of the judicial system.

B: The *Bundesgerichtshof* [Federal Court of Justice] under its president Weinkauff stood for this direction. One manifestation was the decision on procuration.[6] [VIII]

G: Is your article also directed against this?

B: Not really. The general relationship between ethics and law, that law is a system for maintaining the coexistence among human beings, not a system for perfecting it, was not yet the theme here. This was more about the narrowed focus on the political and the failure to recognize what the *bonum commune* really is. That is what I wanted to instruct the Church officials and my fellow believers about. When they spoke about the *bonum commune* they always meant the sphere of natural law rights, but when it comes to the totality of

[6] Bundesgerichtshof, *Entscheidungen in Strafsachen* (St. 6, 46ff.).

[VIII] In 1954, the criminal division of the Federal Court of Justice (the highest appellate court for civil and criminal law) ruled that sexual intercourse between fiancés is fornication and that its toleration by relatives is to be regarded as procuration, thus amounting to criminal behaviour. The Court stressed that this applies regardless of any changed attitudes among the public, since the norms of the meta-positive moral law may claim meta-temporal validity. See BGH, decision 17 February 1954, Az.: GSSt 3/53 (https://www.jurion.de/urteile/bgh/1954-02-17/gsst-3_53/).

the common good these are only *bona particularia*, however important they might be. These were put in place of the whole.

G: How were these articles received? It is my understanding that of all those we have talked about ['German Catholicism in 1933' and its rejoinder, see note 3] were the ones that attracted the most attention and also drew the strongest opposition.

B: Yes and no, there was also agreement from many people. It came from older people who were involved at the time and understood the circumstances. The official reaction got quite heated. The publishers reprinted 3,000 copies right away, because the edition had sold out after three weeks. Then came the criticism from Hans Buchheim and others, in part very polemical. It certainly was a medium-sized earthquake, because the facts had been largely repressed. People said this could not be, we—the Church—had always been opposed, this had to be fake. Things had truly been repressed. When this defence failed, the Catholic Committee for Contemporary History was established.[IX] My essay and the subsequent discussion were the impetus behind it, that is something Konrad Repgen, the co-initiator of this Committee, also conceded. On the whole the Committee did solid historical work in the many blue volumes. As I see it, 80% of what I had written, on the basis of source material that encompassed at best 10 to 15%, was confirmed in the process. It is remarkable that the theses had been correctly laid out on this narrow basis.

G: With your article you thus set in motion a research activity within the Catholic Church that overwhelmingly confirmed your theses?

B: That is my impression, others may contest that, but I still claim credit for this today. I was able to persuade Catholicism that one's own freedom can be defended only as part of the general freedom.

THE 'BÖCKENFÖRDE DICTUM'

G: The period of the 1970s and early 80s, which is what we are talking about, also saw the beginning of the triumphal march of a dictum for which you have become famous.[X] It rounds off this section of our conversation, undergirds it, in a sense. It is sometimes called the 'Böckenförde Paradox'. You developed it in the 1964 Ebrach lecture (published in 1967) about the rise of the state as a process of secularization. The dictum states: 'The liberal,

[IX] The Committee for Contemporary History was founded in 1962 as a non-university research institute. Its purpose is to support, conduct, and publish research on the history of German Catholicism. The Committee also maintains one of the largest archives on German Catholicism with files of Catholic organizations and literary estates of individuals.

[X] Note that in this section, two different parts of the biographical interview (pp. 482ff. and 469ff.) have been merged.

secularized state is sustained by conditions it cannot itself guarantee. That is the great gamble it has made for the sake of liberty.'[7] This statement is found in the first volume of essays that Suhrkamp published, and it has made its way into the theoretical political thinking of nearly all relevant disciplines.

This sentence is quoted time and again, sometimes it is wrongly quoted, in some cases it is perhaps also misunderstood. But it stands for you, as it were, for you as a person and for you as a thinker. You picked up this sentence in your Reuchlin Prize lecture about ten years later.[XI] You confirmed it or found it confirmed also on the basis of more recent reflections. Could you say something again on how these reflections came about? Were they born from a very specific situation, 1964, when you delivered this lecture in Ebrach? Is there something that preceded it, perhaps also in the circumstances at the time, that prompted you to come up with this pithy formulation? Or was it more like the sum of fundamental reflections?

B: Both factors were probably at work. The Vatican Council was debating religious freedom at that very time, and the issue was not yet decided. But it was a sign that the Christian state as such was a thing of the past. This led to fundamental reflections, the result of which was quite simple: the state and secularization belong together. In its origin and telos, the state is a secularized and then secularizing state, which was realized in history step by step, also in a back and forth. This gives rise to the structural problem and this question: What next if religion no longer forms the binding foundation of the state and the liberal state is legitimized through secular basic rights that are independent of religion?

Beyond that, for me the question arose of how Catholics should deal with this new, altered situation. There were passionately waged struggles for confessional schools in Oldenburg/Lower Saxony, as well as in North Rhine-Westphalia. The last section should be read as an appeal chiefly to Catholics to see the secularized state no longer as a potential enemy and at a great remove. Rather, they should accept it and become part of it, as an opportunity for them, as well, and because it depends also on the energy they can contribute to it.

G: To that extent there is a close substantive connection to the 1957 essay 'Ethos of Modern Democracy and the Church'.

B: Yes, you can say that. The thrust of the essay was that one should no longer entertain reservations and mourn the Christian state, which will not exist again. That thrust was then given legitimacy by the Second Vatican Council, in that religious freedom was recognized as grounded in the dignity of

[7] Ernst-Wolfgang Böckenförde, 'Die Entstehung des Staates als Vorgang der Säkularisation', in his *Staat, Gesellschaft, Freiheit. Studien zur Staatstheorie und zum Verfassungsrecht* (Frankfurt/M., 1976), pp. 42–64, quote p. 60. Included in this volume as Chapter V, p. 167.

[XI] 'The State as an Ethical State' (1978), included in volume I of this edition.

human nature. If one takes this seriously, there is really no option but to accept the open and neutral state in which various currents of faith have the possibility of realizing themselves—of course, on the basis of the recognition of a universal order. An order, however, which no longer necessarily is or can be a substantively Christian one, but rather one that makes it possible for Christians as well as other religious communities to live their faith privately and publicly.

G: This aspect of the essay is directed also—and perhaps especially—at devout Catholic citizens, though naturally it is formulated much more broadly. Although you still speak of the secularized state, and in that regard about a state that withdraws from religion or at least sets itself apart from religion, the word 'condition' is broader in this context, it means not only religious condition.

B: This appeal was in part understood to mean that only religion can guarantee a state-sustaining ethos and a relative homogeneity. But that is not so. I am talking about the lived, living culture; religious aspects flow into it, and it often has religious roots, though these can also wane and be overlaid with other things. . . We are talking primarily about culture, a cultural foundation, from which the state-sustaining ethos and community spirit grow. Religion participates in this and, I believe, plays an important role, but not the only one. You simply have to see what happens when religion dies off as a living force and a power with social efficacy. That can happen. In that case culture is no longer grounded in a lived religion, but must find other foundations and traditional dispositions that fulfil this function. . . I repeatedly tried to make this clear against many an attempt at appropriating my views.

Then there is another misunderstanding. The sentence is often quoted to say that the state is sustained by conditions it cannot itself *create*. But it says: which it cannot itself *guarantee*. That is something else, it is aimed at sovereign instruments. But the state can support and protect the existing ethos and basic convictions, and affirm them and keep them alive especially through education in schools, so that they will be passed on to subsequent generations. It must not simply wait and see what is left over by media society.[XII] If I had the time, it would be worth examining the permanent neglect of the state's educational mandate, which is explicitly recognized in the Basic Law (Article 7) when it comes to schools. Shaping consciousness, transmitting and keeping alive the ethos that exists, none of that happens by itself. The view of the 1968ers was 'we are all OK', one simply has to set nature free, everything else will then happen by itself. In my contribution to Erwin

[XII] 'Media society' is a term that came into usage in West Germany after the state monopoly on TV and radio broadcasting was phased out in the 1980s and private channels opened up. There was a general sense that the heavy slant on entertainment lowered the quality of TV and radio, and that the state had forfeited part of its public education function by enabling this development. Böckenförde here presumably intends to remind the reader that the state nevertheless still retains powerful instruments of public education and does not need to leave the entire field to private actors.

Teufel's anthology *Was hält die moderne Gesellschaft zusammen?* [What holds modern society together?],[8] I pointed out that experience has now demonstrated that humans are neither good nor bad by nature, but ambivalent. They carry both within themselves as a possibility. The task that arises from this for child-raising and education, especially for that part carried out by the state, is to subdue the one and promote the other as much as possible. This is where there is a great void today, because one practically proceeds on the assumption 'we are all OK' and seeks only the lowest common denominator. It should then come as no surprise when elements of an ethos evaporate.

G: Where do you think these elements could be held on to more firmly without endangering freedom?

B: It has been my thesis for some time already to establish obligatory classes on ethics in school—alongside religion classes, not instead of them. It is not difficult to create a reasonable curriculum, after all, we have so many classic and modern texts. In and of themselves, these texts already have an effect of stimulating thought and inner reflection, without the need to impose them as a prescription or commandment.

G: That would be one suggestion. Can you think of other measures?

B: Yes, for example a critical reflection about a media freedom that is getting out of hand. One would have to commit the public institutions, which are financed by fees, more strongly to a cultural and educational mission circumscribed by law, the fulfilment of which would also be subject to oversight. It is more than regrettable to what extent public institutions are becoming like private broadcasters, where only money and ratings matter. One relative exception is still the Bayerischer Rundfunk. Added to this are computer games, most of which are hideous [*unsäglich*]. Nobody wants to think about—age-based—prohibitions, even if it is blatantly obvious that computer games promote a propensity to violence. The only answer one ever hears, in the sense of a knockout argument, is: the freedom of the media. As though the promotion of a sense of community, the building and strengthening of culture, and the defence against a propensity to use violence do not have their own, by no means insignificant, value. This also shapes the entire mental climate, the spirit of community, which then becomes rather spiritless and is reflected in light, shallow entertainment—mediocrity.

G: But you would say that the liberal, secularized state could also do more to secure its substrate, its survival, without endangering freedom? That is to say, there are possibilities that are not being used.

B: Yes, precisely that.

. . .

[8] Ernst-Wolfgang Böckenförde, 'Fundamente der Freiheit', in Erwin Teufel (ed.), *Was hält die moderne Gesellschaft zusammen?* (Frankfurt/M.: Suhrkamp, 1996), pp. 89–99.

G: The paradox . . . may well have become the most important epigram of state theory in the history of the Federal Republic. How do you explain the potent and lasting effect of this statement?

B: Perhaps because this sentence succeeded in capturing a fundamental phenomenon of the liberal order under the conditions of the modern liberal state. The success could not be foreseen, the sentence stood as a kind of theoretical summation at the end of an essay that dealt primarily with constitutional history. Here I must always think of Goethe's lines: 'And what you do, was it for ill or good, only the next day will tell.'[9] That it spread like that completely surprised me. This sentence presupposes, for one, the recognition of the modern state with its claim to sovereignty and comprehensive regulation, for another, its elaboration as a liberal state that guarantees basic rights, and how the two things can coexist. The modern state as a liberal, democratic *Rechtsstaat* is an achievement of political culture, an outstanding achievement. Perhaps this realization has prevailed a little also through the paradox of my statement. It is therefore important to ponder the preconditions on which the liberal state rests and how we can continue to preserve it.

FREEDOM OF RELIGION

G: Let us move on to another point where the problem of the liberal, secular constitutional state is dealt with, namely the foundations and the very scope of the claim of religious freedom.[XIII] We have talked about this in many places. It is a leitmotif of your constitutional-legal, philosophical-legal, as well as historical thinking, and it relates to the sphere both within and outside the Church. Would you like to summarize the importance that the issue of religious freedom has in your scholarly thinking?

B: I would say the impetus for a closer engagement was my realization that the Church did not recognize religious freedom as an institution of the law. Religious freedom was opposed with the right of truth, with the claim that it alone possesses full freedom and should assert itself. Especially as a jurist I could not understand how someone can claim more for himself than he is willing to concede to others. The core issue was the recognition of the equality of individuals and of the personal dignity of every human being. A gradual evolution within the Church became apparent with John XXIII.[XIV]

[9] Johann Wolfgang Goethe, *Hamburger Ausgabe*, 7th ed. (Munich, 1964), vol. I, p. 110 (Ilmenau, 3 September 1783).

[XIII] Note that in this section two separate sections of the biographical interview have been merged.

[XIV] Angelo Giuseppe Roncalli (1881–1963) was made cardinal in 1953 and was unexpectedly elected pope in 1958. As Pope John XXIII, he appointed the first cardinals from Africa, Japan, and the Philippines in the history of the church, and reached out to the Eastern Orthodox churches and to Eastern European communist governments. Politically, he prohibited Italian bishops from advocating for a particular political party and helped the Christian Democrats to cooperate with the

I welcomed this very much; I also became involved myself and tried to promote this development.[10] And later, after the declaration on religious freedom had been adopted, I tried to interpret it and to explain what it had achieved.[11] I still regard the declaration on religious freedom as the most important document of the Second Vatican Council, because it placed the relationship of the Church to the world on a new foundation, without people being aware of it right away. It cleared away a number of positions that had become cherished and had been handed down as immutable. This was not an entirely easy development within the Church itself. The religiously neutral state was strengthened by the declaration, something I deeply welcomed. It was no longer something that one had to tolerate and put up with because those were the circumstances, but something that had its own inherent justification if religious freedom is grounded in the dignity of the human person. It was an epochal change for the Church to recognize that one can always freely practise what one recognizes as true for oneself, and not only what is objectively true according to the judgment of the Church. It led to the acceptance of pluralism in society and shaped how one dealt with it. For me personally it was a relief that one no longer suffered an inner conflict as a jurist and a Catholic Christian. The tension was now resolved.

G: And now there was also the possibility of competing truths.

B: Yes, there are competing truths, then, in the shared existence of people, because the notion of what is true differs. But this does not change the fact that the Catholic Church can say that the revelation that was bestowed upon us in and through Jesus Christ is *the* truth and not merely a truth. In the coexistence of human beings, every person must be able to practise and carry out what he considers true, the prerequisite being the framework of an order that is compatible with everyone.

. . .

G: (T)he question of religious freedom and the freedom to profess a religious creed has become very virulent again since the 1990s—especially from the new and changed coexistence of various religions in the Federal Republic, from a very strong growth in the number of Muslim believers, who have also become much more visible in the public space alongside the two Christian denominations and the Jews. I am referring, for example, to the building of mosques, but also the wearing of openly religious symbols like the headscarf for women in public and beyond that also in public institutions like schools.

Socialists. By convening the Second Vatican Council (1962–1965), Pope John XXIII initiated one of the Catholic Church's most important periods of renewal.

[10] Ernst-Wolfgang Böckenförde, 'Religionsfreiheit als Aufgabe der Christen. Gedanken eines Juristen zu den Diskussionen auf dem Zweiten Vatikanischen Konzil', *Stimmen der Zeit* 90(9) (1964/65), pp. 199–213, (most parts of which are included in Chapter IV in this volume).

[11] Second Vatican Council, *Erklärung über die Religionsfreiheit. Lateinisch und deutsch. Mit einer Einleitung von Ernst-Wolfgang Böckenförde* (Münster/W., 1968).

This is a new problem, because we are no longer dealing with the Christian religion and the Jewish religion, which have had equal status for a long time, but with a different religion, one against which strong reservations exist for historical and cultural reasons. This gives rise to a new potential for conflict, which you have addressed.

B: Indeed. The issue for me was to make clear that religious freedom, as guaranteed by the Basic Law, applies not only to certain denominations. Christians cannot lay claim to full religious freedom for themselves, and others are only more or less tolerated. Instead, religious freedom applies to all religious convictions and creeds. And it is not subject to cultural reservations. If we take in people of the Muslim faith and allow them to settle, they live with us with their human rights garments, not without them.

My second concern was that the neutrality of the state is correctly perceived and understood, namely, in the sense of an open, encompassing—not a strictly distancing—neutrality toward the various religions and worldviews. This is the concept that I believe has found expression in the Basic Law, as distinct from the French *laïcité*. According to our view, the public space, too, should remain open for religious profession, for example, when appearing in public or in school. That also shapes my basic attitude towards the headscarf question. If Muslim women see the wearing of the headscarf as tradition or a commandment, they must be allowed to wear it, as long as it does not conjure up a concrete danger, say, to the peace in school. If Catholic nuns are allowed to wear their habits while they are teachers at state schools, as for example in Baden-Baden Lichtental, how can Muslim teachers not be allowed to wear a headscarf? I was always against issuing a blanket prohibition or even making giving up the headscarf a requirement for the teaching profession. In North Rhine-Westphalia there are ten to fifteen female Muslim teachers, some of whom have been teaching for decades with a headscarf, and there has never been a complaint. Still, North Rhine-Westphalia enacted a law that more or less copied the law in Baden-Württemberg, and now the legal cases are making their way through the courts. If it continues this way, the end result in Germany, too, will be the full privatization of religion.[XIV]

[XIV] A school board in Baden-Württemberg denied a Muslim woman who applied for a teaching position the appointment, because, so the board argued, her insistence on wearing a headscarf in school indicated that she lacked the 'personal aptitude' required of civil servants. The intention to wear a headscarf, according to the board, should be read as 'an expression of cultural separation, incompatible with the requirement of state neutrality, and an interference with the rights of pupils and their parents' (quoted in Kommers and Miller (annotation V), p. 586). Whereas later administrative court rulings upheld the school board decision, the Second Senate of the Federal Constitutional Court decided in 2003 that the woman's then filed constitutional complaint was well founded. The Court held that, in general, different rights of religious freedom have to be weighed against each other—here the right of the woman to wear a religious symbol, there the right of pupils and parents to a religiously neutral state, represented in the teachers as civil servants. The judges did not decide whether a headscarf ban would violate the religious freedom of teachers, but rather held that a statutory law is required which regulates the nature and scope of conflicting constitutional freedoms and obligations. The Court thus passed the ball on to the

G: But for political reasons you are against the general prohibition? You do believe that a legislator can issue such a general and universally applicable prohibition on the use of religious symbols in the public space?

B: No, I don't believe that. This is more than merely a restriction. After all, those affected are deprived a priori of their fundamental right. I also consider the decision of the Constitutional Court as inherently contradictory. On the one hand, it affirms the encompassing, open neutrality, not the distancing neutrality; on the other hand, it says that the legislator can bar the wearing of the headscarf generally, merely on the basis of an abstract danger, thus making its renunciation an eligibility characteristic for the teaching profession. The two don't go together. If there is a concrete threat, for example to the peace in a local school, one must see to finding an acceptable solution, through a balancing mediation or a local and/or time-limited renunciation or a prohibition to that effect. But one cannot try to simply rid oneself of the problem in this way.[XV]

G: That is also why you are against seeing the headscarf of Muslim teachers less as a religious than a political symbol.

B: The headscarf has religious roots and is cultural tradition. But there is no denying that here in Germany it can also be perceived, and is perceived,

legislature. Since not the federal level but the German federal states hold sovereignty on educational and cultural matters (*Kulturhoheit*), each state now has its own regulations on whether teachers may wear religious symbols in the classroom. Until 2015, eight (of sixteen) Länder enacted a headscarf ban for teachers in classrooms. These regulations differ in their extent: in Berlin all religious and philosophical symbols are prohibited; Bavaria allows for Christian symbols as they are regarded as symbols of a long-standing cultural tradition; in North Rhine-Westphalia only those religious symbols are prohibited that may conflict with the state's neutrality towards students and parents or jeopardize school peace. The law specifies that this would be particularly the case if the impression could arise that teachers agitate against human dignity, equal rights under Article 3 of the Basic Law, or the liberal and democratic constitutional order. The laws in both North Rhine-Westphalia and Bavaria have to be reformed, however, following the decision of the Federal Constitutional Court in January 2015 (BVerfG, Order of the First Senate of 27 January 2015—1 BvR 471/10, paras. (1–31), see also next annotation).

XV In 2015, the First Senate of the Federal Constitutional Court ruled against the statutory law in North-Rhine-Westphalia. The Court held that a general ban on religious statements by teachers, without proof that they form a concrete threat to the school's peace, is unconstitutional: 'The Court rules that a statutory prohibition based on the mere abstract potential to endanger the peace at school or the neutrality of the state is disproportionate if this conduct [to cover the head] can be plausibly attributed to a religious duty perceived as imperative. An adequate balance between the constitutional interests at issue—the educational staff's freedom of religion, the pupils' and parents' negative freedom of religion, the fundamental right of parents and the educational mandate of the state—can only be struck via a restrictive interpretation of the prohibitive provision, i.e. that there must be at least a sufficiently specific danger to the protected interests.' Furthermore, the Court held that there can be no privilege for Christian symbols: 'If expressions of religious belief by outer appearance made by educators in interdenominational comprehensive state schools are prohibited by law for the purposes of protecting the peace at school and the neutrality of the state, in principle, this must apply to all religions and ideologies without distinction.' (http://www.bverfg.de/e/rs20150127_1bvr047110en.html). Although this decision deviates from the Second Senate's decision of 2003, it was not referred to the joint Senate. In light of this decision, some of the states' regulations will have to be reformed.

politically. That does not justify a general prohibition, though. Above all, I cannot abstract from the person who is wearing the headscarf. If this person herself does not have an open, neutral attitude towards the students, but seeks to proselytize them, she is unsuited to the job of a teacher from the outset, whether with a headscarf or without.

CARL SCHMITT AND POLITICAL THEOLOGY

G: I would like to touch on a topic that you have repeatedly picked up, namely, the interpretation of the work of Carl Schmitt as political theology. You have written in a number of passages that this is something that will remain well beyond the person, also beyond his entanglement as well as participation in terrible events. But Schmitt as a political theologian—if I understand it correctly, is that something about which there is already consensus? Or do you see this connection more strongly than others do?

B: The discussion about this is very much ongoing, especially on the part of Heinrich Meier, who has now written a very interesting afterword to the third edition of his *Lehre Carl Schmitts*.[12] He points out how Schmitt fluctuates with the concept [theology], uses it with changing content, and never completely clarifies it. He often does this deliberately, for if a concept is fully transparent, has reached rational clarity, no efficacy radiates from it any longer. For one, we are dealing with the transfer of theologically shaped concepts into state law doctrine, for example, sovereignty, omnipotence, unboundedness, which came to fruition in the French Revolution. For another, the issue is that theology translates a revealed religion into political consequences and to that extent leads to patterns of behaviour, to commandments and prohibitions which have repercussions for politics. Both of these things occur in Schmitt.

I myself believe that religion, especially a revealed religion, certainly gives rise to commandments and prohibitions, as well as principled pronouncements that have consequences for political behaviour and also for political systems. Let us take, for example, the story of creation, the creation of man: 'God created man in his image.' Of course, grounded in this, from an ideological perspective, are consequences for the political system, because one can derive from it the recognition of the equal dignity of all humans. This in turn has repercussions for the recognition of the legal equality of people.

G: Of equality amongst one another?

B: What I mean is legal equality. Take, as a counter image, the caste system in India. Do you know this lovely song of the peasants in the fourteenth century in England: 'When Adam delved and Eve span, who was then the

[12] Heinrich Meier, *Die Lehre Carl Schmitts. Vier Kapitel zur Unterscheidung politischer Theologie und politischer Philosophie. Mit einem Rückblick: Der Streit um die politische Theologie*, 3rd ed. (Stuttgart, 2009).

gentleman?' Something like this reverberates into politics, delegitimizes estate-based systems.

G: Is it not the case that we also have from him position statements and writings as a Catholic, as a Catholic thinker, so to speak?

B: Yes, there is, for one, the work *Römischer Katholizismus und politische Form* [Roman Catholicism and Political Form]. It is a piece of apotheosis to show, in the Catholic Church, a connection of rationality and theological substance. However, he draws no consequences from this for constitutional law. For another, he probably believes that the state as such is not viable and capable of making decisions without a final metaphysical anchoring. When Schmitt says in 1963 that the state is finished, no further word need be wasted about it, behind it is a notion of the state according to which the state is still truly empowered, embodies its own, consensus-independent authority, and exists not only as the functional mode of societal forces. For this to be sustained and accepted this way is for him, as I have said, not possible without metaphysical anchoring. 'And I will put enmity between you and the woman, and between your offspring and hers'—for him this is also a statement of political theology. Evil exists in this, as does the engagement from the basis of faith for the confrontation with evil, with the enemy. On the whole, the issue is whether it is seen and accepted at all that there is something like Evil, or, to put it differently, the Devil as the progeny of Lucifer. Augustine's theology of history is also based on this. For Schmitt, if I see it correctly, it is also a point of reference from faith that he accepts the existence of enmity.

G: I ask myself whether you differentiate more strongly than Schmitt does between ecclesiastical-religious commandments, whether of natural law or not, on the one hand, and an independent democratic ethos of the modern state, on the other. I have the impression that Schmitt perhaps places the Catholic notion of a world order more strongly into the modern, also secular state, and wants to assert the Christian-religious commandments more strongly. Perhaps that is not correct, it is an open question.

B: I'm rather sceptical about that. With me the situation is that I make a distinction. The traditional Christian natural law, as it is part of the Church's self-understanding, presupposes a self-contained Christian ordo, which today is no longer given that way. Part of that, as elaborated in the Church's doctrine of the state by Pope Leo XIII, is that the state must serve the true religion and make it the foundation of its order. For me the question was how, on this basis, a democratic state order is possible, one that is based on the equality of all citizens and has the majority principle as its basic rule. Can this be accepted, and to what extent, by the Church or on the basis of religious faith? These are the disputes that I engaged in during the second half of the fifties. They concerned, first of all, the ethos of democracy and the acceptance of freedom and equality as an ethical foundation of democracy, from which the limits on the majority principle then arise. By now, I believe, quite a bit has been clarified also in the discussion within the Church. Today, if I see it correctly, there is broad consensus that natural law is a question of the ethics of law, that it cannot be postulated as already valid law, but as an ethical demand to the law. As such it has an important function. It can legitimize positive law, it can be a spur to reform, and it can delegitimize it if positive law fundamentally contradicts its demands.

G: … under the condition that there is a significant portion of the population which, out of this faith, brings to the political secular order what is not subject to a vote.

B: Yes, exactly. The situation has by now also eased on the other side. The latest statements by Habermas in recent years contain a relevancy of the stock of religious tradition for the stabilization of the democratic-discursive order.[XVI] He goes quite far in this regard. In this area I see a convergence of the positions, his and mine.

B: That is remarkable, considering that in the past you have had strong discrepancies with Habermas, though I don't know the details. Habermas, for his part, took your intellectual closeness to Carl Schmitt as a reason to understand you differently or perhaps not at all, no?

B: Yes, that was very clear. Habermas supposedly said once that he suffered very much under Koselleck and me. Evidently, he felt that the way I kept my distance within the discussion over the domination-free discourse [*herrschaftsfreier Diskurs*] represented a contrary position, which it in fact did. After all, domination-free discourse will hardly produce an order, since the discourse itself never ends. In opposition to Habermas, Robert Spaemann has defined domination as anticipated consensus.[XVII] One must decide and cannot wait until consensus occurs at some point, but must anticipate it. If it does not happen, one is voted out of office or has to resign. I think that Habermas no longer disputes this now.

[XVI] Jürgen Habermas, 'Faith and Knowledge: Acceptance Speech'. Peace Prize of the German Booktrade (2001), (https://www.friedenspreis-des-deutschen-buchhandels.de/sixcms/media.php/1290/2001%20Acceptance%20Speech%20Juergen%20Habermas.pdf); Jürgen Habermas, 'Pre-political Foundations of the Democratic Constitutional State?', in Jürgen Habermas and Joseph Ratzinger, *The Dialectics of Secularization: On Reason and Religion*, trans. Brian McNeil (San Francisco: Ignatius Press, 2006), pp. 19–52; Jürgen Habermas, 'Religion in the Public Sphere: Cognitive Presuppositions for the 'Public Use of Reason' by Religious and Secular Citizens', in his *Between Naturalism and Religion: Philosophical Essays* (Cambridge: Polity Press, 2008), pp. 114–147; Jürgen Habermas, 'Religious Tolerance as Pacemaker for Cultural Rights', in his *Between Naturalism and Religion: Philosophical Essays*, trans. Ciaran Cronin (Cambridge: Polity Press, 2008), pp. 251–269.

[XVII] Robert Spaemann (1927–2018) was a German moral philosopher. Like Böckenförde, he was a member of the Collegium Philosophicum in Münster, a discussion circle organized by Joachim Ritter, one of the most influential German philosophers of the post-war period. Spaemann became a frequent interlocutor and an occasional co-author of Böckenförde's.

CONSTITUTIONAL JUDGE: ETHOS, OFFICE, DECISIONS

G: Before we talk about individual decisions, let me begin with an issue that has attracted considerable public attention. I mean your understanding of exercising the office of a constitutional judge as a Christian. In an essay of 1999, which was written as a retrospective of your work as a constitutional judge, you explain your own criteria, and in addition develop criteria that deserve to be considered and perhaps accepted by others, as well.[13] These are criteria that arise from the stance as a Catholic or Protestant Christian, or in general from that of a person of faith who is placed into the highest judicial office of a religiously neutral, secular state. In the process you address very practical implications that arose for you when you assumed the office in 1983: you resigned from the Central Committee of German Catholics.[XVIII] You suspended the privileges of your membership in the SPD. You report that this was the first and only oath of office that you swore with a religious affirmation.

B: The only oath of office, yes.

G: But why did you not do this when you were sworn in as a professor, but specifically as a constitutional judge?

B: Because I believe that especially this entirely independent and unchecked office depends on the morality of the individuals who exercise it. That is why I consider it legitimate that the religiously neutral state in this case lays claim to a person's inner powers of commitment, even if this is formally voluntary. The oath for regular civil service positions does not have this specific meaning. That is also why I left out the religious affirmation when I was sworn in as a professor.

G: But does that mean that a direct link exists between the decision to make this religious affirmation as a constitutional judge and your core thesis of 1967? According to this thesis, the liberal secular state is sustained by conditions it cannot guarantee itself. It follows from this that a state depends all the more on the fact that a person who joins it and assumes a special responsibility also brings along his inner powers of commitment.

B: Yes, in this sense that is consistent.

[13] Ernst-Wolfgang Böckenförde, 'Als Christ im Amt eines Verfassungsrichters', in his *Kirche und christlicher Glaube in den Herausforderungen der Zeit*, 2nd ed. (Münster: LIT Publishing House, 2007), pp. 415ff [included in this volume as Chapter XI].

[XVIII] The Central Committee of German Catholics is elected by an assembly of Catholics representing the different groups and branches of lay Catholicism. Its tasks include organizing the biennial Catholic *Kirchentag* (Church Day), discussing pending issues with the Conference of German Bishops, and representing lay Catholicism in public. Böckenförde served as an advisor to the Committee for many years.

G: Later you also had to engage in internal and external struggles in this duality as a believing Christian and judge of a state required to be neutral in religious matters. This includes the problem of terminating a pregnancy. Was this the point where the strongest conflicts existed?

B: Yes, there were strong tensions.

G: The major decision of 1993 concerning the termination of pregnancy, in which you were involved, triggered an impassioned public and political discussion. Could you speak to the political context of this decision? The *Bundestag* had passed a law that stipulated a first trimester solution [*Fristenlösung*],[XIX] and an appeal had been made to the court.

B: Yes, that is correct. The law was prompted, in the wake of reunification, by the necessary harmonization with the prevailing law in the GDR. This was supposed to happen by 1992. A kind of term-solution [*Fristenlösung*] carried the day in the law that was passed. Although it included obligatory counselling, the core was that if a woman decided to terminate her pregnancy after counselling, she could legally do so within the first twelve weeks of pregnancy. At the same time, a constitutional review against the law of 1975, pursued by the state government of Bavaria, was pending before the court. Essentially the issue was whether the term solution of 1974, which the constitutional court had declared invalid,[14] would, in slightly modified form, take the place of the indication solution agreed upon following the court's decision. The basic problem up for debate was the question of how to handle the protection of life for the embryo. To what extent is it protected by the constitution, also vis-à-vis the mother? Of course, this presupposes the question of whether the embryo should be seen as an unborn child, that is, a human being who is the bearer of human dignity and therefore has the right to life. What follows from this is not invariably an absolute right to life, since that right is not unlimited, as Article 2 Section 2 of the Basic Law demonstrates, but can be restricted in situations of conflict. On the other side stands the woman's and mother's right to personality and self-determination. How can and must this

[XIX] The abortion debate in 1970s West Germany oscillated between two approaches: according to the *Fristenlösung*, abortion would not be penalized if it was performed by a licensed physician with the consent of the pregnant woman, within the first trimester. By contrast, the more restrictive *Indikationslösung* provided that abortion would not be penalized only when certain narrow conditions [*Indikationen*] were met (for example, criminal or medical reasons). In the first abortion decision of the Federal Constitutional Court in 1975, four such conditions were recognized: 1) medical reasons: if the mother's life is endangered due to the pregnancy; 2) embryonic reasons: if the child's health is considerably threatened; 3) social reasons: if there is a grave social situation, under which the mother cannot be expected to continue the pregnancy, and which cannot be resolved otherwise; and 4) criminal reasons: if the pregnancy is the result of a crime. See for a summary, interpretation, and an English translation of the main passages, Kommers and Miller (annotation V), pp. 373–386.

[14] BVerfGE 39,1.

be incorporated, which approaches can the legislator take to do justice to both? As a background one must also realize that the indication rule, which has been in effect again since 1975, is not very effective. A practice has taken hold that has expanded the conditions [*Indikationen*] very broadly. This raises the fundamental question of what the law can and should achieve here. The views within society in this regard were not only diverse, but in opposition. One position declared that the child in the womb was also a human being and that human rights must therefore be protected in its case. Terminating a pregnancy could be contemplated only in extreme situations of conflict. By contrast, the other position took the view that it was up to the mother to decide whether she wanted to accept and carry to term a child she had conceived. This position invoked primarily the woman's right to self-determination and freedom. These were two diametrically opposed views. Society was deeply divided and probably is to this day. This situation accounted for the special difficulties. Law has the task of ordering and regulating human coexistence in a binding way. To exert its socially ordering force, the law depends on statutes usually being followed voluntarily, for sanctions, too, are effective only if they need to be employed not on a mass scale, but only occasionally and against a certain section of the people. The law shatters against a statute that is adhered to and implemented only when there is a policeman standing behind virtually every citizen. These were our difficulties.[xx]

G: Your Senate was tasked with rendering a decision, and you were called on to take a position within the college of judges. You thus had to somehow combine your own positions as judge and Christian, without being split apart in the process.

B: For me it was clear that as a judge I had to decide the way I believe the Basic Law settles this conflict, independent of whether or not that accorded with

[xx] In the second abortion decision of 1992, the Federal Constitutional Court ruled that the 'Pregnancy and Family Assistance Act', which had reformed the abortion law after German reunification in 1990, was partly unconstitutional. The Act had aimed to find a compromise between the legal situation in the Federal Republic (*Indikationslösung*) and the former GDR (*Fristenlösung*). It provided a *Fristenlösung* combined with obligatory counselling and a variety of social support programmes for pregnant mothers and their families, such as the provision of day care and financial support. Against the Act, the court ruled that '(a)bortions performed at any point during a pregnancy [even in the first trimester] must be fundamentally considered a wrong and thus unlawful' (Head Note 4, BVerfGE 203, Engl. transl. in Kommers and Millers (annotation V), p. 387), except in the event of either medical or criminal indications: here an abortion could be considered justified because it may be unreasonable to insist on the general duty of the pregnant woman to carry out the pregnancy (Head Note 7). But the court also famously declared: if an abortion is undertaken in the first trimester and none of the indications apply, the abortion is unlawful, but may go without punishment if ethical counselling has taken place: 'The legislature acts constitutionally when it adopts a regulatory scheme for the protection of the unborn that uses counselling as a means of inducing pregnant women in conflict during the early stage of the pregnancy to carry their pregnancy to term. The legislature also acts within constitutional bounds when it dispenses with criminal prosecution for indicated abortions as well as the determination of such indications by third parties.' (Head Note 11, ibid., p.388). This idea is summarized in the 'illegal but exempt from punishment' formula, for which the court decision has become widely known.

my personal beliefs as a Catholic Christian. After all, that is why I swore an oath on the Basic Law. To that extent there is a difference to the situation in which a member of parliament votes in favour of a law.

G: Is that why you would feel less of a burden compared with a member of parliament who has to decide this question, since you apply 'only' the criterion of the constitution to a law? To that extent, would you consider the issue of individual conscience that is naturally tied to this a lesser problem compared to the member of parliament?

B: Certainly. As a member of parliament, I could say that I cannot accept this term solution and everything that departs from the indication regulation. I would then act accordingly in parliament. Within the parliamentary context, this also raises the problem of the capacity for compromise, its possibilities and limitations. As a judge I am relieved of all of that. The legislator has decided the matter this way, and now I must examine whether or not the law violates the constitution. I must fulfil this task independent of the fact that as a member of parliament I might have never voted in favour of such a law.

G: Did this become clear to you over the course of the process, or had you already anticipated precisely this problem in your mind?

B: No, it became clear only in the course of this process. But when it became relevant, it was for me not a problem I still had to resolve with myself. Some may think that this is a piece of dialectics. But for me it was clear: I had sworn my oath of office, namely with a religious affirmation, on the Basic Law and on the duties of the office of judge.

G: But for yourself you interpreted this formula of religious affirmation to mean *not* that you should insert Christian ideas into the interpretation of the constitution, but that as a Christian you should respect the secular order.

B: Precisely that, if I commit myself to that.

G: You are then acting from a Christian responsibility when you preserve and interpret the secular order of the Basic Law?

B: Yes. Taking advantage of the position on the constitutional court as a Catholic actor would have been to me an abuse of office.

G: Many would feel legitimated by a religious affirmation in their oath of office to introduce their religious conviction into their official actions. That is precisely what you are not doing. You pull back your religious attitude.

B: Yes, but that is the very object of the oath. I swore an oath on the constitution and that I would preserve it against everybody. If the constitution contains any shortcomings with respect to my convictions as a Catholic Christian, I must accept that. I may not attempt to undermine it, and to seek to become active as a Catholic vanguard, so to speak. If one has a problem with this and concerns of conscience, one may not in honesty assume such an office. For me that is part of it.

ON SOCIAL EQUALITY AND THE *RECHTSSTAAT*

G: Finally, let us pick up a topic that incorporates some of the aspects we have just talked about. This is the problem of the *Rechtsstaat*, especially in its relationship to democracy and to the social foundations of what is called the social state. In a number of writings, you repeatedly dealt with the *Rechtsstaat* and the history of the *Rechtsstaat* as a concept, but also as a form of constitutional law. Could you explain once more why this form of the *Rechtsstaat* became so central for you in your scholarly thinking?

B: Because the *Rechtsstaat* is about securing liberty and guaranteeing a liberal order. This is central for an orderly and beneficial coexistence of human beings. Democracy, by contrast, has a different goal. It is concerned with establishing and legitimizing authority [*Herrschaft*] as emanating from the people, with the holding of authority. The successful coupling of *Rechtsstaat* and democracy is so important because the two are reciprocally interdependent for a liberal order. A democracy that is not tied to a *Rechtsstaat* can become totalitarian, and the *Rechtsstaat* itself can become automatic and authoritarian if it is not sustained by democracy. *Rechtsstaat* and democracy require a balance. The *Rechtsstaat* establishes the protection of freedom to a large extent through forms and orderly procedures. This includes the separation of power and the fact that the direct access in the name of asserted claims or truths is blocked. If the state wishes to limit and interfere in freedom, it needs a basis in law. This seems more important to me than materially endowing the *Rechtsstaat* with values. The *Rechtsstaat* is aimed primarily at the orderly guarantee of freedom, and only then—and also within this framework—at the realization of justice. What is or may be just can only be realized, and must be realized, in the forms and under the conditions of freedom. The link between the *Rechtsstaat* and the social state, or with the social balancing as such, arises from the fact that the securing of freedom is not already adequate if it manifests itself only on the legal level through the guarantee of rights of freedom, such as the freedom to enter into contracts, the freedom to engage in gainful activity, and the guarantee of property. For precisely these guarantees set in motion a process that leads inherently to social inequalities. Human beings are simply not equal by nature, one person is more active, the other more lackadaisical, one has a lot of energy, the other has less, and they are also not equal in terms of talent. The exercise and the fruit of freedom therefore engenders social inequality, and it consolidates across generations, especially through the guarantee of property and inheritance rights. Social inequality can then turn into social unfreedom, because some lack the social preconditions to make real use of the legal freedoms. The best example of this is wage workers in the nineteenth century. That is why the social preconditions to make use of freedom are part of the guarantee of freedom. Freedom is true freedom only in the person who possesses its conditions, the material and intellectual goods, as the precondition of self-determination, as we read in Lorenz von Stein. To work towards that end and to moderate social inequality is a continuous task of the state. To that extent, *Rechtsstaat* and social state belong together.

G: Into what tradition of theoretical thinking about the state does this place you?

B: It's the name Lorenz von Stein that belongs here, who really laid this out brilliantly, these processes and this dialectical development. Many still do not fully recognize this. If they did, many controversies could be resolved, and one would pose the question about the scope of the social state, but no longer the question of 'whether' it should exist.

G: And Marx?

B: Yes, I would say the analyses of Marx and Lorenz von Stein are virtually identical. Marx's proposed remedies are unacceptable, but there is little to be said against his analysis. He conceptualized how capitalism develops out of its own premises. Years ago, I said: Karl Marx is becoming topical again.

G: As you look over this scholarly as well as politically engaged life, what was for you the greatest disappointment, measured against the ambitions of scientific analysis and of the political implementation of what you considered correct?

B: I might say that which we just spoke about. The fact that this necessary interconnection of *Rechtsstaat* and social state, namely from the basis of freedom, has not been understood, that was a disappointment. In other areas I did also have successes.

G: That is the next question. Where do you see those successes?

B: In the areas we have spoken about: the general acceptance of the secularized, religiously neutral state, the acceptance of democracy and religious freedom by the Church, and not least the closer elaboration of *Rechtsstaat* and democracy in the democratic constitutional state. Here I was able to make contributions that had an impact. It was also a success to have given Carl Schmitt's concepts a liberal reception. I think that I was able to achieve and effect a good deal here. And when I look back over my professional life, it is a great pleasure that I was allowed to hold the office of constitutional judge for twelve-and-a-half years.

G: Thank you very much, Mr. Böckenförde.

Appendix 1
List of Original Titles

The articles included were originally published in the following publications:

- *The Ethos of Modern Democracy and the Church*—Das Ethos der modernen Demokratie und die Kirche. Published in: *Hochland*, 50(1) (1957), pp. 4–19.
- *German Catholicism in 1933: A Critical Examination*—Der deutsche Katholizismus im Jahre 1933. Eine kritische Betrachtung. Published in: *Hochland*, 53(3) (1961), pp. 215–239.
- *Types of Christian Conduct in the World during the Nazi-Regime*—Formen christlichen Weltverhaltens während der NS-Herrschaft. Lecture given in 1965, published in: *Kirche und christlicher Glaube in den Herausforderungen der Zeit. Beiträge der politisch-theologischen Verfassungsgeschichte 1957–2002*, (Münster/W.: LIT-Verlag, 2004), pp. 181–191.
- *Religious Freedom Between the Conflicting Demands of Church and State*—Religionsfreiheit zwischen Kirche und Staat. Lecture given in 1979, published in: *Gewissen und Freiheit* 22 (1984), pp. 13–31. This text was a combination of large parts of two previously published articles: 'Religionsfreiheit als Aufgabe der Christen. Gedanken eines Juristen zu den Diskussionen auf dem Zweiten Vatikanischen Konzil,' in *Stimmen der Zeit* 90(9) (1964/65), pp. 199–213; and 'Einleitung zur Textausgabe der 'Erklärung über die Religionsfreiheit'', in *Erklärung über die Religionsfreiheit (lateinisch und deutsch)* (Münster, 1968), pp. 5–21. The present translation is based on the slightly revised version 'Die Religionsfreiheit im Spannungsfeld zwischen Kirche und Staat', in Ernst-Wolfgang Böckenförde, *Religionsfreiheit. Die Kirche in der modernen Welt* (Freiburg: Herder, 1990), pp. 33–58, with updated references.
- *The Rise of the State as a Process of Secularization*—Die Entstehung des Staates als Vorgang der Säkularisation. Published in: *Säkularisation und Utopie. Ebracher Studien. Ernst Forsthoff zum 65. Geburtstag* (Stuttgart etc.: Kohlhammer, 1967), pp. 75–94.
- *The Fundamental Right of Freedom of Conscience*—Das Grundrecht der Gewissensfreiheit. Published in: *Veröffentlichungen der Vereinigung der Deutschen Staatsrechtslehrer* 28 (1970), pp. 33–88.
- *Remarks on the Relationship between State and Religion in Hegel*—Bemerkungen zum Verhältnis von Staat und Religion bei Hegel. Published in: *Der Staat* 21 (1982), pp. 481–503.
- *The Secularized State: Its Character, Justification, and Problems in the Twenty-First Century*—*Der säkularisierte Staat. Sein Charakter, seine Rechtfertigung und seine Probleme im 21. Jahrhundert* (Munich: C.F. von Siemens Stiftung, 2007).
- *Political Theory and Political Theology: Comments on their Reciprocal Relationship*—Politische Theorie und politische Theologie. Bemerkungen zu ihrem gegenseitigen

Verhältnis. Published in: *Revue Européenne des Sciences Sociales et Cahiers Vilfredo Pareto* XIX (1981), Nos. 54–55 (Etudes en l'honneur de Julien Freund), pp. 233–243. Reprinted in: *Der Fürst dieser Welt. Carl Schmitt und die Folgen*. Ed. by Jacob Taubes (Paderborn etc.: Schöningh/Fink, 1983), pp. 16–25.

- *Reflections on a Theology of Modern Secular Law*—Überlegungen zu einer Theologie des modernen säkularen Rechts. Vortrag anlässlich der Ehrenpromotion am 12. Mai 1999 (1999). Published in: *Universitätsreden*—New Series—Nr. 9 der Ruhr-Universität Bochum, pp. 27–50.
- *A Christian in the Office of Constitutional Judge*—Als Christ im Amt eines Verfassungsrichters. Published in: E.-W. Böckenförde and A. Schavan (eds.), *Salz der Erde* (Stuttgart: Schwabenverlag, 1999), pp. 14–28.
- *On the Authority of Papal Encyclicals: The Example of Pronouncements on Religious Freedom*—Über die Autorität päpstlicher Lehrenzykliken am Beispiel der Äußerungen zur Religionsfreiheit. Published in: *Theologische Quartalsschrift* 186 (2006), pp. 22–39.
- *Abolition of Section 218 of the Criminal Code? Reflections on the Current Debate about the Prohibition of Abortion in German Criminal Law*—Abschaffung des § 218 StGB? Überlegungen zur gegenwärtigen Diskussion um das strafrechtliche Abtreibungsverbot. Published in: *Stimmen der Zeit*, 188 (1971), pp. 147–167.
- *Human Dignity as a Normative Principle: Fundamental Rights in the Bioethics Debate*—Menschenwürde als normatives Prinzip. Published in: *Juristenzeitung* 58 (2003), pp. 809–815.
- *Will Human Dignity Remain Inviolable?*—Bleibt die Menschenwürde unantastbar? Published in: *Blätter für deutsche und internationale Politik*, 49 (2004), pp. 1216–1227.
- Selections from the 170-page biographical interview that legal scholar and historian Dieter Gosewinkel conducted with Böckenförde in 2009/2010 on issues related to religion, law, and democracy. Published in: *Wissenschaft, Politik, Verfassungsgericht. Aufsätze von Ernst-Wolfgang Böckenförde. Biographisches Interview von Dieter Gosewinkel* (Berlin: Suhrkamp, 2011).

Appendix 2
*Ernst-Wolfgang Böckenförde: List of Publications**

A. Books
B. Journal Articles and Chapters in Edited Volumes
C. Analysis of Cases
D. Book Reviews
E. Book Announcements
F. Published Panel Contributions
G. Edited Volumes and Journals (as Single Editor or Co-Editor)
H. Interviews
I. Translations and Foreign Language Contributions

A. Books

1. *Gesetz und gesetzgebende Gewalt. Von den Anfängen der deutschen Staatsrechtslehre bis zur Höhe des staatsrechtlichen Positivismus* (Berlin: Duncker & Humblot, 1958). First book in newly founded series 'Schriften zum Öffentlichen Recht'. Revised edition with a new postscript published in 1981.
2. *Die deutsche verfassungsgeschichtliche Forschung im 19. Jahrhundert. Zeitgebundene Fragestellungen und Leitbilder* (Berlin: Duncker & Humblot, 1961). First book in newly founded series 'Schriften zur Verfassungsgeschichte". Revised edition with a new preface published in 1995.
3. *Die Organisationsgewalt im Bereich der Regierung. Eine Untersuchung zum Staatsrecht der Bundesrepublik Deutschland* (series 'Schriften zum Öffentlichen Recht') (Berlin: Duncker & Humblot, 1964). 2nd edition published in 1998.
4. *Die Rechtsauffassung im kommunistischen Staat* (Munich: Kösel, 1967). 3rd edition published in 1968.
5. *Kirchlicher Auftrag und politische Entscheidung* (Freiburg: Rombach, 1973).
6. *Die verfassungstheoretische Unterscheidung von Staat und Gesellschaft als Bedingung der individuellen Freiheit* (Opladen: Westdeutscher Verlag, 1973).
7. *Verfassungsfragen der Richterwahl. Dargestellt anhand der Gesetzentwürfe zur Einführung der Richterwahl in Nordrhein-Westfalen* (Berlin: Duncker & Humblot, 1974). 2nd edition published in 1998.
8. *Staat, Gesellschaft, Freiheit. Studien zur Staatstheorie und zum Verfassungsrecht* (Frankfurt: Suhrkamp, 1976).

* The structure of this bibliography goes back to Böckenförde. It has been updated for present purposes and details have been completed where previously missing. Section I. (translations) has been updated since the publication of the hardback.

9. *Der Staat als sittlicher Staat* (Berlin: Duncker & Humblot, 1978).
10. *Demokratie und Repräsentation. Zur Kritik der heutigen Demokratiediskussion* (Hanover: Niedersächsische Landeszentrale für politische Bildung, 1983). Also published in A 17.
11. *Die verfassunggebende Gewalt des Volkes. Ein Grenzbegriff des Verfassungsrechts* (Frankfurt: Metzner, 1986). Also published in A 17.
12. *Schriften zu Staat, Gesellschaft, Kirche. Vol. 1 Der deutsche Katholizismus im Jahre 1933. Kirche und demokratisches Ethos* (Freiburg: Herder, 1988).
13. *Schriften zu Staat, Gesellschaft, Kirche. Vol. 2 Kirchlicher Auftrag und politisches Handeln. Analyse und Orientierungen* (Freiburg: Herder, 1989).
14. *Schriften zu Staat, Gesellschaft, Kirche. Vol. 3 Religionsfreiheit. Die Kirche in der modernen Welt* (Freiburg: Herder, 1990).
15. *Zur Lage der Grundrechtsdogmatik nach 40 Jahren Grundgesetz* (Munich: Carl Friedrich von Siemens-Stiftung, 1990).
16. *Recht, Staat, Freiheit. Studien zur Rechtsphilosophie, Staatstheorie und Verfassungsgeschichte* (Frankfurt: Suhrkamp, 1991). 3rd edition published in 2000. Expanded edition published in 2006.
17. *Staat, Verfassung, Demokratie. Studien zur Rechtsphilosophie, Staatstheorie und Verfassungsgeschichte* (Frankfurt: Suhrkamp, 1991). 2nd edition published in 1992.
18. *Welchen Weg geht Europa?* (Munich: Carl Friedrich von Siemens-Stiftung, 1997). Also published in A 19.
19. *Staat, Nation, Europa. Studien zur Staatslehre, Verfassungstheorie und Rechtsphilosophie* (Frankfurt: Suhrkamp, 1999). 2nd edition published in 2000.
20. *Vom Wandel des Menschenbildes im Recht* (Münster: Rhena, 2001).
21. *Recht, Sittlichkeit, Toleranz* (Ulm: Humboldt Studienzentrum, 2001).
22. *Geschichte der Rechts- und Staatsphilosophie. Antike und Mittelalter* (Tübingen: Mohr Siebeck, 2002) 2nd revised and expanded edition published in 2006.
23. *Kirche und christlicher Glaube in den Herausforderungen der Zeit. Beiträge der politisch-theologischen Verfassungsgeschichte 1957–2002* (Münster: LIT Verlag, 2004). 2nd expanded edition published in 2007.
24. *Sicherheit und Selbsterhaltung vor Gerechtigkeit. Der Paradigmenwechsel und Übergang von einer naturrechtlichen zur positivrechtlichen Grundlegung des Rechtssystems bei Thomas Hobbes* (Basel: Schwabe, 2004).
25. *Der säkularisierte Staat. Sein Charakter, seine Rechtfertigung und seine Probleme im 21. Jahrhundert* (Munich: C.F. von Siemens Stiftung, 2007). 2nd edition published in 2015.
26. *Vom Ethos der Juristen* (Berlin: Duncker & Humblot, 2010). 2nd revised edition published in 2011.
27. *Wissenschaft, Politik, Verfassungsgericht. Aufsätze von Ernst-Wolfgang Böckenförde. Biographisches Interview von Dieter Gosewinkel* (Berlin: Suhrkamp, 2011). 3rd edition published in 2019.

B. Journal Articles and Chapters in Edited Volumes

1. 'Das Ethos der modernen Demokratie und die Kirche', *Hochland* 50:1 (1957), pp. 4–19. Also published in Heinz Dieter Wendland and Theodor Strohm (eds.), *Politik und Ethik* (Darmstadt: Wissenschaftliche Buchgesellschaft, 1969), pp. 218–240. Also published in A 5, A 12.
2. 'Noch einmal: Das Ethos der modernen Demokratie und die Kirche. Erwiderung', *Hochland* 50:5 (1958), pp. 409–421.
3. 'Naturrecht auf dem Hintergrund des Heute', *Archiv für Rechts-und Sozialphilosophie* 44 (1958), pp. 94–102.
4. Co-authored with Robert Spaemann, 'Die Zerstörung der naturrechtlichen Kriegslehre. Erwiderung an P. Gustav Gundlach', in Rudolf Fleischmann et al. (eds.), *Atomare Kampfmittel und christliche Ethik. Diskussionsbeiträge deutscher Katholiken* (Munich: Kösel, 1960), pp. 161–196. Also published in A 5, A 13.
5. 'Der deutsche Katholizismus im Jahre 1933. Eine kritische Betrachtung', *Hochland* 53:3 (1961), pp. 215–239. Also published in A 5, A 12.
6. Co-authored with Robert Spaemann, 'Christliche Moral und atomare Kampfmittel', *Militärseelsorge. Zeitschrift des Katholischen Militärbischofsamts* 3 (1961), pp. 267–301.
7. 'Der deutsche Katholizismus im Jahre 1933. Stellungnahme zu einer Diskussion', *Hochland* 54:3 (1962), pp. 217–245. Also published in A 5, A 12.
8. Co-authored with Robert Spaemann, 'Noch einmal. Atomare Kampfmittel und christliche Ethik', *Militärseelsorge. Zeitschrift des Katholischen Militärbischofsamts* 4 (1962), pp. 213–229.
9. 'Lorenz von Stein als Theoretiker der Bewegung von Staat und Gesellschaft zum Sozialstaat', in Historisches Seminar der Universität Hamburg (ed.), *Alteuropa und die moderne Gesellschaft. Festschrift für Otto Brunner* (Göttingen: Vandenhoeck & Ruprecht, 1963), pp. 248–277. Also published in A 8 and in Ernst Forsthoff (ed.), *Lorenz von Stein. Gesellschaft – Staat – Recht* (Frankfurt: Ullstein, 1972), pp. 513–547.
10. 'Die Historische Rechtsschule und das Problem der Geschichtlichkeit des Rechts', in Ernst-Wolfgang Böckenförde and Joachim Ritter (eds.), *Collegium Philosophicum. Studien. Joachim Ritter zum 60. Geburtstag* (Basel: Schwabe, 1965), pp. 9–36. Also published in A 8, A 16.
11. 'Religionsfreiheit als Aufgabe der Christen. Gedanken eines Juristen zu den Diskussionen auf dem Zweiten Vatikanischen Konzil', *Stimmen der Zeit* 90:9 (1964/65), pp. 199–212. Also published in A 5, A 14.
12. 'Religionsfreiheit und öffentliches Schulgebet. Eine Auseinandersetzung mit dem Urteil des Hessischen Staatsgerichtshofes vom 27.10.1965', *Die Öffentliche Verwaltung* 19 (1966), pp. 30–38.
13. 'Kirche und Politik. Zu einigen Neuerscheinungen über das Verhalten der katholischen Kirche zum Dritten Reich', *Der Staat* 5 (1966), pp. 225–238.
14. 'Die Eingliederung der Streitkräfte in die demokratisch-parlamentarische Verfassungsordnung und die Vertretung des Bundesverteidigungsministers in der militärischen Befehlsgewalt (Befehls- und Kommandogewalt)', in Hochschule

für Politische Wissenschaften (ed.), *Stellvertretung im Oberbefehl. Referate und Diskussionsbeiträge auf einer Arbeitstagung der Hochschule für politische Wissenschaften* (Munich: Universis-Verlag, 1966), pp. 43–59.

15. 'Stabsorganisation und Haushaltsplanung', in Hochschule für Verwaltungswissenschaften Speyer (ed.), *Die Staatskanzlei. Aufgaben, Organisation und Arbeitsweise auf vergleichender Grundlage* (Berlin: Duncker & Humblot, 1967), pp. 149–154.
16. 'Bonn ist nicht Weimar', *Archiv des öffentlichen Rechts* 92 (1967), pp. 253–254.
17. 'Die Entstehung des Staates als Vorgang der Säkularisation', in s. ed., *Säkularisation und Utopie. Ebracher Studien. Ernst Forsthoff zum 65. Geburtstag* (Stuttgart: Kohlhammer, 1967), pp. 75–94. Also published in A 8, A 16.
18. 'Vorwort', in s. ed. *Lorenz von Stein. Die Lehre vom Heerwesen. Als Theil der Staatswissenschaft* (Osnabrück: Biblio-Verlag, 1967), pp. IX–XVI.
19. 'Der deutsche Typ der konstitutionellen Monarchie im 19. Jahrhundert', in Werner Conze (ed.), *Beiträge zur deutschen und belgischen Verfassungsgeschichte im 19. Jahrhundert* (Stuttgart: Klett, 1967), pp. 70–92. Also published in A 8, A 16. Also published as: 'Der Verfassungstyp der deutschen konstitutionellen Monarchie', in G 3.
20. 'Einleitung', in s. ed., *Zweites Vatikanisches Ökumenisches Konzil. Erklärung über die Religionsfreiheit* (Münster: Aschendorff, 1968) pp. 5–21. Also published in A 23. Also published in Heinrich Lutz (ed.), *Zur Geschichte der Toleranz und Religionsfreiheit* (Darmstadt: Wissenschaftliche Buchgesellschaft, 1977), pp. 401–421.
21. 'Die Teilung Deutschlands und die deutsche Staatsangehörigkeit', in Hans Barion et al. (eds.), *Epirrhosis. Festgabe für Carl Schmitt zum 80. Geburtstag. Vol. 2* (Berlin: Duncker & Humblot, 1968), pp. 423–463.
22. 'Der Rechtsbegriff in seiner geschichtlichen Entwicklung. Aufriß eines Problems', *Archiv für Begriffsgeschichte* 12 (1968), pp. 145–165.
23. 'Entstehung und Wandel des Rechtsstaatsbegriffs', in Horst Ehmke, Carlo Schmid, and Hans Scharoun (eds.), *Festschrift für Adolf Arndt zum 65. Geburtstag* (Frankfurt: Europäische Verlagsanstalt, 1969), pp. 53–76. Also published in A 8, A 16.
24. 'Rechtsfragen der Neuordnung des Schulwesens im Lande Nordrhein-Westfalen', in s. ed., *Rechtsgutachten zur Neuordnung von Grundschule und Hauptschule* (Wuppertal: Aloys Henn, 1969). pp. 4–109.
25. 'Der Westfälische Friede und das Bündnisrecht der Reichstände', *Der Staat* 8 (1969), pp. 449–478.
26. 'Politisches Mandat der Kirche?', *Stimmen der Zeit* 184 (1969), pp. 361–373. Also published in A 5, A 13, A 23.
27. Co-authored with Rolf Grawert, 'Sonderverordnungen zur Regelung besonderer Gewaltverhältnisse', *Archiv des öffentlichen Rechts* 95 (1970), pp. 1–37.
28. 'Das Grundrecht der Gewissensfreiheit', *Veröffentlichungen der Vereinigung der Deutschen Staatsrechtslehrer* 28 (1970), pp. 33–88. Also published in A 8, A 17.

29. 'Wendung zu einer rechtlosen Politik?',
    a. *Frankfurter Allgemeine Zeitung*, 27 October 1970, p. 12.
    b. Also published in *Bulletin der Bundesregierung* 171, 8 December 1970, pp. 1826–1829.
    c. Slightly revised version published as 'Ostpolitik steht auf neuer Rechtsgrundlage', *Die Neue Gesellschaft* 18 (1971), pp. 36–41.
30. Co-authored with Rolf Grawert, 'Kollisionsfälle und Geltungsprobleme im Verhältnis von Bundesrecht und Landesverfassung', *Die Öffentliche Verwaltung* (1971), pp. 119–127.
31. 'Abschaffung des § 218 StGB? Überlegungen zur gegenwärtigen Diskussion um das strafrechtliche Abtreibungsverbot', *Stimmen der Zeit* 188 (1971), pp. 147–167. Also published in A 13, A 23.
32. 'Verfassungsprobleme und Verfassungsbewegung des 19. Jahrhunderts. Ein Überblick', *Juristische Schulung* (1971), pp. 560–566. Also published in A 8.
33. 'Die Bedeutung der Unterscheidung von Staat und Gesellschaft im demokratischen Sozialstaat der Gegenwart', in *Rechtsfragen der Gegenwart. Festgabe für Wolfgang Hefermehl zum 65. Geburtstag* (Stuttgart: Kohlhammer, 1972), pp. 11–36. Also published in A 8, A 16. Also published as a shortened preprint in *Aus Politik und Zeitgeschichte. Beilage zur Wochenzeitung Das Parlament* B 49, 4 December 1971, pp. 3–17.
34. 'Wider die Bauland-Spekulation. Vorschläge zu einer Reform des Bodennutzungsrechts', *Die Zeit* 19, 12 May 1972, p. 54.
35. 'Eigentum, Sozialbindung des Eigentums, Enteignung', in Konrad Duden et al. (eds.), *Gerechtigkeit in der Industriegesellschaft. Rechtspolitischer Kongreß der SPD, Mai 1972 in Braunschweig. Dokumentation* (Karlsruhe: C. F. Müller, 1972), pp. 215–231. Also published in A 8.
36. 'Zum Verhältnis von Geschichtswissenschaft und Rechtswissenschaft', in Werner Conze (ed.), *Theorie der Geschichtswissenschaft und Praxis des Geschichtsunterrichts* (Stuttgart: Klett, 1972), pp. 38–43.
37. 'Planung zwischen Regierung und Parlament. Ernst Forsthoff zum 70. Geburtstag', *Der Staat* 11 (1972), pp. 429–458.
38. 'Die Einheit von nationaler und konstitutioneller Bewegung', in Ernst-Wolfgang Böckenförde (ed.) with assistance from Rainer Wahl, *Moderne deutsche Verfassungsgeschichte (1815–1918)* (Cologne: Kiepenheuer & Witsch, 1972), pp. 27–39. The article contains excerpts of A 2.
39. 'Bemerkungen aus verfassungsrechtlicher und verfassungspraktischer Sicht', in Hochschule für Verwaltungswissenschaften Speyer (ed.), *Aktuelle Probleme der Ministerialorganisation. Referate und Diskussionsbeiträge der internationalen verwaltungswissenschaftlichen Arbeitstagung der Hochschule für Verwaltungswissenschaften Speyer 1971* (Berlin: Duncker & Humblot, 1972), pp. 65–74.
40. 'Ernst Rudolf Huber zum 70. Geburtstag', *Archiv des öffentlichen Rechts* 98 (1973), pp. 255–259.
41. 'Qualität des Lebens – Aufgabe und Verantwortung des Staates?', *Die Neue Gesellschaft* (1973), pp. 261–265. Revised and expanded version published in

Ernst-Wolfgang Böckenförde (ed.), *Lebensqualität? Von der Hoffnung Mensch zu sein* (Cologne: Wissenschaft und Politik, 1974), pp. 165–184.

42. 'Kirchliches Naturrecht und politisches Handeln', in Franz Böckle and Ernst-Wolfgang Böckenförde (eds.), *Naturrecht in der Kritik* (Mainz: Matthias Grünewald, 1973) pp. 96–125. Also published in A 13, A 23.
43. 'Wie verhält sich der Staat neutral? Religionsfreiheit als Prinzip des Verhältnisses von Kirche und Staat', *Publik-Forum*, 20 November 1973, pp. 12–14.
44. 'Organ, Organisation, Juristische Person. Kritische Überlegungen zu Grundbegriffen und. Konstruktionsbasis des staatlichen Organisationsrechts', in Christian-Friedrich Menger (ed.), *Fortschritte des Verwaltungsrechts. Festschrift für Hans J. Wolff* (Munich: C. H. Beck, 1973), pp. 269–305.
45. 'Vorläufige Bilanz im Streit um das Schulgebet. Zum Urteil des BVerwG v. 30.11.1973 – VII C 59.73', *Die Öffentliche Verwaltung* Vol. 27 (8) (1974), pp. 253–257.
46. '"Integrierte Wahl" – verfassungsgemäß?' *Zeitschrift für Rechtspolitik* Vol. 7(6) (1974), pp. 134–137.
47. 'Grundrechtstheorie und Grundrechtsinterpretation', *Neue Juristische Wochenschrift* Vol. 27 (1974), pp. 1529–1538. Also published in A 8, A 17, A 27.
48. 'Kreuze (Kruzifixe) in Gerichtssälen? Zum Verhältnis von staatlicher Selbstdarstellung und religiös-weltanschaulicher Neutralität des Staates', *Zeitschrift für evangelisches Kirchenrecht* Vol. 20 (1975), pp. 119–147.
49. 'Freiheitssicherung gegenüber gesellschaftlicher Macht', in Diether Posser and Rudolf Wassermann (eds.), *Freiheit in der sozialen Demokratie. 4. Rechtspolitischer Kongreß der SPD vom 6. bis 8.6.1975 in Düsseldorf. Dokumentation* (Karlsruhe: C. F. Müller, 1975), pp. 69–76. Also published in A 8, A 17, A 27. Shortened preprint published as 'Sicherung der Freiheit vor neuen Gefahren', *Frankfurter Allgemeine Zeitung*, 3 June 1975, p. 9.
50. 'Grundrechtsgeltung gegenüber Trägern gesellschaftlicher Macht?' in Diether Posser and Rudolf Wassermann (eds.), *Freiheit in der sozialen Demokratie. 4. Rechtspolitischer Kongreß der SPD vom 6. bis 8.6.1975 in Düsseldorf. Dokumentation* (Karlsruhe: C. F. Müller, 1975), pp. 77–89.
51. 'Keine Chance für eine gemeinsame Regelung? Gedanken zur abschließenden Beratung der Reform des Abtreibungsstrafrechts', *Stuttgarter Zeitung*, 12 February 1976, p. 6.
52. 'Die Methoden der Verfassungsinterpretation – Bestandsaufnahme und Kritik', *Neue Juristische Wochenschrift* (1976), pp. 2089–2099. Also published in A 17, A 27.
53. 'Die politische Funktion wirtschaftlich-sozialer Verbände und Interessenträger in der sozialstaatlichen Demokratie. Ein Beitrag zum Problem der "Regierbarkeit"', *Der Staat* 15 (1976), pp. 457–483. Also published in A 17.
    a. Shortened preprint published in *Frankfurter Allgemeine Zeitung*, 22 December 1976, p. 11.
    b. Also published in
    – Wilhelm Hennis, Peter Graf Kielmansegg, and Ulrich Matz (eds.), *Regierbarkeit. Studien zu ihrer Problematisierung* (Stuttgart: Klett-Cotta, 1977), pp. 223–254; and

- Rudolf Steinberg (ed.), *Staat und Verbände. Zur Theorie der Interessenverbände in der Industriegesellschaft* (Darmstadt: Wissenschaftliche Buchgesellschaft, 1985), pp. 305–340.

54. 'Einleitung', in Ernst-Wolfgang Böckenförde (ed.), *Staat und Gesellschaft* (Darmstadt: Wissenschaftliche Buchgesellschaft, 1976), pp. XI–XVI.

55. 'Zum Verhältnis von Kirche und moderner Welt', in Reinhart Koselleck (ed.), *Studien zum Beginn der modernen Welt* (Stuttgart: Klett-Cotta, 1977), pp. 154–177. Also published in A 14.

56. 'Die stufenweise Auflösung der Einheit von geistlich-religiöser und weltlich-politischer Ordnung in der Verfassungsentwicklung der Neuzeit', in Gerhard Dilcher and Norbert Horn (eds.), *Sozialwissenschaften im Studium des Rechts. Vol. 4 Rechtsgeschichte* (Munich: C. H. Beck, 1977), pp. 43–53.

57. 'Laudatio auf Prof. Dr. Niklas Luhmann (217. Sitzung der Rheinisch-Westfälischen Akademie der Wissenschaften am 15.12.1976)', in s. ed., *Jahrbuch 1976 der Rheinisch-Westfälischen Akademie der Wissenschaften* (Opladen: Westdeutscher Verlag, 1977), pp. 70–73.

58. 'Überlegungen und Empfehlungen der Enquete-Kommission Verfassungsreform zur demokratisch-parlamentarischen Verfassungsorganisation', in Ernst-Wolfgang Böckenförde and Klaus Stern (eds.), *Überlegungen zur Verfassungsreform. Empfehlungen der Enquete-Kommission des Deutschen Bundestages* (Hanover: Niedersächsische Landeszentrale für Politische Bildung, 1977), pp. 7–40. Also published as 'Überlegungen und Empfehlungen der Enquete-Kommission. Verfassungsreform im Hinblick auf die demokratisch-parlamentarische Verfassungsorganisation', in Ernst-Wolfgang Böckenförde and Klaus Stern (eds.), *Die Ergebnisse der Enquete-Kommission Verfassungsreform und die verfassungsrechtliche Fortentwicklung der Bundesrepublik* (Cologne: Grote, 1977), pp. 23–50.

59. 'Parlamentarische Untersuchungsausschüsse und kommunale Selbstverwaltung', *Archiv des öffentlichen Rechts* 103 (1978), pp. 1–42.

60. 'Der Staat als sittlicher Staat', *Neue Zürcher Zeitung*, 29 April 1978, p. 29. The article contains excerpts of A 9.

61. 'Der vernünftige Staat – Aufgaben und Grenzen', *Deutsches Allgemeines Sonntagsblatt* 20, 14 May 1978, p. 10. The article contains revised excerpts of A 9.

62. 'Verhaltensgewähr oder Gesinnungstreue? Sicherung der freiheitlichen Demokratie in den Formen des Rechtsstaats', *Frankfurter Allgemeine* Zeitung, 8 December 1978, pp. 9–10. Also published in A 17. Also published in Hans Koschnick (ed.), *Der Abschied vom Extremisten-Beschluß* (Bonn: Verlag Neue Gesellschaft, 1979), pp. 76–80.

63. 'Der Staat als Organismus. Zur staatstheoretischen Diskussion in der Vormärzzeit', *Neue Zürcher Zeitung*, 16./17 December 1978, p. 61. Also published in A 16.

64. 'Organ, Organismus, Organisation, politischer Körper (Abschnitt VI–IX)', in Otto Brunner et al. (eds.), *Geschichtliche Grundbegriffe. Historisches Lexikon zur*

politisch-sozialen Sprache in Deutschland. Vol. 4 (Mi–Pre) (Stuttgart: Klett-Cotta, 1978), pp. 561–622.

65. 'Der verdrängte Ausnahmezustand. Zum Handeln der Staatsgewalt in außergewöhnlichen Lagen', *Neue Juristische Wochenschrift* (1978), pp. 1881–1890.
66. 'Elternrecht – Recht des Kindes – Recht des Staates', in Jospeh Krautscheidt and Heiner Marré (eds.), *Essener Gespräche zum Verhältnis von Staat und Kirche. Vol. 14* (Münster: Aschendorff, 1980), pp. 54–98 (comments on pp. 104–127). Partly published in *Internationale Katholische Zeitschrift* issue 4 (1979), pp. 320–336.
67. 'Zur verfassungsrechtlichen Beurteilung der Unverjährbarkeit des Mordes', *Zeitschrift für die gesamte Strafrechtswissenschaft* 91 (1979), pp. 889–901. Shortened version published as 'Wo das Grundgesetz den Verjährungsstreit begrenzt. Zur Verfassungsmäßigkeit der von der SPD und von Prof. Maihofer gewünschten Regelung', *Frankfurter Allgemeine* Zeitung, 30 June 1979, p. 6.
68. 'Das neue politische Engagement der Kirche. Zur "politischen Theologie" Johannes Pauls II', *Stimmen der Zeit* issue 4 (1980), pp. 219–234. Also published in A 13, A 23. Shortened version published in *Neue Zürcher Zeitung*, 26/27 January 1980, p. 67.
69. 'Rechtsstaat und Ausnahmerecht. Eine Erwiderung', *Zeitschrift für Parlamentsfragen* 4 (1980), pp. 591–595.
70. Co-authored with Franz Böckle, Bernhard Stöckle, and Hans F. Zacher, 'Der "Wahlhirtenbrief" 1980. Eine Anfrage an die deutschen Bischöfe', *Herder-Korrespondenz* 34:11 (1980), pp. 570–573.
71. 'Zum Ende des Schulgebetsstreits. Stellungnahme zum Beschluß des BVerfG vom 16.10.1978', *Die Öffentliche Verwaltung* (1980), pp. 323–327.
72. 'Sozialer Bundesstaat und parlamentarische Demokratie. Zum Verhältnis von Parlamentarismus und Föderalismus unter den Bedingungen des Sozialstaates', in Jürgen Jekewitz, Michael Melzer, and Wolfgang Zeh (eds.), *Politik als gelebte Verfassung. Aktuelle Probleme des modernen Verfassungsstaates. Festschrift für Friedrich Schäfer* (Opladen: Westdeutscher Verlag, 1980), pp. 182–199. Also published in A 19.
73. 'Die sozialen Grundrechte im Verfassungsgefüge', in Ernst-Wolfgang Böckenförde, Jürgen Jekewitz, and Thilo Ramm (eds.), *Soziale Grundrechte. Von der bürgerlichen zur sozialen Rechtsordnung. 5. Rechtspolitischer Kongreß der SPD, 1980. Dokumentation Teil 2* (Heidelberg: C. F. Müller, 1981), pp. 7–16. Also published in A 16. Shortened preprint published as 'Was nützen soziale Grundrechte? Etwas anderes als Freiheitsrechte – und nicht nur ein "Programm guter Politik"', *Frankfurter Allgemeine Zeitung*, 27 February 1980, p. 11.
74. 'Politische Theorie und politische Theologie. Bemerkungen zu ihrem gegenseitigen Verhältnis', *Revue européenne des sciences sociales* 19:54/55 (1981), pp. 233–243.
    a. Shortened version published as 'Politische Theologie – Begriff und Bedeutung', *Neue Zürcher Zeitung*, 30/31 May 1981, p. 69.
    b. Also published in Jacob Taubes (ed.), *Der Fürst dieser Welt. Carl Schmitt und die Folgen* (Paderborn: Schöningh/Fink, 1983), pp. 16–25. Also published in A 13, A 23.

75. 'Ausnahmerecht und demokratischer Rechtsstaat', in Hans-Jochen Vogel, Helmut Simon, and Adalbert Podlech (eds.), *Die Freiheit des Anderen. Festschrift für Martin Hirsch* (Baden-Baden: Nomos Verlag, 1981), pp. 259–272.
76. 'Ethische und politische Grundsatzfragen zur Zeit', *Herder Korrespondenz* issue 7 (July 1981), pp. 342–348. Also published in A 13, A 23.
77. 'Rechtsstaatliche politische Selbstverteidigung als Problem', in Friedrich-Ebert-Stiftung (ed.), *Extremisten und öffentlicher Dienst. Studie der Friedrich-Ebert-Stiftung* (Baden-Baden: Nomos Verlag, 1981), pp. 9–33.
78. 'Weimar – Vom Ende einer zu früh gekommenen Demokratie', *Die Öffentliche Verwaltung* 34 (1981), pp. 946–949.
79. 'Zur Diskussion um die Totalrevision der Schweizerischen Bundesverfassung', *Archiv des öffentlichen Rechts* 106 (1981), pp. 580–603.
80. 'Nekrolog. Ulrich Scheuner (1903-1981)', *Historische Zeitschrift* 234 (1982), pp. 251–254.
81. 'Mittelbare / repräsentative Demokratie als eigentliche Form der Demokratie. Bemerkungen zu Begriff und Verwirklichungsproblemen der Demokratie als Staats- und Regierungsform', in Georg Müller et al. (eds.), *Staatsorganisation und Staatsfunktionen im Wandel. Festschrift für Kurt Eichenberger* (Basel: Helbing & Lichtenhahn, 1982), pp. 301–328.
82. Co-authored with Joachim Wieland, 'Die "Rundfunkfreiheit" – ein Grundrecht? Überlegungen zu den verfassungsrechtlichen Vorgaben in Art. 5 Abs. 1 GG für die Organisation des Rundfunks', *Archiv für Presserecht* 13 (1982), pp. 77–85.
83. 'Staat – Gesellschaft – Kirche', in Ernst-Wolfgang Böckenförde and Konrad Deufel (eds.), *Christlicher Glaube in moderner Gesellschaft. Vol. 15* (Freiburg: Herder, 1982), pp. 5–120. Also published in A 14.
84. 'Über die Schwierigkeit, ein Versprechen einzulösen', *Badische Zeitung*, 16 November 1982, p. 6.
85. 'Bemerkungen zum Verhältnis von Staat und Religion bei Hegel', *Der Staat* 21 (1982), pp. 481–503. Also published in A 16.
86. 'Die Eigenart des Staatsrechts und der Staatsrechtswissenschaft', in Norbert Achterberg, Werner Krawietz, and Dieter Wyduckel (eds.), *Recht und Staat im sozialen Wandel. Festschrift für Hans Ulrich Scupin zum 80. Geburtstag* (Berlin: Duncker & Humblot, 1983), pp. 317–331. Also published in A 17.
87. 'Das "C" ist kein Papiertiger! Wenn ein Christ Politik macht', *Publik-Forum* 5, 4 March 1983, pp. 3–5.
88. 'Garantie für Recht und Freiheit', *Badische Zeitung*, 11 April 1983.
89. 'Geschichtliche Entwicklung und Bedeutungswandel der Verfassung', in Arno Buschmann et al. (eds.), *Festschrift für Rudolf Gmür zum 70. Geburtstag am 28.7.1983* (Bielefeld: Gieseking, 1983), pp. 7–19. Expanded and revised version published in *Juristische Arbeitsblätter* 1984, pp. 325–332. Also published in A 17.
90. 'Steuergerechtigkeit und Familienlastenausgleich', *Frankfurter Rundschau* 24 October 1983, p. 14. Also published in *Stimme der Familie* 11 (1983), pp. 129–132; and *Steuer und Wirtschaft* 63 (1986), pp. 335–340.

91. 'Die Ausgestaltung der Souveränität. Demokratie und Repräsentation in der Gegenwart', *Neue Zürcher Zeitung*, 26/27 November 1983, pp. 69–70. Preprint of excerpts of A 10.
92. 'Religionsfreiheit zwischen Kirche und Staat', *Gewissen und Freiheit* 22 (1984), pp. 13–31. Slightly expanded and slightly revised version published as 'Die Religionsfreiheit im Spannungsfeld zwischen Kirche und Staat', in A 14.
93. 'Johannes Popitz. Der Staatsbegriff als allgemeingültiger Begriff. Eine Dokumentation. Einleitung', *Der Staat* 23 (1984), pp. 227–232.
94. 'Normativismus', in Joachim Ritter and Karlfried Gründer (eds.), *Historisches Wörterbuch der Philosophie. Vol. 6* (Basel: Schwabe, 1984), pp. 931–932.
95. 'Ordnungsdenken, konkretes', in Joachim Ritter and Karlfried Gründer (eds.), *Historisches Wörterbuch der Philosophie. Vol. 6*,,B(asel: Schwabe, 1984), pp. 1311–1313.
96. 'Das Bild vom Menschen in der Perspektive der heutigen Rechtsordnung', in Krzysztof Michalski (ed.), *Der Mensch in den modernen Wissenschaften. Castelgandolfo-Gespräche 1983* (Stuttgart: Klett-Cotta, 1985), pp. 91–99. Also published in A 16.
97. 'Der Zusammenbruch der Monarchie und die Entstehung der Weimarer Republik', in Kurt G. A. Jeserich, Hans Pohl, and Georg-Christoph von Unruh (eds.), *Deutsche Verwaltungsgeschichte. Vol. 4* (Stuttgart: Deutsche Verlagsanstalt, 1985), pp. 1–23. Also published in A 16.
    a. Excerpts published as 'Brückenbauer zwischen Revolution und Legitimität', *Frankfurter Allgemeine* Zeitung, 26 November 1983, p. 11.
    b. Slightly revised version published in Karl Dietrich Bracher, Manfred Funke, and Hans-Adolf Jacobsen (eds.), *Die Weimarer Republik 1918–1933. Politik – Wirtschaft – Gesellschaft* (Bonn: Bundeszentrale für politische Bildung, 1987), pp. 17–44.
98. 'Widerstand', in Thomas Meyer et al. (eds.), *Lexikon des Sozialismus* (Cologne: Bund-Verlag, 1985), p. 712.
99. 'Die Bedeutung der Konzilserklärung über die Religionsfreiheit. Überlegungen 20 Jahre danach', *Stimmen der Zeit* issue 5 (1986), pp. 303–312. Also published in A 14. Slightly shortened version published in *Neue Zürcher Zeitung*, 12/13 July 1986, p. 58; and in *Deutsche Tagespost*, 18 April 1987, p. 21.
100. 'Gerhard Anschütz – 1867–1948', in Wilhelm Doerr (ed.), *Semper Apertus. Sechshundert Jahre Ruprecht-Karls-Universität Heidelberg 1386–1986 –Festschrift in sechs Bänden. Vol. 3* (Berlin: Springer, 1986), pp. 167–175. Also published in A 16.
101. 'Kirche und modernes Bewußtsein', in Peter Koslowski, Robert Spaemann, and Reinhard Löw (eds.), *Moderne und Postmoderne? Zur Signatur des gegenwärtigen Zeitalters* (Weinheim: VCH Verlag, 1986), pp. 103–129. Also published in *Internationale katholische Zeitschrift Communio* 15:2 (1986), pp. 153–168.
102. 'Freiheit und Recht. Freiheit und Staat' (with assistance from Christoph Enders), in Görres-Gesellschaft (ed.), *Staatslexikon. 2. Vols.* (Freiburg: Herder, 1986), pp. 704–713. Also published in A 16.

103. 'Recht und Liebe', in Ulrich Ruh, David Seeber, and Rudolf Walter (eds.), *Handwörterbuch religiöser Gegenwartsfragen* (Freiburg: Herder, 1986), pp. 386–390.
104. 'Die Krise in der Rechtsordnung: Der Ausnahmezustand', in Krzysztof Michalski (ed.), *Über die Krise. Castelgandolfo-Gespräche 1985* (Stuttgart: Klett-Cotta, 1986), pp. 183–191.
105. 'Kritik der Wertbegründung des Rechts. Überlegungen zu einem Kapitel "Rechtsphilosophie" ', in Reinhard Löw (ed.), *Einwohnung. Festschrift für Robert Spaemann* (Weinheim: VCH Verlag, 1987), pp. 1–21.
    a. Revised and expanded version published as 'Die Begründung des Rechts auf Werte oder auf das von Natur Rechte', in Richard Brinkmann, Alfred Gierer, Walter Jens (eds.), *Natur in den Geisteswissenschaften. Erstes Blaubeurer Symposion. Vol. 1* (Tübingen: Attempto, 1988), pp. 181–202.
    b. Excerpt of (a) published as 'Die Begründung des Rechts auf Werte. Eine Kritik aus juristischer Sicht', *Neue Zürcher Zeitung*, 17/18 December 1988, p. 65.
    c. Revised and expanded version published as 'Zur Kritik der Wertbegründung des Rechts', in Ralf Dreier (ed.), *Rechtspositivismus und Wertbezug des Rechts. Vorträge der Tagung der deutschen Sektion der internationalen Vereinigung für Rechts- und Sozialphilosofie (IVR) in der Bundesrepublik Deutschland* (Stuttgart: Franz Steiner Verlag, 1990), pp. 33–46. Also published in A 16.
106. 'Demokratie als Verfassungsprinzip', in Josef Isensee and Paul Kirchhof (eds.), *Handbuch des Staatsrechts der Bundesrepublik Deutschland. Vol. 1 Grundlagen von Staat und Verfassung* (Heidelberg: C. F. Müller, 1987), pp. 887–952. Revised version published in A 17.
107. 'Demokratische Willensbildung und Repräsentation', in Josef Isensee and Paul Kirchhof (eds.), *Handbuch des Staatsrechts der Bundesrepublik Deutschland. Vol. 2 Demokratische Willensbildung. Die Staatsorgane des Bundes* (Heidelberg: C. F. Müller, 1987), pp. 29–48.
108. 'Der Begriff des Politischen als Schlüssel zum staatsrechtlichen Werk Carl Schmitts', in Helmut Quaritsch (ed.), *Complexio Oppositorum. Über Carl Schmitt. Vorträge und Diskussionsbeiträge des 28. Sonderseminars 1986 der Hochschule für Verwaltungswissenschaften Speyer* (Berlin: Duncker & Humblot, 1988), pp. 283–299 (comments on pp. 302–303, 314–318). Expanded version published in A 16.
109. 'Erinnerungen an Franz Schnabel', in Historische Kommission bei der Bayerischen Akademie der Wissenschaften (ed.), *Franz Schnabel – zu Leben und Werk (1887–1966). Vorträge zur Feier seines 100. Geburtstages* (Munich: Oldenbourg, 1988), pp. 15–25.
110. 'Staat und Gesellschaft', in Görres-Gesellschaft (ed.), *Staatslexikon. Vol. 5* (Freiburg: Herder, 1989), pp. 228–235.
111. 'Stellung und Bedeutung der Religion in einer "Civil Society" ', *Internationale katholische Zeitschrift Communio* 18:6 (1989), pp. 584–597. Also published in A 19.
112. 'Die sozialen und politischen Ordnungsideen der Französischen Revolution', *Neue Zürcher Zeitung*, 16/17 September 1989, p. 66. Slightly revised version published in Krzysztof Michalski (ed.), *Europa und die Civil Society. Castelgandolfo-Gespräche 1989. Vol. 4* (Stuttgart: Klett-Cotta, 1991), pp. 103–117. Also published in A 18.

113. 'Grundrechte als Grundsatznormen. Zur gegenwärtigen Lage der Grundrechtsdogmatik', *Der Staat* 1 (1990), pp. 1–31. Also published in A 17, A 27.

114. Co-authored with Dieter Grimm, 'Nachdenken über Deutschland', *Der Spiegel* 10 (1990), pp. 72–77.

115. 'Religionsfreiheit', in Hans Gasper, Joachim Müller, and Friederike Valentin (eds.), *Lexikon der Sekten, Sondergruppen und Weltanschauungen* (Freiburg: Herder, 1990), pp. 880–885.

116. 'Freiheit und Recht. Einige Überlegungen zu ihrem Verhältnis', *Neue Zürcher Zeitung*, 22/23 September 1990, p. 69. Also published as 'Freiheit und Recht sind nicht selbstverständlich', in Zentralkomitee der deutschen Katholiken (ed.), *Wie im Himmel so auf Erden. 90. Deutscher Katholikentag. Berlin, Dokumentation I* (Paderborn: Bonifatius, 1991), pp. 401–404.

117. 'Die Schweiz – Vorbild für Europa?', *Neue Zürcher Zeitung*, 13 December 1991, p. 37. Also published in A 17.

118. Co-authored with Edward Shils, 'Introduction', in Ernst-Wolfgang Böckenförde and Edward Shils (eds.), *Jews and Christians in a Pluralistic World* (London: Weidenfeld & Nicolson, 1991), pp. xi–xv.

119. 'Nationen und Nationalstaaten. Die Ordnung Europas am Scheideweg', in Hilmar Hoffmann and Dieter Kramer (eds.), *Das verunsicherte Europa. Römerberggespräche Frankfurt 1992* (Frankfurt: Anton Hain, 1992), pp. 77–88.

120. 'Erinnerung an die Kurator-Verfassung', in Andreas Dress et al. (eds.), *Die humane Universität Bielefeld 1969–1992. Festschrift für Karl Peter Grotemeyer* (Bielefeld: Westfalen Verlag, 1992), pp. 151–159.

121. 'Der Beitrag politischen Handelns zur Verwirklichung von Gerechtigkeit', in Wilhelm Ernst (ed.), *Gerechtigkeit in Gesellschaft, Wirtschaft und Politik* (Fribourg: Universitäts-Verlag, 1992; Freiburg: Herder, 1992), pp. 149–173. Partly published in *TRANSIT. Europäische Revue* issue 4 (1992), pp. 28–45.
    a. Revised and shortened version published as 'Nicht Machterhalt ist das Ziel der Politik, sondern Gerechtigkeit', *Frankfurter Allgemeine Magazin* issue 676, 12 February 1993, pp. 22–28.
    b. Also published in U. Wickert, *Das Buch der Tugenden* (Hamburg: Hoffmann und Campe, 1995), pp. 347–360.

122. 'Autorität – Gewissen – Normfindung. Thesen zur weiteren Diskussion', in
    a. Josef Römelt and Bruno Hidber (eds.), *Christus zum Leben befreit. Für Bernhard Häring* (Freiburg: Herder, 1992) pp. 131–138. Also published in A 23.
    b. Also published in *Neue Zürcher Zeitung* 247, 23/24 October 1993, p. 59.

123. 'Anmerkungen zum Begriff Verfassungswandel', in Peter Badura and Rupert Scholz (eds.), *Wege und Verfahren des Verfassungslebens. Festschrift für Peter Lerche zum 65. Geburtstag* (Munich: C. H. Beck, 1993), pp. 3–14. Also published in A 19. Also published in Bernd Guggenberger and Thomas Würtenberger (eds.), *Hüter der Verfassung oder Lenker der Politik? Das Bundesverfassungsgericht im Widerstreit. Interdisziplinäres Forum: Bürger und Recht 2000. Vol. 1* (Baden-Baden: Nomos Verlag, 1998) pp. 44–56.

124. 'Rechtsstaat', in Joachim Ritter and Karlfried Gründer (eds.), *Historisches Wörterbuch der Philosophie. Vol. 8 (R–Sc)* (Basel: Schwabe, 1993), pp. 332–342.

125. 'Begegnungen mit Adolf Arndt', in Claus Arndt (ed.), *Adolf Arndt zum 90. Geburtstag. Dokumentation der Festakademie in der Katholischen Akademie Hamburg* (Bonn: Friedrich-Ebert-Stiftung, 1995), pp. 32–39.

126. 'Zur Funktion des Rechts für die Reform staatlicher Institutionen', in Georg Müller et al. (eds.), *Zur Funktion des Rechts für die Reform staatlicher Institutionen. Symposium zum 70. Geburtstag von Kurt Eichenberger. Referate und Diskussionen vom 11./12. Juni 1992 in Lenzburg* (Basel: Helbing & Lichtenhahn, 1993), pp. 34–57.

127. 'Die Nation – Identität in Differenz', in Krzysztof Michalski (ed.), *Identität im Wandel. Castelgandolfo-Gespräche. Vol. 6* (Stuttgart: Klett-Cotta, 1995), pp. 129–154. Also published in A 19.
    a. Also published in *Universitas* 50:592 (1995), pp. 974–991.
    b. Revised and shortened version published as 'Die Nation. Jenseits von Herkunft, Muttersprache und Religion: Über ein Phänomen, das selbst die Merkmale bestimmt, die es bestimmen', *Frankfurter Allgemeine Zeitung* 228, 30 September 1995, p. 15. Also published in
    – Thomas Brose (ed.), *Deutsches Neuland. Beiträge aus Religion und Gesellschaft* (Leipzig: Benno, 1996), pp. 17–29; and
    – Dieter Gutzen (ed.), *Les repercussions de l'unification en Allemagne* (Paris: Presses Universitaires de France, 1996), pp. 17–29.

128. 'Staatliches Recht und sittliche Ordnung', in Hermann Fechtrup, Friedbert Schulze, and Thomas Sternberg (eds.), *Aufklärung durch Tradition. Symposion der Josef Pieper Stiftung zum 90. Geburtstag von Josef Pieper (Mai 1994 in Münster)* (Münster: LIT Verlag, 1995), pp. 87–107. Revised version published in A 19.

129. 'Von welchen Ressourcen leben wir? Erfolg und Herausforderungen der Aufklärung', *Neue Zürcher Zeitung* 116, 20/21 May 1995, p. 66.
    a. Also published as 'Erfolge und Grenzen der Aufklärung. Acht Thesen', *Universitas* 50:8 (1995), pp. 720–726.
    b. Revised version published as 'Fundamente der Freiheit', in Erwin Teufel (ed.), *Was hält die moderne Gesellschaft zusammen?* (Frankfurt: Suhrkamp, 1996), pp. 91–99.

130. 'Demokratie', in Walter Kasper et al. (eds.), *Lexikon für Theologie und Kirche. Vol. 3* (Freiburg: Herder, 1995), pp. 83–87.

131. 'Was heißt eigentlich "politisch"?' in Jürgen Manemann et al. (eds.), *Jahrbuch Politische Theologie. Vol. 1 Demokratiefähigkeit* (Münster: LIT Verlag, 1996), pp. 2–5.

132. 'Religion im säkularen Staat', *Universitas* 51:604 (1996), pp. 990–998.

133. 'Die Überlastung des Bundesverfassungsgerichts', *Zeitschrift für Rechtspolitik* 29 (1996), pp. 281–284. Shortened preprint published as 'Dem Bundesverfassungsgericht droht der Kollaps', *Frankfurter Allgemeine Zeitung*, 24 May 1996, pp. 8–9.

134. 'Zur Idee der Verfassungsgerichtsbarkeit im demokratischen Staat', *Justizblatt* 50:10, 3 July 1996.

135. 'Das Unwahrscheinliche wollen', *Frankfurter Allgemeine* Zeitung, 2 May 1996, p. 6.

   a. Expanded version published as 'Ist die Demokratie eine notwendige Forderung der Menschenrechte?', in Georg Lohmann and Stefan Gosepath (eds.), *Philosophie der Menschenrechte* (Frankfurt: Suhrkamp, 1998), pp. 233–243. Also published in A 19.

   b. Preprint published in *MUT – Forum für Kultur, Politik und Geschichte* issue 353 (1997), pp. 50–55.

136. 'Christliche Werte in der Politik', *IWM-Newsletter* (Institut für die Wissenschaft vom Menschen) issue 55 (1996), pp. 4–5.

137. 'Juristenausbildung – auf dem Weg ins Abseits?', *Juristen-Zeitung* 52 (1997), pp. 317–326.

   a. Preprint in excerpts published as 'Weniger büffeln, mehr begreifen', *Frankfurter Allgemeine Zeitung*, 26 October 1996, p. 12.

   b. Also published in Dieter Strempel (ed.), *Juristenausbildung zwischen Internationalität und Individualität. Auch ein Problem der Gesetzgebung* (Baden-Baden: Nomos Verlag, 1998), pp. 63–88.

138. 'Die Verfolgung der deutschen Juden als Bürgerverrat', *Merkur* 51:575 (1997), pp. 165–70. Slightly expanded version published in *MUT – Forum für Kultur, Politik und Geschichte* 363 (1997), pp. 36–45. Also published in A 19.

139. 'Recht setzt Grenzen. Warum Entgrenzungen freiheitswidrig sein können', *Neue Zürcher Zeitung* 32, 8/9 February 1997, p. 70.

   a. Reprinted as 'Recht setzt Grenzen', in Ernst Ulrich von Weizsäcker (ed.), *Grenzen-los? Jedes System braucht Grenzen – aber wie durchlässig müssen diese sein?* (Berlin: Birkhäuser, 1997), pp. 272–284.

   b. Slightly expanded version published as 'Kein Spiel ohne Grenzen', *Die politische Meinung* 43:340 (1998), pp. 5–13.

   c. Also published as 'Recht als Bedingung der Freiheit. Grenzen im Prozeß der Globalisierung', *MUT – Forum für Kultur, Politik und Geschichte* issue 379 (1999), pp. 6–17. Slightly shortened version published in A 19.

140. 'Auf dem Weg zum Klassiker. Carl Schmitt in der Diskussion: Politische Theologie als Fluchtpunkt seines Werks', *Frankfurter Allgemeine Zeitung* 158, 11 July 1997, p. 35.

141. 'Wenn der europäische Stier vom goldenen Kalb überholt wird', *Frankfurter Allgemeine Zeitung* 169, 24 July 1997, p. 30. Shortened preprint of A 18.

142. 'Begriff und Probleme des Verfassungsstaates', in Rudolf Morsey, Helmut Quaritsch, and Heinrich Siedentopf (eds.), *Staat, Politik, Verwaltung in Europa. Gedächtnisschrift für Roman Schnur* (Berlin: Duncker & Humblot, 1997), pp. 137–149. Also published in A 19.

143. 'Ebert, die Räte und die alten Gewalten', *Das Parlament* 3–4, 16 January 1998, p. 15. Partial reprint of B 95 b.

144. 'Die Zukunft politischer Autonomie. Demokratie und Staatlichkeit im Zeichen von Globalisierung, Europäisierung und Individualisierung', in Martin Meyer and Georg Kohler (eds.), *Die Schweiz – für Europa? Über Kultur und Politik*, Munich: Carl Hanser Verlag, 1998, pp. 63–90. Also published in A 19.

145. 'Regierungsfähigkeit zwischen Verfassung und politischer Verantwortung', in Bertelsmann Stiftung (ed.), *Demokratie neu denken. Verfassungspolitik und Regierungsfähigkeit in Deutschland* (Gütersloh: Verlag Bertelsmann Stiftung, 1998) pp. 83–94.
146. 'Verfassungsgerichtsbarkeit. Strukturfragen, Organisation, Legitimation', *Neue Juristische Wochenschrift* 52:1 (1999), pp. 9–17. Also published in A 19.
147. 'Organisationsgewalt und Gesetzesvorbehalt (Besprechung von NWVerfGH, Urteil vom 9.2.1999, VerfGH 11/98)', *Neue Juristische Wochenschrift* issue 17 (1999), pp. 1235–1236.
148. 'Als Christ im Amt eines Verfassungsrichters', in Ernst-Wolfgang Böckenförde and Annette Schavan (eds.), *Salz der Erde. Christliche Spiritualität in der Welt von heute* (Stuttgart: Schwabenverlag, 1999), pp. 14–28. Also published in A 23.
149. 'Rechtsstaat', in Michael Buchberger et al. (eds.), *Lexikon für Theologie und Kirche. Vol. 8* (Freiburg: Herder, 1999), pp. 914–916.
150. 'Überlegungen zu einer Theologie des modernen säkularen Rechts. Vortrag anlässlich der Ehrenpromotion am 12. Mai 1999', in s. ed., *Universitätsreden. Neue Serie 9* (Bochum: Ruhr-Universität, 1999), pp. 27–50. Also published in A 23.
    a. Slightly shortened version published as 'Zur Theologie des modernen säkularen Rechts', *Stimmen der Zeit* 217:9 (1999), pp. 579–596.
    b. Excerpt published as 'Die Macht der Entzweiung. Überlegungen zu einer Theologie des säkularen Rechts', *Neue Zürcher Zeitung* 139, 19/20 June 1999, pp. 53–54.
151. 'Toleranz – Leidensgeschichte der christlichen Kirchen', *MUT – Forum für Kultur, Politik und Geschichte* issue 386 (1999), pp. 54–63.
152. 'Stellungnahme zu: "Der freiheitliche, säkularisierte Staat lebt von Voraussetzungen, die er selbst nicht garantieren kann" (Beitrag von Frau Ursula Neumann)', *Ethik und Unterricht* 1 (1999), p. 43.
153. 'Vier Thesen zur Kommunitarismusdebatte', in Peter Siller and Bertram Keller (eds.), *Rechtsphilosophische Kontroversen der Gegenwart* (Baden-Baden: Nomos Verlag, 1999), pp. 83–86.
154. 'Kommentar zu Ulrich K. Preuß. Auf der Suche nach Europas Verfassung', *TRANSIT. Europäische Revue* issue 17 (1999), pp. 175–179.
155. 'Wie viel Staat die Gesellschaft braucht', *Süddeutsche Zeitung*, 8 November 1999, p. 12. Also published in A 27.
156. 'Die Krise unserer Demokratie verlangt eine Rückbildung des Parteienstaates', *Frankfurter Allgemeine* Zeitung, 14 February 2000, p. 3. Also published in Günther Nonnenmacher (ed.), *Die gespendete Macht* (Berlin: Alexander Fest Verlag, 2000), pp. 55–62.
157. 'Notwendigkeit und Grenzen staatlicher Religionspolitik', in Wolfgang Thierse (ed.), *Religion ist keine Privatsache* (Düsseldorf: Patmos Verlag, 2000), pp. 173–184.
158. 'Schmitt, Carl', in Michael Buchberger et al. (eds.), *Lexikon für Theologie und Kirche. Vol. 9* (Freiburg: Herder, 2000), pp. 183–184.
159. 'Józef Tischner (Nachruf)', *Tygodnik Dowszechny*, 16 July 2000, p. 11.
160. ' "Kopftuchstreit" auf dem richtigen Weg?' *Neue Juristische Wochenschrift* 54:10 (2001), pp. 723–728.

161. 'Reichtum – mehr als Wohlstand', in Markus Schächter (ed.), *Was kommt, was geht, was bleibt* (Freiburg: Herder, 2001), pp. 263–266.
162. 'Recht und Gewissen', *Konradsblatt. Wochenzeitung für das Erzbistum Freiburg* 13, 1 April 2001, p. 21.
163. 'Der Verlust des Standhaften in jeder Hinsicht. Das Bild vom Menschen im gegenwärtigen Recht', *Frankfurter Allgemeine Zeitung* 172, 27 July 2001, p. 7. Preprint in excerpts of A 20.
164. 'Bedürftigkeit und Selbstbestimmung. Recht und Menschenbild in historischer Perspektive', *Neue Zürcher Zeitung* 103, 5/6 May 2001, p. 50. Preprint in excerpts of A 20.
165. 'Die Frucht einer verbotenen Tat. Wie weit reicht der Achtungsanspruch der Menschenwürde?', *Süddeutsche Zeitung* issue 23, 28 January 2002, p. 9. Also published as 'Unscheinbare Konsequenz. Embryonenforschung: Wie weit reicht die Achtung vor der Würde des Menschen', *MUT – Forum für Kultur, Politik und Geschichte* issue 416 (2002), pp. 10–17.
166. 'Hat das geltende Recht seine Orientierung verloren?', *Akademische Monatsblätter* issue 1 (2002), pp. 7–8.
167. 'Mehr als die Abwesenheit von Krieg. Der Westfälische Frieden als Modell einer Friedensordnung', *Neue Zürcher Zeitung* 213, 14/15 September 2002, p. 74.
168. 'Schutzbereich und Eingriff. Zur Kritik gegenwärtiger Grundrechtsdogmatik', in Ernst-Wolfgang Böckenförde, David Edward, and Erich Schumann (eds.), *Grundrechte in Deutschland und Europa* (Münster: LIT Verlag, 2002), pp. 11–28. Revised and expanded version published as 'Schutzbereich, Eingriff, verfassungsimmanente Schranken – Zur Kritik gegenwärtiger Grundrechtsdogmatik', *Der Staat* 42 (2003), pp. 165–192. Also published in A 27.
169. 'Gemeinwohlvorstellungen bei Klassikern der Rechts- und Staatsphilosophie', in Herfried Münkler and Karsten Fischer (eds.), *Gemeinwohl und Gemeinsinn im Recht. Konkretisierung und Realisierung öffentlicher Interessen* (Berlin: Akademie Verlag, 2002), pp. 43–65.
170. 'Einführung', in Ulrich Ruh (ed.), *Johannes Paul II., Gewissen der Welt* (Freiburg: Herder, 2002), pp. 9–21.
171. 'Der freiheitliche säkularisierte Staat . . . ', in Susanna Schmidt and Michael Wedell (eds.), *Um der Freiheit willen . . . ! Kirche und Staat im 21. Jahrhundert. Festschrift für Burkhard Reichert* (Freiburg: Herder, 2002), pp. 19–23.
172. 'Religion im säkularen Staat', in Rainer Isak and Hansjörg Schmid (eds.), *Christen und Muslime in Deutschland. Religion – Gesellschaft – säkularer Staat* (Freiburg: Verlag der Katholischen Akademie, 2003), pp. 11–25.
173. 'Die Bedeutung der Geisteswissenschaften im politischen Leben', in Florian Keisinger, Steffen Seischab, and Angelika Steinacher (eds.), *Wozu Geisteswissenschaften? Kontroverse Argumente für eine überfällige Debatte* (Frankfurt: Campus, 2003), pp. 48–50.
174. 'Menschenwürde als normatives Prinzip', *Juristenzeitung* issue 58 (2003), pp. 809–815. Shortened preprint published as 'Menschenwürde – Dasein um seiner selbst willen', *Deutsches Ärzteblatt* issue 100 (2003), pp. 1246–1249.

175. 'Die Würde des Menschen war unantastbar', *Frankfurter Allgemeine Zeitung* 204, 3 September 2003, pp. 33–35. Also published in Deutscher Hochschulverband (ed.), *Glanzlichter der Wissenschaft 2003. Ein Almanach* (Bonn: Lucius und Lucius, 2003), pp. 25–31. Also published in A 16.

176. 'Was ist sozial gerecht?', *Frankfurter Rundschau* 126, 2 June 2003, p. 7.

177. 'Bedingungen der europäischen Solidarität', *TRANSIT. Europäische Revue* issue 26 (2003/04), pp. 16–28. Shortened preprint published as 'Grundlagen europäischer Solidarität', *Frankfurter Allgemeine Zeitung* 140, 20 June 2003, p. 8.

178. 'Ver(w)irrung im Kopftuchstreit', *Süddeutsche Zeitung* 12, 16 January 2004, p. 2. Also published as 'Bekenntnisfreiheit als Menschenrecht. Bemerkungen zum Kopftuchstreit in Deutschland', in Volkmar Deile et al. (eds.), *Jahrbuch Menschenrechte* (Frankfurt: Suhrkamp, 2005), pp. 314–317.

179. 'Vorwort', in Joseph H. H. Weiler (ed.), *Ein christliches Europa. Erkundungsgänge* (Salzburg: Pustet, 2004), pp. 8–14.

180. ‚Bekenntnisfreiheit in einer pluralen Gesellschaft und die Neutralitätspflicht des Staates', *Zur Debatte. Themen der Katholischen Akademie in Bayern*, 34:4 (2004), pp. 26–28. Revised version published as 'Mit dem Unvertrauten vertraut werden', *Frankfurter Allgemeine Zeitung* 164, 17 July 2004, p. 41. Partly expanded version published in *Una Sancta, Zeitschrift für ökumenische Begegnung,* issue 3 (2005), pp. 235–249.

181. 'Wahrheit und Freiheit. Zur Weltverantwortung der Kirche heute', *Zur Debatte. Themen der Katholischen Akademie in Bayern* 34:6 (2004), pp. 5–6. Expanded version published in *MUT. Forum für Kultur, Politik und Geschichte* 474 (2007), pp. 76–87. Also published in A 23.

182. 'Anmerkung zum Urteil des Bundesverwaltungsgerichts vom 24.6.2004 – 2C45.03', *Juristenzeitung* 59 (2004), pp. 1181–84.

183. 'Wie werden in Deutschland die Grundrechte im Verfassungsrecht interpretiert', *Europäische Grundrechte Zeitschrift* 31:20–21 (2004), pp. 598–603.

184. 'Bleibt die Menschenwürde unantastbar?', *Blätter für deutsche und internationale Politik* 49 (2004), pp. 1216–1227

185. 'Europa und die Türkei. Die europäische Union am Scheideweg?' *Forum Kommune* 23:1 supplement (2005), pp. X–XI, XIII–XX. Also published in *MUT, Forum für Kultur, Politik und Geschichte* issue 454 (2005), pp. 14–27; and in *Internationale Katholische Zeitschrift Communio* 34 (2005), pp. 270–285. Shortened preprint published as ' "Nein" zum Beitritt der Türkei. Eine Begründung', *Frankfurter Allgemeine Zeitung* 289, 10 December 2004, pp. 35, 37.

186. 'Religionsfreiheit (revised version)', in Harald Baer, Hans Gasper, and Joachim Müller (eds.), *Lexikon neureligiöser Gruppen, Szenen und Weltanschauungen* (Freiburg: Herder, 2005), pp. 1080–1086.

187. 'Einleitung zur achten Auflage', in Georg Meyer and Gerhard Anschütz (eds.), *Lehrbuch des deutschen Staatsrechts, 8. Vols.* Reprint of the 7th ed. from 1919 (Berlin: Duncker & Humblot, 2005), pp. V–XVI.

188. 'Demokratische Willensbildung und Repräsentation (revised version)', in Josef Isensee and Paul Kirchhof (eds.), *Handbuch des Staatsrechts der Bundesrepublik*

Deutschland. Vol. 3, Demokratie – Bundesorgane (Heidelberg: C. F. Müller, 2005), pp. 31–53.

189. 'Was kennzeichnet das Politische und was ist sein Grund? Bemerkungen zu einer Kommentierung von Carl Schmitts "Begriff des Politischen,"' *Der Staat* 44 (2005), pp. 595–607.
190. 'Die Garantie der Menschenwürde', *Blickpunkt Bundestag* issue 4 (2006), p. 53.
191. 'Über die Autorität päpstlicher Lehrenzykliken am Beispiel der Äußerungen zur Religionsfreiheit', *Theologische Quartalsschrift* 186 (2006), pp. 22–39. Also published in A 23. Shortened preprint published as 'Rom hat gesprochen – die Debatte ist eröffnet', *Frankfurter Allgemeine Zeitung* 285, 7 December 2005, p. 39.
192. 'Haus und Hof – die Gefährdung', Bausparkasse Schwäbisch Hall Stiftung (ed.), *Kultur des Eigentums* (Berlin: Springer, 2006), pp. 9–15.
193. 'Säkularer Staat und Religion', *MUT. Forum für Kultur, Politik und Geschichte* 484 (2007), pp. 24–35. Also published in Franz Sommerfeld (ed.), *Der Moscheestreit. Eine exemplarische Debatte über Einwanderung und Integration* (Cologne: Kiepenheuer und Witsch, 2008), pp. 130–146.
194. 'Menschenwürde und Lebensrecht am Anfang und am Ende des Lebens. Aufriß der Probleme', *Stimmen der Zeit* 226 (2008), pp. 245–258.
195. 'Zum Briefwechsel zwischen Ernst Forsthoff und Carl Schmitt', *Archiv des öffentlichen Rechts* 133 (2008), pp. 261–266.
196. 'Woran krankt der Kapitalismus? Ein Gegenmodell zum inhumanen Kapitalismus', *MUT. Forum für Kultur, Politik und Geschichte* 500 (2009), pp. 96–104. Also published as 'Woran der Kapitalismus krankt', *Süddeutsche Zeitung* 94, 24 April 2009, p. 8.
197. 'Stellungnahme (zu Hartmut Kress, Religion, Staat und Toleranz angesichts des heutigen Pluralismus: Kritische Bemerkungen zum Böckenförde-Dictum)', *ETHIKA* 16 (2008), pp. 369–371.
198. 'Das unselige Handeln nach Kirchenraison', *Süddeutsche Zeitung* 98, 29 April 2010, p. 2.
199. 'Der Glaube der Muslime und die Pluralität der Religionen', *Konradsblatt. Wochenzeitung für das Erzbistum Freiburg* 24, 13 June 2010, p. 23.
200. 'Kennt die europäische Not kein Gebot?', *Neue Züricher Zeitung* 140, 21 June 2010, p. 33.
201. 'Die Reinigung des Glaubens', *Frankfurter Allgemeine Zeitung* 215, 16 September 2010, p. 32.
202. 'Warum nicht PID? Einspruch im Namen der Menschenwürde', *Frankfurter Allgemeine Zeitung* 61, 14 March 2011, pp. 27–28.
203. 'Wie weit müssen wir Muslims entgegenkommen?', in Thorsten Gerald Schneiders (ed.), *Verhärtete Fronten. Der schwere Weg zu einer vernünftigen Islamkritik* (Wiesbaden: Springer, 2012), pp. 53–56. Also published as 'Ver(w)irrung im Kopftuchstreit', *Süddeutsche Zeitung* 12, 16 January 2004, p. 2; and as

'Bekenntnisfreiheit als Menschenrecht. Bemerkungen zum Kopftuchstreit in Deutschland', *Jahrbuch Menschenrechte* 173 (2005), pp. 314–317.

204. 'Vorwort', in Martin Rhonheimer (ed.), *Christentum und säkulare Staat. Geschichte, Gegenwart, Zukunft* (Freiburg: Herder, 2012), pp. 9–14.

205. 'Franz-Xaver Kaufmann – Stationen eines Lebenswerks', *Stimmen der Zeit* issue 3 (March 2013), 147–155. Also published in Stephan Goertz und Hermann-Josef Große Kracht (eds.), *Christentum – Moderne – Politik: Studien zu Franz-Xaver Kaufmann* (Paderborn: Ferdinand Schoeningh, 2014), pp. 177–186.

C. Analysis of Cases

1. 'Lösung eines Klausurfalls aus dem öffentlichen Recht', *Die Fortbildung. Studien- und Mitteilungsblatt der deutschen Verwaltungs- und Wirtschaftsakademie* 5 (1960), pp. 39–41.
2. 'Der Stellvertreter-Fall', *Juristische Schulung* 6:9 (1966), pp. 359–367.
3. 'Der Honnef-Fall ("Der praktische Fall", Öffentliches Recht)', *Juristische Schulung* issue 8 (1968), pp. 375–380.
4. 'Sandwich-Träger: Öffentlich-rechtliche Aufsichtsarbeit, Frühjahr 1980', *Verwaltungsblätter für Baden-Württemberg* 7/8 (1981), pp. 230–231, 265–271.

D. Book Reviews

1. Weilenmann, Heinz, *Untersuchungen zur Staatstheorie Carl Ludwig v. Hallers*, 1955, in: *Zeitschrift für die gesamte Staatswissenschaft* 114 (1958), pp. 376–377.
2. Guradze, Heinz, *Der Stand der Menschenrechte im Völkerrecht*, 1955, in: *Archiv für Rechts- und Sozialphilosophie* 44 (1958), pp. 139–143.
3. Hesse, Konrad, *Die normative Kraft der Verfassung*, 1959, in: *Zeitschrift für die gesamte Staatswissenschaft* 118 (1962), pp. 172–174.
4. Gneist, Rudolf, *Der Rechtsstaat und die Verwaltungsgerichte in Deutschland*, 1958, in: *Zeitschrift für die gesamte Staatswissenschaft* 118 (1962), pp. 176–178.
5. Wilhelm, Walter, *Zur juristischen Methodenlehre im 19. Jahrhundert*, 1958, in: *Archiv für Rechts- und Sozialphilosophie* 48 (1962), pp. 249–254.
6. Huber, Ernst Rudolf, *Dokumente zur deutschen Verfassungsgeschichte. Vol. 1*, 1960, in: *Zeitschrift für die gesamte Staatswissenschaft* 118 (1962), pp. 571–574.
7. de Vattel, Emer, *Le droit de gens ou principes de la loi naturelle. German Translation by W. Euler. Introduction by G. Guggenheim*, 1959, in: *Zeitschrift für die gesamte Staatswissenschaft* 118 (1962), pp. 574–576.
8. Maier, Hans, *Revolution und Kirche*, 1959, in: *Theologische Revue* 59 (1963), pp. 43–47.
9. von Stein, Lorenz, *Geschichte der sozialen Bewegung in Frankreich von 1789 bis auf unsere Tage*. 3 Vols. 1959;

   von Stein, Lorenz, *Movimientas sociales y Monarquia*. Traducide par Enriques Tierno Galvan, 1957;

   von Stein, Lorenz, *The History of the Social Movement in France 1789-1850*, edited by Kaethe Mengelberg, 1964;

von Stein, Lorenz, *System der Staatswissenschaft. Vol. 1 System der Statistik, der Populationstechnik und der Volkswirtschaftslehre. Vol. 2 Die Gesellschaftslehre*, reprint of the 1852–1856 edition, 1964;

von Stein, Lorenz, *Die Verwaltungslehre. 8 Parts in 10 Volumes*, Reprint of the 1st and 2nd edition, 1866–1884, 1962, all in: *Der Staat* 4 (1965), pp. 489–492.

10. Huber, Ernst Rudolf, *Dokumente zur deutschen Verfassungsgeschichte. Vol. 2 Deutsche Verfassungsdokumente 1851–1918*, 1964, in: *Der Staat* 4 (1965), pp. 502–505.
11. Leder, Joseph, *Geschichte der Religionsfreiheit im Zeitalter der Reformation. Vol. 1–2*, transl. by Elisabeth Schneider, 1965, in: *Die Welt der Bücher. Beihefte zur Herder-Korrespondenz* 3:5 (1966), pp. 237–238.
12. Hofmann, Hasso, *Legitimität gegen Legalität. Der Weg der politischen Philosophie Carl Schmitts*, 1964, in: *Die öffentliche Verwaltung* (1967), pp. 688–690.
13. Grundmann, Siegfried et al. (eds.), *Evangelisches Staatslexikon*, 1966, in: *Der Staat* 6 (1967), pp. 513–517.
14. Quaritsch, Helmut and Hermann Weber, *Staat und Kirche in der Bundesrepublik. Staats- und kirchenrechtliche Aufsätze 1950–1967*, 1967, in: *Neue Juristische Wochenschrift* (1968), p. 1322.
15. Albrecht, Dieter (ed.), *Der Notenwechsel zwischen dem Heiligen Stuhl und der deutschen-Reichsregierung. Vol. 1 Von der Ratifizierung des Reichskonkordats bis zur Enzyklika,Mit brennender Sorge*, 1965, in: *Der Staat* 8 (1969), pp. 265–268.
16. Schneider, Burkhardt, Pierre Blet, and Angelo Martini (eds.), *Die Briefe Pius' XII. an die deutschen Bischöfe 1939–1944*, 1966, in: *Der Staat* 8 (1969), pp. 265–268.
17. Leibholz, Gerhard and Hans Rinck, *Grundgesetz für die Bundesrepublik Deutschland. Kommentar an Hand der Rechtsprechung des Bundesverfassungsgerichts*, 3rd edition, 1968, in: *Der Staat* 8 (1969), pp. 533–536.
18. Hennis, Wilhelm, *Verfassung und Verfassungswirklichkeit. Ein deutsches Problem*, 1968, in: *Der Staat* 9 (1970), pp. 533–536.
19. Hintze, Otto, *Regierung und Verwaltung. Gesammelte Abhandlungen zur Staats-, Rechts- und Sozialgeschichte Preußens. Vol. 3*, 2nd edition, edited by Gerhard Oestreich, 1967, in: *Historische Zeitschrift* 213 (1971), pp. 128–131.
20. Quaritsch, Helmut, *Staat und Souveränität. Vol. 1*, 1970, in: *Neue Juristische Wochenschrift* 24 (1971), p. 2060.
21. Friedrich, Manfred, *Zwischen Positivismus und materialem Verfassungsdenken. Albert Hänel und seine Bedeutung für die deutsche Staatsrechtswissenschaft*, 1971, in: *Die Öffentliche Verwaltung* 21 (1972), p. 763.
22. Makarov, Alexander, *Deutsches Staatsangehörigkeitsrecht. Kommentar*, 2nd revised edition, 1971, in: *Rabels Zeitschrift für ausländisches und internationales Privatrecht* 37 (1973), pp. 184–188.
23. Maier, Hans, *Kirche und Gesellschaft*, 1973, in: *Frankfurter Allgemeine Zeitung* 4 October 1973, p. 231.
24. Hermann, Horst, *Ein moralisches Verhältnis. Bemerkungen eines Betroffenen zur Lage von Staat und Kirche in der Bundesrepublik Deutschland*, 1974, in: *Vorwärts* 30, 24 July 1975, p. 14, under the title 'Streitschrift eines Betroffenen. Wie realistisch ist Horst Hermanns Kritik?'

25. Huber, Ernst Rudolf and Wolfgang Huber (eds.), *Staat und Kirche im 19. und 20. Jahrhundert. Dokumente zur Geschichte des deutschen Staatskirchenrechts. Vol. 1 Staat und Kirche vom Ausgang des alten Reiches bis zum Vorabend der bürgerlichen Revolution*, 1973, in: *Der Staat* 14 (1975), pp. 576–578.
26. Kunst, Hermann, Roman Herzog and Wilhelm Schneemelcher (eds.), *Evangelisches Staatslexikon*, 2nd revised and expanded edition, 1975, in: *Der Staat* 16 (1977), pp. 413–415.
27. Martiny, Martin, *Integration oder Konfrontation? Studien zur sozialdemokratischen Rechts- und Verfassungspolitik*, 1976, in: *Frankfurter Allgemeine Zeitung* 87, 15 April 1977, p. 9, under the title 'Rechtspolitik als politischer Kampf ums Recht. Die Haltung der SPD zu Recht und Verfassung in Kaiserreich und Weimarer Republik'.
28. Köhler, Michael, *Die Lehre vom Widerstandsrecht in der deutschen konstitutionellen Staatsrechtstheorie der 1. Hälfte des 19. Jahrhunderts*, 1973, in: *Der Staat* 16 (1977), pp. 599–601.
29. *Corpus Constitutionnel, Recueil universelle des constitutions en vigueur. Vol. 1 Afghanistan à Brasil*, 1968–72. *Vol. 2/1 Bulgarie – Ceylon (Sri-Lanka)*, 1974, *Supplement 1 Afghanistan – Burundi*, 1976, in: *Der Staat* 17 (1978), pp. 631–633.
30. Huber, Ernst Rudolf and Wolfgang Huber (eds.), *Staat und Kirche im 19. und 20. Jahrhundert. Dokumente zur Geschichte des deutschen Staatskirchenrechts. Vol. 2 Staat und Kirche im Zeitalter des Hochkonstitutionalismus und des Kulturkampfes 1848–1890*, 1976, in: *Der Staat* 17 (1978), pp. 635–636.
31. von Simson, Werner, *Die Verteidigung des Friedens. Beiträge zu einer Theorie der Staatengemeinschaft*, 1975, in: *Der Staat* 18 (1979), pp. 283–285.
32. Möser, Justus, *Sämtliche Werke. Historisch-kritische Ausgabe in 14 Bänden. Vol. 13 Osnabrückische Geschichte. Vol. 14/1 Historische Aufsätze 1753–91. Historische Handschriften*, edited by Paul Göttsching, 1971/1976, in: *Der Staat* 18 (1979), pp. 629–631.
33. Quaritsch, Helmut, *Probleme der Selbstdarstellung des Staates*, 1977, in: *Die Öffentliche Verwaltung* issue 478/479 (1979), p. 725.
34. Bornhalt, Conrad, *Preußische Staats- und Rechtsgeschichte*, reprint of the 1903 edition, 1979, in: *Die Öffentliche Verwaltung* (1980), p. 147.
35. Leibholz, Gerhard (ed.), *Jahrbuch des öffentlichen Rechts der Gegenwart. Vol. 27*, 1978, in: *Der Staat* 19 (1980), pp. 304–306.
36. Winkler, Heinrich August, *Die Sozialdemokratie und die Revolution 1918/19. Ein Rückblick nach 60 Jahren*, 1979, in: *Der Staat* 19 (1980), pp. 315–317.
37. Kleinheyer, Gerd and Paul Mikat (eds.), *Beiträge zur Rechtsgeschichte. Gedächtnisschrift für Hermann Conrad*, 1979, in: *Der Staat* 20 (1981), pp. 142–144.
38. Hirsch, Ernst E., *Zur juristischen Dimension des Gewissens und der Unverletzlichkeit der Gewissensfreiheit des Richters*, 1979, in: *Deutsches Verwaltungsblatt* (1980), pp. 206–207
39. Miehsler, Herbert et al. (eds.), *Ius Humanitatis. Festschrift zum 90. Geburtstag von Alfred Verdroß*, 1980, in: *Der Staat* 20 (1981), pp. 478–480.

40. Thümmel, Hans-Wolf (ed.), *Arbeiten zur Rechtsgeschichte. Festschrift für Gustaf Klemens Schmelzeisen*, 1980, in: *Der Staat* 21 (1982), pp. 313–314.
41. Leibholz, Gerhard (ed.), *Jahrbuch des öffentlichen Rechts der Gegenwart. Vol. 29*, 1980, in: *Der Staat* 22 (1983), pp. 314–316.
42. *Corpus Constitutionnel. Recueil universelle des constitutions en vigueur. Vol 2/2 Chili – Coree*, 1979, in: *Der Staat* 22 (1983), pp. 316–317.
43. Scholder, Klaus (ed.), *Die Mittwochsgesellschaft. Protokolle aus dem geistigen Deutschland 1932-1944*, 1982, in: *Der Staat* 23 (1984), pp. 314–316.
44. Arndt, Claus, *Widerstand in der Demokratie*, 1983, in: *Recht und Politik* issue 2 (1984), pp. 110–111.
45. Huber, Ernst Rudolf and Wolfgang Huber (eds.), *Staat und Kirche im 19. und 20. Jahrhundert. Dokumente zur Geschichte des deutschen Staatskirchenrechts. Vol. 3 Staat und Kirche von der Beilegung des Kulturkampfes bis zum Ende des Ersten Weltkrieges*, 1983, in: *Der Staat* 23 (1984), pp. 631–633.
46. Salzmann, Rainer (ed.), *Die CDU/CSU im Parlamentarischen Rat. Sitzungsprotokolle der Unionsfraktion. Vol. 2*, 1981, in: *Der Staat* 24:4 (1985), pp. 635–636.
47. Huber, Ernst Rudolf and Wolfgang Huber (eds.), *Staat und Kirche im 19. und 20. Jahrhundert. Dokumente zur Geschichte des deutschen Staatskirchenrechts. Vol. 4 Staat und Kirche in der Zeit der Weimarer Republik*, 1988, in: *Der Staat* 29:3 (1990), pp. 441–444.
48. Gatz, Erwin (ed.), *Die Bischöfe des Heiligen Römischen Reiches 1648–1803. Ein biographisches Lexikon*, 1990, in: *Der Staat* 31:2 (1992), pp. 319–320.
49. Heinrichs, Helmut (eds.), *Deutsche Juristen jüdischer Herkunft*, 1993, in: *Frankfurter Allgemeine Zeitung* 284, 7 December 1993, p. L21.
50. Möser, Justus, *Sämtliche Werke. Historisch-kritische Ausgabe in 14 Bänden. Vol. 11 Patriotische Phantasien und Zugehöriges. Vol. 14/2 Osnabrückische Geschichte und historische Einzelschriften*, edited by Paul Göttsching, 1988/1990, in: *Der Staat* 33:3 (1994), pp. 486–488.
51. Brubaker, Rogers, *Staats-Bürger. Deutschland und Frankreich im historischen Vergleich*, transl. by Wiebke Schmaltz, 1994, in: *Frankfurter Allgemeine Zeitung* 86, 11 April 1995, p. L32 under the title 'Wer ist das Volk? Rogers Brubakers Vergleich französischer und deutscher Staatsangehörigkeit'. Also published in A 19, under the title 'Staatsbürgerschaft und Nationalitätskonzept'.
52. Göbel, Andreas, Dirk van Laak, and Ingeborg Villinger (eds.), *Metamorphosen des Politischen. Grundfragen politischer Einheitsbildung seit den 20er Jahren*, 1995, in: *Frankfurter Allgemeine Zeitung* 55, 5 March 1995, p. 39, under the title 'Das Politische im Zeitalter der Systemtheorie. Eine neue Generation übernimmt die Carl-Schmitt-Debatte: Zu einer Sammlung bemerkenswerter Studien'.
53. Stolleis, Michael, *Recht im Unrecht. Studien zur Rechtsgeschichte des Nationalsozialismus*, 1994, in: *Frankfurter Allgemeine Zeitung* 24 March 1995, p. 17.
54. Kerber, Markus, *Wachstum und Konsolidierung. Ein Vorschlag zur Reform von Wirtschaft und Staatsfinanzen*, 1997, in: *Süddeutsche Zeitung* 79, 7 April 1997, p. 9, under the title 'Ausweg aus der wirtschaftspolitischen Zwickmühle. Eine herausfordernde Streitschrift: Wie sich staatliche Vermögensreserven produktiv mobilisieren lassen'.

55. Friedman, Michel et al. (eds.), *Religionsfreiheit. Jahrestagung der Deutschen Sektion der Internationalen Juristen-Kommission vom 29.9. bis 2.10.1995 in Erfurt. Rechtsstaat in der Bewährung*, 1996, in: *Zeitschrift für Rechtspolitik* issue 4 (1998), p. 150.
56. Arndt, Claus, *Amt und Mandat. Ausgewählte Reden und Schriften aus drei Jahrzehnten. Vol. 3*, 1996, in: *Der Staat* 37 (1998), p. 653.
57. Gatz, Erwin (ed.) with assistance by Clemens Brodkrob, *Die Bischöfe des Heiligen Römischen Reiches 1448-1648. Ein biographisches Lexikon*, 1996, in: *Der Staat* 37 (1998), pp. 660–661.
58. Gosewinkel, Dieter, *Einbürgern und Ausschließen. Die Nationalisierung der Staatsangehörigkeit vom Deutschen Bund bis zur Bundesrepublik Deutschland*, 2001, in: *Frankfurter Allgemeine Zeitung* 301, 28 December 2001, p. 8.
59. Siehr, Angelika, *Die Deutschenrechte des Grundgesetzes. Bürgerrechte im Spannungsfeld von Menschenrechtsidee und Staatsmitgliedschaft*, 2001, in: *Frankfurter Allgemeine Zeitung* 83, 10 April 2002, p. 8.
60. Gatz, Erwin (ed.) with assistance from Clemens Brodkorb, *Die Bischöfe des Heiligen Römischen Reiches 1198-1448. Ein biographisches Lexikon*, 2001, in: *Der Staat* 41 (2002), pp. 642–644.
61. Jakobs, Günther, *Staatliche Strafe. Bedeutung und Zweck*, 2004, in: *Frankfurter Allgemeine Zeitung* 179, 4 August 2004, p. 30, under the title 'Warum soll man bestrafen?'
62. Pawlik, Michael, *Person, Subjekt, Bürger. Zur Legitimation von Strafe*, 2004, in: *Frankfurter Allgemeine Zeitung* 293, 15 December 2004, p. 38, under the title 'Den Täter als Bürger ehren'.
63. Kersting, Wolfgang, *Kant über Recht*, 2004, in: *Frankfurter Allgemeine Zeitung* 215, 15 September 2004, p. 34, under the title 'Wie frei macht der Sozialstaat?'
64. Günther, Frieder, *Denken vom Staat her. Die bundesdeutsche Staatsrechtslehre zwischen Dezision und Integration 194–1970*, 2004, in: *Rechtsgeschichte* 6 (2005), pp. 220–224.
65. Uertz, Rudolf, *Vom Gottesrecht zum Menschenrecht. Das katholische Staatsdenken in Deutschland von der Französischen Revolution bis zum II. Vatikanischen Konzil (1789–1965)*, 2005, in: *Frankfurter Allgemeine Zeitung* 95, 25 April 2005, p. 42, under the title 'So ist Autonomie nicht gemeint'.
66. Offenloch, Werner, *Erinnerung an das Recht. Der Streit um die Nachrüstung auf den Straßen und vor den Gerichten*, 2005, in: *Frankfurter Allgemeine Zeitung*, 24 October 2005, p. 29, under the title 'Wir saßen und blockierten'.
67. Hollerbach, Alexander, *Katholizismus und Jurisprudenz. Beiträge zur Katholizismusforschung und zur neueren Wissenschaftsgeschichte*, 2004, in: *Stimmen der Zeit* 223 (2005), pp. 862–864.
68. Grothe, Ewald, *Zwischen Geschichte und Recht. Deutsche Verfassungsgeschichtsschreibung 1900–1970*, 2005, in: *Frankfurter Allgemeine Zeitung* 20, 24 January 2006, p. 7.
69. Lenz, Sebastian, *Vorbehaltlose Freiheitsrechte*, 2006, in: *Frankfurter Allgemeine Zeitung* 48, 26 February 2007, p. 37, under the title 'Zerbrecht nicht das Recht'.
70. Koenig, Matthias and Jean Paul Willaime (eds.), *Religionskontroversen in Frankreich und Deutschland*, 2008, in: *Frankfurter Allgemeine Zeitung* 263, 10 November 2008, p. 32.

71. Honnefelder, Ludger, *Woher kommen wir? Ursprünge der Moderne im Denken des Mittelalters*, 2008, in: *Frankfurter Allgemeine Zeitung* 279, 28 November 2008, p. 47, under the title 'Mein Wille will nicht so, wie ich es will'.
72. von Ungern-Sternberg, Antje, *Religionsfreiheit in Europa*, 2008, in: *Frankfurter Allgemeine Zeitung* 72, 26 March 2009, p. 34.
73. Wick, Lutz, *Islam und Verfassungsstaat. Theologische Versöhnung mit der Moderne*, 2009, in: *Frankfurter Allgemeine Zeitung*, 22 April 2009, under the title 'Religionsfreiheit ist kein Gottesgeschenk'.
74. Nolte, Paul, *Religion und Bürgergesellschaft. Brauchen wir einen religionsfreundlichen Staat?*, 2009, in: *Frankfurter Allgemeine Zeitung* 266, 16 November 2009, p. 28.
75. Kaufmann, Franz Xaver, *Kirchenkrise. Wie überlebt das Christentum?*, 2011, in: *Badische Zeitung*, 24 February 2011, p. 11.

E. Book Announcements

1. Bachof, Otto, *Verfassungsrecht, Verfahrensrecht in der Rechtsprechung des Bundesverwaltungsgerichts. Part 1 and 2*, 1963, in: *Der Staat* 3 (1964), pp. 126–127.
2. Dahm, Georg, *Deutsches Recht. Die geschichtlichen und dogmatischen Grundlagen des geltenden Rechts*, 1963, in: *Der Staat* 3 (1964), p. 260.
3. Viehweg, Theodor, *Topik und Jurisprudenz*, 1963, in: *Der Staat* 3 (1964), p. 517.
4. Hering, Carl Joseph and Hubert Lentz (eds.), *Entscheidungen in Kirchensachen seit 1946*: *Vol. 1 (1946/1952)*, 1963, in: *Der Staat* 4 (1956), p. 127.

   Vol. 2 (1953/1954), vol. 3 (1955/1956), 1964/65, in: *Der Staat* 5 (1966), p. 267.

   Vol. 4 (1957/1958), 1966, in: *Der Staat* 6 (1967), pp. 135–136.

   Vol. 5 (1959/1961), 1967, in: *Der Staat* 8 (1969), p. 542.

   Vol. 6 (1962/1963), 1969, in: *Der Staat* 9 (1970), p. 547.

   Vol. 7 (1964/1965), 1970, in: *Der Staat* 11 (1972), p. 575.

   Vol. 8 (1966), Vol. 9 (1967), Vol. 10 (1968/69), 1971/74, in: *Der Staat* 15 (1976), pp. 149–150.
5. Conrad, Hermann, *Deutsche Rechtsgeschichte. Vol. 1 Frühzeit und Mittelalter*, 2nd expanded and revised edition, 1962, in: *Der Staat* 4 (1965), pp. 127–128.
6. Meisner, Heinrich Otto, *Verfassung, Verwaltung. Regierung in neuerer Zeit*, 1962, in: *Der Staat* 4 (1965), p. 128.
7. Verdross, Alfred, *Abendländische Rechtsphilosophie. Ihre Grundlagen und Hauptprobleme in geschichtlicher Schau*, 2nd expanded and revised edition, 1963, in: *Der Staat* 4 (1965), pp. 391–392.
8. Fuller, John Frederick Charles, *Die entartete Kunst, Krieg zu führen 1789–1961*, 1964, in: *Der Staat* 4 (1965), p. 524.
9. Miller, Susanne, *Das Problem der Freiheit im Sozialismus. Freiheit, Staat und Revolution in der Programmatik der Sozialdemokratie von Lassalle bis zum Revisionismus*, 1964, in: *Der Staat* 5 (1966), p. 401.
10. Carstens, Carl, Hans Peters, *Hochschulrechtliche Aufsätze. Aus der Festschrift für Hermann Jahrreiß*, 1965, in: *Der Staat* 5 (1966), p. 541.

11. Maier, Hans, *Revolution und Kirche. Studien zur Frühgeschichte der christlichen Demokratie (1789–1901)*, 2nd expanded and revised edition, 1965, in: *Der Staat* 6 (1967), p. 135.
12. Bussmann, Walter, *Otto von Bismarck: Geschichte – Staat – Politik*, 1966, in: *Der Staat* 6 (1967), p. 268.
13. Hauriou, Maurice, *Theorie der Institution und zwei andere Aufsätze*, transl. by Hans Jecht and Jutta Jecht, 1965, in: *Der Staat* 6 (1967), p. 402.
14. Heinrich Pesch-Haus (ed.), *Civitas. Jahrbuch für christliche Gesellschaftsordnung*, (published from Vol. 8 onwards under the title *Jahrbuch für Sozialwissenschaften*):
    Vol. 3 (1964), *Vol. 4* (1965), in: *Der Staat* 6 (1967), p. 403.
    Vol. 5 (1966), *Vol. 6* (1967), in: *Der Staat* 7 (1968), pp. 541–542.
    Vol. 7 (1968), *Vol. 8* (1969), *Vol. 9* (1970), in: *Der Staat* 11 (1972), p. 283.
    Vol. 10 (1971), *Vol. 11* (1972), in: *Der Staat* 12 (1973), p. 578.
    Vol. 12 (1973), in: *Der Staat* 15 (1976), p. 144.
15. Jahn, Hans Edgar, Kurt Neher, and Lothar Roske (eds.), *Taschenbuch für Wehrfragen 1966/67*, 1966, in: *Der Staat* 6 (1967), p. 408.
16. Herrmann, Günter, *Rundfunkgesetze*, 1966, in: *Der Staat* 6 (1967), p. 539.
17. Leibholz, Gerhard (ed.), *Jahrbuch des öffentlichen Rechts der Gegenwart. Vol. 15*, 1966, in: *Der Staat* 6 (1967), pp. 537–538.
18. Zoltón Petéri (ed.), *Etudes en droit comparé. Essays in comparative law*, 1966, in: *Der Staat* 7 (1968), pp. 132–133.
19. Conrad, Hermann et al. (eds.), *Gedächtnisschrift Hans Peters*, 1967, in: *Der Staat* 7 (1968), p. 402.
20. Randelzhofer, Albrecht, *Völkerrechtliche Aspekte des Heiligen Römischen Reiches nach 1946*, 1967, in: *Der Staat* 8 (1969), pp. 541–542.
21. Huber, Ernst Rudolf (ed.), *Dokumente zur Deutschen Verfassungsgeschichte. Vol. 3 Dokumente der Novemberrevolution und der Weimarer Republik*, 1966, in: *Der Staat* 9 (1970), p. 284.
22. Bornhak, Conrad, *Deutsche Verfassungsgeschichte vom Westfälischen Frieden an*, 1934, reprint 1968, in: *Der Staat* 9 (1970), p. 430.
23. Schmitthemmer, Friedrich, *Grundlinien des allgemeinen oder idealen Staatsrechts (Zwölf Bücher vom Staate, oder systematische Encyklopädie der Staatswissenschaften, 3. Vol.)*, 1845, reprint 1966, edited by Herbert Krüger, in: *Der Staat* 9 (1970), pp. 430–431.
24. Peters, Hans, *Geschichtliche Entwicklung und Grundfragen der Verfassung*, edited by Jürgen Salzwedel and Günter Erbel, 1969, in: *Der Staat* 9 (1970), pp. 570–571.
25. Rürup, Reinhard, *Probleme der Revolution in Deutschland 1918/19*, 1968, in: *Der Staat* 9 (1970), p. 567.
26. Otruba, Gustav, *Gesellschaft und Herrschaft. Forschungen zu sozial- und adelsgeschichtlichen Problemen vornehmlich in Bayern. Festgabe für Karl Bosl zum 60. Geburtstag*, 1969, in: *Der Staat* 9 (1970), p. 567.
27. Imboden, Max Friedrich et al. (eds.), *Festschrift für Adolf J. Merkl zum 80. Geburtstag*, 1970, in: *Der Staat* 10 (1971), p. 429.

28. Mayer-Scheu, Hans-Josef, *Grundgesetz und Parität von Kirchen und Religionsgemeinschaften*, 1970, in: *Der Staat* 11 (1972), p. 141.

29. Bosl, Karl, *Franken um 800. Strukturanalyse einer fränkischen Königsprovinz*. 2nd expanded edition, 1969, in: *Der Staat* 11 (1972), p. 143.

30. Spranger, Eduard, *Staat, Recht und Politik*, edited by Hermann Josef Meyer, 1970, in: *Der Staat* 11 (1972), p. 281.

31. Arndt, Adolf et al. (eds.), *Konkretionen politischer Theorie und Praxis. Festschrift für Carlo Schmid zum 75. Geburtstag*, 1972, in: *Der Staat* 12 (1973), p. 138.

32. von Stein, Lorenz, *Proletariat und Gesellschaft*, edited by Manfred Hahn, 1971, in: *Der Staat* 12 (1973), p. 139.

33. Suerbaum, Werner, *Vom antiken zum frühmittelalterlichen Staatsbegriff*, 2nd revised and expanded edition, 1970, in: *Der Staat* 12 (1973), p. 285.

34. Pawlowski, Hans-Martin and Franz Wieacker, *Festschrift für Karl Michaelis zum 70. Geburtstag am 21. Dezember 1970*, 1972, in: *Der Staat* 12 (1973), p. 577.

35. Freiherr von Kruedener, Jürgen, *Die Rolle des Hofs im Absolutismus*, 1973, in: *Der Staat* 13 (1974), pp. 150–151.

36. Paulus, Gotthard, Uwe Diederichsen, and Claus-Wilhelm Canaris (eds.), *Festschrift für Karl Larenz zum 70. Geburtstag*, 1973, in: *Der Staat* 13 (1974), p. 301.

37. Hollerbach, Alexander, Werner Maihofer, and Thomas Wurtenberger (eds.), *Mensch und Recht. Festschrift für Erik Wolf zum 70. Geburtstag*, 1972, in: *Der Staat* 13 (1974), p. 301.

38. Achterberg, Norbert (ed.), *Öffentliches Recht und Politik. Festschrift für Hans-Ulrich Scupin zum 70. Geburtstag*, 1973, in: *Der Staat* 13 (1974), p. 601.

39. von Oertzen, Hans-Joachim (ed.), *Demokratisierung und Funktionsfähigkeit der Verwaltung. Vorträge und Diskussionen auf der verwaltungswissenschaftlichen Fachtagung der Deutschen Sektion des Internationalen Instituts für Verwaltungswissenschaften in Regensburg vom 10.–12. Oktober 1973*, 1974, in: *Der Staat* 13 (1974), pp. 602–603.

40. Ellscheid, Winfried and Günter Hassemer (eds.), *Interessenjurisprudenz*, 1974, in: *Der Staat* 14 (1975), p. 151.

41. Schneider, Hans and Volkmar Götz (eds.), *Im Dienst an Recht und Staat. Festschrift für Werner Weber zum 70. Geburtstag*, 1974, in: *Der Staat* 14 (1975), pp. 296–297.

42. Malkoff, Johan, *Recht, Mensch und Gesellschaft. Zur Transformation gesellschaftlicher Kräfte in Rechtsnormen*, 1972, in: *Der Staat* 14 (1975), p. 453.

43. Schnatz, Helmut (ed.), *Päpstliche Verlautbarungen zu Staat und Gesellschaft. Originaldokumente mit deutscher Übersetzung*, 1973, in: *Der Staat* 14 (1975), p. 608.

44. Hollerbach, Alexander, *Neuere Entwicklungen des katholischen Kirchenrechts*, 1974, in: *Der Staat* 15 (1976), p. 145.

45. Reich, Norbert and Hans-Christian Reichel, *Einführung in das sozialistische Recht*, 1975, in: *Der Staat* 15 (1976), p. 602.

46. von Münch, Ingo (ed.) with assistance from Ondolf Rojahn, *Dokumente des geteilten Deutschlands. Quellentexte zur Rechtslage des Deutschen Reiches, der Bundesrepublik Deutschland und der Deutschen Demokratischen Republik. Vol. 2*, 1975, in: *Der Staat* 16 (1977), p. 148.

47. Klose, Alfred et al. (eds.), *Ordnung im sozialen Wandel. Festschrift für Johannes Messner zum 85. Geburtstag*, 1976, in: *Der Staat* 16 (1977), p. 149.
48. Krautscheidt, Joseph and Heiner Marré (eds.), *Essener Gespräche zum Thema Staat und Kirche. Vol. 10*, 1976, in: *Der Staat* 16 (1977), p. 463.
49. Delbrück, Jost and Dietrich Rauschning (eds.), *Recht im Dienst des Friedens. Festschrift für Eberhard Menzel zum 65. Geburtstag am 21.1.1976*, 1975, in: *Der Staat* 16 (1977), p. 457.
50. s. eds., 'Völkerrecht als Rechtsordnung. Grundlagen und Quellen. Beiträge zum Fünfzigjährigen Bestehen des Max-Planck-Instituts für Ausländisches Öffentliches Recht und Völkerrecht, 1924–1974', *Zeitschrift für ausländisches öffentliches Recht und Völkerrecht* 36:1–3 (1976), in: *Der Staat* 16 (1977), pp. 457–458.
51. Schambeck, Herbert (ed.), *Kirche und Staat. Fritz Eckert zum 65. Geburtstag*, 1976, in: *Der Staat* 16 (1977), p. 612.
52. König, Klaus, Hans Laubinger, and Friedo Wagner (eds.), *Öffentlicher Dienst. Festschrift für Carl Hermann Ule zum 70. Geburtstag am 26.2.1972*, 1977, in: *Der Staat* 17 (1978), p. 158.
53. Drath, Martin, *Rechts- und Staatslehre als Sozialwissenschaft. Gesammelte Schriften über eine soziokulturelle Theorie des Staates und des Rechts*, edited by Ernst Eduard Hirsch, 1977, in: *Der Staat* 17 (1978), pp. 637–638.
54. Wilke, Dieter and Harald Weber (eds.), *Gedächtnisschrift für Friedrich Klein*, 1977, in: *Der Staat* 18 (1979), pp. 315–316.
55. *Annuaire Suisse de science politique (Schweizer Jahrbuch für Politische Wissenschaft). Vol. 16 (1976), 17 (1977), 18 (1978)*, (editor-in-chief: Raimund E. Germann), 1976–1978, in: *Der Staat* 18 (1979), pp. 643–644.
56. Winkler, Günther, *Orientierungen im öffentlichen Recht. Ausgewählte Abhandlungen*, 1979, in: *Der Staat* 19 (1980), pp. 323–324.
57. Lieberwirth, Rolf, *Der Staat als Gegenstand des Hochschulunterrichts in Deutschland vom 16. bis zum 18. Jahrhundert*, 1978, in: *Der Staat* 19 (1980), pp. 482–483.
58. Püttner, Günther, *Staatsverschuldung als Rechtsproblem. Ein verfassungsrechtliches Plädoyer gegen die Kreditfinanzierung der öffentlichen Haushalte*, 1980, in: *Der Staat* 21 (1982), pp. 156–157.
59. Thümmel, Hans-Wolf (ed.), *Arbeiten zur Rechtsgeschichte. Festschrift für Gustaf Klemens Schmelzeisen*, 1980, in: *Der Staat* 21 (1982), pp. 313–314.
60. Rottleuthner, Hubert, (ed.) *Recht, Rechtsphilosophie und Nationalsozialismus. Vorträge auf der Tagung der Deutschen Sektion der Internationalen Vereinigung für Rechts- und Sozialphilosophie (IVR) in der Bundesrepublik Deutschland vom 11. und 12. Oktober 1982 in Berlin (West)*, 1983, in: *Der Staat* 23 (1984), p. 475.
61. Vezina, Birgit, *Die 'Gleichschaltung' der Universität Heidelberg im Zuge der nationalsozialistischen Machtergreifung*, 1982, in: *Der Staat* 23 (1984), p. 476.
62. Häberle, Peter (ed.), *Jahrbuch des öffentlichen Rechts der Gegenwart. Vol. 32*, 1983, in: *Der Staat* 24 (1985), p. 642.
63. Gatz, Erwin (ed.), *Die Bischöfe der deutschsprachigen Länder 1785/1803–1945. Ein biographisches Lexikon*, 1983, in: *Der Staat* 24 (1985), p. 643.

64. Avenarius, Hermann et al. (eds.), *Festschrift für Erwin Stein zum 80. Geburtstag*, 1983, in: *Der Staat* 25 (1986), p. 641.

F. Published Panel Contributions

1. 'Der Bürger und das Recht. Rechtspolitischer Kongreß der SPD am 26./27.03.65 in Heidelberg', Vorstand der SPD (ed.), *Dokumentation: 'Der Bürger und das Recht'* (Mannheim: Erich-Ollenhauer-Haus AZ-Druck, 1967), pp. 109 ff.
2. 'Der Schießbefehl an der Mauer. Jahrestagung des Königsteiner Kreises am 4. November 1967 in Königstein im Taunus', *Mitteilungsblatt der Vereinigung der Juristen, Volkswirte und Beamten aus der Sowjetischen Besatzungszone e. V.* 12 (1967), pp. 88–91.
3. 'Das Staatsoberhaupt in der parlamentarischen Demokratie', *Veröffentlichungen der Vereinigung der Deutschen Staatsrechtslehrer* 25 (1967), pp. 220, 232.
4. 'Die Kirchen unter dem Grundgesetz', *Veröffentlichungen der Vereinigung der Deutschen Staatsrechtslehrer* 26 (1968), pp. 123–124, 144.
5. 'Das Grundrecht der Gewissensfreiheit', *Veröffentlichungen der Vereinigung der Deutschen Staatsrechtslehrer* 28 (1970), pp. 102–106, 109–112, 125, 141–146.
6. 'Grundrechte im Leistungsstaat', *Veröffentlichungen der Vereinigung der Deutschen Staatsrechtslehrer* 30 (1972), pp. 162–165.
7. 'Staatsrechtliche Stellung der Ausländer in der BRD', *Veröffentlichungen der Vereinigung der Deutschen Staatsrechtslehrer* 32 (1974), pp. 134–135, 142–144.
8. 'Vertrauensschutz im Verwaltungsrecht', *Veröffentlichungen der Vereinigung der Deutschen Staatsrechtslehrer* 32 (1974), pp. 244–245.
9. 'Parlamentarisches Regierungssystem des Grundgesetzes', *Veröffentlichungen der Vereinigung der Deutschen Staatsrechtslehrer* 33 (1975), pp. 132–134.
10. 'Organisierte Einwirkungen auf die Verwaltung', *Veröffentlichungen der Vereinigung der Deutschen Staatsrechtslehrer* 33 (1975), pp. 297–300.
11. 'Die Funktion von Glaube und Kirche angesichts der Sinnproblematik in Gesellschaft und Kirche heute', *Essener Gespräche zum Thema Staat und Kirche* 11 (1977), pp. 37–39.
12. 'Über die Moralität staatlicher Normsetzung', *Essener Gespräche zum Thema Staat und Kirche* 11 (1977), pp. 82–84.
13. 'Kirchliche Präsenz in Hörfunk und Fernsehen', *Essener Gespräche zum Thema Staat und Kirche* 12 (1978), pp. 35–36, 52–53.
14. 'Positionen, Erfahrungen und Erwartungen im Verhältnis der Kirchen zu den öffentlich-rechtlichen Rundfunkanstalten in der Nachkriegsentwicklung', *Essener Gespräche zum Thema Staat und Kirche* 12 (1978), pp. 81–83.
15. 'Verfassungstreue und Schutz der Verfassung', *Veröffentlichungen der Vereinigung der Deutschen Staatsrechtslehrer* 37 (1978), pp. 138–141.
16. 'Deutschland nach 30 Jahren GG', *Veröffentlichungen der Vereinigung der Deutschen Staatsrechtslehrer* 38 (1980), pp. 118–120.
17. 'Sozialstaat, Besitzindividualismus und die Uneinholbarkeit der Hegelschen Korporation', in Peter Koslowski, Philipp Kreuzer, and Reinhard Löw (eds.),

Chancen und Grenzen des Sozialstaats. Staatstheorie – Politische Ökonomie – Politik (Tübingen: Mohr Siebeck, 1983), pp. 248–250.

18. 'Die Jugendreligionen und die Grenzen der Religionsfreiheit', *Essener Gespräche zum Thema Staat und Kirche* 19 (1985), pp. 156–158.
19. 'Untitled Panel Contributions', in Bundesministerium der Justiz (ed.), *Vierzig Jahre Dritte Gewalt unter dem Grundgesetz. Festveranstaltung am 5.10.1989 in der Paulskirche Frankfurt* (Bonn: Bundesministerium der Justiz, 1989), pp. 20–22, 26–27, 33–36, 41–44, 48.
20. 'Der Gleichheitssatz', *Veröffentlichungen der Vereinigung der Deutschen Staatsrechtslehrer* 47 (1989), pp. 95–96.
21. 'Die Verantwortung der Kirche für den Staat', *Essener Gespräche zum Thema Staat und Kirche* 25 (1991), pp. 96–98.
22. 'Die Einigung Deutschlands und das deutsche Staat-Kirche-System', *Essener Gespräche zum Thema Staat und Kirche* 26 (1992), pp. 32, 35, 101, 129–130.
23. 'Erziehungsauftrag und Erziehungsmaßstab der Schule im freiheitlichen Verfassungsstaat', *Veröffentlichungen der Vereinigung der Deutschen Staatsrechtslehrer* 54 (1995), pp. 125–127.
24. 'Untitled Panel Contributions', in Klaus Grupp and Michael Ronellenfitsch (eds.), *Kommunale Selbstverwaltung in Deutschland. Symposium zum 65. Geburtstag von Prof. Dr. Willi Blümel* (Berlin: Duncker & Humblot, 1995), pp. 52–53, 61–62, 96–97, 117–118, 119–120.
25. 'Das christliche Freiheitsverständnis und seine Bedeutung für die staatliche Rechtsordnung', *Essener Gespräche zum Thema Staat und Kirche* 30 (1996), pp. 71–73.
26. 'Die Staat-Kirche-Ordnung im Blick auf die Europäische Union', *Essener Gespräche zum Thema Staat und Kirche* 31 (Münster, 1997), pp. 43–45.
27. 'Empfiehlt es sich, die Juristenausbildung nach Abschluß des Studiums neu zu regeln?', in s. ed., *Verhandlungen des 62. Deutschen Juristentages, Bremen 1998* (Munich: C. H. Beck, 1998), pp. N 120–N 123.
28. 'Arbeitsmarkt und staatliche Lenkung. Staat und Religion', *Veröffentlichungen der Vereinigung der Deutschen Staatsrechtslehrer* 59 (2000), pp. 148–149, 315–319.
29. 'Untitled Panel Contributions', in Der Präsident des Landtags Rheinland-Pfalz (ed.), *Volk und Parteien – Wer ist der Souverän? Podiumsdiskussion im Landtag Rheinland-Pfalz am 20. Juni 2000* (Mainz: Schriftenreihe des Landtags Rheinland-Pfalz, 2000), pp. 17–22, 50–51.
30. 'Untitled Panel Contributions', in Friedhelm Boll (ed.), *Wir gewähren Vergebung und bitten um Vergebung. 40 Jahre deutsch-polnische Verständigung* (Bonn: Friedrich-Ebert-Stiftung, 2006), pp. 82–91.

G. Edited Volumes and Journals (as Single Editor or Co-editor)

1. Böckenförde, Ernst-Wolfgang et al. (eds.), *Der Staat. Zeitschrift für Staatslehre, öffentliches Recht und Verfassungsgeschichte* (Berlin: Duncker & Humblot, published since 1967)

2. Barion, Hans, Ernst-Wolfgang Böckenförde, Ernst Forsthoff, and Werner Weber (eds.), *Epirrhosis. Festgabe für Carl Schmitt zum 80. Geburtstag. 2 Volumes* (Berlin: Duncker & Humblot, 1968). 2nd edition published in 2002.
3. Böckenförde, Ernst-Wolfgang (ed.) with assistance from Rainer Wahl, *Moderne deutsche Verfassungsgeschichte (1815–1918)* (Cologne: Kiepenheuer & Witsch, 1972). 2nd revised edition published in 1981, Königstein: Athenäum, Hain, Scriptor, Hanstein.
4. Böckle, Franz and Ernst-Wolfgang Böckenförde (eds.), *Naturrecht in der Kritik* (Mainz: Matthias-Grünewald, 1973).
5. Böckenförde, Ernst-Wolfgang (ed.), *Staat und Gesellschaft* (Darmstadt: Wissenschaftliche Buchgesellschaft, 1976).
6. Böckenförde, Ernst-Wolfgang and Lewald Walter (eds.), *Adolf Arndt. Gesammelte juristische Schriften. Ausgewählte Aufsätze und Vorträge 1946–1972* (Munich: C. H. Beck, 1976).
7. Böckenförde, Ernst-Wolfgang, Jürgen Jekewitz, and Thilo Ramm (eds.), *Soziale Grundrechte. Von der bürgerlichen zur sozialen Rechtsordnung. 5. Rechtspolitischer Kongreß der SPD 1980, Dokumentation Teil 2* (Heidelberg: C. F. Müller, 1981).
8. Böckenförde, Ernst-Wolfgang, Christian Tomuschat, and Dieter C. Umbach (eds.), *Extremisten und öffentlicher Dienst. Rechtslage und Praxis des Zugangs zum und der Entlassung aus dem öffentlichen Dienst in Westeuropa, USA, Jugoslawien und der EG* (Baden-Baden: Nomos Verlag, 1981).
9. Böckenförde, Ernst-Wolfgang (ed.), *Staatsrecht und Staatsrechtslehre im Dritten Reich* (Heidelberg: C. F. Müller, 1985).
10. Böckenförde, Ernst-Wolfgang and Robert Spaemann (eds.), *Menschenrechte und Menschenwürde. Historische Voraussetzungen – säkulare Gestalt – christliches Verständnis* (Stuttgart: Ernst Klett, 1987).
11. Böckenförde, Ernst-Wolfgang and Edward Shils (eds.), *Jews and Christians in a Pluralistic World* (London: Weidenfeld & Nicolson, 1991).
12. Böckenförde, Ernst-Wolfgang and Annette Schavan (eds.), *Salz der Erde. Christliche Spiritualität in der Welt von heute* (Stuttgart: Schwabenverlag, 1999).

H. Interviews

1. 'Ist der deutsche Katholizismus systemkonform? Ein Gespräch aus Anlaß des 40jährigen Bestehens der Bundesrepublik', *Herder-Korrespondenz* 43 (1989), pp. 260–266.
2. 'L'Allemagne, le Concile et la politique', *Catholica* 17 (1989), pp. 28–35. (No published German original.)
3. 'Sécularisation, ou démission du politique?', *Catholica*, June (1994), pp. 16–26. (No published German original.)

4. 'Sobre el Derecho y el Estado. Conversación con el Profesor Ernst-Wolfgang Böckenförde', Interview by Jose Juan Gonzalez Encinar, *Anuario de Derecho Constitucional y Parlamentario* 7 (1995), pp. 7–32. (No published German original.)
5. 'Religion im freiheitlichen Staat, anläßlich der Konferenz "Demokratische Politik: Die Agenda der Zukunft" des Instituts der Wissenschaften vom Menschen, Wien', *Inter Medias* 6, 20 June 1997.
6. 'Warum wird dem Volk die Politik egal, Herr Professor Böckenförde?' *Frankfurter Allgemeine Magazin* issue 918, 2 October 1997, pp. 58–59.
7. 'Prawo stwarza wolnos', *Tycodnik Powszechny* 22, 31 May 1998, p. 4. (No published German original.)
8. 'Verfassungsänderung unnötig', *Der Tagesspiegel*, 7 January 1999, p. 2.
9. 'Der Staat ist für die Menschen da. Interview anlässlich des 50. Jahrestages des Grundgesetzes', *Badische Zeitung*, 30 April 1999, Magazin, p. III.
10. 'Die Ungleichheit darf ein gewisses Maß nicht überschreiten', *Süddeutsche Zeitung* 172, 29 July 1999, p. 11.
11. 'Verfassungsurteil gegen Embryonenforschung', *Financial Times Deutschland*, 9 May 2001, p. 12.
12. 'Das Tor zur Selektion ist geöffnet', *Süddeutsche Zeitung* 112, 16 May 2001, p. 11. Also published in Christian Geyer (ed.), *Biopolitik. Die Positionen* (Frankfurt: Suhrkamp, 2001), pp. 112–115.
13. 'Religionsfreiheit ist nicht teilbar', *Herder-Korrespondenz* 58 (2004), pp. 286–291.
14. 'Das Kopftuchverbot trifft auch Kreuz und Kippa', *Süddeutsche Zeitung*, 16 October 2004, p. 6.
15. 'La Constitutión: Entre los Historia y el Derecho, Historia Constitutional', *Revista electrónica* 5 (2004), pp. 319–324. (No published German original.)
16. 'Uns verbindet etwas', *Die Furche. Die österreichische Wochenzeitung* 15, 13 April 2006, p. 9.
17. 'Im Staat sind die Gedanken zollfrei', *Der Tagesspiegel*, 16 July 2007, p. 5.
18. 'Nadal papiestwu ludzka twarz', *Gazeta Wyborcza*, 29/30 November 2008, pp. 16–17. (No published German original.)
19. 'Ich sehe kein Demokratiedefizit', *Der Sonntag*, 24 May 2009, p. 1.
20. 'Freiheit ist ansteckend', *Die Tageszeitung* 31, 23 September 2009, p. 4.
21. 'Il paradosso della laicità', *Avvenire*, 3 November 2009, p. 23. (No published German original.)
22. 'Nie dajmy sie przestraszyć', *Tygodnik Powszechny* 46, 15 November 2009, p. 5. (No published German original.)
23. 'Freiheit ist ansteckend', *Frankfurter Rundschau* 255, 2 November 2010, p. 32.
24. 'Ernst-Wolfgang Böckenförde: "Ich war kein hundertprozentiger Sozi" ', *Badische Zeitung*, 3 May 2017.

I. Translations and Foreign Language Contributions

Note: Translators and editors are listed whenever they could be identified.

I. Arabic

1. 'Demokratie als Verfassungsprinzip' (Part A. Die Anknüpfung an das Prinzip der Volkssouveränität, (pp. 291–296) and Part B. Demokratie als Staats- und Regierungsform (pp. 297–343) from A 17), translated by Dalal Arsuzi-Elamir, Rule of Law Programme Middle East/North Africa, Konrad-Adenauer-Stiftung, 2020. For the German original, see A 17.

II. Czech

1. 'Das Bild vom Menschen in der Perspektive der heutigen Rechtsordnung', in *Člověk v moderních vědách. Castel Gandolfo Gespräche*, 1983, translated and edited by Jiří Pechar, Filozofický Ústav (Prague: ČSAV, 1992). For the German original, see B 96.
2. 'Die Entstehung des Staates als Vorgang der Säkularisation', in Jiří Hanuš (ed.), *Vznik státu jako proces sekularizace: diskuse nad studií Ernsta-Wolfganga Böckenförde* (Brno: Centrum pro studium demokracie a kultur, 2006). For the German original, see B 17.

III. Danish

1. 'Forord [Preface]', in *Carl Schmitt. Det politiskes begreb*, transl. by Lars Bo Larsen and Christian Borch (Copenhagen: Hans Reitzels Forlag, 2002), pp. 7–12. (No published German original.)

IV. English

1. 'German Catholicism in 1933 (Der deutsche Katholizismus im Jahre 1933. Eine kritische Betrachtung)', *Cross Currents* 11 (1961), pp. 283–304. For the German original, see B 5.
2. *State, Society and Liberty. Studies in Political Theory and Constitutional Law (Staat, Gesellschaft, Freiheit)*, transl. by Jim Underwood (Berg, 1991). Includes the following articles:
   a) 'Die Historische Rechtsschule und das Problem der Geschichtlichkeit des Rechts.' For the German original, see B 10.
   b) 'Die Entstehung des Staates als Vorgang der Säkularisation.' For the German original, see B 17.
   c) 'Entstehung und Wandel des Rechtsstaatsbegriffs.' For the German original, see B 23.
   d) 'Der deutsche Typ der konstitutionellen Monarchie im 19. Jahrhundert.' For the German original, see B 19.

e) 'Lorenz von Stein als Theoretiker der Bewegung von Staat und Gesellschaft zum Sozialstaat.' For the German original, see B 9.

f) 'Die Bedeutung der Unterscheidung von Staat und Gesellschaft im demokratischen Sozialstaat der Gegenwart.' For the German original, see B 33.

g) 'Grundrechtstheorie und Grundrechtsinterpretation.' For the German original, see B 47.

h) 'Das Grundrecht der Gewissensfreiheit.' For the German original, see B 28.

i) 'Freiheitssicherung gegenüber gesellschaftlicher Macht. Aufriss eines Problems.' For the German original, see B 49.

3. 'Carl Schmitt revisited (Auf dem Weg zum Klassiker. Carl Schmitt in der Diskussion: Politische Theologie als Fluchtpunkt seines Werks, expanded version)', *Telos* 109 (1996), pp. 81–86. For the German original, see B 138.

4. 'The Concept of the Political: A Key to Understanding Carl Schmitt's Constitutional Theory (Der Begriff des Politischen als Schlüssel zum staatsrechtlichen Werk Carl Schmitts)', transl. by Heiner Bielefeldt, *The Canadian Journal of Law and Jurisprudence* 10:1 (1997), pp. 5–19. For the German original, see B 108.

5. 'Conditions for European Solidarity (Bedingungen der europäischen Solidarität, shortened and revised version)', in Krzysztof Michalski (ed.), *What Holds Europe Together?* (Budapest: Central European University Press, 2005) pp. 30–41. Also published in *Europa PL*, 3 February 2006. For the German original, see B 177.

6. Künkler, Mirjam and Tine Stein (eds.), *Constitutional and Political Theory. Selected Writings*, transl. by Thomas Dunlap (Oxford: Oxford University Press, 2017). Includes the following articles:

a) 'Sicherheit und Selbsterhaltung vor Gerechtigkeit. Der Paradigmenwechsel und Übergang von einer naturrechtlichen zur positivrechtlichen Grundlegung des Rechtssystems bei Thomas Hobbes'. For the German original, see A 24.

b) 'Der Begriff des Politischen als Schlüssel zum staatsrechtlichen Werk Carl Schmitts'. For the German original, see B 108.

c) 'Der Staat als sittlicher Staat'. For the German original, see A 9.

d) 'Der verdrängte Ausnahmezustand. Zum Handeln der Staatsgewalt in außergewöhnlichen Lagen'. For the German original, see B 65.

e) 'Begriff und Probleme des Verfassungsstaates'. For the German original, see B 142.

f) 'Geschichtliche Entwicklung und Bedeutungswandel der Verfassung'. For the German original, see B 89.

g) 'Die verfassunggebende Gewalt des Volkes. Ein Grenzbegriff des Verfassungsrechts'. For the German original, see A 11.

h) 'Verfassungsgerichtsbarkeit. Strukturfragen, Organisation, Legitimation'. For the German original, see B 146.

i) 'Zur Kritik der Wertbegründung des Rechts'. For the German original, see B 105.

j) 'Grundrechte als Grundsatznormen. Zur gegenwärtigen Lage der Grundrechtsdogmatik'. For the German original, see B 113.

k) 'Grundrechtstheorie und Grundrechtsinterpretation'. For the German original, see B 47.

l) 'Freiheitssicherung gegenüber gesellschaftlicher Macht. Aufriss eines Problems'. For the German original, see B 49.
m) 'Die Verfolgung der deutschen Juden als Bürgerverrat'. For the German original, see B 138.
n) 'Staatsbürgerschaft und Nationalitätskonzept'. For the German original, see D 51. Also published in A 19.
o) 'Die Zukunft politischer Autonomie: Demokratie und Staatlichkeit im Zeichen von Globalisierung, Internationalisierung und Individualisierung'. For the German original, see B 144. Also published in A 19.
p) 'Welchen Weg geht Europa?' For the German original, see A 18.
q) 'Biographisches Interview mit Ernst-Wolfgang Böckenförde [Excerpts]'. For the German original, see A 27.

7. Künkler, Mirjam and Tine Stein (eds.), *Religion, Law, and Democracy. Selected Writings*, transl. by Thomas Dunlap (Oxford: Oxford University Press, 2020). Includes the following articles:
a) 'Das Ethos der modernen Demokratie und die Kirche'. For the German original, see B 1.
b) 'Der deutsche Katholizismus im Jahre 1933. Eine kritische Betrachtung'. For the German original, see B 5.
c) 'Formen christlichen Weltverhaltens während der NS-Herrschaft'. For the German original, see A 23.
d) 'Die Religionsfreiheit im Spannungsfeld zwischen Kirche und Staat'. For the German original, see B 92.
e) 'Die Entstehung des Staates als Vorgang der Säkularisation'. For the German original, see B 17.
f) 'Das Grundrecht der Gewissensfreiheit.' For the German original, see B 28.
g) 'Bemerkungen zum Verhältnis von Staat und Religion bei Hegel'. For the German original, see B 85.
h) 'Der säkularisierte Staat. Sein Charakter, seine Rechtfertigung und seine Probleme im 21. Jahrhundert'. For the German original, see A 25.
i) 'Politische Theorie und politische Theologie. Bemerkungen zu ihrem gegenseitigen Verhältnis'. For the German original, see B 74.
j) 'Überlegungen zu einer Theologie des modernen säkularen Rechts'. For the German original, see B 150.
k) 'Als Christ im Amt eines Verfassungsrichters'. For the German original, see B 148.
l) 'Über die Autorität päpstlicher Lehrenzykliken am Beispiel der Äußerungen zur Religionsfreiheit'. For the German original, see B 191.
m) 'Abschaffung des § 218 StGB? Überlegungen zur gegenwärtigen Diskussion um das strafrechtliche Abtreibungsverbot'. For the German original, see B 31.
n) 'Menschenwürde als normatives Prinzip'. For the German original, see B 174.
o) 'Bleibt die Menschenwürde unantastbar?' For the German original, see B 184.
p) 'Biographisches Interview mit Ernst-Wolfgang Böckenförde [Excerpts]'. For the German original, see A 27.

V. French

1. 'Les juifs et la trahison allemande (Die Verfolgung der deutschen Juden als Bürgerverrat)', *Le Monde*, 8 November 1997, p. 15. For the German original, see B 138.
2. Olivier Jouanjan (ed.), *Le Droit, l'État et la Constitution Démocratique. Essais de théorie juridique, politique et constitutionnelle [Law, the State, and the Democratic Constitution. Essays in Legal, Political, and Constitutional Theory]*, transl. by Olivier Jouanjan (inter alia on the basis of two previous article translations by Willy Zimmer and one previous article translation by Olivier Beaud) (Paris: LGDJ, Bruylant, 2000). Includes the following articles:
   a) 'Die historische Rechtsschule und das Problem der Geschichtlichkeit des Rechts'. For the German original, see B 10.
   b) 'Zur Kritik der Wertbegründung des Rechts'. For the German original, see B 105.
   c) 'Die Entstehung des Staates als Vorgang der Säkularisation'. For the German original, see B 17.
   d) 'Der Staat als Organismus. Zur staatstheoretischen Diskussion in der Vormärzzeit'. For the German original, see B 63.
   e) 'Entstehung und Wandel des Rechtsstaatsbegriffs'. For the German original, see B 23.
   f) 'Lorenz von Stein als Theoretiker der Bewegung von Staat und Gesellschaft zum Sozialstaat'. For the German original, see B 9.
   g) 'Die Bedeutung der Unterscheidung von Staat und Gesellschaft im demokratischen Sozialstaat der Gegenwart'. For the German original, see B 33.
   h) 'Die verfassunggebende Gewalt des Volkes. Ein Grenzbegriff des Verfassungsrechts'. For the German original, see A 11.
   i) 'Die Methoden der Verfassungsinterpretation – Bestandsaufnahme und Kritik'. For the German original, see B 52.
   j) 'Grundrechtstheorie und Grundrechtsinterpretation'. For the German original, see B 47.
   k) 'Prinzipien der Demokratie als Staats- und Regierungsform'. (No published German original, published only in Japanese and French.)
   l) 'Demokratie und Repräsentation. Zur Kritik der heutigen Demokratiediskussion'. Also published in *Trivium. Revue franco-allemande de sciences humaines et sociales* 6 (2014). For the German original, see A 10.
3. 'L'Europe et la Turquie (Europa und die Türkei)', transl. by Jochen Hoock, *Le Débat* 137:5 (2005), pp. 60–72. For the German original, see B 185.

VI. Italian

1. *La storiografia costituzionale tedesca nel secolo decimonono. Problematica e modelli dell'epoca (Die deutsche verfassungsgeschichtliche Forschung im 19. Jahrhundert. Zeitgebundene Fragestellungen und Leitbilder)*, translated and with an introduction by Pierangelo Schiera (Milan: Giuffrè, 1970). For the German original, see A 2.

2. 'La pace di Westfalia e il diritto di alleanza dei ceti dell'impero (Der Westfälische Friede und das Bündnisrecht der Reichsstände)', transl. by Ettore Rotelli and Pierangelo Schiera, in Ettore Rotelli and Pierangelo Schiera (eds.), *Lo stato moderno* (Bologna: Il Mulino, 1974), pp. 25–34. For the German original, see B 25.
3. 'Commissioni parlamentari d'inchiesta e autonomia comunale (Parlamentarische Untersuchungsausschüsse und Kommunale Selbstverwaltung)', transl. by Girolamo Sciullo, *Problemi di amministrazione pubblica* (1979), pp. 126–182. For the German original, see B 59.
4. ‚Democrazia e rappresentanza (Demokratie und Repräsentation. Zur Kritik der heutigen Demokratiediskussion)', transl. by Pasquale Pasquino, *Quaderni costituzionali* 2 (1985), pp. 227–63. Also published in: Michele Nicoletti and Omar Brino (eds.), *Stato, costituzione, democrazia (Staat, Verfassung, Demokratie)* (Milan: Giuffrè, 2006). For the German original, see A 10.
5. 'La formazione dello stato come processo di secolarizzazione (Die Entstehung des Staates als Vorgang der Säkularisation)', in Paolo Prodi and Luigi Sartori (eds.), *Cristianesimo e potere. Atti del seminario tenuto a Trento il 21–22 giugno 1985* (Bologna: EDB Edizioni dehoniane, 1986), pp. 101–122. Also published in Michel Nicoletti (ed.), *La formazione dello stato come processo di secolarizzazione*, transl. by Corrado Bertani and with a new introduction by Michele Nicoletti (Brescia: Morcelliana, 2006). Also published in Geminello Preterossi (ed.), *Diritto e secolarizzazione. Dallo Stato moderno all'Europa unita (Recht und Säkularisierung. Vom modernen Staat zum vereinten Europa)*, transl. by Mario Carpitella (Rome: Editori Laterza, 2007). For the German original, see B 17.
6. *Il potere costituente del popolo. Un concetto limite del diritto costituzionale (Die verfassunggebende Gewalt des Volkes. Ein Grenzbegriff des Verfassungsrechts)*, in Gustavo Zagrebelsky, Pier Paolo Portinaro, and Jörg Luther (eds.), *Il futuro della costituzione* (Turin: Einaudi, 1996), pp. 231–252. Also published in Michele Nicoletti and Omar Brino (eds.), *Stato, costituzione, democrazia (Staat, Verfassung, Demokratie)* (Milan: Giuffrè, 2006). For the German original, see A 11.
7. 'II rapporto tra Chiesa e Mondo Moderno. I contorni di un problema (Zum Verhältnis von Kirche und moderner Welt)', transl. by Antonio Furlanetto, in Reinhart Koselleck (ed.), *Gli inizi del Mondo Moderno* (Milan: Vita e Pensiero, 1997), pp. 199–230. For the German original, see B 55.
8. 'Teoria politica e teologia politica. Osservazioni sul loro rapporto reciproco (Politische Theorie und politische Theologie. Bemerkungen zu ihrem gegenseitigen Verhältnis)', transl. by Giulio Colombi, *Hermeneutica - Annuario di Filosofia e Teologia fondato da Italo Mancini - Nuova Serie* (Brescia: Morcelliana, 1998), pp. 65–80. Also published in Michele Nicoletti (ed.), *Cristianesimo, libertà, democrazia (Christentum, Freiheit, Demokratie)* (Brescia: Morcelliana, 2007), pp. 339–352. For the German original, see B 74.
9. 'Teologia e politica. Responsabilità della Chiesa nel mondo d'oggi (Wahrheit und Freiheit. Zur Weltverantwortung der Kirche heute)', transl. by Giancarlo Caronello, *Il Regno* 20 (2004), pp. 721ff. For the German original, see B 181.
10. 'Roma ha parlato, la discussione è aperta (Shortened preprint of: Über die Autorität päpstlicher Lehrenzykliken am Beispiel der Äußerungen zur

Religionsfreiheit)', transl. by Giancarlo Caronello, *Il Regno* 22 (2005), pp. 739–744. For the German original, see B 191.

11. Nicoletti, Michele and Omar Brino (eds.), *Stato, costituzione, democrazia [State, Constitution, Democracy]* (Milan: Giuffrè, 2006). Includes the following articles:
   a) 'Das Grundrecht der Gewissensfreiheit'. For the German original, see B 28.
   b) 'Grundrechtstheorie und Grundrechtsinterpretation'. For the German original, see B 47.
   c) 'Freiheitssicherung gegenüber gesellschaftlicher Macht'. For the German original, see B 49.
   d) 'Die politische Funktion wirtschaftlich-sozialer Verbände und Interessenträger in der sozialstaatlichen Demokratie. Ein Beitrag zum Problem der "Regierbarkeit"'. For the German original, see B 53.
   e) 'Die Methoden der Verfassungsinterpretation – Bestandsaufnahme und Kritik'. For the German original, see B 52.
   f) 'Verhaltensgewähr oder Gesinnungstreue? Sicherung der freiheitlichen Demokratie in den Formen des Rechtsstaates'. For the German original, see B 62.
   g) 'Sozialer Bundesstaat und parlamentarische Demokratie'. For the German original, see B 72.
   h) 'Die sozialen Grundrechte im Verfassungsgefüge'. For the German original, see B 73.
   i) 'Demokratie und Repräsentation. Zur Kritik der heutigen Demokratiediskussion'. For the German original, see A 10.
   j) 'Die Eigenart des Staatsrechts und der Staatsrechtswissenschaft'. For the German original, see B 86.
   k) 'Geschichtliche Entwicklung und Bedeutungswandel der Verfassung'. For the German original, see B 89.
   l) 'Die verfassunggebende Gewalt des Volkes. Ein Grenzbegriff des Verfassungsrechts'. For the German original, see A 11.
   m) 'Grundrechte als Grundsatznormen. Zur gegenwärtigen Lage der Grundrechtsdogmatik'. For the German original, see B 113.
   n) 'Anmerkungen zum Begriff Verfassungswandel'. For the German original, see B 123.
   o) 'Begriff und Probleme des Verfassungsstaates'. For the German original, see B 142.
   p) 'Verfassungsgerichtsbarkeit. Strukturfragen, Organisation, Legitimation'. For the German original, see B 146.
   q) 'Demokratie als Verfassungsprinzip'. For the German original, see B 106.

12. Bertani, Corrado and Sara Bignotti (eds.), *Cristianesimo, libertà, democrazia [Christianity, Freedom, Democracy]*, transl. by Alberto Anelli (Brescia: Morcelliana, 2007). Includes the following articles:
   a) 'Das Ethos der modernen Demokratie und die Kirche'. For the German original, see B 1.
   b) 'Religionsfreiheit als Aufgabe der Christen'. For the German original, see B 11.

c) 'Die Religionsfreiheit im Spannungsfeld zwischen Kirche und Staat'. For the German original, see B 92.

d) 'Politisches Mandat der Kirche?' For the German original, see B 26.

e) 'Kirchliches Naturrecht und politisches Handeln'. For the German original, see B 42.

f) 'Zum Verhältnis von Kirche und moderner Welt'. For the German original, see B 55.

g) 'Das neue politische Engagement der Kirche. Zur "Politischen Theologie" Johannes Pauls II'. For the German original, see B 68.

h) 'Ethische und politische Grundsatzfragen zur Zeit. Überlegungen aus Anlass von 90 Jahren "rerum novarum"'. For the German original, see B 76.

i) 'Politische Theorie und politische Theologie. Bemerkungen zu ihrem gegenseitigen Verhältnis'. For the German original, see B 74.

j) 'Kirche und modernes Bewußtsein'. For the German original, see B 101.

k) 'Der Beitrag politischen Handelns zur Verwirklichung von Gerechtigkeit'. For the German original, see B 121.

l) 'Autorität – Gewissen – Normfindung. Thesen zur weiteren Diskussion'. For the German original, see B 122.

m) 'Religion im säkularen Staat'. For the German original, see B 132, B 172.

n) 'Wahrheit und Freiheit. Zur Weltverantwortung der Kirche heute'. For the German original, see B 181.

o) 'Über die Autorität päpstlicher Lehrenzykliken am Beispiel der Äußerungen zur Religionsfreiheit'. For the German original, see B 191.

13. Preterossi, Geminello (ed.), *Diritto e secolarizzazione. Dallo Stato moderno all'Europa unita [Law and Secularisation. From the Modern State to a United Europe]*, transl. by Mario Carpitella (Rome: Editori Laterza, 2007). Includes the following articles:

a) 'Die historische Rechtsschule und das Problem der Geschichtlichkeit des Rechts'. For the German original, see B 10.

b) 'Die Entstehung des Staates als Vorgang der Säkularisation'. For the German original, see B 17.

c) 'Die Bedeutung der Unterscheidung von Staat und Gesellschaft im demokratischen Sozialstaat der Gegenwart'. For the German original, see B 33.

d) 'Bemerkungen zum Verhältnis von Staat und Religion bei Hegel'. For the German original, see B 85.

e) 'Der Begriff des Politischen als Schlüssel zum staatsrechtlichen Werk Carl Schmitts'. For the German original, see B 108.

f) 'Die Nation – Identität in Differenz'. For the German original, see B 127.

g) 'Staatsbürgerschaft und Nationalitätskonzept'. For the German original, see D 51. Also published in A 19.

h) 'Welchen Weg geht Europa?' For the German original, see A 18.

i) 'Die Zukunft politischer Autonomie. Demokratie und Staatlichkeit im Zeichen von Globalisierung, Europäisierung und Individualisierung'. For the German original, B 144. Also published in A 19.

14. 'Libertà religiosa e diritto: Lo stato secolarizzato e i suoi valori (Der säkularisierte Staat. Sein Charakter, seine Rechtfertigung und seine Probleme im 21. Jahrhundert)', transl. by Giancarlo Caronello, *Il Regno* 18 (2007), pp. 637–648. For the German original, see A 25.
15. 'L'uomo funzionale. Capitalismo, proprietà, ruolo degli stati (Woran der Kapitalismus krankt)', transl. by Giancarlo Caronello, *Il Regno* 10 (2009), pp. 289–291. For the German original, see B 196.
16. 'Dignità umana e bioetica (Menschenwürde und Bioethik)', edited and transl. by Sara Bignotti (Brescia: Morcelliana, 2009. For the German original, see H 12 and B 174.
17. 'Di cosa soffre il capitalismo (Woran der Kapitalismus krankt)', transl. by Sara Bignotti and Ilario Bertoletti, in Michele Nicoletti (ed.), *Chiesa e capitalismo (Kirche und Kapitalismus)* (Brescia: Morcelliana, 2010, pp. 21–32. For the German original, see B 196.
18. 'Quel senso pre giuridico di "communanza"', *Reset* 104 (2007), pp. 16–17. (No published German original.)
19. *Lo Stato come Stato etico* (Der Staat als sittlicher Staat), edited and transl. by Elisa Bertò (Pisa: Edizioni ETS, 2017). For the German original, see A 9.

VII. Japanese

1. Shiyake, Masanori (ed.), *Gendai Kokka to Kempo, Jiyu, Minshusei [The Modern State, Constitution, Freedom, and Democracy]* (Tokyo: Fukosha, 1999). The volume contains articles from Böckenförde's books *Recht, Staat, Freiheit* and *Staat, Verfassung, Demokratie* as well as manuscripts of lectures Böckenförde held during his trip to Japan in 1996, specifically:
   a) 'Die Eigenart des Staatsrechts und der Staatsrechtswissenschaft'. For the German original, see B 86.
   b) 'Entstehung und Wandel des Rechtsstaatsbegriffs'. For the German original, see B 23.
   c) 'Die Bedeutung der Unterscheidung von Staat und Gesellschaft im demokratischen Sozialstaat der Gegenwart'. For the German original, see B 33.
   d) 'Freiheit und Recht, Freiheit und Staat'. For the German original, see B 102.
   e) 'Geschichtliche Entwicklung und Bedeutungswandel der Verfassung in Deutschland und Europa'. For the German original, see B 89.
   f) 'Begriff und Probleme des Verfassungsstaates'. For the German original, see B 142.
   g) 'Die verfassunggebende Gewalt des Volkes. Ein Grenzbegriff des Verfassungsrechts'. For the German original, see A 11.

h) 'Verfassungsgerichtsbarkeit. Strukturfragen, Organisation, Legitimation'. For the German original, see B 146.
i) 'Prinzipien der Demokratie als Staats- und Regierungsform'. (No published German original, published only in Japanese and French.)
j) 'Demokratie und Repräsentation. Zur Kritik der heutigen Demokratiediskussion'. For the German original, see A 10.
k) 'Grundrechtstheorie und Grundrechtsinterpretation'. For the German original, see B 47.
l) 'Die sozialen Grundrechte im Verfassungsgefüge'. For the German original, see B 73.
m) 'Freiheitssicherung gegenüber gesellschaftlicher Macht. Aufriss eines Problems'. For the German original, see B 49.
n) 'Zur Lage der Grundrechtsdogmatik nach 40 Jahren Grundgesetz'. For the German original, see A 15.
o) 'Probleme des normativen Gehalts der Grundrechte'. Published only in Japanese.

2. 'Der deutsche Typ der konstitutionellen Monarchie im 19. Jahrhundert', in Osamu Naruse (ed.), *Dento Shakai to Kindai Kokka* (Tokyo: Iwanami-shoten, 1982), pp. 487–522. For the German original, see B 19.
3. 'Der Begriff des Politischen als Schlüssel zum staatsrechtlichen Werk Carl Schmitts', in Masanori Shiyake and Keita Koga (eds.), *Carl Schmitt no Isan* (Fukosha, 1993), pp. 282–308. For the German original, see B 108.
4. 'Religionsfreiheit als Aufgabe der Christen', in *Shakai to Rinri, Vol. 7*, (Nagoya: University of Nanzan, 1999), pp. 159–173. For the German original, see B 11.
5. 'Die Religionsfreiheit im Spannungsfeld zwischen Kirche und Staat', in *Shakai to Rinri. Vol. 7* (Nagoya: University of Nanzan, 1999), pp. 174–194. For the German original, see B 92.
6. 'Die Entstehung des Staates als Vorgang der Säkularisation', in *Ho no Riron. Vol. 22* (Tokyo: Seibundo, 2003), pp. 49–74. For the German original, see B 17.
7. 'Bleibt die Menschenwürde unantastbar?' *Hikaku Hogaku, Waseda* 42:2 (2009), pp. 267–288. For the German original, see B 184.
8. 'Book review: Konrad Hesse, *Die normative Kraft der Verfassung*', in Toyoaki Furuno and Yuhiko Miyake (eds.), *Kempo no Kihanryoku, Vol. 1: Kihanryoku no Kannen to Joken* (Tokyo: Shinzansha, 2013), pp. 219–222. For the German original, see D 3.

VIII. Korean

1. 'Entstehung und Wandel des Rechtsstaatsbegriffs', transl. by Hyo-Jeon Kim, *Wolgangoshi* 12:1 (1985), pp. 28–44, 80–91. Also published in *Verfassung, Staat, Freiheit. Studien zur Verfassungstheorie und Staatstheorie*, transl. by Hyo-Jeon Kim (Seoul: Bŏbmun-Sa, 1992). For the German original, see B 23.
2. 'Der deutsche Typ der konstitutionellen Monarchie im 19. Jahrhundert', transl. by Hyo-Jeon Kim, *Wolgangoshi* 14:4 (1987), pp. 129–155. Also published in *Verfassung, Staat, Freiheit. Studien zur Verfassungstheorie und Staatstheorie*, transl. by Hyo-Jeon Kim (Seoul: Bŏbmun-Sa, 1992). For the German original, see B 19.

3. 'Die verfassungstheoretische Unterscheidung von Staat und Gesellschaft als Bedingung der individuellen Freiheit', transl. by Hyo-Jeon Kim, *DongaBobhak/Dong-A Law Review* 4 (1987), pp. 143–217. Also published in *Die verfassungstheoretische Unterscheidung von Staat und Gesellschaft als Bedingung der individuellen Freiheit*, transl. by Hyo-Jeon Kim (Seoul: Bŏbmun-Sa, 1989). For the German original, see A 6.
4. 'Die sozialen Grundrechte im Verfassungsgefüge', transl. by Hyo-Jeon Kim, *Koshi Yonku* 16: 4 (1989), pp. 199–211. Also published in *Verfassung, Staat, Freiheit. Studien zur Verfassungstheorie und Staatstheorie*, transl. by Hyo-Jeon Kim (Seoul: Bŏbmun-Sa, 1992). For the German original, see B 73.
5. 'Die verfassunggebende Gewalt des Volkes. Ein Grenzbegriff des Verfassungsrechts', transl. by Hyo-Jeon Kim, *Koshikye* 34:12 (1989), pp. 165–172 and 35:6 (1990), pp. 153–165. Also published in *Verfassung, Staat, Freiheit. Studien zur Verfassungstheorie und Staatstheorie*, transl. by Hyo-Jeon Kim (Seoul: Bŏbmun-Sa, 1992). For the German original, see A 11.
6. *Die verfassungstheoretische Unterscheidung von Staat und Gesellschaft als Bedingung der individuellen Freiheit*, transl. by Hyo-Jeon Kim (Seoul: Bŏbmun-Sa, 1989). 3rd edition published in 2020. For the German original, see A 6. Includes the following articles:
    a) 'Die verfassungstheoretische Unterscheidung von Staat und Gesellschaft als Bedingung der individuellen Freiheit'. For the German original, see A 6.
    b) 'Staat und Gesellschaft'. For the German original, see B 108.
    c) 'Die Bedeutung der Unterscheidung von Staat und Gesellschaft im demokratischen Sozialstaat der Gegenwart'. Also published in *Verfassung, Staat, Freiheit. Studien zur Verfassungstheorie und Staatstheorie*, transl. by Hyo-Jeon Kim (Seoul: Bŏbmun-Sa, 1992). For the German original, see B 33.
7. 'Grundrechtstheorie und Grundrechtsinterpretation', transl. by Hyo-Jeon Kim, in *Gegenwärtige Aufgabe der öffentlichen Rechtstheorie. Festschrift für Byung-Sack Koo* (Seoul, 1991), pp. 97–124. Also published in *Verfassung, Staat, Freiheit. Studien zur Verfassungstheorie und Staatstheorie*, transl. by Hyo-Jeon Kim (Seoul: Bŏbmun-Sa, 1992). Also published in *Staat, Verfassung, Demokratie*, transl. by Hyo-Jeon Kim and Tae-Ho Chung (Bŏbmun-Sa, 2003). For the German original, see B 47.
8. 'Freiheitssicherung gegenüber gesellschaftlicher Macht', transl. by Hyo-Jeon Kim, *Wolgangoshi* 18:9 (1991), pp. 58–70. Also published in *Verfassung, Staat, Freiheit. Studien zur Verfassungstheorie und Staatstheorie*, transl. by Hyo-Jeon Kim (Seoul: Bŏbmun-Sa, 1992). Also published *in Staat, Verfassung, Demokratie*, transl. by Hyo-Jeon Kim and Tae-Ho Chung (Seoul: Bŏbmun-Sa, 2003) For the German original, see B 49.
9. *Constitution, State, Freedom. Essays on Constitutional Theory and Theories of the State*, transl. by Hyo-Jeon Kim (Seoul: Bŏbmun-Sa, 1992). Includes the following articles:
    a) 'Die verfassunggebende Gewalt des Volkes. Ein Grenzbegriff des Verfassungsrechts'. For the German original, see A 11.
    b) 'Geschichtliche Entwicklung und Bedeutungswandel der Verfassung'. For the German original, see B 89.

c) 'Entstehung und Wandel des Rechtsstaatsbegriffs'. For the German original, see B 23.

d) 'Der deutsche Typ der konstitutionellen Monarchie im 19. Jahrhundert'. For the German original, see B 19.

e) 'Die Bedeutung der Unterscheidung von Staat und Gesellschaft im demokratischen Sozialstaat der Gegenwart'. For the German original, see B 33.

f) 'Grundrechtstheorie und Grundrechtsinterpretation'. For the German original, see B 47.

g) 'Die sozialen Grundrechte im Verfassungsgefüge'. For the German original, see B 73.

h) 'Eigentum, Sozialbindung des Eigentums, Enteignung'. For the German original, see B 35.

i) 'Freiheitssicherung gegenüber gesellschaftlicher Macht'. For the German original, see B 49.

j) 'Demokratie und Repräsentation'. For the German original, see A 10.

k) 'Der verdrängte Ausnahmezustand'. For the German original, see B 65.

10. 'Der Begriff des Politischen als Schlüssel zum staatsrechtlichen Werk Carl Schmitts', transl. by Hyo-Jeon Kim, in *Carl Schmitt. Der Begriff des Politischen* (Seoul: Bŏbmun-Sa, 1995), pp. 183–209. For the German original, see B 108.

11. 'Zur Lage der Grundrechtsdogmatik nach 40 Jahren Grundgesetz', transl. by Hyo-Jeon Kim, *Dong-A Bobhak/Dong-A Law Review* 21 (1996), pp. 217–271. Also published in *AnamBobhak/Anam Law Review* 4 (1996), pp. 235–294, transl. by Hee-su Choi. Also published in *Staat, Verfassung, Demokratie*, transl. by Hyo-Jeon Kim and Tae-Ho Chung (Seoul: Bŏbmun-Sa, 2003). For the German original, see A 15.

12. 'Die Eigenart des Staatsrechts und der Staatsrechtswissenschaft', transl. by Hyo-Jeon Kim, *Kyung HeeBobhak/Kyung Hee Law Journal* 35:1 (2000), pp. 245–262. Also published in *Staat, Verfassung, Demokratie*, transl. by Hyo-Jeon Kim and Tae-Ho Chung (Seoul: Bŏbmun-Sa, 2003). For the German original, see B 86.

13. 'Verfassungsgerichtsbarkeit. Strukturfragen, Organisation, Legitimation', transl. by Hyo-Jeon Kim, *Dokilhak Yonku* 17 (2001), pp. 103–122. Also published in *Staat, Verfassung, Demokratie*, transl. by Hyo-Jeon Kim and Tae-Ho Chung (Seoul: Bŏbmun-Sa, 2003). For the German original, see B 146.

14. 'Begriff und Probleme des Verfassungsstaates', transl. by Hyo-Jeon Kim, *Koshi Yonku* 29:9 (2002), pp. 134–148. Also published in *Sungkyunkwan Law Review* 14:2 (2002), pp. 321–333. Also published in *Staat, Verfassung, Demokratie*, transl. by Hyo-Jeon Kim and Tae-Ho Chung (Seoul: Bŏbmun-Sa, 2003). For the German original, see B 142.

15. 'Die Methoden der Verfassungsinterpretation – Bestandsaufnahme und Kritik', transl. by Hyo-Jeon Kim, *Honbobhak Yonku* 8:2 (2002), pp. 443–483. Also published in Hyo-Jeon Kim (ed.), *Quellen zur deutschen Verfassungslehre* (Busan: Sanzini, 2018), pp. 179–207. For the German original, see B 52.

16. 'Religionsfreiheit im Spannungsfeld zwischen Kirche und Staat', transl. by Hyo-Jeon Kim, *Honbobhak Yonku* 8:4 (2002), pp. 529–561. Also published in Hyo-Jeon Kim (ed.), *Quellen zur deutschen Verfassungslehre* (Busan: Sanzini, 2018), pp. 622–644. For the German original, see B 92.
17. *State, Constitution, Democracy*, transl. by Hyo-Jeon Kim and Tae-Ho Chung (Seoul: Bŏbmun-Sa, 2003). Includes the following articles:
    a) 'Die Eigenart des Staatsrechts und der Staatsrechtswissenschaft'. For the German original, see B 86.
    b) 'Begriff und Probleme des Verfassungsstaates'. For the German original, see B 142.
    c) 'Freiheit und Recht, Freiheit und Staat'. For the German original, see B 102.
    d) 'Grundrechtstheorie und Grundrechtsinterpretation'. For the German original, see B 47.
    e) 'Die sozialen Grundrechte im Verfassungsgefüge'. For the German original, see B 73.
    f) 'Zur Lage der Grundrechtsdogmatik nach 40 Jahren Grundgesetz'. For the German original, see A 15.
    g) 'Freiheitssicherung gegenüber gesellschaftlicher Macht'. For the German original, see B 49.
    h) 'Verhaltensgewähr oder Gesinnungstreue? Sicherung der freiheitlichen Demokratie in der Form des Rechtsstaates'. For the German original, see B 62.
    i) 'Demokratie als Verfassungsprinzip'. For the German original, see B 106.
    j) 'Die politische Funktion wirtschaftlich-sozialer Verbände und Interessenträger in der sozialstaatlichen Demokratie'. For the German original, see B 53.
    k) 'Ist die Demokratie eine notwendige Forderung der Menschenrechte?' For the German original, see B 135.
    l) 'Verfassungsgerichtsbarkeit. Strukturfragen, Organisation, Legitimation'. For the German original, see B 146.
18. 'Religionsfreiheit als Aufgabe der Christen', transl. by Hyo-Jeon Kim, *Honbobhak Yonku* 9:1 (2003), pp. 487–509. Also published in Hyo-Jeon Kim (ed.), *Quellen zur deutschen Verfassungslehre* (Busan: Sanzini, 2018), pp. 645–658. For the German original, see B 11.
19. 'Die Entstehung des Staates als Vorgang der Säkularisation', transl. by Hyo-Jeon Kim, *Honbobhak Yonku* 10:4 (2004), pp. 589–615. Also published in Hyo-Jeon Kim (ed.), *Quellen zur deutschen Verfassungslehre* (Busan: Sanzini, 2018), pp. 287–303. For the German original, see B 17.

IX. Polish

1. 'Nowy Sposób Politycznego. Zaangażowania Kościoła - o "Teologii Politycznej" Jana Pawła II (Das neue politische Engagement der Kirche. Zur "politischen Theologie" Johannes Pauls II.)', in *Znak Miesięcznik*, Kraków, Rok XXXVII, Marzec 3 (1985), pp. 3–24. For the German original, see B 68.

2. 'Wizerunek człowieka w świetle dzisiejszego porządku prawnego (Das Bild vom Menschen in der Perspektive der heutigen Rechtsordnung)', in *Człowiek w nauce współczesnej. Rozmowy w Castel Gandolfo* (Krakow: Znak, 1988), pp. 115–126. 2nd edition published in 2006. For the German original, see B 96.
3. *Wolność-państwo-Kościół [Freedom, State, Church]*, transl. by Paweł Kaczorowski and Grzegorz Sowinski Wstęp ks. Józef Tischner (Krakow: Znak, 1994). Includes the following articles:
   a) 'Das Ethos der modernen Demokratie und die Kirche'. For the German original, see B 1.
   b) 'Religionsfreiheit im Spannungsfeld zwischen Kirche und Staat'. For the German original, see B 92.
   c) 'Stellung und Bedeutung der Religion in einer "Civil Society"'. For the German original, see B 111.
   d) 'Die Entstehung des Staates als Vorgang der Säkularisation'. For the German original, see B 17.
   e) 'Zur Kritik der Wertbegründung des Rechts'. For the German original, see B 103.
   f) 'Freiheit und Recht, Freiheit und Staat'. For the German original, see B 102.
   g) 'Der Staat als sittlicher Staat'. For the German original, see A 9.
   h) 'Zum Verhältnis von Kirche und moderner Welt'. For the German original, see B 55.
   i) 'Kirche und modernes Bewußtsein'. For the German original, see B 101.
   j) 'Der Beitrag politischen Handelns zur Verwirklichung von Gerechtigkeit'. For the German original, see B 121.
   k) 'Kirchliches Naturrecht und politisches Handeln'. For the German original, see B 42.
4. 'Idee ładu społecznego i politycznego w Rewolucji Francuskiej (Die sozialen und politischen Ordnungsideen der Französischen Revolution)', in *Europa i społeczenstwo obywatelskie. Rozmowy w Castel Gandolfo* (Krakow: Znak, 1994). For the German original, see B 112.
5. 'Wartości chrześcijańskie w polityce (Christliche Werte in der Politik)', *Transit* 3 (1997), pp. 21–24. For the German original, see B 136.
6. 'Historyczny rozwój i różne znaczenia pojecia konstytucji (Geschichtliche Entwicklung und Bedeutungswandel der Verfassung)', *Civitas* 1 (1997), pp. 11–35. For the German original, see B 89.
7. 'Etos nowoczesnej demokracji a Kościół (Das Ethos der modernen Demokratie und die Kirche)', *Civitas* 3 (1999), pp. 23–45. For the German original, see B 1.
8. 'Raz jeszcze: etos nowoczesnej demokracji a Kościół. Polemika między Hermannem-Josefem Spitalem i Ernstem-Wolfgangiem Böckenförde (Noch einmal: Das Ethos der modernen Demokratie und die Kirche. Kontroverse zwischen Hermann-Josef Spital und Ernst-Wolfgang Böckenförde)', *Civitas* 3 (1999), pp. 47–77. For the German original, see B 2.

9. 'Jaką drogą podąża Europa? (Welchen Weg geht Europa? gekürzte Fassung)', in Aniela Dylus (ed.), *Europa. Drogi integracji* (Warsaw: Studium Generale Europa, UKSW, 1999), pp. 11–23. For the German original, see A 18.
10. Stawrowski, Zbigniew (ed.), *Państwo prawa w jednoczącej się Europie [Rule of Law in a United Europe]*, transl. by Paweł Kaczorowski (Warsaw: Instytut Studiów Politycznych PAN, 2000). Includes the following articles:
    a) 'Recht schafft Freiheit, indem es Grenzen setzt'. For the German original, see D 139. Also published in A 19.
    b) 'Begriff und Probleme des Verfassungsstaates'. For the German original, see B 142.
    c) 'Verfassungsgerichtsbarkeit. Strukturfragen, Organisation, Legitimation'. For the German original, see B 146.
    d) 'Welchen Weg geht Europa?' For the German original, see A 18.
11. 'Einführung, in *Johannes Paul II., Gewissen der Welt*', *ZNAK* issue 581 (October 2003), pp. 10–21. For the German original, see B 170.
12. 'Oswoić religię ze świeckim państwem (Religion im säkularen Staat)', *FAKT Europa* 20, 18 August 2004, pp. 8–9. For the German original, see B 132, B 172.
13. 'Teoria polityki a teologia polityczna. Uwagi na temat ich wzajemnego stosunku (Politische Theorie und Politische Theologie. Bemerkungen zu ihrem gegenseitigen Verhältnis)', transl. by Magdalena Kurkowska, *Teologia polityczna* 3 (2005–2006), pp. 301–309. For the German original, see B 74.
14. 'Warunki mieszkedne dla europejski(ej) solidarności (Bedingungen der europäischen Solidarität, shortened and revised version)', *FAKT Europa*, Special Issue, 3 February 2006, p. 30. For the German original, see B 177.

X. Portuguese

1. 'O Contributo do agir Politico para a realizaçao da Justiça (Der Beitrag politischen Handelns zur Verwirklichung von Gerechtigkeit)', *Brotéria* 134:3 (1992), pp. 239–258. For the German original, see B 121.
2. 'Dignidade humana como princípio normativo: os direitos fundamentais no debate bioético (Menschenwürde als normatives Prinzip)', in Ingo Wolfgang Sarlet and George Salomão Leite (eds.), *Direitos Fundamentais e Biotecnologia* (São Paulo: Editora Metodo, 2008), pp. 59–76. For the German original, see B 174.
3. *História da filosofia do direito e do Estado: Antiguidade e Idade Média (Geschichte der Rechts- und Staatsphilosophie. Antike und Mittelalter)*, transl. by Adriana Beckman Meirelles (Porto Alegre: Sérgio Antônio Fabris, 2012). For the German original, see A 22.
4. *Estado de direito e democracia [State, Constitution, Democracy]*, transl. by Marcelo Oliveira da Silva (Curitiba: Instituto Atuação, 2017). Includes the following articles:
    a) 'Begriff und Probleme des Verfassungsstaates'. For the German original, see B 142.
    b) 'Demokratie als Verfassungsprinzip'. For the German original, see B 106.
    c) 'Demokratie und Repräsentation'. For the German original, see A 10.

d) 'Die Verfassunggebende Gewalt des Volkes. Ein Grenzbegriff des Verfassungsrechts'. For the German original, see A 11.

e) 'Anmerkungen zum Begriff Verfassungswandel'. For the German original, see B 123.

XI. Russian

1. Demokratiya kak konstitutsionniy princip [Democracy as Constitutional Principle]. In *Gosudarsvennoye pravo Germanii [State Law of Germany]*. Vol. 1. Moscow: Institute of State and Law RAS, 1994, pp. 33-44. For the German original, see B 106.
2. 'Methoden der Verfassungsinterpretation. Bestandsaufnahme und Kritik', in Georgi Khubua and Angelika Nussberger (eds.), *Interpretacija konstitucionnych norm v postsovetskich stranach: Teorija i praktika*, (Tiflis, 2007), pp. 18–52. For the German original, see B 52.
3. Ponyatiye politicheskogo kak kluch k rabotam Karla Schmitta po gosudarstvennomu pravu [The Concept of the Political as a Key to Carl Schmitt's works on state law]. *Logos 5(89)*, 2012, pp. 158-177. For the German original, see B 108.

XII. Slovenian

1. 'Država kot nravna država (Der Staat als sittlicher Staat)', transl. by Jani Šumak, *Tretji dan: verski časopis študentov in izobražencev. Letn.* 37:1/2 (2008), pp. 4–20. For the German original, see A 9.

XIII. Spanish

1. *Escritos sobre Derechos Fundamentales [Writings on Fundamental Rights]*, transl. by Juan Luis Requejo Pagés and Ignacio Villaverde Menéndez (Baden-Baden: Nomos Verlag, 1993). Includes the following articles:
   a) 'Die Methoden der Verfassungsinterpretation – Bestandsaufnahme und Kritik'. For the German original, see B 52.
   b) 'Grundrechtstheorie und Grundrechtsinterpretation'. For the German original, see B 47.
   c) 'Die sozialen Grundrechte im Verfassungsgefüge'. For the German original, see B 73.
   d) 'Freiheitssicherung gegenüber gesellschaftlicher Macht'. For the German original, see B 49.
   e) 'Zur Lage der Grundrechtsdogmatik nach 40 Jahre Grundgesetz'. For the German original, see A 15.
2. *Estudios sobre el Estado de Derecho y la democracia [Studies of the Rule of Law and Democracy]*, transl. by Rafael de Agapito Serrano (Madrid: Editorial Trotta, 2000). Includes the following articles:

a) 'Entstehung und Wandel des Rechtstaatsbegriffs'. For the German original, see B 21.
b) 'Demokratie als Verfassungsprinzip'. For the German original, see B 106.
c) 'Demokratie und Repräsentation. Zur Kritik der heutigen Demokratiediskussion'. For the German original, see A 10.
d) 'Die verfassunggebende Gewalt des Volkes. Ein Grenzbegriff des Verfassungsrechts'. For the German original, see A 11.
e) 'Anmerkungen zum Begriff "Verfassungswandel" '. For the German original, see B 121.

3. "¿Por qué se debe penar? Günther Jakobs se pregunta qué posición ocupa el enemigo en el Ordenamiento jurídico [Why should one punish? Günther Jakobs inquires into the legal standing of the enemy]', Review of Jakobs, Günther, *Staatliche Strafe. Bedeutung und Zweck*, 2004, *Cuadernos de política criminal* 93 (2007), pp. 251–254. For the German original, see D 61.
4. 'Honrar al delincuente como ciudadano. Michael Pawlik responde a la pregunta de por qué pena el Estado [Honouring the culprit as citizen. Michael Pawlik explains why the state punishes]', Review of Pawlik, Michael, *Person, Subjekt, Bürger. Zur Legitimation von Strafe*, 2004, *Cuadernos de política criminal* 94 (2008), pp. 289–294. For the German original, see D 62.

XIV. Swedish

1. 'Johannes Paulus II's "politiska teologi" (Das neue politische Engagement der Kirche. Zur "politischen Theologie" Johannes Pauls II, shortened version)', *Signum. Katolsk orientering om kyrka, kultur & samhälle* 4 (1980), pp. 105–108. For the German original, see B 68.
2. 'Efterskrift (Postscript)', in *Carl Schmitt. Det politiska som begrepp*, transl. by Svenja Hums (Gothenburg: Daidalos, 2010). (No published German original.)

XV. Ukrainian

1. Chy ye demokratiya neobhidnoyu vymogoyu prav lyudyny [Is Democracy Essential for Human Rights], in Stefan Gosepath and Georg Lohmann (eds.) *Filosophiya prav lyudyny [Philosophie of Human Rights]*, transl. by Olesksandr Judin & Larissa Doronitschewa. Kyiv: Nika-Tsentr, 2012 [2008], pp. 163-171. For the German original, see B 135.

Appendix 3

*Address given by Federal President Joachim Gauck on the Occasion of Awarding the Grand Cross of the Order of Merit of the Federal Republic of Germany to Prof. Dr. Ernst-Wolfgang Böckenförde on 29 April 2016 at Schloss Bellevue**

Welcome to an extraordinary award ceremony for an extraordinary individual. Every award ceremony is actually special, we all know that, particularly those who have already received awards. But today's honour has an extraordinary history, which should not be left untold: When you, dear Mr. Böckenförde, were to be honoured in 1996 for your work as a judge at the Federal Constitutional Court, you pointed out to the fact that you merely performed duties emanating from the office entrusted to you. Such modesty is striking. Indeed, it is truly remarkable!

But to anyone who has known you for a long time—as most of the guests gathered here today have—your decision at the time hardly came as a surprise: it reflects the ethos of a legal scholar and thinker who, despite the great impact of his words, has always remained a person of great personal restraint. Against this background, I am particularly delighted about this ceremony with you, your dear wife, your children, and the guests to whom you feel particularly connected. I am personally pleased with this recognition of you and your life's work.

Many of your students and assistants are now highly respected figures who play a key role in shaping our constitutional state. You can be proud of that. When I use the term pride here, I am referring to what legal scholars like you have done for our country. I am a Protestant pastor by profession, and I had got out of the habit of using the word 'pride'. But as a result of my political biography, I have learned to associate the Germany of our time with the word 'pride'. And when I reflect on why this association works well, great political achievements come to mind. There is also an amazing inner change that has given this country back its very own own identity marked by decency. And then there is the imposing edifice of the law. The fact that honour, dignity, and the role of the law have returned to this country after everything had been lost is something truly special. And that's why I would ask you to call to mind how little our democracy

* Original available at http://www.bundespraesident.de/SharedDocs/Reden/DE/Joachim-Gauck/Reden/2016/04/160429-Ordensverleihung-Boeckenfoerde.html. We thank the Bundespräsidialamt for the permission to reproduce the speech here.

would be worth if it were not for the reassurance which the great institutions of our legal system give us.

Many people did not have the opportunity to grow accustomed from an early age to the importance and dignity of law. It was often other values, moral values, that guided them. All of this has its place in life. But the fact that it has evolved this way, that in addition to various elements that provide certainty in this country, we can always ultimately rely on the guarantees provided by the law, does indeed endow this country with a very special and outstanding dignity and above all, credibility. We have to be able to believe in what we want to rely on. And you, Prof. Böckenförde, and your predecessors, your students, all of you, ladies and gentlemen, have played a decisive, formative role in this. You see before you today a president who—perhaps because he is not a lawyer—is able to feel great admiration for the legal profession.

When I talk about the edifice of the law, I do not mean something perfect. And I see certain parallels to another institution that is part of the 'fallen world', as the theologians would say, and that is the Church. One would like it to be a perfect embodiment of all that is humanly possible. But it is not. It is, to put it in theological terms, part of the fallen world. And I believe that we can treat the law with respect, even though it is partly flawed and in need of improvement in its concrete form. Especially when we know that, we come to value the positive developments. They should inspire us not only with gratitude but also happiness—happiness and pride.

I do not make such statements often, but here, in your presence, I feel an urge to say this—it is basically an additional honour that I, as a citizen and as a President, would like to add to the one you are about to receive. Prof. Böckenförde, people like you have allowed me in a special way to combine the word 'pride' with a feeling of gratitude and humility.

Prof. Böckenförde, I was told that you were reluctant to found a school of thought. Instead it was more important to you that your doctoral and other postgraduate students developed arguments and approaches independently and with courage. In this discursive manner, you have actually brought into being a 'Böckenförde school' with its own particular stamp: a school of free intellectual self-development.

While others mention your achievements, Prof. Böckenförde, you prefer to simply speak of 'contributions that have had an effect'. I would like to add: with these contributions you have enriched our country—as a bridge-builder between the Church and the state, as a pioneer and supporter of our liberal-democratic order, sometimes as a strict admonisher when you saw fundamental rights and principles at risk, and as a guardian of the constitution.

The young Federal Republic was still in its early democratic phase and you were at the start of your legal career, when you raised your voice and criticized the distance that you perceived between German Catholics—in your Church—and democracy. At the same time, you initiated a critical examination of the role of leading German Catholics when the National Socialists seized power. As a committed Christian and passionate democrat, it was a matter close to your heart to convince Christians in post-war West Germany to support the democratic order, the 'ethos of freedom and equality'. You have made a significant contribution towards the successful development of our constitutional state in the face of some resistance and the conflict-ridden efforts to find our identity.

This success can give us the courage to confront current challenges. In times of upheaval and uncertainty, the rise of radical forces and dwindling cohesion, in some quarters we are experiencing distrust, even hostility, towards our liberal, secular state. Once again, it is important to convey that a pluralistic society is an opportunity and a task for all citizens, regardless of their religious, political, or ideological beliefs. It is important to remember our shared responsibility for the success of democracy. This is the groundbreaking mandate, which I do everything in my power to support, that I take from your famous dictum.

Most of us here know it by heart: 'The liberal, secularized state is sustained by conditions that it cannot guarantee itself. That is the great gamble it has made for the sake of liberty.'

We know the history of this dictum and we also know the debates that followed. And it is always interesting to ask again in critical phases: Is what you said at the time still true today? Do we want it to be true? Would it be a problem for us it it were true? We still grapple with your dictum today, and few sentences are quoted as often in intellectual debates about the state and society in our country. And yet your dictum is not a one-off for me. For it is embedded in your work, work that has strengthened our public realm as a whole: our sense of history, our sense of freedom and our ethical sense of responsibility. All of these are the fruits of your learning, your intellectual acumen and your political instinct.

But there is something to add. That is your affection—your affection for people and for the society that these people have built.

A look at your work would be incomplete without a look at its ethical foundation. I am thinking, for example, of your concern about how the weak in our society can realize their potential and thus experience freedom. I am also thinking of your interventions to protect human dignity. They show that the individual is the focus of your attention, the individual who is always both capable and fallible. Ideally, humanity, intellect, and integrity merge into one and form a whole. And we, your admirers, see that this is the case with you. Our country thanks you for that and I too, thank you—not only as a Christian, as a citizen, but here and now as the President of this free country.

And in this spirit, ladies and gentlemen, we are now honouring one of the greats, Prof. Böckenförde. It gives me great pleasure to present you with the Great Cross of the Order of Merit.

Index

abortion 4, 8, 18, 26, 41, 243–44, 275–76, 284–87
  criminal indications 312, 390
  ethical counselling 276, 286, 310–313, 318, 329, 330–31, 335, 389–90
  ethical indications 334
  eugenics 335, 352
  German unification and 311–12
  indication solution 308–10, 318, 334
  law reform 311–12, 329–36
  medical counselling 308
  medical indications 276, 308, 310–12, 318, 328–29, 334, 335, 389
  Section 218 308–9, 318–20, 322–28, 330–38
  term solution 308–10, 318, 329, 389, 391
  time-restricted exemptions from punishment 329–32, 335–36
  see also protection of the unborn child; right to life
Adenauer, Konrad 8, 88, 281, 370–71
agnosticism 128, 140, 239–40, 295
Aquinas, Thomas 57, 116, 126, 152, 248, 260, 263, 268–69, 278–79, 376
Aristotle 19, 61, 152, 167, 221, 241–42, 272, 278
Arndt, Adolf 12–13, 188, 372
asylum 8, 41, 144, 192–93
atheism 125–26, 129, 140, 149, 162–63, 226, 239–40, 249–50
Augustine of Hippo 268–69, 277, 386
  civitas terrena and civitas Dei 239, 252

Basic Law (*Grundgesetz*)
  Art. 1 (human dignity) 16, 26–27, 179, 217, 224, 276, 313–17, 323, 334, 340–41, 344–45, 354–55, 358, 359–61, 362, 364
  Art. 2 (right to life) 143, 191–92, 276, 309–10, 315, 318, 320–23, 334, 348, 356, 359–61, 389
  Art. 3 (equality before the law) 384
  Art. 4 (freedom of belief and conscience) 135, 141–43, 168–69, 170, 177–86, 191–93, 197–98
    freedom of belief 141, 169, 170
    freedom of conscience 135, 141–43, 168–69, 170–98
    freedom to profess 142, 178, 180, 181
    freedom of worship 181–82
  Art. 6 (protection of marriage and family) 217
  Art. 7 (school system) 379–80
  Art. 14 (property, inheritance, expropriation) 9, 16–17
  Art. 20 (constitutional principles) 16, 64, 317
  Art. 79 (amendment, eternity clause) 362
  Art. 140 (law of religious denominations) 285
  Forsthoff-Abendroth Controversy 16–17, 392– 93
Berning, Hermann Wilhelm (Bishop of Osnabrück) 86–87
Bertram, Adolf (Cardinal) 54, 80, 83–84, 86, 88, 107, 374,
Bhargava, Rajeev 42–43
bioethics 26–27, 308–9, 313
  embryo-consuming research 347–49
  human dignity 313–17
  importation of stem cells 349
  pre-implantation diagnosis 315, 339, 347, 350–52, 360
  therapeutic cloning 352–53
  see also human dignity
biomedical / biotechnological advances 339–40, 358
  see also bioethics; human dignity
blasphemy 57, 115–18
Böckenförde Dictum (also *Böckenförde* Paradox) 3, 33, 42, 139, 145, 167, 198, 228, 243, 317, 377–81, 447
Bornewasser, Franz Rudolf (Bishop of Trier) 87, 89
Brandt, Willy 8, 14, 18–19
Brauer, Theodor 91–92
Brecht, Arnold 239–40, 249–50
Brüning, Heinrich 81–82, 83, 85, 88, 99

Calvin, John 57, 117–18
Calvinism 64–65, 69, 141
canon law
  Code of Canon Law 1917 (CIC 1917) 28, 87, 125, 246, 291, 303
  Code of Canon Law 1983 (CIC 1983) 28, 246, 290, 291–92, 303– 6
capitalism 2–3, 17, 393
  Sozialstaat-Rechtsstaat Controversy 15–17, 392–93
  social state 3, 15, 17–18, 392–93
Catholic Church
  authoritarianism of the Church 54–55, 70, 72, 73– 75, 87, 90, 108
  attitude towards parental rights 131, 230, 372
  Catholic state 29, 104, 123, 124, 127, 149, 235, 243, 282, 298

Catholic Church (*cont.*)
complicity with Nazi regime 48–52, 78–104
democracy, approach to 1–2, 29, 48–49, 73–76
duty of obedience of the intellect and will 28, 163, 303
ecclesiastical sovereignty 156–57, 174–75
encyclicals *see* Papal Encyclicals
freedom of religion, approach to 1, 29, 56–58
individual conscience, relationship with 4
internal reform 11–12, 29–33
nuclear armament 8, 29, 52–53 *see also* canon law; *Declaratio de Libertate Religiosa*
Second Vatican Council Popes *see Popes*
theory of tolerance (1315) 32, 56–57, 58
Catholic natural law 11, 54, 150–51, 240– 42
ecclesiastical sovereignty 156–57, 174–75
Catholic opposition to National Socialism 77–78, 79–80, 81–2, 88, 95–96
Catholicism and modern democratic ethos 369–73
Central Committee of German Catholics 8, 243, 284, 312, 375, 388
Central Council of Muslims in Germany 150, 234
Centre Party 31, 78–88, 98–99, 101, 107, 110–11, 374
Christian Democratic Union of Germany (CDU) 8, 47, 61, 79, 149, 232, 285, 309, 310, 318, 324,
Cicero 199, 248
civil religion 150, 229–30
civil service 8, 41–43, 280–87, 388–92
civic society 203, 221–22
civis simul et christianus (a democratic citizen while also a Christian), 4, 40, 41–43, 46, 242, 281–83
Committee for Contemporary History 32, 52, 77, 377
common good
Catholic Church and common good 30–31, 50
democracy and 3, 25, 42, 61–63, 66, 68–69, 76, 127, 140, 145, 323, 325
individual freedom, relationship with 241–42, 264, 323
religion and 34, 38, 48, 86, 98, 106, 122, 132, 145, 376–77
communism 15
law in communism 14, 53, 372
conditio humana 273–75, 277
confessional wars 139, 158–64
French Revolution 163–64
Peace of Augsburg 57, 120, 141
secularisation of the state 139, 158
see also reformation
conscientious objection to military service 8, 144–45, 186–87, 189–90
constitutionalism 6, 12–15, 21, 39
cuius regio eius religio (whose land, his religion) 57–58, 119, 141, 159
cura animarum 107–8

Dahrendorf, Ralf 34–35
de l'Hôpital, Michel 121, 153, 160, 221
Declaratio de Libertate Religiosa 56–57, 59, 115–16, 126
achievements 126–33
conflict with 296–98
history of religious freedom 116–22
individual rights 126–27
legal and moral dichotomy 128–30
Papal Encyclicals, conflict with 296–98
religious truth / human freedom dichotomy 116, 126–27
right of religious freedom 126–27
state and religion, relationship between 126–27, 130–32
Déclaration des droits de l'homme et du citoyen de 1789 (Declaration of the Rights of Man and of the Citizen of 1789) 13, 163, 166, 224, 271
democracy and democratic theory
autonomy and individualism 64–65, 67
Catholic Church's, approach to 1–2, 48–49, 73–76
characterisation of democracy 63–69
common good, relationship with 61–63
constitutional democracy 66–67
democratic ethos 3, 70, 75 76, 369–73, 386 *see also* ethos of modern democracy
equality 47–48, 65–66, 67–68
liberty 63–65, 67–68
social and political equality 47–48
unity and identity of governed and governing 63–64
distancing neutrality
open encompassing neutrality compared 37, 138, 222–23, 383
'dowry' theory 358, 359–60, 362
Dreier, Horst 359–60
Dürig, Günter 323, 354–56
see also Maunz-Dürig commentary
duty
duty of civic education, not indoctrination 38, 148
duty to protect life 323, 334 *see also* Basic Law -> Article 1
duty to respect human dignity 323, 334, 341, 344
see also Basic Law -> Article 1

East Germany *see* German Democratic Republic
ecclesiastical sovereignty 156–57, 174–75
economic inequality 15, 17–18, 41, 42–43
embryo-consuming research 347–49
embryonic stem cells 313–15, 347–49
importation of stem cells 349
therapeutic cloning 352–53
emergency
emergency and rational state [Hegel] 215
emergency powers of the Nazi regime 20, 86
state of emergency 8, 20, 21, 24

Enlightenment 206, 295
Catholic opposition 70, 101
law of reason 271
religious freedom 58, 121, 172, 226–27
Erasmus of Rotterdam 40, 57–58, 115, 118–19
ethics of conviction (Weber) 55, 110
ethics of responsibility (Weber) 55, 110
ethos 3, 4–5, 33–36, 39–41
Böckenförde's personal ethos 35–36, 284
ethos of modern democracy 29, 30, 46–47, 369–73
autonomy and individualism 64–65, 67
Catholicism and 369–73
Christian values and modern democracy 1–2, 70–76
common good 3, 35, 38, 42, 48, 61–63
eugenics 335, 352
European Convention on Human Rights (ECHR) 169–70
European integration 24–26
euthanasia 55, 111–12, 331
Nazi regime 55, 88, 111– 12, 331–32

Faulhaber, Michael von (Cardinal) 50–51, 86, 97, 98, 374
Federal Constitutional Court
Böckenförde's personal experience 8, 41–43, 280–87, 388–92
constitutional interpretation 143–44, 316–17
freedom of conscience 197–98
non-partisan/non-bias 243, 283–84, 391
Decisions
Abortion 243–44, 276, 285, 308, 310, 311, 312, 314, 318, 389, 390
Concordat 49
Headscarf 147, 383–84
KPD (Communist Party) 67, 372
Lüth 23, 141, 143, 187
Rag Collection 192
Tobacco-Atheist 187
Forsthoff-Abendroth Controversy 16–17, 392–93
freedom of assembly 142, 173
freedom of association 37, 142, 173
freedom of belief 36, 147, 163, 165, 189–90, 225
Basic Law 141, 169, 170
Paulskirche Constitution 176
Prussian Civil Code (1794) 142, 172–73
Protestant reformers 116–17
Weimar Constitution 175, 176, 181
freedom of conscience 12–13, 141, 144–45, 168–70
Basic Law 141–43, 168–70
individual liberty 177–81, 193
limitations 186–91
substance 181–83
unconditional guarantees 183–86, 192
concept of conscience 193–94, 196–97
limitations and restrictions 195–96
personal nature 194–95
constitutional interpretation 197–98
defensive right 171
expansion of scope
freedom of assembly 173
full freedom of worship 173
recognised denominations 172–73
historical background 170–77
open encompassing neutrality 141, 143–44
origins as a legal concept 170–71
state and society distinguished 141, 143
freedom of religion 1, 32–33, 42, 57–58, 120, 132, 142, 163–65, 174, 177, 181, 183, 224, 234, 265, 273, 277, 381–85
cuius regio eius religio (whose land, his religion) 57–58, 119, 141, 159
Declaratio de Libertate Religiosa see *Declaratio de Libertate Religiosa*
ethical minimum, law as 273
freedom of conscience 12–13, 141
general intolerance 115–19
historical background 115–22, 141–43
Church reaction to 122–26
human dignity, relationship with 58, 265
humanist position 57–58, 118–19
limits 132–33
Papal Encyclicals 289–90
authority 290–93
consequences 299–302
Declaratio de libertate religiosa, conflict with 296–98
Patent of Toleration (1781) (Austria) 120, 172
political theology 263–67
Protestant position 57, 116–18
Prussian Civil Code (1794) 58, 120–21, 142
recognition by Catholic Church 1, 29, 32–33, 56–58
Reformation 116–18
Second Vatican Council 56, 115–16
state secularism, relationship with 36–37, 381–85
theory of tolerance (1315) 56–57
freedom of the individual 1–2, 7–8, 139–40, 168–69, 174, 184–85, 238, 320
freedom of worship 36, 123, 125–26
Basic Law 181–82
Declaratio de libertate religiosa 133
French Constitution 161, 163
Libertas praestantissimum 294
Paulskirche constitution 142, 173
Weimar Constitution 173
freedom to profess 36, 120, 124, 131–32, 147, 225, 382–83
Basic Law 142, 178, 180, 181
freedom of conscience distinguished 176–77
Prussian Constitution (1850) 216
Weimar Constitution 181
French Revolution 69, 139, 152, 163–64, 295, 385
Fulda Conference of Bishops 83–84, 86, 107

Galen, Clemens August, Graf von (Bishop of Münster) 55, 85, 88, 97, 110–11
Galen, Franz, Graf von (politician) 55, 85, 99, 110
Gelasian doctrine of the two swords 248, 252
Gentilis, Albericus 40, 122
German Democratic Republic 14, 53–54, 105, 109, 280, 311, 389–90
  abortion 311, 389–90
  authoritarianism 54
  Christian comportment 54–55
  Nazi crimes, prosecution of 53–54
Gröber, Conrad (Archbishop of Freiburg) 84, 86–87
Grundwertedebatte (debate on core values) 18, 200
guilt 53–54, 114, 247, 311, 332, 334, 337
Gundlach, Gustav 29, 52–53, 88, 91, 210

Habermas, Jürgen 16, 27, 33–34, 38, 42, 145, 274, 387
Hegel, Georg Wilhelm Friedrich 2, 3, 6–7, 21–22, 25, 39, 57, 103, 130, 138, 145–47, 165, 167, 201–2
  civic society 203, 221–22
  concept of 'state' 202–204
  foundation of the state 146, 204–5
  individual conscience 146
  political Christology 252
  right of conscience 213–15
  state and reason 204
  state and religion, relationship between 146, 167, 204–5
    abstract notion 205, 206
    concrete reality 205–13, 216–19
    inseparability of 146–47, 212–13
    religious fanaticism 208–9
    spiritual hierocracy 209–10
    state rationality and ethical substance 210–11
Heller, Hermann 2, 13, 15–16, 34–35, 39, 152, 197, 199, 227
Herdegen, Matthias 27, 315–17, 354, 356–58, 360–61
heresy 28, 116–19, 159–61, 303
Herwegen, Ildefons (Abbot of Maria Laach) 92–93
Hobbes, Thomas 39, 139
  auctoritas non veritas facit legem 122
  political theology 239, 252–53
  secular state 156–57, 159, 162–63
Hofmann, Hasso 358–59
Hommes, Jakob 90–91
Hufen, Friedhelm 362–63
human dignity 16, 26–27
  Basic Law 313–17, 340–41
  bioethics 313–17, 339–40
  'dowry' theory 358, 359–60, 362
  freedom of religion, relationship with 58, 265
  Nazi regime and 340–41, 354–55
  philosophical origins 316–17
  pre-natal dignity 314–16, 341–42, 344–47, 355–56, 357, 364–65
    personhood debate 343
    scientific realities and moral/ethical considerations 342–43
    status of embryos 342–43, 364–65
  scope of guarantee of human dignity 357–61
    evolution 361–64
  social recognition theory 358–59
  Universal Declaration of Human Rights 340–41
human rights 43
  autonomous and individual freedom 139–40, 166, 179, 241, 271–72
  courts' duties 271–72
  criticisms of Catholic Church 29
  freedom of conscience 36
  French Revolution 163–64
  secularisation of the state 139, 148–49, 224
  states' duties 184, 224
  see also Basic Law, individual right
humanism and humanists 40–41, 57–58, 118–19, 121

individual conscience 4, 146, 168–69, 183, 391
  see also freedom of conscience
inequality *see* economic inequality, social inequality
Investiture Controversy 139, 154–57, 256

Jellinek, Georg 171, 199, 273, 320
just war theory 29, 52–53

Kaas, Ludwig (Prelate) 81–82, 99
  negotiations with Hitler 82–83
Kaller, Maximilian (Bishop of Ermland) 87
Kant, Immanuel 12–13, 62, 64, 173–74, 262, 268, 314, 316, 344–45, 362, 364
Kartellverband deutscher katholischer Studentenvereine (Union of German Catholic Student Associations) 94–95
Keller, Michael (Bishop of Münster) 282, 374
Kulturkampf 30–31, 50, 73, 78–79, 97, 99, 101, 121

law *see* legal system; *Rechtsstaat*; rule of law
law as the ethical minimum 273, 320
legal equality 385–86
legal ethics 242, 361–62
legal system 129, 131, 135, 148, 167, 177, 198, 208, 222–23, 232, 272–74, 283
  Basic Law 355, 364
  ethical and moral basis 275
  foreign legal systems 276–77
  justification of 320
  legal good 323
  prescriptions and commandments 274–75
  purpose of the law 320–21
  social validity 326–29
Lerche, Peter 358
liberal state 2, 3, 19, 133, 150, 167, 177, 282, 378, 381
Lortz, Josef 89–90
Luhmann, Niklas 144–45
  function of conscience 189, 194–97
  performance theory 358

Lüth *see* Federal Constitutional Court Decisions
Luther, Martin 57, 116–17, 158, 242, 268–69, 277–78
  two-kingdom theory 252, 255, 296

Maaßen, Johannes 96
Maastricht Treaty (1992) 25
Markl, Hubert 361–62
Marx, Karl 17, 146, 208, 217, 268, 393
  'opium of the masses' 208
  religion 121, 163–65, 174, 221, 248–49
marxism 67, 92, 102–103, 268
Maunz-Dürig commentary 26–27, 315, 354–55
Melanchthon, Philip, 40, 57, 116–17
Metz, Johann Baptist 254
Michalski, Krzysztof 24–25, 34
modern democracy *see* democracy
moral, morality 19, 55, 105–6, 110–12, 123–25, 128, 272–73, 277, 282–83, 287, 295–97, 299, 300, 310, 319–320, 326–27, 329, 333, 335, 341–42, 376, 446
  law and morals, law and morality 4, 244, 262–67, 295–96
  moral natural law 262–63, 274–75, 277, 299
  see also *Sittlichkeit*
More, Thomas 39–41
Mörsdorf, Klaus 123–24, 235, 305

National Socialist German Workers' Party (NSDAP) 80–84, 88, 93, 95, 113
natural law
  Catholic natural law 11, 150–51, 240–42, 260, 267–70, 386–87
  human natural law 277–78
  moral natural law 262–64, 274–75, 277, 299
  secular law, conflict with 264–65, 386–87
  sittliche Weltordnung 261–62
Nazi regime 53–54
  Catholic Church's complicity 13, 48–52, 78, 97–104, 374
  Catholic opposition to 77–78
  Christian conduct 105–14, 374–77
  Enabling Act 20, 79, 81–83, 107, 110
  human dignity concept, impact on 340–41, 354–55
  leadership of Catholic Church 79, 81–88
    Berning, Hermann Wilhelm (Bishop of Osnabrück) 86–87
    Bertram, Adolf (Cardinal) 84, 86
    Bornewasser, Franz Rudolf (Bishop of Trier) 87
    Faulhaber, Michael von (Cardinal) 86
    Fulda Conference of Bishops 83, 86
    Galen, Clemens August, Graf von (Bishop of Münster) 55, 85, 88, 97, 99, 110– 11
    Gröber, Conrad (Archbishop of Freiburg) 84, 86
    Kaas, Ludwig (Prelate) 81–83
  persecution of Christians 77, 79, 105–14
  persecution of Jews 51, 88, 183
  programmatic joint pastoral letters 84–85, 88
  Reich Concordat 49–51, 54, 82–108, 374
nuclear (dis)armament 8, 29, 52–53
  Catholic Church's position 52–53

open encompassing neutrality 5, 28–29, 36–39, 141, 143, 147–48, 194, 233
  courtrooms 38, 148
  Gemeinwesen (polity) and *Hoheitsgewalt* (sovereign activity) distinguished 37–38, 144, 148
  distancing neutrality compared 37, 138, 222–23, 225, 383
  schools 38, 148
Ottaviani, Alfredo (Cardinal) 122–24, 132, 225

Papal Encyclicals 27, 28, 244, 289–90
  Immortale Dei (1885) 297
  Libertas praestantissimum (1888) 59, 133, 293, 294
  Mirari vos (1832) 293–94
  Pacem in Terris (1963) 126, 283
  Quanta Cura (1864) 293, 294, 295
  Quadragesimo anno (1931) 91, 210
  Rerum Novarum (1891) 91, 283
  see also *Declaratio de libertate religiosa*: conflict with
Papen, Franz von 80–81, 93
Parliamentary Council 16, 143–44
  freedom of belief and conscience 178, 180, 183
  human dignity 313, 316, 340–41, 344–45, 355, 356, 358–59, 362
  parental rights regarding religious education 281–82, 372
  right to life 321
Paulskirche Constitution (1849)
  freedom of assembly 142
  freedom of belief and conscience 176
  freedom of worship 142, 173
Peace of Augsburg (1555) 57, 119–120, 141, 171
Peterson, Erik 253
Pieper, Josef 91
Plato 157, 203, 248, 361
Podlech, Adalbert
  Gemeinwesen (polity) and *Hoheitsgewalt* (sovereign activity) distinguished 37–38, 144, 148
political Christology 252
political theology
  appellative political theology 239, 254–55
  Catholic/Christian natural law 260
  Carl Schmitt 238–39, 251–52, 257, 385–87
  conceptual sociology 251–52
  Hegel, Georg Wilhelm Friedrich 21, 252
  institutional political theology 239, 253, 254–56
  legal political theology 254
  modern secular law 259–60, 270–77

political theology (*cont.*)
theological status 277–79
natural law principles 260–70
origins 248–49
political and social conduct of Christians 253–54
political theory, relationship with 238–40, 248–51
Pope John Paul II 256–58
state and religion, relationship between 252–53
Thomas Hobbes 156, 159
Pope Benedict XVI 226–27, 236, 290, 300
Pope Boniface VIII 156
Pope Gregory VII 155–56
Pope Gregory XVI 290
Pope John XXIII 33, 57, 126, 282–83, 381–82
Pope John Paul II 21, 149, 226, 239, 256–58, 274–75, 301–2, 376
Pope Leo XIII 51, 99–100, 123, 128, 226, 235, 252–53, 255, 262, 266, 281–82, 386
Pope Pius IX 289, 290
Pope Pius XII
Bellum iustum 52
Tolerance Address (1953) 122, 124, 264, 282, 297–98
popular sovereignty 6, 26, 101, 251, 254
pouvoir constituant 22, 254
pouvoirs constitués 22
pre-implantation diagnosis 315, 339, 347, 350–52, 360
pre-natal dignity 314–16, 341–42, 344–47, 355–56, 357
personhood debate 343
status of embryos 321, 342–43, 364–65
private property 2, 16, 67, 271
protection of the unborn child 275–76, 285–86, 308–12, 315, 321
see also abortion; right to life; Section 218
Prussian Civil Code (1794)
freedom of belief 142, 172–73
freedom of religion 58, 120–21, 142
Prussian Constitution (1850)
freedom of religion 175, 213, 216
freedom to profess 216

Ranke, Leopold von 159
Ratzinger, Joseph Aloisius (Cardinal) 33–34, 149, 231–32, 272, 295, 301, 387
Rechtsstaat 2–3, 12–13, 17
freedom, concept of 178–79, 184, 198
democracy, relationship with 66–67, 69, 168–69, 198, 381
Rechtsstaat-Sozialstaat debate 15–17, 392–93
Red Army Faction (RAF) 8, 18
threat to state order 20–21
reformation 57, 116, 118, 122, 139, 157, 207, 223
Calvin, John 57, 117–18
Erasmus of Rotterdam 40, 57–58, 115, 118–19
freedom of religion 57, 122
Luther, Martin 57, 116–17, 158, 242, 268–69, 277–78
Melanchthon, Philip 40, 57, 116–17
Reuchlin, Johannes 40, 57–58, 118–19
secularisation of the state 122, 139, 158–64, 207, 223
see also Confessional wars
Reich Concordat 49–51, 54, 82–108, 374
religion *see* Catholic Church; Christian state; freedom of belief; freedom of conscience; freedom of worship; freedom to profess; natural law; political theology, religious law; secularization
religio-natural law *see* natural law
religious law *see* canon law; natural law
religious truth/human freedom dichotomy 116, 126–27
Repgow, Eike von 248
Reuchlin, Johannes 40, 57–58, 115, 118–19
right to life 309, 313–15, 320, 340–41, 348
see also abortion; Basic Law (Art.2); human dignity; protection of the unborn child; Section 218
Ring katholischer deutscher Burschenschaften (Ring of German Catholic Fraternities) 94–95
Ritter, Joachim 6, 12–13, 145–46
Rousseau, Jean-Jacques 62, 64–65, 68–69, 150, 229–30
rule of law 2, 8, 12, 15–16, 18–21, 39, 41–42, 53–54, 66–67, 133, 145, 170, 179, 184–86, 192–93, 198, 271
see also *Rechtsstaat*

Schmauz, Michael 89–90
Schmidlin, Josef 88
Schmidt, Helmut 8, 18–19, 200
Schmitt, Carl 7, 8, 10, 13–4, 21, 39, 63–64, 93, 178, 238–9, 251–2, 257, 385–87, 393
identity theory 14
legal-political concepts of modern state theory 251
political theology 238–39, 251–52, 256–57, 385–87
Schnabel, Franz 13, 63–64, 95, 208
schools 37, 48, 68, 82, 84, 98–99, 109, 131–32, 148, 150, 195, 232–33, 281, 372–73, 380, 383–84, 446
crucifix 38, 148
denominational 47, 72, 74–75, 131–32, 281
Enabling Act 82
ethos of democracy 72, 74–75, 372
headscarf 42, 147, 231, 382–385
open encompassing neutrality 38, 148, 222
parental rights regarding religious education 131, 281–82, 372
Schreiber, Georg 88
Schwarzer, Alice 285
Second Vatican Council 1, 11, 30–32, 46, 50, 56, 58–59, 70, 115, 124, 127, 140, 150, 207, 212, 225, 235–36, 238–39, 241–42, 245, 252–53, 264–66, 288, 291, 297, 299, 304–5, 309, 382

De Libertate Religiosa see *Declaratio de Libertate Religiosa*
  human dignity 265
  religious freedom 56, 225, 235, 239, 245, 266, 378–79
  theological justifications for secular state 225–27, 252–53
Section 218 (German Penal Code)
  abortion offences 324–25
  illegal abortions 324
  negative effects 325–26
  rape 285, 308, 310, 334
  relationship to social reality 326–29
  see also abortion; human dignity; protection of the unborn child; right to life
secular state
  distancing neutrality 222–23
  justifications 148–49, 223
    human rights principles 224
    resisting ecclesiastical-religious claims of supremacy 223–24
    Second Vatican Council and theological justification 225–27
  open encompassing neutrality *see* open encompassing neutrality
  state secularism 3–4, 12–13
    characteristics of secular states 221–22
    civis simul et christianus 4, 41–43, 46, 280–87
    constitutionalisation of human and civil rights 139
    demanding loyalty to state law over religion 234–35
    Gemeinwesen (polity) and *Hoheitsgewalt* (sovereign activity) distinguished 37–38, 144, 148
    human and civil rights, emergence of 165–67
    legitimacy 227–31
    open encompassing neutrality *see* open encompassing neutrality
    religious freedom, relationship with 36–37, 381–85
    state neutrality *see* open encompassing neutrality
secularisation 36–39, 207, 223
  Confessional wars 119, 122, 139, 141, 158–64
  desacralization / secularization / despiritualization 165–67
  French Revolution 69, 139, 152, 163– 64, 295, 385
  Investiture Controversy 139, 154–57, 256
  open encompassing neutrality 138–39
  secular law 127, 129
  understanding from theological perspective 240–42, 259–79, 371
  see also confessional wars; distancing neutrality; freedom of conscience; freedom of religion; open encompassing neutrality; reformation; secular state
self-realization 2, 19, 102–3, 132, 145–46, 248–49, 314, 332, 344–45
Sieyès, Emmanuel Joseph
  pouvoir constituant and *pouvoirs constitués* 22
Sittlichkeit 33–36, 143, 146–47, 166, 179, 195, 210–11, 262–63
  see also moral, morality
Smend, Rudolf 10, 15–16, 187
societal cohesion v, 34–35, 149–50, 166, 227, 447
Social Democratic Party of Germany (SPD) 8, 14, 19, 53, 80, 82, 243, 308–9, 318, 372, 375
  Böckenförde's membership 14–15, 284, 388
social inequality 3, 17–18, 392–93
social state 3, 15–18, 392–93
Soviet Union
  inversion of tolerance principle 59, 125
Spaemann, Robert 7, 29, 52–53, 261, 322, 387
Spann, Othmar 91–92, 102
state neutrality *see* open encompassing neutrality
state organisation 23, 152–53
state power 129, 157, 162, 209, 251
  emergency powers 20
  freedom, relationship with 1–2, 7–8, 263
  political authority 251, 254
  securing human rights 148–49, 224, 263
  states' duties towards religion 127–29
  see also secular state
state sovereignty 36, 71, 152, 157, 182–83, 190, 238–39, 251–52, 254, 381
Stein, Lorenz von 13, 15–17, 63, 163, 393

therapeutic cloning 314, 339–40, 352–53
Tischler, Peter 123
tolerance
  religious tolerance 277, 282, 387
  theory of tolerance (1315) 32, 56–57, 58
transitional justice policies 53–54
  Treaty of Westphalia (1648) 57, 141–42, 170–71
two-kingdom theory 252, 255, 296

unborn child, protection of 275–76, 285–86, 308–12, 321
  personhood debate 343
  pre-natal dignity 314–16, 341–42, 344–47, 355–56, 357
  scientific realities and moral / ethical considerations 342–43
  status of embryos 321, 342–43, 364–65
  see also abortion; human dignity
Union of Utrecht (1579)
  freedom of belief and conscience 57, 141–42, 170–71
Universal Declaration of Human Rights 271, 340–41

value-based grounding of law 23–24, 140–41, 200
Vatican I 261, 292, 304
Vatican II *see* Second Vatican Council

we-consciousness 33–35, 42, 145, 227–28, 230–34
Weimar Church Compromise 284

Weimar Constitution 20, 80–81, 93, 98–99, 135, 142, 169, 178, 187
freedom of assembly 173, 176
freedom of belief and conscience 170, 174–75, 176, 181, 183
freedom of worship 173
freedom to profess 176, 181
Weimar Republic 6, 30–31, 50, 79, 329
failure of 49, 50–51, 85, 98–99
Wöllner, Johann Christoph von 172–73

Zypries, Brigitte 360, 363

Printed and bound by CPI Group (UK) Ltd, Croydon, CR0 4YY